VOLUME TWO

GIAC Certification Series

SANS Immersion Training™

SANS Security Essentials with CISSP CBK

Version 2.1

VOLUME TWO

Eric Cole
Jason Fossen
Stephen Northcutt
Hal Pomeranz

SANS Security Essentials with CISSP CBK Version 2.1

Document Legalities

Cover Photo © Diana Ong/Superstock

Cover Designer: José Ellauri

International Standard Book Number: 0-9724273-6-8

Library of Congress Control Number: 2003101189

Printed in the United States of America

First Printing: February 2003

Second Printing: April 2003

Warning and Disclaimer

Every effort has been made to make this book as complete and as accurate as possible, but no warranty of fitness is implied. The information provided is on an "as is" basis. The authors and the publisher shall have neither liability nor responsibility to any person or entity with respect to any loss or damages arising from the information contained in this book.

Table of Contents

Volume One

Volume Two

About the Authoring Team

Primary Authors

Eric Cole is a graduate of the New York Institute of Technology with Bachelor's and Master's degrees. He is finishing up his Ph.D. from Pace University. Eric is a speaker at national and international conferences on network security. An information security expert for more than 10 years, Eric holds several professional certifications and helped develop several of the SANS GIAC certifications and corresponding courses. Eric is currently chief scientist for The Sytex Group's Information Warfare Center, where he heads cutting edge research in technology and various areas of network security. He is the author of *Hackers Beware* and co-author of *SANS GIAC: Security Essentials Toolkit.*

Jason Fossen is the founder and president of Fossen Networking & Security, which provides consultation for Microsoft Windows 2000/XP/.NET solutions and security. In addition to the consulting practice, Jason is also a prolific author and guest speaker at national security conferences on a variety of topics, including cryptography, PKI deployment, firewall design, Web server security, IPSec, and Virtual Private Networking. Jason graduated from the University of Virginia and received his master's degree from the University of Texas at Austin. He currently lives in Dallas, Texas.

Stephen Northcutt is a graduate of Mary Washington College. Before entering the field of computer security, he worked as a Navy helicopter search and rescue crewman, white water raft guide, chef, martial arts instructor, cartographer, and network designer. Stephen is author/co-author of *Incident Handling Step-by-Step, Intrusion Signatures and Analysis, Inside Network Perimeter Security* and *Network Intrusion Detection*. He was the original author of the Shadow Intrusion Detection system before accepting the position of Chief for Information Warfare at the Ballistic Missile Defense Organization. Stephen currently serves as Director of Training for the SANS Institute.

Hal Pomeranz is founder and principal consultant for Deer Run Associates, a systems management and security consulting firm. He has spent more than fifteen years managing systems and networks for some of the largest commercial, government, and academic organizations in the United States. Hal participated in the first SANS conference and designed the SANS Step-by-Step course model. He is a top-rated instructor and author, and a recipient of the SAGE Outstanding Achievement Award for teaching and leadership in his field.

Author Coordinator

Karen Kent is a Senior Intrusion Detection Analyst working in northern Virginia. She holds a bachelor's degree in computer science from the University of Wisconsin-Parkside and a master's degree in computer science from the University of Idaho. Karen has over 10 years of experience in technical support, system administration, programming, and information security. She holds several certifications including MCSE+Internet, GCIA, GCIH, GCUX and GSEC; she is also on the GSEC and GCIA Advisory Boards. Karen is one of the authors of *Intrusion Signatures and Analysis* and *Inside Network Perimeter Security*. She also frequently writes articles for `SecurityFocus.com`.

Contributing Authors

David J. Bianco has been a Unix administrator for more than a decade. He got his start lurking around his university's computer science lab in his freshman year, forcing the staff to either call security or give him a job. Fortunately for him, they chose the latter. He spent four years as a security consultant, first for IBM/Transarc and then for a smaller information security vendor. He is currently a system administrator for a US nuclear physics lab. David is a member of the GSEC Advisory Board and is Vice Chair for the GCUX Advisory Board.

Tony Cole is currently responsible for Symantec Corporation's Critical Infrastructure Protection Program. His responsibilities include assisting the Federal government in security architecture design and implementation. He is retired from the military and has over 20 years of experience in IT systems, security, and technical project management. For the last seven years, Tony has focused on security and very much enjoys assisting organizations like SANS to make our networks more secure.

William Curd, Ph.D., has over 15 years of experience as a technology leader, system architect, and certified security, quality and project management professional. He has managed all aspects of computer and network security for a Fortune 100 corporation. In the information security field, he is an author, training developer, and speaker. He started his career as a software engineer, became a network architect, managed a computing center, coordinated corporate-wide security and network activities, and pioneered network, security, collaboration and product data management systems. Bill has a Ph.D. in electrical engineering and an M.S. in system engineering from SMU. He is a CISSP, GCFA, Project Management Professional, Six Sigma Green Belt, Malcolm Baldrige and European Foundation for Quality Management examiner. He is also a member of HTCIA, ISSA, FBI InfraGard, FISSEA, AZSAGE, PMI, and the IEEE.

Mark Edmead, CISSP, SSCP, TICSA, Security+, is an information security consultant and trainer for MTE Software, Inc., and has more than 22 years experience in software development, product development, and network systems security. He was contributing editor of *SANS Digest* (SysAdmin, Audit & Network Security) and contributing editor to the *SANS Step-by-Step Windows NT Security Guide*. Mark previously worked for KPMG Information Risk Management Group and IBM's Privacy and Security Group, where he performed network security assessments, security system reviews, development of security recommendations, and ethical hacking. Other projects included assisting companies in developing secure and reliable network system architecture for their Web-enabled businesses. Mark is co-author of the book *Windows NT: Performance, Monitoring and Tuning* published by New Riders and developed the

SANS Business Continuity/Disaster Recovery Plan Step-by-Step Guide.

Gary C. Kessler is an Associate Professor and program director of the Computer Networking major at Champlain College in Burlington, VT, where he also is the director of the Vermont Information Technology Center security projects. He is also an independent consultant specializing in issues related to computer and network security, Internet and TCP/IP protocols and applications, e-commerce, and telecommunications technologies and applications. Gary is a frequent speaker at industry conferences, has written two books and over 60 articles on a variety of technology topics. He is a frequent contributor to *Information Security Magazine*, is an instructor for the SANS Institute, and is the chair of the Vermont InfraGard chapter (`http://www.vtinfragard.org`). He holds a B.A. in mathematics and an M.S. in computer science. Gary has two children in college and lives in Colchester, Vermont. More information can be found at `http://www.garykessler.net`.

Andrew J. Korty started as a programmer at the age of 10 and participated in various coding projects and system administration duties throughout high school and college. After receiving a bachelor's degree in honors physics from Purdue, he stayed on with the department as a systems programmer and later became director of the departmental computer network. Later, Andrew's interests turned to information security, and he has held the position of Principal Security Engineer at Indiana University ever since. Soon after he started at IU, he had the privilege of extracting the first known copy of the mstream DDoS zombie-master source code from the raw disk of a compromised system. Though he has focused mostly on developing security tools for use at IU, lately he has also been involved in promoting awareness by teaching short courses and developing a more useful Web site. In fall 2003, he will teach a course in advanced computer security for the Purdue School of Engineering and Technology. Andrew holds a GCIA certification and is working on his GCFA.

Adelle McIlroy is the Principal Consultant for International Network Services (INS) in Washington, DC. She has responsibility for the metro-area Security Practice, including security assessment, policy development, infrastructure and design, and awareness and training services. She received her bachelor's degree in mathematics and physics from the University of Miami, is certified as a CISSP, GCIA, and CBCP, and has experience with information security audit and control in the telecommunications and banking industries. McIlroy has also authored material for publication by INS, *Disaster Recovery Journal*, and the SANS Institute.

Ronald W. Ritchey is avidly interested in secure network design and network intrusion techniques. He gets to exercise this interest regularly by leading penetration-testing efforts for Booz Allen Hamilton. He has had the opportunity to learn first-hand the real-world impact of network vulnerabilities. He is also an active researcher in the field with peer-reviewed publications in the area of automated network security analysis and is one of the co-authors of *Inside Network Perimeter Security*, published by New Riders in association with the

SANS Institute. Ron has authored courses on computer security that have been taught across the country and periodically teaches master's level courses on computer security. Ron holds a master's degree in computer science from George Mason University and is currently pursuing his Ph.D. in information technology at their School of Information Technology and Engineering. His doctoral research involves automating network security analysis.

Darrin Wassom is currently a Technical Architect for Spectrum Health, in Grand Rapids, Michigan. He is responsible for HIPAA compliance in the areas of network and systems' security. Prior to his work at Spectrum Health, he was responsible for the Internet infrastructure design and security for a large Midwestern retail and grocery chain with yearly sales exceeding $9 billion. In early 2002, Darrin started a consulting company, Essential Security, which offers services relating to information security. He currently holds the CCSA, CCNA, GSEC and GSNA certifications. In addition to being a member of the GSEC and GSNA Advisory Boards, he is active with the GSEC Local Mentor Program and is an Authorized Grader for the GSEC Certification. Darrin is a veteran of the United States Army Signal Corps and a graduate of Michigan State University with a degree in telecommunications, information technology and systems management. Darrin is currently working on obtaining his GCIA certification.

Scott Winters has been working in all aspects of networking and computer security for over 13 years. He has been an instructor, author, network engineer, consultant and systems administrator and has worked with various perimeter security solutions, firewalls, and infrastructure designs. He currently works as a consultant for Unisys at the Commonwealth of Pennsylvania Enterprise Server Farm. Scott has SANS GIAC Firewalls and Incident Handling certifications, as well as MCSE, CNE, Cisco CCNP and CCDA and other technology certifications. Other accomplishments include the authoring and editing of SANS GIAC Training and Certification course and exam content. He has also been involved in the SANS GIAC Mentoring program, and has served on the SANS GCFW Advisory Board.

Lenny Zeltser's work in information security draws upon experience in system administration, software architecture, and independent research. Lenny consulted to a major financial institution, co-founded a software company, and is now the Director of Information Security at Kiodex, Inc. He produced and co-authored *Inside Network Perimeter Security* (New Riders, 2002), and has written and presented coursework for the SANS Institute. Lenny is an active member of several security workgroups and advisory boards, and holds a number of professional certifications, including: CISSP, GCFW, GCUX, GCWN, GCIH and GCIA. He earned a B.S.E. degree in computer science engineering from the University of Pennsylvania. More information about Lenny's projects and interests is available on his Web site at `http://www.zeltser.com`.

Editors

Gregory W. Price's first "PC" was an Adam, which remains in a box but close. While pursuing his master's in English, Greg concentrated on every bit of technology he could squeeze into his schedule. While teaching English, he took networking courses in Novell and NT and immediately was recruited from the classroom into a networking environment, working his way quickly to network administrator. From there, he moved to network planner and security specialist for an insurance company and continues to pursue security issues diligently. In his free time, he teaches college English; works as a freelance editor; and composes poetry and fiction, for which he has won many awards.

Sharon J. Ritchey loves putting words on paper and making publications come alive. She began working as a writer, editor, and researcher 10 years ago while living in the Netherlands, where she became the Benelux queen of frozen food news. She has editorial credits in the food industry, direct marketing, and computer fields. Her byline has appeared in numerous trade publications and consumer magazines and she is a frequently sought after editor and writer. She lives in Northern Virginia and spends her free time chasing after her daughter Renee, editing her husband Ron's work, and is currently working on a master's of fine arts in creative non-fiction writing from George Mason University.

Other Acknowledgments

Zoe Dias, Suzy Northcutt, Deb Tuttle and Katherine Webb Calhoon of the SANS Institute—for all of their assistance with this project, and most importantly, their patience.

Eric Cole, Tony Cole, Clement Dupuis, Mark Edmead and Adelle McIlroy—for adding the CBK material to the course.

John Stone—for his review and feedback on the malware chapter.

John Bambenek—for updating the glossary and URL listing.

Preface

More people have taken the SANS Security Essentials course than any other information security course in the world and the numbers are rapidly growing. Today, security is so complex that each of us must realize there is a lot we don't know and understand. SANS' Security Essentials has been developed to fill these gaps. A few people have filled notable roles in developing the courseware, though it is also the product of several hundred security practitioners in the defensive community working together, and it continues to evolve to meet the needs of the students.

Security Essentials was born at the SANS '99 annual conference in Baltimore, Maryland. Alan Paller, Director of Research for SANS, had been trying to develop a program that covered only the things you needed to know about information security and nothing you didn't. However, it had been slow going. Everyone who worked on the project ended up giving up after a couple of weeks. Alan would tell me what he had tried and why it hadn't worked and I would nod and express my condolences being careful not to volunteer since I was really busy at the time. I wanted to help, but it sounded like a tremendous amount of effort, possibly thousands of hours. However, I too was frustrated. I was a manager for the Department of Defense and it was hard to hire people with the skills to do the jobs we needed to have done. At best, they understood the theory of security and that theory tended to be from the mainframe era. I thought if I could just hire people that met a minimum standard, my life would be ten times better. Prior to departing for Baltimore, I knew that for better or worse, I was going to take the lead for the Security Essentials project—it was too important a project to leave drifting.

I wasn't scheduled to teach on the third day of the conference and Alan and I got in a harbor taxi boat so we could get away from the noise and excitement of the conference. We had a set of index cards and we started brainstorming about what people needed to know, what was critical, what wasn't, and what were the essentials of information security for the practitioner. When we got back to the conference, Fred Kerby took the cards and started a list. Michele Guel, Hal Pomeranz, and other instructors took shots at the list too. Dr. Eugene Schultz helped us with an hour-long conference call. He expressed his concerns and gave us his suggestions. Soon we were up to the 21st revision and the fact that we were not yet at a working first version tells you how far we felt we needed to go. We ran the objectives and domains of knowledge past the CIO Institute to get feedback from senior management and from as many system, network, and security admins in the trenches as we could find.

We started developing the first course modules, the really obviously needed ones like cryptography, malicious code, how IP works, and threat and risk assessment. At the time we were hoping to partner with ISC2, the folks that produce the CISSP. We shared the design, objectives and courseware we developed and asked for guidance on what they thought might be missing, or what needed to be covered differently. Eventually, after 99 revisions, we finally reached the point we had version 1.0 of Security Essentials. Before the first person outside the development team ever saw the courseware, over a hundred security experts from fifteen countries had invested in the creation of Security Essentials.

The goal from the beginning was for this to be the consensus of the global community. Special thanks should be offered to Philip Boyle from New Zealand, Guy Bruneau from Canada, Andrew Sturman from the United Kingdom, and Dean White from Australia. The only way to reach out globally that we could see was to offer an online version of the course. Jennifer Kolde is best known as director of the GIAC Certification, but she was instrumental in formatting the early courseware. Dave Turley, building on work started by Rob Kolstad, wrote the software delivery system for both the courses and exams. John Green created the powerful database that tracks registration and accounting for both live and online training. Doug Austin developed the system we use for digital audio and Karen Ellrick, a musician and missionary in Japan, helped us with a huge breakthrough. She suggested we convert from our audiotapes to minidisks as our sound source. The higher quality source material meant better sound files, one of the biggest problems we had to overcome.

Eric Cole was involved with the project since the early days and is one of the best instructors of the courseware. When we realized that we were going to have to expand the program from three to six days to cover the material properly, he took the lead role in the conversion. Today, Kimie Reuarin is managing the online version of the course material. Almost weekly the course is being taught somewhere in the world, in conferences, private onsite courses, or in the form of the local mentoring project. As an example, next week the courseware will be taught in Orlando, Sydney and Honolulu. Zoe Dias takes the lead on getting the printed materials ready, and staffing the conferences with SANS Certified Instructors. Vicki Irwin of incidents.org fame also helped drive the content to the next level; Security Essentials must continue to improve.

I am thankful to have had the best spot in the house, watching this course grow. I have met a lot of wonderful people and know that together we are making a difference. I thank God for giving me the courage to work on this project. It is by far the most challenging project I have ever worked on. I missed out on a lot of sleep and way too many swims off the beaches of Kauai with my wife and son, but I feel it was and is worth the sacrifice. I know Eric Cole also put in very long hours with the tightest deadlines I have ever seen on a book project. Karen Kent, a co-author on several previous books, did the heavy lifting of getting this book created. Algis Kibirkstis took the lead on helping us remove some of the “Americanisms” in the book. He got involved late in the project, so there is more work in this area to be done, but we are learning.

The day is soon coming when it will be hard to be considered a credible information security practitioner without holding a GIAC Security Essentials Certification. This book is a very positive step forward in the evolution of the program. We care deeply about your experiences, what works for you, what doesn’t, and the things you know that we do not, so, don’t be a stranger.

Essentially yours,

—Stephen Northcutt
The SANS Institute

Section IV

Secure Communications

NOTES

Secure Communications

SANS Security Essentials IV

Secure Communications Agenda

SANS Security Essentials – Secure Communications

Chapter 19

Encryption 101

NOTES

Encryption 101

SANS Security Essentials IV:
Secure Communications

Encryption 101

Cryptography, the science of secret writing, helps us communicate without revealing information to adversaries and also protects our identities. It can protect any kind of data, from very sensitive information, such as Internet-based commerce and banking transactions, to harmless messages you would just rather no one else knew about, such as a letter to a friend. Strong cryptography, also referred to as crypto, can provide a great deal of protection. But it is not a silver bullet, and it can lead to a tremendous false sense of security unless used properly. Cryptography should always be a part of a larger defense-in-depth strategy, providing just one layer of the security onion.

NOTES

Course Objectives

- Case Studies
- The Challenge That We Face
- Cryptosystem Fundamentals
- Types of Cryptosystems
- Real-World Implementations

We will begin our study with some examples that illustrate the importance of sound cryptographic practices. We will then take a closer look at the basic reasons cryptography, despite its potential power, is easy to implement poorly. Then we will dive into the technical material with a discussion of how it all works, building a foundation for the cryptosystems covered in the next chapter. Finally, we will close by examining some cryptosystems we use in real life. But first, we will define some basic terms and discuss why every security professional should care about cryptography.

NOTES

What is Cryptography?

- Cryptography means "hidden writing."
- Encryption is coding a message in such a way that its meaning is concealed.
- Decryption is the process of transforming an encrypted message into its original form.
- Plaintext is a message in its original form.
- Ciphertext is a message in its encrypted form.

SANS Security Essentials – Secure Communications

Why Use Cryptography?

Cryptography is vitally important to information security. One of the main goals of cryptography is to help fend off eavesdroppers. The idea is that communicating over any kind of medium has the inherent risk that an unauthorized third party could be listening in, and we want to minimize that risk. So, in its most basic form, cryptography garbles text in such a way that anyone who intercepts the message cannot understand it. Although there are many ways to perform cryptography, most follow similar methodologies.

Nearly every cryptographic algorithm performs two distinct operations: encryption and decryption. *Encryption* is the practice of coding a message in such a way that its meaning is concealed. How the message is transformed depends on a mathematical formula called an *encryption algorithm* or a *cipher*. Once a message has been transformed with a cipher, the resulting message is called *ciphertext*. Since ciphertext contains the message in its encrypted form and not its native form, it is unintelligible. For the recipient of the ciphertext to read the message, the recipient must *decrypt* it. *Decryption* is the process of transforming an encrypted message back into its original *plaintext* or *cleartext* form.

Who creates these encryption algorithms? Computer scientists called *cryptographers*, who are well trained in several different fields of mathematics and usually work in groups, take many years to invent and refine ciphers. But with so much depending on cryptography, there are also individuals called *cryptanalysts*, who dedicate their lives to *breaking* ciphers. Some cryptanalysts work for the military and for governments; others are just interested in the study of ciphers and want to find weaknesses in ciphers to ensure they cannot be broken by others. The generic term for the study of both cryptography and cryptanalysis is called *cryptology*.

NOTES

Note

David Kahn's *The Code Breakers* is an excellent source that would give anyone a better appreciation for the field of cryptography. Starting with the Pharaohs, this book chronicles hidden writing throughout history. Cryptography has always been popular—perhaps one of history's most famous cryptographers was Julius Caesar, who invented the Caesar cipher. He used a basic substitution similar to the encryption schemes that are used on the back of some kids' cereal boxes. But cryptography has come a long way since then. An indisposable reference for modern ciphers and techniques is *Applied Cryptography: Protocols, Algorithms and Source Code in C* by Bruce Schneier. At over 750 pages, it is a comprehensive guide to modern algorithms and is written by someone who understands that the quality of a cryptosystem requires more than just a good algorithm.

NOTES

Why Do I Care About Crypto?

- It is part of a defense-in-depth strategy.
- It is a critical component and enabler of e-commerce / e-business.
- The "bad guys" are using it.
- Security professionals should keep abreast of cipher standards because they change and new weaknesses are found.

SANS Security Essentials – Secure Communications

Cryptography Motivation

Since cryptography is a critical component of information security, practitioners must be competent in its application. Bruce Schneier applies a fitting proverb to the study of cryptography: "The devil's in the details." Remember, one of the golden rules of information security is *Defense in-Depth*. Never rely on a single mechanism to protect the security of your site, but use several defense mechanisms in conjunction. A firewall is a good starting point, but it needs to be combined with good system administration practices, enforced policies, intrusion detection systems, virtual private networks, strong authentication, and encryption.

Listening to the news, you may have noticed how important cryptography has become. US encryption export regulations have been relaxed. The National Institute for Standards and Technology (NIST) announced the winning cipher for its Advanced Encryption Standard (AES). The patent on the popular RSA public-key cipher has expired. And the US Department of Commerce no longer supports the Data Encryption Standard (DES).

Almost every bank uses DES hardware to protect its financial transactions. These systems have been in place for years, and all of a sudden the encryption hardware is useless! What happened? Well, it was not all that sudden—plans have been available on the Internet for years to build near-real-time DES decryption engines. For $200,000, you can build your own out of Intel chips. Most criminals would agree that $200,000 is a worthwhile capital investment for stealing billions and billions of dollars. So perhaps the first target that comes to mind is the banks. How exposed are they?

Security professionals, especially those minding our money in the banks and any other institution, need to keep abreast of cryptography practices. In 1997, it became clear that high-priority targets were not safe when Rocke Verser, with the help of tens of thousands of Internet-connected computers, was able to decrypt a message encrypted with 56-bit DES. But even with all that power, the cryptanalysis took four months to complete, so DES still seemed safe. But in 1998, the Electronic Freedom Foundation's custom-built cracking engine broke the same cipher in 56 hours. Without a community of cryptographers seeking out stronger ciphers, we would be at the mercy of old, weak ciphers that no longer offer protection.

NOTES

Crypto and E-Commerce

Customers need to be sure that:

- They are communicating with the correct server.
- What they send is delivered unmodified.
- They can prove that they sent the message.
- Only the intended receiver can read the message.
- Message delivery is guaranteed.

Vendors need to be sure that:

- They are communicating with the right client.
- The content of the received message is correct.
- The identity of the author is unmistakable.
- Only the purported author could have written the message.
- They acknowledge receipt of the message.

SANS Security Essentials – Secure Communications

We demand secure communications for electronic commerce (e-commerce), government, military, diplomatic, and other applications. Cryptography is one of several technologies absolutely essential to e-commerce. In particular, cryptography helps to assure customers that:

- They are communicating with the correct server, not a spoofed one set up by an imposter.
- Messages they send are actually delivered.
- Messages cannot be altered without the recipient's knowledge.
- They can prove that someone else did not send messages they sent.
- Only the intended recipient can read the message.

Similarly, crypto helps assure e-commerce vendors that:

- They are communicating with the right client, not an imposter.
- The contents of the received message are correct and unaltered.
- There is no question about the identity of the sender.
- Only the individual purporting to be the author could have sent the message.

In the meantime, the underground uses cryptography to conceal their malicious activities. For instance, the Distributed Denial of Service (DDoS) network—protected by Blowfish, a scrambling algorithm—was used to attack numerous online businesses, such as Yahoo, and employed encryption to protect its covert communications channels. If the bad guys are using it to break into sites, shouldn't the good guys be using it to protect their sites? For defenders and attackers alike, the cyberscape of the new century will rely on cryptography.

Case Studies

Now that we have examined the basic principles of cryptography and our motivation from a security and privacy perspective for using cryptography, we will examine some case studies of how cryptography is used today. The next few sections will focus on specific situations that illustrate the importance of good practices in cryptography. First, we will review the lesson the recording industry learned the

NOTES

hard way when it invented a proprietary cipher implementation for DVDs. We will learn not to put our trust in large key lengths, even though they are generally stronger than small ones. Finally, we will take a quick look at cryptography's role in e-commerce.

NOTES

Security by Obscurity is No Security!

- Case-in-point: DVD "encryption"
- Proprietary algorithms are high risk.
- "Tamper-proof" hardware can be defeated with sufficient effort.
- Technical solutions usually do not satisfactorily address legal issues.

SANS Security Essentials – Secure Communications

The DVD Protection that Failed

Everyone loves DVDs. Never before have we been able to see our favorite movies in such breathtaking detail on our home televisions. But not everyone is aware of the lessons in cryptography best practices that lurk behind the scenes of DVD mania:

- Never believe in a secret or proprietary cryptographic algorithm (even if you work for the US National Security Agency). The algorithm will be eventually discovered, and if knowing the algorithm makes it trivial to decrypt a message without the appropriate key, all communications encrypted with that algorithm are compromised.
- Never rely on a single technology (or any other measure) as your only line of defense. Defense in-Depth is layering countermeasures for completeness and redundancy. Just encrypting everything is not enough.
- Above all, never attempt to write your own encryption system. There are plenty of superb algorithms with free implementations available. Unless you are a seasoned cryptographer, and you think you can improve on AES, Blowfish, RSA, etc., do not bother trying.

So what happened with DVDs? The motion picture industry spent years secretly developing its own standard for encryption—the Contents Scrambling System (CSS). CSS attempted to prevent unauthorized duplication of DVDs by encrypting the data on the DVDs. Each DVD included a key that could be used to decrypt the data and a hash (fixed-length value computed from the plaintext) to verify that the data was correctly decrypted. That key was encrypted and could only be decrypted with one of the player keys, which were built into every DVD player. Instead of submitting the CSS standard for review, which would have taken advantage of the collective brainpower of cryptologists worldwide, they implemented the standard themselves, and released a product (DVDs) that relied on the cipher.

According to Frank Stevenson, who published a cryptanalysis of CSS in November 1999, the cipher was designed with a 40-bit key length (inadequate in itself) to meet US export regulations. However, only 225 keys are necessary in a brute-force attack. He estimates it would take less than 18 seconds on a 450 MHz PC to recover a disk key from the hash. According to Stevenson, "If the cipher was intended to get security by remaining secret, this is yet another testament to the fact that security through obscurity is an unworkable principle."

NOTES

Soon after, a couple of technologists, Canman and SoupaFr0g, decoded that magic algorithm and released a program that became very popular. DeCSS 1.2b pulls the decrypted data off the DVD disk and stores it so it can be played like any other multimedia file. Don't want to pay $20 for a movie DVD? No problem! Just "borrow" it from a friend. And what can the movie industry do now? Sue Canman and SoupaFr0g for quadrillions of dollars?

Professional cryptanalysts spend their time looking for tiny flaws and often tinier clues in encrypted messages, so as to break the cipher. Canman was a very good amateur, and he broke an under-scrutinized crypto algorithm. For an algorithm to be good, it has to be objectively examined by people whose job it is to find flaws. The motion picture industry thought they would be clever, but with crypto, clever it is not sufficient. There is no substitute for public scrutiny of a cipher.

NOTES

Beware of Overconfidence

- Case-in-point: Large key lengths
- Simply using popular cryptographic algorithms with large key lengths does not make your system secure.
- What's the weakest link?
- Cryptanalytic compromises usually originate from totally unexpected places.

SANS Security Essentials – Secure Communications

Large Key Lengths May Not be Key

Our second case study explores the risks of being overly confident of cryptographic solutions. All aspects of cryptosystems are subject to attack, especially the keys. Despite their importance, keys are seldom adequately protected. There are many situations that threaten key integrity. Once a workstation is compromised (or under surveillance by the FBI or other law enforcement), capturing keystrokes is trivial. A faulty cipher implementation may temporarily expose keys. But perhaps the most likely cause of key compromise is the tendency of humans to fail to protect their keys, storing them on sticky pieces of paper under the keyboard or blurting them out to anyone who telephones and claims to be with "Security" or "Technical Support."

In 1998, Stephen Northcutt served as the technical analyst to support a team of law enforcement agents to detect, investigate, apprehend, and convict a child pornographer. Interestingly, the perpetrator used cryptography to transmit the data right past Northcutt's intrusion detection systems (IDS). Since IDS uses pattern matching to detect anomalies, the encrypted data did not trigger any warnings.

How did he get caught? It was not hard. The first clue was that too much data was being transmitted. Top talkers on a network are conspicuous. The next clue is that even though the encrypted traffic slipped by the IDS, it *does* have a signature: white noise. You can detect an encrypted byte stream simply by counting the bytes that are the same. An even distribution indicates random, and therefore probably encrypted, data. A good encryption algorithm enforces randomness to be resistant to known-plaintext and chosen-plaintext attacks (explained further in this chapter). But if you examine the *content*, the payload data in a normal connection, it is probably anything but random. So detection was easy. How did Northcutt detect the cryptography?

At this point, the law enforcement agents were ready to give up and bring in the suspect for questioning, assuming they could not possibly recover the cleartext data. But by examining other machines the suspect was using, Northcutt eventually found the key hard-coded in cleartext. Game over! Key-protection discipline is everything in this sport.

NOTES

Simplicity is a "Good Thing"

- Case-in-point: E-commerce / E-business
- Morphing your business into an online business can be a complex undertaking.
- Taking shortcuts in **any** aspect of the development of your e-commerce systems can introduce weak links.
- Security is a "process"...not a product.

SANS Security Essentials – Secure Communications

Think about the Weakest Link

Any security solution is only as strong as its weakest link, so it is important for cryptography to be designed and implemented with as high a degree of quality as possible. The US military uses cryptography developed by the National Security Agency (NSA) for all classified and some additional communications. NSA provides more than just encryption hardware—they provide the keys and the rules. They have developed an entire cryptosystem infrastructure because they know there is more to protected communications than cryptanalysis-resistant algorithms.

Then there are the rest of us, many of whom strive to take our business online and offer a ".com" business avenue. Traditional catalog retailers are rushing to establish an Internet presence, universities to offer online courses and exams, and so on. Just like the previous example of the criminal investigation, a number of things can go wrong when protecting information in transit and at rest. Cryptography provides us with a suite of tools that can help us with *confidentiality*, *integrity*, *authentication*, and *non-repudiation* (we will examine these later). Somehow, people feel safer when using HTTPS—a more secure protocol—rather than HTTP, and are more willing to use their credit cards. But consider the clerical worker earning minimum wage to process all the orders at the end of the day with access to thousands of credit card numbers. It is probably less likely that an attacker will sniff your network connection than bribe or threaten that clerical worker.

The moral: Security is accomplished through technologies or products you deploy once and forget about, and by creating systems and processes that are ongoing. Encryption needs to be built into systems and processes from the beginning—not tacked on later. Secure Sockets Layer (SSL) technology alone is no substitute for a comprehensive security system. Security involves the whole system—the processes, human behaviors, and risk management, as well as infrastructure. It is a never-ending activity.

Credit Cards Over the Internet

- Case-in-point: How many people will use their credit cards to buy merchandise on the Internet? How many people will pay for a meal with a credit card?
- Which is riskier?
  - Perception vs. reality
- Real risk is back-end database that possibly stores credit cards unencrypted.
- Understanding the threat is key.

SANS Security Essentials – Secure Communications

Credit Card Numbers Over the Internet

If you ask a classroom of adult US students how many of them use their credit cards to buy merchandise over the Internet, approximately 60 to 70 percent would raise their hands. If you then asked how many would pay for a meal in a restaurant with a credit card, usually at least 90 percent of the class responds. Is paying for a meal more secure? Actually, no. It is just that people have been doing it for longer and for smaller amounts, so they perceive it to be more secure. But perception and reality can be two different things.

Let's examine these two scenarios. The next time you pay for a meal with a credit card, look down at your watch when the waitperson takes your card to process it. Normally, a total stranger takes your card into a back room and returns a few minutes later—long enough to secretly copy down your number. When the waitperson scans your credit card at the terminal, your number can be stored there for up to a week! Anyone with access to that terminal can retrieve your credit card information, and if you left a signed receipt, they have your signature, too.

On the other hand, when you buy something on the Internet, you enter the credit card information from the comfort of your own home, and the chance of someone intercepting it as it traverses the Internet is very slim. Even if someone does, the data is encrypted (when using SSL), so an attacker would not be able to read it.

Another threat to using credit cards in either scenario is associated with how the numbers are stored once the credit card company receives them. Many e-commerce businesses claim your information is secure because they use SSL to protect the data. That might be true, but maybe they store it in plaintext on an Internet-connected server. An attacker can try to intercept an encrypted number, which would take a lot of work (if not an infinite amount of time) to crack. If successful, the attacker would have access to one credit card. Or, the attacker could break into the server—possibly much easier—and gain access to many, many credit cards.

NOTES

NOTES

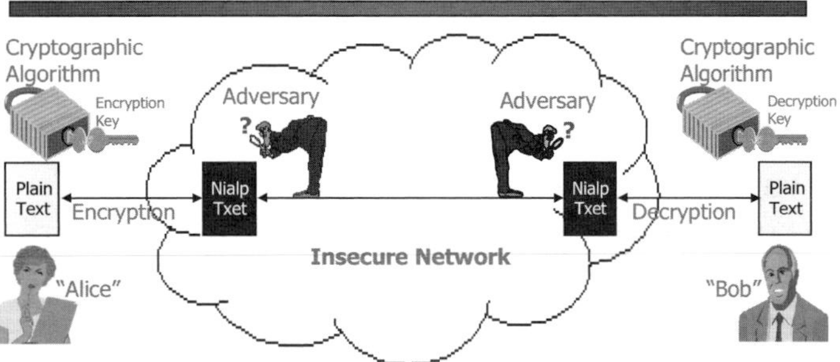

The Challenge that We Face

So far, we have discussed the need for cryptography and introduced practical applications in our case studies. We will now take a closer look at what are the real user requirements.

The diagram portrays the challenge of communicating over an insecure network. Alice and Bob wish to exchange information securely. Their cipher is built on basic transformations, permutations, and substitutions. The result of the cipher is that the message is transformed so that without knowledge of the cipher and the key system, it is unreadable. They hope.

The User's Perspective...

The diagram implies that Alice and Bob have successfully navigated the real-world challenges of incompatible systems, different algorithms, key management, personnel training, and behavior. These issues are especially prone to occur with inter-company (and even inter-division) communications, and require forethought and coordination.

Both Alice and Bob have a number of requirements, but let's restate one of them: The algorithm used must be a well-known, established, scrutinized, tested, accepted method of encryption. When a programmer who is also a wanna-be cryptographer implements an inferior cryptosystem and includes it in a vended product, most consumers using it unwittingly think it is secure. Even security vendors are guilty—one very popular firewall product has a proprietary cipher. By learning about the major systems, we can help avoid false assumptions and claims. Using a proper algorithm is your responsibility as an educated consumer. When you do choose your approach to encryption, you take something on faith—that an adversary listening on an untrusted network cannot intercept your communications, reverse-engineer your key, and recover your original information. A one-way mathematical function makes any attacker's job difficult. If we have message x, we can compute $f(x)$, but if the attacker has $f(x)$, it should be very hard to retrieve x. The concern is whether the one-way function really is computationally difficult to reverse.

NOTES

NOTES

Goals of Cryptography

- "Alice" and "Bob" need a cryptosystem which can provide them with:

Confidentiality	Integrity of Data
Authentication	Non-repudiation

- *"Cryptography is about communications in the presence of adversaries" (Rivest, 1990)*

SANS Security Essentials – Secure Communications

Like many of us, Alice does not care *how* the cryptography works, as long as it works. She needs to send a message to Bob with the same level of integrity it would have if she walked up and handed it to him. In addition to being unreadable by adversaries (*confidentiality*), we may have the following requirements:

- Authentication: If Alice walks up to Bob and hands him a message, he positively knows the message is from Alice. Alice may require the cryptosystem to provide an equivalent service for her—Bob must hand deliver messages to her.
- Integrity: It should be possible to prove the message has not been tampered with, that this message is exactly the same as the one Alice sent to Bob.
- Non-repudiation: The system should be able to prove that Alice, and only Alice, sent the message and that it has not been falsified or subsequently altered. In essence, this is a requirement that both authentication and integrity be provable.

The technology to do this is available, but for this system to work in practice, the non-technical issues are also important. Alice and every user of the system must be trained in its use and its limitations and have access to the keys, yet keep them protected and current. Processes must be as foolproof as practical. Think about *social engineering*, human error, and operator efficiency, accuracy, and understanding.

Basic Terms

We already defined the four most common cryptographic terms: *encryption*, *decryption*, *plaintext*, and *ciphertext*. Encryption and decryption must use the same algorithm. Those operations are also managed by the choice of the *key*. It is the key that changes periodically (for example, daily, hourly, or per-message) so that the same algorithm can be used for years on end while communications remain secure. We will discuss key length in detail later in this chapter; in general, longer keys are more secure from attack than shorter keys.

In the following discussion, weaknesses with crypto schemes will be mentioned. While this is not a focus of the chapter, there are several ways to defeat even a good crypto algorithm, including to exhaustively search every possible key or to exploit a mathematical weakness in the algorithm.

One common attack on crypto algorithms is a *brute-force attack*, whereby the analyst tries every possible key (the *keyspace*) to see if a meaningful message emerges from some ciphertext. This type of attack is feasible with short keys; a key length of 40 bits translates to about a trillion (2^40) possible keys, a keyspace that is easily searched by a modern computer in just hours. Long keys make this type of attack fruitless because it may take years to find the key.

Many crypto algorithms never find their way into products or common use because they are found to be mathematically weak. Once a mathematical flaw is found, a cryptanalyst will exploit it to weaken the crypto scheme. One famous example of this is the Enigma cipher, used by the Germans during World War II. The Enigma machines had several million possible keys, far too many to search by brute-force methods at the time. But Enigma had several flaws. For example, when encrypting a given character, it never produced the same character as ciphertext. This and other weaknesses provided sufficient clues to cryptanalysts, making brute-force attacks feasible.

One last comment is due. In general, one never wants to encrypt multiple messages using the same key. It is important, therefore, to change keys often, particularly if the algorithm uses short keys.

The Players

In this chapter, we have followed the convention of assigning human names to the participants in secure communications. We give the names "Alice" and "Bob" to two communicating parties.

Although these names personalize our situations involving crypto, we need to remember they are just metaphors. While we might say, "Alice decides to use crypto algorithm X," keep in mind that users of crypto rarely make these kinds of deliberate, conscious choices. Alice probably bought some crypto product that selects a cipher from a set of available ones. The point is that users are generally not encumbered with the details of the cryptography.

Essential Mathematics

Now we turn our attention from Alice and Bob to bits and bytes. Cryptography is a mathematical specialty that includes aspects of probability theory, information theory, complexity theory, number theory, abstract algebra, and more. Our discussion of crypto, however, will not require delving into these fields. Nevertheless, there are a few mathematical operations that are necessary for understanding our subsequent discussion, namely the OR, exclusive OR (XOR), and modulo functions. These are discussed in the following sections.

NOTES

NOTES

Digital Substitution

(Encryption)

21- Bit Key
1010011 1010010 1001110

\+ Plaintext in ASCII
C = 1000011
A = 1000001
T = 1010100

1010011 1010010 1001110
1000011 1000001 1010100

0010000 0010011 0011010

XOR Operation:

0 if the compared bits are the same

1 if they are different

SANS Security Essentials – Secure Communications

Symmetric encryption

OR and Exclusive OR

George Boole, a mathematician in the late 1800s, invented a form of logic algebra that provides the basis for electronic computers and microprocessor chips. His logical operations were a set of *truth tables*, in which each of the inputs and outputs were either TRUE or FALSE.

The Boolean Exclusive OR (XOR) function is one of the fundamental operations used in cryptography. The output of an XOR is TRUE if exactly one of the inputs is TRUE; otherwise the output is FALSE. For example:

- "The sky is blue XOR the world is flat" is TRUE.
- "The sky is blue XOR the world is round" is FALSE.

Computations require numbers, so we use 0 and 1 instead of TRUE and FALSE. The output of an XOR operation (denoted by the ⊕ symbol) is 0 if both inputs are the same, and the output is a 1 if the two inputs differ.

These properties of XOR make it very useful to cryptographers for two reasons. First, any value XORed with itself is 0 ($0 \oplus 0 = 0$, $1 \oplus 1 = 0$). Second, any value XORed with 0 is just itself ($0 \oplus 0 = 0$, $1 \oplus 0 = 1$). Why are these properties important? Consider the following example.

Suppose Alice has a secret message to send to Bob, comprising the three-character message "Buy". This translates to a standard 7-bit ASCII bit stream as:

1000010 1110101 1111001

Now, suppose that Alice and Bob have already shared the following 21-bit secret key:

0101101 1100111 1000101

Alice converts the plaintext into ciphertext by XORing the message with the key:

```
  1000010 1110101 1111001
⊕ 0101101 1100111 1000101
  ======= ======= =======
  1101111 0010010 0111100
```

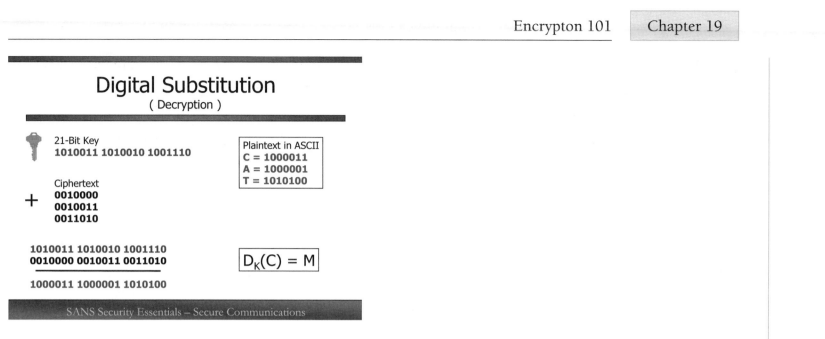

NOTES

Digital Substitution

(Decryption)

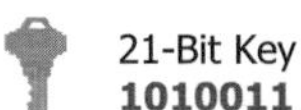

21-Bit Key
1010011 1010010 1001110

Plaintext in ASCII
C = 1000011
A = 1000001
T = 1010100

\+ Ciphertext
0010000
0010011
0011010

1010011 1010010 1001110
0010000 0010011 0011010

1000011 1000001 1010100

$D_K(C) = M$

SANS Security Essentials – Secure Communications

Bob receives the ciphertext from Alice and, in turn, XORs it with the secret key:

  1101111 0010010 0111100

⊕ 0101101 1100111 1000101

  ======= ======= =======

  1000010 1110101 1111001

The recovered plaintext is Alice's original message. So XOR naturally acts as a cipher: The original message XORed with a key yields a jumble of bits; XORing that jumble with the key again yields the original message.

Another Boolean function sometimes seen in cryptography is OR. The output of an OR is TRUE if either of the inputs is TRUE; otherwise the output is FALSE. Using binary digits, the output is a 1 if either or both inputs are a 1; the output is a 0 only if both inputs are 0.

Digital Substitution

(Your Turn)

21-Bit Key
1010011 1010010 1001110

Plaintext in ASCII
+ **D = 1000100**
O = 1001111
G = 1000111

XOR Operation:

0 if the compared bits are the same

1 if they are different

1010011 1010010 1001110
1000100 1001111 1000111

SANS Security Essentials – Secure Communications

Modulo Arithmetic

Many of the mathematical operations in cryptography are based on modulo arithmetic. The modulo function is, simply, the remainder function. It is commonly used in programming and is an important operation in crypto algorithms. To calculate “X modulo Y” (usually written “X mod Y”), you merely determine the remainder of Y divided by X. The value X mod Y will be in the range from 0 to Y-1.

Here are some examples of the modulo operator in action:

- 15 mod 7 = 1
- 25 mod 5 = 0
- 33 mod 12 = 9
- 203 mod 256 = 203

Modulo arithmetic is useful in crypto because it ensures that numbers never get too large. This property is important when using computers with registers of limited size that would overflow for large numbers. Modulo arithmetic is used by various encryption techniques, as you shall see shortly.

NOTES

General Encryption Techniques

- Goal: Garble the original message so its meaning is concealed.
- Basic techniques:
  - Substitution
  - Permutation
  - Hybrid
- These techniques are used by single-key systems.

SANS Security Essentials – Secure Communications

Essential Operations

The main goal of encryption is to garble text so someone cannot understand it. Two basic methods of encrypting or garbling text are *substitution* and *permutation*. A third approach is actually a hybrid, a mixture of both. There are also two basic types of key encryption systems, one-key and two-key systems. The first methods we will discuss are for one-key systems. As you will see later, two-key systems are much more complex. In this section, you will learn that one-key systems are very effective, despite being based on high school mathematics.

NOTES

Arbitrary Substitution

- Uses a one-to-one substitution of characters.
- Replace x with y
- For example:
  - A B C D E.....
  - W K M P D.....
  - So CAB becomes MWK
- Very easy to break using character frequency analysis

SANS Security Essentials – Secure Communications

Substitution

Substitution involves exchanging one character (or byte) for another. Simple substitution schemes use mapping so that one character would be substituted with another character to encrypt a message, with decryption being the inverse action. The mapping function is the key—that is, anyone who knows how the characters were mapped to encrypt the message can decrypt the message.

Consider a very simple example. Suppose we define the following mapping (only a portion of the alphabet is shown):

Plaintext: A B C D E ...

Ciphertext: W K M P D ...

To encrypt the word "CAB", Alice would substitute characters and send the string "MWK". Bob, in turn, would reverse the substitution to recover the plaintext.

For substitution to work, there has to be a unique one-to-one mapping from plaintext character to ciphertext character. A many-to-one or one-to-many mapping would make decryption difficult or impossible. For example, if both A and C were replaced with W, you would still be able to encrypt the message, so CAB would become WWK. But now when we tried to decrypt it, we would not know if the W should be an A or a C since they are both mapped to the same letter.

Rotation Substitution

- Also uses a one-to-one substitution of characters. Also very easy to break.
- "Rotate" the alphabet by *N* characters.
- Easy to remember. For example:
  - Plaintext: A B C D E.....
  - Ciphertext: D E F G H.....
  - So "CAB" becomes "FDE"
- Caesar Cipher was ROT-3.
- USENET uses ROT-13 (symmetric).

SANS Security Essentials – Secure Communications

An alternate substitution method that does not require mapping is *rotation*. In this type of substitution, we shift every character a set number of spaces. For example, if we shift A three spaces, it becomes D, B becomes E, and so on. The Caesar Cipher, invented by Julius Caesar to encode messages to his generals, is a famous rotation cipher. If Alice were using this "ROT-3" scheme, she would encrypt her message as "FDE". In its day (roughly 50-60 BC), the Caesar Cipher was considered good enough to fool almost anyone because very few people could read, even fewer could write, and couriers would rather kill a snooper than let him capture a message. Caesar was no fool, though—he did not use just one encryption tool. He also transliterated Latin into Greek and used other forms of subterfuge.

Though many people believe the Caesar cipher is the earliest cipher, cryptography actually goes back nearly 2000 years earlier to ancient Egypt and China. For more information, look at the Crypto Timeline found at `http://emmy.nmsu.edu/crypto/public_html/Timeline.html`.

Although character rotation is a trivial scheme, rotation ciphers came back into vogue in the early 1980s, primarily in the form of ROT-13. Shortly after USENET newsgroups and electronic mailing lists became popular, subscribers realized they did not always want to see the contents of a message. Some messages contained jokes that might offend some subscribers. Other messages might contain riddles or puzzles complete with answers that the recipients may not have wanted to see before reading the riddle or puzzle.

The answer was to encrypt (or obscure) jokes and answers using ROT-13. ROT-13 was never meant to be a strong cipher—it is trivially breakable. The point was for the reader to make a deliberate effort to decipher the message. No one could later claim accidental discovery, nor could anyone ruin a puzzle by accidentally glimpsing at the solution. ROT-13 eventually became part of newsreader software and a common function of the UNIX operating system. ROT-13 had another nice feature. Because there are 26 letters in the English alphabet, ROT-13 is a symmetric operation; the same implementation will both encode plaintext and decode ciphertext.

These one-to-one forms of character substitution are very weak because they can be defeated with frequency analysis. Cryptanalysts long ago made tables showing the relative frequency with which

NOTES

NOTES

letters, letter pairs (*bigraphs*), and letter triples (*trigraphs*) appear in a variety of languages. In all character-based languages, some letters occur with a greater frequency than others. In the English language, the letter "E" occurs approximately 13% of the time, and the letter "T" occurs approximately 9.3% of the time (see `http://www.trincoll.edu/depts/cpsc/cryptography/caesar.html` for details on this and other ciphers, and `http://www-math.cudenver.edu/~wcherowi/courses/m5410/exsubcip.html` for a tutorial on how to crack them). So by looking at the enciphered message, we can see which letter appears more often than most, and assume that the enciphered letter is an "E". The next most frequently occurring letter would probably be a "T", and so on. By looking at letter pairs (instead of just single letters), we can achieve an even more accurate guess.

Another flaw with substitution encryption is its predictability. If you use only one set of substitution rules, the encrypted message is easy to crack. Cryptographers responded by inventing more complicated substitution schemes.

Permutation

- Keeps the same letters, but changes the position within the text.
- Change the order from `xyz` to `zxy`.
- For example:
  - Change `1 2 3 4 5` to `3 5 2 1 4`
  - So `order` becomes `drroe`
- Very easy to break.
- Substitution and permutation can be combined together.

SANS Security Essentials – Secure Communications

Permutation

Permutation, also called *transposition*, shuffles the order in which characters (or bytes) appear rather than substituting one for another. Consider this simple example. Suppose that Alice and Bob chose the key word "SCUBA" to determine the character permutation order. If we alphabetize the letters in the key word, we obtain the string "ABCSU". Since "A is the first letter, it is assigned the number 1 and "U" is assigned the number 5; the string "43521" then determines the way in which we will move around letters. Alice takes her message, breaks it into blocks of five characters (since that is the length of the key word), and then moves the characters within each block accordingly. If Alice wanted to send the message:

DINNER TONIGHT OK

she would encrypt it into the following ciphertext:

NNEID NOITR OTKHG

Unfortunately, permutation is also relatively easy to break. Remember, however, that while a few thousand or million combinations is nothing for a computer, it can defeat an adversary using pencil and paper. Today's computer-based methods still use substitution and permutation, but in combination, applied many times. Let's take a look at the mechanics of current encryption methods.

NOTES

NOTES

Ways to Encrypt Data

- Two general ways to encrypt information:
  - Break the data into blocks and encrypt each block
  - Encrypt the entire stream on a bit-by-bit basis

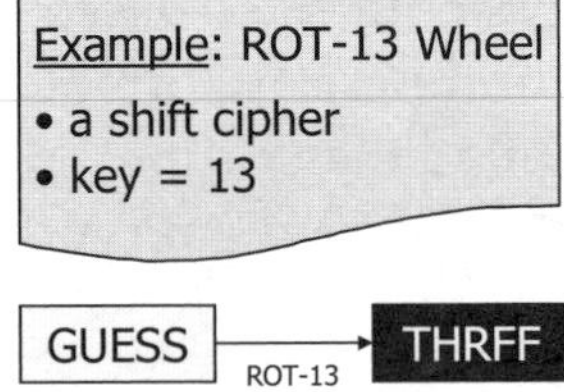

SANS Security Essentials – Secure Communications

Ways to Encrypt Data

There are two ways to manipulate the data while encrypting and decrypting: you can break up the data into blocks and encrypt each block, or you can encrypt a stream bit–by–bit (or byte–by–byte). Hence, crypto schemes are generally classified as either *stream ciphers* or *block ciphers*, depending on how much information they manage at once and how the key is generated.

NOTES

Stream Ciphers

- A "keystream" is generated first; successive plaintext elements are encrypted using elements of *keystream.*
- Good for real time audio and video.

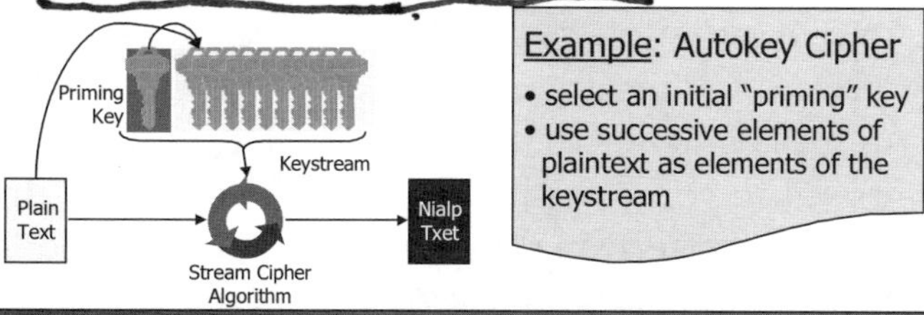
Priming Key
Keystream
Plain Text
Stream Cipher Algorithm
Nialp Txet
Example: Autokey Cipher
• select an initial "priming" key
• use successive elements of plaintext as elements of the keystream

SANS Security Essentials – Secure Communications

Stream Ciphers

Stream ciphers operate on a single bit, byte, or (computer) word at one time and implement some form of feedback mechanism so that the key is constantly changing. Ideally, the key in a stream cipher is at least as long as the plaintext being encrypted.

A *keystream* is generated first at both the sending and receiving ends. Both ends must be kept in synchronization with each other and produce identical keystreams. The keystreams also must be unpredictable by an outside observer; therefore, they must use keys. At the sending end, the keystream and plaintext stream are merged (for example, using XOR) to produce a stream of ciphertext that is transmitted. At the receiving end, the identical keystream is extracted from the ciphertext stream, recreating the original plaintext stream. Stream ciphers are highly dependent on the randomness of the keystream, and have vulnerabilities to noise during transmission. Imagine a bit being dropped or an extra bit being inserted during transmission!

While there are a variety of stream ciphers, two are worth mentioning here. An *auto key* or *self-synchronizing* stream cipher calculates each bit in the keystream as a function of the previous N bits in the keystream. It is named for its ability to keep the decryption process synchronized with the encryption process merely by knowing how far it is into the N-bit keystream. One problem is error propagation; a garbled bit in transmission will result in N garbled bits at the receiving end.

Synchronous stream ciphers generate the keystream in a fashion independent of the message stream by using the same keystream generation function at both ends. It is important that the key generation function appears unpredictable to an eavesdropper.

Stream ciphers are not the most commonly used scheme today in strong cryptographic applications. For that reason, only one example of stream ciphers is offered next, before we discuss block ciphers, which are far more prevalent today than stream ciphers.

NOTES

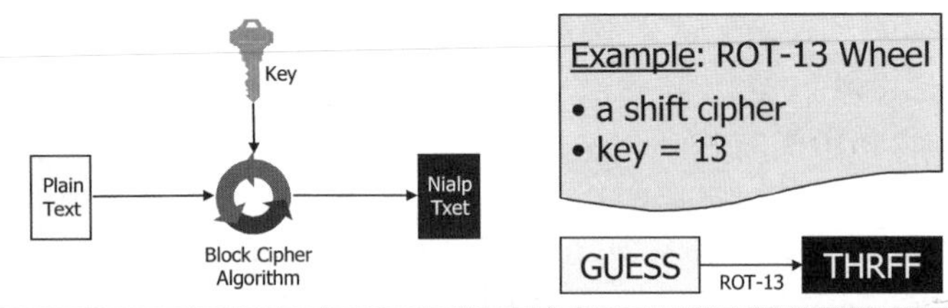
Block Ciphers
• Successive plaintext elements are encrypted using the *same* key.
– E.g., Caesar Cipher, Shift Cipher, Substitution Cipher, Vigenere Cipher, Permutation (Transposition) Cipher
Key
Plain Text
Block Cipher Algorithm
Nialp Txet
Example: ROT-13 Wheel
• a shift cipher
• key = 13
GUESS
ROT-13
THRFF
SANS Security Essentials – Secure Communications

Block Ciphers

Most crypto schemes used today are *block ciphers*, meaning that the scheme encrypts one block of data at a time. Block ciphers can operate in one of several modes. The *mode* you select for a block cipher directly affects the strength and performance of the cryptosystem. The following four modes are the most important:

- Electronic Codebook (ECB) mode is the simplest, most obvious application; the key is used to encrypt the plaintext block to form a ciphertext block. Two identical plaintext blocks will always generate the same ciphertext block. Although this is the most common mode of block ciphers, it is susceptible to a variety of brute-force attacks.
- Cipher Block Chaining (CBC) mode adds a feedback mechanism to the encryption scheme. In CBC, the plaintext is XORed with the previous ciphertext block prior to encryption. In this mode, two identical blocks of plaintext never encrypt to the same ciphertext.
- Cipher Feedback (CFB) mode is a block cipher implementation as a self-synchronizing stream cipher. CFB mode allows data to be encrypted in units smaller than the block size, which is useful in some applications, such as encrypting interactive terminal input. A 1-byte CFB mode, for example, would place each incoming character into a shift register the same size as the block, encrypt the character, and send the block. At the receiving end, the ciphertext is decrypted and the extra bits in the block (that is, everything above and beyond the one byte) are discarded.
- Output Feedback (OFB) mode is a block cipher implementation conceptually similar to a synchronous stream cipher. OFB prevents the same plaintext block from generating the same ciphertext block by using an internal feedback mechanism that is independent of both the plaintext and ciphertext bit streams.

Block ciphers can be implemented as stream ciphers and vice versa; the difference is how you apply the cipher. If you have a hardware device, such as a hardware-based Virtual Private Network (VPN), streaming ciphers are easy to implement in hardware and may be ideal, especially for never-ending streams, such as communications links. If the encryption is accomplished in software, such as encrypting a file, block ciphers will be much more efficient. To implement stream ciphers in software requires a tremendous amount of bit masking, which can result in programmer errors and performance penalties.

With block ciphers, plaintext is broken into fixed-length blocks (often 64-bit) and processed one block at a time. As necessary, the last block may be padded. A fixed transformation—same algorithm and key—is applied to each block. Typically, a considerable number of repetitive operations are performed on each block. For most algorithms, the same key is used to encrypt each block at the sending end and to decrypt each block at the receiving end. At the receiving end, the blocks are decrypted (often a nearly identical process as encryption) one block at a time, using the same algorithm and key on each block, to recreate the original plaintext.

The Data Encryption Standard (DES) is a very common block cipher. It uses 64-bit blocks and a 56-bit key. In 1976, the US government adopted DES, followed by the International Standards Organization (ISO) 11 years later. It has been used worldwide for financial transactions ever since.

NOTES

NOTES

Goals of Cryptography

- "Alice" and "Bob" need a cryptosystem which can provide them with:

Confidentiality	Integrity of Data
Authentication	Non-repudiation

- *"Cryptography is about communications in the presence of adversaries"* *(Rivest, 1990)*

SANS Security Essentials – Secure Communications

Modern Cryptographic Algorithms

Now that you know the basics of cryptographic methods, you are ready to examine the characteristics and qualities, good and bad, of modern cryptographic algorithms. Remember that no cryptographic algorithm is known to be totally secure (except for a one-time pad with truly random data). Our first case study discussed a well-known cryptosystem that was defeated. The strength of a cryptosystem is its ability to withstand attacks. There are a number of attacks against cryptosystems, most of which use some piece of known unencrypted information (*known plaintext*). A trustworthy algorithm is one that can withstand an attack when the cryptanalyst knows or can choose the text to be encrypted. The latter is known as a *chosen plaintext* attack.

The strongest statement we can make regarding our trust in a cryptographic algorithm is that it is not yet known to have been broken! You can prove that a system is not secure—you just cannot prove that it *is* secure.

Today's cryptographic methods and cryptosystems use all of the functions, methods, and modes discussed earlier. We are particularly concerned with providing secure communications and transactions on the Internet, so today's crypto schemes have a number of necessary functions:

- *Authentication*: The process of proving one's identity. Traditional host-to-host authentication schemes on the Internet were name-based or address-based, both of which are notoriously weak because they can be easily spoofed or imitated. If you think you are communicating with a specific Internet company, you should be able to authenticate that you are really communicating with them, not a perpetrator spoofing their site.
- *Message integrity*: Assuring the receiver that the message has not been altered in any way from the original.
- *Non-repudiation*: Mechanism to prove that the sender really sent the message so that the sender cannot later deny sending it. This attribute is critical for the success of e-commerce. If I electronically order 50 widgets at $100 each, and five days later the market drops on widgets so that now I can get the same widget for $1 each, I might deny I ever sent the order or specified that quantity. For e-commerce to work, the supplier

NOTES

must be able to prove I actually sent the order in such a matter that I cannot deny it.

- *Privacy/confidentiality*: This is the classic reason for crypto: ensuring that no one can read the message except the intended receiver(s).

Another function of cryptography, but one that is not obvious, is that of key exchange. In the earlier discussion, the fact that Alice and Bob had to share a key before any secret message could be exchanged was mentioned several times. As it happens, the key exchange problem is a huge one—one solution is to use crypto to exchange crypto keys.

NOTES

Types of Cryptosystems

- 3 general types of crypto algorithms:
  - Secret Key
    - Symmetric
    - Single or 1-key encryption
  - Public Key
    - Asymmetric
    - Dual or 2-key encryption
  - Hash
    - One-way transformation
    - No key encryption

SANS Security Essentials – Secure Communications

Types of Cryptosystems

In today's cryptosystems, there are three general types of crypto algorithms: *secret key* or *symmetric*, *public key* or *asymmetric*, and the *hash*.

Each is used because they provide a different function from other algorithms. These schemes are usually distinguished from one another by the number of keys employed. The remainder of this section will discuss these different types of algorithms.

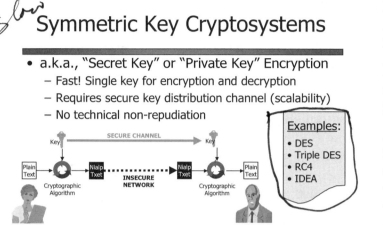

Symmetric Key Cryptosystems

- a.k.a., "Secret Key" or "Private Key" Encryption
  - Fast! Single key for encryption and decryption
  - Requires secure key distribution channel (scalability)
  - No technical non-repudiation

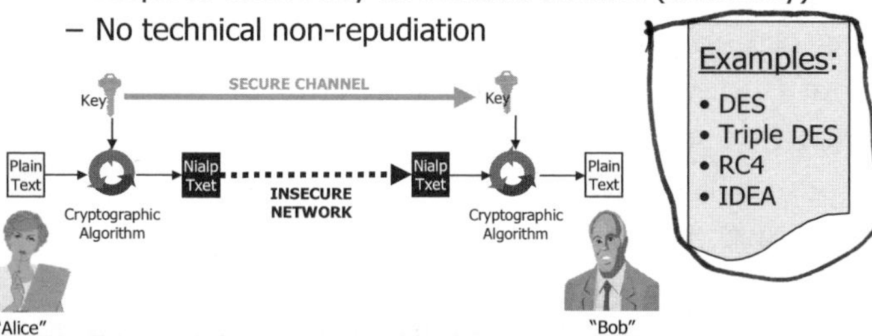

SANS Security Essentials – Secure Communications

Secret Key Cryptography

Secret key cryptography (SKC) uses a single key for both encryption and decryption; this key is the shared secret between sender and receiver. Because SKC uses only one key for both encryption and decryption, it is also called *symmetric cryptography*. The primary application of SKC is privacy, where only the parties with the key can encrypt and decrypt messages for each other.

Given an adequate SKC algorithm, the basic attack is brute force. Until 1998, this has mostly been a joke and the product of a few Internet research efforts to harness loosely coupled parallel attacks. Now anyone with a six-figure budget can build a specialized DES cracker. Those willing to attack systems and steal their computing power may not even need money! The RingZero and the DDoS attacks of February 2000 beg the question, "If an encrypted message were worth, say, $20 million, and you could assign, say, a thousand Trojanized zombie systems to work on the problem, how long would the symmetric key length need to be?" In 1997, a 40-bit RSA challenge key fell in 3.5 hours using 250 computers. Keep Moore's law in mind—computating power doubles every 18 months. So 40 bits is inadequate for today's threat model.

All that said, the bigger issue with secret keys is managing the key creation and exchange to avoid key compromise. Also, the greater the number of parties that share the secret key, the greater the exposure of the key. Bottom line: Because symmetric-key cryptosystems are so much faster than asymmetric-key systems but lack the latter's key management and digital signatures, the two are often combined to achieve the best of both worlds.

There are a number of SKC schemes in common use today, all believed to be mathematically strong. If a cryptanalyst cannot defeat the ciphers by finding a weakness in the mathematical algorithms, then the remaining approach is a brute-force attack to guess all possible keys. In SKC, key size does matter, as explained in a paper by Matt Blaze, Whitfield Diffie, Ron Rivest, Bruce Schneier, and others in the cryptographic community. The paper, *Minimal Key Lengths for Symmetric Ciphers to Provide Adequate Commercial Security* (`http://www.counterpane.com/keylength.html`), describes brute-force attacks that are within the cost and computing means of a variety of attackers, and the key lengths necessary to keep such attackers at bay.

Examples of SKC schemes in common use today are the Advanced Encryption Standard (AES), Blowfish, the Data Encryption Standard (DES), Triple DES, and the International Data Encryption Algorithm (IDEA).

NOTES

NOTES

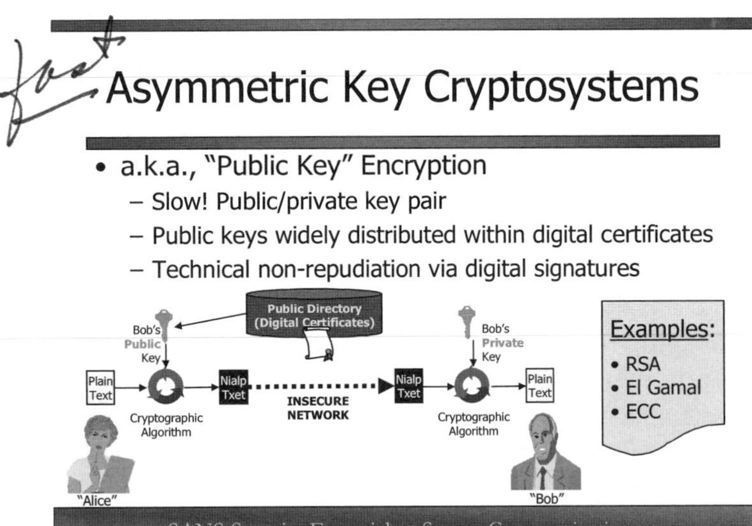
Asymmetric Key Cryptosystems
• a.k.a., "Public Key" Encryption
– Slow! Public/private key pair
– Public keys widely distributed within digital certificates
– Technical non-repudiation via digital signatures
Public Directory (Digital Certificates)
Bob's Public Key
Bob's Private Key
Plain Text
Nialp Txet
INSECURE NETWORK
Nialp Txet
Plain Text
Cryptographic Algorithm
Cryptographic Algorithm
"Alice"
"Bob"
Examples:
• RSA
• El Gamal
• ECC
SANS Security Essentials – Secure Communications

Public Key Cryptography

The management problems associated with symmetric keys are so overwhelming that they virtually preclude their use by themselves in commerce. But we can use public key computation to develop a shared message key. Also, algorithms like Diffie-Hellman can be used to exchange a secret key. Again, the general idea is to exchange keys securely, perhaps only once, to secure a given session, such as a visit to a Web page to execute a credit card transaction.

Public key cryptography (PKC) methods have two keys: one used for encryption and the other for decryption. Because two keys are used, making the encryption and decryption process different, PKC is also called *asymmetric cryptography*. PKC has many applications, but the primary ones today are key exchange (for SKC), authentication, and non-repudiation.

Stanford University professor Martin Hellman and graduate student Whitfield Diffie first described modern PKC publicly in 1976. Their paper described a two-key cryptosystem in which two parties could engage in a secure communication over a non-secure communications channel without sharing a secret key. The mathematical trick of PKC depends on the existence of so-called *trapdoor functions*, or mathematical functions that are easy to calculate, whereas their inverse is difficult to calculate. Here are two very simple examples:

- *Multiplication vs. factorization:* Multiplication is easy; given the two numbers 9 and 16, it takes almost no time to calculate the product of 144. But factoring is harder; it takes longer to find all of the pairs of integer factors of 144, and then to determine the *correct* pair that was actually used.
- *Exponentiation vs. logarithms:* It is easy to calculate, for example, the number 3 to the 6th power to find the value 729. But given the number 729, it is much harder to find the set of integer pairs, x and y, so that $\log_x y = 729$ and then, again, to determine which pair was actually used.

The examples above are trivial, but they are examples of the concept; namely, the ease of multiplication and exponentiation versus the relative difficulty of factoring and calculating logarithms, respectively. Actual PKC algorithms use integers that are prime and may be several hundred digits in length. Multiplying two 300-digit primes, for example, yields a 600-digit product; finding the two prime factors of a 600-digit number is beyond the capabilities of today's known methods. In this case, then, factoring is said to be *intractable* because of the difficulty of solving the problem in a timely fashion.

PKC keys are derived in pairs and are mathematically related, although knowledge of one key by a third party does not yield knowledge of the other key. One key is used to encrypt the plaintext, and the other key is used to decrypt the ciphertext; it does not matter which key is applied first, but both keys are required for the process to work.

In PKC, one of the keys is designated as the *public key* and may be advertised as widely as the owner wants. The other key is designated as the *private key* and is never revealed. If Alice wants to send Bob a message, she merely encrypts the plaintext using Bob's public key; Bob decrypts the ciphertext using his private key.

This two-key scheme can also be used to prove who sent a message. If Alice, for example, encrypts some plaintext with her private key, Bob (or anyone else) can decrypt the ciphertext using Alice's public key. The benefit here is that Bob (or whoever successfully decrypts the ciphertext) knows for sure that Alice encrypted the message (authentication), and Alice cannot subsequently deny having sent the message (non-repudiation).

In the real world, how are these asymmetric key systems used? Two examples, Pretty Good Privacy (PGP) and the Secure Sockets Layer (SSL), will be discussed later in this chapter's summary and in Chapter 21. We use PGP at SANS when we send exam information among people working on exam development. The so-called web of trust is simply our small community—we each have each others' public keys, so we can encrypt documents for safe transmission. In general, we use 2048-bit keys. We recommend that you use PGP and exchange keys with those you have to do business with in an expedited manner. It is always best to exchange keys in person, or verify them (out-of-band) by comparing the keys' hashes (fingerprints). Otherwise, you risk an intermediary, or man-in-the-middle attack.

Bottom line: Despite being much slower than symmetric-key cryptosystems, asymmetric-key systems are widely used because of their powerful key management and digital signatures—often in concert with symmetric-key systems to attain the best of both worlds. In the next section, you will read a case study of a well-known asymmetric-key system, the Diffie-Hellman Key Exchange.

NOTES

NOTES

Asymmetric for Key Exch.
Symmetric for confidentiality

Who Invented Public-Key Crypto?

The true history of PKC—and answering the question of its invention—is somewhat murky. There is no question that Diffie and Hellman were the first to publicly publish on the topic. Their classic paper, *New Directions in Cryptography*, appeared in the November 1976 issue of *IEEE Transactions on Information Theory*. Diffie and Hellman were not trying to solve the key exchange problem, per se, but were trying to make the problem obsolete by inventing a scheme that used a split key; that is, one key for encryption and a second key for decryption. They published their *concept* of split-key crypto, but did not identify a function that would work. Rivest, Shamir, and Adleman described their implementation in the paper *A Method for Obtaining Digital Signatures and Public-Key Cryptosystems,* which was published in the February 1978 issue of the *Communications of the ACM* (*CACM*).

Some sources, however, credit Ralph Merkle as the first to describe a system that allows two parties to share a secret using what is now called a Merkle Puzzle. His early work was largely misunderstood, and although he submitted a paper to *CACM* some years earlier, his description did not appear until April 1978. He certainly was not the first to publish, but did he have a workable idea before Diffie and Hellman?

The true invention of public key cryptography probably does not belong to anyone in the US, however. The article *The Open Secret* in the April 1999 issue of *WIRED Magazine* reports that PKC was probably first invented by James Ellis of the UK's Government Communications Headquarters (GCHQ) in 1969. Ellis' work was classified until the late 1990s, so there was no public mention of it, and it is possible that Ellis influenced the work of Diffie and Hellman. The US National Security Agency (NSA) claimed to have knowledge of this type of split-key crypto as early as 1966, but there is no known documentation.

Diffie-Hellman Key Exchange

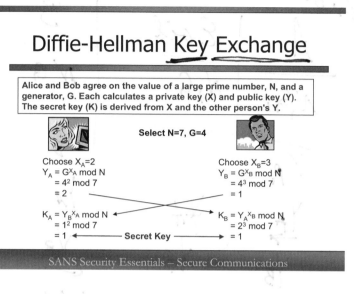

Alice and Bob agree on the value of a large prime number, N, and a generator, G. Each calculates a private key (X) and public key (Y). The secret key (K) is derived from X and the other person's Y.

Select N=7, G=4

Choose $X_A=2$
$Y_A = G^{X_A} \bmod N$
$= 4^2 \bmod 7$
$= 2$

Choose $X_B=3$
$Y_B = G^{X_B} \bmod N$
$= 4^3 \bmod 7$
$= 1$

$K_A = Y_B^{X_A} \bmod N$
$= 1^2 \bmod 7$
$= 1$

$K_B = Y_A^{X_B} \bmod N$
$= 2^3 \bmod 7$
$= 1$

Secret Key

SANS Security Essentials – Secure Communications

Case Study: Diffie-Hellman Key Exchange

Diffie and Hellman first published the concept of two-key crypto in 1976, but it was some time later that they developed the Diffie-Hellman PKC algorithm, which is referred to today as the "Diffie-Hellman" and is used only for key exchange. This method provides a mechanism for Alice and Bob can determine the *same* secret key, even on a network with someone observing all of their communications.

Alice and Bob start by agreeing on a large prime number, N. They then choose a generator number, G, where G<N, and G also meets some other conditions. Alice and Bob then each follow these same steps:

1. Each chooses a large, random number, X < N. X is the private key.
2. Each calculates the value $Y = G^X \bmod N$. Y is the public key and is sent to the other party.
3. Each computes the secret key $K = Y'^X \bmod N$, where Y' is the other party's public key.

Note that each party's Y is openly shared, but X is kept secret; these are the public and private keys, respectively. For that matter, N and G might also be well known. This scheme works because the secret key values (K) that Alice and Bob compute independently are the same; namely, $K = G^{XX'} \bmod N$, where X is their own private key and X' is the other party's private key (derived from the value of Y'). Since both X values are private, an eavesdropper cannot discover G except by brute-force methods. And if N is large enough, this cannot be accomplished *in a reasonable amount of time*.

For purposes of checking (and proving), note that we used G=4 and two private keys with the values 2 and 3. Therefore, our shared secret key should be $4^{2*3} \bmod 7 = 4096 \bmod 7 = 1$. *Voila!*

The figure shows a Diffie-Hellman example where N=7 and G=4. As shown, Alice and Bob choose private key (X) values of 2 and 3, respectively, from which they calculate public key (Y) values of 2 and 1, respectively. After swapping their Y values, both independently compute a secret key (K) value of 1.

NOTES

N + G must be very large #'s

N, G sent in clear - everyone has it

NOTES

This scheme works because Alice and Bob are using the same computation to calculate the secret key, namely:

$$K = Y'^{X} \bmod N$$
$$= (G^{X'} \bmod N)^{X} \bmod N$$
$$= G^{XX'} \bmod N$$

where X and Y are their own private and public keys, and Y' is the other party's public key. In this example, Alice and Bob used N=7, G=4, and two private keys with the values 2 and 3; therefore, their shared secret key should be 4^{2*3} mod 7 = 4096 mod 7 = 1, which is exactly what they both got. Since the X values are private, an eavesdropper cannot determine K except by brute force, even if G, N, and both Y values are known. And if N and G are large enough, this cannot be done *in a reasonable amount of time*.

Hash Functions

hash function
plaintext ⟶ ciphertext

- No key
  - Plaintext (and length of plaintext) is not recoverable from the ciphertext
  - Examples: HMAC, MD2, MD4, MD5, RIPEMD-160, SHA
  - Also called *message digests* or *one-way encryption*
- Primary use: Message integrity

SANS Security Essentials – Secure Communications

Hash Functions

Remember that there are three types of cryptography algorithms: secret key, public key and hash functions. Unlike secret key and public key algorithms, *hash functions*, also called *message digests* or *one-way encryption*, have no key. Instead, a fixed-length hash value is computed based on the plaintext that makes it impossible for either the contents or *length* of the plaintext to be recovered.

The primary application of hash functions in cryptography is message integrity. The hash value provides a digital fingerprint of a message's contents, which ensures that the message has not been altered by an intruder, virus, or other means. Hash algorithms are effective because of the extremely low probability that two different plaintext messages will yield the same hash value.

There are several well-known hash functions in use today:

- Hashed Message Authentication Code (HMAC): Combines authentication via a shared secret with hashing.
- Message Digest 2 (MD2): Byte-oriented, produces a 128-bit hash value from an arbitrary-length message, designed for smart cards.
- MD4: Similar to MD2, designed specifically for fast processing in software.
- MD5: Similar to MD4 but slower because the data is manipulated more. Developed after potential weaknesses were reported in MD4.
- Secure Hash Algorithm (SHA): Modeled after MD4 and proposed by NIST for the Secure Hash Standard (SHS), produces a 160-bit hash value.

NOTES

NOTES

Real-World Implementations

- Kerberos
- Digital Substitution
- Diffie-Hellman
- PGP
- SSL

Today's Cryptosystems

The previous section described a number of cryptography algorithms that are employed for different applications that enable secure communications. In today's environment, computers come in many varieties—from desktop systems to mobile communications devices to home appliances. The Internet, now nearly ubiquitous, is the ultimate insecure communications medium. Hence, increasingly, so is cryptography.

So how are these types of cryptosystems deployed in the real world? In this section, we will examine Pretty Good Privacy (PGP) and the Secure Sockets Layer (SSL). These public key systems are arguably the de facto standards worldwide in their respective niches. SSL is built into virtually every Web browser, and PGP is widely used to encrypt or digitally sign documents and e-mail. We will also discuss a single sign-on system for client/server authentication called Kerberos, which was invented at MIT. The university has deployed it in their high-risk environment for over 15 years. Microsoft has incorporated Kerberos into recent versions of some of its operating system products.

In today's crypto products, what appears to the user as a single system actually comprises multiple algorithms used in conjunction to form a hybrid *cryptosystem*. Multiple algorithms are employed because each is optimized for a specific purpose.

For example, Alice wants to send a message to Bob. The message needs to be private, the message integrity verified, and Alice's identity confirmed. Alice knows several things, including the message, her own private key, and Bob's public key. Alice starts by passing the message through a hash function to obtain a hash value. She encrypts the hash value with her private key using a PKC (asymmetric) algorithm. This forms the *digital signature*.

Alice also creates a random session key for the secret key (symmetric) encryption of the message. The secret key, itself, is encrypted with Bob's public key using PKC. The encrypted message and encrypted session key form a *digital envelope*. The digital envelope and digital signature are sent to Bob.

Bob obtains the SKC session key by decrypting it with his private key using PKC. The session key is then used to decrypt the message. The decrypted message is run through the hash function, and the value is compared to the digital signature's hash value that was decrypted with Alice's public key.

At this point, Bob knows:

- The contents of the private message (SKC).
- That the message was intended for him (because he was able to obtain the secret key).
- That the message was not altered (because his hash value matched Alice's hash value).
- That the message was sent by Alice (because he was able to recover the hash value using Alice's public key).

But why do we need all of these crypto algorithms? Why not just use PKC for everything? The answer is processing speed: SKC is about 1000 times faster than PKC for bulk encryption, particularly important in the 1980s when several teams were trying to implement this in products aimed at the emerging market for personal computers. Diffie-Hellman and RSA were originally seen by their inventors as a way to encrypt and decrypt information using a split key, thereby eliminating the key exchange problem of SKC methods. In the mid-1980s, Lotus Notes' designer Ray Ozzie and PGP developer Phil Zimmermann independently observed that PKC was so much slower than SKC that using PKC for large volumes of data would be infeasible. They designed their software to use SKC for encryption of data, and RSA for SKC key exchange. Other algorithms were added, such as hash values for integrity and signed hash values for authenticating the sender.

In the next few sections, we will examine some commonly employed cryptosystems—PGP, SSL and Kerberos—in greater detail.

NOTES

NOTES

Pretty Good Privacy (PGP)

- Public key cryptography (DH/DSS, RSA) to encrypt/sign e-mail and files
- Developed by Philip Zimmermann (1991)
- Confidentiality: CAST, IDEA, Triple-DES,
- Integrity: MD5, SHA
- Authentication: Knowledge of private-key
- Non-repudiation: Digital signature

SANS Security Essentials – Secure Communications

Case Study: PGP

Pretty Good Privacy (PGP) is one of today's most widely used public-key cryptography products. PGP was developed by Philip Zimmermann in 1991, and was the subject of controversy and debate for a long time because it made strong cryptography available to virtually anyone, in possible conflict with the laws governing the export of crypto products at the time. PGP is available as a plug-in for many e-mail systems, including Claris E-mailer, Microsoft Outlook/Outlook Express, and Qualcomm Eudora.

PGP can be used to sign or encrypt e-mail messages with a mere click of the mouse. Depending on the version, PGP's crypto algorithms include:

- SHA-1 or MD5 for message hashing.
- DES, CAST, Triple DES, or IDEA for encryption.
- RSA or DSS/Diffie-Hellman for key exchange and digital signatures.

The PGP distributed web-of-trust model is based on the concept of trusted introducers or CAs. In this model, each party can independently decide who it will trust to introduce other parties to it. A PGP user can sign the PGP public key of any other PGP user. By signing another person's public key, the signer asserts that the public key belongs to that person, and that person understands how to use PGP. What does this mean to a person who is presented with a signed PGP public key? The recipient can examine the public key he or she has been presented with to determine exactly who has signed it. Based on the number of people who have signed the key, as well as the quality of these signers, the recipient can decide whether or not to trust that particular key. The quality of a signer is a subjective decision that is made on a case-by-case basis by the key recipient.

When PGP is first installed on a computer, the user creates a public/private key pair. The public key can be advertised and widely circulated, while the private key is protected by a passphrase that the user enters every time the private key is used.

```
-----BEGIN PGP SIGNED MESSAGE-----

Hash: SHA1

Hi Bob.

What was that pithy Groucho Marx quote?

Thanks!

Alice

-----BEGIN PGP SIGNATURE-----

Version: PGP for Personal Privacy 5.0
```

```
Charset: noconv

iQA/AwUBNFUdO5WOcz5SFtuEEQJx/ACaAgR97+vvD
U6XWELV/GANjAAgBtUAnjG3Sdfw2JgmZIOLNjFe7j
P0Y8/M

=jUAU

-----END PGP SIGNATURE-----
```

The listing above shows a signed message sent from Alice to Bob. Messages are signed using the sender's private key, so Alice had to enter her passphrase before this message could be transmitted. Upon receipt, Bob uses Alice's public key to confirm that the message contents were not altered in transit and that Alice (or someone knowing her passphrase!) really sent it. Note that this message is not encrypted at all; signing merely provides integrity and authentication.

```
-----BEGIN PGP MESSAGE-----

Version: PGP for Personal Privacy 5.0

MessageID:DAdVB3wzpBr3YRunZwYvhK5gBKBXOb/m

qANQR1DBwU4D/TlT68XXuiUQCADfj2o4b4aFYBcWu
mA7hR1Wvz9rbv2BR6WbEUsyZBIEFtjyqCd96qF38s
p9IQiJIKlNaZfx2GLRWikPZwchUXxB+AA5+lqsG/E
LBvRac9XefaYpbbAZ6z6LkOQ+eE0XASe7aEEPfdxv
ZZT37dVyiyxuBBRYNLN8Bphdr2zvz/9Ak4/OLnLiJ
Rk05/2UNE5Z0a+3lcvITMmfGajvRhkXqocavPOKii
n3hv7+Vx88uLLem2/fQHZhGcQvkqZVqXx8SmNw5gz
uvwjV1WHj9muDGBY0MkjiZIRI7azWnoU93KCnmpR6
0VO4rDRAS5uGl9fioSvze+q8XqxubaNsgdKkoD+tB
/4u4c4tznLfw1L2YBS+dzFDw5desMFSo7JkecAS4N
B9jAu9K+f7PTAsesCBNETDd49BTOFFTWWavAfEgLY
cPrcn4s3EriUgvL3OzPR4P1chNu6sa3ZJkTBbriDo
A3VpnqG3hxqfNyOlqAkamJJuQ53Ob9ThaFH8YcE/V
qUFdw+bQtrAJ6NpjIxi/x0FfOInhC/bBw7pDLXBFN
aXHdlLQRPQdrmnWskKznOSarxq4GjpRTQo4hpCRJJ
5aU7tZO9HPTZXFG6iRIT0wa47AR5nvkEKoIAjW5Ha
DKiJriuWLdtN4OXecWvxFsjR32ebz76U8aLpAK87G
ZEyTzBxdV+lH0hwyT/y1cZQE5USePP4oKWF4uqquP
ee1OPeFMBo4CvuGyhZXD/18Ft/53YWIebvdiCqsOo
abK3jEfdGExce63zDI0=

=MpRf

-----END PGP MESSAGE-----
```

The listing above shows the PGP-encrypted message sent from Bob to Alice. In this scenario, Bob's PGP software has chosen the session secret key and sent it to Alice encrypted with her public key and PKC; the message itself, of course, is encrypted using the session secret key and SKC.

When Alice receives the message, she uses her passphrase to access her private key, which is required to extract the session secret key to successfully decrypt the message:

```
Hi Alice,

"Outside of a dog, a book is man's best
friend.

Inside of a dog, it's too dark to read."

Bob
```

As a side note, suppose that Bob sent this message to Alice, Carol, and Dave. The resulting PGP transmission would not be three times the length of the message to only one recipient. The reason is that the message has to be encrypted only one time using a single-session secret key. It is the secret key that has to be present three times, encrypted using Alice's, Carol's, and Dave's public keys.

NOTES

PGP users can easily maintain their own key pairs on computers they have access to, but how do they obtain the public keys of others? The most common method is for each user to maintain a *public keyring* with the set of all known and trusted public keys. Alice can obtain Bob's public key in a number of ways:

- Ask Bob for his public key, which he might supply in an e-mail, in a file, or on a floppy disk.
- Ask Carol for Bob's public key. Alice needs to determine how much she trusts Carol and Carol's key management skills before being sure that this key is really Bob's.
- Download Bob's key from a public PGP key server, such as `http://pgp.mit.edu/`.
- Download the key from Bob's Web site.

Again, it is totally up to Alice to determine the trustworthiness of any of these sources.

Well-known PGP servers on the global Internet serve as repositories for publishing PGP public keys and digital certificates. The procedures for revoking PGP public keys and digital certificates are informally handled. In general, key negotiation is the weakest part of all existing cryptosystems. It is also a weakness of the PGP program because once key negotiation has been compromised, the underlying encryption algorithm is worthless.

NOTES

Secure Socket Layer (SSL)

- Encryption at TCP/IP transport layer
- *De facto* standard by Netscape in 1994
- Where is the key stored?
- https://[host].[enterprise].com/
- Confidentiality: Triple-DES, RC4
- Integrity: MD5, SHA-1
- Authentication: RSA, Diffie-Hellman
- Non-repudiation: Digital signature

SANS Security Essentials – Secure Communications

Case Study: SSL

The *Secure Sockets Layer (SSL)* protocol was developed by Netscape Communications in 1994 to provide application-independent secure communications over the Internet. SSL procedures are most commonly employed on the Web with the Hypertext Transfer Protocol (HTTP) for e-commerce transactions, although SSL is not limited to HTTP. SSL uses cryptography to provide message privacy, message integrity, and client and server authentication.

The oldest version of SSL in use today is version 2 (SSL v2), although SSL version 3 (SSL v3) is far more commonly employed. The Internet Engineering Task Force (IETF) updated SSL v3 when they created the non-proprietary Transaction Layer Security (TLS) protocol (RFC 2246). All operate in essentially the same manner. TLS is advertised as SSL v3.1.

SSL/TLS employs two protocols. The Handshake Protocol allows the client and server to mutually authenticate each other, exchange certificates, and negotiate the crypto algorithms to be used for hashing, SKC, and PKC. The Record Protocol is then used to exchange encrypted data.

SSL and TLS support a variety of crypto protocols:

- SSL v2 supports RC2 and RC4 with 40-bit keys for privacy. SSL v3 added support for DES (40- and 56-bit keys), RC4 (128-bit key), and 3DES.
- MD5 and SHA-1 are used for message integrity.
- RSA is used for key exchange and digital signatures in SSL. TLS added support for Diffie-Hellman and DSS.

The most popular use of SSL and TLS is to ensure Web users that they are not communicating with a spoofed or fake server, or that their network connection is being monitored. The server keeps a certificate, signed by a trusted third party (for example, VeriSign or Thawte). Web browsers are shipped with embedded certificates for these signing authorities, and can prove the server certifications were signed by them. Although this technique has been very convenient and successful for deploying wide-scale use of cryptography, it is a bit of a placebo. Many Web servers do not have valid certificates (they are either expired or not signed by a bona fide authority), and the security of the sensitive data (for example, credit card numbers) is arguably more dependent on the security of the Web server than the network connection. The security of the communications between the business and the bank when processing credit card transactions is

NOTES

also a concern. Still, SSL and TLS help guard against DNS spoofing, which would allow an attacker to set up a fake server and collect all the credit card numbers that fly by. Besides, encryption of the network connection *is* a requirement. We just need to remember it is necessary, but not sufficient.

Kerberos

- Secret-key protocol and distributed service, for third-party authentication
- Kerberos KDC is a trusted intermediary
- Confidentiality: DES (CBC mode), ...
- Integrity: Cryptographic hash algorithms
- Authentication: Login password (local)
- Non-repudiation: Knowledge of a password

SANS Security Essentials – Secure Communications

Case Study: Kerberos

Kerberos is a trusted third-party scheme that allows a user to log on to a system once and use any available services without re-authenticating to many different servers. Developed by Massachusetts Institute of Technology's (MIT's) Project Athena, Kerberos is named for the three-headed dog from Greek mythology that guards the entrance of Hades. Kerberos version 4 was released in 1987, and is still in use in select locations, although version 5, described in IETF's RFC 1510 and released in 1990, is far more common. Meanwhile, Microsoft incorporated Kerberos in Windows 2000, although that version contains some proprietary extensions to version 5. While there are significant differences between the three versions, they have many conceptual similarities. Despite its complete approach to providing a cryptographic infrastructure for communications, Kerberos is still far from ubiquitous, mainly because Kerberized applications used to be rare. Now that Windows 2000 has built-in support for Kerberos, the scheme has become much more popular.

Kerberos provides authentication based on secret key technology (DES for V4, DES, Triple DES, or other schemes for V5). Users on the network have conventional passwords that are effectively their secret keys. In addition, every *service* on the network (for example, Telnet, IMAP, etc.) has *its* own secret key, called a *service key*. In Kerberos parlance, we call these services *application services* to differentiate from services offered by the KDC. Instead of users authenticating to services, users and services (also called *principals*) authenticate *to each other*. Servers can detect and thwart imposters, and users can be assured they are not talking to spoofed servers.

When authenticating or encrypting data, both the client and the server must share a secret, randomly generated session key. As we have discussed, the difficulty with secret key cryptography is in the key exchange. Principals could use their own secret keys to secure the key exchange, but then every principal would have to know every other principal's secret key, which introduces another, much bigger, key exchange problem.

Instead, Kerberos employs a secure, trusted server known as a *Key Distribution Center (KDC)* that stores every principal's secret key. When a new service (such as Telnet or IMAP) is brought online, only the KDC and the new service need to be configured with the service's key, which can be

NOTES

NOTES

distributed physically or by some other secure means. As Jeff Schiller, who managed this type of system for years at MIT points out, Kerberos is only viable if the KDC is physically secured in such a manner that MIT engineering students cannot pick the lock! KDCs must also be protected at all costs against compromise via the network, lest all the keys stored there be stolen.

If deployed incorrectly, the KDC could be a potential performance bottleneck and a single point of failure. But read-only replicas of the KDC are deployed at various locations in large networks to maximize the availability of remote resources.

Control of the KDC has important political considerations because whoever manages the KDC can access every user's secret key. In large enterprises, it can be politically and practically unacceptable for a single user or team to wield this much power. Typically, this problem is addressed by logically subdividing the enterprise network into distinct *realms*, each with its own independent and locally managed KDC.

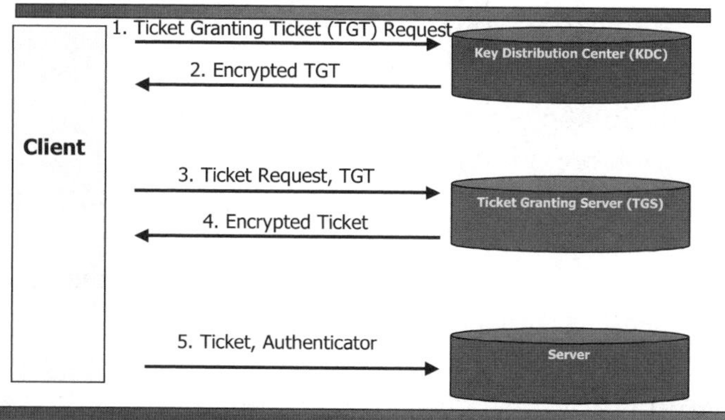

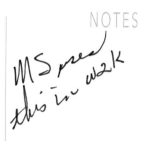

When a participating entity wishes to communicate in a trusted manner with another participating entity over the insecure network, the KDC issues it a ticket that becomes the basis for the establishment of trust between the two participating entities. Kerberos principals use encrypted timestamps to prove to the KDC that they posses the correct secret keys. Hence, the clocks of all participating entities on the network must be synchronized.

The KDC comprises two distinct services: the *authentication service* (AS) and the *ticket-granting service* (TGS). In Kerberos terms, *application services* refer to services such as Telnet and IMAP, so they are not confused with the AS and TGS. The steps in establishing an authenticated session between a client and server are:

1. The Kerberos client software establishes a connection with the AS. The AS authenticates the client and then provides the client with a secret key for this login session (the TGS session key) and a ticket-granting ticket (TGT), which gives the client permission to talk to the TGS. The ticket has a finite lifetime (for example, ten hours) to reduce the chances of it being stolen while still valid. Because the TGT expires, the authentication process must be repeated periodically if the login session has a long duration.
2. The client now requests from the TGS a *service ticket* for the application service it wants to contact. To make this request, the client must supply the TGS with the TGS session key and TGT it obtained in step 1. The TGS responds with two copies of a randomly generated session key: one encrypted with the application service's secret key (this is the *service ticket*) and one encrypted with the client's key.
3. The client can now prove its identity to the application service by supplying the service ticket. The application server responds with encrypted information to authenticate itself to the client. At this point, the client can initiate the intended service requests (for example, Telnet, FTP, HTTP, etc.).

NOTES

NOTES

Summary

Cryptography, the science of secret writing, is an essential component of computer and network security at all levels. Information security professionals must be comfortable with at least the basic terms and concepts associated with this field so that they can understand products, services, and vendor claims.

While the crypto methods used today are vastly stronger and more complex than algorithms used even 30 years ago, the same two fundamental operations still form the basis of all schemes used to encrypt messages for privacy, namely *substitution* and *permutation*. Substitution is the method of replacing, or substituting, characters in a message with other characters, while permutation (transposition) moves characters around within the message. Today's algorithms tend to employ many rounds of both.

Crypto schemes that operate on a single bit or byte at one time are usually called *stream ciphers*, while those that work on larger collections of bits and bytes are called *block ciphers*. Block ciphers are most common, although there are a number of stream ciphers used in the field.

A crypto key exactly governs the transformation of the plaintext into ciphertext. Modern crypto algorithms can be broadly classified into three categories based on the number of keys employed. Each of these methods is used for specific applications.

- Secret-key crypto algorithms use a single key for both encryption and decryption. SKC key lengths between 128 and 256 bits are generally thought to be adequate; shorter keys are deemed weak. SKC algorithms such as AES (Rijndael), DES, 3DES, IDEA, RC4, and RC5 are used for privacy.
- Public-key cryptography algorithms use a pair of very large, mathematically related keys. PKC is a two-key system, whereby one of the keys is used to encrypt data, and the other is used for decryption. PKC depends on the existence of so-called *trapdoor functions* that are easy to calculate whereas the inverse function is very difficult (intractable). With trapdoor functions, one key does not yield knowledge of the other key. One of the keys, therefore, can be widely distributed and is called the *public key*; the other key is kept secret and is called the *private key*. PKC schemes such as Diffie-Hellman, RSA, and ECC may be used for such functions as key exchange, user authentication, and digital signatures. RSA is a public key algorithm invented in 1977 by Rivest, Shamir, and Adleman. RSA and Elliptic Curve Cryptography (ECC) are discussed further in the next chapter.
- Hash functions are one-way encryption; they employ no key, and the hash operation cannot be reversed to recover the original plaintext from the hash value. Hash functions such as MD5 and SHA are used for message integrity.

In today's environment, it is rare to find only one of these algorithms in use; it is far more common to find a set of these protocols used together to form a cryptosystem. PGP is such a cryptosystem, and can provide privacy, message integrity, and authentication for e-mail applications. In the same manner, SSL/TLS is used as a cryptosystem for secure e-commerce transactions.

While cryptography is necessary for security, it is not sufficient by itself. There are bad crypto schemes, bad implementations of good crypto schemes, and misuse of good implementations. Just as security is a process, so is the management and use of crypto; thus, security administrators—and users—need to be trained in the art of cryptography.

NOTES

NOTES

Chapter 20

Encryption 102

NOTES

Encryption 102

SANS Security Essentials IV: Secure Communications

SANS Security Essentials – Secure Communications

Encryption 102

The last chapter was a quick tour of some of the important issues and concepts in the field of cryptography. It showed that encryption is real, it's crucial, it's a foundation of much that happens in the world around us today, and most of all, it is completely transparent to us.

One of this chapter's goals is to show you how some of the world's most popular ciphers, which are in constant use in many different sectors, operate under the covers. Along the way, we'll share some pragmatic lessons we've learned the hard way, hoping our experience will be of help to you in the future.

We begin by examining the conceptual underpinnings of today's major ciphers. In particular, we'll cover Triple DES, a good alternative for the now obsolete and relatively easy-to-crack DES algorithm. Then we'll discuss the new standard for encryption, the Advanced Encryption Standard (AES).

Our next stop will be the widely deployed RSA public-key algorithm. RSA was released from its patent in September 2000. To demonstrate RSA, we'll walk through a highly simplified version of the mathematical algorithm it's based on.

We'll wrap up the chapter with an overview of emerging Elliptic Curve Cryptosystems (ECC). ECCs, whose processing power and storage requirements are relatively low, are rapidly growing in popularity due to the proliferation of small electronic devices with limited power and storage.

NOTES

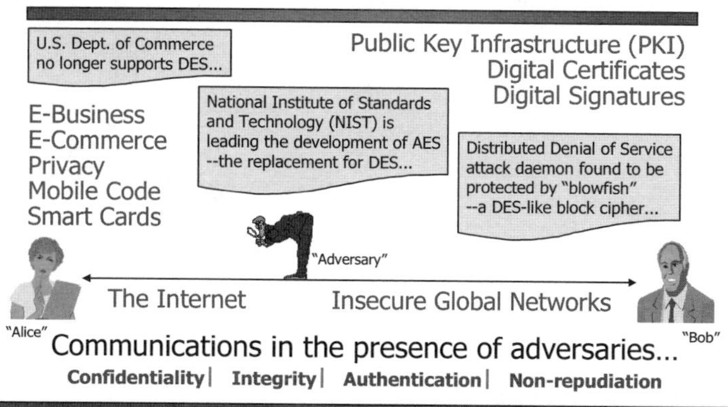
Why Do I Care About Crypto?
U.S. Dept. of Commerce no longer supports DES...
Public Key Infrastructure (PKI)
Digital Certificates
Digital Signatures
E-Business
E-Commerce
Privacy
Mobile Code
Smart Cards
National Institute of Standards and Technology (NIST) is leading the development of AES --the replacement for DES...
Distributed Denial of Service attack daemon found to be protected by "blowfish" --a DES-like block cipher...
"Adversary"
The Internet
Insecure Global Networks
"Alice"
"Bob"
Communications in the presence of adversaries...
Confidentiality | Integrity | Authentication | Non-repudiation
SANS Security Essentials – Secure Communications

Why Cryptography is Useful and Necessary

Without cryptography, there is no e-business, no viable e-commerce infrastructures, no military presence on the Internet, and no privacy for the citizens of the world. Cryptography is used in more situations every day, at work, and at play, often without the participants even realizing it. Often, the underlying cryptographic infrastructure is so seamless we only take notice when it is absent or implemented incorrectly.

For example, when you use a secure mobile telephone, your conversation is rapidly encrypted and decrypted on the fly, preventing eavesdroppers from listening in. Every once in a while, we hear about some public figure whose sensitive communications were intercepted. Such a compromise of privacy can be embarrassing or damaging, but it can usually be avoided by using cryptography-enabled products.

It's best to consider the Internet and any other networks you don't control to be insecure. Any and all of your communications could be under surveillance by adversaries—business competitors, criminals, terrorists, or script kiddies hoping to earn credibility in the culture of system cracking. A strong enough cipher lets us always communicate in the presence of adversaries without fear that our data will be compromised.

One of the more important emerging uses for cryptography is to protect e-commerce transactions on the Internet. Businesses can use a *Public Key Infrastructure (PKI)* model to allow an unlimited number of customers to interact with them without revealing transaction data to eavesdroppers as it traverses across the Internet. Since PKI is supported by most Web browsers and relies on a trusted third party, customers and merchants need never have met to be assured their communications are relatively safe.

When businesses support PKI on an enterprise-wide scale, a whole suite of new products and services becomes available, leading to new business opportunities, new capabilities being delivered to consumers, new functionality provided by organizations to their shareholders, fundamental changes in the way entire industries function, new legislation, global opportunities, and so on. The effects of cryptography can be far reaching.

NOTES

Course Objectives

- Concepts in Cryptography
- Secret (Symmetric) Key Systems
  - Triple DES
  - AES
- Public (Asymmetric) Key Systems
  - RSA
  - ECC

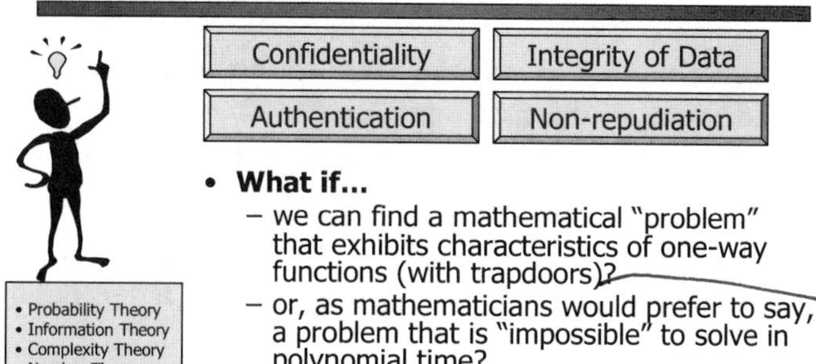

Concepts in Cryptography

The last chapter defined the four main characteristics of a cryptosystem: *confidentiality*, *integrity of data*, *authentication*, and *non-repudiation*. But how do we construct a cipher that enforces these characteristics? Mathematics has fields such as probability theory, information theory, complexity theory, number theory, abstract algebra, and finite fields that are all rich in ideas that could contribute to our cipher.

The last chapter also introduced one-way mathematical functions. Such functions can have trapdoor properties that make them well suited for public-key cryptography, in which the trapdoor allows a message to be decrypted using a different key than the one used to encrypt the message. If the public key were used to encrypt the message, the trapdoor in this case is the corresponding private key.

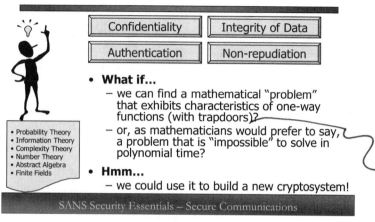

One-way functions that are computationally hard—that is, impossible to solve in polynomial time—can make things very difficult for an adversary eavesdropping on our communications, say over an insecure public network like the global Internet. At the same time, the existence of a trapdoor could be used to provide an easy solution to the intractable problem for use by the sender or the recipient.

NOTES

NOTES

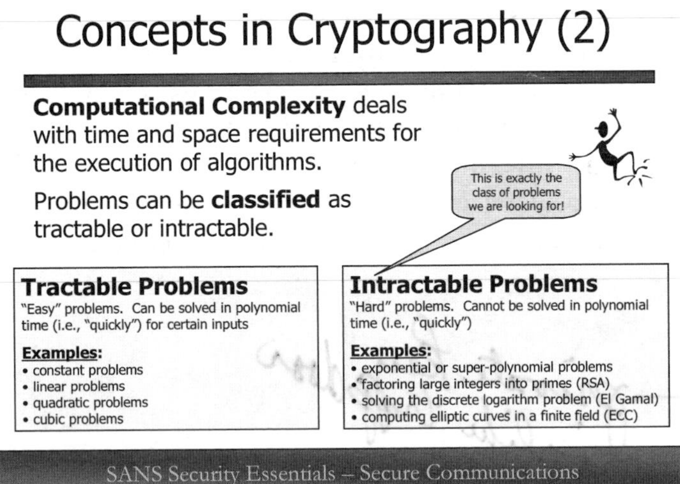

Concepts in Cryptography (2)
Computational Complexity deals with time and space requirements for the execution of algorithms.
Problems can be classified as tractable or intractable.
This is exactly the class of problems we are looking for!
Tractable Problems
"Easy" problems. Can be solved in polynomial time (i.e., "quickly") for certain inputs
Examples:
• constant problems
• linear problems
• quadratic problems
• cubic problems
Intractable Problems
"Hard" problems. Cannot be solved in polynomial time (i.e., "quickly")
Examples:
• exponential or super-polynomial problems
• factoring large integers into primes (RSA)
• solving the discrete logarithm problem (El Gamal)
• computing elliptic curves in a finite field (ECC)
SANS Security Essentials – Secure Communications

Computational Complexity

Mathematics is filled with intractable problems. So a cipher designer can start by just picking one and trying it out. Evaluating an algorithm's *computational complexity* will reveal the time and space required to execute it and help us classify the problem as either tractable (easy) or intractable (hard).

When computers are used to solve problems, we don't care about the exact number of operations—we're more interested in how the amount of input to the problem (or program) affects the number of operations it takes to solve (or execute). *Big-O notation* is used to give a general idea of how many operations a problem takes relative to the input size n. The big-O function isn't usually specifically defined; it's mostly used as a notational shorthand to indicate a problem's complexity.

Relatively easy problems can be solved in *polynomial time*—that is, the relationship between the input size and the number of operations required to solve the problem is constant, linear, quadratic, cubic, *etc.* *Constant time*, $O(1)$, means they take the same number of operations to solve regardless of the input size. *Linear time*, $O(n)$ means the number of operations increases linearly with the input size—when the input size is doubled, the problem takes twice as long to solve. *Quadratic time* is $O(n^2)$, *cubic time* is $O(n^3)$, *etc.*

Problems are considered intractable (or hard) when they can't be solved in polynomial time. Examples are *exponential*, $O(2^n)$, and *superpolynomial* (somewhere between polynomial and exponential), which are considered so complex as to be hard or intractable. A cubic-time algorithm might take thousands of years to solve, whereas an exponential-time algorithm might take longer than the universe is expected to last.

It can be hard to prove whether a problem is intractable or not. Someone might prove a particular problem can be solved in superpolynomial time, only to have someone later discover it can be solved a different way in polynomial time. So it's more accurate to state that the problems we use in cipher algorithms are *believed to be* intractable by most researchers in complexity theory. There's always the chance that easier solutions have been overlooked or just haven't been discovered yet.

Three well-known examples of intractable problems include: factoring certain large integers into their two prime factors (the basis for RSA), solving the discrete logarithm problem over finite fields (the basis for ElGamal), and computing elliptic curves over finite fields (the basis for Elliptic Curve Cryptosystems). Now, let's examine each of these three important classes of intractable problems in greater detail, as each one of them forms the basis of important cryptosystems, which are widely used all over the world today.

NOTES

NOTES

Concepts in Cryptography (3)

An Example of an Intractable Problem...
Difficulty of factoring a large integer into its two prime factors

- A "hard" problem
- Years of intense public scrutiny suggest intractability
- No mathematical proof so far

Example: RSA

- based on difficulty of factoring a large integer into its prime factors
- ~1000 times slower ~~than DES~~
- considered "secure"
- *de facto* standard
- patent expired in 2000

SANS Security Essentials – Secure Communications

Perhaps the most popular public-key algorithm today, RSA, takes advantage of the intractability of the integer factorization problem. We'll cover RSA in depth later in the chapter.

Prime Factorization of Large Integers

Factoring integers doesn't seem that hard. It doesn't take much thought to figure out that 15 can be factored into 1 x 15 and 3 x 5. So why is it on our list of intractable problems?

The operative word here is *large*. The larger the integer, the harder it is to factor. In fact, there is no known recipe for factoring other than trial and error: keep multiplying primes together until you arrive at the number. Remember that even though most researchers in complexity theory believe factoring large integers is a hard problem, there is no unequivocal proof to that effect. It's only the years of public scrutiny of the problem that lead us to conclude the problem cannot be solved in polynomial time.

Concepts in Cryptography (4)

Another Intractable Problem...
Difficulty of solving the discrete logarithm problem --for finite fields

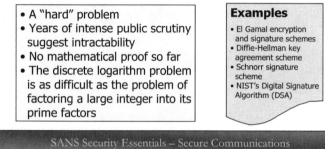

- A "hard" problem
- Years of intense public scrutiny suggest intractability
- No mathematical proof so far
- The discrete logarithm problem is as difficult as the problem of factoring a large integer into its prime factors

Examples

- El Gamal encryption and signature schemes
- Diffie-Hellman key agreement scheme
- Schnorr signature scheme
- NIST's Digital Signature Algorithm (DSA)

SANS Security Essentials – Secure Communications

The Discrete Logarithm Problem for Finite Fields

Another intractable problem is the *discrete logarithm problem for finite fields*. The discrete logarithm is based on a statement of the form $a^x \bmod n = b$, where a, b, n, and x are integers and a and n are known. The *mod* operator just means we take the remainder of the first number (a^x) when divided by the second number (n). Finding b when we know x is easy, but not the other way around.

For example, it's easy to calculate $8^3 \bmod 7$—since $8^3 = 512$ and the next lowest multiple of 7 is 511, the remainder must be $512 - 511 = 1$. But it takes trial and error to discover that $8^x \bmod 7 = 1$ is satisfied only by $x = 3$. This problem is the discrete logarithm. Just as with prime factorization, the problem *really* gets hard when x is a hundred- or thousand-bit number.

Again, the notion that discrete logarithms are intractable is the consensus of computational complexity researchers, and there is no unequivocal proof that this problem cannot be solved easily. It's the years of public scrutiny of the problem that leads us to conclude that it is a hard problem that cannot be solved in polynomial time. But how does it compare with the previous intractable problem we looked at—the factorization of large integers into two primes? Evidence shows the discrete logarithm problem is just as difficult.

So we should be able to use the discrete logarithm problem in building a cipher. In fact, several ciphers in use today are built upon the intractability of the discrete logarithm problem over finite fields: the ElGamal encryption and signature schemes, the Diffie-Hellman key agreement scheme, the Schnorr signature scheme, and the Digital Signature Algorithm (DSA) by the US Department of Commerce's National Institute of Standards and Technology (NIST).

NOTES

RSA website challenge

NOTES

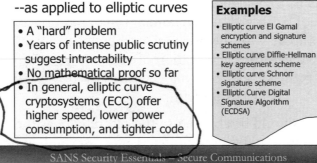

Concepts in Cryptography (5)

Yet Another Intractable Problem...
Difficulty of solving the discrete logarithm problem
--as applied to elliptic curves

- A "hard" problem
- Years of intense public scrutiny suggest intractability
- No mathematical proof so far
- In general, elliptic curve cryptosystems (ECC) offer higher speed, lower power consumption, and tighter code

Examples

- Elliptic curve El Gamal encryption and signature schemes
- Elliptic curve Diffie-Hellman key agreement scheme
- Elliptic curve Schnorr signature scheme
- Elliptic Curve Digital Signature Algorithm (ECDSA)

SANS Security Essentials – Secure Communications

The Discrete Logarithm Problem for Elliptic Curves

The ciphers we named in the last section use the discrete logarithm problem, but only for certain sets of numbers that belong to what are known as *finite fields*. It turns out this problem also makes for a good cipher algorithm when applied to *elliptic curves*.

This class of problem is considered every bit as intractable as the previous two. Plus, it lends some additional useful features to our algorithm: high security levels even at low key lengths, high speed processing, and low power and storage requirements. These characteristics are very useful in crypto-enabling the many new devices that are rapidly appearing in the marketplace, *e.g.*, mobile telephones, information appliances, smart cards, and even the venerable ATM.

Building a Cryptosystem

This chapter began by describing the problem of communicating in the presence of adversaries and how to solve it by constructing a cryptosystem that can provide confidentiality, data integrity, authentication, and non-repudiation. We then briefly examined some of the well-known intractable mathematical problems that could be used as building blocks upon which to construct our cryptosystem. But how do we make the connection between complex and abstract mathematical concepts to crypto-enabled products we use routinely every day?

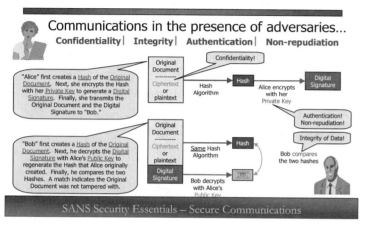

While each type of cryptosystem addresses specific details in its own unique way, the fundamental concepts behind their mechanics are quite similar in practice. The slide puts it all together from the perspective of a message being sent by Alice over an insecure public network (like the global Internet) to Bob. The mechanisms shown in the diagram (*hash*, *digital signature*, *keys*, *etc.*) are at the foundation of many cryptosystems. The users of the cryptosystem automatically benefit from the confidentiality, integrity of data, authentication, and non-repudiation offered by these mechanisms.

NOTES

NOTES

Milestones in Cryptography

Origins of Cryptography (traced as far back as 4000 years!	RSA (Rivest, Shamir, Adleman, 1978)	AES: Advanced Encryption Standard (sponsored by NIST, 2002)
Index of Coincidence (Friedman, 1918)	Public-Key Encryption (Rabin, 1979)	
Vernam Cipher (Vernam, 1926)	Public-Key Encryption & Signature (ElGamal, 1985)	
Secure Communications (Shannon, 1949)	Elliptic Curve Cryptography (Miller, 1986 & Koblitz, 1987)	
Lucifer Cryptosystem (Feistel, 1974)	ECA: Elliptic Curve Algorithm (Lenstra, 1987)	
Public-Key Cryptography (Diffie and Hellman, 1976)	Differential Cryptanalysis (Biham and Shamir, 1993)	
Key-Exchange Method (Diffie and Hellman, 1976)	X.509 v3 Digital Certificates (ITU-T, 1993)	
DES: Data Encryption Standard (U.S. FIPS-46, 1977)	Linear Cryptanalysis (Matsui, 1994)	
Public-Key Cryptography (Merkle, 1978)	...	

...built upon the work of giants!

SANS Security Essentials – Secure Communications

Milestones in Cryptography

We noted earlier in our discussion that a number of researchers have made important contributions over the years, advancing the mathematical ideas that serve as the foundation of cryptosystems in use today. We also noted that each of the three classes of intractable problems we discussed were successfully employed as building blocks for constructing cryptosystems.

There is a long, rich history behind modern cryptosystems. The slide lists a few (but by no means all) of the leading cryptographers whose work and ideas have been successfully incorporated into everyday products we use routinely. Modern day cryptosystems are truly built upon the shoulders of giants!

The mathematics behind cryptosystems can be abstract and complex. The process of developing new ciphers works best when the details behind the algorithms are available to everyone rather than kept secret. A good cryptosystem places all its security in the keys; knowing the algorithm should not be enough for a cryptanalyst to break the cipher. Ciphers under development must be open to intense scrutiny by cryptologists worldwide to achieve the trust required for use in our growing e-commerce infrastructure.

NOTES

Crypto History

- The history of Cryptography is long and interesting
- In the next couple of slides we will discuss some of the highlights

Cryptography dates back to the ancient Egyptians when they began using secret writing called *hieroglyphics*, as early as 3000 BC. The term comes from the ancient Greek word *hieroglyphica*, meaning *sacred carvings*. The Egyptians used this writing to hide messages from unintended recipients.

By the fifth century BC, the Spartans were using a *scytale*, a wooden staff of prescribed thickness with a strip of cloth or parchment wrapped around it. The cleartext message was written along the length of the rod so that when the cloth was unwrapped, it appeared to contain a stream of random letters. The recipient would then wrap the cloth on an identical scytale, thereby decrypting the message.

NOTES

Key Events

- Jefferson Disk Cipher system
- Japanese Purple Machine
- German Enigma Machine
- Vernam Cipher

SANS Security Essentials – Secure Communications

Thomas Jefferson invented a wheel cipher in 1790 using a spindle containing 26 adjacent wooden disks that could be independently rotated. The letters of the alphabet were etched in random order around each disk's outer edge. The cleartext message (of 26 letters or fewer) could be spelled out along the length of the spindle by rotating the disks. Any of the other rows could then be used as the ciphertext. The recipient of the enciphered message could use an identical machine to spell out the ciphertext by rotating the disks and then finding the row that spelled out a sensible message.

World War II impressed upon the world the importance of cryptography. The Japanese military used a code called *Purple* to transmit orders and intelligence. Cryptanalysts stationed in Pearl Harbor broke the code in 1942. US Navy Commander Joseph Rochefort's team intercepted and deciphered a Japanese message referring to a planned attack on an island in the Pacific referred to as *AF*. Although Rochefort thought this to be Midway Island, he could not convince his superiors. To prove his point he sent a message in the clear in a poor cipher and stated that Midway Island was having water problems. Sure enough, the US Navy intercepted an enciphered message from the Japanese shortly afterwards stating that AF was having water problems. When the Japanese Navy launched their attack on Midway, the US was prepared.

In the European theater, the Germans used a cryptosystem called *Enigma*. The Engima machine is one of the most famous cryptographic devices ever built. The British, French, and Americans worked for decades to break the cipher, which used two types of substitution cipher. A monoalphabetic cipher always uses one particular letter to replace another. With a polyalphabetic cipher, one of several letters could replace any given plaintext letter.

Perhaps the most difficult-to-break cipher is the Vernam Cipher, or the *one-time pad*, developed by AT&T. The key for a one-time pad consists of a truly random set of non-repeating characters. A key letter is added modulo 26 to a letter of the plaintext, creating a message the same length as the plaintext. One letter of the key gets used up for every letter of plaintext, making for a very long key, and the key can never be reused. The big disadvantage of the one-time pad is that a new lengthy key must be shared with the recipient for every message.

NOTES

DES: Data Encryption Standard

- Released March 17, 1975
- Rather fast encryption algorithm
- Widely used; a *de facto* standard
- Symmetric-key, 64-bit block cipher
- 56-bit key size → Small 2^{56} keyspace
- Today, DES is not considered secure

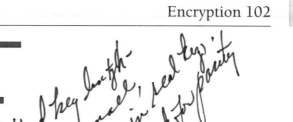

SANS Security Essentials – Secure Communications

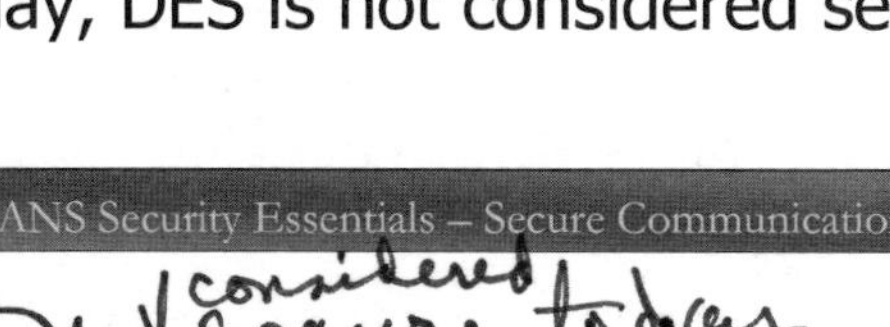

Data Encryption Standard (DES)

DES is the most commonly used encryption algorithm in the world. The United States government proposed its adoption as a national standard on March 17, 1975, for use with unclassified computer data. Based on IBM's Lucifer cipher, DES is specified in Federal Information Processing Standard (FIPS) 42. The American National Standards Institute (ANSI) adopted DES as a standard (ANSI X3.92) in 1981, calling it the Data Encryption Algorithm (DEA).

Due to the internal bit-oriented operations in the design of DES, software implementations are slow, while hardware implementations are faster. The National Institute of Standards and Technology (NIST) standardized four different DES operation modes for use in the US: electronic codebook (ECB) mode, cipher block chaining (CBC) mode, output feedback (OFB) mode, and cipher feedback (CFB) mode.

NOTES

DES Weaknesses

- DES is considered non-secure for very sensitive encryption. It is crackable in a short period of time.
- See the Cracking DES book by O'Reilly.
- Multiple encryptions and key size will increase the security.
- Double DES is vulnerable to the meet-in-the-middle attack and only has an effective key length of 57 bits.
- Triple DES is preferred.

SANS Security Essentials – Secure Communications

Strength of DES

From the very beginning, concerns were raised about the strength of DES, due to the rather small key length of 56 bits (a 64-bit ciphertext block minus 8 bits for parity), resulting in a keyspace containing only 2^{56} possible different keys. The effectiveness of attacks based on brute force searches depends upon keyspace size. Because of DES's relatively small keyspace, brute force attacks are feasible. DES was first (publicly) cracked in the RSA Challenge, a program that offers monetary rewards for breaking ciphers and solving computationally intensive mathematical problems. The DES challenge took only five months for the public to solve, and subsequent attempts are taking less and less time.

Consequently, DES is no longer considered secure because of its key size. In fact, anyone can build a DES cracking engine these days. All the information you need, including sample code, is available in a book called *Cracking DES*. But with the global e-commerce infrastructure build-out proceeding at a furious pace, due to all the new e-business initiatives that are sprouting up all over the world, the need for a fast, symmetric block cipher is extremely urgent. If DES can no longer be considered to be secure, what can we do in the interim?

Again, DES was already widely deployed in both hardware and software products, and it had withstood unbridled cryptanalysis for decades. It didn't take long to realize what a great advantage it would be to somehow increase DES's key size and use the existing implementations until a new standard was built. One way to effectively increase the key length is to perform the encryption more than once. That is, encrypt the cleartext, then encrypt the resulting ciphertext, and so on. But this only works if the cipher algorithm is not a *group*.

We say the function E is a group if E(K2, E(K,M)) = E(K3, M). In other words, encrypting once with key K and then again with key K2 is equivalent to encrypting once with K3. Thus, if a cipher algorithm is a group, encrypting multiple times is no stronger than encrypting once.

NOTES

DES

- In 1992 it was proven that DES is not a group. This means that multiple DES encryptions are not equivalent to a single encryption. THIS IS A GOOD THING.
- If something is a group then
  - E(K2,E(K,M)) = E(K3,M)
- Since DES is not a group, multiple encryptions will increase the security.

SANS Security Essentials – Secure Communications

Whether an algorithm is a group is an important statistical consideration. If it is a group, then applying the algorithm multiple times is a waste of time. In 1992, it was proven that DES is not a group, in fact, so encrypting multiple times with DES is not equivalent to encrypting once. That's good news; it means that encrypting more than once with DES could increase the security of the ciphertext.

NOTES

totally different from "man in the middle"

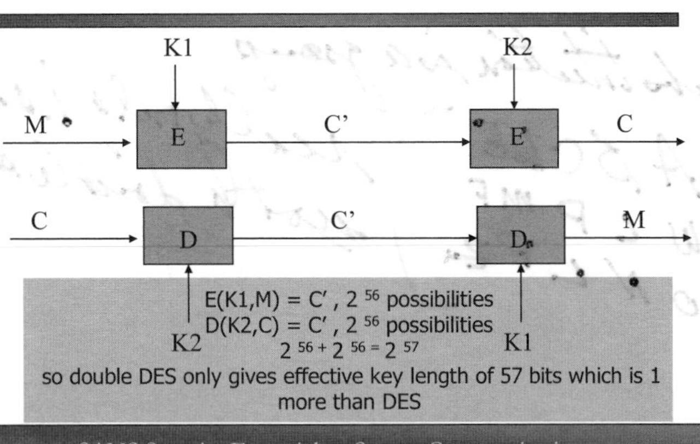

But encrypting twice with DES (Double DES) does not increase the effective key size significantly. If a cryptanalyst is able to obtain both a cleartext message (M) and its corresponding ciphertext (C), she can perform a *meet-in-the-middle attack.*

We already mentioned that brute force attacks on DES are feasible, which means we can attempt to decrypt a message with every possible key until we find the one that gives us sensible cleartext. For a meet-in-the-middle attack, we first encrypt the cleartext M with every possible key K1:

C' = E(K1, M)

giving us 2^{56} values of intermediate ciphertext C'. Then we decrypt the ciphertext C with every possible key K2:

C' = D(K2, C)

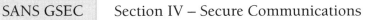

again giving us 2^{56} values of C'. The values of K1 and K2 that yield the same C' in the above equations are the two keys used for the double DES encryption. The number of operations, and therefore the resulting key length, is only $2^{56} + 2^{56} = 2^{57}$.

NOTES

Triple DES

USAGE	VULNERABILITIES
Supported in latest releases of Web clients, such as Microsoft Internet Explorer & Netscape Communicator Prefer Triple DES over DES (which is – officially – no longer considered to be secure)	Cracking Triple DES means examining all possible pairs of crypto-variables (a task considered to be beyond today's technology) So far, there have been no public reports claiming to have cracked Triple DES...

SANS Security Essentials – Secure Communications

Triple DES

To thwart meet-in-the-middle attacks, Triple DES adds a third round of encryption. Thus, when performing the two steps of the meet-in-the-middle attack, a cryptanalyst ends up with two sets of ciphertext that won't be comparable—they're separated by another encryption step. Triple DES is well-known and widely implemented, and it has been intensely scrutinized by the global community of cryptologists. Furthermore, it uses the same tried and true DES algorithm, and all existing DES implementations can be used to perform Triple DES. See the ANSI X9.52 standard for additional information on Triple DES encryption.

Support for Triple DES is built right into popular Web clients, such as Microsoft Internet Explorer and Netscape Communicator. Using Triple DES from the end user perspective is often as simple as reconfiguring the Web browser's SSL version 3 support to prefer Triple DES over DES. SSL version 2 should be disabled altogether, or else the user could unwittingly communicate with a site using only DES, and those communications could be intercepted.

NOTES

Triple DES (2)

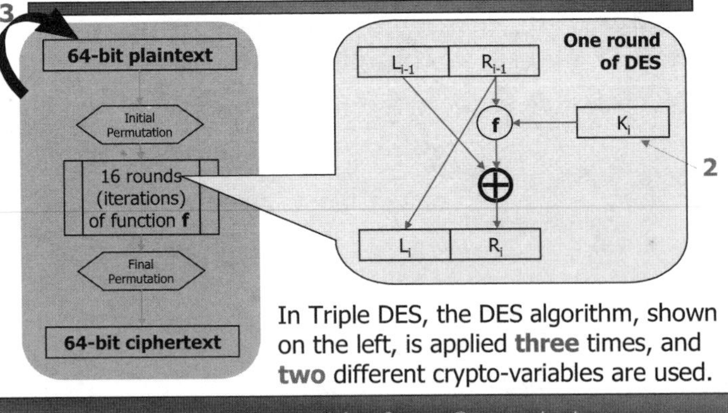

This slide shows the mechanism of the Triple DES algorithm. Note, that it looks (not surprisingly) quite similar to the DES algorithm. It is the unique way in which the DES algorithm is applied three times, using two or three different keys, that makes Triple DES secure enough to use in the interim between DES and a new standard.

NOTES

AES

- Advanced Encryption Standard
- AES is a new encryption algorithm(s) that is being designed to be effective well into the 21st century

THE FIVE "AES" FINALISTS !

- **MARS** IBM
- **RC6™** RSA Laboratories
- **Rijndael** Joan Daemen, Vincent Rijmen
- **Serpent** Ross Anderson, Eli Biham, Lars Knudsen
- **Twofish** Bruce Schneier, John Kelsey, Doug Whiting, David Wagner, Chris Hall, Niels Ferguson

Significance

Developing "good" cryptographic algorithms that can be trusted is hard. The only practical way to develop such algorithms is to perform the development process in an open manner, and under intense public scrutiny of the global cryptographic community. Can you think of a recent example in which this was not followed?

Countdown to AES !

- 1/2/1997, the quest for AES begins...
- 8/9/1999, five finalist algorithms announced
- Announced winner – Rijndeal
- 12/26/2001 – AES approved!

SANS Security Essentials – Secure Communications

Advanced Encryption Standard (AES)

On January 2, 1997, NIST announced the initiation of an effort to develop the Advanced Encryption Standard (AES). A formal call for algorithms was made on September 12, 1997. The call stipulated that AES must specify unclassified, publicly disclosed encryption algorithm(s), available royalty-free, worldwide. In addition, the algorithm(s) would implement symmetric key cryptography as a block cipher and (at a minimum) support a block size of 128 bits and key sizes of 128, 192, and 256 bits. The evaluation criteria were divided into three major categories: *security*, *cost*, and *algorithm and implementation characteristics*.

NIST selected the five AES finalists shown in Table 20.1 on August 9, 1999. In October 2000, Rijndael (pronounced "Rain Doll" or "Rhine Dahl") was announced as the winner and was approved as the official AES cipher. The two Belgian researchers who developed Rijndael are Dr. Joan Daemen (YO-ahn DAH-mun) of Proton World International and Dr. Vincent Rijmen (RYE-mun) of Katholieke Universiteit Leuven.

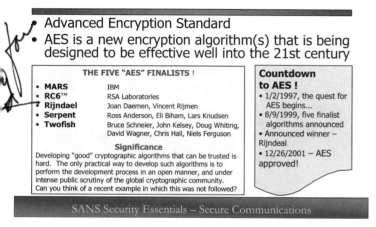

Table 20.1: AES Finalists

Cipher	Developers
MARS	IBM
RC6ä	RSA Laboratories
Rijndael	Joan Daemen, Vincent Rijmen
Serpent	Ross Anderson, Eli Biham, Lars Knudsen
Twofish	Bruce Schneier, John Kelsey, Doug Whiting, David Wagner, Chris Hall, Niels Ferguson

On December 26, 2001, NIST announced the approval of FIPS 197, which describes AES as an offical government standard, by the US Secretary of Commerce. FIPS 197 became effective on May 26, 2002. See the official AES Web site for more information: `http://www.nist.gov/aes/`.

The AES has supplanted the inadequate 56-bit DES, which is to be used only in legacy systems. AES has three key sizes: 128-bit, 192-bit, and 256-bit. Testing of the algorithm was performed by NIST and the Canadian Communications Security Establishment (CSE).

NOTES

AES Algorithm

```
Cipher (byte in[4*Nb], byte out[4*Nb], word w[Nb*(Nr+1)])
begin
  byte state[4,Nb]

  state = in

  AddRoundKey(state, w)

  for round = 1 step 1 to Nr-1
    SubBytes(state)
    ShiftRows(state)
    MixColumns(state)
    AddRoundKey(state, w+round*Nb)
  end for

  SubBytes(state)
  ShiftRows(state)
  AddRoundKey(state, w+Nr*Nb)

  out = state
end
```

SANS Security Essentials – Secure Communications

The AES Algorithm

Pseudo-code for the AES algorithm appears in the slide. Let's discuss it briefly.

- *in[]* is an array containing the block of plaintext. In general, *in[]* is 4 * *Nb* bytes in size—16 bytes in the current AES specification.
- *out[]* is an array containing the ciphertext and is also 4 * *Nb* bytes in size.
- *w[]* is the array containing the expanded key and is *Nb* * (*Nr* + 1) words in size.

The code also shows one additional data structure, *state[]*, a two-dimensional array containing the current value of the transformed ciphertext. The transformations themselves are defined by four function calls: *AddRoundKey()*, *SubBytes()*, *ShiftRows()*, and *MixColumns()*. The specifics of these transformations are described in the next section.

The rest of the code is rather straightforward:

1. The plaintext is moved into the *state[]* array.
2. The first round key is applied.
3. There are then *Nr* - 1 rounds that apply all four transformations.
4. The final round applies to all but the *MixColumns()* transformation.
5. The *state[]* array is moved into the ciphertext data structure.

NOTES

AES Basic Functions

- AES algorithm employs four basic transformations:
  - *AddRoundKey:* XOR Round Key with State
  - *SubBytes:* Substitute bytes in State s to form State s' on a byte-for-byte basis using S-box
  - *ShiftRows:* Left circular shift of rows 1-3 in State s by 1, 2, and 3 bytes, respectively
  - *MixColumns:* Apply mathematical transformation to each column in State s to form State s'

SANS Security Essentials – Secure Communications

AES Basic Functions

The AES algorithm employs four basic transformations:

- *AddRoundKey()*: Takes the appropriate round key and performs a bit-by-bit XOR with the current state
- *SubBytes()*: Using a substitution box (S-box) defined in the specification, substitutes each 8-bit quantity in the State array to a different 8-bit value
- *ShiftRows()*: Circularly shifts left the contents of state array rows 1, 2, and 3 by 1, 2, and 3 bytes, respectively. A left circular shift of one byte, for example, means that the bytes in columns 1, 2, and 3 move to positions 0, 1, and 2, respectively, and the value in byte position 0 moves to position 3.
- *MixColumns()*: Another byte value substitution, but in this case performed on a column (32-bit) basis; i.e., rather than perform an S-box substitution on a per byte basis, this transformation applies a polynomial transformation on four bytes at a time.

NOTES

AES

USAGE	VULNERABILITIES
The AES algorithm has been developed to replace DES, which is no longer officially considered to be secure. DES/Triple DES is very widely used throughout the world today, and AES is expected to be just as popular...	Too early to tell... Lets see how it stands the test of time. So far so good.... The NIST has a winner! AES will be the new standard for encryption effective May 26, 2002.

SANS Security Essentials – Secure Communications

The AES development process has given us a splendid opportunity to see first-hand what it takes to develop a cryptographic algorithm. The process is inherently complex, and the only realistic way to reduce the risk of producing a weak algorithm is to open up the development activity to all interested parties and to the intense scrutiny by the global community of cryptologists.

Contrast the AES development process with that of DVD encryption. The DVD algorithm was developed in relative secrecy, and soon after DVDs began to use it, it was cracked. This embarrassing episode should be remembered by anyone developing a new cipher.

NOTES

RSA

USAGE	VULNERABILITIES
Wide-spread support in major web clients, such as Microsoft Internet Explorer & Netscape Communicator. Expected to become even more popular after it comes off-patent later in 2000...	Cracking RSA generally means compromising poor implementations, or those using small key lengths. So far, there have been no public reports claiming to have compromised the RSA algorithm itself...

SANS Security Essentials – Secure Communications

RSA

The RSA algorithm has been widely implemented all over the world in all kinds of cryptography-enabled applications. It can be used to support both encryption and digital signature schemes. A central part of the Secure Sockets Layer (SSL), it is also included in major Web clients such as Microsoft Internet Explorer and Netscape Communicator.

Although there have been a large number of claims to having cracked the RSA algorithm, they have all turned out to be false. Vulnerabilities have been found in certain RSA implementations, however. Poor implementations of the RSA algorithm can be compromised, but as in the case of other cryptographic algorithms, it does not mean the algorithm itself has been cracked.

The working mechanism of most public-key (asymmetric) cryptographic algorithms is generally openly published and widely known. The security of the cryptosystem comes from the secrecy and size of the private key and not from the secrecy of the algorithm itself. As for other cryptographic algorithms, it is important to ensure that the key size is not so small that brute force attacks become feasible due to the small size of the resulting keyspace.

NOTES

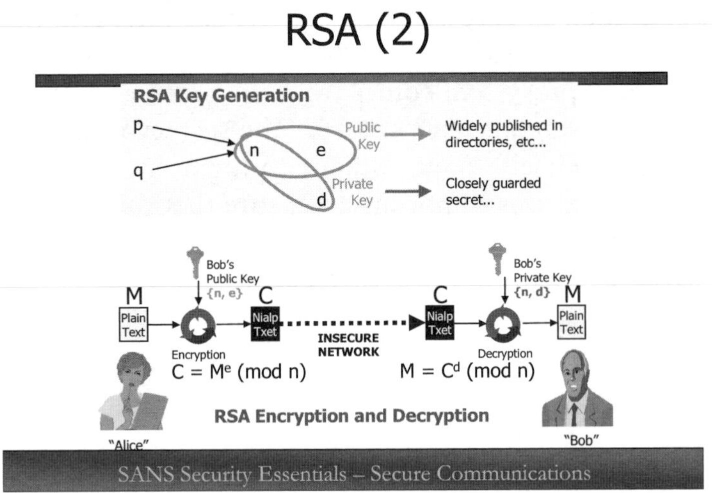

Communicating Using RSA

The slide shows how Alice and Bob can communicate using RSA and Bob's public and private key pair. First, Alice gets a copy of Bob's public key {**n**, **e**} from a public directory. Next, she uses Bob's public key to encrypt her plaintext message M to get the ciphertext $C = M^e \pmod{n}$. This ciphertext is then communicated to Bob over a possibly insecure network with adversaries present. When Bob receives the ciphertext, he uses his (trapdoor) private key {**n**, **d**} to regenerate the plaintext by calculating $M = C^d \pmod{n}$. Any eavesdropper would not have a trapdoor and must solve the intractable problem of factoring a large integer. It's the large key length that makes this integer so large as to be infeasible to attempt factoring.

NOTES

Generating RSA Keys

- p and q are large primes
- n = p * q
- e is relatively prime to (p-1) *(q-1)
- d = e^{-1} mod (p-1) * (q-1)
- Public Key: **{n,e}**
- Private key: **{n,d}**
- Large primes can be found using probalistic algorithms due to Solvay and Strassen

SANS Security Essentials – Secure Communications

Generating RSA Keys

The following are the main steps that are performed to generate an RSA key pair:

1. Choose two large primes p and q
2. Calculate n = p * q
3. Choose e so it is relatively prime to (p - 1) * (q - 1); that is, the only common factor between e and (p - 1) * (q - 1) is 1
4. Compute d = e^{-1} mod (p - 1) * (q - 1)
5. Publish the public key {**n**, **e**}
6. Keep the private key {**n**, **d**} **secret**

Large primes can be found using the Solovay-Strassen algorithm.

NOTES

RSA Example

- Select p=3, q=5
- n = pq = 15
- Choose e=11, relatively prime to (p-1)(q-1) = 8
- (11d-1)/8 must be an integer; choose d=3
- M = 8384 (0x8384)
- Encrypt
  - Public key value is (e,n) = (11,15)
  - $C_i = M_i^{11}$ mod 15
  - C = 0x2c24
- Decrypt
  - Private key value is (d,n) = (3,15)
  - $M_i = C_i^3$ mod 15
  - M = 0x8384

SANS Security Essentials – Secure Communications

RSA Example

Now the description of RSA might look complex and, indeed, the calculations take a lot of computer power given the large size of the numbers; since P and Q may be 100 or more decimal digits or more in length, D and E will be about the same size, and N may be well over 200 digits in length. Nevertheless, a simple example may help. In this example, the values for p, q, e, and d are purposely chosen to be very small.

1. Select $p = 3$ and $q = 5$.
2. The modulus $n = pq = 15$.
3. The value e must be relatively prime to $(p - 1)(q - 1) = 2 \bullet 4 = 8$. We choose $e = 11$.
4. The value d must be chosen so that $(ed - 1)/[(p - 1)(q - 1)]$ is an integer. Thus, the value $(11d - 1)/8$ must be an integer. One possible value is $d = 3$.
5. Let's say we wish to encrypt the hex value 8384. For this example, we will encrypt each hex digit individually.
6. The sender encrypts each digit of M one at a time using the public key value $(e, n) = (11, 15)$. Thus, each ciphertext character $C_i = M_i^{11}$ mod 15. The input string M = 0x8384 will be transmitted as C = 0x2c24.
7. The receiver decrypts each digit using the private key value $(d, n) = (3, 15)$. As above, each plaintext character $M_i = C_i^3$ mod 15. The input string C = 0x2c24 will now yield M = 0x8384.

NOTES

RSA vs. DES (Asymmetric vs. Symmetric)

- Fastest implementation of RSA can encrypt kilobits/second
- Fastest implementation of DES can encrypt megabits/second
- It is often proposed that RSA can be used for secure exchange of DES keys
- This 1000-fold difference in speed is likely to remain independent of technology advances
- In software, DES is about 100 times faster than RSA

SANS Security Essentials – Secure Communications

RSA Versus DES (Asymmetric Versus Symmetric)

Symmetric cryptography is generally much faster than asymmetric. Whereas the fastest hardware RSA implementation can encrypt on the order of kilobits per second, hardware DES is on the order of megabits per second. (DES was designed to run slowly in software, so in software it is only about 100 times faster). The major drawback to symmetric cryptography is that, since both the sender and receiver use the same key, the key has to be exchanged via a secure mechanism before the two parties can communicate. Therefore, RSA is often used for the initial exchange of a symmetric session key. Once the session key has been securely transmitted, Triple DES or some other symmetric cipher is used for the remainder of the session. So we take advantage of the speed of a symmetric cipher without the worry of a shared key getting misplaced or stolen.

NOTES

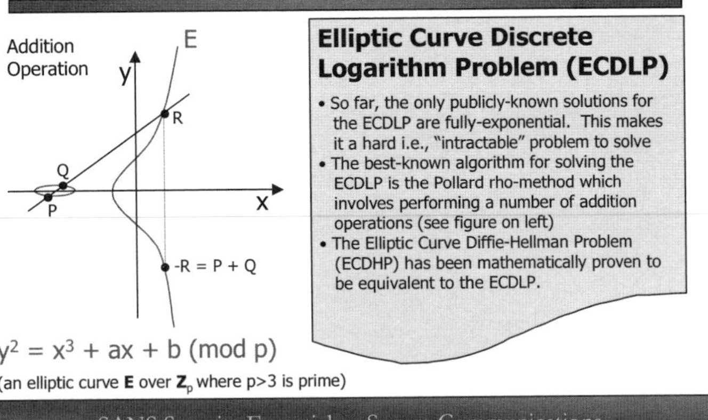

Elliptic Curve Cryptosystem
Addition Operation
E
y
R
Q
P
x
-R = P + Q
y2 = x3 + ax + b (mod p)
(an elliptic curve E over Zp where p>3 is prime)
Elliptic Curve Discrete Logarithm Problem (ECDLP)
• So far, the only publicly-known solutions for the ECDLP are fully-exponential. This makes it a hard i.e., "intractable" problem to solve
• The best-known algorithm for solving the ECDLP is the Pollard rho-method which involves performing a number of addition operations (see figure on left)
• The Elliptic Curve Diffie-Hellman Problem (ECDHP) has been mathematically proven to be equivalent to the ECDLP.
SANS Security Essentials – Secure Communications

Elliptic Curve Cryptosystems (ECCs)

In 1985, Neil Koblitz and Victor Miller independently proposed the Elliptic Curve Cryptosystem (ECC). Its security depends on the intractability of solving the discrete logarithm problem over points on an elliptic curve.

The slide depicts a general form of an elliptic curve, $y^2 = x^3 + ax + b \pmod{p}$. An interesting property of elliptic curves is that the sum of two points on the curve (P and Q) is always another point (-R) on the curve.

What exactly is the elliptic curve discrete logarithm problem (ECDLP)? For a given (fixed) prime number p and an elliptic curve in the general form $y^2 = x^3 + ax + b \pmod{p}$, let xP represent the point P added to itself x times. Further, let Q be a multiple of P, such that $Q = xP$ for some x. Then, the ECDLP is to determine x, given known values of P and Q.

So far, the only publicly known algorithms for solving the ECDLP are of exponential-time complexity. The best-known is the Pollard rho-method algorithm, which involves performing a number of addition operations (like the $P + Q = -R$ operation).

NOTES

Elliptic Curve Cryptosystem

USAGE

Where high speed, low power consumption, low storage requirements, and high security at small key lengths is critical, e.g., in wireless communications, electronic cash, and ATMs

Growing in popularity...

VULNERABILITIES

Cracking ECC generally means compromising poor implementations, or those using small key lengths.

So far, there have been no public reports claiming to have cracked the ECC algorithm itself...

SANS Security Essentials – Secure Communications

Like RSA, ECCs are capable of supporting both encryption and digital signature schemes. In addition, the ECC has some very interesting characteristics: high security even at relatively small key lengths (*i.e.*, a higher strength per bit), high-speed implementations, low processing power requirements, and low storage requirements. These properties make ECCs particularly attractive for use in resource-constrained computing environments, such as mobile telephones, PDAs, information appliances, smart cards, and ATMs. We expect to see increasing deployments of ECC-enabled applications in our e-commerce-enabled environments.

Cryptanalysis Attacks

When developing a cipher, it helps to be aware of the types of attacks cryptanalysts employ when trying to break ciphers. Each type of attack has to do with what pieces of information a cryptanalyst has in her possession. We assume the cryptanalyst always has full knowledge of the cipher algorithm.

NOTES

Crypto Attacks

- Known plaintext attack
- Chosen plaintext attack
- Adaptive chosen plaintext attack

Cipher Attacks

A cryptanalyst with access to both the ciphertext and the plaintext of a message can mount a *known-plaintext attack*. The goal is to find the key used to encrypt the ciphertext or an alternate algorithm to decrypt *any* message with a key the cryptanalyst knows.

Similar to the known-plaintext attack is the *chosen-plaintext attack*. For this attack, the cryptanalyst is able to choose what plaintext gets encrypted and see the resulting ciphertext. Sometimes being able to choose what gets encrypted can reveal information about the key.

An *adaptive-chosen-plaintext attack* is a special case of the chosen-plaintext attack. After choosing the plaintext that gets encrypted, the cryptanalyst can choose other blocks to be encrypted as well. This attack allows even more analysis based on the results of each encryption step.

The above attacks all require the cryptanalyst to have plaintext and ciphertext versions of a message. They can be guarded against by keeping plaintext secret and deleting it when it is no longer needed. You must also guard against mechanisms that allow an attacker to encrypt arbitrary messages using your secret key. Even if the attacker does not know the key, he could use an adaptive-chosen-plaintext attack by encrypting his own crafted messages.

NOTES

More Crypto Attacks

- Ciphertext only attack
- Chosen ciphertext attack
- Chosen key attack

SANS Security Essentials – Secure Communications

A *ciphertext-only attack* requires only encrypted messages—no plaintext is available. The goal is to recover one or more plaintext messages or the key used to encrypt the messages.

In a *chosen-ciphertext attack*, cryptanalyst can choose the ciphertext to be decrypted. Thus, the cryptanalyst has ciphertext and plaintext for messages he chooses. This attack is mainly used against public-key ciphers.

In a *chosen-key* attack the cryptanalyst knows something about specific relationships between the keys. Contrary to what the name would suggest, the cryptanalyst does not choose the key—that wouldn't leave much to reveal!

NOTES

Birthday Attack

- It is a surprising fact that when 23 people are put together the odds are greater than ½ that 2 or more people will share a birthday
- Our attack is related to that probability

SANS Security Essentials – Secure Communications

The Birthday Attack

Cryptanalysts can sometimes use a phenomenon known as *the birthday paradox* to attack hash signatures. People in large groups often find that at least two of them share the same birthday. They're usually astonished at the coincidence, thinking that the odds must be very slim that two people could be born on the same day of the year. It's true that it would be rather unusual to find a person with your exact birthday unless the group were very large. The odds of finding someone born on a particular day are 1 in 365 (assuming all days of the year are equally likely birthdays and nobody was born on February 29).

But just specifying that any two people have the same birthday, without specifying who, improves the odds considerably. For a group as small as 23 people, the odds are greater than 50% that two or more of them will share a birthday. If each of the 23 people compares birthdays with another, you'd have 253 comparisons. The odds, then, that *none* of the 23 have the same birthday are $(364/365)^{253} = 0.4995$. Thus, the odds that two of them share a birthday are $1 - 0.4995 = 0.5005$.

Just as pairs of people in a group might have the same birthday, pairs of messages might have the same hash signature. Of course, there are many more possibilities for hash signatures than birthdays, but the same logic applies. If an attacker can find any two messages that generate the same hash value, that is, a *collision*, she could substitute one message for the other at will. For example, maybe she has a list of password hashes but not the cleartext. If she can hash enough of her own generated cleartext to cause a collision, she has a password that works just as well as the real thing.

The entire attack is a statistical probability problem. Using the birthday attack against MD5 is improbable due to processing power limitations with our PCs. A machine processing a billion messages per second would take 586 years on average to identify the inputs. We hope our users would have changed their passwords by then!

NOTES

Course Objectives

- Concepts in Cryptography
- Symmetric (Private) Key Systems
  - Triple DES
  - AES
- Asymmetric (Public) Key Systems
  - RSA
  - ECC

SANS Security Essentials – Secure Communications

Summary

Cryptography is essential for e-commerce, military communications, and the privacy of individuals on the Internet and other networks. A cryptographic algorithm must provide confidentiality, integrity of data, authentication, and non-repudiation. To achieve these goals, mathematical problems with a suitable computational complexity are used to create a cipher that takes too long to break using brute force methods to be practical. Such problems are considered *intractable*, and though they can't usually be proven to be hard to solve, years of research and scrutiny leads us to believe they are.

Cryptography has been around for at least five millennia. Over the years, substitution and transposition ciphers have been used with increasing complexity. The German Enigma machine employed a very sophisticated substitution cipher. The Vernam one time pad is perhaps the most difficult to crack ciphers, but the fact that the key must be as long as the message makes it very difficult to use.

The Data Encryption Standard (DES), introduced in 1975, is the most commonly used cipher today. Its small 56-bit key makes it too easy to brute force for serious use today, but Triple DES effectively lengthens that key size. Triple DES employs the already available DES implementations and takes advantage of DES's decades of public scrutiny. Triple DES is considered secure enough for serious use today.

A permanent replacement for DES was needed to last for decades to come, and that was chosen as the Advanced Encryption Standard (AES) in October 2000. Rijndael, chosen from one of five finalists, is a symmetric cipher with three possible key sizes: 128-bit, 192-bit, and 256-bit.

Symmetric ciphers aren't right for every application. When the two parties, such as a merchant and a customer, have never met, secure key exchange is not easy. Public-key cryptography solves this problem by allowing for separate keys for encryption and decryption. The famous RSA algorithm is one such cipher, and it is used by the Secure Sockets Layer (SSL) to provide secure communications on the Internet. Since symmetric cryptography is much faster, RSA is often used to exchange a session key for Triple DES, which then encrypts the transaction.

NOTES

Proposed in 1985, elliptic curve cryptosystems (ECCs) offer the possibility of strong cryptography with low overhead. Thus, ECCs lend themselves to embedded applications in which memory and processing speed are at a premium.

When attacking a cipher, a cryptanalyst takes advantage of what information he has. Plaintext, ciphertext, and relationships between keys can all be useful. Being able to choose the text that gets encrypted or decrypted can be even more useful, as the cryptanalyst can deduce information based on his own input. For attacking hash algorithms, the birthday paradox makes it surprisingly likely to find collisions, two messages that hash to the same value. Strong hash algorithms like MD5, however, would take impractically long to attack this way.

Perhaps the most important lesson in this chapter is that ciphers should be developed in the open, taking advantage of the collective brainpower of cryptologists throughout the world. This kind of scrutiny reduces the likelihood that a weak algorithm is used and encourages cipher designers to place all of a cryptosystem's security in the key rather than the algorithm itself.

References

Menezes, Alfred J., Paul C. van Oorschot, and Scott A. Vanstone. *Handbook of Applied Cryptography*. Boca Raton: CRC Press, 1997.

Schneier, Bruce. *Applied Cryptography*. New York: John Wiley & Sons, Inc., 1996.

Singh, Simon. *The Code Book*. New York: Doubleday, 1999.

Chapter 21

Applying Cryptography

NOTES

Applying Cryptography

SANS Security Essentials IV:
Secure Communications

SANS Security Essentials – Secure Communications

Applying Cryptography

As was discussed in the previous two chapters, cryptography has many applications in information security. You can consider it the Swiss Army knife of information security since it has so many useful purposes. The top three purposes are Confidentiality, Integrity, and Authentication. By encrypting information with a key that only the rightful users of the information possess, it can be used to protect the information from prying eyes (confidentiality). It can also be used to detect information tampering (integrity) by cryptographically hashing the information then encrypting the hash. If the information is tampered with, the hash will not match proving that the information has been modified. Last, cryptography can be used to prove identity (authentication). This can be done by requesting that the user encrypt a test message. The encrypted test message is then decrypted using the user's stored key. If the message decrypts successfully, the user has proven their identity, or at least that they possess the right key!

Applications of Encryption

- Confidentiality
  - In Transit
  - In Storage
- Authentication & Integrity

SANS Security Essentials – Secure Communications

This last point is critical for all types of authentication. The care taken to issue and protect authentication information (e.g. passwords, tokens, keys) directly determines how confident you should be in the authentication.

The abilities that cryptography offers us are great, but how are they being used in real world networks? In this chapter we discuss some of the practical applications of cryptography, including how cryptography can be used to protect communications across a network, protect information resting in storage, provide authentication services and ensure the integrity of information.

Applying Encryption to Network Communications

Our discussion begins with one of the most common networking uses for cryptography, protecting information as it flows across a network. Information is very exposed when it leaves your PC to travel across a network to another PC or server. At any point between the source and destination of a message, a man-in-the-middle may be able to capture or modify the information contained within the message. What does this mean in the real world? Well, without encryption, an attacker might be able to capture your credit card details as you provide them to an online retailer.

Potentially more damaging, most network protocols do not encrypt their session information. Examples of these are listed in table 21.1. These protocols transmit your username and password information "in the clear." An attacker who can listen in on your network conversations when you use one of these unencrypted protocols will be able to impersonate you, gaining access to all of the network resources you have access to through that protocol. As a last example, consider the damage an attacker could cause by simply modifying the contents of the right network conversation. Changing an account number used during a banking transfer or the ship-to address during an online purchase could defraud you of potentially large amounts of money. Cryptography provides a powerful method to protect against these information security risks.

NOTES

NOTES

Table 21.1 Many common network protocols do not encrypt their network conversations.

Protocol	Purpose
Telnet	Remote login
R* commands (`rlogin`, `rsh`, `rexec`, etc)	Remote login, and command execution
FTP	File transfer
POP, IMAP	Retrieval of e-mail from mail server
SMTP	Transfer of mail between mail servers

Where to encrypt

A basic question when protecting network communications is where should the protection be performed. Should each application be responsible for protecting its own network communications, should cryptography be implemented as a service that applications can optionally use, or should it be included at the network level where all communication from and to particular locations can be protected? In practice, all of these methods are currently in use.

Application Specific

Replacing unencrypted protocols like telnet with secure alternatives can be an easy way to improve security, assuming that a secure replacement exists. Examples include replacing post office protocol (POP) with authenticated post office protocol (APOP), Network File System (NFS) with the Andrew File System (AFS), and (more commonly) telnet and ftp with Secure Shell (SSH). Keep in mind however, that each application can implement different security enhancements and not all replacements protect all conversations. For example, APOP only improves on POP by protecting the authentication messages, not the e-mail messages themselves. APOP prevents casual eavesdropping of usernames and passwords but does not prevent an attacker from listening in or modifying e-mail conversations.

Secure Shell on the other hand, provides several security enhancements to the protocols it replaces. Key among these is its ability to support strong certificate-based authentication, its ability to encrypt all session traffic providing confidentiality, and its ability to authenticate both sides of a connection, server and client. A high quality, free version is available from the OpenSSH organization making its use a no-brainer whenever telnet or ftp like services are required.

Transport Layer

Another option for protecting information transfer is to provide a secure communications service that many applications can use. The advantage of this method is that each application does not have to re-implement the same security services. This is the approach taken by Secure Socket Layer (SSL).

SSL is a protocol created by Netscape Corporation. It was later standardized as the Transport Layer Security (TLS) protocol by the IETF. Quoting from RFC 2246, "The primary goal of the TLS Protocol is to provide privacy and data integrity between two communicating applications." It is comprised of two protocols: the record protocol, which is used to securely transfer application data, and the handshake protocol, which is used to negotiate the details of a secure session. The combination of these two protocols provide, in an application protocol independent way, confidentiality of the communications using symmetric key encryption, integrity of the communications using a cryptographic message authentication code, and mutual certificate-based authentication of client and server.

Many application protocols have been redesigned to utilize SSL security services. There are RFCs that define SSL's use for protecting the transfer of mail from server to server (RFC 2487), for the secure retrieval of mail from a mail server (RFC 2595), and for authentication of PPP sessions (RFC 2716). Its most common use is to protect and authenticate Web sessions.

You most likely have used SSL if you have ever purchased anything from a Web site. Most e-commerce Web sites use SSL to protect communication whenever sensitive information is being requested from you, such as your credit card numbers or your address. You can tell when the Web site you are visiting has activated SSL because a symbol of a locked padlock appears at the bottom of your browser's window whenever an SSL session has been successfully set up.

Even though SSL is application independent, applications must be modified to make use of its services. Just as with application specific cryptography, if the applications you need to use do not support SSL, you cannot make use of its protection. This is where the last type of network cryptographic protection we will discuss comes in.

Network Layer

Network layer encryption protects network conversations whether the application using the network supports cryptography or not. Network layer encryption sits in-between the transmitter and receiver. It accepts in clear-text information, and then encrypts it prior to sending it out. At the receiving end, the information is decrypted and forwarded on to its final destination. This type of network encryption is called a virtual private network (VPN).

NOTES

NOTES

Confidentiality in Transit
• Private Network
– Pro: Dedicated lines and equipment are not shared by others
– Con: Dedicated lines are expensive, grow more so with distance, and are underutilized except at peak
SANS Security Essentials – Secure Communications

Virtual Private Networks

Prior to the popularization of Virtual Private Networks (VPNs), companies wanting to protect network conversations between different locations purchased dedicated leased lines, frame-relay circuits, ATM connections, or other types of private circuits that provided connectivity between the sites from a telecommunications company. They could be reasonably confident that their information could not be intercepted because these circuits only allow the two sides of the connection to exchange information. No third parties should be able to communicate over the private connection. This assumes that you trust the telecommunications provider, which may or may not be a good bet depending upon where in the world you are. While secure, these circuits also tend to be slow and expensive and become more expensive as they get faster, or the distance increases between the sites that need to communicate. There is also a large lead time between the decision to set up one of these connections and getting it running. It can take months for a telecommunications company to fulfill a new circuit order.

Virtual Private Network (VPN)

- Data is encrypted at one end of the VPN from "cleartext" into "ciphertext"
- Ciphertext is transmitted over the Internet
- Data is decrypted at the other end of the VPN from "ciphertext" back into the original "cleartext"

SANS Security Essentials – Secure Communications

VPNs are a perfect alternative to costly, inflexible private circuits. They give companies the option of setting up virtual circuits across public networks, such as the Internet. Encryption provides the confidentiality needed as the private information flows across the public network. This ability allows VPNs to establish secure communication between different remote offices and can also be used to establish remote access to internal network resources by employees from their homes or while they are on travel.

NOTES

NOTES

VPN Advantages

- Improved Flexibility
  - A VPN "tunnel" over the Internet can be set up rapidly. A frame circuit can take weeks.
  - A good VPN will also support Quality of Service (QoS).
- Lowered Cost
  - There are documented cases of a VPN paying for itself in weeks or months.
  - There are also cases where the hidden costs sunk the project!

SANS Security Essentials – Secure Communications

One of the biggest benefits of VPN technology is its flexibility. If you need a secure channel between two hosts only for a day, or even an hour, then a VPN may fit the bill. Once you have all of the components to establish a VPN, setting one up only requires configuration. This makes the technology far more flexible than private circuits, which must be ordered far in advance of their use and may also require additional hardware. This flexibility lends itself to creating new business solutions. For example it's not cost-effective to wire a T1 for every employee who works from home. It's practical, however, to load software on their laptop and let them connect to the home office via a VPN over the Internet.

There are also some disadvantages to VPNs, the primary of which is performance guarantees. Most private circuits, such as leased-lines or ATM, have an ability to guarantee bandwidth and latency. Similar guarantees have been difficult to achieve with VPNs. TCP/IP, the networking protocol for the Internet, was not designed to provide quality of service (QoS) and improvements have been slow in coming. Providing QoS for VPNs is even more difficult because many QoS solutions require the service provider to look into the messages they are passing on to decide whether the message has higher priority than other messages. If the service provider cannot examine the information in a message (because of encryption), it makes it even more difficult to decide which network traffic should get priority.

There are solutions to these problems. Multiprotocol Label Switching (MPLS), an alternative over traditional layer three routing, is used to address these problems. It allows forwarding of messages across the Internet without requiring examination of the message contents. MPLS based VPNs can be purchased from a wide variety of Internet Service Providers, though they are more expensive than standard IP services.

Types of Remote Access

- Client VPN
  - Example: Laptop dial-up connection to remote access server at HQ
- Site-to-Site
  - Example: L.A. office connection to D.C. office location

SANS Security Essentials – Secure Communications

Types of VPNs

There are two primary categories of VPNs to consider, client-to-site, and site-to-site. Client-to-site VPNs provide remote access from a remote client, such as a traveling sales rep or telecommuting employee to the corporate network. Such VPNs are normally established between the client's computer and a gateway device located at the border of the corporate network. The client's computer runs VPN software that allows it to establish the connection to the VPN gateway.

Site-to-site VPNs provide connectivity to networks, such as headquarters and a remote office. In these connections, gateway devices are located in front of both networks. Information needing to flow between the sites is directed to the local gateway, which then encrypts the contents of the message and forwards it to the other site's gateway. The remote site's gateway decrypts the message then sends it onto its final destination.

There is a third, less common type of VPN, the client-to-client VPN. These VPNs establish a protected link between two specific computers. As such, they could be considered the most secure of the VPN types, because in the client-to-site, and site-to-site VPNs, part of the path between the transmitter of a message and the receiver of the message is unencrypted. For instance, in client-to-site VPN, the communication from the client's computer to the VPN gateway is protected, but the message travels unencrypted (and unprotected) from the VPN gateway to the internal corporate server the client is trying to communicate with. If an attacker inserts herself somewhere between the VPN gateway and this server, she would be able to eavesdrop or modify the contents of the message.

If client-to-client VPNs are more secure, why are they not used more often? The majority of the reason is the configuration required. Each pair of hosts wanting to communicate must be specifically configured to allow the communication. The most important part of this configuration is key installation. Each host must have a separate unique key that it can use to encrypt information to a particular destination host. Because of this, client-to-client VPNs between every two hosts would quickly become unmanageable as the number of hosts increases, if manual configuration is used. Public Key Infrastructure, which is discussed later in this chapter, is one way to address this key distribution problem.

NOTES

NOTES

VPN System Components

- Routers
- Firewalls
- Servers & clients
- Encryption
- LDAP server
- QoS
- X.509 digital certificates
- Load balancing
- Failover & redundancy
- Public Key Infrastructure
- Key management schemes

SANS Security Essentials – Secure Communications

Components of a VPN

Chances are, the network components you already have in place have some capability to implement VPN services. For instance, the Microsoft Windows XP operating system comes with software to implement IPSec VPNs, Cisco routers can act as VPN gateways, and most firewalls come with VPN gateway ability. Using existing components can make implementing VPNs affordable.

There is no free lunch though! Adding VPN duties to an already loaded network device may not be the best choice. VPN encryption operations are very performance intensive. Adding this burden to the work already being performed by a router or firewall may cause it to slow down unacceptably. For this reason, many VPNs gateways are implemented using dedicated VPN devices. These devices are designed to efficiently encrypt and decrypt network traffic, making them more suited to high-performance VPNs.

The gateways of the VPN are only part of the VPN solution though. Additional devices may be needed to perform such services as authentication and authorization, key management, load balancing, failover and QoS.

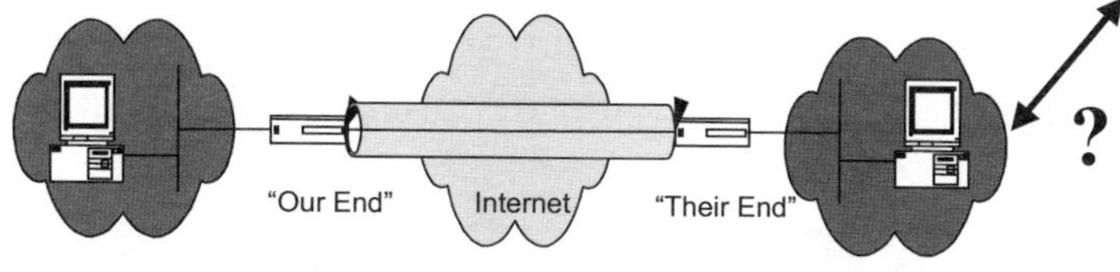
Security Implications
• Bypassing Firewalls, IDS, Virus scanners, Web filters
• Trusting the "Other End"
"Our End"
Internet
"Their End"
?
SANS Security Essentials – Secure Communications

Security Implications

Many sites assume that since they have established a VPN, they are secure. This is a bad assumption, as VPNs bring their own special security concerns into your network. One frequent error made with VPNs is to overly trust the other side of a VPN connection.

With site-to-site VPNs, it is common to see the VPN connection allowed into the network without applying any security restrictions to it. This might be appropriate if the other side of the VPN belongs to the same organization and is controlled by the same security policies and procedures. If the other side of the connection is another organization, such as a business partner, though, access through the VPN should be restricted. Most current VPN gateways include firewall abilities allowing them to limit network traffic across the VPN. It is a best practice to restrict this traffic to the minimum necessary to fulfill the business need of the connection.

Another potential security problem VPNs introduce is caused by the encryption VPNs use to protect the messages they exchange. As mentioned before, this encryption prevents an attacker from eavesdropping, but it also prevents intrusion detection systems and anti-virus tools from examining the packets for malicious or inappropriate content. This reduces or eliminates the effectiveness of these security tools.

Last, client-to-site VPNs suffer from the trusted client problem. Many organizations have strict rules on the type of software allowed on corporate computers. Part of the reason for these controls is that unauthorized software may contain security vulnerabilities. When allowing employees to use a VPN to access the corporate network, the organization may not be in the same position to dictate a tight configuration. In fact, most home computers are insecurely configured. If an attacker discovers the home computer and takes it over, they may be able to use their access to the computer to leverage access to the corporate network over the employee's VPN connection. For this reason, it is a good idea to recommend, or better yet, enforce the use of a personal firewall product and anti-virus software prior to allowing remote users to access client-to-site VPNs.

Now that we've discussed how encryption can be used to protect communications over a network, it's time to introduce some concrete examples of technology that implements these ideas. The first is IP Security (IPSec), the current industry standard for setting up Virtual Private Networks.

NOTES

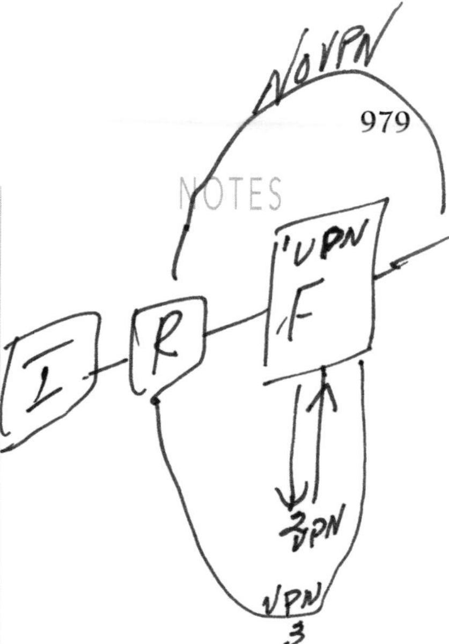

NOTES

IPSec Overview

- Issued by IETF as an open standard (RFC 2401) thus promoting multi-vendor interoperability
- Enables encrypted communication between users and devices
- Implemented transparently into network infrastructure
- Scales from small to very large networks
- Commonly implemented - most VPN devices and clients are IPSec-compliant

SANS Security Essentials – Secure Communications

IPSec

IP Security (IPSec) is an IETF standard for establishing virtual private networks. It is slowly replacing proprietary VPN protocols and becoming the industry standard. Many products on the market now support IPSec natively, such as Checkpoint Firewall-1, Cisco routers, and Windows XP.

Like the application level and transport level techniques we have discussed, IPSec provides data integrity, confidentiality, and authentication. IPSec also offers sophisticated replay attack prevention.

Note

Attackers use replay attacks by copying a message as it goes across the network, then re-transmitting the copy to the destination. Even if the attacker cannot read the encrypted message, he can cause undesired results. For example, if the message was a request to transfer $1,000, the replay might be able to cause an additional transfer making the total transferred $2,000. IPSec includes specific mechanisms to detect and prevent replay.

Types of IPSec Headers

- Authentication Header (AH)
  - Data integrity-no modification of data in transit
  - Origin authentication-identifies where data originated
- Encapsulated Security Payload (ESP)
  - Data integrity-no modification of data in transit
  - Origin authentication-identifies where data originated
  - Confidentiality - all data encrypted

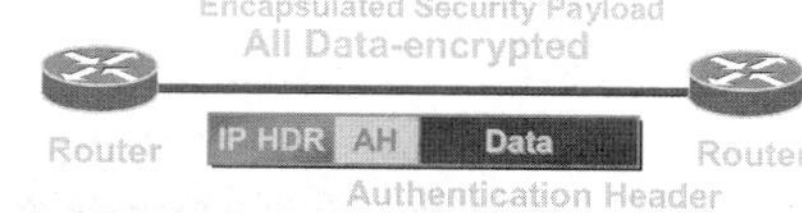

SANS Security Essentials – Secure Communications

The Protocols of IPSec

IPSec is actually a collection of protocols used individually or together to implement its various network security services. Primarily, IPSec is composed of the Authentication Header (AH) protocol, the Encapsulated Security Payload (ESP) protocol, and the Internet Key Exchange (IKE) protocol. To understand how IPSec works, let's examine the abilities offered by each of these protocols.

Authentication Header (AH)

AH provides message integrity, anti-replay, and source authentication. It works by adding authentication information into each IP packet. To see how this works, we need to understand some of the information that goes into an IP packet.

IP packets are composed of many pieces of information, each important. One of the most important, from a security standpoint, is the source IP field. The source IP field is used to tell the recipient who sent the message. In a normal network conversation, the computer that is sending a message uses its own IP address as the source address. This is important to the security of the system because many firewall systems use source IP addresses to determine whether a message should be allowed into a network or not. If an attacker can choose to lie about his IP address, he could potentially use an address that the firewall does allow in fooling the firewall into accepting a message that it should have denied. Without AH there is nothing to prevent an attacker from lying about the source or any other field inside the packet.

To prevent this, AH adds a keyed hash of the message to the packet. This hash is referred to as the Integrity Check Value (ICV). In the ICV computation, AH includes every field that does not change during its trip from source to destination. This includes the source address, destination address, length, and the data. This information is inserted into the packet after the regular IP header, but before the data.

To verify that the packet has not been tampered with, the recipient re-computes the ICV. If any of the hashed fields, including the source address, have been changed, even by a bit, the hash will be different and the integrity check will fail. This provides both integrity checking and authentication. The integrity is guaranteed because the hash must match the message. However, what about the

NOTES

NOTES

authentication? Remember that this is a keyed hash. The key used is negotiated between the sender and recipient prior to the start of communications. You can only compute the hash if you know the right key. Thus, if a recipient can re-compute the hash using the key previously agreed upon with the sender, then the message has been authenticated as originating from that sender.

The algorithm used to create the ICV is configurable. The architects of the IPsec protocol endeavored to minimize any dependency between IPSec and the cryptographic algorithms that it relies upon. This is to prevent the standard from becoming out-of-date if a new cryptographic algorithm needs to be supported. Only two algorithms are required by the IETF for a particular AH implementation to be considered compliant to the protocol. These are MD5 and SHA-1. Both algorithms are used by AH for the same purpose, the creation of a hashed message authentication code (HMAC).

As mentioned earlier, some fields have to be left out of the ICV computation because they change during transmission. An example of this is the time-to-live (TTL) field. The TTL field is used to limit how many different routers (or hops) a packet can pass through before it reaches its destination. Every time a packet arrives at a router, its TTL field is decremented. When it reaches zero, the packet is dropped and an error message is sent back to the source of the packet. You can see why this could never be included inside the hash computation. This field is guaranteed to be different by the time it arrives at the recipient. The recipient's hash computation would always fail!

There is one last feature worth mentioning about AH, its anti-replay capabilities. Notice the sequence number field inside the AH header. AH uses this number to determine whether a packet has been seen before. The way it works is straightforward. When an AH connection is first established, the value is set to zero. Every time a packet is sent out, the number is incremented. So, the first packet has a sequence number of zero, the next 1 and so on. To prevent replay, the receiving system must make sure that it never accepts two messages with the same sequence number.

There is an additional wrinkle to this. The sequence number is a 32–bit value. This allows for over 4 billion different sequence numbers. While this may sound like a large number, it is not inconceivable, given enough time, for it to be exceeded. When this happens, the protocol specifies that the current key in use be renegotiated and that the sequence number value be reset to zero.

Encapsulated Security Payload (ESP)

ESP is the companion protocol to AH. Like AH, it offers message integrity, anti-replay, and authentication features, but it also offers confidentiality by providing the ability to encrypt the contents of the message. Its implementation differs from AH in the area within the packet that it concentrates. ESP does not pay any attention to the IP header of the packet. It concentrates instead on the message contents.

Just like AH, ESP is designed to minimize its dependency on any particular encryption algorithm. To establish compliance with the IETF standard though, an implementation must support the following algorithms: Digital Encryption Standard (DES) for encryption, and HMACs based upon both MD5 and SHA-1 for authentication. Each implementation must also include the NULL algorithm for both encryption and authentication. The reason for the NULL algorithm will be seen momentarily.

As stated above, ESP provides confidentiality and authentication. You don't have to use both though. It is possible to use ESP to only perform authentication, or confidentiality, or both. Here's how.

When encryption is chosen, all of the information in the packet above the network level is encrypted using the selected encryption algorithm. This includes the transport layer protocol header (i.e.,TCP, UDP, ICMP) and all of the message data. The packet is then rewritten by replacing all of the transport data with the payload field of the ESP message.

If you do not need the message to be confidential, you can turn encryption off by using the NULL algorithm. This algorithm, as you might guess from the name, does nothing to the message. When used, an ESP message is still generated and placed into the outgoing packet. The only difference is that the message data contained within the ESP payload is still in its original form (i.e. clear-text).

Authentication is performed similarly to the AH protocol, by creating and then verifying an ICV. The difference is what information is included in the ICV calculation. ESP authentication only includes the information inside the ESP message, so the source and destination of the packet do not enter into the calculation. It does not matter whether the payload of the ESP message is encrypted or not. The calculation is the same.

Just as with ESP confidentiality, a NULL algorithm is available for ESP authentication. This algorithm acts differently than the NULL confidentiality algorithm. When it is called, instead of returning the same message that it was presented, it returns nothing. This results in the authentication field of the ESP message being empty.

There is one caveat worth mentioning about these NULL algorithms. You can use one or the other but not both. Using both would effectively disable ESP and for obvious reasons is not included in the standard.

NOTES

NOTES

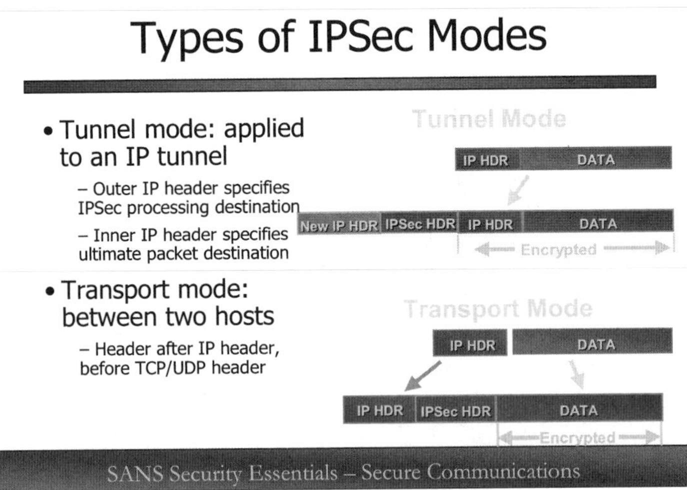

Types of IPSec Modes
• Tunnel mode: applied to an IP tunnel
– Outer IP header specifies IPSec processing destination
– Inner IP header specifies ultimate packet destination
• Transport mode: between two hosts
– Header after IP header, before TCP/UDP header
Tunnel Mode
IP HDR
DATA
New IP HDR
IPSec HDR
IP HDR
DATA
Encrypted
Transport Mode
IP HDR
DATA
IP HDR
IPSec HDR
DATA
Encrypted
SANS Security Essentials – Secure Communications

Modes of IPSec

Both AH and ESP can operate in two modes, transport mode or tunnel mode. Transport mode is used to protect a conversation between two specific hosts on a network. For example, two hosts using ESP in transport mode would be establishing a client-to-client style VPN. Up to now, all of our IPSec examples have been based upon transport mode. Tunnel mode is used to establish site-to-site and client-to site VPNs. Let's take a look at how tunnel mode differs from transport mode for both AH and ESP.

How tunneling works

Tunnel mode, as the name implies, sets up virtual tunnels between gateways. Tunnel mode works by accepting in an entire IP packet, which is then packaged inside an IPSec packet. This new IPSec packet is not addressed to the destination of the packet it is carrying. Instead, its destination address is the address of the gateway system at the other side of the tunnel. When the destination gateway receives a tunnel packet, it un-packages it to get out the original packet. This packet is then routed onward to the host listed in its destination field. From this original packet's point of view, the trip across the tunnel represents just one hop, regardless of how many intermediate routers may have actually existed between the two gateways.

Tunnel Mode and AH

As in transport mode, AH provides authentication and integrity services for the packet. Unlike transport mode though, tunnel mode AH provides these services for the entire packet, including the TTL field. Implementation of tunneling mode AH is straightforward given our description of how tunneling works.

When a packet arrives at a gateway for passage across the tunnel, a new IP packet is created. This tunnel packet's header contains the source address of the gateway and the destination address of the remote side gateway. The data portion of the tunnel packet contains the original packet in its entirety.

Now, AH proceeds exactly the same as transport mode AH. An ICV is computed based upon the fields inside the tunnel IP packet including the data field, which includes our original packet. The ICV is placed just after the new packet header and before the data field. When the packet arrives at the destination gateway, the ICV value is recomputed. If it matches, it proves that the packet has not been tampered with while it traveled through the tunnel. This includes proving that the original packet has not changed, and that the fields of the tunnel packet are genuine. The gateway can now remove the original packet from the data field of the tunnel packet and send it on its way.

Tunnel Mode and ESP

ESP tunnel mode works similarly to AH tunnel mode. When a new packet arrives at a gateway, it is packaged inside a tunnel packet that is addressed to the remote gateway. Encryption and authentication algorithms are then run on this new packet's data field, thus protecting the original packet. Note that this does not protect the header of the tunnel packet. The resulting tunnel packet includes the new IP header addressed to the remote gateway, and an ESP message, which includes the cipher-text and authentication data for the original packet.

Combining Tunnel and Transport Modes

In some cases, it is useful to combine tunnel and transport modes. There are many ways they can be combined. One example of this is using transport mode AH to protect the integrity of an ESP tunnel. When using ESP tunnels, even though the original packet is protected, it is possible that an attacker could modify the ESP packet's header without detection. To prevent this we can use transport mode AH. The transport mode AH prevents any modification of the tunnel packet, while the ESP provides confidentiality of the original packet.

Session Establishment

There are many options available within IPSec. Before an IPSec connection can be created, the two sides of the connection must agree on what options they are going to use. In addition, many of the options require the exchange of other information, such as session keys and sequence numbers. Session establishment negotiates these details. The agreements from these negotiations are called Security Associations.

Security Associations

Security Associations (SA) are a critical part of IPSec. They document the security services (called transforms) that a particular IPSec connection is using. These details include the IPSec protocol being used (AH or ESP), the authentication mechanism that is going to be used (e.g. HMAC-MD5), which cryptographic algorithm to employ (e.g. DES, NULL), the length of the key used in the cryptographic algorithm (e.g. 56–bit), what security services are being applied (e.g. authentication, confidentiality) and any other details necessary to fully describe the security services of the connection. Each IPSec connection must have an SA set up prior to beginning communication.

It is important to note that SAs are unidirectional. A single SA only describes transforms for one side of a network conversation. To establish a two-way conversation, two SAs are required, one to allow packets to be protected from point A to point B, the second to allow packets to be protected from point B to point A. These SAs are normally set to use the

NOTES

NOTES

exact same transforms, but this is not actually required. There is nothing to stop an implementation from using different transforms on each side of the conversation: for instance, encrypting one direction with DES, but leaving the other direction unencrypted. This would normally be undesirable!

Internet Key Exchange (IKE)

Internet Key Exchange (IKE) is the protocol used by IPSec to negotiate the session details of a connection and then document them as SAs. IKE is a hybrid protocol composed of a key management framework and a key exchange protocol. These are the Internet Security Association and Key Management Protocol (ISAKMP) for key management and the Oakley Key Determination Protocol (Oakley) for key exchange. IKE is occasionally referred to as ISAKMP/Oakley. Elements of a third protocol called Secure Key Exchange Mechanism (SKEME) are also used to extend the capabilities of Oakley.

The negotiation occurs in two phases. In phase one, a secure, authenticated connection is established to protect the conversations that will occur next. This is extremely important as the security of all future conversations relies upon the ability of the two sides of the connection to privately exchange keys and other security details. Phase one provides this privacy. The results of phase one are recorded in a special SA (ISAKMP-SA) that is only used to protect ISAKMP conversations. In phase two, the security services and details for an SA are negotiated over the ISAKMP-SA.

There are two methods that can be used to accomplish phase one, referred to as main mode and aggressive mode. The difference between them is that main mode checks the identity of the participants, and aggressive mode does not. Identity protection sounds like a good thing and it is. So why would we go without it? If public key cryptography is used to set up the ISAKMP-SA, identity can be inferred. If side A of a conversation can decrypt side B's messages using side B's public key, we can assume that the message was generated by B as only B should have B's private key. This provides the identity protection indirectly, making it unnecessary for ISAKMP to perform a special operation to check it.

Phase two also has multiple modes but the primary one is quick mode. This is the mode that is used to negotiate the security details for the ESP and AH SAs. This is also the mode that is used to re-key connections when the keys have been in use for too long.

Examples of IPSec Encryption

- Data Encryption Standard (DES)
  - 56-bit algorithm
- Triple DES (3DES)
  - The 56-bit DES algorithm run 3 times
  - 112-bit triple DES includes 2 keys
  - 168-bit triple DES includes 3 keys

When negotiating SAs, the initiator of the connection cannot be sure what IPSec services will be supported by the receiver. To accommodate this, in the initial exchange, the sender is allowed to offer the receiver its choice of several different transforms. For instance, the sender may prefer to use 3DES for ESP confidentiality, but cannot be sure that the receiver supports it. So the sender may offer the receiver transforms for DES and 3DES. Assuming the receiver supports at least one of these, the SA can be established. This capability makes it easier to establish connections between different systems.

Note

Be careful when configuring your IPSec devices that you only allow transforms that meet your security needs. If you allow a transform that provides weaker security than you are comfortable with (e.g. NULL), the receiver just may choose it.

You may be wondering why there are two phases, instead of just combining them. The answer is that phase one requires a lot of effort to set up, so it is much more efficient to only perform it once when multiple SAs need to be negotiated and maintained. After an ISAKMP-SA is established, it can be reused many times over the life of the IPSec connection.

Authentication

In Phase one of IKE, an authenticated connection must be established. There are three methods available to perform this authentication: pre-shared keys, digital signatures, and public key encryption.

NOTES

NOTES

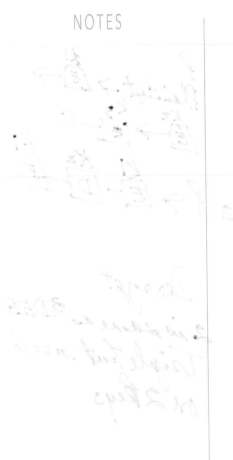

IPSec Key Management

- Internet Key Exchange (IKE)
- Security Association (SA)
- Authenticates peers
  - Pre-shared keys
  - Public key cryptography
  - Digital signatures
- Negotiates policy to protect communication
- Key exchange
  - Diffie-Hellman

IKE 1st
IPSec Next

SANS Security Essentials – Secure Communications

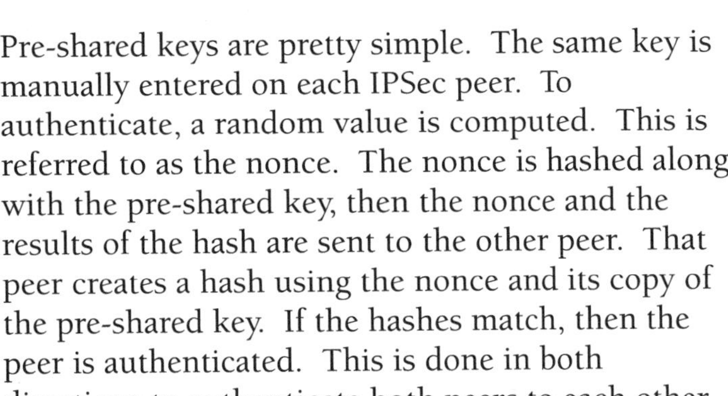

Pre-shared keys are pretty simple. The same key is manually entered on each IPSec peer. To authenticate, a random value is computed. This is referred to as the nonce. The nonce is hashed along with the pre-shared key, then the nonce and the results of the hash are sent to the other peer. That peer creates a hash using the nonce and its copy of the pre-shared key. If the hashes match, then the peer is authenticated. This is done in both directions to authenticate both peers to each other.

While simple to set up, pre-shared keys do not scale well. For every two peers that want to communicate, a shared secret must be installed on each of them. For a small number of peers, this is no problem, but this quickly becomes unmanageable with larger numbers.

The next method available is digital signatures. This method hashes a nonce along with some additional IKE information, including a shared secret derived from a Diffie-Hellman exchange. The sender then cryptographically signs this information. If the receiver can both recreate the hash and verify the signature on the hash, then the sender is authenticated. The method used to verify the hash depends upon the digital signature algorithm in use. For instance, the RSA digital signature algorithm is public key based. To verify an RSA signature the verifier must know the sender's public key.

The last authentication method is public key encryption. Just like the digital signature method, a nonce is hashed along with some shared information. This hash is then encrypted using the sender's private key. If the receiver can decrypt the hash using the sender's public key, the sender is authenticated. As with RSA digital signatures, the sender's public key must be known to perform the authentication. This method has the advantage of providing non-repudiation. A sender can never deny having sent an authentication message because ONLY the sender can create the message.

The problem with all of these methods is how to get each peer the information it needs to perform the authentication. With pre-shared key, it's obvious and time consuming; an administrator must configure each peer with a secret for every other peer. There is a better option, though, for the digital signature and public key encryption methods. It's called public key infrastructure (PKI), and we'll be describing it in detail before the end of this chapter.

Examples of Non-IPSec VPNs

- Layer 2 Forwarding (L2F)
- Layer 2 Tunneling Protocol (L2TP), combines PPTP and L2F
- PPP Extensible Authentication Protocol (authentication only, RFC 2284)
- SOCKS protocol
- PPP
- SLIP

SANS Security Essentials – Secure Communications

Supporting Other Network Protocols

It is worth mentioning that IPSec is a VPN protocol for IP networks. It was created to be a standard part of IPv6 and an optional capability for IPv4. It was not designed to provide VPN services for other protocols such as Novell's IPX or Microsoft's NetBIOS. It is possible to carry these protocols across an IPSec connection, though. Depending upon the type of connection, this can be done using the Generic Routing Encapsulation (GRE) protocol or the Layer 2 Routing Protocol (L2TP).

If you need to securely bridge two non-IP networks (IPX, Appletalk) over an IP network, you can use GRE combined with IPSec. GRE allows you to set up a tunnel, which will pass arbitrary protocols between two computers connected over an IP network. You can protect this tunnel by establishing IPSec transport mode SAs between the GRE end-point systems.

IPSec can also be used to protect multi-protocol connections between dial-in users and corporate networks by combining IPSec with L2TP. L2TP came out of work performed by Microsoft and Cisco. Each had proprietary protocols to handle multi-protocol tunneling. Microsoft's protocol was the point–to–point tunneling protocol (PPTP) and Cisco's was the Layer 2 Forwarding protocol (L2F). Both extend the point-to-point protocol (PPP), allowing it to be used to tunnel multiple network protocols across an IP network. For example, they both allow a dial-up user to connect from an ISP to a corporate network, while supporting the ability for the dial-up user to send IPX packets to the corporate network. L2TP uses the best features of both protocols and is an IETF standard.

Using our dial-in user as an example, to establish a L2TP connection, the user first uses her modem to dial-in to a remote access concentrator. L2TP is then used to create a tunnel between the dial-in user and a network server. The network server acts as the gateway for the dial-in user into the remote network.

When using L2TP and IPSec together, the L2TP protocol is used to set up the tunnel and IPSec is used to protect the tunnel. This is implemented by establishing an IPSec connection between the remote access server and the network server. By doing this, all traffic passing through the tunnel is protected. You may have noticed that this does not provide end-to-end protection. The connection between the dial-in user and the remote access

NOTES

NOTES

server is still unprotected. If complete end-to-end protection is desired, a GRE tunnel or similar technique would need to be set up across the L2TP tunnel, and IPSec SAs would need to be set up between the dial-in user and the network server.

IPSec and Network Address Translation

Network address translation (NAT), described in Chapter 14, is a useful technique for preserving address space and hiding internal network details. Unfortunately, NAT and IPSec AH are incompatible. To see why, we need to look at what NAT does to a packet.

NAT is normally implemented by a device at the border of a network such as a router or firewall. Computers inside the network are assigned private addresses. When one of these computers needs to send a packet to the outside, it creates a packet with its own private address as the source and the external device's public IP address as the destination. When this packet reaches the NAT device, its IP header is rewritten, by replacing the private source address with a public source address. This new version of the packet is then forwarded on to its destination.

The rewriting of the source address is what breaks AH. Assume for a moment that an IPSec AH SA has been established between our internal, privately addressed computer and an external, publicly addressed computer. When the packet is created, the AH protocol will create a hash of the IP header fields including the source IP address. When this packet reaches the NAT device and gets rewritten, the hash no longer matches the header. The public computer's IPSec implementation will no longer be able to verify the validity of the packet.

IPSec ESP can be used with NAT both in transport and tunnel modes. ESP does not include the IP source address as part of its calculations, so it is not broken by NAT style address rewrites. If you are going to use IPSec across a NAT device, though, you should prefer tunnel mode. ESP transport mode is almost always combined with AH to prevent tampering with the header of the packet. Since AH cannot be used, the only way to protect the packet header is by placing it in a protected tunnel.

This ends our discussion of IPSec and with it our discussion of network layer protection. Now it's time to move on to an example of application specific protection.

Confidentiality in Storage

- Pretty Good Privacy (PGP)
  - Started out in 1991 as a way to bring privacy to a very new, very public communication medium: Email.
  - Freeware accessible at:
    - http://web.mit.edu/network/pgp.html
    - http://www.pgpi.org/

SANS Security Essentials – Secure Communications

Pretty Good Privacy (PGP)

PGP is a great example of an application-specific use of cryptography. The current commercial version of PGP supports encryption and the creation of digital signatures for files, provides IPSec-compliant VPN capabilities and acts as a host firewall, but PGP's original purpose was to protect e-mail.

PGP provides two main protections for e-mail. First, it supports strong encryption of the e-mail message. This encryption is implemented using a combination of public key and symmetric key cryptography. The second protection is digital signature of e-mail messages, providing non-repudiation and integrity verification.

In this section we will concentrate on PGP as an e-mail security tool. We will cover why it was created and how it works. We will also discuss one of the most interesting parts of PGP, how trust is established between PGP participants.

History and Purpose

In 1991, Phil Zimmerman created PGP. He was motivated by the potential passage of a bill that would have forced providers of cryptographic systems to include back doors into their products to allow the Government the ability to decrypt anyone's private messages. While eventually defeated, the bill provided Zimmerman the incentive to create the first version of PGP, a program designed to provide confidentiality for e-mail messages. This political stand was to come at a high price.

The US Government considers cryptographic systems munitions and enforces strict export controls on them. PGP falls into this category. Its export was punishable by up to ten years in jail and a fine of $1 million, but nonetheless, it was exported sometime in 1991. The question though was by whom?

As a protective measure, prior to the vote on the above-mentioned bill, friends of Zimmermann who had copies of PGP given to them began posting PGP on Internet sites and Bulletin Board Systems (BBS). These were US sites, making the activity legal. At some point though, someone downloaded the product and transferred it overseas using the Internet. The cat was out of the bag.

Two years later, in February of 1993, just after the release of PGP version 2.0, US customs got interested in investigating PGP's release to the

NOTES

NOTES

world. A grand jury was created to investigate the charge that Zimmermann allowed his creation to be exported. This was despite the fact that it was clear that Mr. Zimmermann did not perform the (legal) uploading of PGP to the BBSs and did not condone or participate in its eventual transfer outside the country.

The government's investigation caused a huge outcry on the Net. Many people spoke out in support of Zimmermann and a defense fund was set up to help defray the sizable legal costs he incurred. The investigation dragged on for close to three years, but was eventually dropped.

Today, most export restrictions for PGP have been lifted, making PGP legally available both inside and outside the US Commercial versions are available from the PGP Corporation (`www.pgp.com`), which has an export license allowing them to sell to most countries. Open-source versions of PGP are also available (`www.pgpi.org`), including a version called GNU Privacy Guard, which is released under the GNU General Public License making it free for both private and commercial use.

How PGP Protects E-mail

PGP provides two security services for e-mail messages: confidentiality through encryption, and message integrity and source identification through digital signatures.

Encryption

A problem with using encryption for e-mail is that encryption requires some shared information between sender and receiver. Using symmetric key algorithms both participants need to share a secret key. This key needs to be private to the two participants, otherwise a third party would be able to decrypt the exchanges between them. Establishing a shared secret key prior to sending a message can be inconvenient when sending a message to someone you know, but can be impossible if you need to send a message to someone you may never have met. This makes a purely symmetric key system a bad choice for e-mail.

Public key is a better choice for this key exchange. Because public key systems separate the key into two pieces, a public piece, which you can safely distribute to the world, and a private piece, which you do not reveal, it becomes possible to exchange messages with anyone as long as both know each other's public key. Sounds better, but there is a major downside to public key cryptography. It's **slow**!

NOTES

Establishing a Key

- Generate a Public/Private Key Pair
  - Diffie-Hellman/DSS or RSA
  - Key length/size (2048 at minimum)
  - Key expiration

SANS Security Essentials – Secure Communications

To avoid the performance penalty of public key cryptography, while still allowing its use, PGP takes a hybrid approach. It creates a random symmetric key that it uses to encrypt the message, then encrypts this key with the recipient's public key. Upon receipt, the recipient can decode the message by decrypting the symmetric key with his private key, then using the symmetric key to decrypt the message. This provides a fast solution that allows easier establishment of trust between sender and receiver.

Digital Signature

PGP can also digitally sign a message, verifying the integrity of the message, and the identity of who sent it. PGP digital signatures are created in a two-step process. In the first step, the information being signed is submitted to the SHA-1 cryptographic hash algorithm. The resulting hash is then encrypted using the sender's private key. The result is the digital signature, which can be sent with the original message allowing recipients to verify the validity of the message. Verification of the message is performed by decrypting the digital signature using the sender's public key to get the SHA-1 hash. A new hash is then computed on the received message and compared to the decrypted hash. If they match then the message is genuine.

NOTES

Key Management

- Key servers
  - Repositories of public keys
  - Key servers actually make the trust issue more significant, as you send your key to a server to be stored.
- Trust merchants
  - Organizations that validate the keys and add to the trust of a key.

SANS Security Essentials – Secure Communications

Key Management

A critical part of PGP is the features it includes allowing you to share and manage public and private keys. PGP is very flexible, allowing several different sharing strategies to be used. The following section explains what you need to do to create and exchange PGP keys.

Key Generation

The first step to using PGP after installation is the creation of public and private key pairs. You need to provide six pieces of information to PGP prior to the creation of a key record. These are user name, e-mail address, choice of cryptographic algorithms, length of keys, expiration date, and passphrase. The name and e-mail address are used to associate the key to a particular person's e-mail account. It is important that the key be generated with the correct name so that the key will be easy to identify. It is also important to use the correct e-mail address, as it will be bound to the key. It would look suspicious to receive a message from an e-mail address encrypted or signed using a key that was bound to a different e-mail address.

Next is the selection of the cryptographic algorithms. In the commercial version of PGP you have the choice of using either the RSA algorithm or a combination of Diffie/Hellman (DH) and the Digital Signature Standard (DSS). The number of keys PGP will generate is dependent upon which algorithm you choose. When using RSA, only one key pair is required because RSA can be used for both signing and encrypting. The DH/DSS choice requires two keys, one for encrypting with DH, and the other for signing with DSS.

So, which key type should you use? DH/DSS is the current default choice in the commercial version of PGP and should be a safe choice, assuming that you do not need to exchange messages with people running old versions of PGP. The RSA algorithm is supported by some earlier versions of PGP, though the current PGP version will not create messages readable by PGP versions earlier than 2.3a regardless of which algorithm is chosen. From a practical point of view, both algorithms provide strong protection of your messages.

The next choice is how large the keys should be. For both RSA and DH, the length of the key can be set anywhere from 1024 to 4096 bits. The DSS algorithm is not configurable. It is always set to 1024 bits. When choosing the key length, remember that longer is stronger! Many cryptography experts feel that 2048 bits is a good compromise between performance and security.

The length of time the keys should be considered valid is the next piece of information needed. For a personal key, you will probably not set an expiration date, but if you are creating a key for an employee or business partner you may want to limit how long the key is valid. This is similar to the way credit card companies limit how long a card is good for. After the expiration date, a key can no longer be used to encrypt or sign messages, though it can still be used to decrypt and verify signatures.

NOTES

NOTES

Choosing a Passphrase

- Most critical part of key generation
- Use strong password principles
  - many characters
  - mixed case, alphanumeric, special characters
  - easy to remember, hard to guess

SANS Security Essentials – Secure Communications

The last piece of information needed is a passphrase. The private portion of the key, which will be generated, needs to be stored on the disk of the computer that will be sending protected e-mails. Without additional protective measures, anyone with access to the computer would be able to copy it. Compromise of a user's private key would allow the attacker to decrypt every message ever sent using the key. Because of this PGP takes the extra step of encrypting the private key, using the passphrase that you supply. It should be composed of letters, numbers, and symbols and should be fairly long. The rules we talked about in Chapter 9, Access Control and Password Management, about creating strong passwords should apply to your passphrase. Take the time to choose a good passphrase, but take even more time to make sure you are not going to forget it. Without the passphrase, any data you have encrypted with your key will be inaccessible to everyone, including you!

NOTES

Distributing Your Public Key

- Send the key directly to the person you wish to strike up an encrypted conversation with.
  - Export the key
  - Sign it
  - Send it to the intended user as an email attachment
- Send your key to a certificate server or LDAP server.

Digital Certificates

In order to use these newly created keys to send a message to someone, you need to have a way to get your public key to that person. One option is to give it to them directly. This works great if you know in advance who will want to send you encrypted messages. Another alternative is to post your public key on a publicly accessible server. This has the advantage of allowing new contacts to look up your key and send you a message without having to request the key from you. The downside to this is that anyone can create a key with your name and e-mail address and place it in this public place. If someone sent you a private message, but used this phony key, the e-mail could fall into the wrong hands.

NOTES

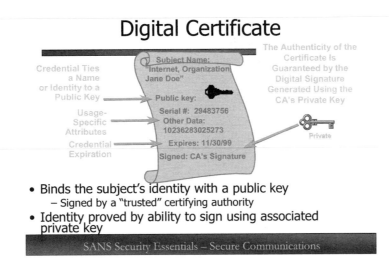

- Binds the subject's identity with a public key
  - Signed by a "trusted" certifying authority
- Identity proved by ability to sign using associated private key

SANS Security Essentials – Secure Communications

To help prevent this problem, PGP uses digital certificates. A digital certificate is a credential used to help someone decide whether a key is genuine. It works by binding a public key with identification information such as name and e-mail address. This information is then signed by at least one third-party. As long as you trust the opinion of one of the third parties that signed the certificate, you should be able to trust the validity of the certificate.

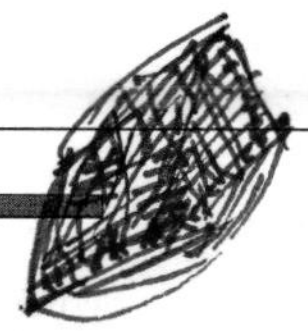

Your Key Ring

- Contains your key and other keys (the public keys of those with whom you correspond)
- Here is an example of your key, and the other 'keys' in your key ring:

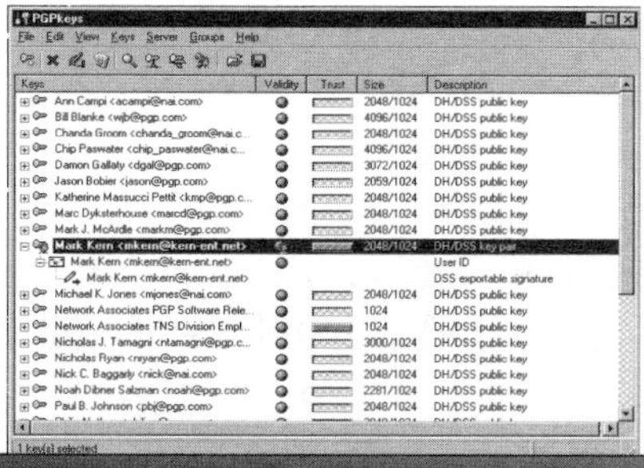

SANS Security Essentials – Secure Communications

Key Rings

As you use PGP, you will collect many digital certificates. To hold them all, PGP uses a structure called the key ring. PGP actually maintains two separate key rings for each user, one for public certificates, and the other for private certificates. Your public key ring holds all of the certificates you know about, including the public version of your own certificates. The private key ring holds your private keys.

NOTES

Adding Keys

- Request a key from the intended recipient
  - Import the key to your key ring
- Search for a key on a key server
  - Use the recipient's email address to search
  - Send a test message to ensure the recipient has the corresponding private key

SANS Security Essentials – Secure Communications

Note

Be extremely careful with your private key ring. Back it up regularly and store the copies in a safe place. If you lose your private key ring, all of the information you have encrypted with it will be lost.

Trust Models

The types of third parties you trust determines what type of trust model you are using. If the only third party you trust is yourself, then you are said to be using direct trust. As mentioned earlier, this works fine when you know everyone you are going to communicate with, but is impractical when you consider all of the individuals on the Internet with whom you might want to exchange messages. There are two other popular trust models used to address distributed trust.

The first is hierarchical trust. In this model, trust flows down from a central authority. This central authority is called the root certificate authority (root CA). The root CA is used to establish a set of systems that are responsible for signing user certificates. These systems are referred to as trusted introducers, or alternatively as certificate authorities (CAs). Any certificate that is signed by a CA can be considered trusted, as long as you trust the root CA's opinion concerning the CA that you are using.

For example, say you are trying to verify Bob's certificate, which was issued by CA-1. To verify the trust, you first verify that the signature on Bob's certificate was produced by CA-1. Next you must verify that CA-1's certificate was signed by the root CA. As long as it verifies correctly, you can consider Bob's certificate as valid. Some CAs are also allowed to have their own CAs. Trust is established by walking up the tree, verifying signatures as you go, until you reach the root CA.

The second type of distributed trust is called the web of trust. In this model, anyone can vouch for anyone else. If you receive a certificate, you check its validity by seeing if it contains a signature from someone you trust. This models how people in the real world establish trust. If Bob trusts Alice, and Alice trusts Greg, Bob may have at least some trust in Greg. Keep in mind when using this model that Bob may trust Greg not because of personal knowledge, but because he trusts someone else who trusts Greg.

NOTES

Validity and Trust

PGP implements trust by allowing each participant to decide whom they are going to trust and by how much. There are four levels of trust available. These are, in order of confidence: implicit, complete, marginal, and none. These levels of confidence are used to determine whether you believe a particular certificate is valid: in other words, that it accurately associates a person's identity with their public key.

Implicit trust is the trust you have in yourself, or in this case your own key. Any certificate signed by your own key is automatically considered valid. This should make sense, as you would not sign another person's certificate without verifying its validity. This is how direct trust is implemented within PGP.

It becomes more complicated when you are trying to take someone else's word about the validity of a certificate. This is where the other trust levels come in. Complete trust is used when you are 100% confident in someone's ability to vouch for other people's certificates. For instance, you may know that Bob always carefully verifies someone's identity before signing his or her certificate. Knowing this, you might decide to automatically validate any certificates that you receive that are signed by Bob. To tell PGP this, you need to have a valid copy of Bob's certificate. You can then tell PGP that you completely trust this certificate. In effect, you have now made Bob a trusted introducer (i.e., certificate authority).

But what if you are not completely confident in Bob? You may believe that he is usually good at checking identities, but not be 100% comfortable in his judgment. In this case it may only be appropriate to have marginal trust in Bob. This means that Bob's signature alone is not enough evidence for you to consider a certificate valid. You would need someone else's opinion that you also trust to verify the certificate. In PGP, before a certificate is considered valid it must either be signed by you, by someone you completely trust, or at least two people that you marginally trust. The underlying theory is that if two people trust a certificate, then even if you don't completely trust either one, the chances that both got it wrong are remote. Your belief in this theory will dictate whether you ever assign anyone marginal trust.

Note

This technique may sound valid, and it is when assuming that all participants are not acting with malicious intent. As soon as you add an adversary to the model though it falls apart. How hard would it really be for an adversary to socially engineer any two people that you know to get them to sign a bogus key? The answer to this may vary in your particular circumstances, but keep in mind that most people are not trained to resist social engineering techniques.

The last level of trust is untrusted. No amount of untrusted signatures will allow PGP to validate a certificate. This is the default level that all certificates have (except your own) until they are signed by a trusted introducer.

NOTES

In addition to the level of trust in a certificate, you can also state how long you want to trust the certificate by setting an expiration date for your signature. This allows you to control how long other people who trust you should trust your opinion of the certificate. For example, imagine that you've hired a summer intern. When signing her certificate, you may want to set an expiration date for the end of the summer so that after she has returned to school, you and everyone using your opinion to trust her, knows that the certificate is no longer valid.

The combination of all of these trust features allows us to implement any of the trust models we've talked about. Direct trust is easy—just don't trust anyone else's signature. This means that you will have to personally sign any certificates that you want to consider valid.

NOTES

Web of Trust

- Sender must have a trusted copy of the intended recipient's public key
- Recipient must have trusted copy of sender's public key
- Middle man exposure – what if someone can intercept the keys and be a middle man, able to decrypt and re-encrypt the data? – Must validate Public keys

SANS Security Essentials – Secure Communications

A web of trust naturally evolves as you start to trust, or marginally trust other people's signatures. Over time, a web forms as linkages among people who trust each other are made. Eventually, assuming no one makes any mistakes, a very large network of trusted certificates can be achieved.

It is possible in PGP to limit how much of this web you trust. You do this by setting a trust depth level for a certificate you are trusting. If you set up Bob as a trusted introducer, but limit his depth to one, then you are saying that you only trust Bob to make introductions for you. Setting it to two, you are saying that people that Bob trusts as trusted introducers can also introduce people to you. You can also limit an introducer's abilities to a particular domain. So, if Bob works for Acme Company, you can set up Bob as a trusted introducer, but only for people with e-mail addresses from `acme.com`.

Hierarchical trust models are also possible within PGP but they need some organization to make them happen. To start, a certificate needs to be created that acts as the root CA. This certificate needs protection, as its compromise would compromise the entire system. Additional certificates can be set up as trusted introducers, and each of these certificates needs to be signed by the root CA. To join the hierarchy, a person needs to create a PGP certificate and have it signed by one of the trusted introducers. In addition, they must sign the root CA's certificate and make it a trusted introducer. In this way, certificates received by a person that has been signed by a trusted introducer that is trusted by the CA will be valid. Remember that the hierarchy would be compromised if people started trusting non-root certificates. In a hierarchical system, trust must always originate at the root. This is one of the main differences between PGP's trust model and a traditional Public Key Infrastructure. PGP does not enforce a hierarchy.

How do you Establish Trust

An important detail to discuss is the steps you need to go through before you decide to trust a certificate. Note that trusting a certificate is not the same as trusting a person. Remember, when validating a certificate, what you are really doing is stating that you believe that the individual whose identity is recorded in the certificate is in sole possession of the private portion of the key included in the certificate. When you receive a certificate for someone you trust, you must still determine whether that person really produced the certificate.

NOTES

One way to do this is to have the person directly hand you their certificate on diskette. Presumably, if they have maintained good physical security of the diskette, you should be able to trust that their certificate is valid. This is not convenient, though. An alternative is to get it from them via e-mail, ftp, or from a public certificate server. The problem here is how can you be sure that the certificate was not tampered with or replaced while it traveled across the network?

PGP's answer is the creation of a certificate fingerprint. The fingerprint is actually a cryptographic hash of the certificate, which results in a unique set of 32 hexadecimal digits that can be used to verify the validity of the certificate. When receiving a certificate from someone, you must get their fingerprint through some other method than was used to get their certificate. This is frequently done by calling them on the telephone and asking them to read their fingerprint to you. As long as you can safely recognize their voice, and the fingerprint matches, you can validate the certificate. Of course, reading 32 hexadecimal digits over the phone can be difficult. For this reason, PGP also translates the hexadecimal digits into a series of twenty words. These words are designed to be easy to pronounce and map back one-to-one with the original hexadecimal fingerprint.

Certificate and Signature Revocation

Remember, when signing a certificate, you have the option of setting an expiration date on the signature. After the expiration date has passed, the signature can no longer be used to validate the certificate.

What happens if you need to invalidate a signature earlier than the expiration date? If an employee quits, or if someone's private key becomes compromised, you need to immediately invalidate the certificate. That's where signature and certificate revocation comes in.

Signature revocation is used when your original opinion about a certificate is no longer valid. This would not necessarily invalidate the certificate's use, though. Remember that PGP allows many different people to sign a certificate. If enough people still believe the certificate is valid, the loss of your signature may not make a difference. From a practical point of view, though, a revoked signature is a strong vote of no confidence.

Revoking entire certificates is also possible within PGP, but it can only be performed by the person who created the certificate (e.g. who possesses the certificate's private key), or someone that has been assigned by the owner of the certificate as a designated revoker. Revoking a certificate immediately invalidates the entire certificate, regardless of how many supporting signatures it contains. There are a couple of reasons that you might want to revoke your own certificate. One is you are retiring an e-mail account. When you get rid of the account, you no longer want anyone encrypting information to the account. Forgetting the passphrase would be another excellent reason to cancel the certificate. This, by the way, is the primary reason for the designated revoker. If you forget your passphrase, you lose access to your private key and its abilities, including the ability to revoke your own certificate. The designated revoker

NOTES

solves this problem by letting someone else revoke your certificate for you.

Using PGP

Once you have the proper certificates in your key ring, using PGP is straightforward. In this section we will demonstrate how to encrypt and decrypt messages, and how to sign and verify signatures for messages. Note that the instructions that follow are specific to the Windows operating system. There are other implementations of PGP for many different operating systems including versions of PGP that work from the command line. While the general practice of using PGP will be the same regardless of which platform you are on, the exact steps you would need to follow may be quite different from what is presented here.

NOTES

Encrypting Outbound Email

- To encrypt or sign email, it is as easy as clicking an icon before you send:

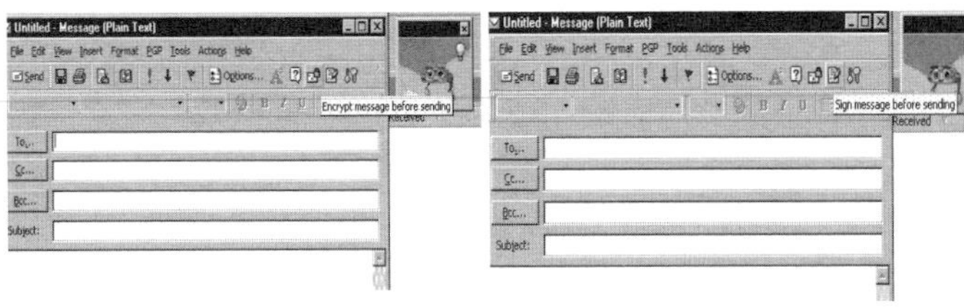

SANS Security Essentials – Secure Communications

Encrypting and Decrypting Mail

Depending upon which e-mail program you use, encrypting mail with PGP can be as simple as clicking a button, or as hard as externally encrypting the message, then pasting the resulting ciphertext into the body of the e-mail. Programs that currently support PGP natively include Microsoft Outlook, Lotus Notes, and Eudora. For these programs, encryption and signing is automatic, as long as you possess valid certificates for the recipients.

Other programs can still be used to send PGP messages. They just do not automatically perform the PGP operations for you. The following steps can be used to encrypt your e-mail messages, regardless of which mail program you are using.

1. Click on the encryption icon of the PGPtools application.
2. Choose encrypt from clipboard.
3. Select and copy the text you want to encrypt into the clipboard. This can be done by highlighting all of the text you want encrypted and selecting Edit->Copy.
4. Select encryption from the PGPtools application by clicking on the encrypt icon (the icon with the envelope covered by a closed lock). PGPtools is part of the commercial release of PGP and is used as its control panel for performing encryption, decryption, signing, and verification.
5. Select encrypt from clipboard on the dialog that will appear after you have selected encryption.
6. Select the certificates of your intended recipients from your public key ring. It is always a good idea to include yourself as one of the recipients.
7. Click the OK button to perform the encryption. PGP replaces the cleartext contents of the clipboard with the encrypted ciphertext.
8. To finish paste the encrypted message into your e-mail document by highlighting all of the text in the e-mail message again and choosing Edit-> Paste. This replaces the original text with the ciphertext. The message can now be mailed normally.

NOTES

Sample PGP-Encrypted Email

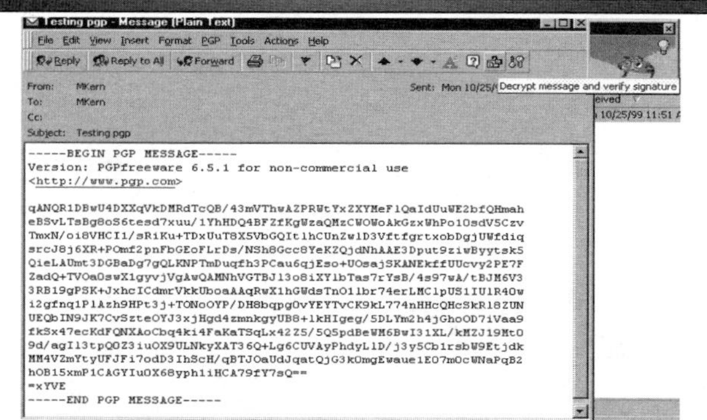

NOTES

Decrypting Inbound Email

- To open an encrypted message, the passphrase is entered
- This permits access to the private key
- The decrypting transformation is applied to the message
- The net of the two actions, the encryption with the public key and decryption with the private key, results in the cleartext message

SANS Security Essentials – Secure Communications

Decrypting the message is performed similarly.

1. Highlight the PGP message and copy it to the clipboard.
2. Using PGPtools, click on the decrypt icon. This icon appears as an envelope covered by a letter and an open lock. Clicking it will open a dialog asking for a file to decrypt/verify.
3. Select the decrypt from clipboard button. Clicking this button brings up a window showing the list of people the message was encrypted to, and a request that you supply your passphrase.
4. Type in your passphrase. Assuming you type your passphrase in correctly, the message will be decrypted and displayed in a new window.

NOTES

Signing Outbound Email

- Use the passphrase to access the private key
- Apply a signature based on that private key

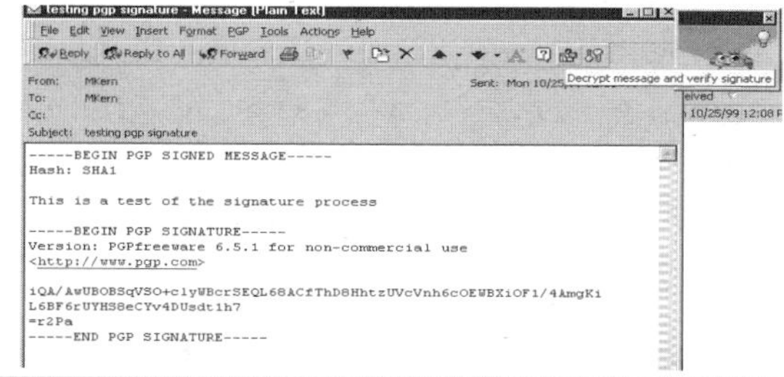

SANS Security Essentials – Secure Communications

Signing and Verifying Mail

Creating a signature for a message follows the same process that you use to encrypt one. The only difference is the result. The message that you want to sign needs to be sent to PGP either through the clipboard or by placing it in a file that PGP can read. Using PGPtools, you sign by clicking on the icon that appears as a letter with a pencil pointing at the bottom. This causes the select file dialog to appear. Choosing the clipboard button causes the passphrase dialog to appear. Typing in the correct passphrase for your certificate will allow PGP to compute a signature for the current contents of the clipboard, which will be replaced by the signed message. The signed message can now be pasted into your e-mail window.

NOTES

Confirming a Signed Email

- Choose to "verify" the signature

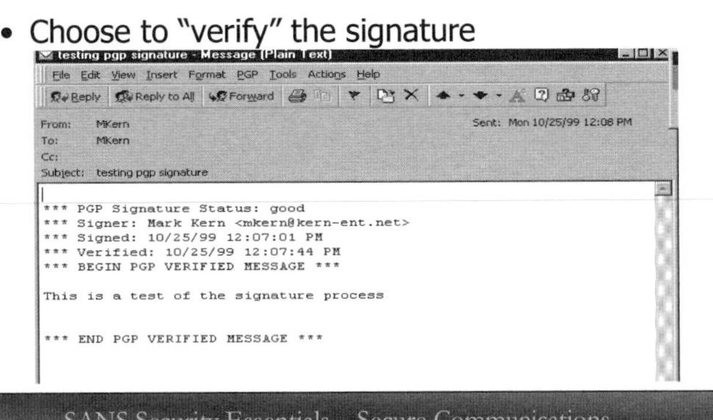

SANS Security Essentials – Secure Communications

Verification occurs just like decryption. It even uses the same PGPtools button. The result is slightly different, though. The resulting window shows the message and information about its validity, including the results of the verification, the name and e-mail address of the sender, the date the message was signed, and the date it was verified by you.

The combination of PGP's ability to protect e-mail (and other) messages while allowing convenient key distribution has made it one of the most popular encryption tools available. It is easy to use, widely available, and secure. If you have not already experienced it, you should strongly consider giving it a test drive.

Public Key Infrastructure

Our last topic in this chapter is Public Key Infrastructure (PKI). PKIs manage the creation and distribution of public keys in a graceful, efficient, and trustworthy manner. PKIs allow trust to be established between any members of the PKI, even if they have not interacted before. This ability is an enabler for many security services, including all of the services discussed in this chapter such as VPNs, application authentication, and secure e-mail exchange.

As we get into our discussion, you may notice that many of the PKI concepts are reflected in PGP. This is natural as PGP implements several elements of a PKI. Both rely upon public key cryptography, and both use certificates to establish trust between an individual's identity and their public key. The major difference between them is PKI exists to provide its trust services to many applications, not just for e-mail exchange. The same PKI can be used by Web browsers to establish trust in a Web server, an application to trust a user, or an individual to trust incoming e-mails. This raises the stakes. It is one thing to have a single application (such as PGP) that may or may not be using valid certificates. It is another when many applications and users count upon the validity of the certificates. When many applications need to rely upon the opinion of the PKI, it becomes imperative that the PKI's opinion on the validity of certificates be trusted. Because of this, most PKIs are based upon the hierarchical trust model, because these models require that the user only trust the opinion of one system, the root CA.

Our discussion of PKI will start by outlining the different components needed to implement a PKI. Next we will discuss how PKIs operate by showing how certificate management is performed. We will finish by talking about some of the problems you may run into when implementing or using a PKI.

NOTES

NOTES

PKI Components

- Public and private encryption keys
- Digital signatures
- Key management protocols
- Digital certificates
- Certificate authorities

SANS Security Essentials – Secure Communications

PKI Components

In its most basic form, a PKI consists of a collection of digital certificates, which have been issued by the PKI, a collection of certificate authorities, which have issued the certificates, and a defined trust hierarchy that is used to verify the validity of the certificates. How these components interoperate allows the members of the PKI to exchange messages securely.

Certificate Authorities (CA)

CAs play a basic and critical role within a PKI. They are responsible for issuing certificates to individuals (or entities such as Web servers). Unlike the PGP model, where anyone can produce a certificate, only CAs are allowed this function within a PKI. When a user wants to join a PKI they must petition a CA for a certificate. The user presents his credentials, which must be validated. Assuming they pass muster, the CA creates a certificate based upon the user's identity information. This certificate is signed by the CA's private key. When someone wants to verify that the certificate is valid, they use the CA's public key to decrypt the signature. If it decrypts successfully, they know that the CA issued the certificate.

NOTES

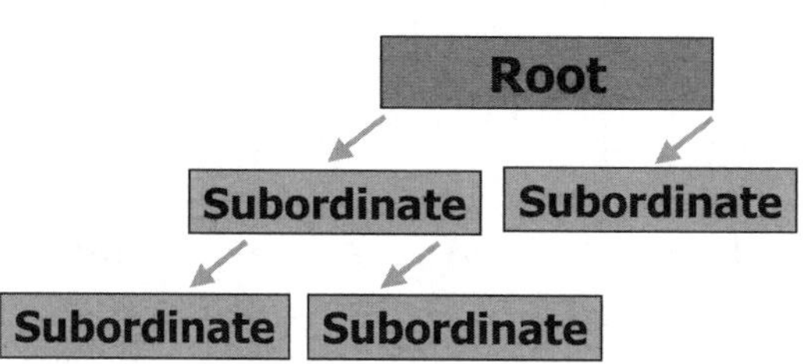

Certificate Authority Hierarchy

PKI CAs are normally organized as a hierarchy with a central root CA used to create an assortment of subordinate CAs. This is done by issuing the CAs certificates, which are signed by the root CA's private key. These subordinate CAs can further delegate their authority by creating CAs subordinate to themselves. These delegations serve a couple of purposes. The first is it allows the CA's role of issuing certificates to be farmed out, spreading the workload. The second is it allows different groups within the PKI to issue their own certificates. Delegation can be important if the number of certificates that needs to be issued is large, policies between different groups on certificate issuance are different, or the organizations are located at different geographic locations.

Verifying a certificate issued by a PKI requires that the verifier know only one public key, that of the root CA. Verification is performed by following the chain of certificates from the issuing CA back up to the root.

One key issue is, who owns the root CA? For a corporation, it is easy to relegate this duty to the corporation's headquarters operation. Different divisions may be granted their own CAs from HQ's root CA. What if you want to exchange certificates with one of your business partners? There are two main ways this is accomplished. The first method is to use an externally agreed third party to host the root CA. There are many companies who offer these services; the most well known is Verisign. In this method, the third party root CA allows each organization to create subordinate CAs that issues certificates for their organization. Should one organization need to communicate with the other, they can verify the authenticity of each other's certificates by following the chain up to the third party root CA. What happens, though, if each organization had already established their own root CAs? The cost to switch to a new third party CA, combined with the loss of management control of their hierarchy, may make the third party solution untenable.

In this case a bridge CA can be set up between two organizations' root CAs. The bridge acts as a trust conduit between the two hierarchies establishing rules of trust. The bridge works by having the two root CAs cross-certify each other. When verifying another organization's certificates, the same process described before is used up to the point that the

NOTES

certificate has been verified up to the other organization's root CA. To complete the verification requires that a cross-certification certificate be located on the home root CA, which verifies that the other organization's root CA is valid.

Digital Certificates

We've already talked about the purpose of digital certificates during our PGP discussion. They bind an individual's identity to the public key. With PKI systems, the purpose is the same, but the process used to produce the certificate is more formal. Most PKI systems do not allow the user to create certificates themselves like PGP does. Instead a certificate authority creates the certificate and issues it to the user. The care at which the CA performs this role directly affects how secure the overall PKI is. If the CA issues a digital certificate to anyone without requesting proof of identity, the confidence you should have in the certificate is low. If instead, the CA requires that you show up, in person, with two forms of government issued ID before issuing you a certificate, your confidence can be high in that CA's certificates.

Most current PKI systems produce certificates in the X.509 certificate format. This specification is published by the International Telecommunications Union (ITU), an international standards body. Each X.509 certificate includes two sections, the data section and the signature section. The data section holds all of the details associated with the certificate, including the following fields:

- X.509 version number
- Serial number
- Identity information of the certificate's owner in the form of a distinguish name (DN)
- Owner's public key, and the algorithm used to generate it
- Period that the key is valid (e.g. 12:00 midnight Nov 1, 2002 through 12:00 midnight Nov 30, 2004)
- Identity information of the issuing CA

The certificate can also include other details, sometimes referred to as certificate extensions that are application dependent. An example is X.509 certificates used in SSL connections. With SSL, the X.509 extensions include a certificate type used to distinguish between certificates issued to browsers and certificates issued to servers.

The signature section of the certificate holds the digital signature generated by the CA when the certificate was issued, and the algorithm that was used to generate the signature. This signature is created by hashing all of the information in the data section of the certificate, then encrypting the hash using the CA's private key. This is one of the main differences between PGP and X.509. In PGP, many different people can sign a certificate. Each is certifying that they trust the certificate. Remember, when you receive a PGP certificate, your decision whether to trust it or not will be based either on it being signed by people you trust, or your personal verification of the certificate. With a PKI, your trust in a certificate is entirely based upon your trust of

NOTES

the CA's signature. Therefore, X.509 certificates only allow (and need) one signature.

Another difference between PGP certificates and X.509 certificates is how the user's identity information is recorded. In PGP, identity information is constructed in a loose format from the user's real name and e-mail address. X.509 certificates are more formal. In X.509, the identity information is in the form of a distinguished name (DN). DNs are a very flexible way of encoding naming information. They are constructed out of a sequence of value-attribute pairs (e.g. CN=Bob Bishop, OU=Security Essentials Division, O=SANS, C=US). The attributes in this example would be typical of a X.509 certificate. These include CN, which is used to specify the user's common name; OU, which specifies the user's organizational unit; O, which specifies the user's organization; and C, which specifies what country the user is from. Other value types are possible, but these are the most common.

NOTES

Certificate Management

- Registration & Initialization
- Certification
- Key Recovery
- Update
- Expiry & Revocation
  - Certificate Revocation List (CRL)

SANS Security Essentials – Secure Communications

Certificate Management

There are many steps along the lifetime of a certificate. Each is important to the maintenance of security within the PKI. The steps are:

- Registration and Initialization
- Certification
- Key Recovery
- Update
- Expiry and Revocation

Registration is the process that occurs before a certificate is issued. It involves the person or entity who wants the certificate to provide their identification information in the form of a DN and (hopefully) some definitive proof that they are indeed the person represented by the DN.

Next comes initialization. This step provides the person the details they will need to communicate with the PKI, including a copy of the root CA's certificate. Initialization is also where the client's public/private key-pair is generated. Depending upon the policy being followed, this key generation may be performed by the person or by the CA. If performed by the person, the public key needs to be sent to the CA. If performed by the CA, the keying material (public and private) needs to be carefully sent to the person.

Certification occurs when the CA actually issues the certificate, which includes the user's DN, public key and certificate details such as validity period, protected by a signature generated by the CA. At this point the certificate can be stored in a certificate server, such as an LDAP, or simply issued to the person to use and share as they wish.

Key recovery is also an important part of many PKIs. Remember that if you lose your private key, all of the information encrypted with that key is lost as well. To prevent this, some CAs store a copy of the person's private key. While this does somewhat undermine the non-repudiation of the key, it does allow the key to be recovered if the person loses it. Key recovery is particularly important in organizational settings where the information that is being protected is owned by the organization, not the individual. If the individual leaves the company, or is simply unavailable, the backup key can be used to recover the materials the individual was working on.

Periodically, it may be necessary to update certificates that have been issued. This could be for

NOTES

a wide variety of reasons, such as a user's name changing, an impending certificate expiration, or because the certificate's private key has been compromised. The update process requires that the person's current certificate be invalidated, and a new certificate issued.

In the case of an expired certificate, the CA need only issue a new certificate for the person. Expired certificates are known by all PKI participants to be invalid. But what about certificates that need to be changed before the expiration date? To revoke a certificate, the CA maintains a Certificate Revocation List (CRL). The CRL consist of a list of the certificate serial numbers for all of the certificates that have been revoked by the CA. This list needs to be regularly updated and sent to each of the PKI participants.

When verifying a certificate, the first check should be to verify that the certificate's serial number is not listed on the latest CRL. One problem with this is the frequency of CRL distribution. When a certificate is revoked, there will be some period of time between its invalidation, and the receipt of all of the PKI members of a CRL, which references the certificate. During this period it is possible that the certificate may be accepted when it should not have been. The solution is to increase the frequency of CRL distributions, but distributing it too much may consume too many network and system resources, so a balance must be made between security and operations.

NOTES

Problems with PKI

- Competing/incomplete standards
- Certification of CAs
  - Important issue but easy to overlook
- Cross-certification between CAs
- Do-it-yourself or outsource?
- User education and/or perception
- Extensive planning requirement

SANS Security Essentials – Secure Communications

Problems with PKI

A basic question when establishing a PKI is who is going to use it. If only a small group is going to share a single CA, management can be relatively simple. Trying to establish a PKI for a large organization can be demanding. Extending it out to other organizations is even more so. As the number of people and groups who will participate increases, so does the need for tight standardization and management, but these agreements will be increasingly difficult to arrive at as there are more participants. Issues that still need to be addressed before wide scale deployment of PKI include the following:

- Competing standards, or standards still in flux. Until most applications support a common PKI standard, interoperability will continue to hamper large PKI deployments. Before a PKI can be useful, the applications that you rely upon need to be able to make use of the PKI.
- Certification of certificate authorities. The policies that a particular CA uses, and how well those policies are enforced, directly affects how secure the entire PKI based upon them will be. Especially when establishing common PKIs with other organizations, common certification standards will need to be agreed to in order to make it possible to understand how trust between different groups should be maintained.
- Cross-certification between CAs. Standards for determining rules of conduct between cross-certifying CAs are still being worked out.
- Do-it-yourself or outsource it is a key question. Allowing a third party who specializes in PKI management to run your PKI infrastructure may be cost effective, but is only possible if you completely trust the third party.
- User education or perception. Any large deployment of software can succeed or fail based upon user reaction to the system. Since a properly implemented PKI may become essential to the operation of the entire network, it is imperative that users understand and accept their role within the PKI.
- Lack of critical mass. PKIs are large systems needing careful planning and deployment to succeed. Getting enough of the components established can be challenging and the PKI will be useless until they are. This can make it difficult to justify the creation of the PKI. The high cost of establishing the PKI prior to

NOTES

receiving any of its benefits has cooled many organizations' interest in establishing their own PKIs.

Even with these problems, it is likely that PKIs will eventually be ubiquitous. Their advantages are too clear for them to remain on the sidelines. Many organizations are working hard to develop technical and management standards for PKI, especially the US government, who is working hard to deploy a government-wide PKI. As these standards evolve and become more robust, the deployment risks will be reduced, encouraging pervasive use of PKI.

NOTES

Summary

As standards related to cryptography become more prevalent, we may reach a day when almost every piece of information that is processed by a computer system is protected by some form of cryptography. In the mean time, this chapter has provided a look at some of the current methods for cryptographic protection of our information systems. To organize our discussion, we showed how cryptography could be applied at several levels of a network including the application level, the transport level, and the network level. Each of these levels brings with it advantages and disadvantages.

At the application level, each application must provide its own cryptographic services. This allows the application developers to closely match the services to the needs of the application. The downside is that each application may need to replicate similar cryptographic services and some applications may have implemented the services better than others. Still, replacing insecure applications such as telnet with applications that support cryptography such as SSH can provide an immediate increase in security.

Applying cryptography at the transport level allows many applications to share a uniform set of cryptographic services, reducing the problem of inconsistency. Applications must still be written to use the transport level services, but since the security services themselves are not being duplicated, there is little possibility of irregularity.

If your application neither supports application level nor transport level encryption, you can still take advantage of network level cryptography. Applying encryption at the network level, referred to as virtual private networking, addresses both consistency and availability issues. Any information that flows across the network can be protected. The downside here is that individual application needs may not be taken into account.

This chapter also included descriptions of current protocols and products that implement cryptographic security. This included a detailed discussion of how IPSec, the current standard for implementing VPNs, can be used to protect all information that flows across an untrusted network. At the application level we described PGP, one of the first widely deployed public key based applications. Finally we discussed what many consider the holy grail of cryptographic protection, PKI systems, and how they can be used to establish trust, even between people who have never interacted with each other before.

While it will be a long time before we reach a point where all of our information assets are protected at all times by cryptography, there are many current applications and protocols available that support cryptography. Using available applications and protocols such as SSH and IPSec can provide an immediate improvement in your organization's security.

Chapter 22

Steganography

NOTES

Steganography

SANS Security Essentials IV:
Secure Communications

SANS Security Essentials – Secure Communications

Steganography

Encryption offers its users data confidentiality, data integrity, and with digital signatures, the non-repudiation of the sending party. However in some cases even these offerings are not enough security. Despite its benefits, encrypted data is still vulnerable to detection and analysis. Even though the data is not available in clear text, it is possible for "information voyeurs" to determine that encryption is being used to protect the data, and in turn attempt to decrypt it. The only way to protect encrypted data from attack is by preventing others from finding it and from even realizing that it is encrypted.

Steganography is one method to disguise such data. It allows users to change the form of the data to appear to be something it is not. In this chapter we will introduce the concepts of steganography and its use, the methods by which steganography is applied to data, some of the tools that are available for its application, as well as ways that steganography can be detected and defeated.

NOTES

Steganography (Stego)

- Steganography (abbreviated as stego), not to be confused with stenography
- Involves concealing the fact that you are sending "sensitive" information
- Data hiding ("steganography" means "covered writing")
- Dates to Ancient Greece, modern awareness relatively new
- Can hide in a variety of formats
  - Images
    - Bmp, Gif, Jpg
  - Word Documents
  - Text Documents
  - Machine Generated Images
    - fractals

SANS Security Essentials – Secure Communications

An Introduction to Steganography

Steganography (stego) is a means of hiding data in a carrier medium. Steganography means, "covered writing". In concept it dates back to ancient Greece. However, as a means of hiding data electronically, it is a new concept.

The modern form of stego can take many forms, though all involve hiding data in something else. This could be the hiding of a document in an image, the hiding of a short message in a document, even hiding an image in a sound file! The applications are only limited by the tool being used, the carrier file, and the imagination of the sender.

Stego can be used for a variety of reasons but most often it is used to conceal the fact that sensitive information is being sent or stored. It can also be used to disguise encrypted data. This helps prevent attacks on encrypted data, or in scenarios where encrypted data is inappropriate for transmissions—for example, in countries where encryption is outlawed.

NOTES

Crypto vs. Stego

- Cryptography (Crypto) provides confidentiality but not secrecy.
- It is fairly easy to detect that someone is sending an encrypted message, it is just very hard for someone to read it.
- With stego, you may not even know someone is sending a message – the true intent is hidden.

SANS Security Essentials – Secure Communications

Cryptography vs. Steganography

Cryptography (crypto) is a tool to protect confidentiality and integrity and provide non-repudiation for the senders of data. However, despite all of these benefits, crypto does not guarantee the secrecy of your data. Scrambling the data into an unintelligible cryptotext may prevent others from reading the file, but it does not keep them from realizing that the data is there. It is easy to detect an encrypted message; it is difficult to read one.

One unwanted side effect of using encryption is that it can mark a user's most important and confidential files. It is similar to keeping valuable items in a bank vault, or an armored car. Encryption keeps the content very safe, but when the bad guys are in hot pursuit they know where to target for the valuables.

An encrypted conversation can also raise suspicions. If two parties suspected of a crime had suddenly started trading extensive encrypted messages the week before the crime occurred, even though we may not know what they were saying, it would definitely raise some flags.

When handling extremely confidential data it would be ideal to obfuscate the information and keep it as undetectable as possible. Secrecy keeps an attacker from even trying to subvert the encryption on these files. They see image or sound files yet have no idea that they are also carriers of encrypted data.

Steganography Doesn't Guarantee Safety

One important thing to keep in mind when using stego is that even though the secrecy provided by stego is great, the data's protection still relies on the encryption algorithm that is being used. Some stego programs use weak, or untested encryption algorithms, or in some cases no encryption at all! Some stego tools have a choice of encryption methods of varying effectiveness that require you to choose between. Users are often duped into a false sense of security while using a stego tool. They think that if the data is hidden, it is safe. However, if stego is detected, the safety of your hidden message is only as good as the encryption that is used to protect it. If the confidentiality of your data is important to you, always verify the stego tool that you are using has a proven encryption algorithm. If it doesn't, or you are unsure, encrypt the data with a tool using a proven algorithm (like PGP) before running it through the steganographic process.

NOTES

Detecting Cryptography

- It is very easy for both humans and computers to detect that a message is encrypted. For example "test" becomes


```
eJrMIedoDcgYmK7/XwY6Q+7RAeuPDSe0FziMLDU1GyUhc0WPcatAaIpw+Urc0MUX
1257b1q11gFZN4S0rXwAKg2Tzqn9ois7+1pJHOdxI2fH9LCQmxtRBpZ79oFh+wFw
cuPV3wW4Mgoh1HL2JQ7SarrJuZixgRoV+IW/HtoWx2Mvop+4CACHtTxbv8SjchhN
FLaQNVQA1o00UgR+m7bJh42bWfR5cdGBYkVTzg1bu5QXzFodk3PmtG+ghqNCz2CZ
5VZv3H581bSeydcM5zjK7DUd4OZEDSa9kF+9xKdyDMCfvFW5Dyh1JkOBUVo8jvQM
n/3nO8vGcx/5CcDVV6MF4xh5hPbV6NfP2OaOyNVXcHwn9n6/swH4OnrBciX8MCgF
JCyXrwn1Y11GK7RBO67zw0imUkBABfAqc+Jwnbv2HJAAU0NDC+Vd+d9I4UZN6QJd
7RN821ID10ScXe1DNiqCq8hxXHJM8qaP5gQp5iC2ExoPfFP18KRsbOKcK5XPP57T
```


- A human can infer that since this is unreadable, it may be encrypted.

SANS Security Essentials – Secure Communications

Detecting Cryptography

Both humans and computers can easily detect encryption because encryption increases file size and mathematically normalizes the occurrence of data. For example, if I take the cleartext sentence:

```
This is a cleartext sentence.
```

and encrypt it with PGP, the resultant output is:


```
qANQR1DDDQQDAwJYfGZiO3aBXGDJNNX7Z6QMR7IbK
l6ljZKj4lrNgHOEv+ZykECoWGdBJ8H1eMnjyZdHV5
jhJkeIkQ2Itrtu4Qs==A9/J
```


The output is several times longer than the original cleartext message and obviously garbled. When viewing a document or e-mail comprised of garbled characters like the example above, one may infer that it is actually encrypted.

NOTES

Detecting Cryptography (2)

- Cryptography effectively randomizes the characters in a message.
- A histogram shows the frequency of characters.
- A normal document has a predictable histogram.
- An encrypted document has a flat histogram, since with randomization, all characters should appear the same amount of times.

SANS Security Essentials – Secure Communications

In the flow of binary communications, encryption may not be as readily noticeable by a human observer. However, computers can still detect the plain characteristics of encrypted data. Because a good encryption algorithm requires a truly random distribution of characters in its output, the resultant file has a predictable frequency of characters throughout.

NOTES

Histograms

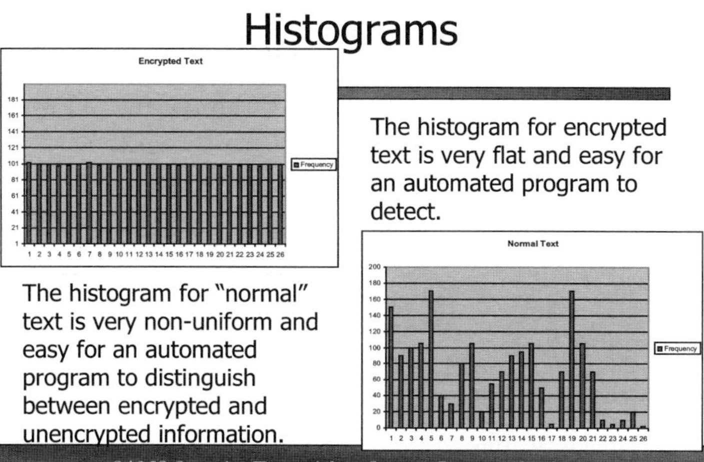

The histogram for encrypted text is very flat and easy for an automated program to detect.

The histogram for "normal" text is very non-uniform and easy for an automated program to distinguish between encrypted and unencrypted information.

Normal Text

Frequency

SANS Security Essentials – Secure Communications

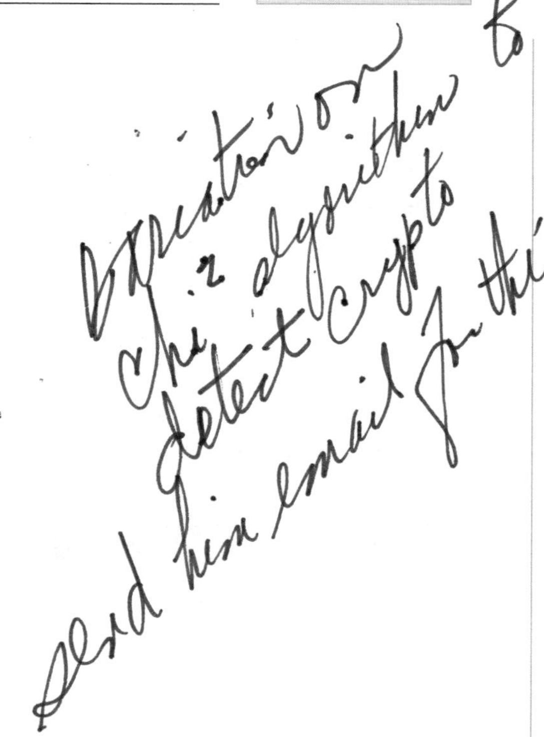

Histograms are graphical representations of the number of occurrences of data in a given distribution of such data. For example, a histogram of a text document would show the number of occurrences of each character that appears in the document. A normal text document would generate a histogram that shows that the frequency of characters varies greatly. In a histogram for an encrypted document, the frequency of characters is normalized. The very same factor that helps prevent encryption from being interpreted makes it easier to detect.

NOTES

How Steganography Works?

- Stego requires a host (to carry the data) and the hidden message.
- Host (usually a file) can be generated on the fly or use existing data.
- Message can be hidden in certain parts of existing file, or can cause a new file to be generated.

SANS Security Essentials – Secure Communications

How Does Steganography Work?

The principle behind steganography is simple—hiding data within data. This can be done in many different ways. The only limiter is the steganographer's creativity. Despite the seemingly endless possibilities for stego, there are some commonalities that can be found in its operation. There are several basic components that are common to all stego and several general types of operations that all stego can be categorized into. In the following sections we will explore these tenants of basic steganography.

Note

For the purposes of this chapter, we will focus on steganography as it relates to files. Other non-file carriers are possible with stego including IP packets, data streams, and correlative messages.

The Components of Stego

There are two general components of standard steganography. The first is the carrier or host. This is the medium used to hold the hidden data. The carrier can be almost any type of file imaginable. Some popular examples of such hosts are:

- Images—bmp, gif, jpeg
- Word Documents
- Sound Files
- Movies—Mpeg
- Text Documents
- Machine Generated Images—Fractals
- HTML Files

Despite the fact that stego can use just about any type of file as a carrier, the best carriers are popularly exchanged files and items that can be altered slightly without being easily detected.

The second component of stego is the hidden data. This data can be almost anything as well, though there are limits to the amount of data you can place in a carrier without causing visible disruption to it. These disruptions could be "noise" in an image, or pops or noticeable echoes in a sound file. Most good steganography tools will limit the amount of data that you can place in a carrier to an amount that should keep the host medium free of such distortions. In any case, assuming that the data that you are placing in a carrier image is no larger than what can be allotted, you could hide anything from

NOTES

a simple text message to an mpeg movie as the payload of a stego host file.

The host or carrier file can take one of two forms. It can either be an existing file of one of the previously listed types, or it can be generated for the sole purpose of carrying the hidden message. When using an existing file as a carrier, the message is inserted into open space in the file, or stored as unnoticeable bit changes in the contents of the file.

In the next section, General Types of Stego, we will go over the ways that stego information is placed into a carrier in greater detail.

NOTES

General Types of Stego

- There are many ways to hide information; lesson in creativity.
- General methods:
  - Injection
  - Substitution
  - Generate new file

Most of the techniques can be summed up in one of three general stego types:

- Injection
- Substitution
- File Generation

General Types of Stego

Information can be hidden in many ways. In ancient times information was placed on wooden tablets that were then covered with wax to hide the message. Messages were also tattooed onto messengers' bare heads. (Hair growth covered the message and their head needed to be shaved so the recipient could read it). In more recent history, messages were written with invisible inks that only appeared after they were heated. Messages were written with these inks in the margins or between lines in false documents to hide the fact that a hidden message existed.

In the information age there are many new creative ways to hide information in an electronic carrier.

NOTES

Injection

- Most file types have ways of including information that will be "ignored".
- For example, hidden form elements or comments in HTML; GIF comments.
- Word documents also have hidden information – holes in the data.
  - Create a large document, save, and then remove data. File size is still very large.

SANS Security Essentials – Secure Communications

Injection

With most file types there are ways to include information within them that will be ignored when the file is processed. This is the basis for injection stego. We place the information into "holes," or unused areas of the file. For example, with HTML, informational tags that tell how it should be processed must precede all characters. Web browsers will ignore data that is formatted with certain HTML tags. However, if you examine the same html file with a text or HTML editor, the added characters will be fully visible. Another example is the comments that can be inserted in files, like those that can be placed in a GIF image or MP3 sound file. These comments do not appear when you view or play the file, though they still physically exist in the body of the file.

Even Microsoft Word documents contain areas (or holes) where information can be hidden. This can be demonstrated by creating a large document, saving it, and then by "cutting" a large portion of the document out. Even after the data is removed the file size is still very large. The slack that is left in the document could also have data inserted into it.

The greatest problem with the injection type of stego is that as data is added, the file size of the carrier increases. This makes detection easy if the original file can be found, or if the size is increased outside of the norm for its type. For instance, if an MP3 file was injected into a document file, the increased size of the document will most likely be noticed.

One example of a tool that utilizes the injection type of steganography is `Snow` (`http://www.darkside.com.au/snow/`). `Snow` is a command line program that allows the encryption and injection of a hidden message into an ASCII text file as "white space," which are extra spaces and tabs. It uses the ICE encryption algorithm which was authored the same person, Matthew Kwan, as Snow and is generally untested and should not be used for high security purposes. Ice supports up to a 1024 byte encryption key. To encrypt a message the command is as follows:

```
snow  -C  -m  "This is the message" -p
"secret password" <input text file name>
<output stego text file name>
```

`-C` compresses the information, `-m` specifies the message to be encoded (in quotes), `-p` specifies the

NOTES

password to encrypt the document (in quotes), followed by the name of the text file to encode the information into and finally the output text file that will hold the stego payload.

To extricate the encrypted payload from the text file simply use the following:

```
snow -C -p "secret password" <stego text
file name>
```

`-C` uncompresses the information, `-p` specifies the password that was used to encrypt the file, and finally the text file name is listed, which holds the stego payload. The hidden message is output directly to the screen. It can be redirected to a file by adding " `> filename.txt`" to the end of the command line.

The data is hidden by adding a series of spaces and tabs to the end of each line, which in turn represents the bits of hidden information. This method can hold approximately 3 bits of information per 8 columns in the document.[1]

When comparing the original document and the stego carrier with most text editors, it is impossible to tell the two apart visually. However, viewing the same document through a file comparison utility or hex editor shows how very different the files actually are.

Injection stego is a viable method to hide small amounts of information in a carrier file. However, because the information is added to the existing contents of the file, an increase in file size can be detected making it typically unsuitable for concealment of larger amounts of data. When large amounts of data need to be concealed, a method of stego where file size is not affected is advisable.

[1] Matthew Kwan *Snow Readme* October Dec 12 1996

NOTES

Substitution

- Data in a file can be replaced or substituted with hidden text.
- Depending on the type of file and/ or the amount of data, it could result in degradation of the file.
- Usually replaces insignificant data in the host file.

SANS Security Essentials – Secure Communications

Substitution

Substitution is the most popular stego method used to hide data in a host file. The concept is that elements are replaced on a bit by bit basis with information that is being hidden in the host document. Because the information is substituted in place of existing information, the file size of the carrier remains the same. However, noticeable file degradation can occur depending on the amount of information placed in the document. It is important to have a suitably large carrier file when great amounts of information are being concealed. Typically, insignificant data is replaced with the information to be hidden. This insignificant data can take many forms, but one of the most common forms is the least significant bits (LSB) in the color table of a graphic.

NOTES

S-Tools

- Embeds data in the LSB of the color table for bmp files.
- Even if you have the original file, the two images look identical.
- S-Tools is available from:
  - ftp://idea.sec.dsi.unimi.it/pub/security/crypt/code/s-tools4.zip

SANS Security Essentials – Secure Communications

One tool that utilizes substitution stego to trade information with the LSB of a carrier file is S-Tools. S-Tools is a GUI based application that allows the steganographic hiding of data in gifs, bitmaps, and wav files. Its graphically based nature makes it intuitive to use. Simply drop a carrier image on the application window.

Then drag and drop the file that you want to hide onto the carrier file. You will be prompted for a passphrase and asked to specify which of the four encryption algorithms you want to use (IDEA, DES, 3DES, or MDC). The resultant image appears in the application window, in a window with the name "hidden data." To save the stego file right click the "hidden data" image and choose "save as" to place it on your local drive.

Note

Be sure to specify the file extension of the file type that you are saving to your local drive. Otherwise the file will be unusable until it is renamed.

To remove the hidden message from the stego carrier, simply drop the stego into the application window and right click it. Choose "reveal" from the context menu that appears. It will prompt for the passphrase and the encryption method that was used. If the correct combination is specified, a window will pop up containing the name of the file that was hidden. Right click the revealed file name and save the file to your local drive.

NOTES

Stego Example

- A common way to embed data in an image is to replace the LSB (least significant bits)
- For an 8-bit file, each pixel is represented by 8 bits:
  - 10001100
  - The most significant bits (MSB) are to the left and the least significant bits (LSB) are to the right.
  - If you change a MSB it will have a big impact on the color. If you change the LSB it will have minimal impact.

SANS Security Essentials – Secure Communications

Now that we have covered how to use S-Tools, let's take a closer look at how S-Tools actually conceal the information. A common means of substitution stego is to replace the least significant bits of color depth in the color table of an image file. This is the way that S-Tools hides information in a carrier image. Images with an 8-bit color depth represent each pixel's color value with an 8-bit value (for example – 10001100). This value represents one of the 256 different color values (anywhere from 00000000-11111111) that any pixel of the image can be.

Note

When dealing with grayscale images, the aforementioned bit depth also applies to the shades of gray of a pixel.

NOTES

Stego Example (2)

- If we change only 1 or 2 LSB's in the image, it will have minimal impact because most human eyes can only detect around 6-7 bits of color.
- Regardless of what the last 2 LSB's are, a human eye can not tell the difference.
- If we take 10001100 and change it to 10001111 or 10001110, it will all seem like the same color.
- This means we can embed data in those bits.

SANS Security Essentials – Secure Communications

2 least sig bits

The most significant bits (MSB) are the digits on the left of the 8-bit value. These values represent the most noticeable elements of the pixel's color. The least significant bits (LSB) are the values on the right of the 8-bit value, which deal with elements of the pixel's color virtually unnoticeable by human eyes. Changes to the most significant bits have a great impact on the color of the pixel, while changes to the LSB should be imperceptible, since most human eyes can only perceive six or seven bits of color. So changes can be made to the last two bits of a pixel's color table value and most humans will not be able to tell the difference.

The colors represented by 10001100 through 10001111 are all shades of the same color that are so close that it is practically impossible to tell them apart with the naked eye. So in turn we can actually hide information in those last two changing bits without detection.

Embedding Data in Pixels

- So if our message converted to binary is 1101 0010, the first 8 pixels will be modified as follows
  - 1100 0101 becomes 1100 01**11**
  - 1111 0010 becomes 1111 00**01**
  - 1010 1111 becomes 1010 11**00**
  - 0010 0010 becomes 0010 00**10**
- To an observer, the image looks normal.

SANS Security Essentials – Secure Communications

If the data that we want to imbed in the LSB of an image's color table is the binary value 11010010, this information could be placed in the LSB of the image as follows:

Color table value 1100 0101 becomes 1100 01**11**

Color table value 1111 0010 becomes 1111 00**01**

Color table value 1010 1111 becomes 1010 11**00**

Color table value 0010 0010 becomes 0010 00**10**

Notice how two bits of the original 8-bit value are placed in each of the four-color table entries. The variations between the original and resultant color values are minute, even though 8 bits of substituted information is hidden in the four 8-bit color values.

In a large picture this could conceal a sizable amount of information. Despite the concealed information, even if you had the original carrier image the two files would visually appear to be exactly the same.

Note

S-Tools version 4.0 is freeware and is available for download from:

ftp://idea.sec.dsi.unimi.it/pub/security/crypt/code/s-tools4.zip

---

Another example of a substitution stego program is `Jsteg`. While it also affects insignificant data, since it deals with jpeg images instead of bitmaps, it doesn't have a color table to work with. It makes changes to the frequency coefficients resulting from the jpeg compression process. It is a command-line utility that places data into Gifs while converting them to jpeg images.

`Jsteg` is actually a conversion of the Jpeg Groups' jpeg compression software. It simply adds a switch (`-steg`) to the program allowing the steganographic input of a text file in the jpeg compression process. The command line to add hidden data is as follows:

```
cjpeg -steg message.txt <Source gif>
<output Stego image>
```

where `-steg` specifies the name of the file to hide, followed by the source gif image file and the name of the jpeg file that will be created. To extract the hidden data run this command:

```
djpeg -steg message.txt <input stego
image> <output file>
```

NOTES

NOTES

where again `-steg` specified the name of the file to extract, followed by the name of the jpeg stego image and then the name of an output file name.

Placing hidden information into jpeg images is a tricky concept. The compression of a jpeg image involves two main steps. The first part of the process called discrete cosine transform (DCT) removes unseen bits from the image, greatly decreasing the image's size. Because this process removes a portion of the image's data, it would also destroy data added via stego substitution.

`Jsteg` solves this by waiting until after this lossy part of the compression process to add the embedded information. The hidden payload is added the same way as S-Tools, by substituting in the embedded information in place of the LSB information for the resulting frequency coefficients (only non-zero coefficients are altered). The embedded information is actually added after two leading length fields. The first is a 5-bit field that describes the length of the 2nd field. The second field tells the length of the third field, which is actually the hidden data. The variation of the 2nd field length helps prevent a recognizable jpeg-jsteg file signature, along with the alternation of a preceding zero on the 2nd field (preventing the sixth bit of information from always being a 1 value). Then the second non-lossy part (Huffman coding) of the jpeg compression process can be completed after the data addition, without a loss of embedded information.[2]

Note

`Jsteg` is available for download from `http://linkbeat.com/files/`.

No matter the tool used for substitution stego, it is plain to see why it is a popular means to hide information. Since file size remains the same and only insignificant information is effected, large amounts of information can be added to a carrier with no visual means of detection.

[2] Derek Upham *JSTEG readme* June 7 1997

NOTES

Generate A New File

- The hidden data can also be used to generate a new file.
- No host file is needed.
- For example, the input text can be used to generate fractals or "human" like text.

File Generation

Another method of stego that is growing in popularity is the actual generation of a new file from the data to be hidden. This is the only form of stego where a carrier isn't needed. It is actually created from the source information to be concealed. This can be used to generate such output as readable text or fractals. With each unique input file, a completely new and unique output file is generated.

NOTES

Spam Mimic

- Hides text in what looks like spam
  - See http://www.spammimic.com/
- "SANS Security" becomes:

Dear Friend ; We know you are interested in receiving cutting-edge info . We will comply with all removal requests . This mail is being sent in compliance with Senate bill 1621 , Title 9 ; Section 304 . This is not multi-level marketing . Why work for somebody else when you can become rich within 39 DAYS . Have you ever noticed people will do almost anything to avoid mailing their bills and most everyone has a cell phone ! Well, now is your chance to capitalize on this . WE will help YOU decrease perceived waiting time by 110% and turn your business into an E-BUSINESS . You can begin at absolutely no cost to you ! But don't believe us ! Mr Simpson who resides in Delaware tried us and says "Now I'm rich, Rich, RICH" . We assure you that we operate within all applicable laws ! We IMPLORE you - act now . Sign up a friend and you'll get a discount of 80% . God Bless !

SANS Security Essentials – Secure Communications

An example of a tool that utilizes stego that generates a new file from user-supplied input is Spam Mimic. Spam Mimic is a Website that allows the creation of what appears to be a Spam-like message from a short text message. The output can be pasted into a text file or e-mailed. The Website is:

`http://www.spammimic.com`

Inputting a message such as:

```
text message
```

Produces the output:

```
Dear Business person ; We know you are interested in

receiving amazing intelligence . This is a one time

mailing there is no need to request removal if you

won't want any more . This mail is being sent in compliance

with Senate bill 1626 , Title 4 ; Section 303 . This

is not a get rich scheme . Why work for somebody else

when you can become rich in 94 MONTHS . Have you ever

noticed society seems to be moving faster and faster

and the baby boomers are more demanding than their

parents . Well, now is your chance to capitalize on

this ! WE will help YOU SELL MORE and turn your business

into an E-BUSINESS . You can begin at absolutely no

cost to you . But don't believe us . Mrs Ames of Michigan

tried us and says "Now I'm rich, Rich, RICH" . We are

a BBB member in good standing . DO NOT DELAY - order

today ! Sign up a friend and you get half off . Thanks
```

Note the length of the output as compared to the input message. The output's length will grow proportionately with the length of the source message, making it impractical for long messages. A password can be added for additional protection of the message. Despite the fact that the output is rather disjointed, and would throw up a red flag to anyone who has seen Spam Mimic before, it will still pass as standard text to most means of electronic monitoring, and many end-users would dismiss it as Spam.

NOTES

NOTES

Mimicry Applet

- Hides text in a baseball announcer's rant
  - See http://www.wayner.org/texts/mimic/
- "SANS Security" becomes (excerpt):

It's time for another game between the Whappers and the Blogs in scenic downtown Blovonia . I've just got to say that the Blog fans have come to support their team and rant and rave . Let's get going ! Another new inning . Ain't life great, Bob ? Yup. Some kind of Ballplayer, huh ? Here we go. Parry Posteriority comes to the plate . The pitchers is winding up to throw. Fans the air ! He's uncorking a smoking gun . Whoa, he's brushing him back . Definitely a ball . It's a bouncing knuckleball . He bounces one of the ground into the first-baseman's glove . One out against the Whappers. Here we go. Mark Cloud adjusts the cup and enters the batter's box . Okay. He's winding up . What a smoking gun . High and too inside. The umpire calls a ball . No wood on that one . He just watched it go by . He waps it into the short-stops glove, but he can't control it . Safe at first . Two more outs to go. Here we go. Sal Sauvignon swings the bat to get ready and enters the batter's box . He's trying the curveball . He pops it up to Harrison "Harry" Hanihan . He's hefting some wood . Now, Herbert Herbertson adjusts the cup and enters the batter's box . Yeah. Here's the pitch It's a rising fast ball . Swings and misses ! And the next pitch is a flaming fast ball . No wood on that one . He's uncorking a fastball with wings . Nothing on that one . Strike out . There goes his batting average . Yowza! End of the inning . Hard to imagine life without baseball? Right, Bob ? Now a message from our sponsors. St. Belch Beer: Especially tailored for men who watch ballgames . Hey! Go green and support the environment . Hey! Live a natural life and drink some more ! We now return to the game between the Blogs and the Whappers . Let's get on with the inning .

SANS Security Essentials – Secure Communications

Note

Spam Mimic is not the only tool that uses grammar generation to conceal a payload. For an applet that hides messages in the monologue of a baseball announcer, see `http://www.wayner.org/texts/mimic/`.

If a password is not used with Spam Mimic, then there is no encryption used at all. And as the makers themselves admit, even when it is used, the encryption is very weak. [3] Also remember that if you aren't using the offered secure connection to the Spam Mimic, your "secret" message is going in the clear from your system to their site. That allows for eavesdropping. However, you don't have to rely on Spam Mimic for your serious steganographic needs.

File generation

Stego offers an interesting way to conceal information in a seemingly innocuous carrier file. Its great advantage is that there is no original host file to compare the output to. However, generated output can be substantially larger then the original information, limiting its effectiveness when substantial amounts of data need to be hidden.

[3] Spam Mimic Encode with Password *Spam Mimic Encode* October 2002 URL: `http://www.spammimic.com/encodepw.shtml`

NOTES

Stego Tools

- There are a wide range of stego tools available from:
  - http://www.stegoarchive.com/
  - http://www.wayner.org/books/discrypt2/links.html
  - http://members.tripod.com/steganography/stego/software.html
- There are over 200 stego tools ranging from different platforms to different techniques.

SANS Security Essentials – Secure Communications

Other Stego Tools

We have just shown a few of the many stego tools that are available online. Many of these tools are freeware or shareware. Some excellent Web resources for these tools are:

- `http://www.stegoarchive.com/`
- `http://www.wayner.org/books/discrypt2/links.html`
- `http://members.tripod.com/steganography/stego/software.html`

The stego tools on these sites cover a variety of host file types, stego techniques, usability options, and a wide range of platforms that they can be run on.

NOTES

Stego Tools Examples

- The following are some example programs:
  - Jsteg – hides in jpeg images using the DCT coefficients
  - MP3Stego – hides in mpeg files
  - S-Mail – hides data in exe and dll files
  - Invisible Secrets – hides data in banner ads that appear on web sites
  - Stash – hides data in a variety of image formats
- As you can see, there are a wide range of tools.

SANS Security Essentials – Secure Communications

Here are a few examples of the many stego programs available:

- MP3Stego—hides information in mpeg files
- S-Mail—hides data in exe and dll files
- Invisible Secrets—hides data in banner ads that appear on Websites
- Mandelsteg—hides data in generated Mandelbrot Fractals
- TextHide—changes text messages grammatically; altering word order, synonyms, perspective and tense to hide data

Defending Against Stego – Steganalysis

Stego is a powerful and useful secrecy tool for addressing today's world of privacy concerns. However, few system administrators and security practitioners will find a day-to-day business use for stego. So why should you be concerned with this technology? Even though your business may not have an application for stego, this doesn't prevent you from being victimized by others' use of this same technology. In this section we will discuss some of the reasons that steganalysis is becoming an important tool of the system administrator, how steganalysis is done, and a practical example of steganalysis in action.

The Importance of Steganalysis

Any system administrator who has responsibility for a network's security may need to protect against hidden data. This data may be placed by inside users, outside users, or posted to publicly accessible Internet resources. So there is a possibility that controversial or even illegal materials could be residing on any network—and no one would know. A business' exposure from the storing of such "contraband" can vary. On a private network you may simply be the storage for employees' illicit behaviors. On a public network you may be an international source for illegal communications, or a point of distribution for illicit or improper information.

So how does one protect their network from such activities? How do we prevent others from hiding data on resources that are ours to defend?

Steganalysis – Detecting and Defeating Stego

There are two aspects to steganalysis—detecting stego and defeating it. Detection involves analyzing a carrier host to determine that information has been hidden in it. This can involve looking for "signatures" left by known stego tools, by comparing original images to carrier images.

Defeating stego is another process altogether. As you may imagine, scanning every image on the Internet is not a viable option for searching for hidden data. Also it is often not possible to gain access to original images, nor is it feasible to have knowledge of every stego tool that may be available for use. So being able to defeat stego without necessarily having to know that it is in use can be helpful. This is particularly useful in situations where you host a publicly available resource where media from outsiders is posted. You may not care what information is hidden in these images, just that it is removed before you post them for the world to see.

NOTES

NOTES

Defending Against Stego

- If the steganographer uses common tools, and you have the original source data, it is easy.
  - Perform a diff or file comparison and see if they are different.
  - Stego might not change the size or make any observable changes, but it does change the data.

SANS Security Essentials – Secure Communications

How do we Detect Stego?

Though it is difficult to detect stego visually, it is possible to detect it electronically. Having the original source image or knowing the stego tool that was used can make this process easier. Even if the files look identical and have the same file size, simply performing a Unix "`diff`" or Windows "`fc`" (file compare) will show all of the differences between them on a bit-by-bit basis (and there will be many).

It may seem ridiculous to imagine having the original image for such comparisons. However, in investigations where home computers, digital cameras, and other devices are taken in to custody, original images may be available or retrievable. Also, since a uniquely created image could give clues to the location or identity of the creator, it is feasible that a stego user may use publicly retrievable files for their carriers. If this is the case, steganalysts may be able to find original images on the Internet using multi-media search engines and the like.

NOTES

Defending Against Stego (2)

- If you do not have the original source file, a variety of checks can be run.
  - Determine "normal" properties of a file and look for changes.
    - Remember S-Tools changes the number of duplicate colors.
    - Not easy to do.
  - Usually requires determining statistics or large number of clean files to come up with unique properties.

SANS Security Essentials – Secure Communications

If you do not have access to the original source files, there are other checks that can be run to detect the likelihood of stego. With less advanced or poorly written stego tools it is sometimes possible to find an obvious signature that can be detected in the output stego image. This is the exception and not the rule. Most often stego must be detected by finding a much less obvious signature. This signature is found through the analysis of the characteristics that separate a "normal" carrier file from a stego file that is generated by the method in question. This process is only limited by the number of files that you have access to for examination and the complexities of the tool used. So knowing the tool that was used and having access to it is an invaluable asset when doing such analysis. Statistical commonalities are found between sets of original files, as well as between sets of processed stego files. Differences are then drawn between the before and after sets. These differences can be used as a fingerprint for stego files created by the tool being studied. This fingerprint is limited strictly to the tool used for the stego process that you are examining (or ones that use a similar method of data concealment). For example, a detection method may determine whether or not a file has stego content as created by S-Tools, but not if it has stego content in general.

Despite these complexities, being armed with the statistical signatures of many popular types of stego tools can be an invaluable aid in detecting the likelihood that there is a hidden stego payload in a given carrier file. Using such detection methods may at least give an analyst some direction, by pointing out possible carrier files that should be scrutinized further.

NOTES

Detecting S-Tools

- Since S-Tools, changes the colors in the color table, it increases the number of near-duplicate colors.
- A normal bitmap (bmp) has very few duplicate colors.
- A bmp with data embedded has a large number of duplicate colors.

SANS Security Essentials – Secure Communications

A Practical Example of Detecting S-Tools

Since S-Tools uses LSB information substitutions in the color table of bitmaps, differences in color variations can be used to help detect a bitmap that has been processed with S-Tools. Due to the way that S-Tools changes colors and adjusts the palette to prevent issues with more color variants being generated than the color palette can hold, it increases the occurrence of near-duplicate colors. An unaltered bitmap should have very few duplicate colors, since only one occurrence of a color in a palette is necessary for an image.

Tools can be constructed to tabulate the number of duplicate colors appearing in the color table of a bitmap file. Running such a tool on known originals and then on the output of the same file after data has been embedded produces noticeable results.

NOTES

Detecting S-Tools (2)

- A small program was written to print out the number of duplicate colors.
- For a normal file, the following is the output:
  - D:\DH\Data\BMP>bmpmap forest.bmp
  - File Name: forest.bmp
  - actual size: 66146 Reported: 66146
  - **Duplicate colors: 2**
- For one with embedded data:
  - D:\DH\Data\BMP\STools>bmpmap forest_h.bmp
  - File Name: forest_h.bmp
  - actual size: 66614 Reported: 66614
  - **Duplicate colors: 1046**

SANS Security Essentials – Secure Communications

A randomly picked example bitmap can be tested and reveals only 2 duplicate colors in the color table. Running the same test on the bitmap after it has had data embedded in it with S-Tools shows that the number of duplicate colors increase to 1046. The difference in the duplicate color values is substantial. Running similar comparisons on a variety of other before and after stego bitmap images will yield similar yet perhaps not such dramatic results. However, differences between the images can help us draw conclusions on which files are more likely to contain stego embedded in them. In this example we can figure that bitmaps with more than 50 duplicate colors are very likely to have been processed by S-Tools. It is important to note that this technique of comparison and analysis can be done for any stego tool, but that excessive duplicate colors in bitmaps is only demonstrative of S-Tools and tools that use a similar substitution technique.

Not all substitution stego tools may result in bitmaps with 50 or more duplicate colors.

How to Defeat Stego

Sometimes it isn't as important to detect the presence of stego, as it is to make sure that it is impossible to retrieve any such hidden information. You may not care what content is contained in a Stego carrier file, just that it cannot be retrieved. If you are the administrator of a Website where you post content submitted from outsiders, it may be in your best interest to assure that there is no hidden content in the media that you are posting.

The key to defeating files with a stego payload is by removing any part of the hidden information. Even removing a small part of the hidden payload can keep it from being properly extricated from the carrier file. This can be accomplished using any method to remove or change the data bits in the stego-affected area of the carrier file. The method's effectiveness can vary based on the type of stego that was used to initially process the file.

One way to remove data from an image is to process it with a lossy compression type, such as jpeg compression. This is especially effective on carriers containing substitution stego, since both jpeg compression and substitution stego act on the LSB of the values in the color table. Therefore, it is very likely that jpeg compression would remove much of the information hidden in a bitmap by a product like S-Tools.

Another means to remove or change file information that can have a negative impact on a stego file is

NOTES

through the application of filters, effects, and other file manipulation techniques. These can be applied to images and sound files, both with similar effect. Anything that can change or remove the data bits in the affected area of the carrier file can be an aid in defeating stego.

A Practical Example of Defeating Stego

Simple filter effects, which may be unnoticeable to the human eye can be destructive to stego payloads in images. The GNU Image Manipulation Program (GIMP) can be used on an image containing a stego payload; applying a sharpen effect at 10% will disrupt the stego but make practically no visible differences in the image.

The image is still viewable with GIMP, MS Paint, and other viewers with no visual changes. However, when trying to reveal the payload of the image using S-Tools, results can be anything from an error that is generated upon processing, to it appearing like you have chosen the wrong passphrase or encryption method. In any event, the payload has been scrambled enough to prevent it from being properly retrieved from the carrier file.

Other filters can be applied with similar results, such as applying a slight blur, de-interlacing the image, applying noise, or other artistic filters. However, growing, rotating, or sizing the graphic will usually have no effect on the stego contents.

So, when dealing with images, it is a worthwhile policy to either translate all submitted media to an alternate or compressed format before posting it, or applying a filter of the types mentioned previously that would cause no visually noticeable changes to the media. It is best for the administrator to experiment with these tools and stego images directly to determine which methods give the best results in their specific situation.

NOTES

Stego Summary

- Reported uses for illicit activity and by terrorist groups.
  - No concrete evidence this was used in 9/11
- Example:
  - I embed data in a picture of a computer
  - I post an ad to eBay selling the computer
  - You browse and select used computers
  - You find my ad and download my image.
  - You extract the secret message.
  - How would one detect that?
  - Is scanning all images on the Internet really practical?

SANS Security Essentials – Secure Communications

Summary

Steganography is a powerful means to protect information. It more than protects the confidentiality and integrity of data; it also makes it truly secret by hiding it within other innocuous files. In process it has been around for a long time, though it has only recently been available and used electronically.

In this chapter we have introduced steganography, and discussed the three main ways that steganography is applied to data- injection, substitution, and file generation. We have also introduced and demonstrated some of the tools that are available for its application. Finally, we have explored steganalysis and ways to detect and defeat stego in your environment, such as analysis, filtering, and compression.

NOTES

Stego Summary (2)

- Stego has been around a long time. It is just starting to become popular.
- As more and more people become concerned with privacy and more and more regulations are being passed, stego will increase in popularity.

SANS Security Essentials – Secure Communications

As privacy concerns rise and regulations are passed, stego will become more and more popular. Despite the fact that there are limited uses for stego in the day-to-day operations of most businesses, many system administrators should still be aware of its use, and versed in means to detect and defeat it. There are reported cases of stego being used for illicit activity by terrorist groups, and awareness by all will help limit the effectiveness of this tool in such criminal activities. In any event, knowledge of steganography is useful as a means of data defense, as well as a means of protecting a business from exposure to risk.

Chapter 23

Viruses and Malicious Code

NOTES

Malicious Software

SANS Security Essentials IV:
Secure Communications

Viruses and Malicious Code

This chapter focuses on the threats and defenses associated with viruses and other types of malicious software (also known as *malware*). Picture this: Security mailing lists are buzzing with warnings of a new killer worm, Child of Nimda. Recall that Nimda struck in September 2001, and affected thousands of systems on the Internet in a matter of hours. How should you assess your company's readiness to combat the new worm? Is this a real threat or a hoax? How can you determine whether any of your systems are already infected? What is the worm capable of? In this chapter we discuss what you can do to prepare for malware attacks, and what you should do if your systems become infected.

Objectives

- Malicious code
- Virus and hoax information
- Virus types and methods
- Organizational AV policy
- Desktop anti-viral care and feeding

Because no security safeguards can offer absolute protection, we go over the ways of detecting an infection as early as possible. We also explain how to implement an action plan that contains and eradicates malware that penetrates your security layers, and discuss information sources that you can use to stay abreast of the latest malware trends and research. Let's begin by examining what characteristics of malware you should be most concerned about.

The Threat of Malware

In this section we look at the most common types of malware, namely viruses, worms, and Trojans, and examine their capabilities. Understanding what malware is, and how it can affect your resources, will help you be effective at defending against malicious code. We begin with the discussion of malware taxonomy by describing popular categories of malicious code. At the end of this section, we look at several malware specimens and discuss their capacity to destroy data, leak information, and establish backdoors into infected systems.

NOTES

NOTES

Malicious Software (Malware)

- Viruses
- Worms
- Trojan horses
- Malicious applets Java problem
- Majority Microsoft-specific

SANS Security Essentials – Secure Communications

Taxonomy

Malware is a generic term that refers to software that was written with malicious intent and performs its actions without the user's permission. There are various ways of classifying malware; however, the majority of specimens that you will encounter will likely belong to one of the following categories:

- Viruses
- Worms
- Trojans

To identify threats associated with malware, let us explore differences and similarities between categories of malicious code. Understanding this taxonomy will help you devise appropriate defenses against malware attacks that we discuss in subsequent sections of this chapter.

Benign Software Used for Malicious Purposes

Our definition of malware refers to code that was specifically written for malicious purposes. This characterization is applicable to entities such as viruses, worms, and Trojans. Keep in mind that it is also possible to use benign applications to cause damage. For example, pcAnywhere is offered by Symantec to grant legitimate access to a system for performing remote administration tasks. However, in a scenario where pcAnywhere is installed on a system to provide an attacker with a backdoor, this benign software becomes a source for malicious purposes. To steer clear of the debate of good vs. evil, this chapter focuses on software written with the goal of causing harm.

Virus

A *virus* is a malware specimen that has the ability to replicate and possesses parasitic properties. A virus is a parasite because it cannot exist by itself; instead, it must attach itself to another program. The *payload* of the virus executes when the user launches the program to which the virus is attached. Instructions in the payload allow the virus to replicate, and give it the opportunity to do its author's bidding. Some viruses do little more than spread and serve as a nuisance. Others can do serious damage, such as destroy data or degrade system performance.

Note

A virus remains dormant until the victim activates its payload by launching the infected program.

NOTES

An example of an especially prolific virus is Melissa, which began spreading on Friday, March 26, 1999. By the following Monday it had reached more than 100,000 computers. Melissa was implemented as a Microsoft Word macro embedded into a Word document. The macro was launched when the victim opened an infected document. Upon execution, the virus inserted itself into the user's normal.dot template file, which ensured that new Word documents created on the system would be infected. Even more insidiously, Melissa's payload contained instructions that sent an e-mail message to the first 50 entries in every Microsoft Outlook address book accessible to the victim. The generated message contained a copy of the infected document as an attachment.[1] This often resulted in sensitive documents being transported outside of the company. According to CERT, one site reported receiving 32,000 copies of e-mail messages containing Melissa within 45 minutes.[2]

Worm

A *worm* is a self-contained malware program that has the ability to spread copies of itself without the victim's participation. If you recall, the payload of a virus was triggered when the victim launched the infected program. A worm, on the other hand, is much more autonomous—it can activate itself without requiring action on the user's part. Also, unlike a virus, a worm is able to function without having to attach itself to another program. The self-sufficient nature of a worm often allows it to spread faster than a virus, infecting a larger number of systems. This trait makes worms very effective attack tools, especially when they are able to propagate over the network. As a result, worms now seem to have surpassed viruses in popularity.

The autonomous nature of worms was particularly evident in Code Red, which surfaced on the Internet in July 2001. Code Red spread by scanning networks for Microsoft Internet Information Servers (IIS) vulnerable to a buffer overflow attack that targeted the indexing service. (`http://cve.mitre.org/cgi-bin/cvename.cgi?name=CAN-2001-0500`) If the worm located a vulnerable Web server, it replicated itself to the machine, and began to scan from there as well. These capabilities allowed the worm to spread without requiring any action on the part of owners of vulnerable systems.

On certain days of the month, Code Red used the infected system to send packets to an IP address that belonged to `www.whitehouse.gov`, in an apparent attempt to perform a distributed denial of service (DDoS) attack against the high-profile Web server. Additionally, if Code Red determined that the default language of the compromised server was US English, it defaced the server's content with a message that was visible for 10 hours after the worm's arrival onto the system:[3]

```
Welcome to http://www.worm.com !

Hacked By Chinese!
```

[1] Carnegie Mellon University. *CERT Advisory CA-1999-04 Melissa Macro Virus*. 31 March 1999. URL: `http://www.cert.org/advisories/CA-1999-04.html` (2 August 2002).

[2] Carnegie Mellon University. *CERT/CC Frequently Asked Questions About the Melissa Virus*. 24 May 1999. URL: `http://www.cert.org/tech_tips/Melissa_FAQ.html` (2 August 2002).

[3] McAfee – AVERT. *W32/CodeRed.a.worm*. 30 July 2001. URL: `http://vil.nai.com/vil/content/v_99142.htm` (3 August 2002).

NOTES

Note

A worm requires no specific action on the victim's part to enable infection and propagation. If the malware specimen cannot propagate unless the user takes action, such as open an e-mail attachment or load a screen saver, then it is generally considered to be a virus.

You may, once in a while, come across terms that refer to different types of computer worms:[4]

- A worm whose components are entirely contained on the infected computer, and that uses the network only to propagate to other systems, is sometimes called a *host computer* worm.
- If the original host computer worm terminates itself after hopping to another system, it is called a *rabbit*. Only a single instance of a rabbit worm runs somewhere on the network at a given time.
- A worm that consists of multiple parts that reside on different machines is called a *network* worm. Network worms may be able to update themselves by obtaining instructions or additional modules from other systems on the network.
- A network worm with one coordinating segment that directs actions of other segments is called an *octopus*.

[4] Nick FitzGerald, et. al. *VIRUS-L/comp.virus Frequently Asked Questions (FAQ) v2.00*. 9 October 1995. URL: `http://www.faqs.org/faqs/computer-virus/faq` (3 August 2002).

Trojan

A *Trojan*, sometimes called a *Trojan horse*, is a malware program whose intended actions are not revealed to the user of the system on which it runs. Additionally, unlike viruses and worms, Trojans do not have the ability to replicate. An attacker may plant a Trojan on a system that she compromised. Other popular distribution techniques for Trojans include e-mail spam messages and tainted Web downloads. Regardless of the distribution mechanism, a Trojan typically masquerades as some other harmless or trusted program.

SubSeven is a common Trojan that embodies many of the characteristics typical to this malware category. With the SubSeven server component running on a system, the attacker can remotely control the victim's machine via easy-to-use client software shown in Figure 23.1. The SubSeven client can connect over the network on a predetermined port to the system infected with the SubSeven server. The following list presents a small subset of the capabilities built into SubSeven:

- Log keystrokes
- Transfer and manipulate files
- Sniff network packets
- Retrieve saved passwords
- Edit the registry
- Execute commands
- Record sound
- Obtain screen captures

NOTES

Figure 23.1 – The SubSeven client application allows attackers to remotely control computers infected with the SubSeven server.

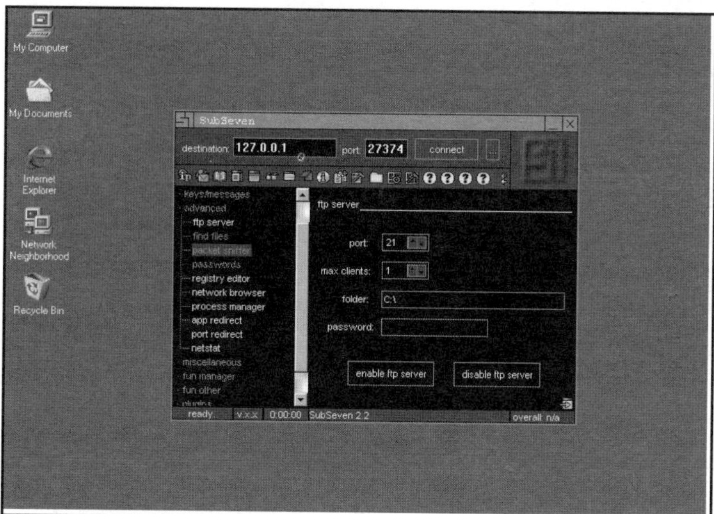

Figure 23.2 – The EditServer utility can be used to customize a SubSeven server before distributing it to potential victims.

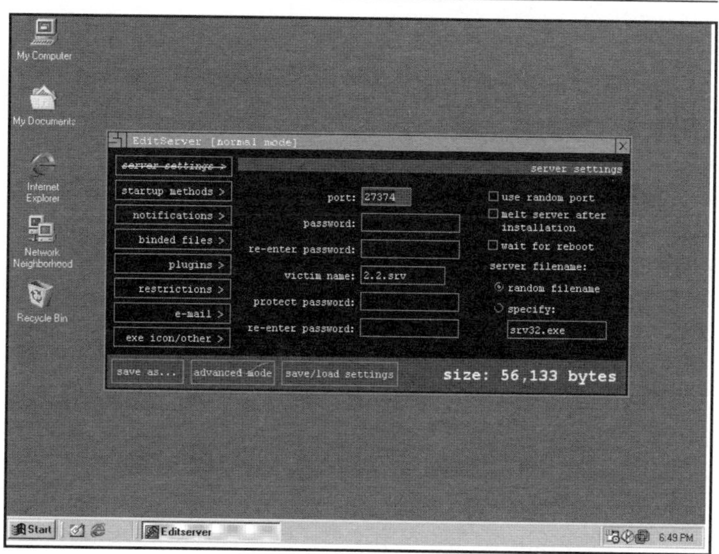

One of the reasons for the popularity of SubSeven is the ease with which it can be customized for a particular purpose. Potential attackers can download the SubSeven kit from the Trojan's Web site, which includes the EditServer utility shown in Figure 23.2. EditServer allows the user of the Trojan to perform actions such as configure the port that the Trojan listens to, password-protect access to the server component, and modify its start-up behavior.

EditServer also has the ability to attach the SubSeven server to another, typically benign program. This allows the attacker to distribute the Trojan together with software that a potential victim may be interested in, increasing the likelihood that the Trojan will be installed, and that the victim will forward the tainted file to somebody else.

Note

Trojans are often bound to other programs before distribution. For example, the infamous Back Orifice Trojan can be attached to other programs using tools such as Silk Rope and SatanWrap.

Web pages with malicious content that execute in the visitor's browser could also be considered Trojans. You could make this classification because such malware performs its actions under false pretenses, assuming the visitor will come to the site with the expectation of encountering useful content. Such Web page Trojans can be implemented as Java applets, ActiveX controls, and JavaScript code segments. A very simple example of a Web page Trojan is Winbomb, which consists of a JavaScript

NOTES

function that attempts to open an unlimited number of browser windows.

An attack based on malicious code embedded into a Web page could involve denial of service, invasion of privacy, or mere annoyance. The possibilities for abuse are almost endless, especially if the malware specimen finds a way to execute arbitrary code on the victim's system. We discuss some of the more common capabilities of malicious code in the next section.

Capabilities

Why do computer users feel threatened by the possibility of a worm or a virus infecting their systems? On a sentimental level, there is something threatening about knowing that an intruder had a chance to go through your data, looking at confidential records and, possibly, retaining them for future use. From a business perspective, there is usually monetary loss associated with losing critical files, revealing sensitive information, or providing unauthorized access to internal systems. These are some of the capabilities often possessed by malware, as we discuss in this section.

Destroying Data

Destroying data is one of the most insidious actions that a malware specimen can take after infecting a system. For example, the CIH virus, which began spreading in June 1998, had a particularly destructive payload. CIH was programmed to activate every year on April 26, at which point it overwrote data on the computer's hard drive. Additionally, the virus attempted to overwrite the flash-BIOS of the infected system, often rendering the computer unusable. (CIH is also known as the Chernobyl virus, because April 26 marks the anniversary of the nuclear plant disaster that occurred in Chernobyl, Ukraine, in 1986.)[5]

If you lose data as a result of a malware infection, your most practical means of recovery is to retrieve files from backup. If backups are not available, and lost data was very valuable, you may be able to restore it via low-level forensic recovery techniques, although such methods tend to be time-consuming and expensive. Unfortunately, destruction of data is only one danger associated with a malware infection.

Leaking Information

The possibility that a malware incident led to information leaking to unauthorized parties can be as devastating as the destruction of data. You may recall that the Melissa virus, which we discussed in the Taxonomy section, often resulted in sensitive Word documents being e-mailed to recipients listed in the victim's address book. The SirCam worm, discovered in July 2001, is another notable example of a mass-mailing malware specimen. SirCam selected a random document from the victim's "My Documents" folder and e-mailed the file, merged with a copy of SirCam, to recipients found in the person's address book and browser cache.

Of course, a document is only one type of information whose confidentiality can be

[5] McAfee – AVERT. *W95/CIH.1003*. 7 September 1999. URL: `http://vil.nai.com/vil/content/v_10300.htm` (4 August 2002).

NOTES

compromised by malware. The Caligula virus, which appeared in January 1999, was programmed to locate the victim's Pretty Good Privacy (PGP) private key file and transmit it to the creator of the virus via FTP. The Marker virus, discovered about half a year later, used a similar technique to obtain information about the infected user from the system's registry, and transferred the data to the author's FTP site. This capability allowed Marker to maintain a trail of infected users, empowering its creator to study relationships between members of the targeted organization.[6]

Trojans can be just as effective at leaking information as worms and viruses. As we mentioned in the discussion of SubSeven, the SubSeven server has the ability to monitor the user's keystrokes, and is capable of retrieving passwords saved on the infected computer. Additionally, various ad-supported applications have been implicated in leaking information without the user's knowledge, often by monitoring the user's browsing habits without permission. Such software is often called *spyware*.

Providing Backdoor Access

Attackers use backdoors to ensure that they retain access to the system after it was compromised. For instance, they might employ a Trojan such as SubSeven or Back Orifice to listen on a pre-determined port of the infected system, allowing the attacker to remotely control the victim's computer at will. The official release of OpenSSH in July 2002, was tainted with a Trojan for a similar purpose. The backdoor was activated during the compilation process of OpenSSH source files, and initiated a network connection to an external server. This enabled the attacker to execute arbitrary commands on the system that compiled the Trojaned version of OpenSSH.

A more elaborate example of using a backdoor can be found in the functionality built into the Leaves worm. By June 2001, Leaves quietly infected nearly 15,000 computers, providing its author with a capable army of zombies that he could centrally control. The Leaves worm spread by scanning for hosts that were already infected with the SubSeven Trojan. When such a system was located, the worm attempted to authenticate to the Trojan using a master password that was known to work with some versions of SubSeven. Once Leaves gained access to the computer through this backdoor, it removed the pre-existing Trojan, presumably to prevent anyone else from getting into the system through such means.

As the next step, Leaves acted to provide its author with a backdoor of his own, by connecting to a channel on a remote Internet Relay Chat (IRC) server. As the worm spread, infected computers logged into the IRC channel, awaiting additional instructions from the worm's creator. This gave the attacker the ability to authenticate to all instances of the worm simultaneously, and issue commands for launching programs, manipulating files, and obtaining system information. Using IRC to access infected computers carried several advantages:

[6] Lenny Zeltser. *The Evolution of Malicious Agents*. April 2000. URL: `http://www.zeltser.com/agents` (4 August 2002).

NOTES

- The attacker could be several network hops away from computers that he was controlling, making it more difficult to trace the attack's origin.
- The attacker could rely on the IRC network to automatically relay commands to all instances of the worm, providing him with a powerful DDoS attack platform.
- Unlike commercial chat services, IRC is not tightly controlled, and, in many ways, continues to be the wild west of chat networks.
- Powerful scripting agents exist for IRC that can provide the attacker with a convenient way to automate tasks for maintaining his army of compromised machines.

Note

IRC is frequently used by malware writers for staying in touch with their creations. If you only block several outbound ports on the firewall at your organization, consider blocking TCP ports 6666 and 6667, which are frequently used for connecting to IRC servers.

In an interesting twist, the Leaves worm took advantage of someone else's backdoors on systems that were compromised earlier, closed them, and established an alternate remote access channel for its creator. Malware writers have numerous options for creating malicious code that meets their objectives, by incorporating different malware types and attack capabilities. Now that we have discussed different types of malware, and examined how it may threaten your computer resources, let's take a closer look at the inner workings of such software.

How Malware Works

Worms, viruses, and Trojans that find their way onto our systems and networks are becoming increasingly complex. Authors of malicious code have numerous choices when it comes to designing mechanisms for malware propagation, infection, and cloaking. This section of the chapter is dedicated to examining inner workings of malware, to help you understand how it works.

Propagation Techniques

Although we may not be able to account for all possible ways in which malicious code penetrates defenses, some propagation techniques are employed much more often than others. The following list presents distribution mechanisms used most frequently—something you should consider in your security policy and architecture:

- Removable media
- E-mail
- Web browsing
- Network vulnerabilities

Removable Media

One of the fundamental properties of a computer virus is the ability to replicate. Within the confines of a single computer, replication involves modifying the system's environment as we discuss Infection

NOTES

Techniques a little later in the chapter. However, the possibility for additional infection within the same system can be quickly exhausted. Malware specimens benefit from the ability to spread to other computers. Removable media such as floppy disks and CDs have provided a time-tested method for malicious code to travel between machines.

As the use of floppy disks diminishes, high-capacity removable media such as Zip disks, CDs, and DVDs continue to be used to distribute files, and therefore to spread malware. If you save infected files onto a removable storage device and later insert it into another computer, you may inadvertently assist in spreading the virus. Official media distributors are as capable of spreading malware as users of Zip disks and home-burned CDs are. For instance, the CIH virus was accidentally disseminated by several gaming companies as part of infected demo CDs.[7] In a similar fashion, the Powerpuff Girls DVD distributed by Warner Bros in October 2001, was accidentally infected with the FunLove virus. FunLove migrated to the victim's computer when contents of the DVD were installed on the PC.[8]

Note

If you are creating custom floppies, CDs, or DVDs for distribution to others, such as customers or internal users, be sure to first scan the contents of the master disk with an up-to-date anti-virus program. Additionally, take advantage of free tools such as md5sum to record cryptographic signatures of all files in the original package. Use the signatures to spot-check duplicated disks to make sure their contents are identical to the original.

When designing network defenses, do not forget to account for the possibility that malicious code may be brought into your environment by foot through the use of removable media. Furthermore, you should not assume that a vendor-installed computer system is malware-free. The CIH virus is known to have been included in a batch of new Aptiva PCs shipped by IBM in March 1999, just a month before the virus activated its payload.[9]

E-mail

It's no surprise that e-mail offers a convenient alternative to using removable media for distributing files. The same viruses that attach to legitimate files and spread via floppies can disseminate through files that are sent as e-mail attachments. Because e-mail messages are usually allowed to leave and enter the organization's

[7] F-Secure. *F-Secure Computer Virus Information Pages: CIH.* URL: `http://www.europe.f-secure.com/v-descs/cih.shtml` (6 August 2002).

[8] Sophos. *Powerpuff Girls Struck Down by FunLove.* 1 November 2001. URL: `http://www.sophos.com/virusinfo/articles/powerpuff.html` (6 August 2002).

[9] ZDNet Reviews. Victor Latona. *CIH: One Year Later.* 21 April 2000. URL: `http://www.zdnet.com/products/stories/reviews/0,4161,2553837,00.html` (6 August 2002).

NOTES

network, malware often uses e-mail as a propagation mechanism.

You've already seen several examples of e-mail borne malware in this chapter. Recall that Melissa and SirCam did not even wait for humans to e-mail infected documents to each other. Instead, they took initiative and automatically mailed copies of themselves from the victim's computer when their payload was activated.

The Klez worm is another prolific malware specimen that used e-mail as one of its distribution mechanisms. It began spreading at the end of 2001. Some versions of Klez spoofed the sender's address when mailing themselves to random recipients from the address book. This made it difficult for the next victim to determine the origin of the tainted e-mail message, and often resulted in false accusations that the person specified in the "From" field had an infected system. Klez also attempted to exploit a MIME header vulnerability known to exist in Internet Explorer, which could automatically launch the attachment simply when the user previewed the worm's e-mail message. (`http://cve.mitre.org/cgi-bin/cvename.cgi?name=CAN-2001-0154`) Interestingly, as part of its payload, Klez contained a copy of the Elkern virus.[10] This relationship between a worm and a virus showcases the potential for innovation in malware distribution techniques.

Web Browsing

Much like e-mail, Web browsing is an activity that takes place at most, if not all, organizations connected to the Internet. A Web browser provides malware with an unobtrusive way of entering the system. In the discussion of Trojans, we already mentioned malicious code based on Java applets, JavaScript, and ActiveX that could be embedded into a Web page. This approach allows Trojans to propagate via the Web when a potential victim connects to the rogue Web site, even though Trojans do not have replication capabilities per se. In another example, the backdoor built into OpenSSH, which we described in the Providing Backdoor Access section, was disseminated when people downloaded tainted version of the program from `ftp.openssh.org` and its mirror sites.

Viruses and worms too can propagate via Web browsing activities. For instance, the good old CIH virus was reported to have been distributed by Yamaha as part of a firmware update for CD-R400 drives. CIH was also included as part of an otherwise legitimate download from a Wing Commander gaming site.[11]

The Nimda worm is yet another example of malware taking advantage of Web browsing activities. If a potential victim browsed to a Web server infected with Nimda, the person was prompted to download a file that contained the worm as an attachment. To make the matter worse, the attachment would be

[10] Symantec Security Response. *W32.Klez.gen@mm.* 2 August 2002. URL: `http://securityresponse.symantec.com/avcenter/venc/data/w32.klez.gen@mm.html` (7 August 2002).

[11] F-Secure. *F-Secure Computer Virus Information Pages: CIH.* URL: `http://www.europe.f-secure.com/v-descs/cih.shtml` (6 August 2002).

NOTES

automatically opened if the user's browser was not patched against a MIME header vulnerability. (That's the same vulnerability that was exploited by Klez.) At its peak, Nimda infected so many IIS servers that the likelihood of a Web surfer stumbling upon an infected server was significant.

Network Vulnerabilities

Yet another way for malware to propagate involves actively probing systems for holes that can be exploited over the network. We've already mentioned such functionality in the discussion of the Leaves worm, which scanned networks looking for systems that contain the SubSeven Trojan. You may also recall that Code Red was programmed to scan for IIS servers that had a remotely exploitable buffer overflow vulnerability. This is a popular attack pattern that is seen over and over again.

A malware specimen does not have to limit itself to a single operating system when propagating through the use of network vulnerabilities. For example, the sadmind/IIS worm spread in May 2001, by targeting unpatched Solaris and Windows systems. The worm took advantage of a two-year-old buffer overflow vulnerability in the sadmind program to compromise Solaris systems. After infecting a Solaris machine, it used a seven-month-old vulnerability to compromise Windows IIS servers.[12]

Taking advantage of overly permissive trust relationships is another way in which malware can exploit network vulnerabilities. This approach dates as far back as 1988, when the Morris worm, also known as the Internet Worm, disrupted most of the major US research centers in a matter of hours. One of the worm's propagation techniques involved examining lists of host names that an infected system was aware of, and attempting to connect to them in hopes that the infected machine is trusted to execute commands on the remote machines. (The Morris worm also attempted to exploit known vulnerabilities in several commonly used network services.) In a somewhat similar manner, one of Nimda's propagation strategies was to locate open file shares that were accessible over the network without login credentials.

Now that you are familiar with some of the most popular malware propagation techniques, let's see how a malware specimen infects an individual system upon arrival.

Infection Techniques

The first steps taken by malicious code after it arrives on the system are usually geared toward establishing its presence on the machine. This may involve altering the machine's configuration so that malicious code is activated every time the system boots up. A malware specimen may also modify installed programs to make sure that it runs whenever they are accessed. It may also attach itself to certain types of documents in a way that triggers a malicious payload when the document is opened. We go over these infection techniques in this section of the chapter.

[12] Carnegie Mellon University. *CERT Advisory CA-2001-11 sadmind/IIS Worm.* 10 May 2001. URL: `http://www.cert.org/advisories/CA-2001-11.html` (7 August 2002).

NOTES

Multiple Propagation Vectors in a Single Malware Specimen

It is common for malware specimens, particularly worms, to possess multiple propagation vectors. This increases the number of targets that the worm might be able to infect. For example, here is a complete list of propagation techniques possessed by Nimda:

- Nimda scanned Internet hosts for vulnerable IIS servers.
- Nimda harvested e-mail addresses from the victim's address book and other files on the infected system.
- When infecting a Web server, Nimda attached a JavaScript code fragment to displayed pages so that a visiting Web browser would automatically attempt to retrieve a copy of the worm.
- Nimda copied itself to local and network folders that the infected user had permissions to access.

Altering System Configuration

When the Nimda worm infected a computer, it copied itself as the file named `load.exe`, and modified the system.ini file by adding the following string after the `SHELL` variable in the `[Boot]` section:[13]

```
explorer.exe load.exe -dontrunold
```

This helped ensure that Nimda would run whenever the PC rebooted. A similar effect can be accomplished by inserting an entry under the `HKLM\Software\Microsoft\Windows\CurrentVersion\Run` registry key, as was the case with the Leaves worm. Another popular technique for loading malware when the OS starts up is to install the malicious executable as a service or a daemon. For example, when the sadmind/IIS worm infected a Solaris machine, it would add an entry to the `/etc/rc2.d/S71rpc` system initialization script.

Another way to have malicious code execute when the machine starts up is to place it in the boot sector of the computer's disk. Every disk has a boot sector, regardless of whether or not it is actually bootable. When a PC is powered up, it looks for boot information in the order dictated by the machine's BIOS. If any of the media in the drives specified by the BIOS has an infected boot sector, the infection will get transferred to the boot drive. Once the infection is complete, malicious code will get loaded into memory at startup. A malware specimen that places malicious code into the boot sector is called a *boot record infector*. Historically, the vast majority of boot record infectors have been viruses. That is why you are much more likely to hear about some "boot record virus," and will rarely (if ever) hear the term "boot record worm."

[13] F-Secure. *F-Secure Computer Virus Information Pages: Nimda.* September 2001. URL: `http://www.europe.f-secure.com/v-descs/nimda.shtml` (9 August 2002).

Note

Boot record infectors lose some of their potency on modern operating systems such as Windows 2000 and Windows XP. In such operating systems, the OS kernel assumes control of the machine in a way that prevents malicious code in the boot record from continuing to execute.[14]

NOTES

[14] Symantec AntiVirus Research Center. *Understanding Virus Behavior under Windows NT.* URL: `http://securityresponse.symantec.com/avcenter/reference/virus.behavior.under.win.nt.pdf` (6 September 2002).

NOTES

Virus Types

- Boot record infectors
  - Floppy boot record (FBR)
  - Master boot record (MBR)
  - DOS boot sector (DBS or PBR)
  - No network spreading potential
- Multipartite
  - Potential to spread over networks

SANS Security Essentials – Secure Communications

Floppy disks contain a *floppy boot record* (FBR), which can harbor malicious code. If a system is booted from such a floppy, the malicious payload will be activated. Hard disks can have a *master boot record* (MBR) and a *partition boot record* (PBR), either of which can become infected. (A PBR is sometimes called a DOS boot sector). The MBR is the first place the BIOS looks when booting from a hard drive. If malicious code is present in the MBR, it can seize control of the hardware before the OS even sees the light of day! Instructions in the PBR are executed after the bootstrap program in the MBR passes on control to the active partition. OS files that are present on a partition are loaded according to instructions in the PBR. Much like in the MBR infection, if malicious code is present in the PBR, it will be loaded before the OS.

Modifying Program Files

Malicious code that infects by attaching itself to existing program files is called a *program infector* (sometimes also known as a *file infector*). As you already know, worms and Trojans are able to operate as stand-alone executables, which is why the term program infector is most often used to describe a virus. A program infector is activated when the executable that hosts malicious code is launched. The malware specimen is then loaded into memory and is ready to perform its author's bidding. Program infectors are usually attached to files with `.com` or `.exe` extensions, but can infect interpretable files as well.

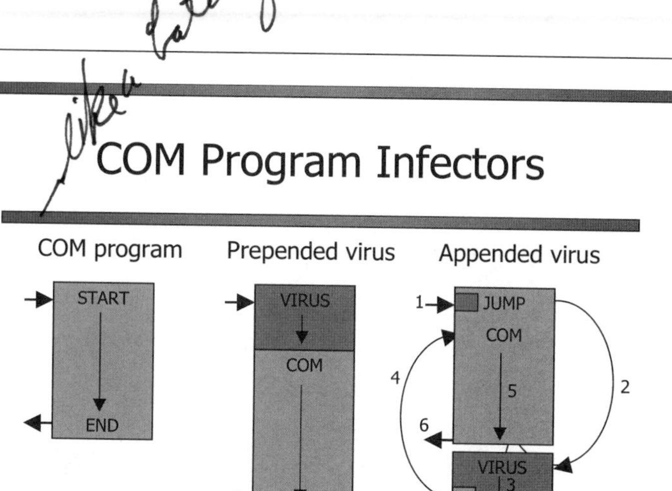

Let's see how program files are actually infected. Viruses that infect COM files (the ones that have the `.com` extension) can attach themselves to the program in one of three ways, as illustrated in the slide:

- By prepending to the beginning of the file—A prepending virus gains control when the first instruction of the infected COM file is executed. The virus runs and then passes control to the original program. Because of this, users may not notice anything different.
- By appending to the end of the file—An appending virus writes its payload to the end of the program file, and inserts a jump instruction as the first instruction in the file. This jump will lead to the execution of the virus, which later returns control to the original COM program. As a result, the functionality of the original program may remain unaltered, hindering the user's ability to detect the incident.
- By overwriting a portion of the file—Overwriting viruses simply write their code to the beginning of the file. These viruses therefore destroy the original program. More sophisticated overwriting viruses will make a copy of the portion that they overwrite so that they can execute it later.

NOTES

NOTES

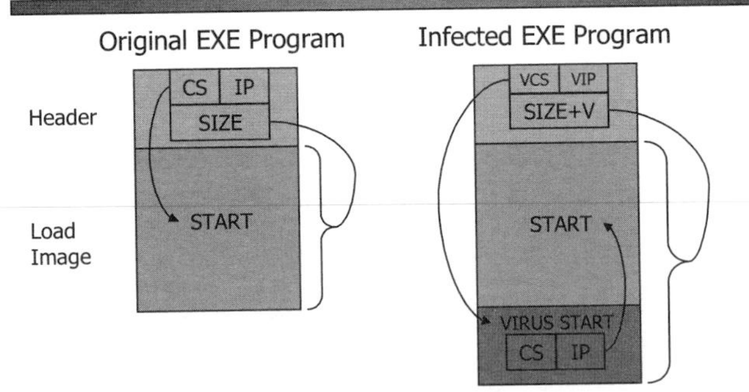

Viruses that infect EXE files (the ones that have the `.exe` extension) operate slightly differently. As you can see in the slide, an EXE file consists of two parts—the header and the load image. The header contains, among other things, a pointer that points to the first instruction to be executed in the load image. This pointer, labeled CS:IP, consists of a pair of values—the code segment (CS) and instruction pointer (IP). A header entry named SIZE stores the size of the load image. When an EXE file is infected, these header entries are altered. The new CS:IP, which we labeled VCS:VIP, now points to the start of the appended viral code. SIZE increases to VSIZE and measures the size of the infected load image. Running the infected program will cause a jump to the virus load image. When completed, the viral code hands execution back to the original program.

Note

Multipartite viruses can infect boot records as well as program files. When executed as a program, they infect the boot sector, and vice versa—if they manage to infect the boot record, they will spread to program files. Multipartite viruses indirectly provide a mechanism by which boot record viruses can get across networks—they travel as program files.

Infecting Document Files

When a virus attaches itself to a file, it usually does this with the expectation that the malicious payload will be triggered when the file is executed. In the good old days, only program files could contain executable instructions, and document files contained only data. However, the line between executable and document files has blurred, particularly on Windows operating systems. For instance, Microsoft Office applications such as Word and Excel have the ability to interpret and execute macros embedded into documents. Such macros are meant to increase the efficiency of application-specific tasks, such as form completion or fax distribution.[15] The Melissa virus was able to take advantage of such capabilities, as we discussed earlier in the chapter.

[15] Denis Zenkin. *Understanding Macro Viruses*. 21 August 2000. URL: `http://online.securityfocus.com/infocus/1278` (10 August 2002).

NOTES

Virus Types (2)

- Macro viruses
  - Targets are data files (e.g., *.doc)
  - Written in 'macro languages' (e.g., Melissa macro virus)
  - Visual Basic Editor
- High network spreading potential!

SANS Security Essentials – Secure Communications

A *macro virus* (or a *macro worm*, for that matter) is implemented using instructions that can be interpreted within applications such as a word processor and a spreadsheet. Unlike program viruses, which target executables, macro viruses usually target document files. Capabilities of a macro infector are limited only by the macro language used to implement it. Microsoft Office macros, written in Visual Basic, are very powerful, and can access all features of the host application, and numerous features of the underlying OS.

Microsoft Office files are not the only document types vulnerable to macro infections. The Peachy worm, discovered in August 2001, embedded its payload inside Adobe Acrobat PDF files. The payload could activate only if the potential victim had a commercial version of Adobe Acrobat version 5 or higher.[16]

Peachy's infection mechanism took advantage of Acrobat's ability to execute Visual Basic scripts embedded in PDF documents.

Malicious payload will not be activated if it is embedded inside a document whose viewer does not support code execution. For example, an unusual proof-of-concept virus called Perrun was discovered in June 2002. Perrun embedded malicious payload in JPEG image files. Because JPEG files do not support macros, opening such a file on a system not infected with Perrun would not trigger the malicious code. In order to execute instructions that it embedded into the image, Perrun changed the program associated with handling JPEG files. As a result, when a user of the infected system attempted to open a JPEG file, the Perrun extractor would run instead of the original viewer.[17] Only machines already infected with this virus through other mechanisms were able to execute commands embedded into infected JPEG files.

In the overview of the inner workings of malware, we have already outlined some of the most common propagation techniques, and examined infection mechanisms that are often employed by malicious code to establish their presence on the compromised system. In the final part of the discussion of how malware works, we would like to tell you about defense mechanisms employed by malware to conceal its presence on the infected system, and to decrease the likelihood that it will be discovered and removed by anti-virus software.

[16] McAfee – AVERT. *VBS/PeachyPDF@MM*. 14 August 2001. URL: `http://vil.nai.com/vil/content/v_99179.htm` (9 August 2002).

[17] McAfee – AVERT. *W32/Perrun*. 19 June 2002. URL: `http://vil.nai.com/vil/content/v_99522.htm` (10 August 2002).

NOTES

Macro Infectors that Build Themselves

We often think of malicious software as code that was written by a particular individual; however, some macro viruses are born as a result of several malware specimens combining themselves into a single entity. Consider a virus that is made up of several macros named OpenDocument, InfectTemplates, and DeleteNetworkFiles. The malicious payload is triggered when an infected document is opened, and is designed to infect the user's template files, and to delete files from the network. Also, consider an unrelated malware specimen created by someone else that includes macros named OpenDocument, InfectTemplates, and EmailPasswords. This specimen is designed to infect files in a manner similar to the first virus, but instead of deleting files, it looks for locally stored passwords, and e-mails them to some Internet address.

If a document is infected with the first virus, and then it is infected with the second one, macros that share names will be automatically merged. This may result in a new virus that is capable of deleting files and stealing user passwords. A process like this generates a malware specimen that was not actually created by any particular individual. Some auto-generated specimens may fail to work properly, while other macro combinations may be more effective at proliferating and causing damage. Mutated macro viruses may possess a signature that does not match previously seen malware, which makes it more difficult for anti-virus software to detect them.

Defenses Employed by Malware

To avoid detection, malicious code may employ sophisticated methods to hide its presence and to establish a stronghold on the conquered system. Here are some examples of malware self-defense techniques at work:

- The Hybris worm, discovered in September 2000, gradually mailed out copies of itself from the victim's computer, instead of instantly sending a flood of messages the way Melissa did. The delay implemented by Hybris was aimed at helping it avoid immediate detection.
- The MTX worm, discovered in August 2000, contained functionality to block access to the Internet sites of major anti-virus vendors. This was meant to preclude the victim from installing anti-virus software, or from updating virus signatures.
- The AceBot worm, discovered in March 2002, was observed to disable personal firewall software installed on the victim's machine. The firewall was disabled to allow the worm to make outbound connections to its author's IRC server.

Frequently, malware self-defense methods can be classified as stealthing or polymorphism. In the following two sections we look at these techniques in some detail, to help you understand what you may be up against when trying to detect malicious code.

NOTES

Virus Protection Techniques

make it harder for us to find it

- Stealthing
  - virus attempts to hide or 'cloak' itself
  - hiding from anti-virus software
  - read stealthing
  - size stealthing
- Need to scan memory to detect

SANS Security Essentials – Secure Communications

Stealthing

Stealthing is a general term that refers to approaches used by malicious code to conceal its presence on the infected system. One popular stealthing technique is called *read stealthing*, which involves intercepting system calls to access files, and responding with false information. For example, if anti-virus software tries to scan an infected file, a memory resident virus may be able to catch this attempt and provide a backed-up copy of the original file to the scanner.

Size stealthing focuses on falsifying the size of the infected file. This can be accomplished by intercepting the system's attempts to inquire about the file's size, or by altering the directory listing to conceal the true size of the file. The Whale virus, which dates all the way back to 1990, implemented this technique by changing the directory entry of the infected file to show 9,216 bytes less than its actual size. (9,216 bytes was the size of the Whale virus.)

A *rootkit* is a collection of tools and utilities designed to conceal evidence of a system compromise, and to allow the attacker to access the system in the future. (A rootkit may also contain programs used to penetrate the system's defenses.) Rootkits frequently implement stealthing by replacing the machine's native tools that may be used to detect the compromise. For example, the t0rn rootkit replaced core Linux system administration programs such as `find`, `ps`, `ls`, and `top`. If the user of the infected system used the t0rn version of `ps`, she would not see processes started by the attacker. In 2001, the Lion worm used the t0rn rootkit to hide the worm's presence on the systems that it infected.

Note

A rootkit may also implement stealthing by running as a kernel loadable module. This technique allows the rootkit to intercept system calls without having to replace any of the system's utilities. As a result, the practice of using tools from a trusted CD when investigating an incident may not be sufficient. If you suspect that a rootkit may be installed on the compromised system, your best bet is to perform the analysis by booting from a trusted bootable CD, or by connecting to the infected hard drive from a pristine machine.

NOTES

Virus Protection Techniques (2)

- Polymorphism
  - poly = many, morph = form
  - encryption/decryption routines
  - mutation engines
- Makes a scanner's job a lot harder

SANS Security Essentials – Secure Communications

Polymorphism

Polymorphism is the process by which malicious software changes its underlying code to avoid detection, usually without affecting its functionality. A virus may modify itself by inserting into its code instructions that do not actually accomplish anything, such as adding 1 to a value, and then subtracting 1. The purpose of this technique is to change the signature of the malware specimen, to make it more difficult for anti-virus software to match it against the database of known viruses.

Another popular way to implement polymorphism is to encrypt malicious code in a way that would allow the malware specimen to decrypt itself into memory during runtime. The way of evading detection in this case is to vary the decryption routine, therefore mutating the executable so that its signature keeps changing. This functionality was incorporated into the Hybris worm, for instance, which was able to encrypt copies of itself before mailing them out.

Metamorphic malware attempts to avoid detection by recompiling portions of itself. This technique significantly complicates the task of detecting such a program through the use of traditional signature-based mechanisms. An example of a powerful metamorphic specimen is the Simile virus, which disassembles its viral code, removes, adds, and rearranges unused instructions, and then reassembles it for future infections.[18]

Authors of malicious code go through considerable efforts to conceal their creations and to make it more difficult for us to recover from an infection. The same degree of care is often put into propagation and infection techniques, as we discussed in the beginning of this section. Now that you know all of this, let's see what you can do to defend your systems against malware attacks.

Defending Against Malware

You should now be familiar with capabilities of several types of malicious code, their propagation and infection mechanisms, and techniques that they can employ in an attempt to thwart detection. If you are feeling powerless against the forces of malware, don't worry; there are practical steps you can take to improve the resilience of your defenses. Historically, methods of preventing infections were heavily

[18] Virus Bulletin. Frédéric Perriot, Peter Ferrie and Péter Ször. *W32/Simile*. URL: `http://www.virusbtn.com/resources/viruses/indepth/simile.xml` (26 September 2002).

focused on the use of anti-virus software on user workstations. Such products are still critical components of a defense infrastructure, but they should not be employed without additional security layers. As we discuss in this section, an effective malware defense strategy should incorporate the following items:

- Anti-virus software at multiple locations
- Up-to-date virus signature files
- A practice of reviewing and installing security patches
- Lock-down of system configuration and dangerous application features

NOTES

NOTES

Anti-virus Software

- Activity monitoring programs
- Scanners
- Integrity checkers
- Remember "defense in depth"

SANS Security Essentials – Secure Communications

Capabilities of Anti-Virus Software

Anti-virus software is one of the most popular measures for fighting malware infections, particularly on Windows systems. When deployed in conjunction with other security mechanisms, it can be reasonably effective in blocking and detecting common malware specimens. There are three primary types of defensive techniques that may be incorporated into an anti-virus product:

- Activity monitors
- Scanners
- Integrity checkers

Note

Software that defends against malware is called *anti-virus* software. This is mainly for historical reasons, even though it can protect against several types of malicious code, including viruses, worms, and Trojans.[19]

Activity monitors, also known as *behavior blockers*, aim to prevent infection by monitoring for malicious activity, and blocking such activity when possible. Activity monitors observe programs that run on the system, and look for attempts to perform actions such as low-level formatting of the hard drive, writing to boot records, and modifying program files. Activity monitors may be able to detect malware specimens that they have not encountered before; however, they are not considered a particularly strong form of defense if deployed alone. Some of the ways of bypassing their restrictions involve directly accessing interrupt handlers on hardware controllers, performing actions that are not being monitored, or disabling the monitoring process altogether.

Scanners are the best-known form of anti-virus defenses. They operate by searching files for content attributable to known malware specimens (signatures). If a scanner detects that a file that is about to be saved or executed matches a malware signature, it may be able to block access to the file. One of the biggest challenges of this approach is that it only detects malware for which the anti-virus vendor has already provided a signature. When

[19] Stephen Northcutt, et. al. *Inside Network Perimeter Security*. New Riders, July 2002.

Nimda struck, for example, signatures were available a day after it first appeared, giving it the opportunity to infect a very large number of systems. Another problem with scanners is that the signature may not be able to match all variants of a particular malware specimen, especially if it has polymorphic properties.

Integrity checkers compute checksums or hash values of original files on the system, and store the results in a baseline database. During subsequent runs, the program compares the current state of the file system with the baseline, warning the administrator if any of the monitored files have changed. Examples of integrity verification software include Tripwire, AIDE, and Intact. These programs may be considered generic detectors because they have the ability to detect activity from previously unknown malware specimens. However, integrity checkers are rarely able to block malicious code from executing—they are usually implemented as infection detectors, not preventors.

No single malware defense technique is effective on its own. It is a good idea to use anti-virus software that employs several approaches discussed above. Luckily, modern anti-virus software usually combines activity monitors and scanners into a single product. For more robust protection, consider also deploying an integrity checker on your critical systems, even if they are already running anti-virus software.

As we discussed in the Propagation Techniques section, malware can spread using a variety of methods such as CD-ROMs, e-mail, Web browsing, and network exploits. It is prudent to install anti-virus software at multiple places in your infrastructure so that it watches as many entry points as possible. Classic locations for anti-virus products include:

- Workstations
- File and print servers
- Mail servers
- Internet gateways

Leading anti-virus products provide software that is able to operate at these locations. You may be tempted to install anti-virus products from different vendors on the same system, to improve the likelihood that a malware infection will be blocked. This is usually a bad idea, as it will rarely result in a stable configuration. Instead, consider using one vendor's product in one location (perhaps for server and workstation scans), and another vendor's product in another location (such as the mail server). Keep in mind that setting up multiple products will increase the solution's cost, and will complicate its maintenance. In the following section we examine considerations for obtaining and maintaining anti-virus software.

NOTES

NOTES

Anti-virus Acquisition

- Single-user purchase
- Multiple users
- What to buy
  - http://www.icsa.net/html/communities/antivirus/certification/certified_products/index.shtml
  - http://www.icsa.net/html/certification/index.shtml

SANS Security Essentials – Secure Communications

Obtaining and Maintaining Anti-Virus Software

Obtaining anti-virus protection for a single computer is relatively simple. You can purchase a single license from your favorite anti-virus vendor, and download the software over the Web or obtain a copy on distribution media. You can follow the same approach if you have several computers to protect; however, it doesn't take a lot of systems for this method to become a burden. For large installations, most anti-virus vendors provide enterprise versions of their products, which support remote installation and maintenance. In this case, anti-virus software is loaded on a central server, which distributes the application and malware signatures to other servers and workstations. The enterprise licensing approach usually allows you to obtain a single physical copy of the product, and pay for licenses according to the number of nodes that will require protection.

Which anti-virus product to buy can be the basis for a great debate, and is beyond the scope of this chapter. It is a good idea to verify that the product you are getting has been tested and certified as having met some objective criteria. ICSA Labs conducts such testing, and makes their results available publicly on its Web site at `http://www.icsalabs.com/html/communities/antivirus`.

Note

The US Department of Defense (DoD) has an agency-wide license for at least two anti-virus product suites. They can be downloaded from DoD servers over the Internet, but only if you are coming from a `.mil` domain. This seems to be a reasonable approach to distributing anti-virus software.

NOTES

Installation

- Self-extracting set-up wizards
- Configure at set-up
- Test that software is running

SANS Security Essentials – Secure Communications

Deploying Anti-Virus Software

Once acquired, installing anti-virus software is relatively straightforward. Most products are set up through the use of a self-extracting program or an installation wizard that provides a certain degree of customization. For example, the software can be configured to perform a hard drive scan at every boot, continually monitor file activity, and scan file downloads, e-mail attachments, and floppy access. Enterprise versions of the products usually give you the ability to enforce these options from a central administration console.

NOTES

Sample Configuration Options

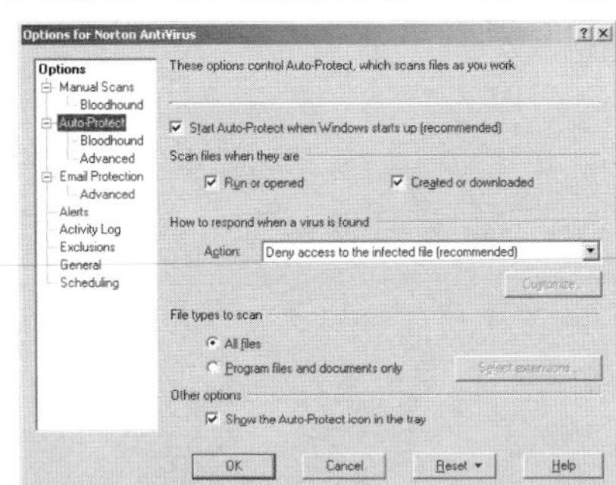

SANS Security Essentials – Secure Communications

The specifics of your configuration should be determined by your anti-virus policy. One way to check the scope of the policy is to take a look at the configuration screen of your anti-virus package, and make sure that the policy addresses settings that you care most about. The slide shows a screenshot of one of the configuration screens for Norton AntiVirus Corporate Edition, which allows you to specify when the program should be started, which files it should scan, and how it should react if malicious code is detected.

Be sure to test anti-virus software after it is installed, to verify that it is indeed active, and that its configuration matches your expectations. Using a real malware specimen to test effectiveness of the software is probably not a good idea; however, most reputable anti-virus products are designed to issue an alert whenever they encounter a file that consists of the following text:

```
X5O!P%@AP[4\PZX54(P^)7CC)7}$EICAR-
STANDARD-ANTIVIRUS-TEST-FILE!$H+H*
```

This text was created by the European Institute for Computer Anti-Virus Research (EICAR) to help troubleshoot anti-virus software. You can download it from `http://www.eicar.org/anti_virus_test_file.htm`. If you copy this string into a new text file and save it with the "`.com`" extension, it will display "EICAR-STANDARD-ANTIVIRUS-TEST-FILE!" when executed. Although there is no malicious code in this file, you should only distribute it to people who clearly understand its purpose. Also, do not store it on production machines that run anti-virus software (except as part of a deliberate test), since it is likely to result in spurious alerts.

Maintaining anti-virus software is generally no more complex than setting it up. Perhaps the most important aspect of anti-virus maintenance is ensuring that it is using the latest virus signatures.

Keeping Signatures Up-to-Date

As we already discussed, the scanning component of anti-virus software operates by examining the contents of a file, and comparing it to the signatures within its database of malware profiles. These profiles may include a string found in the malicious code, a specific set of viral instructions, a routine that gets loaded into memory, or a specific program action. When a new virus appears in the wild, it probably has a novel signature. If researchers have not devised a signature for a new malware specimen, there is a good chance that anti-virus software will not detect it.

NOTES

Whenever a new malware specimen is detected in the wild, anti-virus vendors analyze it and create a signature for it. Signature updates are then distributed to the vendor's clients, usually via a download from its Web or FTP site. Until several years ago, it was recommended that companies obtain and distribute malware signature updates once a week. Nowadays, considering the speed with which network worms are able to propagate across the Net, it is a good idea to check for updates daily.

NOTES

Desktop Care and Feeding

- Configuration
  - Determined by your AV policy
- Updating
  - AV software needs to be told about new viruses

SANS Security Essentials – Secure Communications

The most practical way of making sure that your product's signatures remain up-to-date is to use the scheduled update feature usually provided by anti-virus products. Individual systems that have anti-virus software installed can be configured to download updates directly from the vendor. Enterprise versions of anti-virus products are usually set up so that a scheduled update is obtained by the central management server, which in turn distributes the latest signatures to other servers and workstations. If an automated process does not fit your needs, there is usually a manual way to poll the vendor's site for the latest virus signatures.

Additional Protection Measures

Anti-virus software cannot protect against all threats associated with malware attacks. Therefore, Defense in-Depth is essential to help account for the numerous propagation and infection methods that we discussed in the Threat of Malware section of this chapter. Some of the critical layers that you should add to anti-virus software, to assist its malware defense, are patch management and configuration lock-down.

Patch Management

It is common for software vendors to release an update to an application in the form of a patch, to correct a flaw in the program's logic or implementation. We mention patch management in the chapter devoted to malicious code because malware specimens often take advantage of security vulnerabilities for which patches have already been available. For instance, you may recall that the sadmind/IIS worm exploited a vulnerability in Solaris that was announced two years earlier, and took advantage of a Microsoft IIS vulnerability that was known to exist for seven months. Similarly, holes in IIS and Internet Explorer software exploited by Nimda have been well understood, and could have been closed by applying patches from Microsoft.

Keeping track of vulnerability announcements and making sure that the necessary patches are installed in a timely manner is one of the most effective ways of withstanding malware attacks. Most software vendors maintain mailing lists that they use to distribute vulnerability announcements. Also, consider signing up for the SANS Security Alert Consensus mailing list, which summarizes security announcements each week. (See `http://www.sans.org/newlook/digests`)

NOTES

Configuration Lock-Down

Locking down the configuration of a system is a concept that applies to several areas of computer security, as you have seen throughout this book. In the context of malware defense, it involves disabling access to unnecessary system and application components that may be compromised by malicious code. For example, most of the sites infected by Code Red, which exploited a vulnerability in the IIS indexing service, did not actually use the indexing service. They could have prevented the infection if they followed a policy of disabling software modules that are not in use, even if they did not have a chance to install the applicable patch from Microsoft.

Personal firewalls provide another mechanism for blocking access to potentially vulnerable services. (A personal firewall is usually implemented in software, and is designed to protect the individual system on which it runs.) Personal firewalls are particularly effective in situations where a telecommuting user is connecting to the Internet without the protection of a company-controlled firewall device. Using a personal firewall to block inbound access to the system's file sharing ports, for example, can help protect against worms that spread by locating open file shares. The firewall can block access to file sharing ports even if the shares are configured with overly permissive access control rules.

To help block macro-based malware, make sure that your applications are configured to disable macros embedded in a document. Only digitally signed macros from trustworthy sources should have the ability to execute within your word processor or spreadsheet. To check this setting in Microsoft Word, select the Security option from the Tools/Macro menu.

If your e-mail client supports the execution of code included in an attachment, please consider disabling this functionality. For example, the Outlook 98/2000 SR-1 E-mail Security Update, available from Microsoft, blocks access to attachments that may include executable code. The list of such attachments includes EXE, LNK, CMD, COM, PIF, and SCR files; for a full listing see `http://office.microsoft.com/assistance/2000/Out2ksecFAQ.aspx`. This security update also allows the user to prevent an attached executable from accessing the Outlook Address Book. This feature can significantly inhibit the spread of mass mailing worms such as Melissa and Klez. (Outlook 2002 has similar security features already built-in.)

Note

If possible, develop a standard configuration image for workstations in your organization, complete with anti-virus and personal firewall software. Use centralized management techniques such as Group Policy to distribute security settings to lock down the configuration of your Windows machines.

So far we've talked about malware threats, examined how malicious code operates, and discussed ways of defending against worms, viruses, and Trojans. You will mitigate the most significant risks associated

NOTES

with malware if you install anti-virus software at entrances to your networks and systems, maintain up-to-date malware signatures, and employ additional layers of protection such as path management and configuration lockdown. No security infrastructure can be fault-proof, and you may encounter a situation when a malware specimen slips past your defenses. That is why we devote the next section of the chapter to the best ways of responding to malware infections.

Responding to Malware Infections

There is always a chance that a defense mechanism will fail, and despite multiple layers of security, malicious code will find its way into your network. You should be ready to handle such an event in a timely manner that minimizes the impact of the incident and allows you to resume normal operations as quickly as possible. Dealing with a malware infection should also allow you to fine-tune your defenses to block similar attacks in the future. In this section we cover three facets of responding to infections:

- Indications of an infection
- Infection action plan
- Researching malicious code

Without further ado, let's take a look at some of the indications that a system may contain malicious code.

NOTES

Indications of an Infection

- Computer runs slower
- Disk drive "makes noise"
- Running out of free space
- File sizes change
- Unexplainable files
- Characters dropping from screen

SANS Security Essentials – Secure Communications

Indications of an Infection

You should not rely solely on anti-virus software to alert you when an infection occurs. The software may be misconfigured, it may contain outdated virus signatures, or it may be unable to unravel the latest malware stealthing technique. How do you even stand a chance of detecting infections? Keep an eye open for anomalies. Here are some of the symptoms that you might observe:

- Computer runs slower
- Disk drive activity light is constantly flashing
- The system keeps running out of disk space
- Unexplained files appear on the file system
- Sizes of files unexpectedly change
- Strange visual effects appear on the screen

These are just examples of possible indications, but the idea is that the system starts behaving in an unusual manner. Of course, any of these conditions can have benign explanations, and do not constitute an infection. For instance, persistent disk activity may be attributed to the excessive use of swap space on systems with insufficient amounts of RAM. In any case, such symptoms should alert the administrator that the computer might warrant additional attention.

Intrusion detection systems (IDS) can be very effective at detecting suspicious behavior that may be associated with a malware infection. As we discussed in Chapters 16 and 17, IDS sensors can be dispersed throughout your environment, and can monitor network and system-level activities. System and firewall logs, network usage statistics, and, of course, anti-virus software alerts are all valuable tools for detecting the presence of malicious code within your organization.

If you are responsible for maintaining multiple systems, teach your users about possible signs of a malware infection. Encourage them to notice unusual activity, and thank them for reporting an anomaly even if it turns out to be a false alarm. Usually your users will be pleased to help. Their involvement will allow you to detect malware faster, so that you can begin recovering from the attack sooner.

Ensure that your malware detection mechanisms will be sufficient for discovering the presence of malicious code, and for detecting which systems are infected. You will not be able to get rid of the infection if you cannot locate machines that are causing the problem. In the following section we examine steps for responding to a malware infection.

NOTES

What to do if You're Infected

- Contain the problem
- Fix it
- Share your experiences with others

SANS Security Essentials – Secure Communications

Infection Action Plan

What should you do if you encounter symptoms outlined in the previous section, and believe that they may constitute a malware infection? First, *do not panic*. Your action plan should consist of the following steps, and you should be prepared to execute them in a calm, methodical manner:

1. Contain the problem by isolating the affected computer. This is often as simple as unplugging its network cable. This will allow you to leave the system powered up, and will help prevent malicious code from spreading to other machines over the network.
2. Eradicate malware. Research the cause of the problem based on the symptoms that you observe, as we discuss in section Researching Malicious Code. If you locate eradication instructions from a credible source that are appropriate for your situation, follow them. Install anti-virus software with the latest signatures; it will usually recognize and be able to eradicate common worms, viruses, and Trojans. In case of a Trojan infection, check whether any program files have been replaced or added to the system. If dealing with a rootkit-style attack, you may need to rebuild the whole system to be sure that no tainted files remain on the machine.
3. Recover from the infection. Verify that your actions in the previous step removed the cause of the problem. Restore data and program files that may have been deleted or corrupted. Having a functional tape backup system is likely to come in very handy in this step.
4. Review the incident to determine its root cause, and to see whether you could have responded to it more effectively. Learn from any mistakes that you might have made in setting up your defenses, or in reacting to the infection. Share what you have learned with others, so that they too can benefit from your experience.

Note

There is more to incident response than the steps we were able to provide here. For additional information regarding handling malware and other types of attacks, take a look at the *Computer Incident Handling Step-by-Step* guide by Stephen Northcutt.

The eradication and recovery steps of this action plan are not always easy. You may find yourself in the situation where anti-virus software does not detect anything unusual on the system. In another scenario, it may detect a particular malware specimen, but may not tell you how it found its way to your system, and what damage it inflicted. In the following section we discuss considerations for researching malicious code.

Researching Malicious Code

The Internet offers a wealth of information about commonly seen worms, viruses, and Trojans that you may encounter when defending your systems. You can, and should, use this information when responding to malware infections, to determine the extent of the damage that your system may have suffered, and to research the best way of recovering from the attack. Knowledgebases maintained by anti-virus vendors, combined with Web search engines, provide some of the best ways of learning about popular malware specimens.

Anti-Virus Knowledgebases

While sipping your coffee one morning, you get a phone call from your colleague, who is concerned about a possibly malicious attachment she received in an e-mail message. During the conversation you discover that the e-mail contained no text in its body, and had the subject line "Some advice on your shortcoming". You can use this information to make a quick assessment regarding this threat, to help you determine how to react. We suggest spending a minute or so with your favorite Web search engine to see what you can learn about this potential attack. In fact, searching Google for the subject line of the message in question would inform you that this subject text is often used in e-mail generated by the Klez worm.

NOTES

NOTES

Virus and Hoax Information

http://www.cert.org
http://www.symantec.com
http://www.antivirus.com
http://nai.com
http://www.icsa.net

SANS Security Essentials – Secure Communications

As anti-virus vendors analyze and catalogue new malware specimens, they often incorporate their findings into publicly accessible knowledgebases. Vendors may supply different details in their write-ups, so it is usually advantageous to look at several sites when investigating a particular specimen. Here's a list of some of the sites you may find useful when researching malware:

- F-Secure Computer Virus Info Center—
  `http://www.f-secure.com/v-descs/`
- McAfee Virus Information Library—
  `http://vil.mcafee.com/`
- Sophos Virus Information—
  `http://www.sophos.com/virusinfo/`
- Symantec AntiVirus Research Center—
  `http://www.symantec.com/avcenter/`
- Trend Micro Virus Encyclopedia—
  `http://www.trendmicro.com/vinfo/virusencyclo/`
- Virus Bulletin VGrep Database—
  `http://www.virusbtn.com/resources/vgrep/`

Note

Security mailing lists can be a useful source of information relating to malware, particularly when researching a specimen not listed in anti-virus vendors' knowledgebases. Some of the relevant discussion forums are the SecurityFocus "incidents" list at `http://online.securityfocus.com/archive/75` and the SANS "intrusions" list at `http://www.incidents.org/intrusions`.

Please keep in mind that some threats reported by your friends and colleagues may turn out to be false alarms. Also, sometimes a well-intentioned e-mail message warning you about a new virus that is spreading across the Internet may actually be a hoax.

Hoaxes

One of the classic e-mail rumors, which has been circulating around the Net since 1994, is the Good Times hoax. It consists of a message that warns of a highly destructive virus:

```
Here is some important information. Beware
of a file called Goodtimes.

Happy Chanukah everyone, and be careful
out there. There is a virus on America
Online being sent by E-Mail. If you get
```

NOTES

```
anything called "Good Times", DON'T read
it or download it. It is a virus that will
erase your hard drive. Forward this to all
your friends. It may help them a lot.[20]
```

Several versions of this message have surfaced from time to time, but the basic premise remains the same. In actuality, there is no virus named Good Times. Its only manifestation is the e-mail message aimed at confusing gullible users. People have been forwarding the warning along, propagating the rumor that may have started as a simple prank. In a way, this provided the Good Times hoax with viral properties, because it tricked the user into spreading it around.

An unusual hoax that warned people about the `Sulfnbk.exe` virus appeared in April 2001. The alert explained that if the recipient locates a file named `sulfnbk.exe` on his system, he should delete this file because it is a virus. In reality, `sulfnbk.exe` is a legitimate Windows program that is part of the OS. Having located the strangely named file on their computer, users frequently deleted it in an attempt to eradicate malicious code.

The Honor System Virus

A joke that parodies e-mail hoaxes speaks of the Honor System virus, which relies on the user's good will to spread:

```
Due to budgetary constraints we have
had to let our programming staff go.
We are counting on you to use the
honor system.

Please erase all of the files from
your hard drive and then send this
message to the first 50 people on your
mailing list.[21]
```

[20] *CIAC Notes. Number 94-04c.* 8 December 1994. URL: `http://ciac.llnl.gov/ciac/notes/Notes04c.shtml` (19 August 2002).

[21] Symantec. *Discount Virus Hoax.* 25 August 2000. URL: `http://securityresponse.symantec.com/avcenter/venc/data/discount.hoax.html` (19 August 2002).

NOTES

Virus and Hoax Information (2)

- Viruses
  - http://www.virusbtn.com
- Hoaxes
  - http://www.vmyths.com
  - http://www.hoaxkill.com
  - http://www.snopes2.com

SANS Security Essentials – Secure Communications

Knowing where to turn for information regarding malicious code and virus hoaxes can save you valuable time when responding to an alert, or when following up on symptoms of a potential infection.

Please take care to research symptoms of a potential infection before concluding that it constitutes a legitimate threat. Anti-virus knowledgebases usually include information about popular hoaxes. There are also numerous sites devoted to cataloging hoaxes and related rumors:

- Vmyths Hoaxes—
  `http://www.vmyths.com/hoax.cfm`
- Urban Legends Reference Pages—
  `http://www.snopes2.com/computer/virus/virus.htm`
- Don't Spread that Hoax!—
  `http://www.nonprofit.net/hoax/`
- CIAC Hoax Pages—
  `http://hoaxbusters.ciac.org/`

You Should Be Familiar With:

- Malicious software
- Virus and hoax information
- Organizational AV policy
- Desktop anti-viral principles, care and feeding

SANS Security Essentials – Secure Communications

Summary

This concludes our discussion of malicious software. We began by introducing you to the most common types of malware: worms, viruses, and Trojans. As you saw, they may be capable of performing arbitrary actions on the infected computer, such as destroying data, leaking sensitive information, and providing backdoor access to the system.

We also had a chance to peek at the inner workings of malicious code, and examined how it can use removable media, e-mail, Web browsing, and network vulnerabilities to propagate. Having found its way onto a system, a malware specimen can establish its presence by modifying OS configuration parameters, and infecting boot sectors, program files, and certain types of documents. As we discussed, malware authors may enhance their creations with self-defense capabilities such as stealthing and polymorphism, aimed at concealing evidence of infection.

Anti-virus software provides fundamental protection against malicious code, especially if deployed at key entry points to the organization's network, such as workstations, file servers, mail servers, and Internet gateways. In order for anti-virus software to stand a chance of detecting recent worms, viruses, or Trojans, be sure to keep malware signatures up to date. You should further reinforce your defenses by installing relevant security patches, and locking down the configuration of your systems and applications.

Despite the strictest precautions, malware may find its way into your environment. Pay attention to anomalies in the operation of your systems, since they may indicate the presence of malicious code even if anti-virus software fails to detect it. When responding to infections, design an action plan that allows you to contain the infection, eradicate malicious code, and recover from the attack. To help with carrying out these steps, we examined a number of resources that you can use for researching viruses, worms, Trojans, and hoaxes. To effectively mitigate risks associated with malicious code you should understand malware threats that pertain to your organization, create defenses to combat them, and know how to respond to malware infections.

NOTES

NOTES

Chapter 24

Operations Security

NOTES

Operations Security

SANS Security Essentials IV: Secure Communications

SANS Security Essentials – Secure Communications

In this chapter we will discuss the principles and procedures behind a proper Operations Security (OPSEC) program. OPSEC refers to a process, a specific set of procedures and policies that will keep an organization running with minimal security issues. OPSEC can include components of all the other security disciplines such as physical security, information security, communications security and ties them all together. The term and concept was really popular in the 70s and 80s, but in the past few years people have been moving away from it. As you read through this chapter you will probably agree that while much of this material is basic common sense, it is good to keep the big picture in mind. There is no such thing as a foolproof solution, so you will probably still have an occasional security incident take place within your facility; however, proper OPSEC controls will minimize the amount of incidents and help to quickly identify security events that occur.

Some of the areas we will cover in this chapter are:

- Legal Requirements
- Administrative Management
- Operation Controls
- Monitoring and Auditing
- Roles and Responsibilities
- Problems and Reporting
- Summary

NOTES

Operations Security in a Nutshell

Four basic questions allow you to apply operations security to an organization, system or process. They are shown below.

What is the information or resources that other people might consider important? This question allows you to identify critical information.

What is the value of this information? Is it important to you? Would it be important to someone else? If someone else had access to this information could this be a threat to your company or country?

What are some tricks, methods an adversary could use to get at this information or resource? Or perhaps just to modify it. What are the capabilities of a potential adversary? Could they possibly access the information (if you are connected to a network that is connected to the internet, this is a distinct possibility). If your information is locked in an access controlled vault and the adversary would have to send in a Mission Impossible team, it is less likely.

How likely is it that someone can get at this information? How much work is involved to actually do the tricks you just thought up. *HINT* fix the ones that are very likely and very easy fast!

The answers to these questions begin to make it harder for these tricks to work. Fix problems, put in countermeasures. Make sure your employees and co-workers are aware of what you are doing to improve their job security. That's right, lousy security can lead to the loss of a company's marketshare, or a country's very existence.

`http://www.nswc.navy.mil/ISSEC/Docs/Ref/GeneralInfo/opsec_basics.html`

NOTES

Legal Requirements

- Copyrights
- Retention of records
- Privacy Issues
- Due Care
- Due Diligence

SANS Security Essentials – Secure Communications

Legal Requirements

Operational Security is seen as the continuous maintenance of the organization and the environment in which the organization operates, therefore there is a legal side that must also be considered. There are various legal requirements from your country and state that give specific guidelines to follow. Since requirements vary widely, we will use examples from within the United States. Management must identify the laws their company or organization falls under so that they are aware of their legal responsibilities, particularly what their obligation is toward their customers, shareholders, employees, and the community overall.

There is a new law in the health and medical insurance area that deals with dictating what level of protection has to be in place. It is the Health Insurance Protection Accountability Act (HIPAA), also known as the Kennedy-Kassebaum Act. The law actually covers much more than just security; however, the security requirements within the act are aggressive and require that patient medical data is kept confidential and secure.

In most industrialized nations, the law requires consumers and businesses to respect licenses and copyrights. In accordance with these laws, management must maintain accountability by utilizing proper controls to ensure that actual software usage corresponds with software license agreements. Although many companies are now building software copyright protections into their licenses, unethical people will continue to attempt to overcome these protections and will often be successful in their attempt. It is our job to prevent this activity within our organization. This will keep us out of legal trouble and allow us to develop a good relationship with our software vendors.

Record retention is simply a process for backing up and saving information in accordance with laws or corporate guidance. We would personally never throw out a will or a birth certificate; likewise, many organizations have requirements to save all documents that are created or pass through a facility. Records retention is something that will vary depending on where you are located; different countries, states, and provinces have different guidelines or laws. In many locations, laws have been changed to reflect the computer age; record retention, in addition to paper, includes all kinds of magnetic media, optical media, and maybe even types of media still in development. In the US federal government, e-mail records are retained for three years; of course, this may be a difficult task because of the amount of e-mail generated daily by our government agencies. The point is to be aware of your local laws so that your organization does not find itself liable for destruction of records it was legally required to maintain for a specific period.

The concept of *due care* ensures that a minimum level of protection is in place in accordance with the best practice in the industry. This generally is thought of as the care a normal, prudent citizen would use in a similar situation and position. *Due diligence* is the requirement that organizations must develop and deploy a protection plan to prevent abuse, fraud, and additionally deploy a means to detect them if they occur. Let's examine the difference between due care and due diligence.

If your company has recently changed business practices and now sells items through the Web, you have joined the e-commerce revolution. You can decide as the Chief Security Officer (CSO) to not deploy security devices, such as firewalls and intrusion detection systems to protect the servers until the e-commerce starts to pay for itself. In this instance you have not practiced due care and in some countries you may be held liable if something happens through the Internet connection that you decided did not need protection, such as personal customer information being stolen.

Now you are the CSO for another company, which is also just beginning to practice e-commerce. Your staff has designed a security architecture and put it into place. After this is done, your security team informs you that there may be a hole in the security perimeter and that they think a hacker has penetrated one of the systems. However, you choose to ignore the fact. This time you are not practicing due diligence and may be liable once again. For years this standard of due diligence would have been hard to prove. Today there are generally agreed standards for Cisco routers, Unix and Windows and tools to test whether systems and networks are configured to meet those standards. These standards are available from the Center for Internet Security (`www.cisecurity.org`).

You must remember that the items we have just covered are guidelines. Special requirements may vary from organization to organization, and the requirements may vary between countries and states. They may even vary depending on your organization's structure. Always ensure that you refer to local codes of law and policies in order to properly protect your resources.

NOTES

NOTES

Privacy and Protection

- Code of law
- Use and maintenance
- Protection of data
- Monitoring

SANS Security Essentials – Secure Communications

Privacy and Protection

Privacy is one of the hottest topics today. Whether it is in a virtual world or in our daily life, our privacy is constantly challenged by new technology deployed to track what we are doing. There are video cameras at airports and in public places, photo radar systems, cameras to watch for traffic conditions, and the list goes on and on.

In recent years, the US has seen the enactment of two privacy laws, the Gramm Leach Bliley act (GLB) and, as mentioned before, the Health Insurance Portability and Accountability Act (HIPAA). This laws states that personal financial data and patient medical data must be protected from disclosure by the organization responsible for storing and using that data. Such laws are not only produced in the US; they are currently being introduced in many other countries as well.

The HIPAA privacy laws state that any personal medical information collected by a doctor, hospital, or insurance provider on a patient must be accurately maintained, it will be used only for the purpose for which the information was collected in the first place, it will not be transferred to another entity without the consent of the patient, and finally the patient has a right to correct it. When the information is to be transferred to another entity with patient approval, it must be ensured that the receiving entity can provide the same level of protection; if they can't then the information cannot be transmitted.

As previously stated, the laws vary among jurisdictions, so ensure that you consult your local authorities to become familiar with what you are authorized to do and what protections you must put in place to protect such sources as your employees' data and your customers' data.

NOTES

Illegal Activities

- Fraud
- Theft
- Collusion

SANS Security Essentials – Secure Communications

Illegal Activities

A large part of operations security is the process of detecting any acts of fraud or thefts that take place within your organization. Fraud is sometimes committed due to excessive rights being given to specific individuals within the organization. Sometimes it is also based on collusion that takes place between individuals, who do not have enough privileges by themselves to commit the act. However, by acting as a group, they can access all of the functions needed to commit fraud.

For example, think of a system administrator who has access to most of the major servers in the company, including the HR servers, and who can create and delete accounts; he does not have access to the HR payroll servers. Throughout a one-year period he befriends the HR payroll database administrator and convinces him that together they can create a fictitious employee and collect his paychecks. This is collusion. By themselves they could not do this, but together they can.

Insiders or internal employees commit most fraud and theft cases. There are quite a few factors that can contribute to fraud taking place; some of the most common are pressure, opportunity, and rationalization. Audit trails and proper control are the most efficient deterrents against fraud. You have to ensure that fraud is not tolerated and is prosecuted when it does happen. In the upcoming paragraphs we will see some effective means of fighting fraud and collusion within an enterprise.

NOTES

Administrative Management

- Job requirements
- Background checking
- Separation of duties
- Job rotation
- Vacation and leave
- Terminations

SANS Security Essentials – Secure Communications

Administrative Management

As you have examined in the introduction of this chapter, maintaining the security of your environment includes more than maintaining software and hardware. Proper security also includes the selection and screening of the personnel who are working within your facilities. If a person has physical access to your servers, then there is nothing to stop her from abusing these privileges. Proper security screening and training of your personnel has to start even before they are allowed into your work environment.

The first step is ensuring that your human resource department is doing a thorough verification of someone's past employment before you hire them. Call previous employers and seek information from their human resource department. It is nice to have references on resumes; however, they are frequently the names of people who will talk highly of the person regardless of their history with their previous employer.

As seen in the previous section, often fraud or theft is the result of opportunities. In order to avoid presenting such opportunities, you must carefully select what privileges or access an individual will be assigned. Take the time required to identify jobs that give too much access to one employee and look for ways to reallocate tasks across multiple positions. This can help cut down on opportunities to commit fraud by an individual, but it does not alleviate the chance of collusion between two or more employees. One of the ways to cut down on fraud is to regularly rotate positions within the IT department. This will cause employees to work with new counterparts and give them new skills (cross training), all the while improving security by eliminating opportunities to commit fraud.

Many employees work hard all year and plan for a well-earned vacation; however, you may have some employees that do not wish to take an annual vacation. Although these employees may be some of your most dedicated staff, it could also indicate some type of hidden activities that would quickly come to light if another employee took over while the regular staffer was on vacation. This employee may be abusing your resources, such as selling information or gathering intelligence for a competitor. It may not be in the best interest of your company to create a 'big brother is watching' environment within your work place, but it is important to be aware of this possibility.

NOTES

The Last Lunch

During my active duty days, we had a problem with a contractor that acted as our system administrator for the firewalls in a large classified data security facility. We complained to the contractor in charge and he took the administrator to lunch; we never saw that administrator again. While the lunch was taking place, all the passwords and userids were being changed. This shows someone that knew the proper procedures to follow to ensure there would not be a breach. Of course the repercussion was that after that day, no one would go to lunch with that supervisor when he asked, because everyone was afraid of being fired!

It is important to have a well defined termination policy in place; sabotage, destruction of equipment, or other mischief is sometimes committed after an employee has been made aware of their forthcoming dismissal. This is even more important if the employee is being dismissed for wrongdoing. If this is the case, it should be coordinated with the human resource department, the system and security administrators, and always the employees' supervisor. Do not allow the employee access to records or network resources after being told of their termination. If they must be allowed access again, have someone knowledgeable in the terminated employee's area escort and monitor them.

NOTES

Employment Agreements

- General clauses
- Work Hours/Overtime
- Holidays/Sick Leave/Other leave
- Non-Competition, Non-Solicitation
- Confidentiality
- Non Disclosure Agreement (NDA)

SANS Security Essentials – Secure Communications

Employment Agreements

Considering the extremely competitive market in which IT specialists are performing, the lifelong commitment to a single company is less and less common. Most IT employees are changing jobs regularly as they seek new challenges and opportunities. For these reasons it is important to have strong binding agreements within employee contracts. You do not want an employee to leave with your customer list, your Research and Development (R&D) information, and other valuable data that could give a competitor an unfair advantage.

Below are some important points related to operational security that may be included in a typical contract. These points are to protect the employer as well as the employee. Good negotiation and clear understanding at the offset are key points for a harmonious and long-term relationship.

GENERAL

- Position Title
- Main Duties and Responsibilities
- Immediate Supervisor

SPECIAL PROVISIONS

- Employee's Declarations and Warranties
- Probation
- Exclusivity
- Care and Diligence
- Loyalty and Confidentiality
- Use and Possession of the Employer's Property
- Intellectual Property
- Medical Examination
- Respect of Company Policies
- Undertaking of Confidentiality
- Undertaking Not to Compete
- Notice of Termination or Resignation
- Reasons for Dismissal
- Return of the Employer's Property

Some of the more important points are the non-disclosure agreement, employee declarations, and at will termination clauses. A non-disclosure agreement simply states that you will not talk about the company's research, new products, or anything

NOTES

Non-Compete Clauses

A friend of mine recently learned how important it is to read your contract thoroughly or to write it well, depending if you are on the hiring or being hired side of the fence. He was hired by a company for a specific job on a contract with DoD; he learned the job quickly and became quite proficient at it. After two years, his company lost the contract with DoD and the new company offered him a position in his old job. However, he could not take the new job because his old employer quickly pointed out he had a non-compete clause in his contract and could not work for a competitor competing for the same contract for one calendar year. Read your contract carefully before signing.

that could potentially damage the company by being released. An employee declaration gives the company a list of your previous intellectual property. This list is generally requested from new employees so the company can claim anything you create on their time that did not appear on the original list as of your new hire date. An At Will Termination clause states the company can let you go at any time without notice and you may decide to terminate your employment as well without notice.

NOTES

Individual Accountability

- Own responsibilities
- Act as a deterrent through audits
- Proper mechanisms must be in place
- Must be within the law

Individual Accountability

A company's auditing capabilities ensure that individuals are responsible for their own actions and that they are complying with regulations, policies and guidelines the company put in place. Having an environment where actions are tracked and logged offers an easy means of holding specific users accountable. It acts as a valid deterrent and if people know they are monitored, they will think twice before attempting an illegal action. Accountability can be applied toward internal users but also against external users that may be attempting to abuse your system and its network resources.

All monitoring or auditing should be done in accordance with local laws to avoid further prosecution or accusation of invasion of privacy on the employee's part. Usually employees can be subject to monitoring for security, performance, or other reasons, as long as they are informed of the mechanisms that are in place before the monitoring begins. It is a great idea to have the policy in the HR hiring forms that all new employees are required to read and sign when they begin employment. From that point on, all you need to do is add it into your security awareness plan. You do have one, right?

NOTES

Need to Know

- Only when necessary
- Only to what is necessary
- Only where it is necessary
- A business requirement
- Usually combined with the 'least privilege' principle

SANS Security Essentials – Secure Communications

"Need to Know"

The "need to know" concept ensures that only people that have a need to access certain information or resources will be authorized to do so. This access can be further restricted to specific hours, days, or a timeframe. Access is granted based on a business requirement and not simply because someone has a desire to see specific information.

Often we also talk about the least privilege principle, which is similar to the need to know. The least privilege principle ensures that only the minimum required access is given at any time. The difference between the two is subtle; least privilege could mean someone gets only user rights and not administrator rights to their workstation, while with need to know, they might have access to all of the development data but none of the HR data.

NOTES

Sensitive Information

- Marking
- Handling
- Storage
- Destruction

SANS Security Essentials – Secure Communications

Sensitive Information

All sensitive information should be clearly marked in accordance with the organization's security policy and security guidelines. Some companies mark all information as proprietary or sensitive, but a far better course is to explicitly mark sensitive information by level. This should be done for all information, whether it is in electronic form or the media that contains the data, such as a floppy disk or hard drive. Marking is used in systems that must enforce a mandatory security policy; information is marked with a classification or other sensitivity label. The two most common categories are management only for human resources information and proprietary for trade secrets. The system must ensure that these classifications or sensitivity labels are maintained while the information is flowing through the systems.

Electronic labels and paper labels should be used the same way. Paper, media, and any other items that contain sensitive information should be marked with the appropriate sensitivity label, and the label should remain clearly visible. This will insure that you do not erase or destroy important information by error and also that you do not transfer classified information to unauthorized persons.

NOTES

Operations Controls

- Resource protection
- Privileged-entity controls
- Hardware controls
- Input/output controls
- Media controls
- Admin controls

missing backup tapes

SANS Security Essentials – Secure Communications

Operation Controls

Operations control means controlling the access to our computer facility, the entire site housing the computer facility, and the movement of data within our networks. We implement operation controls to protect resources that our organization has designated sensitive or business critical. These resources must be protected to keep an organization operating. Auditing is one way to determine if resources have been tampered with.

NOTES

Control Types

- Directive controls
- Preventive controls
- Detective controls
- Corrective controls
- Recovery controls

SANS Security Essentials – Secure Communications

Control Classification

Gene Kim, the CTO of Tripwire did a study of hundreds of organizations in late 2002 and early 2003. He found that many organizations were struggling with patch management, and were struggling with system administrator to server ratios of one admin to five or six servers. Other organizations were humming along with ratios like one administrator to a hundred servers. These organizations also had strong security. The difference between the strong organizations and the ones that were simply struggling to survive were controls. There are different ways of classifying controls. Some organizations like to classify them by their nature, such as administrative controls (policies, HR actions), technical controls (IDS, single sign-on) and physical controls (mantraps, fences). Another way of classifying controls is based on actions, such as directive, preventive, detective, corrective, and recovery.

Directive controls are the equivalent of administrative controls. In this category are items such as policies, standards, guidelines, personnel screening, and security awareness training. Directive controls are important and form the foundation for enterprise security.

Preventive controls are the equivalent of technical controls. These contain all the methods, tools, practices, and the techniques used to ensure that systems remain secure and highly available. It also contains logical access control, encryption, security devices, identification, authentication, firewalls, antivirus, separation of duties, access rights, data classifications, physical access controls, and a whole lot more.

Detective controls are used to validate that the preventive controls and the directive controls are performing adequately. This is where computer abuse, fraud, or crime would be detected with both automated and manual tools. This type of control area contains log review, surveillance, auditing, and integrity checkers, to name a few.

Corrective controls provide information, procedures, and instructions for correcting detected shortcomings. These shortcomings could be attacks that have been detected, errors, or system misuse. In this category are procedures, instruction manuals, audit trails, and many more.

Recovery controls are in place to facilitate restoration of systems and services after an interruption took place. They insure that proper planning and tools are ready so an organization can quickly recover in case of a disaster; these controls permit continuity of operations. In this category we would find backups, backup site, high availability systems, restore, and restart procedures.

The different categories of control can easily be shown in an example. A disgruntled employee is passed over for a promotion and decides to change his pay in the HR database. Once he made this decision, directive controls failed (he knew he wasn't supposed to try and access the HR system). The employee scans the HR database server and finds a userid with no password. Preventive controls have failed. He accesses the HR database remotely and the IDS began to alarm, warning of his indiscretions. The detective controls did not fail! Since this was identified, corrective controls can be used to fix the HR database problem (and perhaps fire the disgruntled employee). The recovery controls may not be needed at all in this case.

Some other controls are *hardware controls*, which are usually linked to systems. They include how systems are protected, how they will be maintained, who will maintain them, and what to do in case of emergency. They also give procedures on who can perform hardware maintenance, when this maintenance can be performed, procedures for emergency repairs, procedures used to control remote maintenance, and more.

Input/output controls describe the controls that are used for the marking, handling, processing, storage and disposal of input/output of information from a system. These are the controls that are used to monitor and deploy updates and patches as well as procedures that are used for change control.

We have previously touched on *media controls*, so let's make one brief point: all the markings we place on our media to protect it has little importance if someone can walk off with the media. Store your media securely, and ensure it is properly labeled.

NOTES

Resource Protection (1)

- Communications
- Processing equipment
- Application libraries
- Application source code
- Vendor software
- OS
- System utilities

SANS Security Essentials – Secure Communications

Resource Protection (2)

- Address tables
- Proprietary packages
- Main storage
- Critical data
- Violation reports
- Sensitive forms

SANS Security Essentials – Secure Communications

Resource Protection

Operation controls are implemented to protect resources, and resources are not just systems and network access. This list is not all-inclusive but does include most of the resources we are trying to protect.

- Communications
- Processing Equipment
- Application Libraries
- Application Source Code
- Vendor Software
- OS
- System Utilities
- Address Tables
- Proprietary Packages
- Main Storage
- Critical Data
- Violation Reports
- Sensitive Forms
- People

Monitoring and Auditing

Monitoring is an all-inclusive term that can mean many things. In this context it means to review, to watch, and to audit the network. The network is monitored to identify access attempts to the data or resources, and although this is really one of the operation controls previously discussed, it is important enough to go into more depth and look at the types of monitoring available today. It is also important to look at what can be done with the data collected by the monitoring devices and how configuration management can help network administrators identify when someone else has placed an unauthorized monitor on their network.

Auditing is closely related to monitoring; some smaller organizations that monitor the network security devices also audit the network and security device data as well. The relation is simple between the two. A team monitors the network for suspicious activity; if activity is detected and a possible compromise of a system is suspected, then an audit team could be asked to review the system in question, physically and electronically. This would include the system logs and critical files for any anomalies.

The security device that detected the activity does not usually show all the details on the console being monitored. This means someone must audit the security data being saved to a database. It is also important to have regular scheduled audits of the saved security device data and the critical systems on a network. The data from the audits and our monitoring devices can be crucial to a criminal investigation if someone successfully breaches our security.

Note

If you are responsible for monitoring your network, then it is important for all security professionals worldwide that you attempt to do your job well. Gather the evidence and prosecute the criminals. Hopefully in the long run, this will mean there are fewer criminals attacking systems worldwide.

NOTES

NOTES

Monitoring

- Keystroke
- Illegal software
- Traffic Analysis
- Trend Analysis

SANS Security Essentials – Secure Communications

Types of Monitors

Keystroke monitoring is a technique that records all keys, and in some cases, all mouse clicks and menu selections while a user is at a computer. It is generally used with legal permission in a criminal investigation to monitor the activity of suspected criminals. In most countries it is only used under the permission of a judge. This is a very effective means of collecting all information from a user. The monitoring tools used to record the keystrokes can be either software or hardware based.

Software tools are well made and usually have a blind mode where they will not show in your list of processes. You will not see them on your application bar or system tray and in most cases, there is no simple way of knowing that they are active on your machine. Sometimes these tools are distributed by a Trojan that entices you to look at a new software piece (a game or utility).

The hardware tools used to record keystrokes are in the form of a keyboard adaptor. In most cases you install this device at the back of the computer and then connect your keyboard to it. The device will record and store all keys pressed at the keyboard and later on you simply pick the device up and have access to all passwords that were entered on the keyboard while the device was in place. This is a technique that was previously used in some criminal cases where cryptography was being used and the secret passphrase was needed by the authorities to break the encrypted information.

NOTES

Monitoring Tools and Techniques

- Real time
- Ad hoc
- Passive

SANS Security Essentials – Secure Communications

Monitoring tools are used to ensure that security devices, resources, and usage are as per the policies that have been put in place. Monitoring is essential to ensure availability, security, and proper care of resources. There are different types and categories of monitoring. Three popular ones in widespread use are, real time, ad hoc, and passive monitoring. It is not accurate to use the words 'real time' while referring to monitoring, because activities cannot be reported until they have actually happened or been identified. Monitoring is not truly real time, but is immediate as possible after the fact. Intrusion detection systems (IDS) are sometimes called real time, this is because they have the ability to react to specific events identified on the network. This can be based on exploit signatures that an IDS is monitoring for or a threshold that is crossed, such as a certain amount and type of traffic across the network.

The ad hoc monitoring technique is performed at regular intervals or whenever a need arises. This category contains tools such as vulnerability checkers, file integrity checkers, network sniffers, and log consolidation tools.

Some monitoring tools are passive on the network; they have no active role and cannot interfere with passing traffic, unlike a firewall that cannot be configured to stop traffic. Some IDS devices can be set up to "reset" traffic connections. This means that if a system connected to the network exhibits a sign of suspicious activity then the connection can be terminated with the IDS device. Many devices are not set up to automatically reset connections due to false positives, activity that looks suspicious yet is actually normal traffic. It is not a good idea to automatically terminate what may be an important link. This is why we have trained analysts to review the alarms and data.

Traffic/Trend Analysis

One of the more interesting things you can do with the data being collected from your security monitors is analysis of the traffic traversing your network. The fundamental basis of traffic analysis is in the detection of a message passed from A to B. Even if it is encrypted, the simple fact the message was sent has meaning. For instance, if the message was from an intrusion detection sensor, an attacker could craft a packet and send it to the sensor. If the sensor had a rule for that packet, it would respond with an alert. This would allow an attacker to determine the security policy of a sensor. Packets have numerous fields and any one of these fields may yield

NOTES

information that allows a skillful analyst to gather clues about the message. As an example, the IP Identification field of an IP packet is usually sequential. So if a number of packets were observed with static IP Identification fields, then the packets are probably crafted. Traffic analysis consists of building statistics of traffic on your network. After a while you will have an established baseline and you will know what is normal for your environment. A quick glance over the stats will allow you to detect anomalies.

Trend analysis is another technique related to traffic analysis. The difference is that you look for more general indicators during a longer time period. This may allow you to see that a specific type of traffic is continually increasing and that more resources need to be assigned to meet the increased demand. A sharp increase of FTP traffic from a specific user might indicate that he is using the FTP protocol to tunnel other types of traffic, such as a streaming audio feed or some messaging software, which might not be authorized in your environment.

NOTES

Auditing

- Compliance checks
- Internal and external
- Frequency of review
- Standard of due care

SANS Security Essentials – Secure Communications

Auditing

Auditing is a function that will verify the security of systems and resources and also whether or not a system has been compromised or misused. This also tests the effectiveness of the operation controls implemented throughout the network and can help to determine where more controls might be needed. This is an important step in the accountability process as well. If you don't audit your systems, then it will be extremely difficult to make your users responsible for their actions. Auditing is a broad topic. In this instance it covers the review of data gathered from security devices (log reviews), and the security assessment of devices connected to the network with an assessment tool. There are many types of assessment tools, all of them gather similar data; they generally gather information on a specified list of vulnerabilities built into the tool against the weaknesses in the operating system or application. This gives a list of what must be fixed to keep someone from compromising the vulnerability. The tools are run either automatically at pre-determined times or manually by the auditing team members.

There are normally two types of audits, internal audits and external audits. Internal employees perform internal audits and external audits are performed by a third party or outside trusted firm. It is important to regularly use both audit types, even though this could be cost prohibitive. It is not a good idea to use your network administrator to audit your network. This would create a situation where a person is both the accused and the judge. It's likely they would find themselves innocent. Audits are normally conducted through the use of a very detailed checklist. This is a nice way of remaining consistent and results can be compared from time to time.

The frequency at which audits take place depends on multiple factors, such as the complexity of your environment, regulations and policies. In some cases, an audit may occur after major changes have been implemented or an incident has taken place. Although audits are usually conducted at regular intervals, it is also a good idea to conduct surprise audits once in a while. This ensures that security is maintained throughout the year and not only when there is an upcoming audit announced.

The whole audit process is a verification to ensure that due care is being carried out in according with best practices of the industry. This is what is sometimes referred to as the Prudent Man rule.

NOTES

Configuration Management

Configuration management is a process to control all changes to the network, which is important to the auditing and monitoring team. If someone changes the configuration of a network without informing the auditing and monitoring teams then many anomalies discovered may be of no significance yet they may tie up the security teams for hours or even days.

Configuration management is done to keep someone from crashing a network while adding or moving equipment on a network they don't completely understand. This configuration management process is also very important to the security of the network as well. Any changes to the network must be fully reviewed to determine the effects on the security perimeter and internal security devices. The aim of configuration management is control, not to prevent needed modifications. Changes are fine, as long as they are planned, and their impact properly evaluated. Of course all changes should be documented; this could be critical if a major disaster struck and the disaster recovery plan had not been updated to reflect the current network design.

Crashing Your Own Network

Being competent is very important. I remember an agency calling us when they were in the middle of an audit they were conducting on themselves. Each time they ran the vulnerability assessment tool (only a small part of an audit) against their network, most of the network crashed. They did not realize that the way most assessment tools test for a denial of service is to actually execute one! If they had hired this job out or been properly trained, this wouldn't have happened.

Audit Trails

- Must be reviewed
- Must be part of a routine
- Ease task with used of tools
- Ensure tool is working properly

SANS Security Essentials – Secure Communications

Audit Trails

It is fine to collect audit information, but it is useless unless you review this information regularly. Audit trails must be reviewed on a schedule set by policy. This is a very important step in protecting your environment. Often logs will give the first indication that something suspicious is going on with your systems and that abuse might be taking place. It is legally important to be able to demonstrate that audit trails are conducted on a regular basis. This may be the only way that your evidence might be admissible in court.

It is also understood that manual review of audit logs can be cumbersome and quickly become a full-time job. It is strongly recommended that you use a log reduction tool to avoid looking at hundreds of megabytes of information. Such a tool could be used in conjunction with an anomaly detection tool that would notice unusual trends in traffic patterns. A good example is CodeRed. It is abnormal for your Web server to start browsing the Web on port 80 outbound. This type of traffic would be flagged by an anomaly detector tool or by a firewall that is properly configured to only allow the authorized traffic outbound.

Just a word of warning: ensure that the tools that you use are working properly and they do not give you a false sense of security. This is why it is important to manually process part of the logs to ensure they are working.

NOTES

NOTES

Audit Log Backup

- No log, no audit
- Central logging
- Why protect it?
- Covering their tracks
- What time is it?

SANS Security Essentials – Secure Communications

Audit Log Backup

Maintaining a centralized backup copy of your logs is critically important to your monitoring. You must have a means to ensure that the logs were not modified, deleted, altered or changed in order to consider them a reliable source of information. Many attackers know that the last thing to do before exiting a system is to erase all traces of malicious activity by removing logs, shell history, and a few other files that may leave evidence of their visit. This is why you should implement a centralized logging host where a copy of all logs will be sent. This centralized server has to be very secure, as it will contain important information that you will need if something ever goes wrong. By default, syslog does not provide any integrity features that can confirm the authenticity of the logs, but other third party utilities such as Syslog-NG have such features. It is also important to regularly back up your centralized syslog server in order to protect all of the logs that it has stored. In highly critical environments, a copy of logs can be sent to multiple servers at once. This will greatly increase the chances of having a reliable copy of the logs somewhere.

Just as a side note, you must ensure that all of your systems are using a reliable and accurate time source. This will ease log correlation. If the time is erroneous, it will be very difficult to reconstruct the events that took place.

Note

Imagine finding out your systems were hacked and you know the person in your company that did it. Wouldn't it be nice to be able to prosecute them? You won't be able to do it without the logs!

NOTES

Reporting Concepts

- Content
- Format
- Structure
- Hierarchy
- Escalation
- Frequency

SANS Security Essentials – Secure Communications

Reporting Concepts

Audits are of no value unless the information discovered is put together in a structured and organized fashion. The report must be valuable to the high level executive and the system administrator responsible for implementing the fixes and all levels of personnel in between. A high level executive will not want the details, however, a well thought out summary of the security status of the network is vital to a CIO. Most organizations have fairly similar auditing reports. Each report should state at a minimum the purpose of the audit, the scope, and what results were found. Audit reports also typically include the auditor's name, the date and time, what systems were evaluated, the location of the audit, and other pertinent information that may help the auditors.

The reports should be structured in such a way that they are easy to read and understand. Reports are usually distributed to the people that are directly responsible for taking corrective measures. These people should always ensure that the report is given proper consideration. Usually only a summary of the report will be given to upper management, who might not be interested in the technical jargon of the detailed report.

Audit reports are usually produced right after an audit has been completed; however, in case of large audits there may be periodic reports produced to demonstrate the progression of the audit. In case a serious weakness is discovered that may endanger security perimeters, a special report might be prepared immediately to address this shortcoming as quickly as possible.

NOTES

Reporting Mechanisms

- Printed
- On Intranet
- Through newsletter
- Through normal chain of command
- Through company periodical

SANS Security Essentials – Secure Communications

If you are the responsible authority for producing the audit report, remember to ensure its usability. Many times a thousand-page report is given to an overworked system administrator to fix vulnerabilities, and the report doesn't even list which hosts the problems were found on. Imagine trying to find all the vulnerabilities in that mess for each workstation. You need to ensure the report is searchable and available in multiple formats with a good executive summary to explain to senior management what the report means. One nice format is HTML. It allows you to insert some nice graphics for the executives to quickly grasp ("and this graphic shows why we need more people in our department!").

Audit reports can be distributed and disseminated in multiple ways. The best way to distribute them will depend on your company's policies. It is always good to give feedback to the end users as well as upper management. Reports will have to be customized to ensure that they do not reveal sensitive information to unauthorized individuals.

Auditing information is sensitive data and should be given proper care. It is a roadmap of all the vulnerabilities within your network. Any method of disseminating the information within the corporation could lead to a potential compromise of the report and so should be thought out carefully before implementing.

The first means of reporting audit results is the plain, traditional paper method. This is fine for the report if it is a small audit or only the management report. Some companies and organizations use a Web server for the reports. However, if the server were compromised, you would have provided a road map on how to hack your network. One of the best ways is to put the report in HTML format on a CD-Rom, then give the CD-Rom the same protections as any sensitive company information. This method allows CD-Roms to be locked in safes at night and signed out during the day for use by authorized personnel.

NOTES

Reconstruction of Events

- Console messages
- Logs
- Correlation from multiple sources
- Extract data from system
- Not an easy task
- Seek help, again Seek help

SANS Security Essentials – Secure Communications

Reconstruction of Events

Reconstruction of events is sometimes necessary to determine how and why an incident happened. It may allow you to see if this was the result of some abuse or simply an application or subsystem that has failed to perform as expected.

The first thing to look for is error messages on the console that have been generated by the system or its applications. This of course takes for granted that the application or system is built to provide such error or warning messages.

The next location to look for information for the reconstruction of events is from your system logs. If for any reason you believe that your logs may not be reliable, then use the copy on your central logging server. Logs from systems and firewalls can sometimes be gigabytes in size. You will need some log parsing tools to help you in your quest. Once you start putting the puzzle together, you will probably need to correlate information from multiple sources such as firewalls, routers, IDS, and other monitoring tools.

If logs have no indication of what happened, you could dig through some of the system files or temporary space areas to see if there is any information that could help you out.

The reconstruction effort is a puzzle. You will need dedication and patience to succeed, but it can be done. Assistance from a forensic expert might be needed. You will be amazed to see how much information these guys can dig out of a system.

NOTES

Protection Against Alteration

- Use of Integrity Controls
- MAC
- Digital signature

SANS Security Essentials – Secure Communications

Protection Against Alteration

Protection against alterations to your operating systems, applications, and other information is usually achieved by the use of integrity controls. These alterations could be accidental or malicious. The controls that are deployed will give you a high level of assurance that the information has not been modified.

Two cryptographic techniques are usually used to ensure the integrity of information. The first technique is the Message Authentication Code, usually referred to as MAC; the second one is through the use of Digital Signatures that prove the origin of the data, as well as its authenticity. Both techniques use a hashing algorithm that produces a digest of the information. If any modifications are made to the data, the digest will no longer match and changes will be detected. Some of the most popular hashing algorithms are MD5 and SHA1.

Today, the market has a whole series of tools that can help you detect unauthorized alteration. Products such as Tripwire and Veracity are commonly used for detecting changes to files. These products have centralized consoles where alterations are reported. They are fantastic for catching an intruder if malicious activity is not blocked or detected by your network perimeter defenses. Because they are host-based, they are also great to catch the potential insider that may have physical access to the system and is not performing malicious activity across the network itself.

NOTES

Protection Against Unavailability

- Single point of failure
- Redundancy
- Fail-over
- Load-sharing
- Alternate site

SANS Security Essentials – Secure Communications

Protection Against Unavailability

Availability is one of the three tenets on which security is based. It is part of the CIA triangle (confidentiality, integrity, availability) and the opposite of what we continually guard against, DAD (destruction, alteration, and disclosure).

In order to properly protect yourself against unavailability, you must go through the exercise of identifying the single points of failure in your environment. These single points of failure could be hardware, software, or human resources. If you have someone who keeps all information in his head to protect his job (at least he thinks!), then you may be in a lot of trouble if he gets hit by a car and is unable to come to work, or worse, is not able to continue his employment with your company. These are the weakest links that you have to identify in your environment.

How much redundancy is needed will depend on the criticality of the service or resource and also how long is an acceptable downtime for your company. What is the impact of not having Internet access or e-mail, for example? If you have an e-commerce server the impact may be very high.

Once the critical elements have been clearly identified, you should ensure that you reduce the risks by adding redundancy into your environment. If you conduct online commerce and it is your main revenue source, then your connectivity to the Net is crucial and you need redundant links and servers for the e-commerce service.

Fail-over mechanisms refer to when the main component fails and an alternate component takes over immediately. These mechanisms are usually automated and do not require human intervention. There is a heartbeat monitoring the machines so when the primary becomes unavailable, the secondary automatically takes over. Of course, the downside of such a mechanism is that you have a second resource that is not being used until a disaster happen. Another method that makes better use of resources is load sharing.

Load sharing is the use of multiple servers to ensure continuous service. In this case you have more than one server that is providing services and they are all used at the same time. Some firewalls such as CheckPoint and StoneGate allow for very large clustering that can respond to the most demanding environment. Clustering is an easy way to manage a large number of servers by treating them as one with some 3rd party software.

NOTES

Roles and Responsibilities (IS/IT)

- Policy
- Risk Management
- Life Cycle Planning
- Audit and monitoring
- Recovery strategies
- Incident handling
- Awareness

SANS Security Essentials – Secure Communications

IS/IT Functions

- Audit
- Physical Security
- Disaster Recovery
- Monitoring
- Incident Response
- Training and awareness

SANS Security Essentials – Secure Communications

Roles and Responsibilities

The roles and responsibilities for everyone regarding data security in an organization are important; these need to be defined and placed in the security policy to make everyone aware of their security duty. The day to day functions in an IT department is beyond the scope of this chapter; however, there are some basic functions that will be performed by most IS/IT departments regardless of size. Among these are:

- Audit functions. This function will ensure that the controls put in place are offering the proper protection in accordance with policies.
- Physical security. This is sometimes delegated to the building owner or a third party security service. In such a case, you should ensure that they provide proper levels of protection and that access control is properly enforced.
- Disaster recovery. This has taken a life of its own since September 11th, 2001. Disaster recovery used to be overlooked in most environments, but it is now one of the greatest worries for IT/IS managers.
- Monitoring. As previously discussed in this chapter, could be for performance, abuse, or other reasons. Ensure that it is done within the limit of the law and that it is effective.
- Incident response. This is another key point in the numerous IS/IT functions. Without a response capability, deploying controls is not of much value. If you monitor your network, then review the data and take appropriate actions.

NOTES

Last but not least, you have to train your user population at all levels—train them on recognizing threats to their systems and information. By increasing their awareness they will be more receptive to your protection plan and understand why countermeasures are being deployed. Also, there will likely be fewer incidents caused by employees.

NOTES

Roles and Responsibilities (Manager)

- Usually the immediate supervisor of an employee
- Responsible for UserID
- Responsible for contractors
- Looks after termination procedures
- Looks after passwords

SANS Security Essentials – Secure Communications

Roles and Responsibilities (Manager)

A manager is usually a person that has an employee working directly for him. Managers have the ultimate responsibility for information assets owned by the employees working for him. The manager also has to look after the assets of temporary employees such as contractors, consultants, and interns. Here are a few guidelines for managers:

- Ensure that employees are aware of security policies, directives, guidelines, procedures, and standards.
- Receive the initial password for employees under his care; this ensures that an employee will not be granted access without the approval of his manager.
- Notify human resources and the IT security staff immediately when an employee terminates employment or is terminated. This ensures that accounts and access rights will be revoked or suspended in a timely manner.
- Inform the security administrators of any changes in a person's role, to help ensure that only required access in accordance with the role that the employee is playing are granted.

Roles and Responsibilities (Owner)

- Last regards towards security
- Decides what is appropriate
- Ultimately responsible
- Determine what backup to use
- Determine who can access

Roles and Responsibilities (Owner)

Companies often have complicated structures where key information resources have assigned owners. These owners are responsible to define the appropriate protection for the information under their care. They are the ones that will make the ultimate decisions, and they will be accountable as well if a compromise, loss, or abuse happens. Some of their responsibilities include:

- Assigning a classification to the information under their care.
- Ensuring that proper security controls are in place to protect the information for which they are accountable.
- Regularly reviewing who has access to the information under their care.
- Determining what backups are needed.
- Being the main point of contact to approve access to data or information under their care.
- Naming someone else to replace them in case of absence.

NOTES

NOTES

Roles and Responsibilities (User)

- Security involves all personnel
- End user plays a critical role
- They must be aware of their role
- Awareness is key
- Ensure proper training is given

SANS Security Essentials – Secure Communications

Roles and Responsibilities (User)

Security is a matter that should concern everyone in a company. End users must understand what their role toward security is, and how they can contribute to maintaining proper security for the corporation. Often users will notice some strange problems on their computers, if they have been trained well and are security conscious, they will quickly learn to identify problems that might be related to security.

An end user could be anyone within a company, including contractors, vendors, and partners who use the company information resources as part of their daily tasks. Some of their responsibilities are:

- They must not share user IDs and passwords with others.
- They must ensure that they follow proper procedures to protect information under their care.
- They must use company assets only for company related activities.
- They must be conversant with the policies, procedures, guidelines, and standards that they must follow.
- They have a responsibility to report any security incidents that they are aware of.

Note

If you can get senior management to buy-in to a proper security policy and supporting architecture, and then make the employees aware of the policy, then you have won the biggest battle any security professional faces. Your life will be much easier.

Problems and Reporting

All the attempts to educate users, secure the network perimeter, and monitor the network environment will not ensure an incident free network, bad things will happen sooner or later. Any organization hiring many employees will one day get a bad apple. One day the power will go out and the generators won't kick on or a natural disaster will strike.

NOTES

Employee Sabotage

- Destruction of hardware
- Destruction of facility
- Planting bombs
- Deleting or modifying data
- Holding systems hostage
- To avoid it, Be fair and honest

SANS Security Essentials – Secure Communications

A Little Revenge

This reminds me of when we had a system administrator who was fired; right after that he left Europe to move back to the United States. Two months later he had new employment and we were part of a large investigation into some strange events with data disappearing. Yes, you guessed it; he had set up a back door into the network and waited a while to start taking his revenge out upon his old company safely from a continent away. He wasn't quite as safe as he thought, though, since he did get prosecuted.

Employee Sabotage

Sabotage regularly happens but because companies are afraid of negative publicity, you seldom hear anything about it. There have been well-documented cases of employees that have been fired that took great care in causing the maximum amount of disruption before or after they left by using a logic bomb. There have been employees who simply used a fire axe on the wall to cut and destroy data center equipment. Sabotage is real and it can happen to any company.

Protecting against sabotage is not always easy. You have to exercise great care in the way you handle promotions, terminations, or any other matter in your daily dealing with your employees. If employees feel that they are cheated, harassed, or endangered, they may feel like taking a little revenge, and this is when sabotage happens. Most sabotage costs a lot of money due to the privileged access employees have and the intimate knowledge of your systems and networks.

NOTES

Loss of Infrastructure

- Power failures
- Spike and brownouts
- Loss of communications
- Water outage or leaks
- Lack of transportation
- Fire, flood, civil unrest, strike

SANS Security Essentials – Secure Communications

Loss of Infrastructure

Here are some possible examples of loss of infrastructure:

- Power failures
- Spike and brownouts
- Loss of communications
- Water outage or leaks
- Lack of transportation
- Fire, flood, civil unrest, strike

These losses often create a situation where downtime might be experienced. There is little you can do to prevent most of them since they are not easily predictable or are beyond your control. For example, a strike in public transportation is not directly related to your IT systems, but if your personnel cannot get to work then it might become a problem. The same applies for cities that are only accessible through the use of bridges from one shore to the other; if the bridge is closed then you cannot get to work. All of these examples were covered in more detail in Chapter 6, Physical Security.

NOTES

Violations and Reporting

- Policies
- Compliance
- Audit role
- Procedures for reporting
- Part of Security Awareness Training
- Disciplinary/Administrative Actions

SANS Security Essentials – Secure Communications

Violations and Reporting

Even though proper screening is taking place and proper controls are in place, there will always be people that intentionally or unintentionally attempt to trespass in your network. Your policies and acceptable usage agreement should clearly state what employees can and cannot do, what is considered acceptable activity, and what is not. Ensure that the policy is disseminated to all new employees and that they have all agreed and signed the company acceptable use agreement before they are granted access.

Often violations will be discovered while conducting audits or through your monitoring tools. There are cases where a user might notice a violation. Users should be made aware in their security awareness training of what procedures they must follow if they ever discover a violation. There should be a documented procedure that they can follow or refer to if they are in doubt. All violations should be investigated and a motive established. In some cases it might just be a lack of training or a mistake from a user, but in other cases it might be obvious that it was unauthorized activity.

Unauthorized Web Surfing

I had people call me and e-mail me to let me know they went to an inappropriate Web site and that we should not report them. My rule of thumb was the 10-second rule; if they made a mistake then they should have moved on quickly; if they stayed at that site for 10 minutes it was generally not a mistake. Of course this was based on well-known policy for allowable sites and what was not allowed!

NOTES

Summary

We cannot discuss all the issues you may run across in operations security during your tenure as a security professional. We hope we have given you a glimpse into a good security environment and the information you need to build and maintain a good secure stance. Let's run down one more time what we really need to get out of this chapter in security.

We talked about legal requirements for intellectual property, what is due diligence, due care, and why we must care about it. We also discussed how we can interact with our HR department to make sure we do not hire the wrong people and how to have the correct policies in place in case a bad apple slips through the screening process. We also talked about how to mitigate the threat from a potential bad apple with job rotation, mandatory vacations, least privilege, and need to know for specific information.

If our bad apple is successful in doing something malicious on our network, we identified what may be illegal activity and how we can control it through the use of different types of operational controls, including preventive controls, detective controls, corrective controls, and recovery controls. These controls are what allow us to do our job and consist of many things including policies, IDS, firewalls, and recovery tools.

Another area we talked about was the resources that must be protected. Many times some areas are overlooked, and this can be the downfall for a company. Don't spend millions protecting your proprietary development systems and then not spend anything on protecting your backups. Someone could carry off the whole store in plain sight while you stare at the operational network.

The roles and responsibilities for everyone that has access to a system on the network was an issue worth discussing as well. Remember to ensure those roles are clearly defined so everyone knows their responsibilities. This allows them to be well trained in a security awareness program that will help them identify events on your network making your life much easier.

If almost everyone is on your team, then it will be much easier to stop the insider threat and a single disgruntled employee will have a lot of difficulty sabotaging your network. When something is identified ensure the employees know the proper reporting structure and then you can swiftly mitigate the problem.

- OPSEC Professionals Society (`http://www.OPSEC.org/`)
- Operations Security Domain from the Information Security Handbook (`http://www.cccure.org/Documents/HISM/655-661.html`)
- OPSEC definitions (`http://www.peacefulpackers.com/it_solutions/z_is_07.htm`)
- FFIEC Information Systems Examination Handbook (`http://www.fdic.gov/regulations/information/information/contents.pdf`)

Windows Security

NOTES

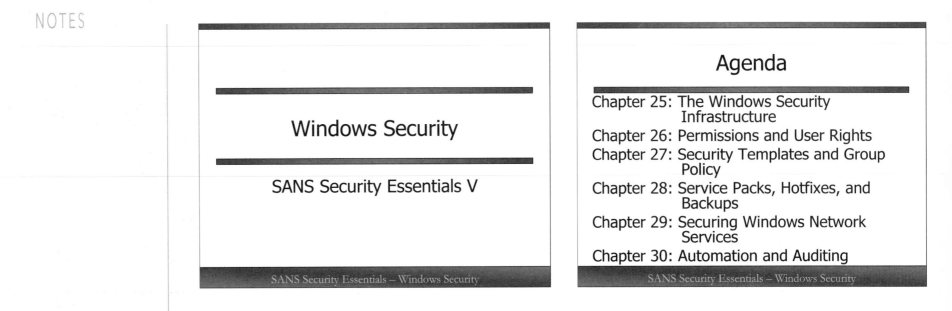

Windows Security

SANS Security Essentials V

Agenda

Chapter 25

The Windows Security Infrastructure

NOTES

The Windows Security Infrastructure

SANS Security Essentials V: Windows Security

SANS Security Essentials – Windows Security

The Windows Security Infrastructure

Remember when Windows was simple? Windows 95 desktops and a Windows NT domain to hold all the user accounts, what could be easier? The Wild World of Windows has changed a lot since then. Now we have Windows 2000, Windows XP, Windows .NET Server, Active Directory, Group Policy, IPSec, PKI, the .NET Framework, etc. This means tackling Unix/Linux head-on and scaling up to provide enterprise-class network services. The trick is to do it securely.

In this chapter we will discuss the infrastructure that supports Windows security. This is the Big Picture overview of the Windows security model, and it provides the background concepts necessary to understand everything else that follows. Because it is the Big Picture, we can't talk about everything, but many of the details will be filled in throughout the chapters that follow.

Specifically, this chapter will answer the following questions:

- Which Windows operating system should I use?
- What is a workgroup?
- What are local users and groups?
- What is a Security ID (SID) number?
- What is a Security Access Token (SAT)?
- What is Active Directory?
- How do I authenticate to the domain?
- What is a forest?
- What is a trust?
- What is Group Policy, and why do people say it is my most important security tool?
- What is this "dot-NET" stuff anyway?

Windows Operating Systems

- Windows 9x/Me
- Windows NT
- Windows 2000
- Windows XP
- Windows .NET

SANS Security Essentials – Windows Security

Windows Family of Operating Systems

Windows 9x and Windows NT were made obsolete by the release of Windows 2000

Many people think of Windows 2000/XP/.NET as just incremental upgrades to Windows NT. Roughly speaking, Windows 2000/.NET domains are ten times more complex than Windows NT 4.0 domains. This makes the learning curve a bit more steep, but, on the brighter side, this complexity comes in part because there are now far better tools for securing the network (like Group Policy) than Windows NT ever had.

If security is a top priority at your organization (and if you have the money), then immediately upgrade to Windows 2000/XP/.NET. To see why this is true, let's look at the different families of operating systems Microsoft provides and see how they relate to each other. This will help us to choose the right Windows operating system for the job. Then, in a latter chapter, we'll talk about how to expose a Windows server to the Internet and *not* get hacked.

NOTES

NOTES

Windows 9x/Me (1 of 2)

- **Not designed for security and cannot be secured, period.**
  - No filesystem security
  - Can't really require initial logon
  - Weak authentication protocol (LM)
  - Extremely vulnerable to DoS attacks
  - Virtually no logging capabilities
  - Prone to lock-ups and crashes
  - Boot into other OS to circumvent *everything*

SANS Security Essentials – Windows Security

Windows 9x/Me

The Windows 9x/Me line of operating systems were never designed for security in the first place and cannot be secured. Period. Install a virus scanner and a personal firewall and there is not much more you can do.

Windows 9x/Me has the following security characteristics:

- Intended for desktop applications like word processors and e-mail clients, hence, they should not be used for high-end workstations or as servers.
- No filesystem security whatsoever, including no built-in file encryption capabilities.
- Almost impossible to enforce user rights restrictions.
- No meaningful security logging.
- Difficult to require successful log on before access to the desktop (there are tricks to get around the System Policy requirement for logon).
- Weak default authentication protocols.
- Extremely vulnerable to Denial of Service (DoS) attacks.
- Simple password-based access control to shared resources in workgroup environments.
- Trivial to boot into another operating system from floppy disk and circumvent all security measures.
- Prone to lock-ups and crashes (a DoS attack from Microsoft against our valuable data).

If your job is to improve network security, the only good reason to have Windows 9x/Me around is because it would be too expensive to upgrade, and management won't financially support the move.

NOTES

Windows 9x/Me (2 of 2)

But if you're stuck with 9x/Me, then:

- Use them as "thin clients" to Terminal Services or Citrix servers
- Keep all mail on Exchange Server, not in local personal storage files (.PST)
- Store all documents on servers
- Install ADCE for NTLMv2 support

SANS Security Essentials – Windows Security

If you're stuck with Windows 9x/Me, a stop-gap measure is to move as much of your users' data onto the servers as possible. For example, use Terminal Services or Citrix MetaFrame; keep all mail on the Exchange Server instead of in local Personal Storage (.PST) files; map a drive letter to the user's home folder, and make that the default (perhaps required) location for all document storage, etc. Also, install the Active Directory Client Extensions (ADCE) upgrade to enable NTLMv2 support (discussed later in this chapter). Having done all this, you can concentrate your attention on the servers. But what operating system should be used for them?

NOTES

Windows NT 4.0

- Windows NT is dead, Dead, DEAD.
- Service Pack 6a is the last one.
- Was at least *intended* to be secure:
  - User-based access control
  - Domain controllers, trusts, and single sign-on
  - NTFS and NTLM
  - Detailed logging
  - Protected memory spaces in OS
  - VMS pedigree

SANS Security Essentials – Windows Security

Great Grandpa: VMS

If you take the letters "VMS" and shift them over one character to the right you get "WNT." Coincidence? David Cutler was the lead developer of the VMS operating system at Digital Equipment Corporation. In 1988, he and 20 other DEC engineers left DEC to go work for Microsoft to build Windows NT. Cutler was NT's chief designer, and the documentation for NT's kernel reads like a VMS white paper. Windows NT was released in April of 1993.

Windows NT 4.0 Workstation and Server

Windows NT 4.0 was designed for security and stems from a different codebase than Windows 9x. Nonetheless, Windows NT was Microsoft's first entry into the secure-OS market and suffers from significant vulnerabilities.

Also, Microsoft has officially declared that Service Pack 6a will be the last Service Pack for Windows NT, ever. Security patches are still being released, but Microsoft has abandoned NT and it is considered a dead product line.

The Workstation version of Windows NT is for desktops, while the Server version is for domain controllers, database servers, e-mail servers, web servers, etc. In general, NT crashes less often than 9x and scales far better. For example, Windows NT supports multiple CPUs, has software-based RAID, can use up to 4GB of RAM, sports a transaction-based filesystem (NTFS), and has a mature thread scheduler and memory management system originally derived from VMS.

Windows NT has the following security characteristics:

- User-based access control to resources
- User-based delegation of rights, e.g., take ownership right
- Filesystem permissions and auditing (NTFS)
- Detailed OS logging capabilities (but no central collection capability like Syslog)
- Stronger authentication protocols than Windows 9x (NTLM), but still weak overall (unless upgraded to NTLMv2)

- User-mode versus privileged-mode process spaces and a kernel designed to keep them separate
- User accounts for every process, perhaps the local System account, and rights/permissions account keying
- Provides a centralized accounts database for single sign-on authentication to all resources in the "domain"
- Provides access to users across domains through "trusts"

Note

A network supports "single sign-on" if all user authentications are invisible to the user once the user has manually logged onto her desktop. The opposite of this is when a user potentially has a different username/password on every machine in the LAN, and, in any case, some username/password is required for every server accessed. Single sign-on also implies an authorization framework common to all the servers; e.g., they can all use the same set of users, groups, rights, and permissions to regulate access.

While NT is more secure than 9x/Me, you should still upgrade to Windows 2000/XP/.NET if finances permit it.

NOTES

NOTES

Windows 2000 (1 of 2)

It's more like Windows NT version 9.0:

- Active Directory
- Group Policy
- Kerberos
- IPSec
- PKI & Smart Cards
- EFS
- Scriptability & CMD Tools

SANS Security Essentials – Windows Security

Windows 2000 Professional and Server

Windows 2000 comes from the same codebase as Windows NT, but it is not an incremental upgrade like the change from NT 3.51 to 4.0. If Windows 2000 were assigned an accurate version number, it wouldn't be NT 5.0; it would be more like NT 9.0 (as though Microsoft had skipped over the versions in between).

A Windows 2000 system out of the box is faster and more secure, than a hardened and optimized Windows NT computer.

Windows 2000 Professional is intended for desktops and replaces Windows NT 4.0 Workstation. Windows 2000 Server replaces Windows NT 4.0 Server. Both support the same security and fault-tolerance features as Windows NT, but with many more features (most will be explained in later chapters) added:

- Active Directory
- Group Policy
- New trust types (transitive, explicit, and shortcut)
- Kerberos authentication
- Extensive Public Key Infrastructure (PKI) support
- Built-in smart card authentication support for logon to the desktop, to dial-up servers, to IIS websites, and to VPN gateways
- Kerberos-authenticated secure dynamic updates to DNS
- IPSec and a built-in IPSec VPN client
- Encrypting File System (EFS)

NOTES

Windows 2000 (2 of 2)

	Standard Server	Advanced Server	Datacenter Server
Max CPUs	4	8	32
Max RAM	4 GB	8 GB	32 GB
Load-Balancing	n/a	32-Node	32-Node
Cluster Nodes	n/a	2-Node	4-Node

SANS Security Essentials – Windows Security

Don't Buy Retail!

You can purchase 100% legal and valid Microsoft licenses through eBay! Often, the price is about one-half to one-fourth what you would pay retail. Just make sure to purchase only from sellers that also are regular companies (not individuals) whose contact information you have verified. Get their guarantee beforehand that the licenses are registerable first. Purchase the licenses one at a time, and, upon receipt, immediately call Microsoft to check and register the licenses in your name. This author once saved a client over $21,000 on the purchase of multiple Advanced Server licenses and CALs, and we got Microsoft's stamp of approval on every one.

Windows 2000 Advanced Server and Datacenter Server

Windows 2000 Advanced Server is intended for enterprise-class servers, which require high availability. It is about four times more expensive than the standard Server (if you buy retail) but has essentially the same security profile. Datacenter Server is intended only for the biggest of the "Big Iron" Windows servers and only can be installed by an OEM vendor. The differences between Server, Advanced Server, and Datacenter Server are mainly for scalability and fault-tolerance.

Windows 2000 Versions:	Standard Server	Advanced Server	Datacenter Server
Max CPUs (SMP)	4	8	32
Max RAM	4 GB	8 GB	32 GB
Network Load-Balancing	N/A	32-Node	32-Node
Fail-Over Clustering	N/A	2-Node	4-Node

If you already have Windows 2000 Server, but you need Advanced Server, go straight to Windows .NET Enterprise Server instead. If you still have Windows NT and you want to upgrade your servers, go straight to Windows .NET Server and skip over Windows 2000.

NOTES

Windows XP

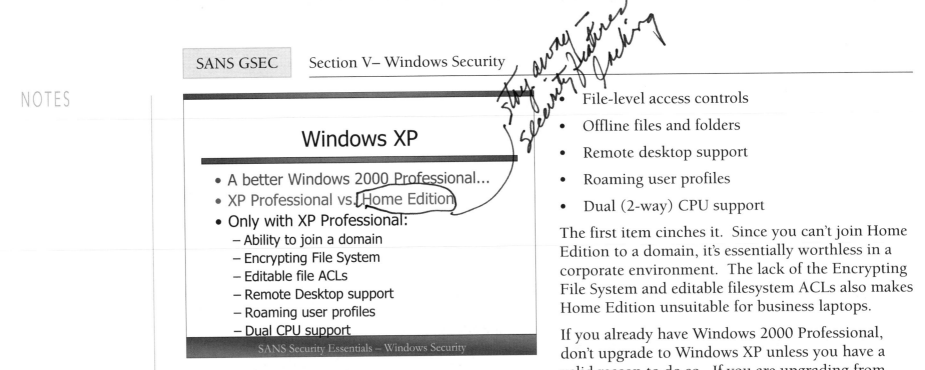

- A better Windows 2000 Professional...
- XP Professional vs. Home Edition
- Only with XP Professional:
  - Ability to join a domain
  - Encrypting File System
  - Editable file ACLs
  - Remote Desktop support
  - Roaming user profiles
  - Dual CPU support

SANS Security Essentials – Windows Security

Windows XP Professional and Home Edition

Windows XP is from the Windows 2000 product line, not the Windows 9x/Me line, despite the graphical interface being "pretty." Every security enhancement in Windows 2000 is in XP, and more.

Windows XP comes in two versions: Professional and Home Edition. It is critical that you don't accidentally order the Home Edition version for use in your organization. This is a common error, so make sure you get the vendor's explicit assurances. Home Edition lacks some very important security benefits only found in the Professional version.

Here are a few of the items you get with Professional but not with the Home Edition:

- The ability to join a Windows domain
- Encrypting File System
- File-level access controls
- Offline files and folders
- Remote desktop support
- Roaming user profiles
- Dual (2-way) CPU support

The first item cinches it. Since you can't join Home Edition to a domain, it's essentially worthless in a corporate environment. The lack of the Encrypting File System and editable filesystem ACLs also makes Home Edition unsuitable for business laptops.

If you already have Windows 2000 Professional, don't upgrade to Windows XP unless you have a valid reason to do so. If you are upgrading from Windows 9x/Me/NT, then go straight to XP, and skip over Windows 2000 Professional.

Windows .NET Server (1 of 3)

- Successor to Windows 2000 Server
  - Not intended for desktops.
  - Mostly an incremental upgrade to Win2000.
  - Scalability and fault-tolerance enhancements.
- Cross-forest trusts.
- You can mix-and-match your Windows 2000 and .NET Servers fairly easily.

SANS Security Essentials – Windows Security

Windows .NET Server domain controllers also support a new type of trust relationship for linking separate Active Directory forests together. These "cross-forest" trusts use Kerberos to cause all domains in the two forests to trust each other transitively even though they are in different forests (more on this later).

NOTES

Windows .NET Server (Standard, Enterprise, Datacenter)

Windows .NET Server is the successor to Windows 2000 Server. You won't find earth-shaking new technologies like Active Directory or Group Policy in it, but there are many important spot-enhancements that make the overall package better than 2000.

Hence, move straight to .NET Server if you are upgrading from Windows NT, but stay with Windows 2000 Server to save money if you already have it, unless, of course, there is some new feature of .NET you just have to have. You can mix-and-match your .NET and 2000 Servers, so it is not the case that you must upgrade every server in one shot or none at all. Piecemeal migration from Windows 2000 to .NET is easy.

NOTES

Windows .NET Server (2 of 3)

	Standard Server	Enterprise Server	Datacenter Server
Max CPUs	4	8	32
Max RAM	4 GB	8 GB	64 GB
Load-Balancing	n/a	32-Node	32-Node
Cluster Nodes	n/a	8-Node	8-Node
64-bit CPU	No	Yes	Yes

SANS Security Essentials – Windows Security

The three versions of Windows .NET Server mainly are for scalability and fault-tolerance, but notice that the numbers have been bumped up considerably. Not only that, but how .NET Server supports clustering and network load-balancing also has been changed significantly.

Windows .NET Enterprise Server represents Microsoft getting serious about trying to take over the very high-end server market, e.g., multi-terabyte-sized databases, 99.999% availability, thousands of simultaneous users, etc.

Windows .NET Versions:	Standard Server	Enterprise Server	Datacenter Server
Max CPUs (SMP)	4	8	32
Max RAM	4 GB	8 GB	64 GB
Network Load-Balancing	N/A	32-Node	32-Node
Fail-Over Clustering	N/A	8-Node	8-Node
64-bit Titanium CPUs	No	Yes	Yes

Windows .NET Server (3 of 3)

- **Windows .NET Web Server**
  - Dedicated-purpose operating system
  - Not available through retail channels.
  - Intended for ISP's and ASP's.
  - Intended for turn-key hardware appliances.
- Only supports two 32-bit CPUs and no more than 2 GB of RAM. *(Why???)*
- Probably better off with Standard Server...

SANS Security Essentials – Windows Security

NOTES

Windows .NET Web Server

Windows .NET Web Server is a fourth member of the .NET Server family. It has no analog in Windows 2000 and is only available through "channel partners;" i.e., it is not available for retail sale. It is a dedicated-purpose server for IIS applications.

Strangely, this Server only supports two 32-bit CPUs maximum and no more than 2GB of RAM. It also can act as a POP3 server.

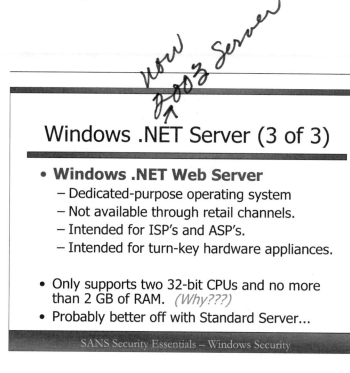

It is unlikely that you will be considering Windows .NET Web Server unless you are an Internet Service Provider (ISP) that provides web hosting, an Application Service Provider (ASP) specializing in .NET Framework distributed XML-based services, or a "network appliance" vendor with pre-configured rack-mountable boxes with Windows .NET Server embedded. Also, the weird 2GB limitation on RAM means you're better off getting Standard Server to accommodate future growth or to re-purpose the box, if the need arises.

NOTES

Workgroups (1 of 3)

- **No domain controllers!**
- Stand-alone computers only.
- Local accounts and local accounts databases only.
- Permissions can be assigned to local users and groups only.
- Local groups cannot have users from other machines.
- User names may be identical across machines, but their SIDs are different (more on this in just a moment).
- Users are typically local administrators of their own machines.
- A "workgroup administrator" simply has a separate administrative account on every machine.
- Workgroups tend to be small, e.g., less than 100 boxes.
- You can have stand-alones or entire workgroups in the midst of domain members, e.g., IIS servers on a service subnet.

SANS Security Essentials – Windows Security

Workgroups and Stand-Alone Computers

Two or more Windows computers that share information in the absence of any domain controllers is called a "workgroup." Even if all the computers are running Windows .NET Enterprise Server, and even if there are thousands of user accounts on each of them, they still only form a workgroup, not a domain.

Because the computer is not a member of a domain, it is called a "stand-alone" computer. This doesn't mean the computer refuses to be a file/print server or to share resources with others, only that it is not a member of a domain.

Characteristics of a Workgroup

Workgroups have the following characteristics:

- There are no domain controllers.
- Each computer has a local accounts database. Users and groups in that database are called "local users" and "local groups" precisely because they exist only in that one database. This database is not shared with or replicated to any other computers.
- When rights or permissions are being assigned to a resource on a workgroup computer, they only can be assigned to local users and local groups defined on that computer. You can't assign permissions or rights to user accounts on other machines.
- A local user account on one machine cannot be made a member of a group on another computer. Conversely, a local group can only contain local users defined on the same computer as the group itself.
- Two computers may each have a local user account with the same name, but these are two different accounts. The accounts will have different Security ID (SID) numbers.
- Typically, the owner or user of a computer in a workgroup is a member of the local Administrators group on that machine, giving him or her full authority over it. But this authority does not extend to any other machine on the network.
- If a person is the administrator of a workgroup, that just means she has a user account on every computer in the workgroup and that that account is in the local Administrators group on each machine. Whether or not all these

NOTES

accounts are named the same or have identical passwords is another issue entirely.

- Workgroups tend to be small, i.e., between one and one-hundred computers. When the number of computers is less than ten, we typically just say "they are all stand-alones" instead of saying "they are a workgroup." The term "workgroup" focuses on the people, while "stand-alones" focuses on the computers, but in both cases neither the computers nor the users are members of a domain.
- You can have stand-alone computers in the midst of other machines that are members of a domain. They are not anathema to each other, and each has its benefits.

NOTES

Workgroups (2 of 3)

- **Benefits of workgroups:**
  - Conceptual simplicity.
  - Lower initial cost.
  - Each computer protects itself.
  - Each user is typically an administrator of his or her own machine, allowing personal creative expression and joy…

SANS Security Essentials – Windows Security

Benefits of Workgroups

Workgroups are not always bad. There often are important security benefits to having stand-alone workstations or servers.

For example, a farm of Microsoft Internet Information Server (IIS) web servers might be better protected if they are all stand-alone servers. Or a public-access kiosk computer might be better off as a stand-alone. For a small group of temporaries working on a project, a little peer-to-peer network may satisfy their needs without exposing the rest of the network to their misdeeds.

Workgroups enjoy the following benefits:

- Conceptual simplicity.
- Lower initial cost.
- Each computer protects itself from the other computers on the LAN. Putting computers into a workgroup is not putting all your eggs into one basket (even though it is easier to manage a basket than an armful of eggs).
- Each infected or compromised computer, if it is a stand-alone, will be somewhat less able to harm other computers on the network precisely because it is a stand-alone. This is because a stolen account on that computer cannot be used to access any other computers.
- Users typically are members of the local Administrators or Power Users groups on their machines. Users enjoy being able to fix their own problems and load programs.

Workgroups (3 of 3)

- **Drawbacks of workgroups:**
  - Users are insane.
  - Workgroup = Anarchy
  - Very difficult to manage a large number of stand-alones (no scalability).
  - No single sign-on without great effort.
  - No consistent permissions or rights.

SANS Security Essentials – Windows Security

Drawbacks of Workgroups

So why isn't every Windows network a workgroup? Why have "domains" at all? Unfortunately, there are some serious drawbacks to having workgroups, especially large ones.

- Users typically are members of the local Administrators or Power Users groups on their machines. Users enjoy doing anything on their computers and potentially destroying their computers. They will then blame you for their problems and demand that you fix them.
- Each computer in a workgroup enforces its own security. In some respects a workgroup is like a miniature replica of the Internet as a whole: *Anarchy*!
- Workgroups lack single sign-on. Potentially, a person might have a differently-named user account on each machine, and the password for each of these accounts might be different, too. On the other hand, single sign-on could be emulated by creating an identical user account with an identical password on every machine, but this is a management and security nightmare in itself when there are more than 100 machines.
- Every computer in a workgroup is a management island. In general, workgroups don't scale to thousands of machines without gallons of elbow grease and lots of summer interns.
- Because local users and groups cannot be made members of groups on other machines, it is very difficult to maintain a consistent assignment of permissions/rights across multiple machines.

NOTES

NOTES

Manage Local Accounts

- Windows NT
  - User Manager
- Windows 2000/XP/.NET
  - User Accounts applet in Control Panel.
  - Computer Management snap-in in Administrative Tools folder.
  - NET.EXE

SANS Security Essentials – Windows Security

And on all these operating systems, you can manage local accounts with the `NET.EXE` command-line tool. Execute "net help user" to see the available switches.

Administrative Tools Folder Missing?

If the Administrative Tools folder is missing, right-click on a blank area of your taskbar > Properties > Start Menu tab > top Start Menu radio button > Customize button > Advanced tab > scroll to the bottom of the list > select System Administrative Tools: Display on the All Programs menu and the Start Menu. While you're there, scroll up again and show the Control Panel too.

Manage Local Accounts

All Windows NT/2000/XP/.NET computers have local accounts and groups, even if the computers are members of a domain. (Local accounts are hidden on Active Directory domain controllers, but they still exist dormant.)

On Windows XP Professional, for example, local users and groups are managed with the User Accounts applet in Control Panel (Advanced tab > Advanced button). On Windows 2000/XP/.NET, you also can get to them through the Computer Management snap-in in the Administrative Tools folder.

On Windows NT 4.0, the User Manager (`USRMGR.EXE`) program can manager either local or domain accounts.

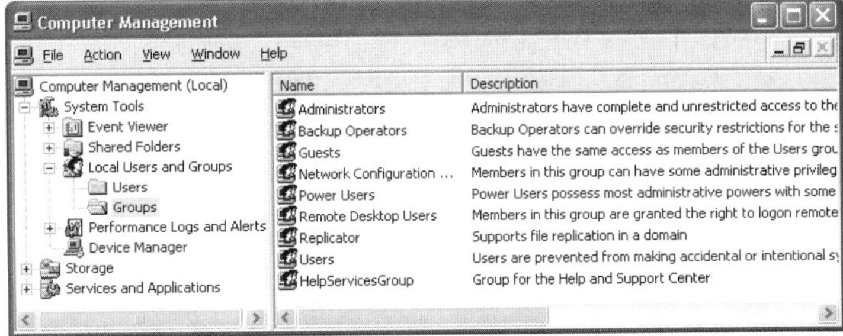

Security ID Numbers (SIDs)

- It's like a Social Security number
  - Every user, computer and group has a unique SID number.
  - Well-known SIDs for certain built-in users and groups.
- Windows only cares about SIDs when enforcing permissions/rights.

SANS Security Essentials – Windows Security

Security ID Numbers (SIDs)

Every user account, computer account, and group has a unique identifying Security ID (SID) number. It's like a Social Security number. For example, here is the SID for a local user account on a Windows XP Professional box:

```
S-1-5-21-501923405-841928246-1347044091-
1003
```

Each computer will create SIDs for its local users and groups. (And domain controllers will do the same for domain accounts.) These SIDs are unique, except for the SIDs of some well-known users and groups, which are shorter and standardized across all boxes. For example:

- S-1-1-0 = Everyone Group
- S-1-5-11 = Authenticated Users Group
- S-1-5-32-544 = Local Administrators Group
- S-1-5-32-547 = Local Power Users Group

The username of an account might be renamed, but the SID stays the same. If a user named "Sam" is deleted, and another user named "Sam" is immediately created, the new Sam will have a different SID number. If there is an account named "Deb" on Computer A, and another local account named "Deb" on Computer B, these are two different accounts. Why? Because their SIDs are different, and that is the only thing that matters. If the two Deb accounts happen to have identical passwords, then the user could log onto one machine and *appear* to access the other computer over the network without being authenticated. In fact, the user's credentials are being locally cached and automatically forwarded to the other box; but at the other box the user actually is logging on with a different user account, i.e., an account with a different SID. The transparency is just an illusion.

Windows actually only cares about SID numbers when it is enforcing rights and permissions. That's because all of your SIDs go into your "ID Card," so to speak, when you log on. And this ID Card is how the computer identifies your programs and regulates your activities. This ID Card officially is called your Security Access Token.

NOTES

NOTES

Your Security Access Token

- It's like your driver's license card.
- SAT attached to every process you start.
- Your SAT contains:
  - The SID number of your user account
  - The SIDs of all your groups
  - A list of all your local user rights
- Windows uses your SAT to check your rights/permissions before allowing actions.

SANS Security Essentials – Windows Security

Security Access Tokens (SATs)

When you log onto your desktop, your computer obtains the SID for your user account and all the SIDs for all the groups to which you belong. Your computer also finds out what your "local rights" are on the machine, e.g., the take ownership right (discussed later).

All these SIDs and rights are written into something like an ID Card and attached to all your processes. This ID Card is called your Security Access Token (SAT). Your SAT identifies you on your computer and is your identity on the network.

Everything the computer needs to know to enforce permissions and user rights restrictions is contained in that one little token. Just like you have to present your military ID or company ID card before you can get onto the base or into secured rooms, the operating system will ask for your SAT before it lets you access any resources. Because every program and process you launch has a copy of your SAT, the OS always can get it easily.

Now, whenever a program you control tries to access a resource or to exercise a user right, the operating system will get the SAT from your process and see if you (and your groups) are permitted to perform the requested action. If yes, the OS lets you. If no, you get an error message. This is made possible by the Access Control Lists (ACLs) on the resources and the fact that certain actions require specially-defined rights before you can execute them (e.g., you must have the "Log On Locally" user right in order to log on at the desktop console).

A More Perfect Workgroup...

- Stand-alone computers do not trust each others' SATs, that is why workgroups don't scale.
- What we need:
  - A central shared database of SIDs that all stand-alone computers agree to use for single sign-on and resource authorization
  - A secure authentication scheme for distributing SID information from this database to computers making SATs

SANS Security Essentials – Windows Security

To Form a More Perfect Workgroup...

Fundamentally, the problem with stand-alone computers in workgroups is that they don't understand, accept, or trust the SATs of each other's users!

It's like a situation where every State in the country issues driver's licenses to its members, but with no State accepting or trusting the driver's license cards other States have issued.

What we need is a way to make the computers in a workgroup all use the accounts and groups defined in the accounts database on just *one* of the computers in the workgroup; a special, designated computer in the workgroup that could be trusted to issue SATs from a *shared* accounts database.

Every user's processes ultimately, then, would get their identifying SATs from this single database that everyone understands, accepts, and trusts. A user at one computer, once authenticated, could present its SAT to another computer, and that remote computer could accept it and use it to authorize requests.

In fact, what a workgroup suffers from is a lack of division of labor. Stand-alones should organize themselves into a true society and institute a Government. If all the computers in a workgroup would just "outsource" their authentication and account management tasks to one (or a few) special computers with a shared accounts database, we could have a *domain*.

We the Computers

in order to form a more perfect Workgroup,

establish justice, and insure domestic tranquility,

do ordain and establish this

Active Directory.

NOTES

NOTES

Active Directory Domains
• Domain Controllers
– The AD database
– Multi-master replication
• What does "being in the domain" mean?
– Domain computers, users and groups
• AD is like a registry for the entire network...
SANS Security Essentials – Windows Security

Active Directory Domains

"Active Directory" is the name of the shared accounts database that gets installed on a Windows 2000/.NET Server when it is promoted to become a domain controller. Again, what is *Active Directory?* It's a database—a database of user accounts that otherwise would have been in the local accounts databases of stand-alone computers. Let's define some terms.

Domain Controllers

A "domain controller" is just a server which helps to manage the Active Directory (AD) database on behalf of the other computers and users in the organization. The AD database contains, among other things, all the SIDs of the users, computers, and groups that have "outsourced" their authentication and account management work to the domain controller. Less formally, a domain controller is like a giant PEZ Dispenser, but it spits out Security Access Tokens instead.

Once a user has her SAT, it is attached to all of her programs like a badge, and every request she makes for local or remote resources is checked against the permissions/rights on that resource with the SAT-badge. How? The resource (file, database, e-mailbox, printer, whatever) will have a list of SIDs attached to it with the permissions that each SID has to the resource. This list of permissions based on user and group SIDs is called an "access control list" (ACL)

Multi-Master Replication

Windows NT 4.0 domain controllers are divided into Primary Domain Controllers (PDCs) and Backup Domain Controllers (BDCs). This is because changes can only be written to the Security Account Manager (SAM) database on the PDC. These changes are then replicated, in a hub-and-spoke pattern, out to each BDC's respective read-only copy of the SAM. This process is called "single-master replication," where the PDC is the "master."

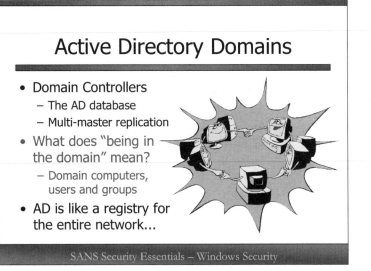

But this PDC/BDC distinction disappears in Active Directory domains (well, almost, but now's not the time to be splitting hairs.). You can make a change to the AD database on any domain controller in an AD domain, and this change will then be replicated to all other domain controllers automatically. This is called "multi-master replication." In a sense, every AD domain controller is a PDC because you can modify its database, and every AD domain

NOTES

controller is a BDC, in a sense, because it receives changes from all the others.

Note

Whenever there is a conflict, the later change overrides the earlier one. AD domain controllers use time-stamps and update sequence numbers on every *property* of every object to keep the replication straight.

Being "In the Domain"

Being "in the domain" has nothing to do with one's physical location or bandwidth. A user in Tokyo and a user in Dallas can both be in the same domain. A cross-legged user sitting on top of a domain controller with a stand-alone laptop is not in the domain.

Strictly speaking, you are "in the domain" if you have an account in the Active Directory database. Your account has your SID and other information about you. That's it! There's not a big mystery about it. A "domain" is all of the users, computers, and groups that have (or, rather, *are*) accounts in the AD database.

Who or what can be "in the domain?" Anything with a SID can be in a domain. Conversely, you must have a SID in order to exist. What can have a SID? All users, groups, and computers have SIDs. Yes, computers have their own accounts, just like human users do. They even have passwords and automatically update them periodically. When a computer which is a member of a domain boots up, it logs into the domain just like a human.

What Else is in the Active Directory Database?

While account information is the most important thing in the AD database, there is *much* more. This is an important difference with the Security Account Manager (SAM) database on Windows NT 4.0 domain controllers, which more-or-less only had account information.

Consider this analogy, because it is the key to understanding what the Active Directory database is intended to be:

Active Directory is like a registry for the entire network.

Windows computers store all their configuration settings in a tiny database called the "registry." It can be edited with `REGEDIT.EXE`. Active Directory can store many of the configuration settings for all users and computers too. It stores these settings in the form of "Group Policy Objects" that modify registries and other things.

Discussing everything that can be stored in the Active Directory database is beyond the scope of this chapter, but here is a partial list of what can be stored:

- User account properties and passwords
- Groups and their memberships
- Computer properties and passwords
- Domain names and trust relationships
- Kerberos master keys
- Digital certificates and Certificate Trust Lists
- Organizational Units and their members

NOTES

- LANs and IP subnets in the organization
- AD replication links and their settings
- Shared printer locations (UNC paths)
- Exchange 2000 Server directory information
- Group Policy Objects for managing virtually every aspect of a computer's configuration and its users' desktops
- And any custom data third-party developers would like to be accessed through LDAP

Just as the registry on a computer stores the configuration settings that affect just that one computer, Active Directory can store the configuration settings that affect the entire domain.

Active Directory, unlike the SAM database on Windows NT, is a general-purpose database and can be accessed through an industry standard protocol, LDAP. Active Directory uses the same database engine as Microsoft Exchange Server and can store millions of objects. Its maximum size is 4000 GB (4TB)!

Domain Users and Groups

Local users/groups still exist in the local accounts databases of computers that have joined the domain. But now the users/groups from the AD database are available to domain member computers as well.

So now a distinction can be made. "Local" users and groups are accounts in the database of non-domain controllers; this is true whether or not that computer is a member of a domain. On the other hand, a "domain" user, computer, or group has its account in the AD database. These domain accounts are available for use by any computer that has joined the domain.

Authentication Protocols (1 of 3)

- A SAT is constructed on-the-fly at the computer where the user is requesting access to a resource.
- The SIDs of domain accounts and groups come from Active Directory, and are conveyed to the computer through the authentication protocol.
- Rights, local account SIDs and local group SIDs come from the target computer itself.

SANS Security Essentials – Windows Security

Authentication Protocols

If a domain controller is like a giant PEZ Dispenser for dispensing Security Access Tokens to users and computers, does it just spew those Tokens out willy-nilly? No. Users and computers have to authenticate to a domain controller first, of course.

Security Access Tokens Revisited

Now that we have a good feel for what Security Access Tokens (SATs) do, let's discuss exactly how they're made. In fact, SATs are never sent over the network. SATs are constructed on-the-fly inside the server, where the user is requesting access. But important *parts* of the SAT *are* sent over the network by the authentication protocol being used.

A SAT can be broken down into four parts, and each part has a source (in parentheses):

1. SID for the user's domain account (AD).
2. SIDs for the domain groups the user is a member of (AD).
3. SIDs for the local groups on the server being accessed that the user is a member of (the server's local accounts database).
4. The list of user rights the user has on the server being accessed (the server being accessed).

It's one of the jobs of the authentication protocol being used to convey to the target server 1) the SID for the user's domain account and 2) the SIDs for the domain groups of which the user is a member. With this information, the target server can construct a SAT to represent the user on the fly. This is because the server already has the last two parts of the SAT: 3) the SIDs for the local groups on the server of which the user is a member and 4) the rights the user has on that machine.

So, how can an authentication protocol convey the user's domain SIDs to the server? Two protocols concern us here: Kerberos and NTLM.

Permissions assigned to objects
rights are what you can do

NOTES

NOTES

Kerberos (2 of 3)

- Default authentication protocol in Windows 2000/XP/.NET.
- Requires Active Directory.
- Uses "tickets" to convey user's account and group SIDs to target servers.
- Ticket encryption based on password
  - Vulnerable to brute-force cracking

SANS Security Essentials – Windows Security

Kerberos Authentication

The default authentication protocol in Windows 2000/XP/.NET is Kerberos (RFC 1510). Windows 9x/Me/NT can't use Kerberos. Kerberos is the "default" in that it will be used if it can be used; otherwise, the computers will fall back to NTLM.

The most important requirement for making Kerberos available is the presence of an Active Directory domain controller. AD domain controllers are all Kerberos "Key Distribution Centers (KDCs)" because they hold every user's and computer's Kerberos master key. Your Kerberos key is derived from your password.

Lets examine the basic idea of Kerberos. Imagine a client named "Kiddo" in a domain named "Disney" and a server named "SpaceMountain." Kiddo wants to access SpaceMountain, so Kiddo has to get a ticket from the Disney ticket booth, i.e., from a domain controller in the Disney domain.

Note

Applications don't have to be "Kerberized" in Windows like they do in Unix. Kerberos is available when any of the following protocols is being used: SMB/CIFS, RPC, LDAP, HTTP, Dynamic DNS secure updates, IPSec IKE, and RSVP. But note what's not on the list: FTP and Telnet!

1. Client Kiddo authenticates to a Disney domain controller with its password used as an encryption key. Only the controller (the KDC) and the client know the client's password, so only they can decipher stuff encrypted with that password.
2. Domain controller sends the Kiddo a "ticket" for getting access to SpaceMountain, the remote server the client wants to access.
3. Kiddo client sends the ticket to the SpaceMountain server. That ticket was encrypted with the *server's* secret key by the domain controller, so only SpaceMountain can decrypt it (not Kiddo). What's inside the ticket? All of Kiddo's domain SIDs! Now the server knows who the client is and can construct a SAT to represent him!

Kerberos is faster than NTLM and scales better in large environments because clients can cache and reuse their tickets (just as though Kiddo managed to keep his ticket to SpaceMountain, so he could go on the ride over and over and over).

NOTES

However, if an attacker can capture the packets of the initial Kerberos exchange (when the user first logs on), then the attacker can mount a brute-force attack to discover the user's password. This is possible because the initial ticket request is encrypted based on the user's password. The shorter and simpler the password, the more likely it will be revealed in a reasonable period of time; long and complex passwords generally cannot be discovered in a usefully short period of time (unless your adversary is extremely well-funded). A brute-force Kerberos cracker for Windows can be found at `http://ntsecurity.nu`.

NOTES

NTLM (3 of 3)

- Windows 9x/NT/2000/XP/.NET, but 9x requires the ADCE add-on.
- User's password information is given to server, which passes it through to a domain controller; controller sends user's SIDs to server.
- NTLMv1 and NTLMv2

SANS Security Essentials – Windows Security

NTLM Authentication

NTLM authentication is supported by Windows NT/2000/XP/.NET natively, but Windows 9x can support it, too, if you install the free Active Directory Client Extensions (ADCE) upgrade from Microsoft.

Note

If you have Windows 9x or Windows NT Workstation clients on your network, make sure to install the ADCE upgrade from Microsoft! This upgrade adds NTLMv2 support, awareness of AD "sites," and a Distributed Filesystem (DFS) client. Download it from `http://www.microsoft.com/windows2000/server/evaluation/news/bulletins/adextension.asp`. Also see KnowledgeBase articles Q288358 and Q295166.

NTLM is "I need to ask your mother" authentication. The client wants to access a server, so the client sends to the server the client's encrypted password information. The server passes this information through to a domain controller, which checks the password. If the password is good, the domain controller sends the server all of the client's domain SIDs. Now the server can construct a SAT to represent the client.

As we all probably know, however, NTLM protection of password data is dreadful, and the password data itself (the password hashes) are not well-protected either. Using a password-sniffing tool like L0phtCrack, a hacker can listen in on these NTLM exchanges and extract password hashes. These hashes then usually can be cracked in less than a day (often in less than ten minutes).

NOTES

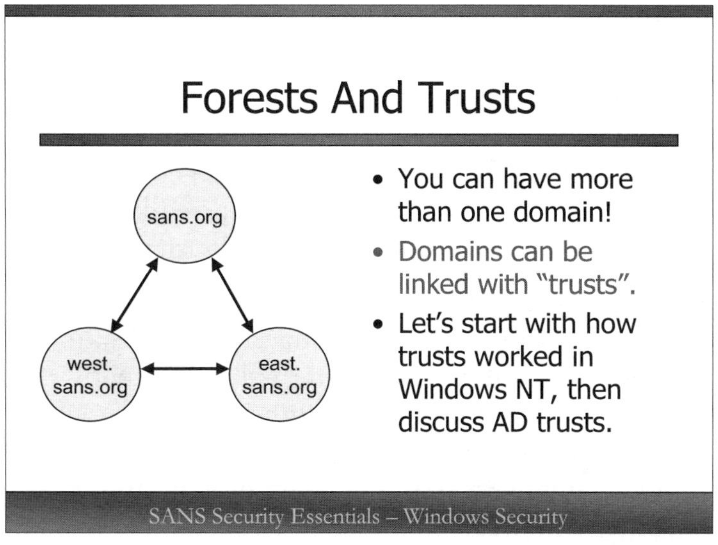

Forests and Trusts

You can have more than one domain! If you do have multiple domains, they will be linked together by "interdomain trusts."

A lot has changed since Windows NT, though, so let's first discuss having multiple Windows NT domains; then we'll talk about having multiple Active Directory domains.

NOTES

NT Trusts (1 of 2)

- **Without an interdomain trust:**
  - Can't assign rights/permissions to users or groups in the other domain.
  - No single sign-on when accessing resources in the other domain.
  - Can't log on to your desktop with an account in the other domain.

SANS Security Essentials – Windows Security

Windows NT Domains and Trusts

Let's say that you had two Windows NT 4.0 domains. By default, there would be no trusts between them. Having no trusts between two domains means that:

- You can't assign rights or permissions to resources in your domain to users/groups in the other domain. For example, when setting NTFS permissions, you simply won't be able to select the other domain in the permissions dialog box to see all the users and groups from the other domain.
- There's no single sign-on when accessing resources in the other domain. You log onto your desktop with your own domain account. When you access a server in the other domain, you are prompted for a username and password, i.e., a username and password valid in the *other* domain! If you happen to know the username and password to an account in the other domain, you can access resources *as* that person; hence, you will have the rights/permissions of that person. This isn't single sign-on; it's like the other domain is just a mega-workgroup.
- You can't log onto your desktop with a user account from the other domain. Your desktop has a computer account in the local domain. The user account is in the other domain. But because there is no trust, your computer doesn't trust any users from the other domain to log onto it interactively.

A trust link between the two domains solves all these problems. With a two-way trust you can log onto your desktop with an account in the other domain; you can access resources in either domain as yourself (single sign-on); and you can assign rights/permissions on resources to any user or group you want, no matter from what domain they come.

NOTES

NT Trusts (2 of 2)

- **Windows NT trusts are one-way:**
  - A "two-way" trust is just two one-way trusts in opposite directions.
  - Direction of trust determines the direction of possible resource access.
  - Trusts are **in**transitive.
- **No interdomain replication of data.**

SANS Security Essentials – Windows Security

Windows NT Trusts Are One-Way

A "two-way trust" is just two one-way trusts going in opposite directions. They are reflexive, that is, each end point refers to the other. All Windows NT trusts are one-way. Trust is an important concept in security architecture, never create a two-way trust unless it is needed. With Windows NT you can establish a one-way trust between domains.

The direction of trust determines *who* can logon *where*. By analogy, if I trust you, then you could borrow my motorcycle. It is my trusting you that gives you the opportunity to come back to me and ask for the bike. Hence, access to resources goes in the *opposite* direction as the direction of the trust: I trust you; therefore, you can ride my bike. The same goes for domains.

In the diagram, users in domain A can access servers in domain B. But users in domain B cannot access servers in domain A. B trusts A; therefore, users in A can access servers in B (but not vice versa).

What does "access" mean here? It means that, if you were an administrator in domain B, and you were setting share/NTFS permissions on a server, you could select users and groups from domain A and assign them permissions. On the other hand, if you were an administrator in domain A doing the same, then all the users and groups in B would be unavailable to you: A doesn't trust B, so you can't give rights/permissions to people in B on servers in A!

No Inter-Domain Replication

Another important fact about Windows NT trusts is that they do not cause any replication of accounts (or other data) between the two trusting domains. Even with two one-way trusts there is no replication between the domains, as there is within each domain. The PDC in each domain replicates changes to the accounts database to the BDCs in that domain, but the PDCs in the two domains do not replicate anything to each other (i.e., there is no PDC-to-PDC replication). This is not true with Active Directory.

NOTES

Active Directory Forests
• A "forest" is a set of AD domains:
– AD data are multi-master replicated across all domains in the forest.
– Two-ways trusts between all domains.
– Trusts are transitive.
– Other trust types are possible to domains within and outside the forest.
SANS Security Essentials – Windows Security

Active Directory Forests and Trusts

A "forest" is composed of Active Directory domains that replicate their AD databases with each other. Think how different that is from Windows NT!

Forest-Wide Replication

If you have two AD domains in a forest, the domain controllers in these domains replicate changes to their AD databases across the domain boundary. Because AD uses multi-master replication, a modified user or new group on any domain controller in one domain is replicated to all the other domain controllers in the entire forest, including the domain controllers in the other domain. That data in the Active Directory database which is replicated to all domains is called the "Global Catalog."

In many respects, there is just one Active Directory database in a forest no matter how many domains there are. It's definitional; in fact, a shared accounts database across the domains is what makes them a "forest" instead of just "a bunch of mutually trusting domains." A collection of Windows NT domains could all be made to trust each other, but this would not turn them into a forest.

For more information on Global Catalog, Schema, and Configuration Naming Context, see `http://www.microsoft.com/activedirectory/`.

Two-Way Transitive Trusts

All domains in a forest have two-way transitive trusts between them. This is the "complete trust" model. This means any user can log on at any computer and access any resources in any domain in the forest (assuming the user has the necessary permissions, of course).

Other trust types are possible, such as explicit trusts, shortcut trusts, cross-forest trusts. Please see `http://www.microsoft.com/activedirectory/` or the Windows 2000 *Resource Kit* for more information. However, as a word to the wise, the more complex your trust model, the greater the risk your security design will enter unexpected states.

Group Policy

- Group Policy manages:
  - Password policy
  - Lockout policy
  - NTFS permissions
  - User rights
  - Event logs
  - Registry settings
  - IPSec settings
  - And *much* more

SANS Security Essentials – Windows Security

Group Policy

Group Policy Objects are some of the most important data replicated through Active Directory. Group Policy is a technology that you can use to configure virtually every security option on every Windows 2000/XP/.NET computer in your enterprise.

Group Policy is used to manage the following:

- Password policies
- Account lockout policies
- Kerberos policies
- Audit policies
- Custom user rights assignments
- Security options, e.g., authentication protocols
- Event log sizes and wrapping options
- Custom memberships in important groups
- Startup options and permissions on services
- Registry key permissions and audit settings
- NTFS permissions and audit settings

NOTES

NOTES

How Group Policy Works
• GPOs are like complex scripts stored in the AD database.
• GPOs are applied automatically:
– At boot-up
– At logon
– 90-minute intervals
• Your local GPO applies just to your machine.
• Domain GPOs can be applied to individual OUs, if desired.
SANS Security Essentials – Windows Security

How Does Group Policy Work?

Think of Group Policy Objects (GPOs) as special logon scripts that, when run, can reconfigure almost anything on the computer, including the user's desktop.

When a computer boots up it will download the GPOs assigned to it and execute them automatically. Every 90 minutes thereafter the computer will check to see that none of its GPOs have been changed, and, if any have, then the computer will download the edited GPOs and run them automatically too, even if the computer has not been rebooted.

Similarly, when a user logs on, his or her computer will obtain the GPOs for that user and execute them automatically to reconfigure the user's desktop. Every 90 minutes the computer will check for any newly edited GPOs and reapply them. Some settings do not take effect until after the user logs back on again, but many settings apply immediately.

If you want to see a Group Policy Object on Windows XP, click on Start > All Programs > Administrative Tools > Local Security Policy. This is your "local GPO." It applies only to your computer, not to other machines in the domain, and it applies even if your machine is a stand-alone. It defines your local security policies, which may then be overwritten by domain GPO policies.

On an AD domain controller, you can see a domain-wide GPO by going to Start > Programs > Administrative Tools > Default Domain Policy. To see the entire GPO, open the "Active Directory Users and Computers" snap-in tool > right-click on the name of your domain > Properties > Group Policy tab > highlight Default Domain Policy > Edit. This is the same "Default Domain Policy" GPO, but the snap-in shows all of its properties.

Domain GPOs are stored in the AD database and replicated to all domain controllers. Each Organizational Unit in AD can have completely different and separate GPOs linked to it. When a domain GPO is linked to an OU instead of to the domain, it only applies to the users and computers in that OU.

What Is ".NET" Anyway?

"Dot NET" means three things:

1. Windows .NET Server
2. The .NET Framework
   - Common Language Runtime (CLR)
   - Framework Class Library
3. XML Web Services

SANS Security Essentials – Windows Security

What Is ".NET" Anyway?

What the heck is this "dot-NET" stuff anyway? How does it relate to network security? Why does Microsoft put out such weird TV commercials that don't tell you anything about it?

As you've probably guessed, ".NET" is a marketing term that is intended to group together different things under one umbrella concept. There are three technologies that fall under the rubric of .NET:

- Windows .NET Server
- The .NET Framework
- XML Web Services

Note

There is more information in this section on .NET than can be discussed in seminar. It is here for your reference because there are always so many questions about it.

Windows .NET Server

Think of Windows .NET Server as "Windows XP Server," except that Microsoft changed its name as part of its .NET advertising campaign. This OS comes with the .NET Framework installed by default, but you can easily install the Framework on Windows 2000 or Windows XP too. You can largely ignore Windows .NET Server *per se* when discussing what ".NET" is.

Note

The .NET Framework is installed by default on Windows .NET Server, but it must be installed on Windows 98/Me/NT/2000/XP manually (it's a 21MB file). Get it for free from `http://www.microsoft.com/net/`.

The .NET Framework

When talking about the .NET Framework, we're talking about things that interest programmers: interfaces, object models, garbage collection, threading, handling exceptions, memory leaks, buffer overflows, etc.

So, when we're interested in the security of the Framework, we're really talking about the low-level security of code written for, and executed in, the

NOTES

NOTES

.NET Framework. This is security inside of applications. Almost always, we're talking about code written in C# or VB.NET, but any language can be ported over to run as "Framework-managed code," even COBOL, Perl, and C++. Visual Studio .NET is Microsoft's tool for writing programs using the .NET Framework. The .NET Framework has two core pieces: the Common Language Runtime (CLR) and the Framework Class Library.

Common Language Runtime (CLR)

The CLR is similar to the Java Virtual Machine (JavaVM) in purpose and design but with important differences. The CLR compiles program code *twice*: when the software is built it is compiled into byte-code; and when this byte-code is executed on a particular computer, it is compiled again on-the-fly into the native binary format understood by that platform (and not in a Virtual Machine). Similar to Java byte-code, though, the Framework's byte-code can be copied simply to another machine with a CLR and executed there without modification.

Currently, the CLR only works on Windows machines, but there's no reason that a Unix/Linux/ Solaris version of the CLR couldn't be developed. Indeed, such a CLR is part of Microsoft's long-term strategy to kill off Linux (or at least profit from it), but Microsoft has not yet seriously begun developing it.

Note

See `http://www.go-mono.com` for an open source version of the CLR and Class Library for Unix/ Linux!

Both the JavaVM and the Framework's CLR enhance application security by preventing execution code from getting unregulated access to the operating system, to hardware, to memory, or to other processes. (This is sometimes called "sandboxing" software.) Memory leaks, buffer overruns, kernel-killing code faults, and other issues are all *supposed to* be eliminated when an application runs in the CLR using 100% managed code.

Most OS experts agree that roughly the same security benefits of running code in the JavaVM also will be enjoyed by running code through the CLR. For example, Foundstone has published a white paper that is positive on the security of the .NET Framework (`www.foundstone.com/microsoft/dotnet/`).

Framework Class Library

When the .NET Framework is installed, thousands of classes and interfaces become available to managed applications in the form of the "Class Library." The Class Library includes functionality for such functions as accessing databases, managing threads, accessing Active Directory, handling XML data, and using sockets. What we care about here, though, are the classes related to application security.

NOTES

The Class Library includes extensive cryptographic services for encryption, hashing, signing, certificate management, and authentication. There also is an extensive programmatic infrastructure for tracking the identities of local/remote users, enforcing role-based security restrictions within the application, and authorizing requests for access to sensitive objects such as the registry. In short, the Framework provides the "plumbing" for secure communications, authentication, role-based permissions, authorization of requests, and auditing in a way that attempts to hide the low-level details from the developer. This security "plumbing" is essential if anyone is going to trust using XML Web Services at all.

XML Web Services

The future of the Internet is going to be fancier web pages displayed in ever more complex browsers for humans to look at. Applications will also use the Internet to communicate directly and independently *among themselves* to provide useful services *for* human beings.

For example, an airline might make all of its real-time departure/arrival/gate information available as a query service (kind of like a DNS server for the gates and times of all the particular airplanes the carrier has in the air at any given time). The consumers of this data are all the travel agencies, taxi services, hotel chains, and anyone else who wants to provide this information as a service to augment her own products or services. An end user could also use this data when she, for example, double-taps a travel date in her calendar program on her wireless PDA or GUI cellphone, which will then list the gate and departure time (including real-time delay information) next to the little airplane icon on that day in the calendar. Indeed, why double-tap it? The PDA will just refresh that data automatically every few minutes, along with dozens of other flights, stock prices, weather forecasts, or whatever else the user cares about.

But to make a service like this work, Microsoft needs a "glue" that can make interoperability among different software packages, platforms, operating systems, and databases all work together as transparently as possible. That's where XML comes in. *Extensible Markup Language* (XML) is used to format data in a way that is easy to work with, even when that data is sent back-and-forth between different applications on different hardware platforms running different operating systems.

Note

If you have Windows XP/.NET, you'll have some example XML files on your hard drive. Just do a search for "*.xml" in My Computer, and double-click any file to open it in the Internet Explorer XML parser. The colored HTML-looking tags are the XML. The file itself is just ASCII text.

Built into the .NET Framework is functionality to make web services like the above not only possible but also relatively easy to develop. XML support is built into more-or-less everything .NET-ish. Visual Studio .NET greatly simplifies the development process. The .NET Enterprise Servers (like BizTalk

NOTES

Server) and the Class Library provide the "plumbing" to make it scalable and secure.

Billions of dollars are at stake. The entire .NET project at Microsoft will stand or fall depending on its security and reliability. Who would trust their business to an application model like this if hackers could compromise it or take down the servers at will? *Now* we see why Microsoft has gotten so serious about security lately.

Summary

- Windows Operating Systems:
  - Windows 9x
  - Windows NT
  - Windows 2000
  - Windows XP
  - Windows .NET
- Workgroups
- Local Accounts
- SIDs and SATs
- Active Directory
- Authentication:
  - Kerberos
  - NTLM
- Trusts
- Group Policy
- ".NET"

SANS Security Essentials – Windows Security

NOTES

Summary

The purpose of this section was to provide the necessary background information to be able to understand what follows.

We started with an overview of the many different operating systems available from Microsoft. If security is your prime concern, and if your organization has the money, upgrade to Windows 2000/XP/.NET. Windows 9x and Windows NT are obsolete. Next, we talked about how Windows computers can be made to share resources with each other and be managed.

Workgroups are composed of stand-alone computers, each with its own separate user accounts database. A domain is a set of computers which all use a shared accounts database called Active Directory. Domain controllers are the servers which manage this database on behalf of the other computers in the domain. A user must authenticate to a domain controller before being permitted to logon to his or her desktop, and domain controllers authenticate users when they attempt to access other servers over the network.

The two main authentication protocols used on Windows networks are Kerberos, which is the default, and NTLM, which is retained for backwards compatibility and used when Kerberos is unavailable. Both Kerberos and NTLMv1 authentication traffic can be sniffed to extract crackable information, but NTLMv1 is trivial to crack in comparison to the difficulty of brute-forcing Kerberos passwords.

A theme throughout this section has been the authorization mechanisms providing the security infrastructure. Every user, computer, and group is uniquely identified by a Security ID (SID) number. Your identity on the network is defined by your Security Access Token (SAT) which lists your SIDs and user rights on any given machine. Every program you run gets a copy of your SAT so that the operating system can know who is behind each program's requests and actions. Hence, the operating system can enforce permissions and user rights restrictions.

Next, we compared Windows NT domains with Active Directory domains. Windows NT uses single-master replication, while Windows 2000/.NET uses multi-master replication. Windows NT domains do not replicate data between them, but Active Directory domains do. We also saw that Active Directory domains in a forest always have two-way transitive trusts between them, forming the "complete trust" domain model.

We briefly talked about Group Policy, perhaps the most important security tool in your arsenal for locking down your network. And finally we talked about ".NET."

Websites Mentioned

- L0phtCrack (`www.atstake.com`)
- Windows NT (`www.microsoft.com/ntserver/`)
- Windows 2000 (`www.microsoft.com/windows2000/`)
- Windows XP (`www.microsoft.com/windowsxp/`)
- Windows .NET (`www.microsoft.com/windows.netserver/`)
- Citrix MetaFrame (`www.citrix.com`)
- Terminal Services (`www.microsoft.com/terminalservices/`)
- Kerberos (`web.mit.edu/kerberos/www/`)
- Kerberos Cracker (`ntsecurity.nu`)
- eBay (`www.ebay.com`)
- Intel 64-bit Itanium Processors (`www.intel.com`)
- .NET Framework (`www.microsoft.com/net/`)
- Foundstone (`www.foundstone.com/microsoft/dotnet/`)

Chapter 26

Permissions and User Rights

NOTES

Permissions And
User Rights

SANS Security Essentials V:
Windows Security

SANS Security Essentials – Windows Security

NOTES

Permissions and User Rights

Why have user accounts at all? Why go through all the trouble of Active Directory, Kerberos, NTLM, SIDs, SATs, mandatory user logons, and the rest of the machinery for user authentication? The payoff comes in three forms:

- Permissions
- User Rights
- Auditing

Permissions on files, folders, printers, registry keys, and other items allow you to regulate access to these objects. Some users will only have Read access to an object, while others will be given Full Control. This kind of *selective access control* is possible only if users are authenticated first; otherwise, how would the operating system know *who* was trying to read or change the object?

Indeed, authentication and authorization are two sides of the same coin. On the one side, you can't authorize access to an object if you don't know who is requesting the access, and you can't know who someone is without authenticating him first. On the other side of the coin, there's no point in authenticating users if you can't regulate or audit their activities based on their unique identities. As discussed earlier, a user's identity is represented by his or her Security Access Token (SAT), which lists the Security ID number (SID) of the user's account and all the SIDs of the groups to which the user belongs. A SAT also lists all of a user's rights on the computer where he or she is sitting.

If you have a user right, then you have a general capability that may apply to many different objects or to no "object" at all. For example, if you have the "Take Ownership Right," you can take ownership (discussed later) of *any* object on the computer, and if you have the "Change System Time" right, you can edit the BIOS clock through a variety of tools.

Auditing and logging will be discussed in Chapter 30, but the authentication-auditing connection should be clear. If you don't authenticate users, then the logs merely will show that *someone* did this or that action, but not exactly *who* performed the action. This makes logging much less useful.

Hence, this chapter explains why there is a point to authenticating users and forcing them to memorize long passphrases. In this chapter we will discuss:

NOTES

- NTFS Permissions
- Shared Folder Permissions
- The Encrypting File System (EFS)
- Printer Permissions
- Registry Key Permissions
- Active Directory Permissions
- User Rights

NOTES

NTFS Overview

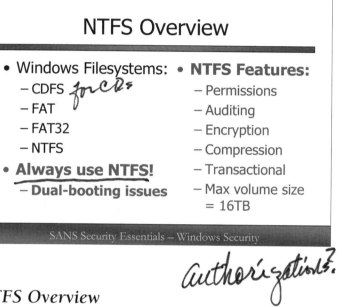

- Windows Filesystems:
  - CDFS
  - FAT
  - FAT32
  - NTFS
- **Always use NTFS!**
  - **Dual-booting issues**
- **NTFS Features:**
  - Permissions
  - Auditing
  - Encryption
  - Compression
  - Transactional
  - Max volume size = 16TB

SANS Security Essentials – Windows Security

NTFS Overview

Windows 2000/XP/.NET supports a variety of file systems, including CDFS, FAT, FAT32, and NTFS. CDFS is only for CD-ROMs. FAT and FAT32, though they can be used for hard drive partitions and are faster than NTFS on volumes smaller than 400MB, provide no auditing, access control, or fault tolerance.

Note

Another file system, NPFS, is for use with "named pipes," a networking technology that leverages the Server Message Block (SMB) protocol for inter-process communications across a network. Even though no drives are formatted with NPFS, only buffer areas, NPFS is still a true file system. It's kind of like a RAM drive with a shared folder in it!

> *Boot From The System Partition*
>
> The computer boots from the "system partition," usually the C: drive or a floppy disk, while the operating system is installed into the "boot partition." If these terms seem reversed, that's because they are. They were accidentally switched in the publication of the first Windows NT *Resource Kit*, and over the years the names have just stuck! Also, make sure your system partition has at least 20MB of free space when you install Windows XP/.NET, or else the OS might refuse to install!

The Windows NT File System (NTFS) should be used on every hard drive. The exceptions are when you must retain the ability to boot into other operating systems or when you want the system partition to be formatted with FAT to aid in certain disaster recovery situations, e.g., when your recovery software must be installed into a FAT-formatted C: drive. Beyond this rare exception, NTFS always should be used.

The NTFS file system has the following characteristics:

- Permissions
- Auditing
- Encryption (EFS)
- Compression
- Transaction-oriented processing
- Maximum volume size: 16,000 GB (with 4KB-sized clusters)

NOTES

The transaction-oriented processing of write requests helps to ensure that the file system stays in a consistent state even after an abrupt power failure or Blue Screen of Death (BSOD). The `CHKDSK.EXE` program runs automatically after a failure or BSOD, and you can use it to schedule a full volume or sector-level scan at the next reboot (see `chkdsk.exe /?`).

Compression is handled by the NTFS driver itself (not a separate application like WinZip), which makes the compression transparent to the user. To compress a folder or file, right-click it > Properties > General tab > Advanced button > check the Compress box. You can show compressed files/folder in a blue font, if desired, by opening Windows Explorer > Tools menu > Folder Options > View tab.

Encryption, auditing, and the other features of NTFS will be discussed later in this chapter. For now, let's talk about the most important feature of NTFS for security: Discretionary Access Control Lists (DACLs).

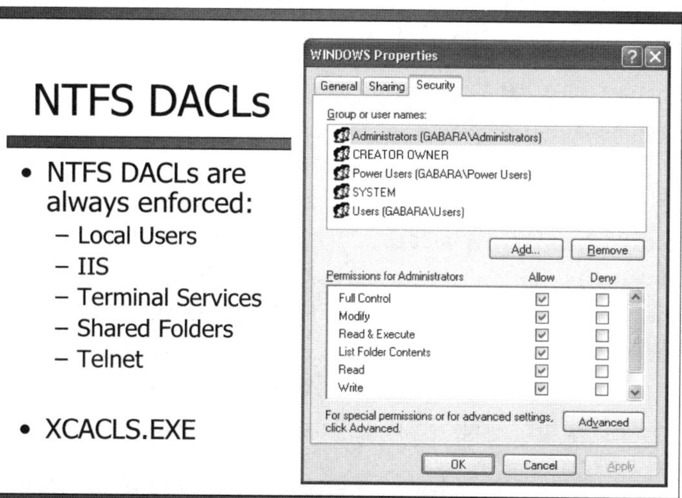

NTFS Discretionary Access Control Lists

A set of NTFS permissions on a folder or file is called a "Discretionary Access Control List (DACL)." Individual permissions in the DACL are called "Access Control Entries (ACEs)."

The permission ACEs are accessed through Windows Explorer > right-click on the folder or file > Properties > Security tab. You can also manage NTFS permissions through custom scripts or command-line tools like `XCACLS.EXE` from the *Resource Kit*.

NOTES

Note

If you have no Security tab on the property sheet of an NTFS folder/file, then pull down the Tools menu in Windows Explorer > Folder Options > View tab > uncheck the box at the bottom labeled "Use simple file sharing." This will show the Security tab.

The important thing to understand about NTFS permissions is that they *always* are enforced, no matter how the files are being accessed: via a shared folder, FTP, HTTP, Telnet, direct console access, a thin client with Terminal Services, etc. It doesn't matter; NTFS permissions always are enforced by the operating system.

Standard ACEs (Security Tab)

On the Security tab of an NTFS folder or file you will see the "standard" or generic permission ACEs. Each ACE consists of a user or group and the permissions assigned to that user/group as represented by the boxes checked below. Highlight a user/group to see which permission boxes are checked just for it. If no boxes are checked for a particular user or group, or the "Special Permissions" box is checked, there may be custom individual ACEs that don't translate into any standard ACEs.

NOTES

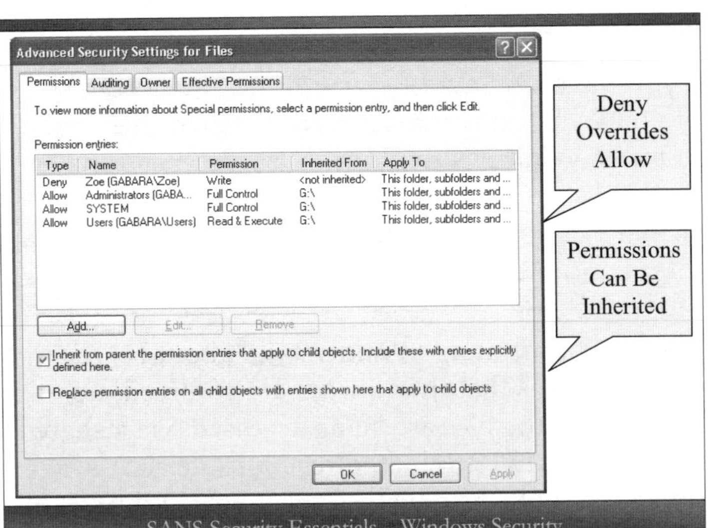

Individual ACEs (Advanced Button)

The standard permissions are just collections of one or more "individual" permission ACEs. Individual permissions are the low-level, detailed, atomic ACEs that actually make up the DACL. If you happen to configure a set of individual permissions that do not equal the definition of a standard permission, the Security tab shows the "Special Permissions" box checked. Standard permissions are nothing but collections of individual permissions, just like water molecules are nothing but collections of hydrogen and oxygen atoms.

To manage the individual ACEs on a folder/file, right-click on it > Properties > Security tab > Advanced button > Permissions tab. Highlight a permission and click Edit to see the low-level, individual permissions that are available.

Deny Overrides Allow

A user can be a member of multiple groups. These groups might have different and conflicting permissions on a single folder or file. For example, the user might be a member of two groups, one group has Allow:Read access to a file and the other group has Deny:Read access permission to the same file. What is the user's final, effective permission? The user will be denied Read access. Whenever there is a conflict between Allow and Deny permissions, the Deny permission always takes precedence.

Explicit vs. Inherited Permissions

On the Security tab, notice that some ACEs are represented by checkboxes that are somewhat gray and cannot be altered. Other ACEs have solid-colored checkmarks and can be altered. The gray-checked ACEs are inherited permissions, while the solid-checked ACEs have been assigned explicitly to that folder or file. On Windows XP/.NET, the list of individual ACEs also includes an "Inherited From" column to help diagnose DACL problems (Windows 2000 doesn't have this).

NTFS permissions on a folder/file can be inherited from parent folders anywhere higher up in the directory structure. The root folder of a drive (e.g., C:\) can only have explicit ACEs in its DACL.

You can control whether or not a folder/file inherits any of its ACEs. Inheritance is not mandatory. If you configure a folder/file to not inherit any permissions, only explicit ACEs will exist in its DACL. To exempt a folder or file from any inherited permissions, right-click it > Properties > Security tab > Advanced button > uncheck the box labeled "Inherit from parent the permission entries that apply to child objects." When you do so, you'll be asked if you want to remove the inherited ACEs or copy them as explicit permissions.

NOTES

Apply Onto: Scope of Inheritance

When creating an explicit ACE, you can also configure how and where that ACE will be inherited with the Apply Onto pull-down list in the properties of an individual ACE. You can only set "Apply Onto:This Object Only" on a file, but the Apply Onto field on a folder can be any of the following:

- This folder only
- This folder, subfolders, and files
- This folder and subfolders
- This folder and files
- Subfolders and files only
- Subfolders only
- Files only

Ouch! Watch out, you can really burn yourself with excessively complex inheritance schemes! Complexity is a security threat in itself because it leads to errors and confusion. On the other hand, having this kind of control available allows you to get *exactly* the DACLs you want: if you can think it, you can probably create a permissions scheme to get it. The CREATOR OWNER group gives you even more flexibility.

NOTES

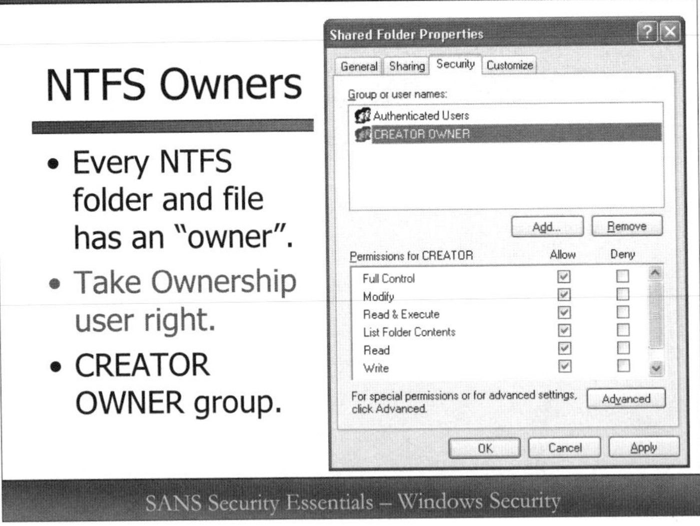

NTFS Owners

Every NTFS folder and file has an "owner" associated with it. You can see the current owner of a folder/file by right-clicking on it > Properties > Security tab > Advanced button > Owner tab. By default, the user who creates a file or folder becomes the owner of that object. Objects created during the installation of the operating system are owned by the local Administrators group.

The owner of a folder/file can always change its permissions, even if its DACL specifies that the owner's account is denied all access. If a user is the owner of an object, that user can change that object's permissions whether you like it or not! The only solution is to take ownership away from the user if you are an Administrator.

The CREATOR OWNER Group

There is a special group, which acts as a stand-in for anyone as the current owner: the CREATOR OWNER group. You can grant permissions to the CREATOR GROUP once, and, even if the owner of a folder or file changes, the permissions you granted will still apply to the new owner. The CREATOR OWNER group should be renamed the "WHOMEVER THE OWNER HAPPENS TO BE *RIGHT NOW*" group. You can't manage the membership of the CREATOR OWNER group; that membership is evaluated on-the-fly for each folder and file being accessed *when* it is accessed.

Here's an example of how the CREATOR OWNER group could be used to create a shared folder that acts as a public bulletin board. If a shared folder has the following DACL, then authenticated users can add files and subfolders and can read each other's files, but only the owner of each file (the one who created it) would have Full Control over it:

- Folder, Subfolders, & Files: Authenticated Users: Read
- Folder and Subfolders: Authenticated Users: Create Files
- Folder and Subfolders: Authenticated Users: Create Folders
- Subfolders and Files: CREATOR OWNER: Full Control

Anyone can add a file to share with others, but only the CREATOR OWNER of each file can delete or modify that file.

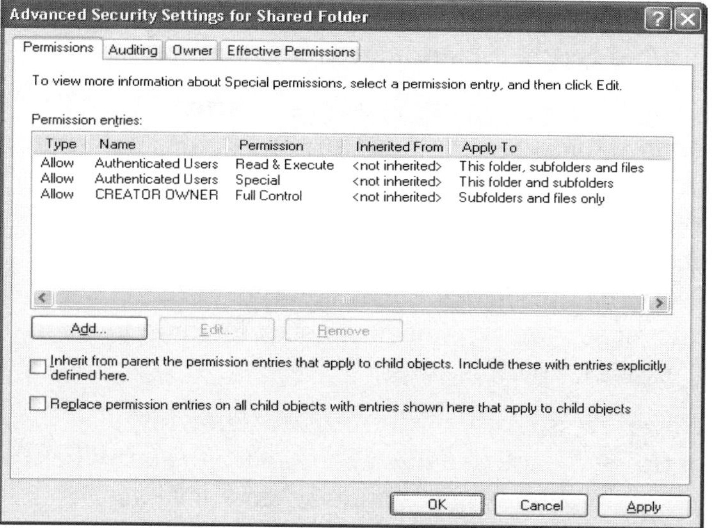
Advanced Security Settings for Shared Folder
Permissions
Auditing
Owner
Effective Permissions
To view more information about Special permissions, select a permission entry, and then click Edit.
Permission entries:
Type Name Permission Inherited From Apply To
Allow Authenticated Users Read & Execute <not inherited> This folder, subfolders and files
Allow Authenticated Users Special <not inherited> This folder and subfolders
Allow CREATOR OWNER Full Control <not inherited> Subfolders and files only
Add...
Edit...
Remove
Inherit from parent the permission entries that apply to child objects. Include these with entries explicitly defined here.
Replace permission entries on all child objects with entries shown here that apply to child objects
OK
Cancel
Apply

NOTES

NOTES

Principle of Least Privilege

- Default DACL = Full Control for Everyone
  - Not configurable.
  - What NTFS permissions should I use?
  - Depends on your "needs analysis".
- A good DACL to start, then apply PoLP:
  - System: Full Control
  - Administrators: Full Control
  - Power Users: Full Control
  - CREATOR OWNER: Full Control
  - Authenticated Users: Read & Execute (or Change)

SANS Security Essentials – Windows Security

Principle of Least Privilege

The default NTFS permission is Full Control for the Everyone group; that is to say, the default NTFS DACL is the worst possible from a security standpoint. Unfortunately, there is no registry value that can be set to change this default for all new folders/files.

If not Full Control for Everyone, then what is the best NTFS DACL to have? No simple answer can be given because of the conflicting demands between the operating system, applications, security, etc.; but you can always count on the Principle of Least Privilege to guide the way.

One way of stating the Principle of Least Privilege is this: Grant users the fewest permissions and rights possible needed to permit them to get their legitimate work done. Said another way: Don't give users more rights or permissions than they currently need to get their legitimate work done.

Hence, before you can start customizing NTFS permissions, you must perform a "needs analysis" of the server or type of resource under consideration. What is it that you don't want certain users to be able to do? What do you want to make sure other users *can* do? Without the answers to these questions, you can't begin to start locking down your NTFS permissions.

However, as a rule of thumb, the following permissions are usually a good place to start when performing your needs analysis and devising DACLs that satisfy the Principle of Least Privilege:

- System: Full Control
- Administrators: Full Control
- Power Users: Full Control
- CREATOR OWNER: Full Control
- Authenticated Users: Read & Execute (or Change)

Often, you'll give Authenticated Users very limited permissions, such as Read & Execute, and then add another ACE for a more-limited group to have Change too. Unless you wish to give some non-administrative users the ability to change NTFS permissions, you don't need to grant Full Control; Change almost always is enough.

However, what's the most efficient way to allocate permissions in environments with hundreds of groups and thousands of users? AGULP!

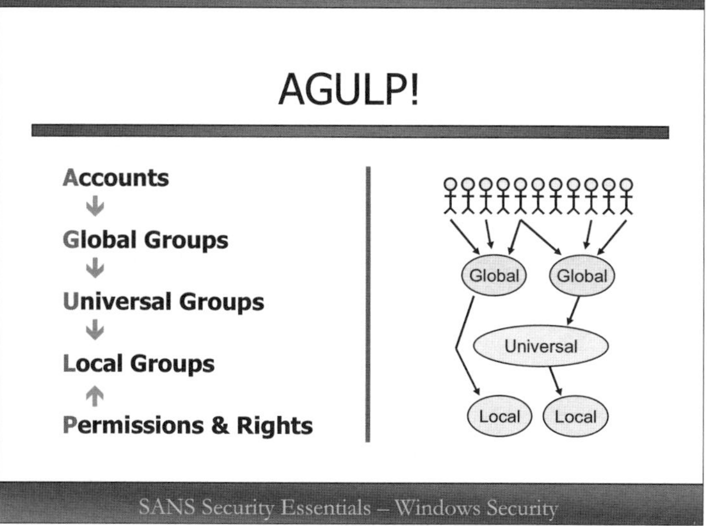

AGULP!

There is a formal model of how rights and permissions should be applied. It is optional, somewhat complex, overkill in small networks, but a useful chaos-fighter in large environments when there are multiple teams of administrators. You can implement some or all of this model as you see fit. The model is known by its acronym, which sounds surprisingly similar to the sound most people make when they first hear the model described: "AGULP!"

Here's the AGULP model:

1. Create a unique Account for each user. Avoid permitting multiple users to log on with the same shared account.
2. Add user accounts to Global groups according to users' geographical locations, job descriptions, and shared needs (e.g., all participants in the company 401k plan might be put into a group because they all share a need to access 401k-related resources). A user can be a member of multiple groups simultaneously.
3. If you are in a native mode Active Directory environment, add Global groups to Universal security groups whenever multiple Global groups from multiple domains all need to be assigned the same rights or permissions. A Global group can only contain members from the same domain where the Global group was created. A Universal group, on the other hand, can contain members from any domain in the entire Active Directory forest. User accounts can be added directly to Universal groups if desired, but this causes unwanted Global Catalog replication traffic.
4. Add Global and Universal groups to Local groups on the computers with the resources that need to be secured. These Local groups can be built-in, but they usually are created just for this purpose.
5. Assign Permissions and rights for these Local groups to the resources/objects that need to be secured. A Local group can be assigned rights/permissions only to resources/objects on the same computer where the Local group exists. And, in this model, rights/permissions should only be granted to Local groups, not to Global groups, Universal groups, or individual user accounts.

If a user is a member of a Global group, and that Global group is a member of a Universal group, and

NOTES

the Universal group is a member of a Local group, then that user inherits all the rights and permissions assigned to the Local group. When groups are nested inside each other, the "inner" groups inherit the rights and permissions assigned to the "outer" groups. In the AGULP model, local groups are "outer" and Global/Universal groups are "inner."

In sum, the purpose of a Local group is to act as the bearer of a set of rights and permissions so that these rights and permissions can be granted more easily to others. The purpose of a Universal group is to gather together many Global groups from multiple domains when those Global groups all happen to need the same rights/permissions; and the purpose of a Global group is to organize users based on their shared needs, job descriptions, or geographical locations. Why organize users like this? Because if one person requires extra rights or permissions, then it is very likely that other users in the same geographical area, or with the same job description, or with the same special needs will also require them. And simplifying the management of rights/permissions is what all this crazy AGULP stuff is about!

Native Mode? Global Catalog?

A "native mode" domain is one in which all the domain controllers have been upgraded to Windows 2000/.NET and all the old NT-style grouping restrictions have been removed. And the "Global Catalog" is that portion of the Active Directory database which is replicated to every domain controller in the forest.

AD Users And Computers

- Active Directory Users and Computers.
- Global, Universal and Local groups.
- Security vs. Distribution groups:
  - Security groups can have rights and permissions, distribution groups cannot.
  - Universal security groups can only be created in native mode.

SANS Security Essentials – Windows Security

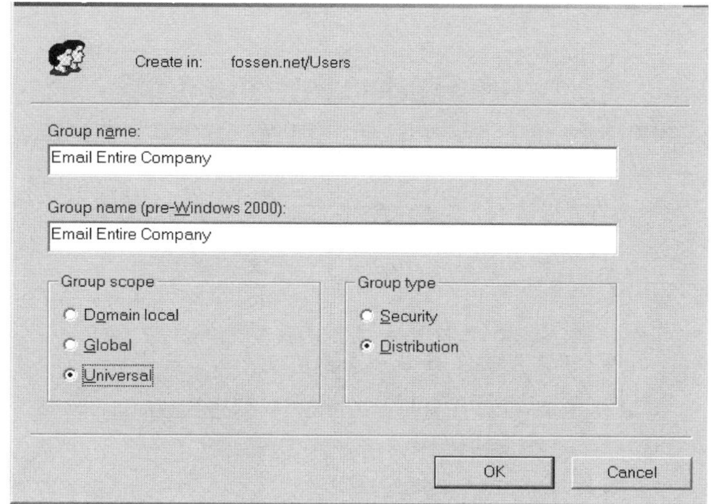

NOTES

Active Directory Users and Computers Snap-In

To create a Global or Universal group in Active Directory, open the Active Directory Users and Computers tool > right-click any Organizational Unit > New > Group. You can create a Local, Global or Universal group. Each group can be marked as either a "distribution" or "security" group; e.g., a "Global distribution group" is not the same thing as a "Global security group."

A distribution group is like an e-mail list, in that you cannot assign rights or permissions to distribution groups. Security groups, on the other hand, are just like groups in Windows NT; i.e., you *can* assign rights/permissions to them. Moreover, Universal security groups are only available in native mode domains, while Universal distribution groups are always available.

To manage the members in a group, simply double-click the group, and go to the Members tab. There you can see the members in the group and add or remove them. What about groups on member servers and standalone systems? To create a Local group on Windows 2000/XP/.NET, open the Computer Management tool > System Tools > Local Users and Groups > right-click on Groups > New Group. You only will be able to create Local groups this way; Global and Universal groups exist in Active Directory.

To manage groups from scripts or the command line, see the list of tools at the end of Chapter 30. To create or manage users and groups in Windows NT 4.0, use the User Manager program (`USRMGR.EXE`).

NOTES

Shared Folder Permissions

- Server Service and SMB/CIFS.
- Share DACLs ignored for local access:
  - Full Control
  - Change
  - Read
- No inheritance of share permissions.
- Multiple share names.
- Net.exe Share

SANS Security Essentials – Windows Security

Shared Folder Permissions

A folder can be shared on the network. This is made possible by the File and Print Sharing service, otherwise known as the Server service, and the Server Message Block (SMB) protocol. You may have heard of the Common Internet File System (CIFS) protocol. But CIFS is not a new protocol; it's just SMB plus a few enhancements. For example, NetBIOS no longer is mandatory for file and print sharing with CIFS like it is with SMB. But SMB and CIFS do the same thing.

Shared folders can be accessed via the following methods:

- My Network Places (i.e., Network Neighborhood)

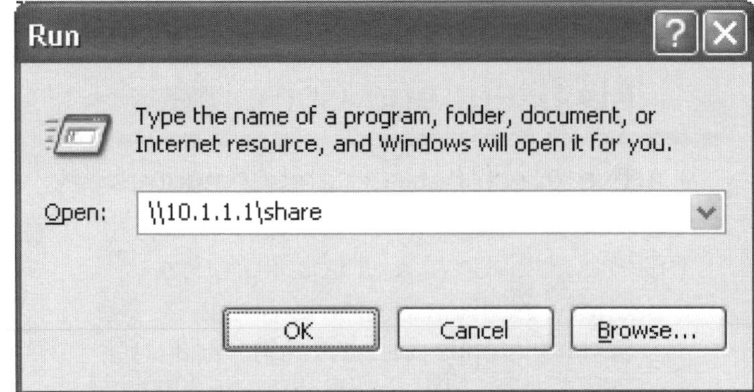
Run
Type the name of a program, folder, document, or Internet resource, and Windows will open it for you.
Open: \\10.1.1.1\share
OK
Cancel
Browse...

- Mapped drive letters (using `NET.EXE` from the command line or using the Tools menu > Map Network Drive option in Windows Explorer)
- Run line (enter `\\ComputerName` or `\\IP-Address` at the Start Menu > Run line)
- Shortcuts (right-click on your desktop or in a folder > New > Shortcut > enter the `\\ComputerName\ShareName` or `\\IP-Address\ShareName` path to the shared folder)

Note

Tip: Create a shortcut to a shared folder in the "\Send" To folder of your profile, then you can right-click on a file and send it to that shared folder in one easy step! To get to the Send To folder in your profile, right-click on the Start button itself and select Explore. This opens up Windows Explorer at your local copy of your profile. You can also place other programs in your Send To folder, such as `NOTEPAD.EXE`, and send files to those programs.

NOTES

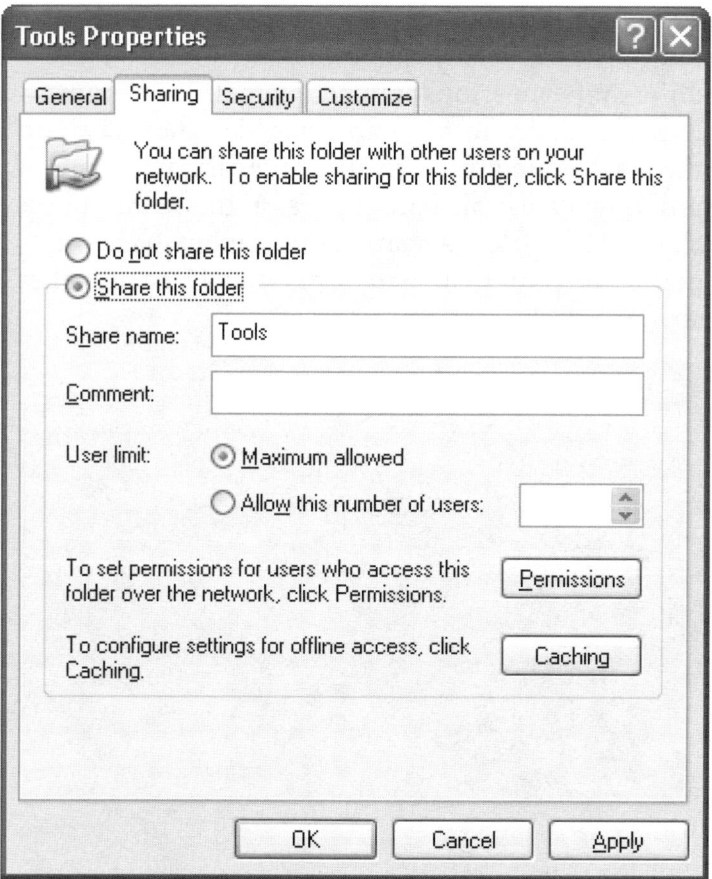

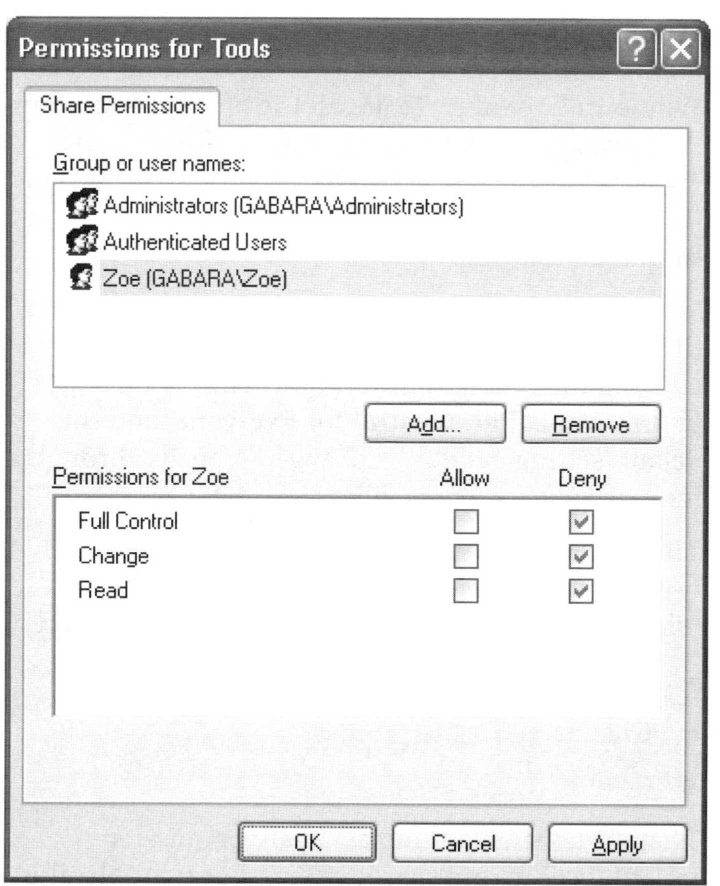

A shared folder has its own Discretionary Access Control List separate from any DACLs in the underlying file system. Shared folder permissions are enforced by the File and Print Sharing Service, not the NTFS file system driver. If a user is sitting locally at a computer and accessing local files with Windows Explorer or `CMD.EXE`, share permissions are simply ignored; share permissions are only enforced when files/folders are being accessed through the SMB protocol, and SMB is not (typically) used during local access.

How to Share Folders

To share a folder with Windows Explorer, right-click the folder > Properties > Sharing tab. To share a folder from the command line, use "`NET.EXE SHARE`" (enter "net help share" for more information). You can also manage shared folders on local or remote systems using the Computer Management tool.

NOTES

Windows XP tries to make folder sharing simpler by hiding configuration options on the Sharing tab in Windows Explorer. To see all the options, including the permissions options, open Windows Explorer > Tools menu > Folder Options > View tab > scroll to the bottom and uncheck the box labeled "Use simple file sharing."

When not using simple file sharing, you can manage the share permissions on a folder's Sharing tab by clicking the Permissions button. The default share permission is Full Control for Everyone, and this default setting cannot be changed globally through a registry value or other switch.

The share permissions are much simpler than the NTFS permissions, and there's no such thing as a "share owner." The possible share permissions are:

- Full Control
- Change
- Read

There is no such a thing as "share permission inheritance" across shares either. For example, if I share the C:\ folder as "C-Drive" with Everyone:Full Control, and I share the C:\Winnt folder as "SystemRoot" with Everyone:Read, when I access the \\Server\SystemRoot share, my share permission is Read, not Full Control. However, beware of overlapping shares! If I access the \\Server\C-Drive share and drill down to the C:\Winnt folder, then my share permission to that folder will be Full Control. It all depends on which sharename I use to access the machine.

A single folder on your hard drive can be shared multiple times using different share names and different permissions for each name! In Windows Explorer, after you've shared a folder once, click on the New Share button to share it again; you can now pull down a list of share names on this folder in the Sharing tab, select a share name, and manage the permissions on that share separately from the other share names.

NOTES

```
Command Prompt

C:\>net share

Share name   Resource                                  Remark

-------------------------------------------------------------------------------
E$           E:\                                       Default share
IPC$                                                   Remote IPC
D$           D:\                                       Default share
IPS$         C:\                                       Inter-Process Sessions
G$           G:\                                       Default share
F$           F:\                                       Default share
ADMIN$       E:\WINDOWS                                Remote Admin
C$           C:\                                       Default share
SharedDocs   E:\DOCUMENTS AND SETTINGS\ALL USERS\DOCUMENTS
The command completed successfully.

C:\>_
```

Hidden Shares

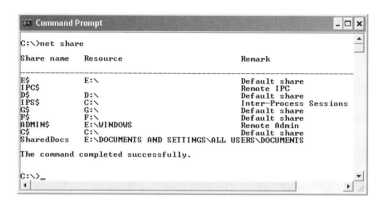

By default, a shared folder is visible in My Network Places and when browsing to the computer through its Universal Naming Convention (UNC) path, e.g., `\\ComputerName` at the Run line. However, if the share name ends with a dollar sign ($), then the share name is not visible in My Network Places. The only way you can access the share is if you enter the full UNC path to it, e.g., `\\ComputerName\HiddenShare$`. You can see a list of all the shares on your computer, both visible and hidden, in both the Computer Management tool and also from the command line using "`NET SHARE`." Looking for unwanted shares, especially hidden shares, should be a part of your regular server audits.

Administrative Shares

By default, the root folder of each drive-lettered volume on a Windows NT/2000/XP/.NET machine has a hidden share. This hidden share is named after the volume itself, e.g., C$, D$, E$, etc. Its permissions are Administrators:Full Control and nothing else. The %SystemRoot% folder also is shared as ADMIN$, but this share also permits read access to the Authenticated Users group. These are all called the "administrative shares," and you can get rid of them on servers if you want by setting a registry value named "AutoShareServer" (REG_DWORD) to zero under the following key:

```
HKEY_LOCAL_MACHINE\System\CurrentControlSet\
Services\LanmanServer\Parameters\
```

There is another built-in share, IPC$, but this is used for inter-process communications and should not be modified. Watch out for hidden shares with names like IPS$ and IPP$ created by malicious users, viruses, or worms that are attempting to avoid notice.

NOTES

Combining NTFS & Share DACLs

- NTFS Permissions:
  - Users: Read
  - Sales: Deny All
  - Amy: Change
- Share Permissions:
  - Everyone: Change
  - Administrators: Read
  - Amy: Read

- Of which groups is Amy a member?
- What are Amy's final permissions then?

SANS Security Essentials – Windows Security

Combining NTFS and Share Permissions

NTFS permissions are always enforced, even when the user is remote. When a folder is shared on an NTFS-formatted volume, both the share permissions and the NTFS permissions must be taken into account when calculating a given user's final, effective permissions to a given share. Calculating a user's effective permissions to a file in a shared folder requires three steps:

1. Assemble a list of all the share permissions the user has to the folder with regards to that user's group memberships. Combine all of these share permissions together. Whenever there is a Deny permission, this Deny permission overrides any other Allow permissions assigned. The permissions left over after this summation and exclusion-by-Deny-permissions are the "final share permissions."
2. Assemble a list of all the NTFS permissions the user has to the file. This includes both explicit and inherited NTFS permissions. Combine all of these NTFS permissions together. Whenever there is a Deny permission, this Deny permission overrides any other Allow permissions assigned. The permissions left over after this summation and exclusion-by-Deny-permissions are the "final NTFS permissions."
3. Examine both the final share and the final NTFS permissions. For any requested action by the user (read, change, delete, etc.) the more restrictive of the two final permissions is the "effective permission." The effective permission is what determines the level of access the user enjoys.

For example, if Amy is a member of three groups, which have the Read, Change, and Full Control share permission, to a folder, then Amy's final share permission to the folder is Full Control. And if Amy also is a member of two other groups which have the Allow:Read and the Deny:Read NTFS permissions, respectively, on a file in that shared folder, then Amy's final NTFS permission to that file is Deny:Full Control. Why is Amy denied *all* NTFS access to the file whatsoever? Because a permission not inherited or explicitly assigned is assumed to be a Deny permission by default. Amy was explicitly assigned Read, but this was overridden by the Deny permission; hence, Amy has no other permissions to the file, inherited or explicit. Finally, Amy's final share permission is Allow:Full Control, and her final NTFS permission is Deny:Full Control, so her effective permission is Deny:Full Control because it is the more restrictive.

NOTES

By combining share and NTFS permissions you can achieve very flexible and precise effective permissions. However, the complexity of the effective permission calculation process is a threat in itself because it is prone to errors. Many administrators, therefore, choose to focus exclusively on NTFS permissions and ignore the share permissions (or view the share permissions as backups to the NTFS permissions).

NOTES

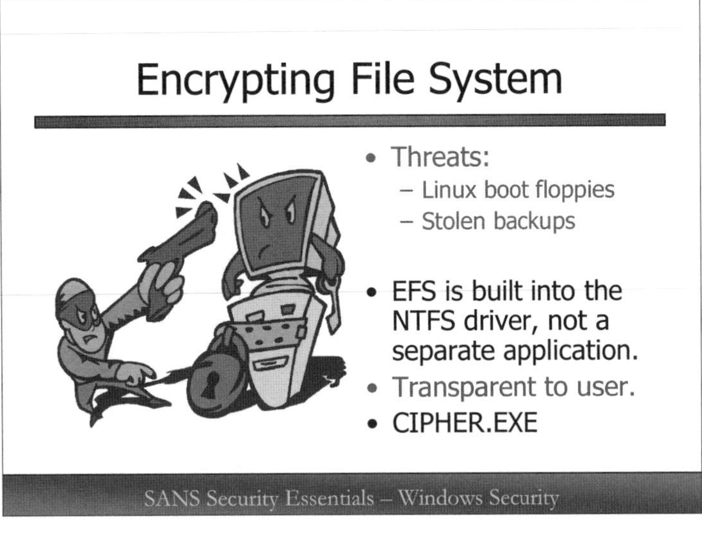

Encrypting File System

NTFS permissions restrict access to files when the computer is booted into Windows, but what if the machine is booted from a Linux floppy disk? What if tape or CD/DVD backups are stolen? What if one's "attacker" is someone with the Full Control permission to one's files? In all these cases, NTFS permissions won't protect the data. What's needed is a form of file encryption that can be combined with NTFS permissions!

The Encrypting File System (EFS) provides encryption of file data on Windows 2000/XP/.NET (it is not available on Windows NT). EFS does not require the installation of any special programs because EFS is built into the NTFS driver itself. EFS is transparent to the user in the same way that NTFS compression is transparent; e.g., if you encrypted a user's My Documents folder, the user wouldn't even know it.

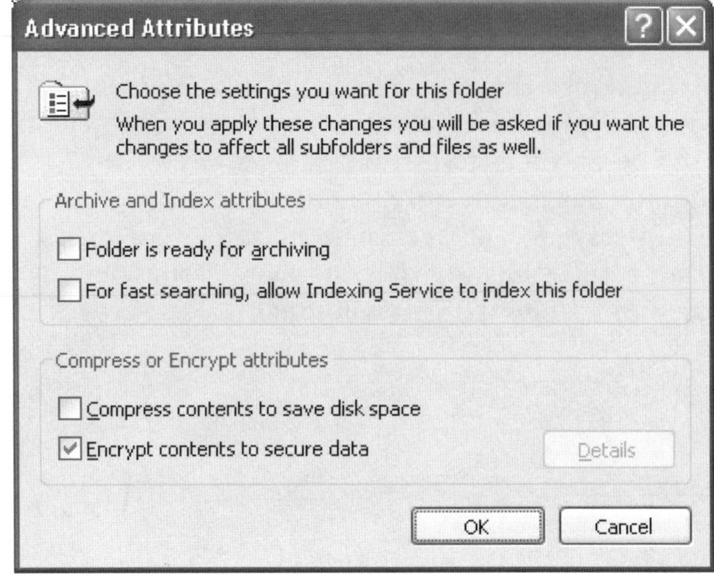

How To Encrypt Files

To encrypt a file or folder, right-click it > Properties > Advanced button > check the Encrypt box. That's it! You can also encrypt/decrypt files from the command line with CIPHER.EXE.

Anything which can be formatted with NTFS by Windows 2000/XP/.NET can use EFS. For example, USB "pen drives" can be NTFS-formatted, mounted with a drive letter, and use EFS. You also can use EFS on any removable drive too, just so long as that drive can be formatted with NTFS.

EFS Implementation Details

- Each file encrypted with its own key:
  - 120-bit DESX (XP/.NET or Win2k+SP2)
  - 168-bit 3DES (with registry change)
  - EFS key stored with file as an attribute.
- EFS key encrypted with user's public key from the user's EFS certificate.
- Certificate created on-the-fly by EFS driver and stored in user's profile.

SANS Security Essentials – Windows Security

EFS Implementation Details

Assuming you've installed Service Pack 2 or later on Windows 2000, or that you have Windows XP/.NET, each encrypted file will have its own randomly-generated 120-bit DESX encryption key (without SP2, Windows 2000 only uses 40-bit keys due to export issues). This DESX key is encrypted with the public key of the user's EFS digital certificate. The user must have the corresponding private key in order to decrypt the DESX key, with which the user can decrypt the file.

Note

If you wish to use 3DES instead of DESX, set the AlgorithmID value (DWORD) to 0x6603 under `HKEY_LOCAL_MACHINE\SOFTWARE\Microsoft\Windows NT\CurrentVersion\EFS\` in the registry. For Windows XP/.NET there also is a Group Policy option to enable this.

How did the user get an EFS certificate? The EFS driver can generate one for the user on-the-fly the first time a file is encrypted. The certificate's private key is itself encrypted, based on the user's password, and stored in the user's profile. If the user has a roaming profile, then her EFS certificate and private key follows her around from machine to machine.

NOTES

NOTES

EFS Recovery (1 of 2)

- Two keys are stored with each file:
  - One is the user's
  - Other is the recovery key
- Either can be used to decrypt the file.
- The recovery key is encrypted with the recovery certificate's public key.
- On Windows 2000, the recovery certificate is in the Administrator's profile.

SANS Security Essentials – Windows Security

Note

With `EFSINFO.EXE` you can see which certificates can be used to decrypt and recover an encrypted file.

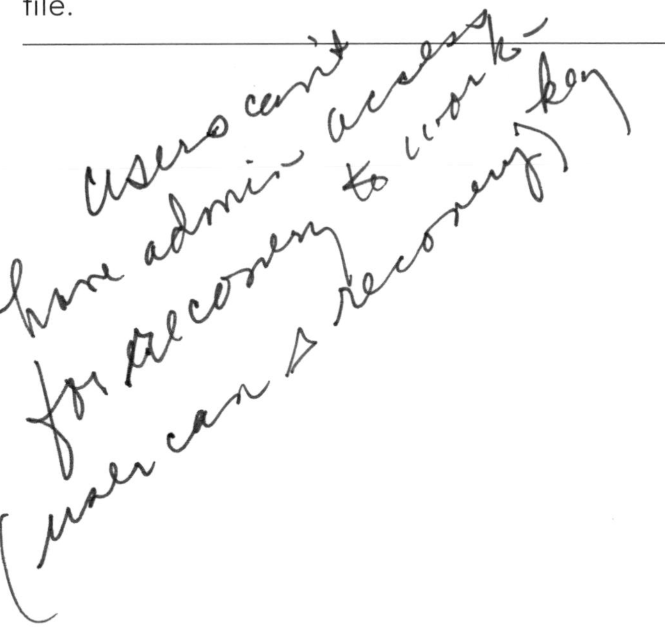

Recovery of Encrypted Data

If a user loses or damages his EFS private key, the user's encrypted data can still be recovered. Each encrypted file actually has two copies of its DESX key attached to it: one copy is encrypted with the user's EFS public key, the second copy is encrypted with the public key of the EFS Data Recovery Certificate. Where did this other certificate come from?

On Windows 2000, the EFS driver generates a Data Recovery Certificate on-the-fly the first time a file is encrypted. This certificate and its private key are deposited into the profile of the local Administrator account. Hence, anyone who can log on as the local Administrator can decrypt any file on that computer.

NOTES

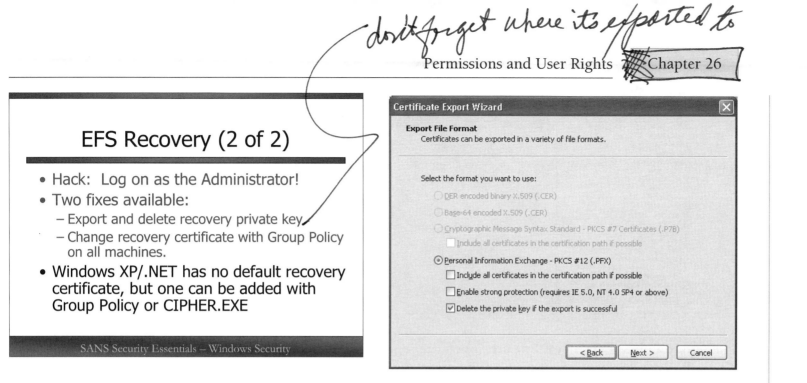

EFS Recovery (2 of 2)

- Hack: Log on as the Administrator!
- Two fixes available:
  - Export and delete recovery private key
  - Change recovery certificate with Group Policy on all machines.
- Windows XP/.NET has no default recovery certificate, but one can be added with Group Policy or CIPHER.EXE

SANS Security Essentials – Windows Security

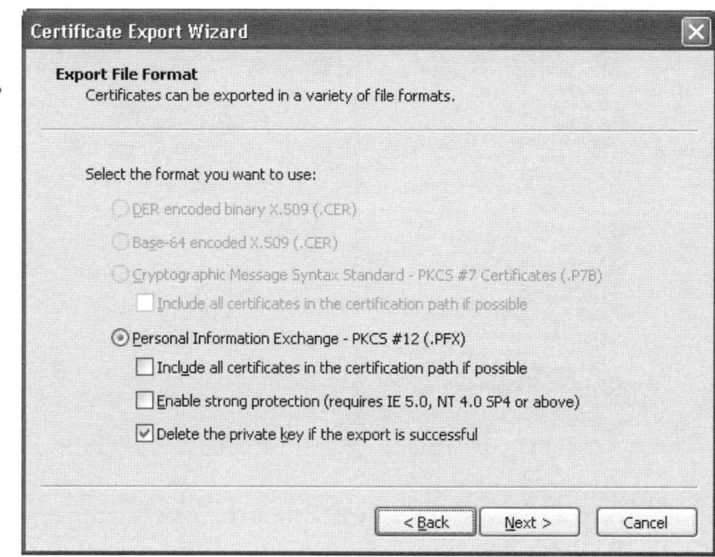

On Windows XP/.NET, there is no Data Recovery Certificate by default (but one can be added using "`CIPHER.EXE /R`"). Why no Recovery Certificate? Because it was discovered that simply deleting the local SAM accounts database file on Windows 2000 caused the computer to create a new one when it was rebooted, that is to say, a new *generic* SAM database with a blank password on the Administrator account. Hence, anyone with physical control of the laptop could reboot it from a Linux floppy disk and do the same! (Actually, this vulnerability wasn't "discovered," it was clearly documented in Windows Help and the Resource Kit, along with the steps necessary to block the attack.)

On Windows 2000, therefore, it is critical to either remove the Recovery Agent's private key from the machine or change the Recovery Agent Certificate entirely (and not put the private key of the new certificate on the computer).

To make a backup copy of the Recovery private key and remove it from the machine, log on as the local Administrator > execute `MMC.EXE` at the Run line > File menu > Add/Remove Snap-In > Add button > double-click the Certificates snap-in > select My User Account > Finish > Close > OK > navigate to the Certificates\Personal container and right-click the Administrator certificate with the File Recovery intended purpose > All Tasks > Export > Next > select Yes > Next > check the box to "Delete the private key if the export is successful" > Next > enter a difficult password > Next > save the file directly to a floppy disk > Next > Finish. Make a copy of the floppy disk.

To change the Recovery Certificate entirely on all Windows 2000/XP/.NET machines throughout the network, use Group Policy. This will push out a new Recovery certificate, but not its private key.

NOTES

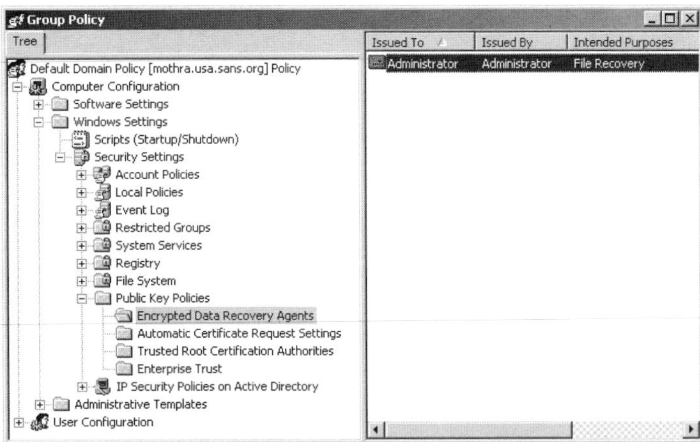

The Group Policy steps in outline are : open the Group Policy Object > Computer Configuration > Security Settings > Public Key Policies > right-click Encrypted Data Recovery Agents > New > Encrypted Recovery Agent. This will launch a Wizard that will help you install the desired recovery agent certificate(s). Select Add instead if a user already has been given an EFS Recovery Certificate. This action will push a new Recovery Certificate out to the machines, but it does not push out its private key, hence, the attack is blocked.

NOTES

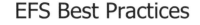

EFS Best Practices

- Strong password policy.
- SYSKEY.EXE protects EFS private key.
- Service Pack 2 or later on Windows 2000.
- Encrypt folders, not files:
  - My Documents
  - %TEMP%
  - Local print spool folder
- Hibernation file cannot be encrypted, but...
- Paging file cannot be encrypted, but...
- Secure the recovery certificate!

SANS Security Essentials – Windows Security

Encrypting File System Best Practices

Keep in mind that password policy is critically important for protecting EFS-encrypted data. Forget all the fancy exploits and off-line cryptanalysis, if an attacker steals your laptop and can guess your password, then all your files can be decrypted simply by opening them! Remember that Windows 2000/XP/.NET support 127-character long passphrases, not just 14-character passwords.

To enhance the protection of all your private encryption keys, including your EFS private key, go to the Run line and execute `SYSKEY.EXE`. The SYSKEY tool is enabled by default and cannot be disabled. The 128-bit RC4 encryption key it manages (the "System Key") not only protects password hashes in the accounts database but also private keys. Click the Update button in the `SYSKEY.EXE` tool, and you can enter a password from which the key is derived. This password must be entered when the laptop reboots, or else the boot-up sequence simply hangs, and no private keys can be decrypted. You also can store the System Key on a floppy disk, but this is inconvenient and somewhat pointless on laptops since the floppy will likely be stolen too. The default is to store the key "locally;" i.e., chop it into pieces and store the pieces in obscure places in the registry, but no password or special floppy disk is required to reboot in this case.

Remember, on Windows 2000, make sure to apply Service Pack 2 or later because without SP2, EFS uses only 40-bit DESX keys.

Encrypt folders instead of individual files. When a file is created in an encrypted folder, the file never exists on the hard drive in cleartext; hence, there are no magnetic traces of the cleartext lurking in forgotten sectors. If you want to wipe the unused sectors of a drive to erase any remnants of cleartext data, use "`CIPHER.EXE /W`." Good folders to encrypt are My Documents, the user's Temp folder, and the local print spool folder.

The hibernation file (`HIBERFIL.SYS`) and the paging file (`PAGEFILE.SYS`) cannot be encrypted, yet they may contain sensitive cleartext data. Consider disabling the use of a paging file (XP) or setting it to its smallest allowed value (2000). But make sure adequate RAM is installed. Also consider disabling the ability to hibernate the system, or, at a minimum, train users to close their sensitive documents before hibernating.

NOTES

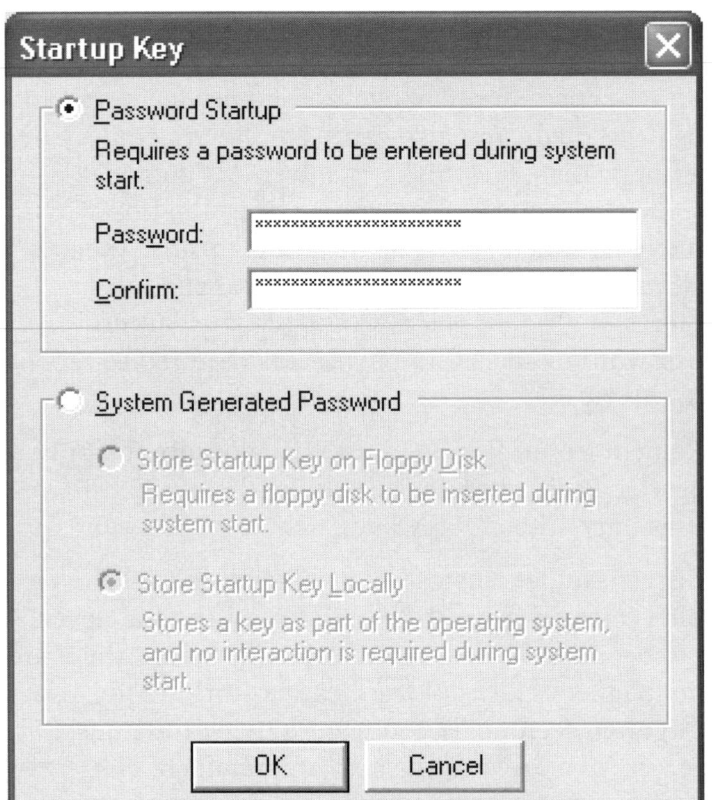

Finally, make sure you change the Recovery Agent Certificate and/or get its private key off your Windows 2000 computers! By far the easiest way to do this is through Group Policy. Remember that Windows XP does not have a default Recovery Certificate, but you can still use Group Policy to add one.

Printer Permissions (1 of 2)

- Everyone: Print
- Delegate authority
  - Manage Documents
- Printer drivers:
  - Any user can install.
  - They run in System context: Trojans!
  - Prevent installation.

SANS Security Essentials – Windows Security

NOTES

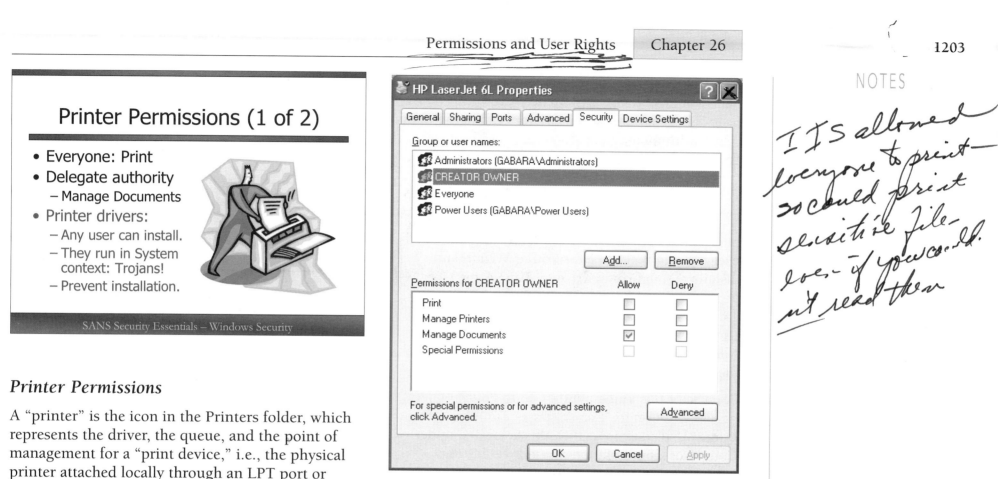

Printer Permissions

A “printer” is the icon in the Printers folder, which represents the driver, the queue, and the point of management for a “print device,” i.e., the physical printer attached locally through an LPT port or directly connected to the network.

Printers can be shared on the network so that other users can send print jobs to them. The risk of denial of service or other attacks is very slight, but the principle of least privilege still applies, so only share the printers you want shared. To control whether a printer is shared, right-click the printer > Properties > Sharing tab.

Printers also have access control lists: go to the Start menu > Settings > Printers > right-click a printer icon > Properties > Security tab. The following are the available permissions:

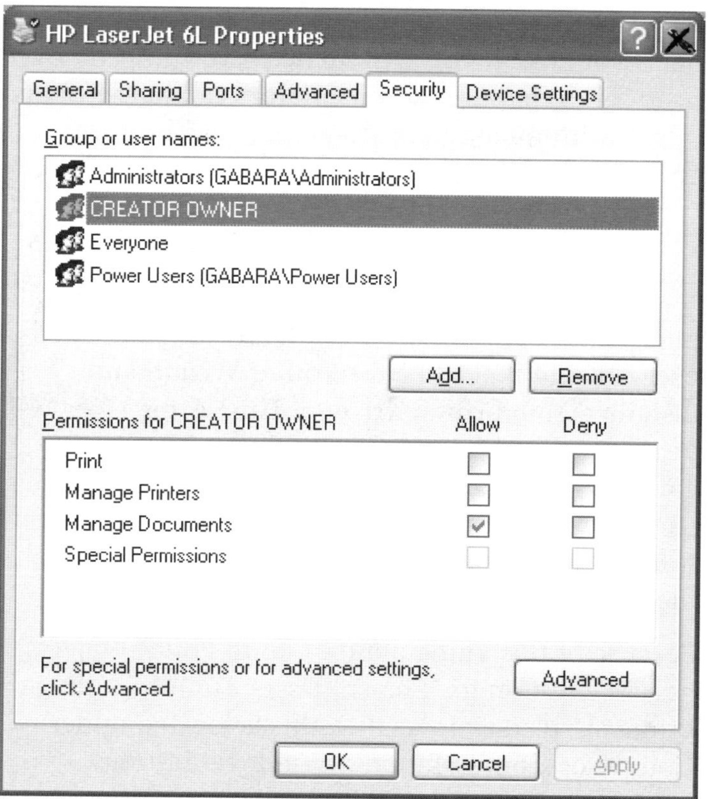

- Print
- Manage Printers
- Manage Documents
- Read Permissions
- Change Permissions
- Take Ownership

One of the default permissions is Everyone:Print. This should be changed to Authenticated Users:Print, or similar. Note that CREATOR OWNER has the Manage Documents permission,

NOTES

which permits each user to pause/cancel only his or her own jobs. If you wish to delegate authority over printers so that non-administrators can pause them, purge print queues, etc., then there is a built-in group named Print Operators for just this purpose.

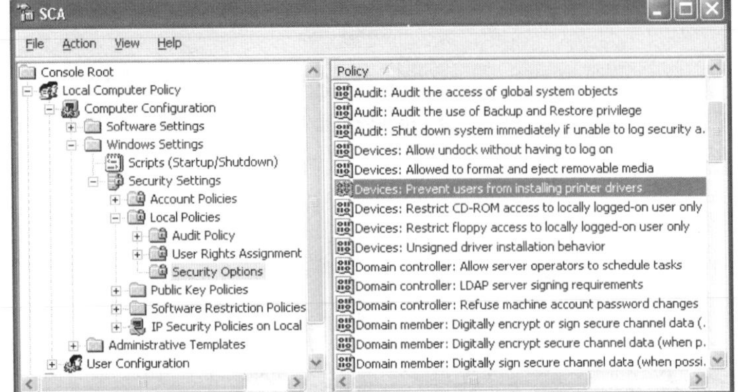

Prevent Users From Installing Printer Drivers

A related permission is the right to be able to install new printer drivers. By default, any authenticated user can run the Add New Printer Wizard and install custom printer drivers. This seems innocuous, but printer drivers run in System context; hence, any user can introduce code of their choice and have it executed with System privileges. A modified printer driver could, for example, add the user to the local Administrators group.

Because of this vulnerability, Group Policy Objects have the option to "Prevent Users From Installing Printer Drivers;" In a GPO, this is located under Computer Configuration > Windows Settings > Security Settings > Local Policies > Security Options. This can be found in both local and domain-based GPOs.

The downside to this, of course, is that users won't be able to install their own printers, or, even more commonly, to fix their printing problems by deleting and reinstalling printer drivers themselves.

NOTES

Printer Permissions (2 of 2)

- Web-Based Printing
  - /Printers virtual folder on IIS
  - Manage printers
  - Submit print jobs over HTTP to IIS
- Removal steps...

SANS Security Essentials – Windows Security

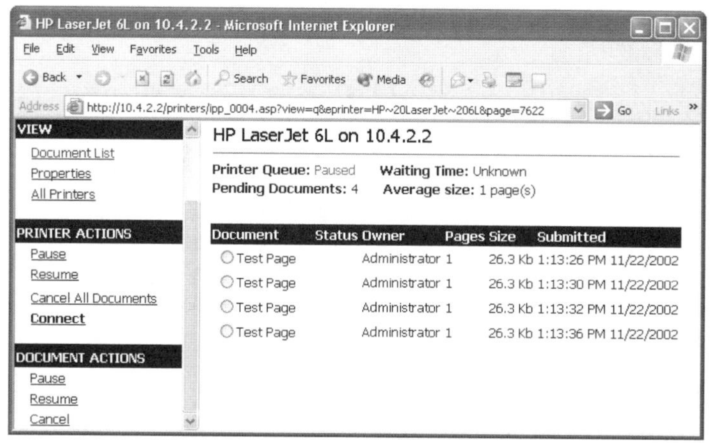

Web-Based Printing

A not-so-benign printing facility can be found on Internet Information Server (IIS). Windows 2000's IIS 5.0 sports a virtual folder named "/Printers" by default. When you browse this folder, its web pages allow you to manage print queues over the Internet just as you can with the Start > Settings > Printers folder (but only printers on the IIS server itself). Moreover, you can even submit print jobs to the IIS server using HTTP! A buffer overflow exploit against this facility was discovered (of course) and fixed with Service Pack 2, but there's no point in waiting around for the next exploit to be published.

Unfortunately, if you remove the /Printers virtual folder in IIS manually, the folder may magically reappear again. Microsoft considers it a mistake on your part to have removed it! To permanently get rid of it, you must edit the Group Policy Object which manages that setting. On a stand-alone IIS server, or in a network that isn't using Active Directory Group Policies, you must edit the local Group Policy Object.

To disable web-based printing support in the local Group Policy Object, go to the Run line > execute `MMC.EXE` > Console menu > Add/Remove Snap-In > Add > highlight Group Policy > Add > Finish > Close > OK > Local Computer Policy > Computer Configuration > Administrative Templates > Printers > double-click Web-Based Printing > select Disabled > OK.

Fortunately, in Windows .NET Server you simply can opt out of web-based printing support when you install IIS. Additionally, IIS is not installed by default on Windows .NET, and the user, upon choosing to install IIS, is forced to run a hardening wizard at install-time.

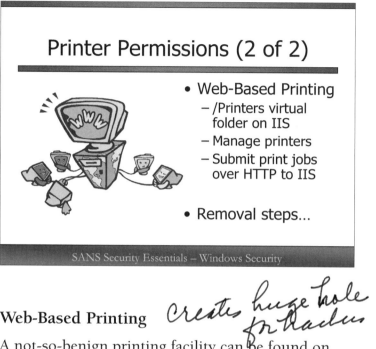

NOTES

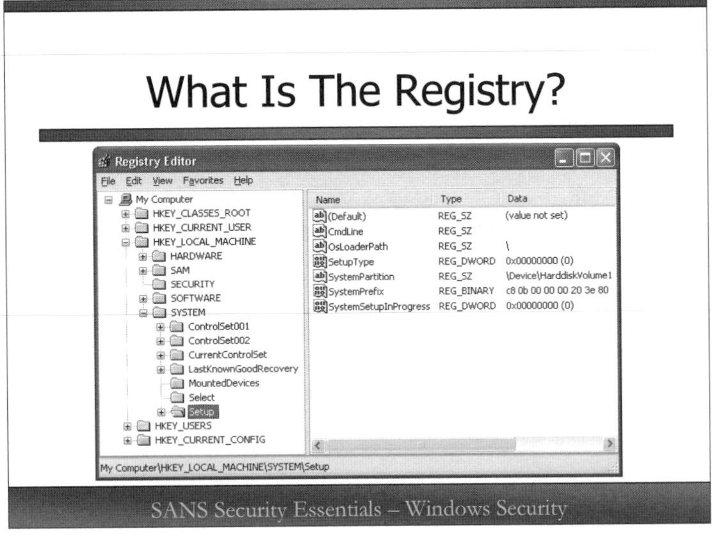

What Is The Registry?

Virtually all configuration settings for the computer's hardware, operating system, applications, and its users' preferences are stored in a special miniature database called the "registry." The registry can be modified directly using scripts, various command-line tools like `REGINI.EXE`, and graphical tools like `REGEDT32.EXE` and `REGEDIT.EXE`.

When using `REGEDIT.EXE`, the registry appears to be structured very similarly to the folders on the hard drive. The yellow-looking folders are called "keys," and the file-looking objects in these keys are called "values." If you double-click a value, a dialog box will display two things: the "type" of value it is (REG_DWORD, REG_BINARY, REG_SZ, REG_MULTI_SZ, or REG_EXPAND_SZ) and the "data" in the value; i.e., to what that value is set equal. You can create your own keys and values using the Edit > New menu option.

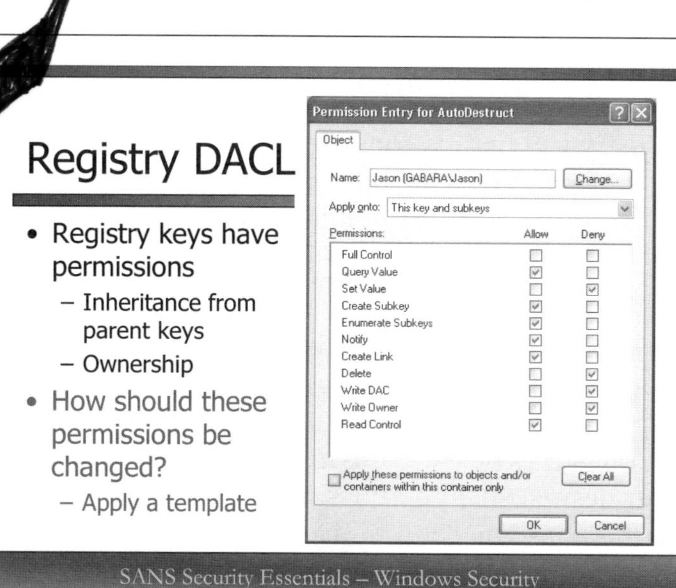

Registry Key Permissions

Because hundreds of security-related values are stored in the registry, it is important to be able to regulate access to it. Each key in the registry has its own owner, auditing SACL, and permissions DACL. The best tool to use to manage these settings is `REGEDT32.EXE`.

To manage the owner, SACL, and DACL of a registry key, open `REGEDT32.EXE` > highlight the key > Security menu > Permissions > Advanced button.

Which Permissions Should Be Changed?

Of the thousands of keys in the registry, which should have their default permissions changed? There is no simple answer. You could spend a couple months reading Microsoft Q-articles, books on hacking, and security bulletins in order to compile a list of keys to be secured, but this would be a Herculean effort. Fortunately, others have already done it for you! And there are tools that can be used to automate the entire process. The next chapter will discuss how to use security templates and Group Policy to solve the problem.

NOTES

NOTES

Remote Registry Service

- Registry is remotely accessible.
- Disable the Remote Registry Service to prevent all access.
- Permissions on the WinReg key are interpreted as the share DACL.
- Registry key and share permissions combine to determine final DACL.

SANS Security Essentials – Windows Security

Remote Registry Service

The registry can be accessed remotely. In REGEDIT.EXE, for example, pull down the Registry menu > Connect Network Registry > enter the name or IP address of a remote system > OK. This is made possible by the Remote Registry Service (REGSVC.EXE); hence, if you wish to prevent all remote registry access, stop and disable this service in the Administrative Tools > Services applet.

Be aware, though, that many management tools require the Remote Registry Service to be running on the target computers. Disable the service to enhance security, but be prepared to enable it again tomorrow. Isn't there another alternative?

Remote Registry Share Permissions

Registry key permissions are always enforced against local or remote users, but you also can restrict who can access the registry remotely at all. In effect, there are share permissions on the registry as a whole!

How you manage these registry share permissions, though, is somewhat strange. There's no special tool or property sheet. Instead, there is a special key in the registry whose permissions are *interpreted as* your desired share permissions. Whatever permissions you set on this key regulate not only access to that single, seemingly-insignificant key but also the share permissions for the registry as a whole. You manage these permissions with REGEDT32.EXE, just like any other key. The name of the key is "winreg," and its full path is

```
HKEY_LOCAL_MACHINE\System\CurrentControlSet\
Control\SecurePipeServers\winreg\
```

Note that the winreg key has a subkey named AllowedPaths. The value(s) in this subkey define the registry paths that will still be remotely readable despite your share permissions on the winreg key! Just disable the Remote Registry Service completely if you're really paranoid.

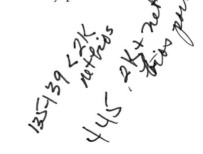

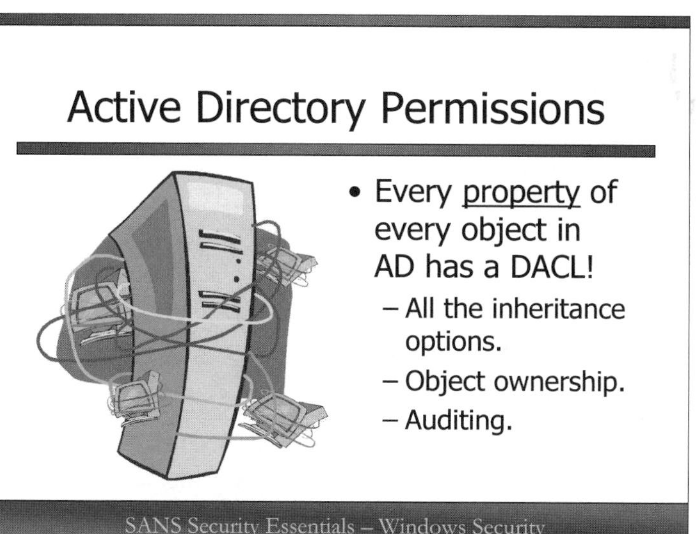

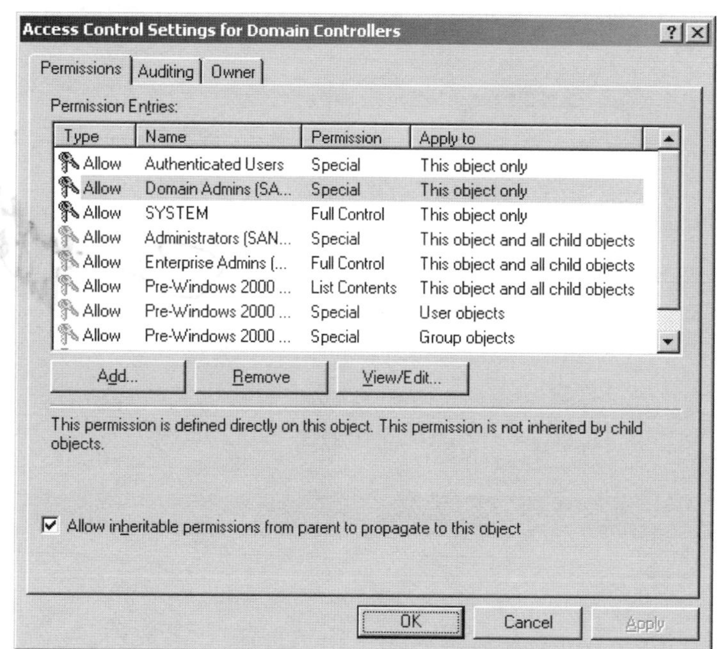

Active Directory Permissions

As discussed before, Active Directory is the accounts-and-everything-else database which is installed on a Windows 2000/.NET Server when it is promoted to become a domain controller. No discussion of permissions would be complete without at least mentioning Active Directory permissions.

Every *property* of every object in the Active Directory (AD) database has its own permissions DACL and auditing SACL! These access control lists also support the full range of inheritance options, just like in NTFS, and every object in AD has an owner for which CREATOR OWNER permissions can be assigned.

It is beyond the scope of this course, but if you have an Active Directory domain controller available to you, you can edit AD permissions by opening the Active Directory Users and Computers snap-in > right-click any OU > View > select Advanced Features > right-click again on any object or container in AD > Properties > Security tab > Advanced button. This will show the familiar Permissions, Auditing and Owner tabs.

NOTES

Delegation of Authority In AD

- AD permissions are the basis for delegation of authority in the domain.
  - Each OU could have its own "OU Admins" group that has Full Control over that OU, but not have authority anywhere else in the domain.
  - Delegation of Authority Wizard

SANS Security Essentials – Windows Security

Delegation Of Authority In Active Directory

Consider an example of how property-level ACLs can be leveraged. A user account has many properties: name, phone, fax, e-mail address, password, etc. Each one of these properties can have its own separate DACL and SACL. Domain Admins could have Full Control over all the properties; the Help Desk group could be given permissions to reset only the password and unlock the account; the Human Resources group could be given exclusive access to sensitive fields like birth date and Social Security number; the Secretaries group could be given Write access to the phone-related fields only; and the user himself might be given the change password permission and nothing else! And because AD supports inheritance, the foregoing permissions could be set for an Organizational Unit (OU) or for the entire domain and then inherited by all the user accounts in that OU or domain.

Just as you can delegate authority over a shared folder through its permissions, so you can delegate authority over user accounts, groups, computer accounts, and everything else in AD through the permissions on the properties of AD objects. And you can track precisely who-is-doing-what because each of these properties has its own audit settings as well.

Collectively, property-level ACLs in Active Directory are one of the most important and least understood security advantages of Windows 2000/.NET, yet they form the foundation for all delegation of authority in AD networks. In fact, to simplify the delegation of authority through AD permissions, there is a Delegation of Control Wizard! To launch the wizard, right-click on any OU > Delegate Control. The wizard will ask you a series of questions and then append additional permissions to the DACL of the OU you selected.

NOTES

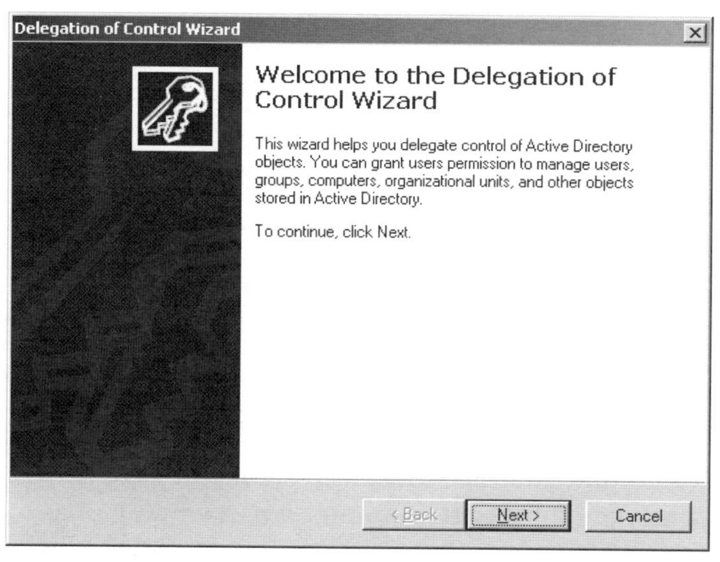
Delegation of Control Wizard
Welcome to the Delegation of Control Wizard
This wizard helps you delegate control of Active Directory objects. You can grant users permission to manage users, groups, computers, organizational units, and other objects stored in Active Directory.
To continue, click Next.
< Back
Next >
Cancel

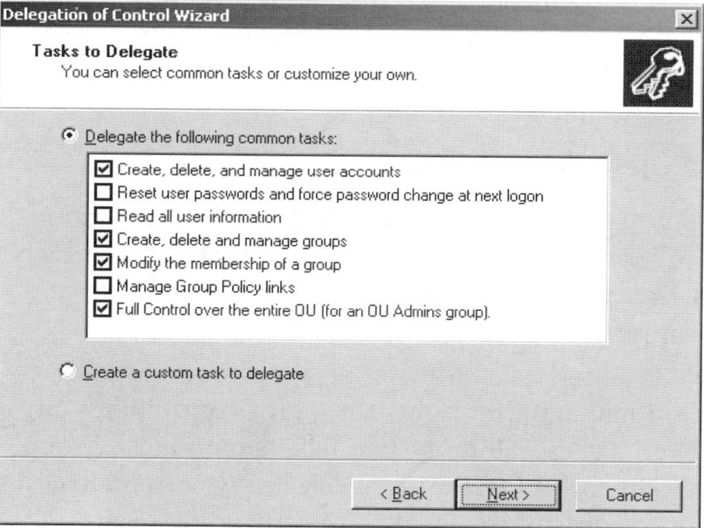
Delegation of Control Wizard
Tasks to Delegate
You can select common tasks or customize your own.
Delegate the following common tasks:
Create, delete, and manage user accounts
Reset user passwords and force password change at next logon
Read all user information
Create, delete and manage groups
Modify the membership of a group
Manage Group Policy links
Full Control over the entire OU (for an OU Admins group).
Create a custom task to delegate
< Back
Next >
Cancel

NOTES

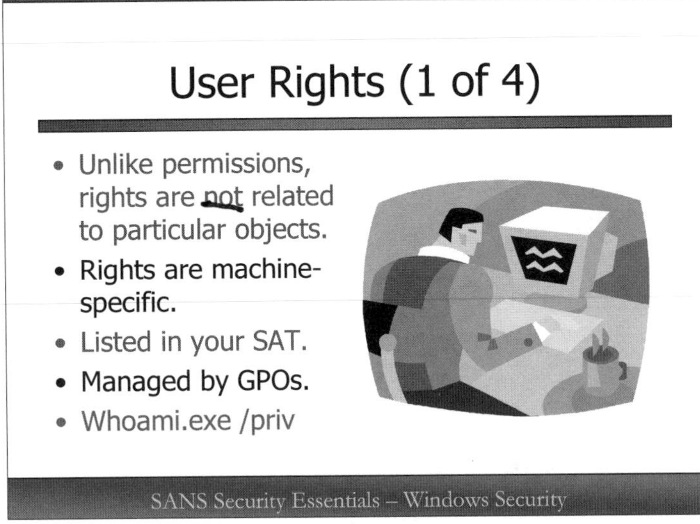

User Rights (1 of 4)
Unlike permissions, rights are not related to particular objects.
Rights are machine-specific.
Listed in your SAT.
Managed by GPOs.
Whoami.exe /priv
SANS Security Essentials – Windows Security

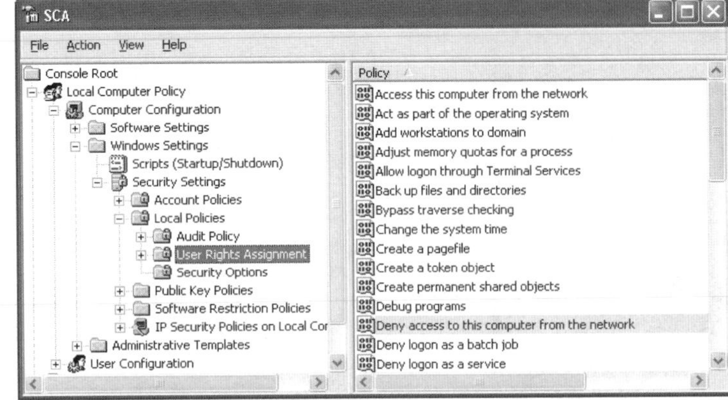

User Rights

A permission always is attached to some particular object, like having Read access to a file or having Full Control over a registry key. A "user right," on the other hand, references a general capability that is not tied to any particular object.

For example, the "Take Ownership" right permits one to take ownership of any object, and the owner of an object can change its permissions in any way the owner desires. How is this possible? Because that capability is hard-wired into the operating system; i.e., it is a "right" which owners enjoy over their objects because Microsoft wants it that way. Another right is "Force Shutdown From A Remote System," which does not refer to any particular object but is a dangerous capability one certainly would want to be able to restrict.

Recall that your Security Access Token (SAT) is constructed by your computer when you log on. Your SAT lists the Security ID numbers (SIDs) of all the groups to which you belong, but your SAT also contains a list of all your user rights on that particular machine. That's an important point: rights are machine-specific, hence, I might have the "Take Ownership" right on one computer but not on another.

Note

If you have the *Resource Kit* installed, you can see what rights you have on your computer by opening a command-prompt window and running `whoami.exe /priv`.

You manage user rights through Group Policy, but even a stand-alone system has its own local Group Policy Object (GPO). The easiest way to manage user rights in the local GPO is by going to the Administrative Tools folder > Local Security Policy > Local Policies > User Rights Assignment. Here, you can double-click on any listed user right and add/

NOTES

remove groups or users from that right. You also can manage user rights with scripts or command-line tools like NTRIGHTS.EXE (see the table of tools in Chapter 30).

What User Rights Exist?

The following is a table of the user rights with a short description of each. Quickly browse the list, and then we'll discuss a few of the more important rights for security.

User Right	Description
Access this computer from the network	Determines who is permitted to connect to the computer over the network using a protocol requiring user authentication. It does not apply to any packets whatsoever.
*Act as part of the operating system	Allows a process to authenticate as any user or to create a SAT with any SIDs and rights desired. **This is an extremely dangerous right.**
Add workstations to domain	Determines who can join workstations to the domain. Authenticated users have this right and can create up to ten computer accounts in the domain, but a modification to an Active Directory property can increase or decrease this number.
Back up files and directories	Determines who can circumvent NTFS permissions for the sake of making backups.
Bypass traverse checking	Determines whether a user can traverse directory trees even though the user may not have NTFS permissions on some of the traversed directories. This privilege does not allow the user to list the contents of a directory, only to traverse it to access subdirectories to which the user does have sufficient permissions.
Change the system time	Determines who can change the time and date on the internal clock of the computer. This right seems trivial, but clock modifications can cause Kerberos authentication to fail or render log data less useful.
Create a pagefile	Determines who can create pagefiles or change their size or locations.
*Create a token object	Allows a process running under the context of an account with this right to create a SAT for the sake of accessing local resources. **This is a dangerous right.**
Create permanent shared objects	Determines which accounts can be used by kernel-mode processes to create an object in the object manager's cache. This is rarely used.
*Debug programs	Determines which users can attach a debugger to any process. **This is a powerful and dangerous user right.**
Deny access to this computer from the network	Determines who is not permitted to connect to the computer over the network using a protocol requiring user authentication. This overrides any other right that would otherwise allow the user to connect.
Deny logon as a batch job	Determines which accounts are denied logons as batch jobs.
Deny logon as a service	Determines which service accounts are prevented from registering a process as a Windows service. This policy overrides any other right that would otherwise permit this action.
Deny logon locally	Determines who is prevented from logging on interactively at the computer. This overrides any other right that would otherwise permit an interactive logon.
Enable computer and user accounts to be trusted for delegation	Determines who can enable the "Trusted for Delegation" value in the properties of a user or computer account.
Force shutdown from a remote system	Determines who is allowed to shut down a computer from a remote location.
Generate security audits	Determines who can write events to the security Event Log.
Increase quotas	Determines which service accounts can increase the processor quota assigned to another process.
Increase scheduling priority	Determines who can change the multitasking priority of a process with Task Manager.

NOTES

Load and unload device drivers	Determines who can load and unload device drivers.
Lock pages in memory	Determines who can keep data in RAM and out of any paging files.
Log on as a batch job	Allows a user account to be used to execute scheduled tasks and to log on for purposes that require neither interactive nor network logons.
Log on as a service	Determines which accounts can register a process as a Windows service.
Log on locally	Determine who can log on at the computer interactively, i.e., at the keyboard.
Manage auditing and security log	Determines who can manage audit settings (SACLs) on NTFS files, registry keys, Active Directory objects, etc. Also determines who can clear the security Event Log.
Modify firmware environment values	Determines who can modify environmental variables that affect the system as a whole. This does not include any user's personal environmental variables.
Profile single process	Determines who can use Performance Monitor and similar tools to monitor user-launched processes.
Profile system performance	Determines who can use Performance Monitor and similar tools to monitor the performance of operating system processes.
Remove computer from docking station	Determines who can gracefully disconnect a laptop computer from its docking station.
Replace a process level token	Determines who can replace the SAT of a subprocess of the current process.
*Restore files and directories	Determines who can circumvent NTFS permissions for the sake of restoring files from backups. **This is a dangerous right because it permits a malicious user, with the right tools, to change any NTFS permissions and to assign (not take) ownership of a file to any desired user account.**
Shut down the system	Determines who can gracefully shut down the computer while logged on locally.
Synchronize directory service data	Not currently used.
*Take ownership of files or other objects	Determines who can make themselves the owner of Active Directory objects, NTFS files and folders, threads, processes, printers, and registry keys. The owner of an object can change the permissions on that object in any way desired. **This is, perhaps, the most dangerous right.**

NOTES

User Rights (2 of 4)

- Allow/Deny Logon Locally
  - Restrict who can log on interactively, i.e., at a computer's keyboard.
- Allow/Deny Logon Over The Network
  - Restrict who can remotely authenticate to a computer.

SANS Security Essentials – Windows Security

Allow/Deny Local and Over-the-Network Logons

To help isolate a server from certain users or groups, you should assign the "Deny Access To This Computer Over The Network" and "Deny Logon Locally" user rights to those users or groups. The deny-style rights are useful for defining exceptions to a general policy.

On the other hand, if you wish to deny everyone access to a server except for a certain group, then assign the "Access This Computer From The Network" and "Log On Locally" rights to just that group. For example, the database servers in the Human Resources department might be restricted only to Administrators and members of the HR group.

NOTES

User Rights (3 of 4)

- Take Ownership of Files and Objects
  - The "owner" of an object can change its permissions in any way desired.
  - Only Administrators have this by default.
  - Objects include files, folders, printers, AD containers, registry keys, processes and threads.

SANS Security Essentials – Windows Security

Very dangerous

Take Ownership of Files or Other Objects

It is worth mentioning again that perhaps the most dangerous user right is "Take Ownership of Files or Other Objects." Again, perhaps the most dangerous user right is "Take Ownership of Files or Other Objects." The owner of an object can change its permissions in any way desired. Objects that have owners include NTFS files and folders, Active Directory objects, printers, registry keys, processes, and threads.

For example, a malicious user with this right could take ownership of an administrator's user account and change its permissions so that that user could reset the password. Similar steps could be taken to plant Trojans on domain controllers, copy or modify database records, hijack privileged processes, and so on. Hence, you should audit regularly who has this right.

User Rights (4 of 4)

- Backup/Restore Files and Directories
  - Think of these as the "circumvent NTFS permissions" rights.
  - Use Group Policy to delegate the Backup right, but reserve the Restore right for Domain Admins only.

SANS Security Essentials – Windows Security

NOTES

Through Group Policy, each OU could have its own "Backup OU" group.

nasty

Backup/Restore Files and Directories

The seemingly innocuous backup/restore rights actually are quite dangerous. Think of these as the "Ignore NTFS Permissions" user rights. Also, if a user has both of these rights, she can assign ownership of a file to anyone she pleases, using well-known hacking tools.

Since rights are configured on a per-machine basis, consider limiting the allocation of these rights to non-administrators only on servers or workstations with low security priorities. Consider creating a custom group with only the "Back Up Files and Directories" right (and not the restore version) so that you can delegate the ability to make backups, but then reserve for Domain Admins the right to restore those files when necessary. Group Policy will simplify greatly the distribution of these custom rights when you have hundreds of machines.

NOTES

Summary

- Why authenticate?
- NTFS Permissions
  - DACLs and ACEs
- Share Permissions
  - Hidden Shares
- EFS Encryption
  - Recovery
- Printer Permissions
  - Driver Installation
- Registry Permissions
  - Remote Access
- Active Directory
  - Permissions
  - Delegation of Authority
- User Rights
  - Group Policy

SANS Security Essentials – Windows Security

Summary

So, why have user accounts at all? Why go through all the trouble of Active Directory, Kerberos, NTLM, SIDs, SATs, and all the rest? The purpose of this chapter was to discuss the two primary benefits of authenticating users: permissions and user rights. (The third benefit, auditing, will be discussed in Chapter 30.) Indeed, selective access control is impossible without authentication, and authentication is pointless unless you intend to use that information for something, i.e., rights, permissions, or auditing.

We started out with a discussion of NTFS and shared folder permissions, including an overview of how they can be combined. NTFS, however, doesn't protect data from hackers who have physical access to computers or who have stolen backup media; for this we need encryption.

The Encrypting File System (EFS) is a feature of NTFS itself and therefore its use is transparent to users. It provides—with Windows 2000 SP2—up to 168-bit 3DES encryption of each protected file, and a recovery facility is provided through Group Policy.

Printer permissions often are overlooked, as well as are registry key permissions, both which are an important part of creating a hardened machine—especially registry key permissions. The registry is the equivalent of the entire /etc directory on a Unix-based system.

Though beyond the scope of this course, Active Directory permissions are critically important for the security of your network. Every property of every object in the AD database has its own ACL. AD permissions are the foundation of all delegation of authority in Windows-based networks.

Finally, the other benefit of user authentication was discussed. User rights define general capabilities not related to particular objects but to system-wide tasks a user might be allowed to perform. The most important of these rights was the "Take Ownership" right.

Chapter 27

Security Templates and Group Policy

NOTES

NOTES

Security Templates
And Group Policy

SANS Security Essentials V:
Windows Security

SANS Security Essentials – Windows Security

Security Templates and Group Policy

This chapter will discuss one of the best tools for automating security configuration changes, Microsoft's Security Configuration and Analysis (SCA) snap-in, and some of the most important changes to make with it, such as password policy, lockout policy, and null user session restrictions. We also will briefly discuss Group Policy Objects and the many security configuration changes that can be made through them throughout the domain.

In particular, this chapter will cover:

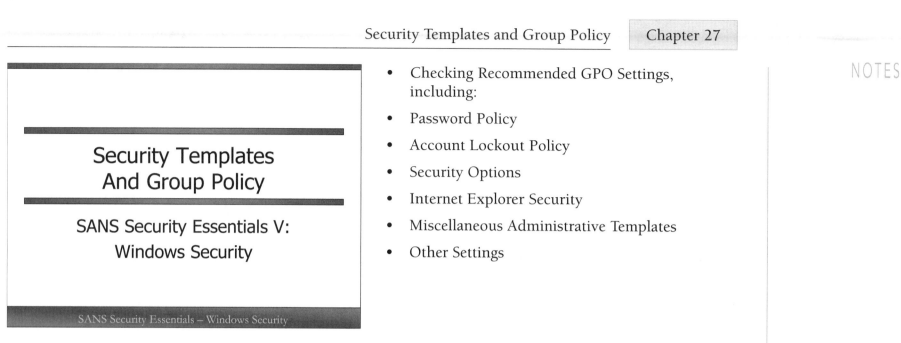

- Applying Security Templates
- Employing the Security Configuration and Analysis snap-in
- Understanding Local Group Policy Objects
- Understanding Domain Group Policy Objects
- Checking Recommended GPO Settings, including:
- Password Policy
- Account Lockout Policy
- Security Options
- Internet Explorer Security
- Miscellaneous Administrative Templates
- Other Settings

NOTES

Security Templates (1 of 3)

- .INF extension
- Stores security settings in an ASCII text file.
- Can be applied like a stamp to multiple machines.

- Password Policy
- Account Lockout Policy
- Kerberos Policy
- Audit Policy
- User Rights Assignments
- Event Log Settings
- NTFS Permissions
- Group Memberships
- Service Startup
- Registry Permissions

SANS Security Essentials – Windows Security

Security Templates

A *security template* is an ASCII text configuration file that can store hundreds of security settings. A computer can be stamped with a template and reconfigured in one shot to match the settings in the template. (Picture a factory with a giant steel press that can stamp security settings into laptops as they pass by on the assembly line.)

A template can store the following security settings:

- Password policies
- Account lockout policies
- Kerberos policies
- Audit policies
- Custom user rights assignments
- Various security options
- Event log sizes and wrapping options
- Custom memberships in important groups
- Service startup options
- Registry key permissions
- NTFS permissions and audit settings

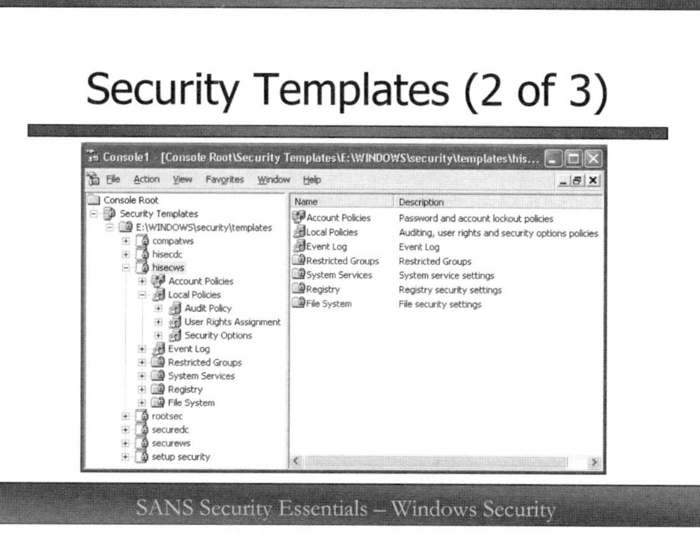

Security Templates MMC Snap-In

Security templates are kept by default in `%SystemRoot%\Security\Templates\`, and they end with the .INF filename extension. Templates can be edited with Notepad, but a much easier method is to use a Microsoft Management Console (MMC) snap-in named "Security Templates."

To load the snap-in and create a new template, go to the Run line and execute `mmc.exe` > pull down the Console menu > Add/Remove Snap-In > Add > Security Templates > Add > Close > OK. In the snap-in, double-click the templates yellow folder to open it. Right-click on the yellow templates folder > New Template > enter "Generic" as the name > OK. This creates a Generic.inf file.

In the Templates snap-in, double-click a template to open it up. Browse through its containers and double-click the policy icons to configure them. When you're done, right-click the edited template and save it. If you wish, browse to that template's folder using Windows Explorer and open the template in Notepad.

NOTES

NOTES

Security Templates (3 of 3)

- *Don't start from scratch!*
- Many pre-configured templates:
  - Freely available (NSA, CIS, MS, etc.).
  - Can be edited to suit your needs.
  - Different templates for different types of servers and security levels.
  - Intended to break as few desired services as possible while securing the rest.

SANS Security Essentials – Windows Security

Where Can I Get Pre-Configured Templates?

You don't have to create your own templates from scratch. Microsoft, SANS, NIST, NSA, CIS, and every other player in the Windows security arena have customized templates free for the download! It is highly recommended that you begin with someone else's templates instead of starting from scratch. The reason for this is that security is bad for usability. In general, the more security options you configure, the more applications you are likely to break. Templates from Microsoft, SANS, CIS and others have been debugged and tested in order to improve security as much as possible while breaking as little as possible.

Consider, out of the thousands of registry key permissions and NTFS permissions which could be changed, which ones should be changed? Which changes will break your favorite applications?

Templates represent the condensed knowledge of experts who have suffered for hundreds of hours to fine-tune them. Hence, start with a template created by a group you trust (Microsoft, NSA, whomever); then customize that template to meet your needs. This is the best answer to the question, "What changes should I make?" Remember, too, that you always can edit a template obtained from someone else in any way you wish.

What Templates Are Available?

Windows 2000 comes with a number of pre-configured templates:

- Default workstation (basicwk.inf)
- Default server (basicsv.inf)
- Default domain controller (basicdc.inf)
- Compatible workstation or server (compatws.inf)
- Secure workstation or server (securews.inf)
- Highly secure workstation or server (hisecws.inf)
- Secure domain controller (securedc.inf)
- Highly secure domain controller (hisecdc.inf)
- Secure Terminal Server (notssid.inf)
- Default initial settings (setup security.inf)

Windows XP includes a few other templates, including:

- Default NTFS permissions on root partition (rootsec.inf)
- Default installation settings (setup security.inf)

NOTES

There are also templates just for securing IIS web servers:

- High security web server (hisecweb.inf)
- IIS Internet (secureinternetwebserver.inf, *Resource Kit*)
- IIS Intranet (secureintranetwebserver.inf, *Resource Kit*)

The National Security Agency (NSA) has an excellent set of whitepapers and security templates for Windows. On their website home page (`http://www.nsa.gov`), click on the link for "Security Recommendation Guides," and follow the links for Windows 2000/XP:

- Windows 2000 domain controller (w2kdc.inf)
- Windows 2000 domain policy (w2k domain policy.inf)
- Windows 2000 Server (w2k server.inf)
- Windows 2000 Workstation (w2k workstation.inf)
- Microsoft ISA Server (isa.inf)

The Center for Internet Security (CIS) not only has security templates available, but also configuration guides and assessment tools to go with them. Get the latest versions from the CIS website:

- `http://www.cisecurity.org`

The CIS templates are particularly good because many different groups (SANS, CIS, NIST, NSA, etc.) all worked together to develop them. These templates represent a consensus of opinion among these organizations.

NOTES

SCA Snap-In

- Security Configuration & Analysis
  - MMC console snap-in.
  - Applies a template to a computer.
- Warning: There is no "undo" feature!
- Cannot apply a template to a computer across the network...

SANS Security Essentials – Windows Security

Security Configuration and Analysis Snap-In

What good is a security template if you can't use it? The Security Configuration and Analysis (SCA) snap-in is used to reconfigure a computer to match the settings in a security template in one easy step (the tool's other uses will be discussed later). The SCA snap-in is the industrial press that applies templates to computers on the assembly line.

Install the SCA snap-in in the same MMC console as the Security Templates snap-in, using the same procedures described above.

When you first click on the SCA snap-in, instructions for using it will appear on the right-hand side of the console. Follow the instructions to create a new database; don't worry, the "database" is just a small temp file. To create a new database, right-click the SCA snap-in > Open Database > enter

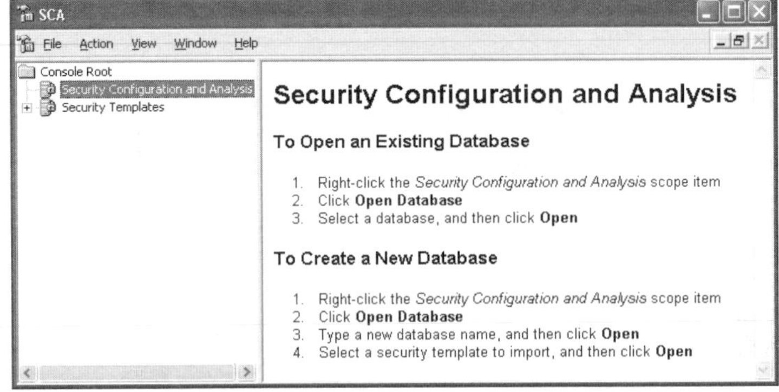
SCA
File Action View Window Help
Console Root
Security Configuration and Analysis
Security Templates
Security Configuration and Analysis
To Open an Existing Database
1. Right-click the Security Configuration and Analysis scope item
2. Click Open Database
3. Select a database, and then click Open
To Create a New Database
1. Right-click the Security Configuration and Analysis scope item
2. Click Open Database
3. Type a new database name, and then click Open
4. Select a security template to import, and then click Open

any database name you wish > Open. If a dialog box does not immediately appear to import a template, then right-click the SCA again > Import Template > double-click an INF template file. This will import the template's settings into the temporary database.

Once a template has been imported into the database, reconfigure the computer to match the template by right-clicking the SCA > Configure Computer Now > OK. That's it!

Note

Warning! There is no "undo" feature in the SCA tool. Test new security settings on non-production systems first, and make a backup of the production server you intend to reconfigure (including the "System State") before you apply the template. You have been warned!

The SCA snap-in has an important limitation, though: it can be used only on the local machine where the tool is being run. However, there is a command-line version of the tool which can be scripted!

NOTES

SECEDIT.EXE

- Command-line version of SCA snap-in.
- Script application of a template from:
  - Shared folder
  - Floppy disk

SANS Security Essentials – Windows Security

SECEDIT.EXE

`SECEDIT.EXE` is a command-line version of the SCA snap-in. Imagine creating a floppy disk with `SECEDIT.EXE` and a simple batch file to run it: you could field a platoon of IT staff with these floppies to quickly reconfigure hundreds of machines! Alternatively, the necessary files could be placed in a shared folder. Other computers would need only map a drive letter to the share and run `SECEDIT.EXE` from there. Or a scheduled batch file could reapply settings on a critical server every night at 3 a.m. from that shared folder.

The `SECEDIT.EXE` tool still cannot be used to apply a template to a machine across the network, but, because it is so easily scriptable, it can make applying templates much easier. To create a floppy with everything you need, follow these steps:

> *Database too big?*
>
> If your database file is too big to put on a floppy, then compress it to a Zip file first. Your batch file should then decompress the Zip file to a temporary folder on the hard drive and apply the database from there. You can use the `COMPRESS.EXE` and `EXPAND.EXE` programs from the *Resource Kit* for this.

1. Use the SCA snap-in to create a database file (let's name it "`dbase.sdb`"), and import the settings from your favorite template(s).
2. Copy the database file to a floppy disk.
3. Create a batch file (let's name it "`apply.bat`") on the floppy disk using Notepad.
4. Add this line to the batch file: "`secedit.exe /configure /db A:\dbase.sdb`."

Now, simply insert the floppy on a Windows 2000/XP/.NET system, and run the `APPLY.BAT` file. You don't have to copy the `SECEDIT.EXE` program to your floppy because it is already in the default path on the hard drive.

But where can one see these settings after they have been applied? NTFS and registry key permissions are easy enough to see in Windows Explorer and `REGEDT32.EXE`, but what about all the other settings? For this we must look at Group Policy Objects.

NOTES

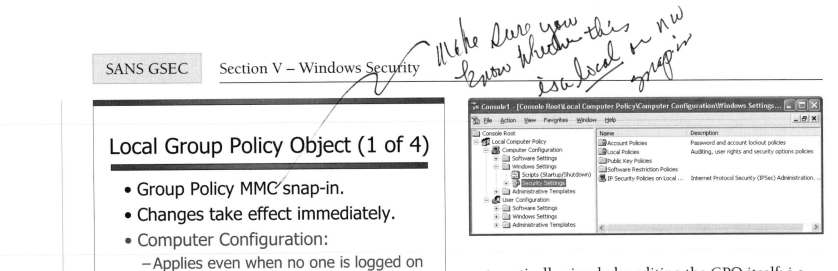

Local Group Policy Object (1 of 4)

- Group Policy MMC snap-in.
- Changes take effect immediately.
- Computer Configuration:
  - Applies even when no one is logged on
- User Configuration:
  - Applies to current user's desktop

SANS Security Essentials – Windows Security

The Local Group Policy Object

A security template stores settings in a form which can be applied to a computer. But applying templates is not the only way to configure security options. Permissions, of course, can be configured with a variety of tools (as discussed in the prior chapter), but there are other options, as well. To change these we need to examine Group Policy Objects (GPOs). We'll start with the local GPO and later discuss domain-based GPOs.

Assume you are working with a stand-alone system (or a system in a Windows NT domain). Your current security settings, except for NTFS and registry key ACLs, can be viewed and edited through your local Group Policy Object. A GPO is similar to a security template, except that GPOs contain even more settings and are applied

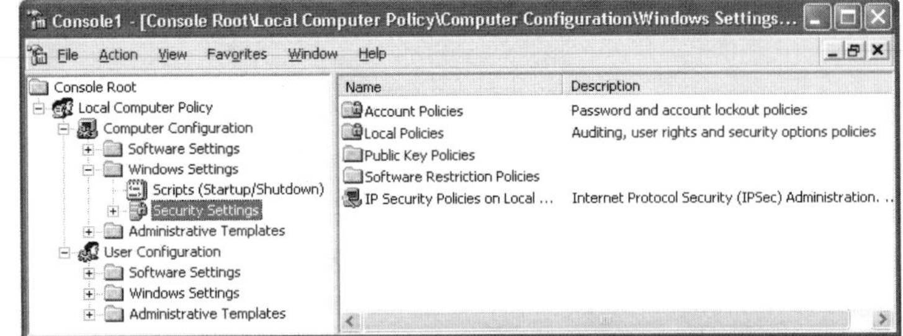

automatically simply by editing the GPO itself; i.e., you don't have to run tools like SECEDIT.EXE or the SCA snap-in to apply these settings.

To access your local GPO, open an MMC.EXE console > Console menu > Add/Remove Snap-In > Add > Group Policy > Add > make sure that "Local Computer" is the selected GPO > Finish > Close > OK. Now, double-click the snap-in to expand it and browse through the many subcontainers and their settings.

The Computer Configuration settings apply even when no one is logged on. The User Configuration settings apply to the user's desktop when a user currently is logged on. Let's browse through some of the more important settings together, but please keep in mind that there are too many to cover in a single chapter.

NOTES

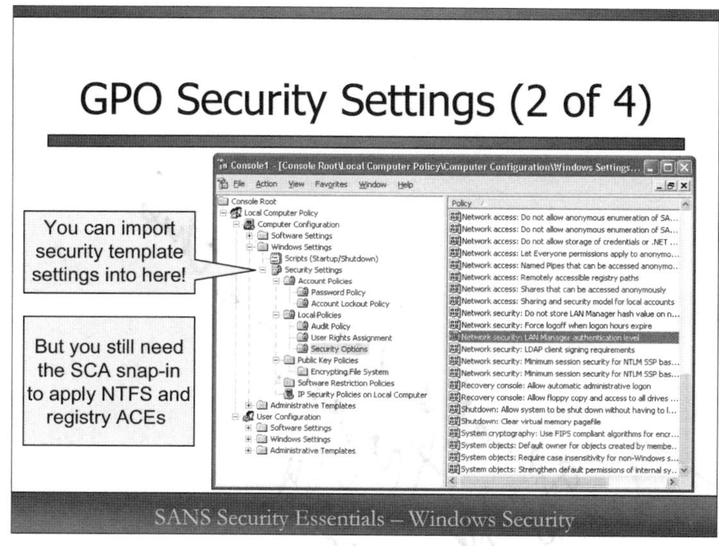

Windows Settings > Security Settings

The Computer Configuration > Windows Settings > Security Settings section bundles together the most important security settings on your system. In fact, this portion of your local GPO looks extremely similar to a security template. This is no accident. You can import a security template into your local GPO! Any settings in the template which are also in the GPO will be overridden by the template; but keep in mind that there are more settings in a template than are available in the local GPO—that's why the SCA snap-in still is needed.

To import a template into your local GPO, right-click the Security Settings container in the GPO > Import Policy. Most changes take effect immediately, but to ensure that all settings have been reapplied, reboot the system after importing a template. Again, just as before, obtain a pre-configured template from an organization you trust; modify that template to match your preferences; and then apply it using the SCA snap-in and/or Group Policy Objects.

But if you wish to edit a setting by hand, you don't have to resort to the importation of an entire template. Simply double-click a policy icon to bring up its dialog box!

NOTES

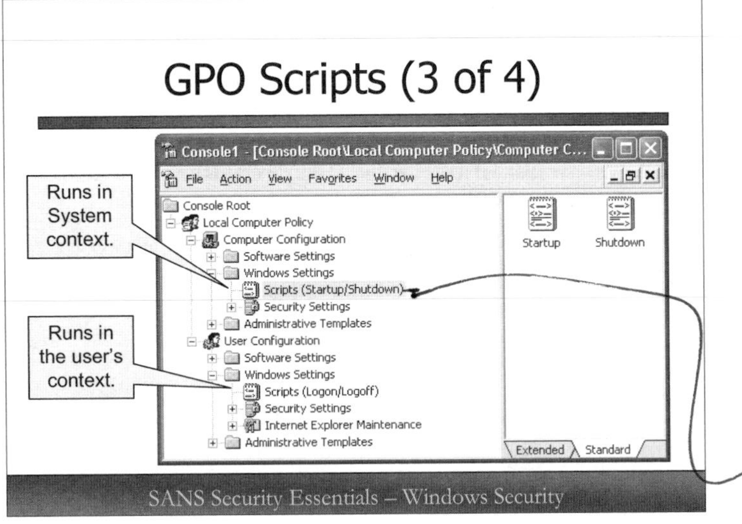

Windows Settings > Scripts

You can assign scripts to be executed through a GPO, as well. These options are found under both Computer and User Configuration > Windows Settings > Scripts.

Scripts can be executed at system startup, shutdown, user logon, or user logoff. Scripts can be written in any language, as long as the necessary Windows Script Host (WSH) interpreter has been installed. By default, scripts only can be written in VBScript, Jscript, or as batch files; but there are free interpreters available for Perl and Python (`www.activestate.com`). Startup/shutdown scripts run in System context, while logon/logoff scripts run in the context of the user. You can have as many of each type of script you wish, and you can mix and match your languages across your scripts as desired.

Virtually every aspect of the operating system can be scripted, including users, groups, NTFS ACLs, shared folders, registry settings, IIS, Office application settings, and more.

NOTES

Administrative Templates (4 of 4)

- A user-friendly registry editor!
  - And the registry controls almost everything of course
- Hundreds of settings are available.
- You can import more ADM templates.
- You can edit these templates to configure any registry value desired.

SANS Security Essentials – Windows Security

Administrative Templates

The registry is the central configuration database for the entire computer. It can be edited with REGEDIT.EXE, of course, but this isn't very user-friendly. Many security settings from the registry are exposed, however, through the Administrative Templates containers in your GPO. Administrative Templates settings are found under both Computer and User Configuration in the GPO; if there is a conflict between the two, the setting from the Computer Configuration container wins (usually).

There are hundreds of settings under Administrative Templates. The best way to become acquainted is simply to browse through the categories. For any setting you wish to configure, double-click its icon to reveal a dialog box. Notice that most items have an Explain tab with some amount of explanation for that setting (sometimes just a sentence, sometimes many paragraphs).

Most aspects of the user's interface can be configured through Administrative Templates. For example, under User Configuration > Administrative Templates > Control Panel, there is an option to restrict which Control Panel applets the user is permitted to open (and another to restrict access to the Control Panel entirely). In that same section is a subcontainer (Display) which can be used to require a password-protected screensaver.

The reason this section mentions "templates" is that you can add more yellow folders and configuration icons. If you right-click on the Administrative Templates folder itself, you can select Add/Remove Templates. These are not INF security templates; these are ADM templates similar to the templates used by the System Policy Editor (SYSPOL.EXE) in Windows 9x/NT. When you import an ADM template, you get more configuration settings available in the GPO. Microsoft has a variety of ADM templates that can be downloaded for free, and you can edit these templates with Notepad to add any registry values you wish. The *Microsoft Office Resource Kit*, for example, has ADM templates to configure almost every setting in Word, Excel, Access, and Outlook.

Now, while it is nice to have these configuration options listed in one tool, it doesn't really help when there are thousands of machines to be hardened. Is there a way to push these settings out automatically across the network to many machines?

NOTES

What About the Others?

Due to time limitations, the other GPO settings cannot be discussed here. Software Settings is for automatic software installation; IP Security Policies is for IPSec; Remote Installation Services is for automatic OS installation; and Internet Explorer Maintenance is for IE configuration management. IPSec, however, will be covered later.

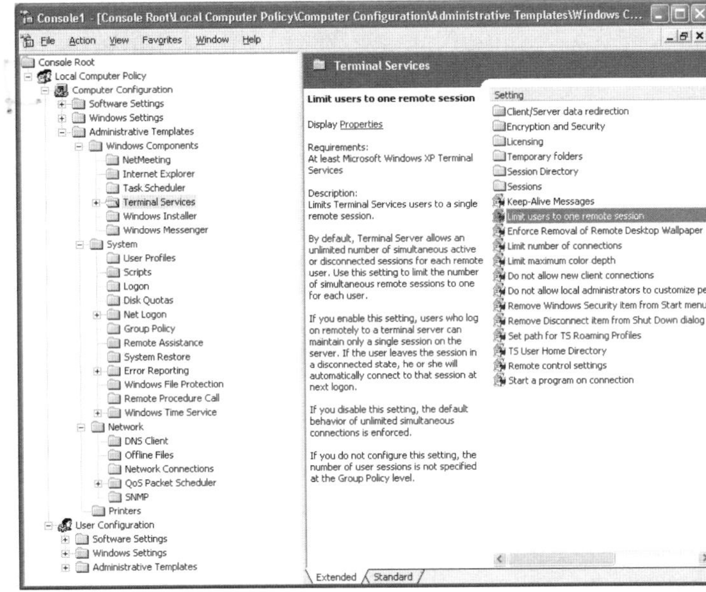

Domain Group Policy Objects
- GPOs stored in Active Directory.
- Downloaded automatically at startup, shutdown, logon and logoff.
- Refreshed every 90 minutes.
- 100% hands-free way of applying security templates to many systems.

SANS Security Essentials – Windows Security

Domain Group Policy Objects

If your computers are running Windows 2000/XP/.NET, and if those computers are members of an Active Directory domain, then *all* the settings in the local GPO (and more) can be pushed out to these computers automatically from your domain controllers. This is 100% hands-free. You are not physically touching any of the target computers or manually editing any user's local GPO. The SCA snap-in is disappointing because it doesn't work over the network, but domain-based GPOs *can* apply security templates over the network.

Domain-based GPOs are stored in the Active Directory database and replicated to all domain controllers. When a computer boots up, it downloads its domain GPO settings automatically (the Computer Configuration settings from the GPO). When a user logs on, the user's GPO settings are downloaded and applied automatically (the User Configuration settings from the GPO). Every 90 minutes thereafter, by default, your computer will check to see if any GPO changes have occurred, and, if so, your computer will download and apply them on-the-fly.

NOTES

NOTES

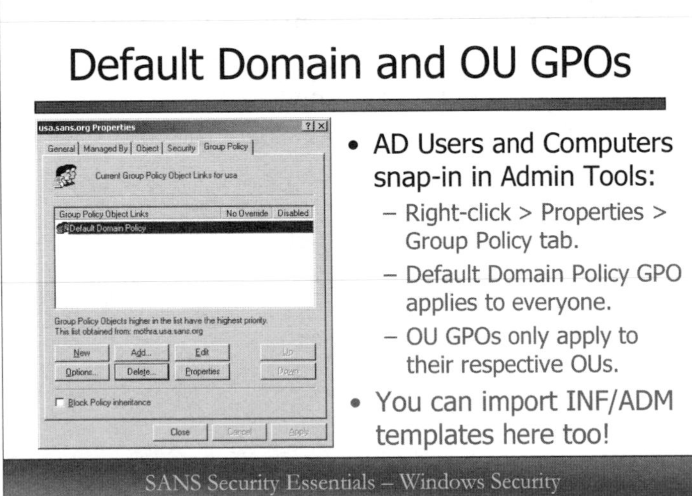

Default Domain and OU GPOs
usa.sans.org Properties
General | Managed By | Object | Security | Group Policy
Current Group Policy Object Links for usa
Group Policy Object Links | No Override | Disabled
Default Domain Policy
New | Add... | Edit | Up
Options... | Delete... | Properties | Down
Block Policy inheritance
Close | Cancel | Apply
• AD Users and Computers snap-in in Admin Tools:
– Right-click > Properties > Group Policy tab.
– Default Domain Policy GPO applies to everyone.
– OU GPOs only apply to their respective OUs.
• You can import INF/ADM templates here too!
SANS Security Essentials – Windows Security

Default Domain and Organizational Unit GPOs

The Default Domain Policy GPO applies to all users and computers throughout the entire domain. To edit the Default Domain GPO, log on to a domain controller as a Domain Admin > click on the Start menu > Programs > Administrative Tools > Active Directory Users and Computers > right-click on the name of your domain > Properties > Group Policy tab > highlight the "Default Domain Policy" > Edit. You will see a GPO just like before.

The Default Domain GPO applies to everyone in the domain, while a local GPO only applies to the computer on which it is found. The settings in the domain-wide GPO override any conflicting settings in the local GPO on each computer; hence, administrators always have the final say-so.

If you wish to restrict the application of a GPO just to the users and computers in a particular Organizational Unit, then create a GPO, and link it just to that OU. The Default Domain Policy GPO is linked at the top-level domain container; that's why it applies to everyone. An OU GPO, on the other hand, is linked only to a particular OU. To create a GPO and link it to an OU, right-click that OU > Properties > Group Policy tab > click the New button > rename the GPO to "OU-GPO." You now can edit that GPO like any other.

Importing Templates Into GPOs

Again, just like with the local GPO, you can import a security template into a domain GPO. Once imported, all of the settings in the template (including the NTFS and registry ACLs!) will be pushed out from the domain controllers automatically. To import a security template into a domain GPO, open the GPO as described above, then open > Computer Configuration > Windows Settings > right-click on Security Settings > Import Policy > Open > close the GPO window > OK.

Note that you don't have to save the GPO explicitly. Simply closing the GPO window will save it. The new GPO settings will be replicated to the other domain controllers within 15 minutes (assuming you don't have any WAN links to remote sites), and workstations and member servers will pick up those new settings within 90 minutes.

Now that we know how to make security configuration changes, what should those changes be? Let's discuss some of the more important security options. The old "80/20 Rule" applies here,

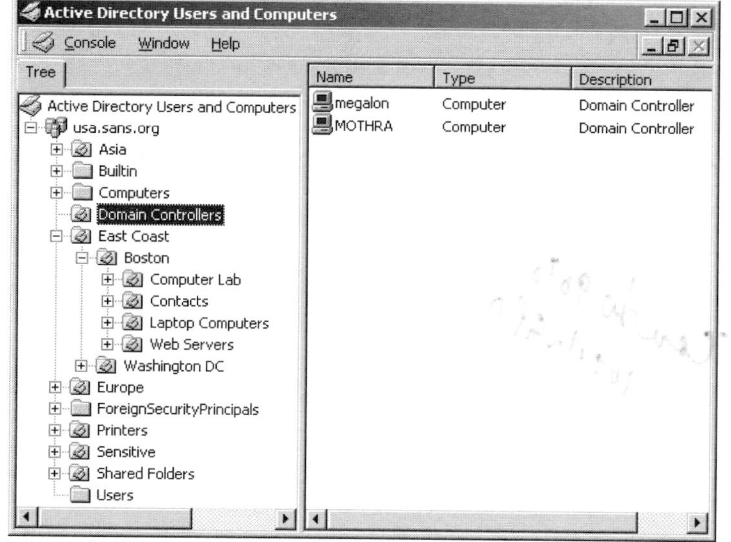

as well: 80% of the security of your system will come from configuring just 20% of these security options, so the following are the ones on which to focus.

Do I Have to Wait?

To force the application of new GPO settings on Windows 2000 immediately, execute `secedit.exe /refreshpolicy machine_policy` for Computer Configuration settings and `secedit.exe /refreshpolicy user_policy` for User Configuration settings. On Windows XP/.NET, just run `gpupdate.exe`. Note that most settings do not require a logoff or reboot, but some do; hence, reboot the system to ensure that all new settings are effective immediately.

NOTES

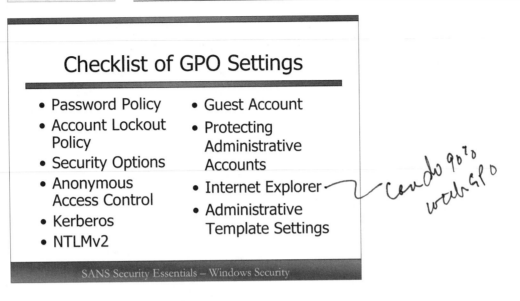

Checklist of GPO Settings

- Password Policy
- Account Lockout Policy
- Security Options
- Anonymous Access Control
- Kerberos
- NTLMv2
- Guest Account
- Protecting Administrative Accounts
- Internet Explorer
- Administrative Template Settings

SANS Security Essentials – Windows Security

Checklist of Recommended GPO Settings

The following is a checklist to use when configuring security templates and Group Policy Objects. The checklist is intended to strike a balance between security and usability, so feel free to harden your settings as you see fit. Also note that the names of these options change somewhat from Windows 2000 to Windows XP to Windows .NET, so the following are the Windows 2000 names with the expectation that the XP/.NET names usually are easy to figure out. Finally, some of these settings will be discussed in detail later, so this is not the end of the story.

NOTES

GPO > Password Policy

- Maximum length: 127 characters
  - Think passphrases, not passwords
- Recommended GPO settings:
  - Enforce password history: 24 passwords
  - Maximum password age: 90 days
  - Minimum password age: 1 day
  - Minimum password length: 8 characters
  - Password must meet complexity requirements: Enabled

SANS Security Essentials – Windows Security

Password Policy

Good security always starts with a strong password policy. Even though users might complain, and management may oppose you, enforcing strong password policy is something about which you should be willing to fight because most of the other security features become moot if weak passwords are permitted. Here are the recommended minimum settings:

- Enforce password history: 24 passwords remembered
- Maximum password age: 90 days
- Minimum password age: 1 day
- Minimum password length: 8 characters
- Password must meet complexity requirements: Enabled

Importantly, remember that you can have 127-character pass*phrases* in Windows 2000/XP/.NET, not just 14-character pass*words*. The length of the passphrase is more important than its complexity, too. Besides, users prefer memorizing meaningful passphrases instead of random-looking passwords, anyway; for example, of the following two passwords, which would you prefer to memorize?

1. %8Hjl@0JaF&LIc
2. Karen's a 100% sweetie-pie!

And the second one is many thousands of times stronger than the first because it contains 27 characters instead of just 14 (and they both satisfy complexity requirements). Unfortunately, Microsoft's password policy only permits the enforcement of 14-character passwords, but users still can be trained and encouraged to use passphrases instead.

Password complexity requires a mixture of three out of the four categories of characters: uppercase, lowercase, numbers, and non-alphanumerics, e.g., punctuation marks. The greater the variety of characters in a password, the more difficult it is to guess it. But password length is still more important than complexity.

Maximum password age prevents a compromised password from being used too long. If a password is crackable, it usually can be cracked in less than 90 days (often less than 90 minutes).

Minimum password age and password history work together. They prevent users from "recycling" their old favorite passwords over and over again. The assumption is that it's too much of a hassle to change one's password every single day for 24 days in a row just to get back to one's favorite password.

NOTES

GPO > Account Lockout Policy

- Prevent brute force password guessing:
  - Account lockout duration: 15 minutes
  - Account lockout threshold: 5 attempts
  - Reset account counter lockout after: 5 minutes

SANS Security Essentials – Windows Security

Account Lockout Policy

If a hacker attempts to use a password-guessing program, then accounts should be locked out temporarily to prevent too many guesses from being checked. The minimum recommended settings are:

- Account lockout duration: 15 minutes
- Account lockout threshold: 5 attempts
- Reset account counter lockout after: 5 minutes

Windows keeps track of how many failed logon attempts have occurred for each user account. But that counter can be reset. For the settings above, tell your users, "Try to guess your password four times. Then wait five minutes, and try four more times, etc." The idea is that a hacker will run up against the five-guess threshold almost instantaneously and trigger the longer lockout timer. If you make the lockout very long or infinite, users will be calling you constantly to reset their accounts.

NOTES

GPO > Security Options

- A variety of security settings are contained in this part of the GPO.
- Recommendations are in the book (long list).
- Let's discuss some of the more important ones:
  - Anonymous Access
  - Kerberos & NTLM
  - Guest Account

SANS Security Essentials – Windows Security

Security Options

The Security Options container lists a variety of security switches that can be turned on. Some are critically important; others are obscure and paranoid. The following are the most important ones to configure, but feel free to enable the others, as well; however, while the other settings may enhance security, beware of their causing widespread interoperability problems without yielding much security advantage (which is perhaps why they are not on the list).

Here is the list of recommended minimum security options on Windows 2000:

- Additional restrictions for anonymous connections: No access without explicit anonymous permissions
- Digitally sign client communication (when possible): Enabled
- Digitally sign server communication (when possible): Enabled
- Disable CTRL+ALT+DEL requirement for logon: Disabled
- LAN Manager Authentication Level: Send LM/NTLMv1 - Use NTLMv2 session security if negotiated
- Message text for users attempting to log on (logon banner): "This system is for the use of authorized users only. Individuals using this computer system without authority, or in excess of their authority, are subject to having all of their activities on this system monitored and recorded by system personnel. In the course of monitoring individuals improperly using this system, or in the course of system maintenance, the activities of authorized users also may be monitored. Anyone using this system expressly consents to such monitoring and is advised that if such monitoring reveals possible evidence of criminal activity, system personnel may provide the evidence of such monitoring to law enforcement officials."
- Recovery Console: Allow automatic administrative logon: Disabled
- Rename administrator account
- Secure channel: Digitally encrypt secure channel data (when possible): Enabled

NOTES

- Send unencrypted password to connect to third-party SMB servers: Disabled
- Smart card removal behavior: Lock workstation

Windows XP/.NET has many overlapping options (even if they have slightly different names) but there are new ones as well. Here is a similar minimum list just for Windows XP/.NET:

- Accounts: Guest account status: Disabled
- Accounts: Limit local account use of blank passwords to console logon only: Enabled
- Rename administrator account
- Interactive logon: Do not require CTRL+ALT+DEL: Disabled
- Interactive logon: Message text for users attempting to log on (logon banner): "This system is for the use of authorized users only. Individuals using this computer system without authority, or in excess of their authority, are subject to having all of their activities on this system monitored and recorded by system personnel. In the course of monitoring individuals improperly using this system, or in the course of system maintenance, the activities of authorized users also may be monitored. Anyone using this system expressly consents to such monitoring and is advised that if such monitoring reveals possible evidence of criminal activity, system personnel may provide the evidence of such monitoring to law enforcement officials."
- Interactive logon: Smart card removal behavior: Lock workstation
- Microsoft network client: Digitally sign communications (if server agrees): Enabled
- Microsoft network server: Digitally sign communications (if client agrees): Enabled
- Network access: Allow anonymous SID/Name translation: Disabled
- Network access: Do not allow anonymous enumeration of SAM accounts and shares: Enabled
- Network access: Do not allow storage of credentials or .NET Passports for network authentication: Enabled
- Network access: Let Everyone permissions apply to anonymous users: Disabled
- Network access: Sharing and security model for local accounts: Classic - local users authenticate as themselves
- Network security: Do not store LAN Manager hash value on next password change: Enabled
- Network security: LAN Manager authentication level: Send LM/NTLMv1 - Use NTLMv2 session security if negotiated
- Recovery console: Allow automatic administrative logon: Disabled

Let's discuss some of these settings and see why they are important.

NOTES

Anonymous Access (1 of 2)

- "Null user sessions" are the source of many Windows vulnerabilities:
  - SMB session with blank username/password
- Open a null session manually:
  - `Net use \\Address\IPC$ "" /user:""`
- Null sessions are not used as much with XP/2000/.NET as with 9x/NT.

SANS Security Essentials – Windows Security

Anonymous Access Control

Null user sessions have been the cause of many Windows security vulnerabilities. For example, through a null user session a remote hacker could download a complete list of all user accounts (and more) from an unfirewalled domain controller. Strictly speaking, a "null user session" is a Server Message Block (SMB) session to a Windows system where both the username and password are blank. Null user sessions were used extensively in Windows NT for legitimate management purposes, but hackers figured out how to leverage them for "other" purposes. To establish a null user session to a Windows system, open a `CMD.EXE` window and execute the following command (where "target" is the IP address of the target computer):

```
net use \\target\ipc$ "" /user:""
```

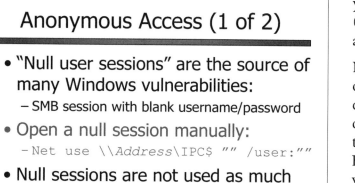

Other auditing tools will create the null session for you. For example, the `DUMPUSERS.EXE` tool (`www.ntsecurity.nu`) can extract a list of all user and group names with a null user session.

Null user sessions are needed much less frequently on Windows 2000/XP/.NET networks because computers can authenticate to each other with their own unique accounts, and trusts are two-way and transitive by default (it's a long story, trust me). Hence, it's a good idea to limit null user session vulnerabilities as much as possible.

NOTES

Anonymous Access (2 of 2)

- Additional Restrictions For Anonymous Connections:
  - No access without explicit anonymous permissions
    - ANONYMOUS LOGON group
    - XP/.NET: Let Everyone Permissions Apply to Everyone Group
  - Do not allow enumeration of SAM accounts and shares
    - Insufficient to block attacks if you only set this.
    - XP/.NET: Allow Anonymous SID/Name Translation

SANS Security Essentials – Windows Security

Block Null User Attacks

On Windows 2000, the GPO setting which can block all forms of this attack is called "Additional restrictions for anonymous connections: No access without explicit anonymous permissions." This has the effect of setting a REG_DWORD registry value named RestrictAnonymous to 2 (the value is found under HKLM\System\CurrentControlSet\Control\Lsa\).

This option also can be set to "Additional restrictions for anonymous connections: Do not allow enumeration of SAM accounts and shares," but this is insufficient. The `DUMPUSERS.EXE` tool, for example, still can get a list of accounts because it can read Security ID numbers (SIDs) over the network and map these SID numbers back to the names of their owners. In fact, in Windows XP/.NET there is another GPO option to handle just this problem: "Network access: Allow anonymous SID/Name translation." This option also should be set to Disabled.

On Windows 2000, when "No access without explicit anonymous permissions" is configured, null user sessions no longer are counted as part of the Everyone group. Hence, permissions granted to the Everyone group are not granted to null users. If you do want to give permissions to null users, then there is a special group named "ANONYMOUS LOGON," to which null users still belong. On Windows XP/.NET there is a separate GPO option to regulate this behavior: "Network access: Let Everyone permissions apply to anonymous users." When enabled, this option causes the OS to treat null users as members of the Everyone group for the sake of ACLs.

Also on Windows XP/.NET there is one last GPO option named "Network access: Do not allow anonymous enumeration of SAM accounts and shares." This should be Enabled, and "Allow anonymous SID/Name translation" should be Disabled.

NOTES

Kerberos & NTLM (1 of 2)

- **Kerberos:**
  - Default protocol, faster, more secure.
  - Requires AD and Windows 2000/XP/.NET
- **NTLM:**
  - Still supported for stand-alones and interoperability with Windows 9x/NT
  - Susceptible to password sniffing, but...

SANS Security Essentials – Windows Security

Kerberos and NTLMv2

The default authentication protocol for Windows 2000/XP/.NET is Kerberos. This means that these operating systems will try to use Kerberos whenever possible, and Kerberos support is built into the drivers for SMB, LDAP, RPC, HTTP, and other protocols for accessing resources over the network (but not Telnet or FTP, surprisingly). This is good because Kerberos is faster and more secure than NTLM. Kerberos uses UDP (mostly), and clients can cache and reuse their "Kerberos tickets," i.e., their authentication tokens, for hours. Kerberos ticket exchanges also cannot be sniffed by L0phtCrack (`www.atstake.com`) or other similar tools to extract password information.

The bad thing about Kerberos, though, is that it requires the computer to be a member of an Active Directory domain. If your domain controllers are Windows NT, then you can't use the built-in Kerberos support of Windows 2000/XP/.NET. But even if you do have an Active Directory domain, your Windows 9x/NT clients and servers still can't use Kerberos.

For the sake of backwards compatibility, Windows 2000/XP/.NET still supports the Windows NT/LAN Manager (NTLM) authentication protocol. But there's a problem. NTLMv1 authentication traffic can be sniffed with tools like L0phtCrack to reveal the user's password hashes! These password hashes then can be loaded into L0phtCrack to reveal (95% of the time) the user's cleartext password.

NOTES

Kerberos & NTLM (2 of 2)

- **NTLMv2:**
  - Not vulnerable to password sniffing.
  - Built into Windows 2000/XP/.NET.
  - Windows 9x/NT need the ADCE add-on.
- LAN Manager Authentication Level:
  - Send LM & NTLMv1 – Use NTLMv2 Session Security If Negotiated
  - Send NTLMv2 Response Only

SANS Security Essentials – Windows Security

Require NTLMv2

Fortunately, NTLMv2 is not vulnerable to this attack. NTLMv2 was redesigned with password-sniffers in mind. Support for NTLMv2 is built into Windows 2000/XP/.NET. Windows NT 4.0 can be made to support it with Service Pack 4 and a registry modification, but make sure to apply the latest Service Pack to deal with other security issues (see Q147706 for more information). Windows 9x also can support NTLMv2 with a free add-on from Microsoft called the "Active Directory Client Extensions (ADCE)." The Windows 9x ADCE is on the Windows 2000 Server CD-ROM in the \Clients\Win9x\ folder. The ADCE for Windows NT 4.0 Workstation can be downloaded from Microsoft's website.

`http://www.microsoft.com/windows2000/server/evaluation/news/bulletins/adextension.asp`

Note

The ADCE should be installed on all Windows NT 4.0 Workstation and Windows 9x systems that are in an Active Directory environment. The ADCE not only includes support for NTLMv2 but also Active Directory site awareness, a DFS client, and other Active Directory integration features. However, the ADCE does not add support for Kerberos or Group Policy.

Both Windows 2000 and Windows XP/.NET have a GPO Security Option named "LAN Manager authentication level." There are a variety of settings for this option, but really there are only two choices worth discussing:

- Send LM & NTLMv1 - Use NTLMv2 session security if negotiated.
- Send NTLMv2 response only/refuse LM & NTLMv1.

The first choice is the best for balancing security and usability; it causes the machine to attempt Kerberos first, NTLMv2 second, NTLMv1 third, and generic LAN Manager authentication last. This is the correct order of preference, yet still allows legacy boxes to communicate with your machines.

The second choice causes the machine to use only Kerberos or NTLMv2 and to reject everything else. This is the more secure option, but it sacrifices backwards compatibility for that security (it all depends on what you want).

The Guest Account

The Guest Account
• Automatic Guest Logon
• Recommendations:
– Disable Guest
– Random password
• Automatic Demotion To Guest:
– Simple File Sharing
SANS Security Essentials – Windows Security

NOTES

The Guest Account

The built-in Guest account can do some strange things. If someone attempts to authenticate to your computer, but the username provided is unknown to your computer or domain controllers (if any), then the remote user simply may be automatically and transparently logged on as guest! For this automatic Guest logon to occur, the Guest account must be enabled and have a blank password.

Therefore, assign a long complex password to your Guest account and disable it! Windows XP/.NET computers support a GPO option to disable the Guest account ("Accounts: Guest account status"). And don't just disable it, either, and not assign a password.

To disable the Guest account and assign it a password, you can use the Administrative Tools > Computer Management snap-in. But a quicker and scriptable way is from the command line:

```
net user guest $5mLb@?49jF&lc /active:no
/times:
```

This disables the account ("/active:no"), sets a complex password ("$5mLb@?49jF&lc" or whatever you want), and prevents logon during all hours of all days ("/times: "—note the blank space after the colon). A simple batch script like this could be pushed out to all Windows 2000/XP/.NET systems through a domain Group Policy Object.

Some people also recommend renaming the Guest account, but the value of this is debatable. Indeed, if the account is renamed, then this may simply make it more difficult to audit the box and verify that the Guest account has been disabled! Also, another administrator might be more inclined to enable an account if it looked like a regular account. Better, perhaps, to just disable it and assign a random password.

There's something else to be aware of, too. If "Simple File Sharing" is enabled on Windows XP, then all remote authentications to the XP box itself will be treated as remote access by the Guest account. This is called "automatic demotion to Guest." To ensure that this is prevented, open Windows Explorer > Tools menu > Folder Options > View tab > uncheck the box labeled "Use simple file sharing." With simple sharing disabled, users authenticate as themselves, and they specifically must be granted permissions to have access. There also is a GPO option to control this feature ("Network access: Sharing and security model for local accounts") which should be set to "Classic - local users authenticate as themselves."

NOTES

Administrative Accounts (1 of 2)

1. Enforce strong password policy.
2. Require smart card authentication.
3. Require Kerberos or NTLMv2.
4. Enable lockout (PASSPROP.EXE).
5. Rename the account.
6. Create a decoy account.

SANS Security Essentials – Windows Security

Protecting Administrative Accounts

The goal of any red-blooded hacker is to acquire an administrative account on your system. Any "lamer script kiddie" can launch DoS attacks, but "the elite" will always try to own your network (or else it's just not worth their time).

An "administrative account" is a user who is a member of any one of these groups, especially the first three: Administrators, Domain Admins, Enterprise Admins, Schema Admins, DnsAdmins, Account Operators, Server Operators, Backup Operators, or Print Operators. Protecting these accounts is roughly equivalent to protecting the entire network! So what should be done to secure the administrative accounts?

- Enforce strong password policy, and encourage administrators to use long (20+ character) passphrases.
- Consider requiring a smart card, biometric, or other "multi-factor" authentication device for logon with administrative accounts. You can require a smart card for interactive logons in the properties of a domain account in Active Directory (Account tab). There also is a GPO option to automatically lock the desktop of users who log on with a smart card and then remove them without logging off first.
- Require Kerberos or NTLMv2 authentication only (see above).

Administrative Accounts (2 of 2)

7. Give them two user accounts:
   - Regular account (regular activities)
   - Administrative account (only as needed)
8. XP: Limit local account use of blank passwords to console logon only.
9. Audit all access to administrative users and groups.

SANS Security Essentials – Windows Security

- By default, the built-in Administrator account cannot be locked out by bad logon attempts. This makes the account an ideal target for brute-force password cracking programs. However, the Windows 2000 Server *Resource Kit* includes a utility named `PASSPROP.EXE` that can be used to enable lockout of the Administrator account when too many bad logon attempts occur. When locked out, though, the account is only locked out from over-the-network logons; the administrator can still sit down at a domain controller and log on locally.
- Rename the built-in Administrator account. There are techniques to reveal the new name, but every extra hurdle helps. There also is a GPO option to do this automatically.
- Create a decoy Administrator account after you've renamed the real one. This account will be named "Administrator" and have the same description field as the original. However, this account will not be a member of any administrative groups, will have a 127-character random password, and will be disabled. It is nothing but bait.
- Administrative users should have two user accounts: their administrative account and a regular account. They should log on with their regular accounts and only launch programs with administrative privileges as necessary. The `RUNAS.EXE` program can be used to launch applications under different credentials than those of the logged-on user, and in the properties of shortcuts is a checkbox to "Run As A Different User." In both cases, when the program is run, the user is prompted to enter the other username and password. In particular, administrators should use their regular account when browsing the Internet or checking e-mail.
- On Windows XP, enable the GPO option called "Accounts: Limit local account use of blank passwords to console logon only." If any local Administrator accounts happen to have blank passwords, then at least they will not be exploitable over the network. This is a good policy to enable for everyone in any case.
- Audit all access to administrative users and groups, especially failed access, and configure one's host-based Intrusion Detection System (IDS) to raise alerts when they are modified. (Auditing is discussed in chapter 30.)

NOTES

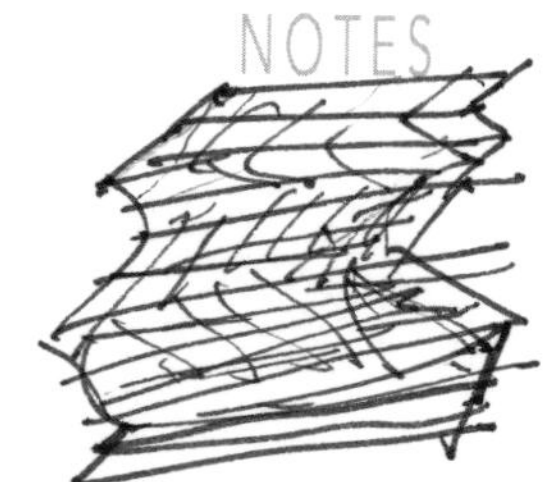

Internet Explorer Security (1 of 3)

- IE has a long history of exploits.
- 95% of IE settings are configurable through Group Policy.
- A few changes will block most of the exploits, even without patches, but these changes break functionality.
- Fortunately, exceptions can be defined…

SANS Security Essentials – Windows Security

Internet Explorer Security

Virtually every aspect of Internet Explorer (IE) can be managed through the "Administrative Templates" and "Internet Explorer Maintenance" containers in Group Policy Objects, which is fortunate because there's been an almost never-ending string of IE exploits since the beginning of the browser's release! It's important to stay on top of IE patches, but patching is always merely reactive. Fortunately, many of these exploits can be blocked through a few simple configuration changes, and these changes are likely to block many future exploits as well. 95% of the configuration options in IE can be managed through Group Policy.

The bad news is that making these changes will break much of the cool functionality in high-end websites. But exceptions can be defined. For example, you can disable client-side scripting, ActiveX controls and Java applets in general, but still allow them when users are accessing intranet sites or when visiting sites whose fully-qualified domain names (FQDNs) you have approved explicitly. In this way, business-critical sites can remain 100% functional while the rest of the Internet can be regarded with more skepticism.

NOTES

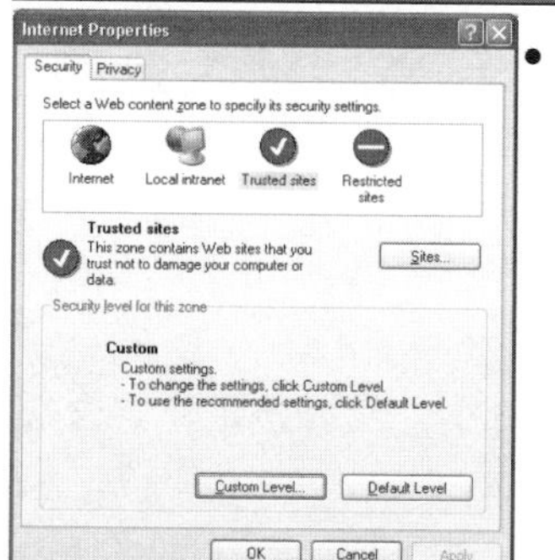

- Configure Internet Zone:
  - Active scripting: Disable
  - Run ActiveX controls and plug-ins: Disable
  - Download signed ActiveX controls: Disable
  - Download unsigned ActiveX controls: Disable
  - Initialize and script ActiveX controls not marked as safe: Disable
  - Script ActiveX controls marked safe for scripting: Disable

SANS Security Essentials – Windows Security

Configure the Internet Zone

In your local or domain GPO, follow these steps to eliminate many IE vulnerabilities: open the desired GPO (see above) > User Configuration > Windows Settings > Internet Explorer Maintenance > Security > Security Zones and Content Ratings > at the top select Import... > Modify Settings button > click on the Internet icon at the top > Custom Level button > and make sure the following options are configured:

- Download signed ActiveX controls: Disable
- Download unsigned ActiveX controls: Disable
- Initialize and script ActiveX controls not marked as safe: Disable
- Run ActiveX controls and plug-ins: Disable
- Script ActiveX controls marked safe for scripting: Disable
- Java permissions: Disable Java (or High Safety, or Custom)
- Launching programs and files in an IFRAME: Disable
- Active scripting: Disable
- Logon: Automatic Logon Only In Intranet Zone

NOTES

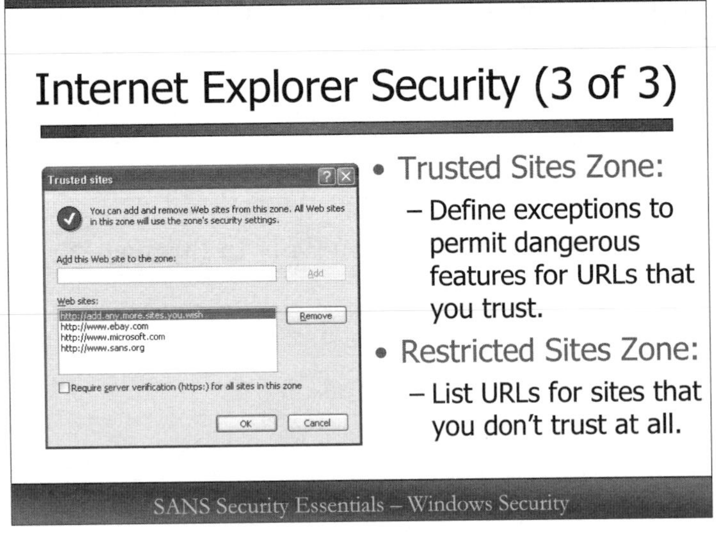

Internet Explorer Security (3 of 3)
Trusted sites
You can add and remove Web sites from this zone. All Web sites in this zone will use the zone's security settings.
Add this Web site to the zone:
Add
Web sites:
http://add.any.more.sites.you.wish
http://www.ebay.com
http://www.microsoft.com
http://www.sans.org
Remove
Require server verification (https:) for all sites in this zone
OK
Cancel
• Trusted Sites Zone:
– Define exceptions to permit dangerous features for URLs that you trust.
• Restricted Sites Zone:
– List URLs for sites that you don't trust at all.
SANS Security Essentials – Windows Security

Remember, if you configure these settings in the domain GPO using the Active Directory Users and Computers tool at your domain controller, these settings will apply to every computer in the domain.

Define Exceptions for Sites You (Don't) Trust

When you click OK to save your custom settings, you are returned to the Security Zones dialog box. You can now select the Trusted Sites zone and, by clicking the Sites button, add any FQDNs for sites on the Internet that you wish to exempt from your new restrictive settings. For example, you may wish to add `www.microsoft.com` to the list because Microsoft's web site uses ActiveX controls and client-side scripting extensively.

The Restricted Sites zone is for the FQDNs of sites that you never wish to trust, no matter what. This might be used instead of altering the Internet Sites zone if there are only a few troublesome sites that you wish to exclude, but you are otherwise comfortable permitting ActiveX controls and active scripting on the rest of the Internet (perhaps because you apply patches quickly and consistently).

Misc ADM Settings (1 of 2)

- Book lists 50+ useful settings available in Administrative Templates:
  - Require password-protected screensaver with a short timeout (15 minutes)
  - Disable auto-complete in IE forms
  - Disable auto-complete in IE for passwords
  - Disable registry-editing tools
    - REGEDIT.EXE and REGEDT32.EXE

SANS Security Essentials – Windows Security

Miscellaneous Administrative Templates Settings

There are *very* many Administrative Template settings that could be used to enhance the security of users' desktops (or at least keep them out of trouble). Here is a sampling of what's possible:

- Require a password-protected screensaver with a 15-minute timeout
- Disable auto-complete of password fields in Internet Explorer pages
- Disable registry editing tools (`REGEDIT.EXE` and `REGEDT32.EXE`)
- Disable the "auto-play" feature on CD-ROM drives

Other settings can be configured to suit your environment. The following is a list of some (not all) of the available security-related options found under the Administrative Templates container in GPOs. We can't discuss them all now, so the list is provided for your browsing convenience later. All of the paths in the GPO begin with "Administrative Templates >."

NOTES

NOTES

Misc ADM Settings (2 of 2)

– Disable auto-play on CD-ROM drive
– Hide specified drives in My Computer
– Prevent access to drives from My Computer
– Disable Control Panel
– Hide specified Control Panel applets
– Disable command prompt
– Etc.

SANS Security Essentials – Windows Security

Administrative Templates >

Windows Components > Internet Explorer:

- Disable changing proxy settings
- Disable changing Automatic Configuration settings
- Disable changing ratings settings
- Disable changing certificate settings
- Disable AutoComplete for forms
- Do not allow AutoComplete to save passwords

Windows Components > Internet Explorer > Internet Control Panel:

- Disable the General page
- Disable the Security page
- Disable the Content page
- Disable the Connections page
- Disable the Programs page
- Disable the Advanced page

Windows Components > Internet Explorer > Browser Menus:

- File menu: Disable closing the browser and Explorer windows
- Tools menu: Disable Internet Options…menu option
- Disable 'Save this program to disk' option

Windows Components > Windows Explorer:

- Remove "Map Network Drive" and "Disconnect Network Drive"
- Hide these specified drives in My Computer
- Prevent access to drives from My Computer
- No "Computers Near Me" in My Network Places
- No "Entire Network" in My Network Places

Windows Components > Microsoft Management Console:

- Restrict the user from entering author mode
- Restrict users to the explicitly permitted list of snap-ins

Windows Components > Task Scheduler:

- Hide Property Pages [of tasks]
- Prevent Task Run or End
- Disable Drag-and-Drop [of .job files into the Tasks folder]

NOTES

- Disable New Task Creation
- Disable Task Deletion
- Disable Advanced Menu
- Prohibit Browse [to schedule arbitrary programs or scripts]

Start Menu & Taskbar:

- Remove common program groups from Start Menu
- Remove Run menu from Start Menu
- Disable and remove the Shut Down command

Control Panel:

- Disable Control Panel
- Hide specified Control Panel applets
- Show only specified Control Panel applets

Control Panel > Add/Remove Programs:

- Disable Add/Remove Programs
- Hide the "Add a program from CD-ROM or floppy disk" option

Control Panel > Display:

- Disable Display in Control Panel
- Hide Background tab
- Disable changing wallpaper
- Hide Appearance tab
- Hide Settings tab
- Hide Screen Saver tab
- Activate screen saver
- Screen saver executable name
- Password protect the screen saver
- Screen saver timeout

Network > Network and Dial-Up Connections:

- Prohibit deletion of RAS connections
- Prohibit access to properties of a LAN connection
- Prohibit access to current user's RAS connection properties
- Prohibit access to properties of RAS connections available to all users
- Prohibit access to the Dial-Up Preferences item on the Advanced menu
- Prohibit access to the Advanced Settings item on the Advanced menu
- Prohibit configuration of connection sharing
- Prohibit TCP/IP advanced configuration

System:

- Custom user interface
- Disable the command prompt
- Disable registry editing tools
- Run only allowed Windows applications
- Don't run specified Windows applications
- Disable Autoplay [on CD-ROM or all drives]

NOTES

System > Logon/Logoff:

- Disable Task Manager
- Disable Lock Computer
- Disable Change Password
- Disable Logoff
- Exclude directories in roaming profile
- Run these programs at user logon
- Disable the run once list
- Disable legacy run list

What About the Other Settings?

There are many other settings that can be found in security templates and GPOs that are important for security, but we can't cover them all here. Many of them will be discussed in the chapters that follow. For example, event log settings will be discussed in Chapter 30 on Windows auditing.

NOTES

Summary

- Security Templates
  - Editable INF text
  - Templates snap-in
  - Where to get them
- SCA Snap-In
- SECEDIT.EXE
- Local GPO
- Domain GPOs
- Recommendations:
  - Password Policy
  - Account Lockout
  - Security Options
  - Internet Explorer
  - Misc ADM Settings

SANS Security Essentials – Windows Security

Summary

The purpose of this chapter was to show how to quickly and easily make numerous security configuration changes. Our primary tools are security templates, the Security Configuration and Analysis snap-in, and Group Policy Objects.

Security templates store most of the settings about which we are really concerned (e.g., password and lockout policies, NTFS permissions, null user session restrictions, etc.), and there are templates free for the download from organizations that have invested a great deal of time and expertise into developing them. These pre-configured templates definitely are the way to begin: don't start from scratch!

The Security Configuration and Analysis snap-in (SCA) is used to apply templates to a system in order to reconfigure that system to match the templates. It is like a giant steel press on an assembly line of computers, and the template is the die-cast. The bad thing about the SCA, though, is that it only works on the local machine.

Group Policy Objects (GPOs), on the other hand, can apply templates to computers throughout the network automatically. And GPOs can be used to accomplish even more! GPOs also can push out a variety of scripts and registry settings, as well. In fact, not much can't be managed through Group Policy.

Next, we considered some recommendations for securing the Guest account, administrative users, null user session vulnerabilities, Internet Explorer, and other items. We could only skim the surface of all the possible issues, however, because there is just too much to talk about! Group Policy, for example, is an entire one-day seminar by itself in the Windows Track at SANS.

And while the security hardening steps in this chapter are important, we are only half-way there. In the next chapter we will discuss the bane of Windows network administrators everywhere (Service Packs and hotfixes), and then we have a chapter on securing network services like Internet Information Server.

NOTES

Chapter 28

Service Packs, Hotfixes, and Backups

NOTES

Service Packs, Hotfixes, And Backups

SANS Security Essentials V: Windows Security

SANS Security Essentials – Windows Security

Service Packs, Hotfixes, and Backups

Security conscious managers of Windows servers and workstations spend a lot of their work time with Service Packs, hotfixes, and backups. Service Packs and hotfixes must be obtained, tested, installed, and checked. The Windows operating system is extremely complex to manage; for instance, "DLL Hell" is Microsoft's term for the problems and vulnerabilities that occur when there are missing, incompatible, or out-of-date Dynamic Link Library (DLL) files on the hard drive. Updating DLLs and other system files is critical for security.

Hotfixes and Service Packs must also be coordinated with one's backups so that successful restores are possible if something goes wrong. If you do anything less than a full restore of the operating system on a machine which has had a later Service Pack applied, chances are the restore will fail to make a viable OS. Backups also are critical for disaster recovery, auditing, forensics, and being able to get back quickly to square one in the lab when testing new changes. Not having good backups is also just the sort of thing that can get you fired, so it's important to talk about having them.

This chapter will discuss techniques for applying Service Packs, installing hotfixes, and managing backups (and not just tape backups). In particular, this chapter will cover:

- Slipstreamed Service Packs
- The Network Security Hotfix Checker (`HFNETCHK.EXE`)
- System and Windows Update
- Software Update Services
- Windows Backup (`NTBACKUP.EXE`)
- Binary Drive Images
- System Restore

NOTES

NOTES

Service Packs (1 of 3)

- A giant patch...
- Mandatory!
- May cause problems.
- Test in lab first
  - Representative systems
  - VMWare, VirtualPC
- Staged deployment
  - Not all at once...

SANS Security Essentials – Windows Security

Service Packs

A Service Pack is a collection of updates and hotfixes rolled up into one large installation package (typically over 100MB in size). It is critical for security that the latest Service Pack be installed on vulnerable systems.

You can get the latest Service Pack for all the Windows operating systems from Microsoft's main download website (`http://www.microsoft.com/downloads/`).

Testing And Staging Deployments

A guaranteed recipe for disaster is to obtain a new Service Pack or patch and install it throughout the enterprise without testing it first. Though it is critical to install the latest Service Pack, doing so can break applications or cause network problems. The applications that break usually can be updated themselves, and the network problems usually can be solved, but you don't want to discover these issues the hard way.

The gentle way of discovering Service Pack problems is by:

1. Testing new Service Packs in a lab.
2. Deploying Service Packs in stages to limited groups of computers, starting with the least important systems and ending with the mission-critical ones (after making full backups of the critical ones).

A testing lab should have at least one representative computer for each type of system found on your network. Hardware and installed software should be as similar as possible to the varieties you actually have. If money is tight, then computer emulation products like VMWare (`http://www.vmware.com`) and VirtualPC (`http://www.connectix.com`) can help, but it's best to have the actual steel and silicon. It usually only takes one bad software rollout to convince management that purchasing a few test systems will actually *save* the company money (besides, you have to have disposable computers anyway when practicing your hacking skills . . . just don't tell that to the MBAs).

Performing staged deployments is just extending the "lab" to the production network a few boxes at a time. Find the least valuable or most despised users on your network and make them your unwilling guinea pigs. If all goes well, then roll out the new software in ever-widening circles until the entire LAN is upgraded. Unless there are red-hot issues that will be fixed by the update, mission-critical servers and the desktops of management should be upgraded last. Ensure you have a full backup of the critical systems first, and consider doing the install during off-peak hours.

NOTES

NOTES

Slipstreaming (2 of 3)
• Install OS and SP at the same time:
1. Copy Windows CD-ROM to a shared folder.
2. UPDATE.EXE –S C:\SharedFolder
– This will merge the SP into the OS installation files.
3. Burn a copy of the shared folder to a CD-ROM
– Can be a bootable CD-ROM if you wish.
4. Install Windows OS from the share or the CD-ROM and the SP will be merged in simultaneously!
SANS Security Essentials – Windows Security

Slipstreamed Service Packs

Wouldn't it be nice to be able to install the operating system and the latest Service Pack in one shot? You can do it if you "slipstream" the Service Pack into the installation process! Here's the recipe:

1. Copy the entire Windows CD-ROM to a folder on the local server where you are sitting.
2. Get the latest Service Pack from Microsoft, and extract its files to another folder (not the folder in the prior step) by running the Service Pack executable with the "`-X`" switch, e.g., "`W2KSP3.EXE -X`". You will be prompted for the target extraction folder.
3. In the extraction folder, go to the \i386\Update\ subdirectory and run the following command: "`UPDATE.EXE -S:PathToInstallFolder`", where *PathToInstallFolder* is the full path to the local folder where you copied the Windows CD-ROM. The "`-S`" switch will merge the files from the Service Pack into the \i386 folder with the OS files, overwriting the older versions of the same files there.
4. Share that installation folder on the network and burn a copy of it onto a CD-ROM. This can be a bootable CD-ROM if you wish (`http://www.nu2.nu/bootablecd/`).
5. Install Windows from either the shared folder or the CD-ROM, and the merged Service Pack will be installed automatically at install time!

NOTES

Hands-Free Service Packs (3 of 3)

- Automate the SP installation:
  - Use the same share in prior slide...
  - Create a batch file there:
    - net use M: *server**sharedfolder* /persistent:no
    - M:\i386\update\update.exe -u -f -o -q
  - Now run batch file from any machine:
    - Run line → *server**sharedfolder*\batch.bat
    - EXEC.VBS or SCHTASKS.EXE
  - Or use Group Policy to push out SP's.

SANS Security Essentials – Windows Security

Installing Service Packs Hands-Free

Slipstreamed Service Packs are convenient when installing a fresh OS, but what about the boxes that are already running? What can be done to make Service Pack installation easier?

The Service Pack installation program (`UPDATE.EXE`) supports command-line switches to make the installation work without user intervention required (execute "`UPDATE.EXE /?`" for the full list of switches). Consider extracting the Service Pack files to a shared folder ("`-X`" switch again) and saving a batch file in the root of the share. When run, the batch file should map a local drive letter back to the share and install the Service Pack automatically. The batch file doesn't have to be more complex than this:

```
net.exe use M: \\server\share /persistent:no

M:\i386\update\update.exe -u -f -o -q
```

Can't Group Policy Do It?

It's beyond the scope of this course, but Group Policy can be used to push out Service Packs to computers automatically. This is possible because Windows 2000/XP/.NET Service Packs come with a file named `UPDATE.MSI`, which can be used by the built-in Windows Installer service on each machine to handle the installation process. In fact, with an application like InstallShield Developer (`http://www.installshield.com`) or Wise for Windows Installer (`http://www.wise.com`), you can create your own MSI files and push out virtually any software you wish to your systems hands-free.

Now, at any computer, you simply can go to the Run line and execute "`\\server\share\batchfile.bat`" and walk away! This command will connect to the share, download the batch file, and run it to install the Service Pack. Using the `EXEC.VBS` script from the *Resource Kit* you can execute the commands from the batch file (or any other commands) on a remote system without having to walk over to it. A batch file or other script could run the `EXEC.VBS` script against a range of systems. Or with the Windows XP/.NET `SCHTASKS.EXE` tool, you can schedule those commands to be executed on remote systems during off-peak hours. There are many options for automating the process . . . if you have Windows 2000/XP/.NET.

There also are third-party tools for pushing out Service Packs; they will be discussed shortly.

NOTES

Hotfixes (1 of 5)

- Hotfix replaces one or a few operating system files; later bundled in next SP.
- **Usually issue- or exploit-specific, but there are cumulative "roll-up" hotfixes too.**
- Obtaining, testing, deploying and auditing hotfixes will consume a great deal of your time as the security administrator.
- http://www.microsoft.com/security/

SANS Security Essentials – Windows Security

Hotfixes

A *hotfix* is a small program from Microsoft which will replace one or a few operating system files currently on the hard drive with updated versions. A hotfix usually is intended to fix a single problem or patch a single hole, but there also are "roll-up" or "cumulative" hotfixes that fix many issues at once. Often a variety of hotfixes will be released to deal with a new spate of related problems, then Microsoft will bundle these patches together into one roll-up hotfix.

Staying on top of the latest hotfixes, testing them, rolling them out to boxes, and auditing their correct distribution will consume a great deal of your time. And, again, it is essential to the security of your network that you test and apply patches soon after their release, especially on Internet-accessible servers.

You can download the latest patches and roll-up hotfixes from Microsoft's security site (`http://www.microsoft.com/security/`). The best way to stay on top of new patches, though, isn't by visiting Microsoft's website four times a day. The easiest way to keep on top of new hotfixes, exploits, viruses, etc., is by subscribing to free e-mail security bulletin services and joining security mailing lists.

E-Mail Security Bulletins (2 of 5)

- Easiest way to stay on top of new patches, SP's, exploits and news.
- Almost impossible to do your job well if you're not subscribing to *something*...
- Many excellent bulletins are free!
  - http://www.microsoft.com/security/
  - http://www.ntbugtraq.com
  - http://www.sans.org
  - http://www.kbalertz.com
  - And many others...

SANS Security Essentials – Windows Security

E-Mail Security Bulletins

Subscribing to e-mail security bulletins and mailing lists is so important that the present author once advised a client to fire his "security administrator" for not having even a single subscription. (The administrator complained: "Our virus scanners update themselves automatically; why do I need to read about it?") Perhaps if one is browsing security and hacking websites every day, then maybe it isn't necessary to subscribe to anything, but it sure makes work more difficult. Besides, many interesting people work in your field; you should get to know them!

Which bulletins to subscribe to? Some of the most popular services and lists can be found at the following websites, and all are free:

- `http://www.microsoft.com/security/`
- `http://www.ntbugtraq.com`
- `http://www.sans.org`
- `http://www.kbalertz.com`

The last site is not for security *per se*: whenever Microsoft publishes new KnowledgeBase "Q-articles" that are of interest to you, the service will send you a summary list. (Q-articles are how-to and help articles.) There are over 100 different categories of interest from which you can select, so you'll only be apprised of items about which you care.

If you'd also like to browse security sites to stay informed, then a good place to start is `http://packetstormsecurity.nl`. The Packetstorm web site is easy to search, contains a variety of articles from different "perspectives" on security, and usually has a link to any hacking/security tool you are likely to try to find.

NOTES

Installing Multiple Hotfixes (3 of 5)

- Windows 2000/XP/.NET patches can usually be installed in any order and you only have to reboot once.
- **-M** switch = hands-free installation.
- **-Z** switch = don't reboot afterwards.
- QCHAIN.EXE and SHUTDOWN.EXE

SANS Security Essentials – Windows Security

Installing Multiple Hotfixes

On Windows NT, hotfixes typically had to be installed in a fixed order, and you often had to reboot after each patch. Windows 2000/XP/.NET hotfixes, on the other hand, usually can be installed in any order—and you don't have to reboot each time, if you use a simple trick.

Hotfix executables support a command-line switch to make their installation hands-free (-M) and another to prevent the automatic reboot of the system (-Z). Multiple hotfixes, therefore, can be installed easily with a single batch file. The last command in the batch file should reboot the system, e.g., with the SHUTDOWN.EXE utility from the *Resource Kit*. The following is a sample batch file:

```
c:\hotfixes\Q423456_w2k_sp3_x86.exe -z -m
c:\hotfixes\Q927324_w2k_sp3_x86.exe -z -m
c:\hotfixes\Q814933_w2k_sp3_x86.exe -z -m
c:\hotfixes\Q745615_w2k_sp3_x86.exe -z -m
c:\hotfixes\Q313789_w2k_sp3_x86.exe -z -m
qchain.exe
shutdown.exe /r
```

Note

If you need to uninstall a patch manually, go to the %SystemRoot%\$NtUninstall*Q555555*$\ folder, where *Q555555* is your patch number, and run "hotfix.exe -y -m" there.

What Does QCHAIN.EXE Do?

A problem occurs when two or more hotfixes both update the same file(s): which hotfix becomes the effective one? Fortunately, the problem is solved if the QCHAIN.EXE utility is run after the patches have been installed but before the system is rebooted. QCHAIN.EXE allows us to install multiple patches in a row without rebooting after each one. Search Microsoft's website for "QCHAIN.EXE" to locate the latest download URL (it seems to change often), or find article number Q296861 to get the URL.

NOTES

Organize Hotfixes (4 of 5)

- Shared folder with all hotfixes and Service Packs

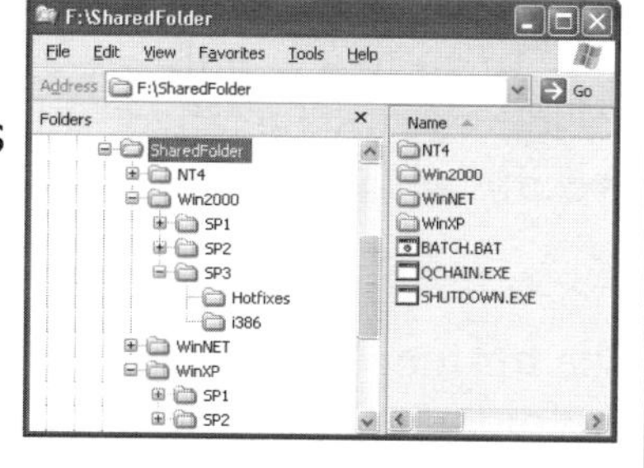

- Dump all new hotfixes into the correct folder.

Use BATCH.BAT file on next slide →

SANS Security Essentials – Windows Security

Organize Hotfixes

A nice way of setting up all this is to have for the operating systems you manage a shared folder with subdirectories for each OS and Service Pack level:

```
\\server\sharedfolder\nt4\sp5\hotfixes\

\\server\sharedfolder\nt4\sp6\hotfixes\

\\server\sharedfolder\win2000\sp2\hotfixes\

\\server\sharedfolder\win2000\sp3\hotfixes\

\\server\sharedfolder\winXP\sp1\hotfixes\
```

You'll extract the appropriate Service Pack source files into the folder named after it; this will create the Service Pack's \i386 folder at the same level as the \hotfixes folder.

NOTES

BATCH.BAT (5 of 5)

- At the Run line on remote system:
  *server**sharedfolder*\batch.bat win2000 sp3
- BATCH.BAT file in shared folder root:

```
net use m: \\server\sharedfolder /persistent:no
m:
cd %1\%2\Hotfixes
For %%x In (Q*.exe) Do %%x -z -m
cd \
qchain.exe
shutdown.exe -r -t 1 -c "Reboot to install hotfixes"
```

SANS Security Essentials – Windows Security

Batch File Automation

Next, into each \hotfixes folder you'll put every available hotfix for that Service Pack level. Copy `QCHAIN.EXE` and `SHUTDOWN.EXE` to the root of the share. Finally, create a batch file similar to the following and place it in the root of the share too:

```
net use m: \\server\sharedfolder /
persistent:no

m:

cd %1\%2\Hotfixes

For %%x In (Q*.exe) Do %%x -z -m

cd \

qchain.exe

shutdown.exe -r -t 1 -c "Reboot to install
hotfixes"
```

When you call the batch script from a remote box, make the first command-line argument to the script the name of the OS (this becomes the "%1" in the script), and make the second argument the Service Pack level (this becomes the "%2"). Hence, if you were to go to a Windows 2000 system with Service Pack 3 already installed, the command you would execute at the Run line would look like this:

```
\\server\share\batch.bat win2000 sp3
```

The for-loop will install any hotfixes in the subfolder as long as the hotfix begins with "Q" (and they do by default). Now you simply can dump new hotfixes into the appropriate shares as the hotfixes are published and keep them organized at the same time. Those same shared folders also could house the slipstreamed installation files too (discussed earlier) and have another batch file for installing Service Packs. If we were using VBScript or Perl, then even more could be automated.

NOTES

The Hotfix Checker (1 of 3)

- **HFNETCHK.EXE**
  - Lists hotfixes that are not installed.
  - Local or remote systems:
    - Windows NT/2000/XP/.NET
    - IIS 4.0 and 5.0
    - SQL Server 7.0 and 2000
    - Internet Explorer 5.01 and later
  - Can scan a range of IP addresses.

SANS Security Essentials – Windows Security

The Network Security Hotfix Checker

While Microsoft's security website and the above e-mail lists are useful for discovering what hotfixes currently are available, it is still a pain to figure out which hotfixes are relevant to a particular computer. For example, a certain patch might have been published two months ago, but has that patch been bundled into any other cumulative patches that already have been applied? How can you know that a particular system has all of the relevant patches for it and that they are still effective (i.e., have not been overwritten or deleted) on the machine? These are questions that no website or bulletin service can answer, and it's not always practical just to reinstall every hotfix every time you're uncertain.

Fortunately, Microsoft has a nice tool named the "Network Security Hotfix Checker" (`HFNETCHK.EXE`), which can check servers to ensure that all the latest hotfixes have been installed. It can check hotfixes for the following products on either local or remote systems:

- Windows 2000
- Windows NT 4.0
- IIS 4.0 and 5.0
- SQL Server 7.0 and 2000
- Internet Explorer 5.01 and later

What makes this tool different is that every time it runs it connects to Microsoft's website, downloads the latest list of hotfixes (in XML format), compares the server's hotfixes against the list, and then reports which hotfixes are missing! Hence, the tool helps alert you to the fact that new hotfixes are available, tells you which hotfixes have not yet been applied to a box, and enables you to perform over-the-network audits of the patch level status of your critical servers. And it's free!

NOTES

Hotfix Checker Database (2 of 3)

- **HFNETCHK.EXE** downloads a database of hotfix information from Microsoft each time it runs:
  - Downloaded with HTTP
  - XML digitally-signed database file
  - Includes patch information, Q-article numbers, file versions, dependencies, file signature data, etc.
  - Can download manually if you prefer

SANS Security Essentials – Windows Security

XML Database of Patch Data

The XML file has information about the files in each hotfix, their version numbers and checksums, which hotfixes are superceded by a given hotfix, which hotfixes are unnecessary after a given Service Pack has been applied, registry values modified, related Q-articles, and other information. When downloaded, the XML file comes in a compressed and digitally-signed CAB file.

An examination of the packets shows that `HFNETCHK.EXE` is doing a simple HTTP download of the database file. If you don't trust Microsoft, or if you don't want your system to have direct contact with the Internet, you can also download the database separately and pass its local path into `HFNETCHK.EXE` with a command-line argument.

Hotfix Checker Usage (3 of 3)

- Can examine the files themselves and ignore the registry data (-z).
- Get the latest version from Shavlik.
- Create a scheduled batch file to scan critical machines every day.
- Why doesn't it list all possible patches?

SANS Security Essentials – Windows Security

Can Examine the Files Themselves

The `HFNETCHK.EXE` tool does not merely inspect data written to the registry about hotfixes. It also verifies that the necessary files do, in fact, exist on the drive and with the correct version number and checksum. In fact, the tool supports a command-line argument ("`-Z`") which will cause it to ignore the registry data and only examine the patched files on the hard drive. If you seem to be getting inconsistent results between `HFNETCHK.EXE` and other tools, make sure to run `HFNETCHK.EXE` with the `-Z` switch.

Get the Latest Version

`HFNETCHK.EXE` originally was developed by Shavlik Technologies (`http://www.shavlik.com`), and new features are being added all the time. Make sure to get the latest version from Microsoft's website (`http://www.microsoft.com/technet/security/tools.asp`). Even better, get the latest version directly from Shavlik! Shavlik has both a free and commercial version of the tool, and enhanced features not offered with Microsoft's version.

Why Aren't All the Patches Listed?

It is not the case that every available patch from Microsoft makes it into the XML database that `HFNETCHK.EXE` uses. And, if a patch does make it into the database, its inclusion may occur weeks after the patch originally was released. We have no control over what goes into the database, and Microsoft adds hotfix information as it sees fit. This is another reason to subscribe to e-mail security bulletins: if you rely completely on `HFNETCHK.EXE`, you may be missing important hotfixes. Unfortunately, this problem of missing hotfixes also is an issue with Windows Update and Automatic Update.

NOTES

NOTES

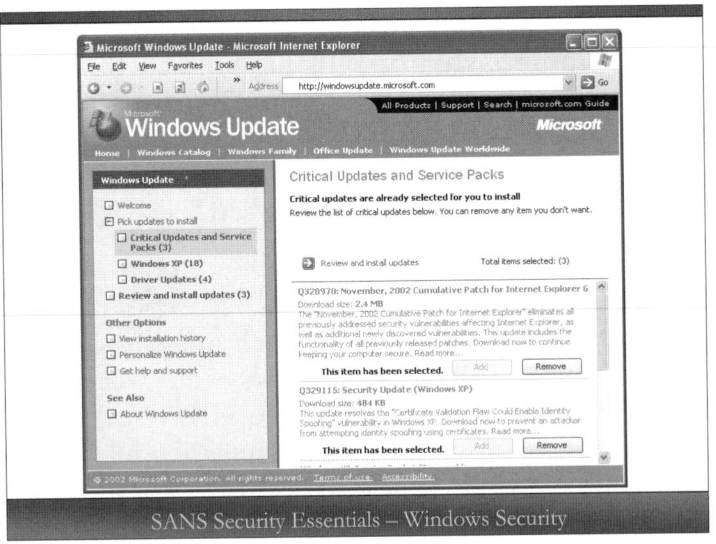

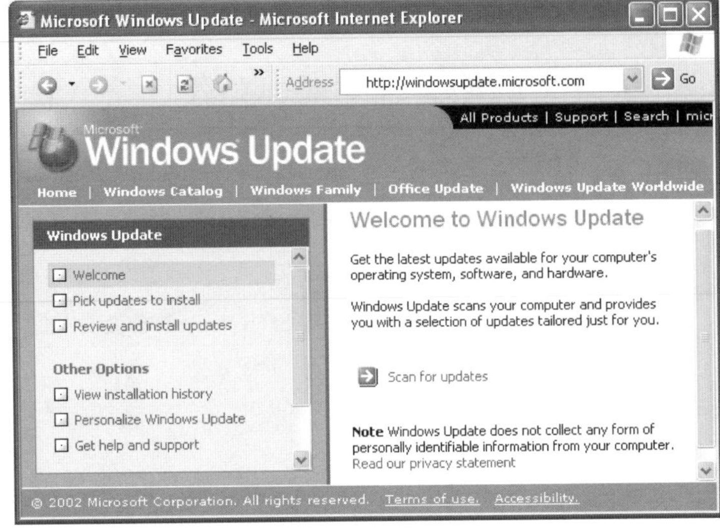

Windows Update and Automatic Updates

Microsoft's `HFNETCHK.EXE` is nice, but it doesn't actually install the patches it lists. We've already discussed the rock-solid way of installing hotfixes (batch files), but there are other options.

Windows Update has been around for a while now. Simply browse to `http://windowsupdate.microsoft.com`, and you will load into Internet Explorer an ActiveX control that scans your system for missing hotfixes.

The page will display a list of the hotfixes and their descriptions where you can select which ones you want installed. Once selected, you click the "Install Now" button on the webpage, and the necessary files are downloaded from Microsoft and installed automatically. Despite the fact that not all patches are available this way, Windows Update is very easy to use, and the bugs in its earlier incarnations mainly have been worked out. This is what most home and small office users depend on and most computer manufacturers ensure a "Windows Update" icon is at the top of the Start menu.

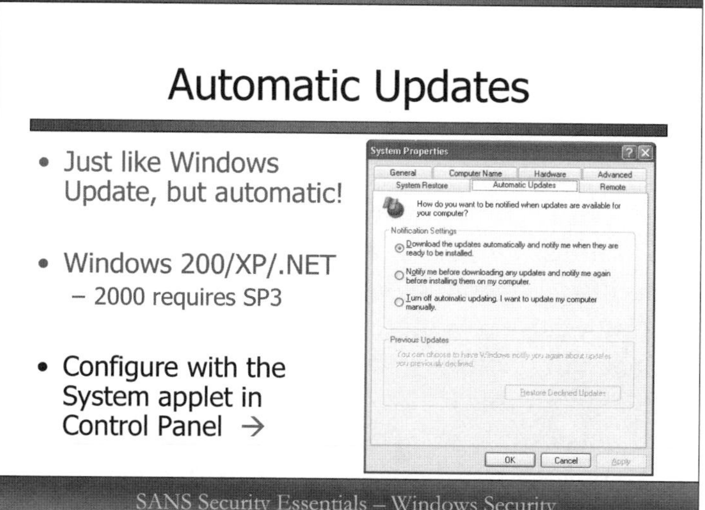

Automatic Updates
• Just like Windows Update, but automatic!
• Windows 200/XP/.NET
– 2000 requires SP3
• Configure with the System applet in Control Panel →
System Properties
General
Computer Name
Hardware
Advanced
System Restore
Automatic Updates
Remote
OK
Cancel
SANS Security Essentials – Windows Security

Automatic Updates

Of course, that's also the weakness of Windows Update: the user has to know about it and choose to go to the website. Automatic Updates, on the other hand, is automatic. It works just like Windows Update, but it connects in the background on a scheduled basis and then only prompts the user to install the hotfixes after they have been downloaded (and user interaction isn't required; see the next section).

Automatic Updates is built into Windows XP/.NET, but it is installed on Windows 2000 with Service Pack 3 or later. To configure your settings in Windows XP/.NET, go to the System applet in Control Panel and click on the Automatic Updates tab. In Windows 2000, after you've installed Service Pack 3 or later, a new applet named Automatic Updates will appear in Control Panel. You can disable Automatic Updates entirely or require your interaction for the hotfixes to be downloaded and/or installed.

The bad news, though, is that neither Windows Update nor Automatic Updates will cause all of the patches listed by `HFNETCHK.EXE` to be installed, and, as we discussed before, `HFNETCHK.EXE` itself doesn't list all possible patches anyway. Is there a solution? Yes, get the patches by hand and use batch files. Is there *another* solution? Well, maybe.

NOTES

Software Update Services (1 of 3)

- Next version of Automatic Updates:
  - Your own local Automatic Updates Server!
- With your own internal SUS Server:
  - Control exactly which hotfixes to deploy.
  - Clients can download from your SUS Server or from Microsoft's servers (your choice).
  - Install hotfixes to machines during off-peak hours, even when no one is logged on at the SUS client machines.

SANS Security Essentials – Windows Security

Software Update Services

Software Update Services (SUS) is the next version of Automatic Updates. Support for SUS is installed automatically with Windows 2000 Service Pack 3 or later, Windows XP Service Pack 1 or later, and is built into Windows .NET Server. (It is not available for Windows 9x/NT.) There are three shortcomings in Automatic and Windows Update which SUS overcomes:

- Administrators cannot centrally control exactly which hotfixes users are permitted to download with Automatic or Windows Update, but this is possible with SUS. The SUS Server administrator chooses exactly which patches to distribute.
- Each computer connects directly to Microsoft itself and downloads its own hotfixes with Automatic or Windows Update, thus consuming a great deal of bandwidth out to the Internet; but this is not necessary with SUS. SUS clients can connect to a local SUS Server and download their hotfixes from there.
- A user must be a member of the local Administrators or Power Users groups in order to install operating system patches through Automatic or Windows Update, or when installing hotfixes manually (like with batch files), but this is not necessary with SUS. SUS clients can download and install updates even if no one is logged on at the machine at all.

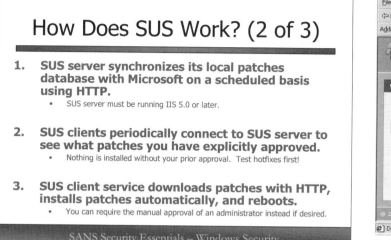

NOTES

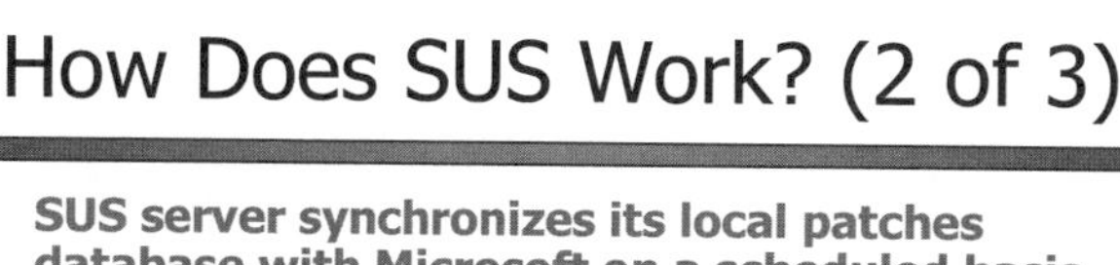

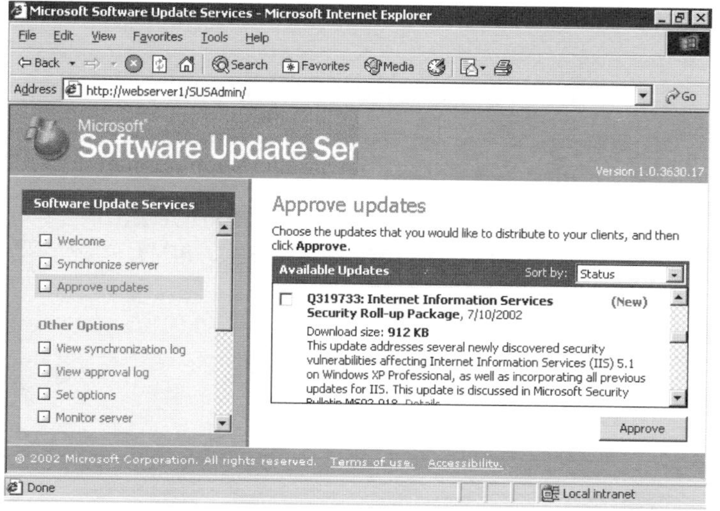

How Does SUS Work?

One or more local "SUS servers" can be installed on Windows 2000/.NET Servers. You can't use Windows 2000 Professional, Windows XP, or Windows NT as an SUS server. The only other requirements are that these boxes have IIS installed and not be domain controllers. The SUS servers will connect to Microsoft and download the latest information about available updates on a scheduled basis (the schedule is determined by the administrator).

Administrators choose exactly which updates they want distributed inside the LAN to SUS clients. Presumably, this is after the administrator has tested the patches in a lab. You select which hotfixes you want deployed by connecting to a special administrative website on the SUS server itself.

The update files from Microsoft can be downloaded to the local SUS server and then downloaded by clients from there, or clients can be directed to download just the approved updates directly from Microsoft. Caching the files locally on the SUS server, of course, will spare Internet bandwidth consumption. Indeed, if you have a very large number clients, you can make your other SUS servers download their files from your "master" SUS server that downloads from Microsoft.

SUS clients download updates using the Background Intelligent Transfer (BITS) service. This "drizzles" the packages down to the client in the background so that other applications are not interrupted, and bandwidth is not monopolized by SUS.

NOTES

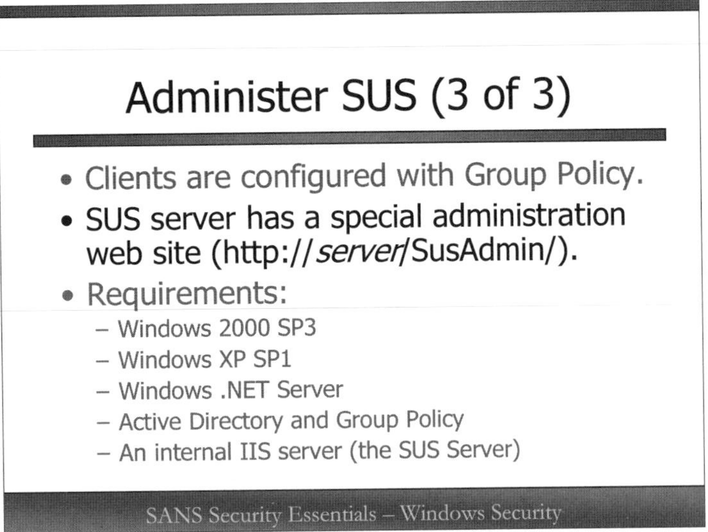

Administer SUS (3 of 3)
• Clients are configured with Group Policy.
• SUS server has a special administration web site (http://server/SusAdmin/).
• Requirements:
– Windows 2000 SP3
– Windows XP SP1
– Windows .NET Server
– Active Directory and Group Policy
– An internal IIS server (the SUS Server)
SANS Security Essentials – Windows Security

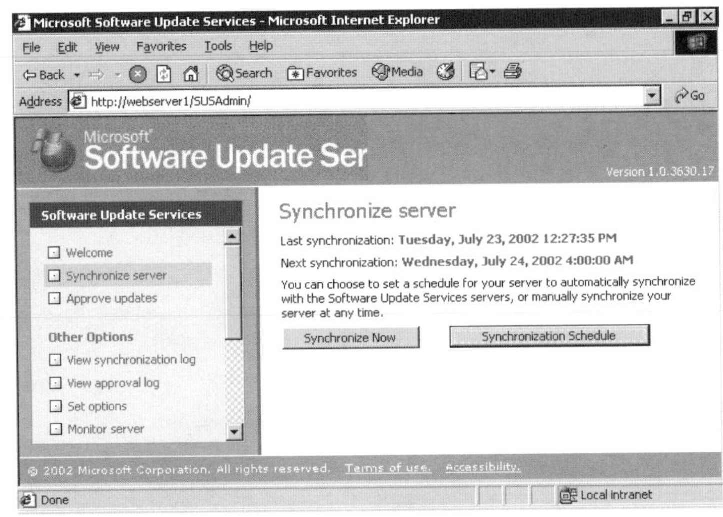

Administer Software Update Services

With Group Policy, SUS clients are informed of their local SUS server, the schedule for checking for new updates, and whether or not the updates should be installed automatically. If not automatically installed, an administrator will have to log on and approve the patch installation. Group Policy, of course, requires that the computers be a member of an Active Directory domain.

The SUS server software (about 50MB) can be downloaded for free from `http://www.microsoft.com/windows2000/windowsupdate/sus/`. Once installed, you manage the download schedule, the list of approved patches, etc. through a website on the SUS server itself (`http://servername/SUSAdmin/`). The configuration of all the clients to the SUS server is accomplished through Group Policy. Group Policy as a whole cannot be discussed here, but, as a quick overview, you import the WUAU.ADM template from the SUS server into your Group Policy Object and configure the settings in the GPO under Computer Configuration > Administrative Templates > Windows Components > Windows Update. (For more information, Microsoft's SUS website above has a detailed whitepaper on SUS administration, and the SANS Windows Track discusses Group Policy and SUS in detail.) Clients download the patches from the local SUS server using HTTP just as they do from Microsoft with Windows Update.

Through Group Policy, SUS clients are configured to connect to their local SUS server on a scheduled basis. Users can be permitted to have full control over the update process (requiring their approval for both download and install of hotfixes), or SUS can work in the background at night to install and reboot machines, even when no one is logged on at them. (If someone is logged on when the installation process begins, the user gets a five-minute warning to save her data and log off.)

NOTES

3rd-Party Patch Management

- Excellent non-Microsoft products available to help manage patches:
  - www.shavlik.com
  - www.bindview.com
  - www.stbernard.com
  - www.pedestalsoftware.com
  - www.polarisgroup.com
  - And many other companies that can't all be listed here...

SANS Security Essentials – Windows Security

Third-Party Patch Management Tools

A variety of non-Microsoft tools exist to help manage hotfixes and patches, too. When comparing products, make sure to ask the vendors if their products can install the hotfix or Service Pack automatically and whether the product requires "agent" software to be installed first. Note, too, that there are vast differences in price between these products.

Shavlik Technologies, for example, jointly developed the XML database of hotfixes used by Microsoft and wrote the `HFNETCHK.EXE` tool (`http://www.shavlik.com`). Shavlik offers their own XML-enabled products, including the free QuickInspector tool, which can scan Windows NT/2000/XP and Microsoft Office products for missing hotfixes and other vulnerabilities. Shavlik also has a COM object for the `HFNETCHK.EXE` tool so that it can be scripted, e.g., logon scripts and more flexible scanning, as well as a GUI enterprise version of the `HFNETCHK.EXE` tool.

Note

The Component Object Model (COM) is a software architecture model developed by Microsoft that allows you to build applications by using binary objects. COM is an architecture that allows you build applications fairly quickly. More information can be found at: `http://www.microsoft.com/com/tech/com.asp`

BindView Corporation is, perhaps, the industry leader in Windows enterprise management and security products (`http://www.bindview.com`). BindView sells the bv-Control and bv-Admin packages for managing Windows NT/2000, Exchange Server, NetWare, Unix, OS/400, and SAP Systems platforms. For security and hotfixes, check out the bv-Control for Internet Security tool and the RAZOR Team's website (`http://razor.bindview.com`). A feature of the bv-Control tool is the Security Advisor, which will analyze the patch level of a Windows system.

St. Bernard Software sells a utility named UpdateExpert (`http://www.stbernard.com`) that will list what Service Packs and hot fixes are installed (or *not* installed) on a system and help to install the missing ones.

Pedestal Software's Security Expressions (`http://www.pedestalsoftware.com`) is similar to the Security Configuration and Analysis tool, but it also allows you to detect missing hotfixes, then

NOTES

download and install them automatically. It works on Solaris and Unix (using SSH for secure communications) and has Group Policy integrated features for the Windows boxes. No agent software must be installed.

The Polaris Group Service Pack & Hotfix Utility (`http://www.polarisgroup.com`) detects missing patches and Service Packs and can apply them automatically. It has both a GUI and command-line version, and either fits on a single floppy disk. A simple .INI file is edited to customize the operation of the utility. Polaris supports Windows NT/2000, IIS, SQL Server, and Exchange Server.

Many other companies provide wonderful patching solutions as well, but they all can't be listed here. If your current solution isn't on the above list, that doesn't mean it's bad or not as good as these.

NOTES

Windows Backup

- Having current backups is needed for:
  - Forensics
  - Performing audits against a baseline
  - Disaster recovery
- You have to assume that *eventually* your servers will get hacked...

SANS Security Essentials – Windows Security

Windows Backup

So, you've got a patched machine with the latest Service Pack—now what? *Back it up!* Windows is not a happy operating system if you restore OS files from archives that pre-date the currently installed Service Pack. Moreover, having adequate backups are indispensable for doing forensics, performing an audit against a prior baseline, and surviving disasters in general. You also need to perform a backup on critical systems right before you apply a new Service Pack or patch so that you quickly can get back to square one if necessary. And you have to assume that *eventually* your servers will be rooted, and your workstations will be infected with data-chomping viruses (Obi-Wan Kenobi is not your only hope), so you should have recent backups, too.

NOTES

A New Hope...

- **NTBACKUP.EXE**
- Back up to tape, archive file or CD/DVD.
- Save archive to remote share.
- Wizard to schedule backups.
- ERD/ASR disks.

- **Can back up:**
  - From shared folders
  - Active Directory
  - Exchange Server
  - Cluster Server quorum
  - Locked/open files
  - Local registry
  - EFS files in their encrypted state

SANS Security Essentials – Windows Security

A New Hope: NTBACKUP.EXE

The Windows NT 4.0 Backup program was more-or-less unusable. Fortunately, Microsoft got rid of it. The new Windows Backup application built into Windows 2000/XP/.NET, `NTBACKUP.EXE`, is a *vast* improvement. It was co-developed with VERITAS of Backup Exec fame (`http://www.veritas.com`) and really is one of the unsung gems of the operating system (*thank you VERITAS!*).

The new Windows Backup can do the following:

- Backup to tape or to an archive file on a local hard drive, in a remote share, or burned directly to a local CD/DVD recorder.
- Backup data from remote shared folders over the network.
- Backup the registry (local only).
- Backup the Active Directory, Exchange Server, Certificate Services, Component Services, and the Cluster Server quorum databases while running on-line with active users (local only).
- Backup open or locked files on running servers, even while users are writing to those files (creates a snapshot at an instant in time of the state of the file when backup begins).
- Backup EFS-encrypted files in their encrypted state.
- Schedule automatic backups with a user-friendly graphical wizard. Scheduled jobs run under the context of whatever username and password are provided.
- `NTBACKUP.EXE` can be run hands-free with command-line switches, as in a scheduled batch file or shortcut icon.
- Create an Emergency Repair Disk (ERD) in Windows 2000 or an Automated System Recovery (ASR) disk in Windows XP Professional. (ERD and ASR disks assist in the recovery of irrecoverably crashed systems that must be booted from the installation CD-ROM or from the setup floppy disks.)
- Runs in either "Wizard Mode" or "Advanced Mode." In Wizard Mode, the program walks the novice user through the entire backup or restore process, hiding the obscure options. In Advanced Mode, the user manages every aspect of the backup/restore process.
- Backs up files currently managed by the Remote Storage System. ("Remote Storage" is a technique for making the contents of remote

archives, in tape or file format, appear as though they are on the local hard drive, and keeping the local cache of these files in sync with that remote archive.)

- Backup files using media pools managed by the Removable Storage System. ("Removable Storage" is the service which manages tape/CD/DVD libraries in robotic "jukebox" changers.)
- Members of the Backup Operators group can use it to back up files even if those members do not have NTFS read access to the files.
- Can erase, format, retension, and catalog tapes.
- Is compatible with mount and junction points. (A "junction point" is a partition that is accessed through or "mounted on" what appears to be a regular folder in the current volume. Junctions are created with `LINKD.EXE` from the *Resource Kit*.)
- Provides detailed per-file logging to a textual log file.

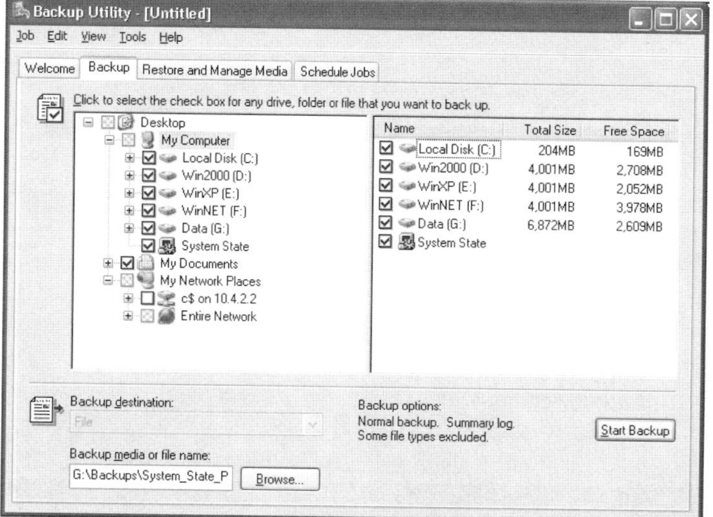

NOTES

NOTES

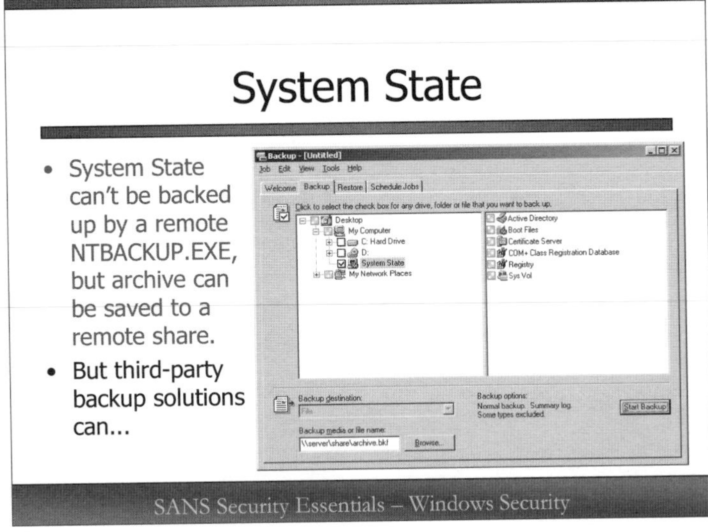

System State
• System State can't be backed up by a remote NTBACKUP.EXE, but archive can be saved to a remote share.
• But third-party backup solutions can...
SANS Security Essentials – Windows Security

System State

Perhaps the most important data for the restoration of your OS is the "System State." There is a checkbox just for this in the Backup program. The System State always includes the local registry and boot-up files, but, depending on what other services are installed on the machine, may also include the Active Directory database, the SYSVOL share on domain controllers, the Certificate Server database, etc.

Very unfortunately, though, the System State cannot be backed up over the network by `NTBACKUP.EXE`, so you'll need to schedule a backup on each machine you wish to protect. You don't have to install a tape drive on each box, but you will have to schedule Backup to run locally. The archive file produced can be written across the network to a share directly, or the archive can be copied or backed up over the network again by some other system, but you don't get a fully centralized backup solution as with third-party commercial products.

Third-Party Backup Solutions

- Many excellent non-Microsoft backup solutions are available:
  - BrightStor ARCserve (www.ca.com)
  - Backup Exec and NetBackup (www.veritas.com)
  - UltraBac (www.ultrabac.com)
  - Legato Networker(www.legato.com)
  - Backup Express (www.syncsort.com)
  - Galaxy (www.commvault.com)
  - OmniBack II and Data Protector (www.hp.com)
  - And others that can't all be listed here...

SANS Security Essentials – Windows Security

Third-Party Backup Solutions

There are many excellent third-party backup products for Windows (they rushed in to fill the void Windows NT 4.0 Backup created). A great place to start your search for better solutions are the following products and manufacturers:

- BrightStor ARCserve (`http://www.ca.com`)
- Backup Exec and NetBackup (`http://www.veritas.com`)
- UltraBac (`http://www.ultrabac.com`)
- Legato Networker(`http://www.legato.com`)
- Backup Express (`http://www.syncsort.com`)
- Galaxy (`http://www.commvault.com`)
- OmniBack II and Data Protector (`http://www.hp.com`)

Just as with third-party patch management solutions, though, these products will scale better, but they're not exactly free.

NOTES

NOTES

Binary Disk Images

- Example: Symantec Ghost®
- Creates an image file of an entire drive or partition.
- Image can be saved to hard disk or burned to CD/DVD.
- Machine must be rebooted.

SANS Security Essentials – Windows Security

Binary Disk Images

A special type of backup involves creating a "binary image" of the desired disk or partition. Symantec Ghost is probably the most famous of these imaging products (`http://www.symantec.com/ghost`), but many of the backup vendors in the list above also sell disk imaging utilities.

A binary disk image can be reapplied to the original machine from which it was made in order to completely restore the machine to its state at that time. You don't have to worry about open files, transaction logs, the registry, or other ephemeral data structures being missed because the image captures all file data. This is a problem with many regular backup programs, even if they claim to be able to backup and restore all files no matter what (including Microsoft's Backup program). A binary disk image also can be applied to another drive on another machine entirely to replicate the original one.

Unfortunately, making a disk image requires rebooting the target machine from a special floppy disk or CD-ROM. Hence, disk imaging is not appropriate for nightly backups of 24x7 servers. The image file itself, though compressed, also can grow very large. Image files can be saved to another hard drive or partition, written to tape, burned to a DVD/CD-ROM, or copied across the network to a server. If the image file is too large for the media chosen, many imaging products will split the file into manageable chunks; during the restore process, the imaging software will request the various chunks as needed to reconstruct the original data. Also, restoring from a disk image usually is faster than restoring from more traditional formats.

Here's an example of when disk imaging can save the day. Design your IIS web servers so that they use removable hard drive cartridges. Once you've configured the operating system and IIS the way you want, create an image on a "stand-by" drive cartridge. If the server is hacked or mysteriously dies, pop in the stand-by cartridge, keep the first drive for forensics analysis, copy the latest web site files over from the webmaster's machine, and you're back up and running in just a few minutes. The more frequently you make an image, then less you'll need to restore.

Again, the real drawback of disk imaging is that you must reboot the machine every time you make an image. It's just too inconvenient for daily use. But if all you want to back up is the registry and drivers database, then Windows XP/.NET can make images of this data on a regular basis automatically.

System Restore (1 of 3)

- Available only on Windows XP/.NET
- It's like a time machine for the registry.
- System Restore points are made:
  - Every 24 hours
  - Just before Automatic Update installs files
  - Just before Backup restores files
  - Just before a prior snapshot is restored
  - Just before a new application/driver is installed
  - Anytime the user manually requests it

SANS Security Essentials – Windows Security

System Restore

"System Restore" is available only on Windows XP and later. It works invisibly in the background, saving snapshots of your computer's configuration. These snapshots are saved for weeks. The good thing is, if you have problems, you can use the System Restore wizard to reinstall one of those saved configurations. It's like a having a time machine for the registry! You launch the wizard by going to the Start Menu > All Programs > Accessories > System Tools > System Restore. Here you can browse through a calendar to select the saved configuration to which you want to return. And there will be many to choose.

The System Restore snapshot, called a "restore point," is created automatically at a variety of times:

- Just after installing the operating system.
- Every 24 hours thereafter.
- Just before Automatic Updates install new files.
- Just before a user installs new software.
- Just before installing a new driver.
- Just before Windows Backup restores any files.
- Just before a restore point is restored.
- Whenever the user manually requests a restore point using the System Restore wizard.

Depending on the amount of free space on the hard drive, there might be checkpoints available for the prior one to three weeks! Importantly, System Restore does not restore user data files; it only restores registry settings, INI configuration files, driver files, and some operating system files.

NOTES

NOTES

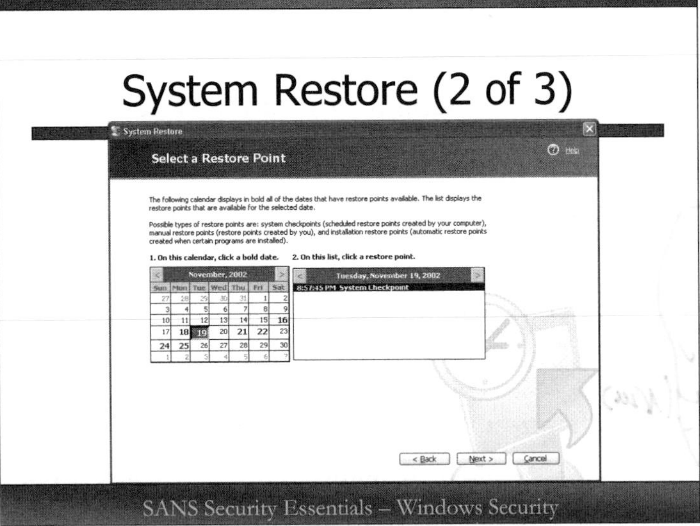

If nothing else, System Restore has the potential to save you hours of drudgery when fixing servers or users' desktops. If you know that the box was working fine yesterday, you can restore the system's configuration to what it was two days ago, and you've got a good chance it will fix the problem. You can even make and restore snapshots over the network with a script!

Making A Restore Point

When you launch the System Restore wizard, you will be able to browse through a calendar to see the available restore points. You simply select the restore point you desire, and your system's configuration will be rolled back to that state. If you regret this action, no worries: another restore point is created automatically right before you restore a prior one.

Note

If you absolutely want to guarantee that a restore point is available at a certain time, then use the System Restore wizard to request an immediate snapshot. This is a good practice whenever you are about to install a new application or device driver, or when about to attempt an uninstall of the same.

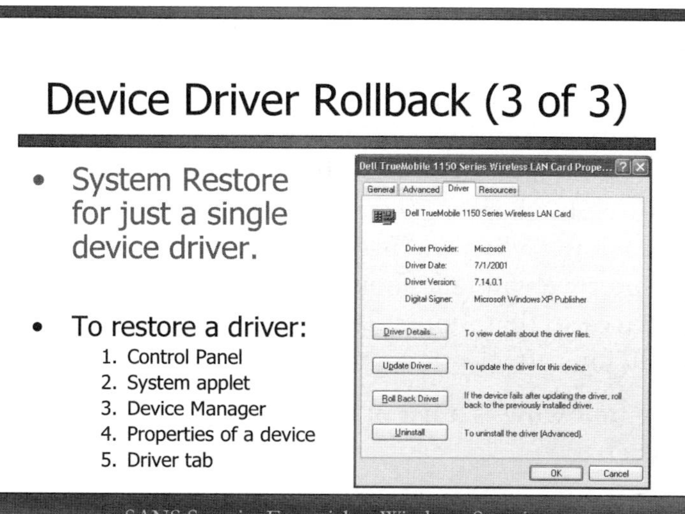

NOTES

Device Driver Rollback

A related System Restore feature is just for device drivers on Windows XP/.NET. After installing a new driver to replace or upgrade a prior one, the new driver may not function correctly. You can roll back the entire system using System Restore, but there is a quicker method. Go the System applet in Control Panel > Hardware tab > Device Manager > go to the properties of the updated driver > Driver tab > click the “Roll Back Driver” button.

NOTES

Summary

- Service Packs
  - Slipstreaming
- Hotfixes
  - Batch installation
- QCHAIN.EXE
- HFNETCHK.EXE
- Windows Update
- Automatic Update
- Software Update Services
- NTBACKUP.EXE
- System Restore
  - Driver Rollback

SANS Security Essentials – Windows Security

Summary

The main purpose of this chapter was to convey the importance of installing the latest Service Packs and hotfixes and to discuss techniques for simplifying the effort. Staying on top of patches is one of the most important duties a security administrator performs, but it can be Herculean task. E-mail security bulletins, Microsoft's security website, and the `NFNETCHK.EXE` tool all help to keep one apprised of new releases. For getting the hotfixes and Service Packs installed, there are batch files, Windows Update, Automatic Updates, and Software Update Services.

This chapter also provided an overview of the new Windows Backup program and the System Restore feature. Maintaining good backups is essential for disaster recovery, forensics, having auditing baselines, and getting back to square one when it all goes to pieces. System Restore and device driver rollback also help to get a system operational again quickly. Disaster recovery often is overlooked as a security precaution, but it is how one survives successful attacks by both hackers and the forces of nature. In chapter 30 we will return to the subject of backups when we discuss auditing. In the next chapter we will talk about how to secure network services so that, hopefully, disaster recovery from malicious attacks never will be necessary.

The following is a list of the websites mentioned in this chapter.

Websites Mentioned

- BindView (`www.bindview.com`)
- BindView RAZOR Team (`razor.bindview.com`)
- Bootable CD-ROMs (`www.nu2.nu/bootablecd/`)
- BugTraq Mailing List (`www.ntbugtraq.com`)
- CommVault Systems (`www.commvault.com`)
- Computer Associates (`www.ca.com`)
- Hewlett Packard (`www.hp.com`)
- InstallShield Developer (`www.installshield.com`)
- KBAlertz Mailing List (`www.kbalertz.com`)
- Legato (`www.legato.com`)
- Microsoft Software Update Services (`www.microsoft.com/windows2000/windowsupdate/sus/`)

NOTES

- Microsoft Windows Update (windowsupdate.microsoft.com)
- Microsoft's Download Center (www.microsoft.com/downloads/)
- Microsoft's Security Homepage (www.microsoft.com/security/)
- Packetstorm (packetstormsecurity.nl)
- Pedestal Software (www.pedestalsoftware.com)
- Polaris Group (www.polarisgroup.com)
- Shavlik Technologies (www.shavlik.com)
- St.Bernard Software (www.stbernard.com)
- Symantec (www.symantec.com)
- SyncSort (www.syncsort.com)
- UltraBac (www.ultrabac.com)
- VERITAS (www.veritas.com)
- VirtualPC (www.connectix.com)
- VMWare (www.vmware.com)
- Wise for Windows Installer (www.wise.com)

NOTES

Chapter 29

Securing Windows Network Services

NOTES

NOTES

Securing Windows
Network Services

SANS Security Essentials V:
Windows Security

SANS Security Essentials – Windows Security

Securing Windows Network Services

Now that you have the latest Service Packs and hotfixes applied, you're *almost* ready to connect your system to the network. Even desktop Windows computers provide a variety of services on the network by default, and a Windows 2000/.NET Server can host dozens more. Applying the latest patches isn't good enough: we want a *bastion host*. A bastion host is a machine which has been hardened specifically *in anticipation of vulnerabilities that have not been discovered yet*. We can't block all possible exploits, of course, but a few basic precautions can reduce our threat exposure greatly. Again, hotfixes are for *yesterday's* exploits; what we're trying to do here is anticipate *tomorrow's* vulnerabilities (which largely involves pretending you're clinically paranoid).

Because we are paranoid, we'll spend extra time talking about how to secure Microsoft Internet Information Server (IIS), which has a dreadful history of exploitation, but the good news is that a few relatively simple changes can improve its security drastically. In fact, these changes can secure your web server against most of the best-known attacks against IIS, *even without the relevant patches*. This includes the Code Red Worm, all variations on the directory traversal ("../..") attack, and a number of miscellaneous buffer overflow exploits.

More specifically, in this chapter we will discuss:

- The Best Way To Secure A Service
- Firewalls And Packet Filtering
- IPSec And Virtual Private Networking
- Wireless Security
- Internet Information Server
- Terminal Services

NOTES

Best Way to Secure a Service

- Uninstall or disable it!
- What's unnecessary?
- Won't disabling service X break Y?
- Answer: Experiment!
- A few dangerous ones to consider...

SANS Security Essentials – Windows Security

The Best Way to Secure a Service

The best way to secure a service is to uninstall or disable it. Even if a zero-day exploit tool—which grants administrative privileges to a remote hacker—is released, if the vulnerable service isn't running, you're immune! Hence, disable all unnecessary services on systems exposed to the Internet. What's unnecessary? Well, that depends on the type of server it is and what functionality you want to keep. For example, an Internet Information Server (IIS) running the HTTP service is only compelled to have the following services running, everything else is unnecessary to being an HTTP server:

- World Wide Web Publishing
- IIS Admin
- Protected Storage
- Remote Procedure Call (RPC)
- Event Log
- Windows NTLM Security Support Provider

How would you know that this is the minimal list? You simply have to experiment with a particular server to see what you can live without. For example, notice that the Remote Registry Service is not on the list above, but perhaps your favorite Enterprise Management System (EMS) uses this service extensively; now you would have to make a choice between functionality and better security. No one can decide what is necessary or unnecessary except for you.

On desktop workstations not exposed to the Internet, you should consider preemptively disabling these services if they are not specifically being used:

- Server (i.e., the File and Printer Sharing service)
- IIS Admin
- World Wide Web Publishing
- FTP Publishing
- Telnet
- Routing and Remote Access (for dial-up/VPN servers)
- Terminal Services
- Universal Plug and Play (for network appliances)

Of these, disabling the Server service will probably have the most undesired consequences. The Server service is what makes shared folders and printers

NOTES

possible, as well as a variety of RPC protocols. On the other hand, the fewer the number of people running their own unauthorized IIS and dial-up servers the better.

NOTES

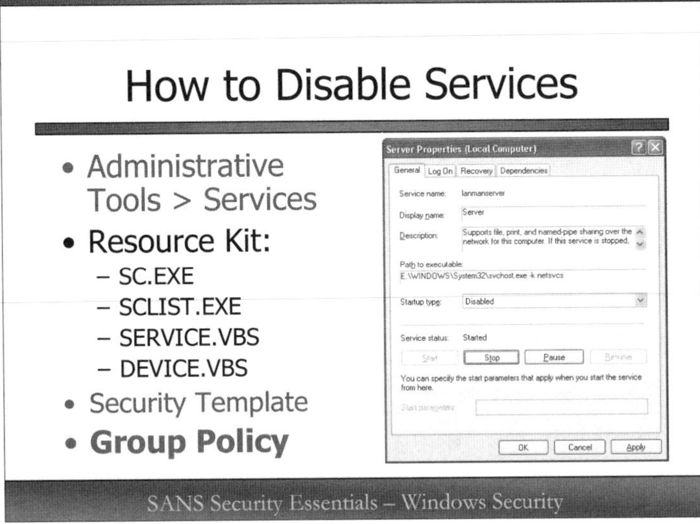

How to Disable Services

The manual way of disabling a service is by going to the Administrative Tools folder off the Start menu and launching the Services applet. For any undesired service, double-click it in the applet, go the General tab, set its startup type to "Disabled", and then stop the service (or reboot).

The *Resource Kit*'s `SC.EXE`, `SCLIST.EXE`, and `INSTSRV.EXE` can be used to query and manage every aspect of installed services on local/remote machines. If you wish to script all this, then see the `SERVICE.VBS` script from the *Resource Kit* as well (it also works against remote machines); the `DEVICE.VBS` script does the same for device drivers.

INF security templates also define service startup settings. You can apply a template to a system with the Security Configuration and Analysis (SCA)

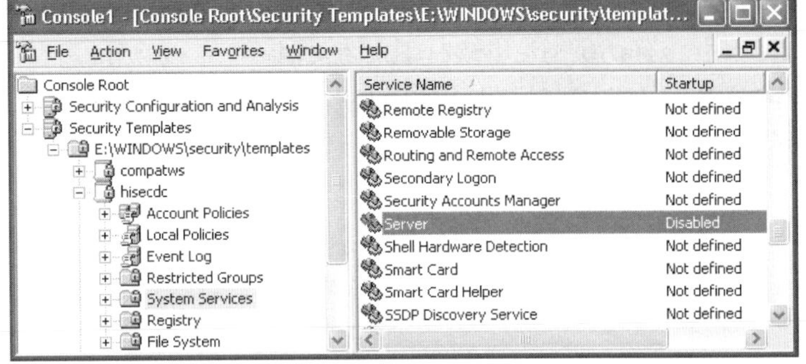

snap-in or `SECEDIT.EXE` to disable all undesired services in one shot.

However, by far the easiest way of disabling services across thousands of machines is with Group Policy. For example, to disable the World Wide Web Publishing service throughout the entire domain, open the Active Directory Users and Computers snap-in > right-click your domain > Properties > Group Policy tab > select the Default Domain Policy > Edit button > navigate to Computer Configuration > Windows Settings > Security Settings > System Services. The "System Services" section of a Group Policy Object (GPO) is more-or-less the Services applet; here you can disable any service you wish, and that service will be disabled on all the systems to which the GPO applies.

NOTES

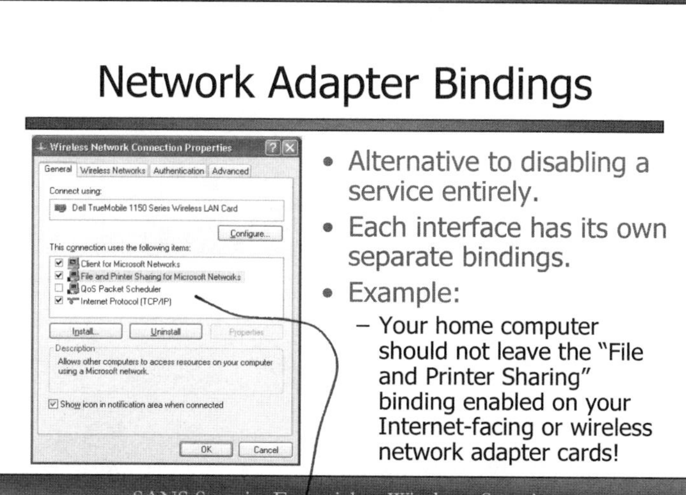

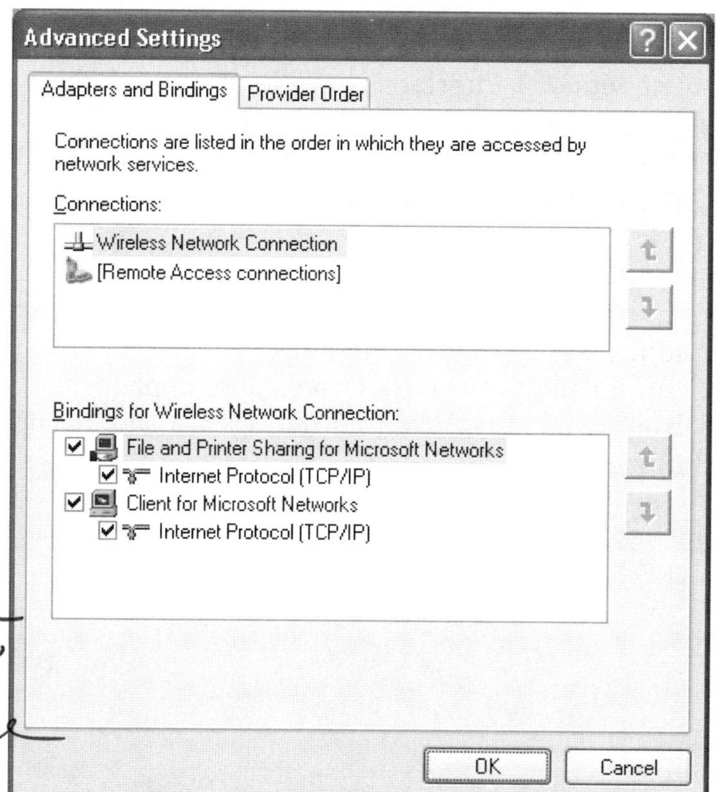

Network Adapter Bindings

Sometimes a service cannot be disabled because of the sacrifices this would entail. A less drastic approach is to keep the service running and instead disable some of its bindings. A "binding" is a path of communications between a networking component (like a service or protocol) and a physical network adapter card. If you break a service's binding to one card, the service can remain accessible over a different card.

Let's work through an example together to make it more concrete. Do you have a 24x7 DSL or cable-modem connection to the Internet at home? If so, it is critical that you break the binding between your Server service and the interface leading out to the Internet; there is no good reason why random people on the Internet need to get to your shared folders and printers!

To do this on your system, go to the properties of the network adapter card that you use for Internet connectivity. If this is a physical interface, then the General tab will show a list of networking components with checkboxes to the left of them; if this is a dial-up or DSL interface, then the Networking tab will show the same list of components. Now, simply uncheck the box next to "File and Printer Sharing on Microsoft Networks," and click OK.

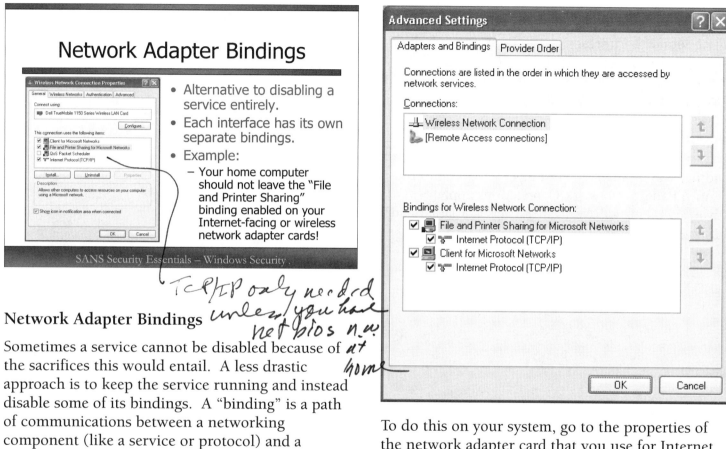

Note

All networking interfaces have bindings like this, including Ethernet cards, Token Ring and FDDI adapters, 802.11 wireless cards, dial-up connections, and even VPN connections. The bindings for each interface can be managed separately from the others.

Another way to manage bindings is by going to the Control Panel > Network Connections applet > Advanced menu > Advanced Settings > Adapters and Bindings tab.

Do I Still Need NetBIOS ?

- NetBIOS is a set of connectionless and connection-oriented protocols.
- On Windows 2000/XP/.NET networks, it can be disabled 95% of the time, but required for backwards compatibility.
- Reconnaissance threat:
  NBTSTAT.EXE –A *IPAddress*
- Disable manually or via DHCP.
- Null user sessions don't require NetBIOS!

SANS Security Essentials – Windows Security

Do I Still Need NetBIOS?

"NetBIOS" is a set of connectionless and connection-oriented protocols that work together to make computers accessible by their user-friendly names instead of their not-so-friendly IP or IPX addresses. NetBIOS often has been wrongly blamed for vulnerabilities that actually reside in the Server service or the Server Message Block (SMB) protocol, but it has weaknesses itself, too. Try this on your own computer, where *IPaddress* is the IP address of the local or a remote Windows system:

```
NBTSTAT.EXE -A IPaddress
```

If the machine is running NetBIOS, you'll get output similar to the following:

```
NetBIOS Remote Machine Name Table
Name                    Type      Status
-----------------------------------------
MOTHRA            <00>  UNIQUE    Registered
MOTHRA            <03>  UNIQUE    Registered
SANS              <00>  GROUP     Registered
SANS              <1C>  GROUP     Registered
ADMINISTRATOR     <03>  UNIQUE    Registered
MOTHRA            <20>  UNIQUE    Registered
SANS              <1E>  GROUP     Registered
SANS              <1D>  UNIQUE    Registered
..__MSBROWSE__.   <01>  GROUP     Registered
```

Each NetBIOS name ends with a code number inside chevrons. These code numbers can be looked up in the following table to reveal what service(s) are running on the target box.

Hence, NetBIOS can be used to gather remote reconnaissance data. The good news is that Windows 2000/XP/.NET systems do not require NetBIOS 95% of the time. NetBIOS is required to maintain full backwards compatibility with older operating systems, like Windows 9x/NT; and a few services and applications still require it, but it can be disabled safely for the most part. Disabling NetBIOS always should be done on Internet-accessible systems, too, if there isn't a compelling reason to leave it on.

To disable NetBIOS on your computer, go to the properties of any physical network adapter card > General tab > highlight Internet Protocol (TCP/IP) > Properties button > Advanced button > WINS tab > select Disable NetBIOS Over TCP/IP. If you wish to disable NetBIOS throughout your network then you

NOTES

NOTES

NetBIOS Name	Type	Service
<computername>00	Unique	Workstation Service
<computername>01	Unique	Messenger Service
<_MSBROWSE_>01	Group	Master Browser
<computername>03	Unique	Messenger Service
<computername>06	Unique	RAS Server Service
<computername>1F	Unique	NetDDE Service
<computername>20	Unique	File Server Service
<computername>21	Unique	RAS Client Service
<computername>22	Unique	Exchange Interchange
<computername>23	Unique	Exchange Store
<computername>24	Unique	Exchange Directory
<computername>30	Unique	Modem Sharing Server Service
<computername>31	Unique	Modem Sharing Client Service
<computername>43	Unique	SMS Client Remote Control
<computername>44	Unique	SMS Admin Remote Control Tool
<computername>45	Unique	SMS Client Remote Chat
<computername>46	Unique	SMS Client Remote Transfer
<computername>4C	Unique	DEC Pathworks TCPIP Service
<computername>52	Unique	DEC Pathworks TCPIP Service
<computername>87	Unique	Exchange MTA
<computername>6A	Unique	Exchange IMC
<computername>BE	Unique	Network Monitor Agent
<computername>BF	Unique	Network Monitor Apps
<username>03	Unique	Messenger Service
<domain>00	Group	Domain Name
<domain>1B	Unique	Domain Master Browser
<domain>1C	Group	Domain Controllers
<domain>1D	Unique	Master Browser
<domain>1E	Group	Browser Service Elections
<Inet~Services>1C	Group	Internet Information Server
<IS~Computername>00	Unique	Internet Information Server
<computername>[2B]	Unique	Lotus Notes Server
IRISMULTICAST[2F]	Group	Lotus Notes
IRISNAMESERVER[33]	Group	Lotus Notes
Forte_$ND800ZA[20]	Unique	DCA Irmalan Gateway Service

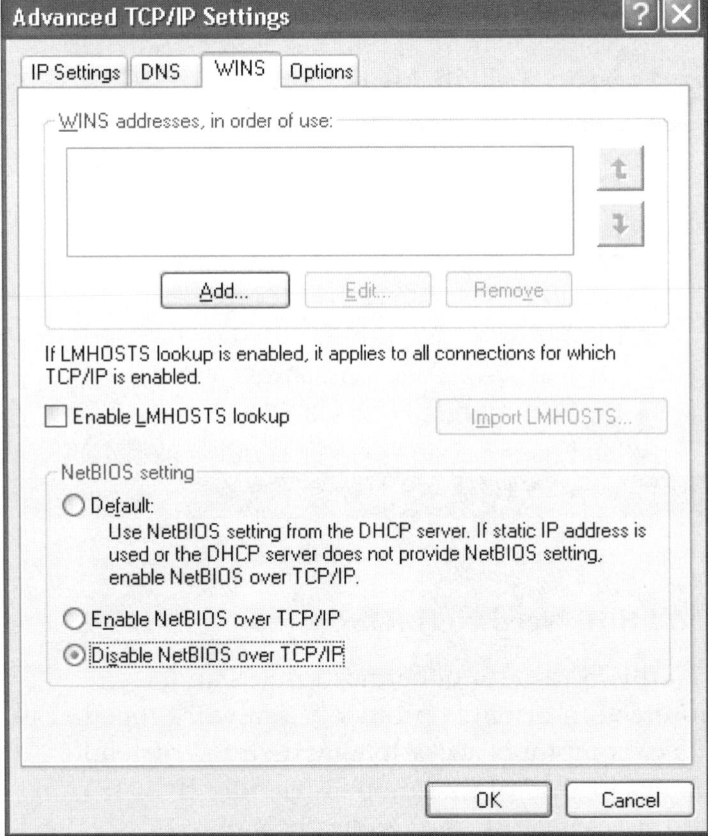

can use Group Policy or your DHCP server. Windows 2000 and later DHCP servers support a scope option to disable NetBIOS on clients. (We'll discuss firewalling NetBIOS traffic in just a few moments too.)

Null User Sessions

What about null user sessions— don't they require NetBIOS? No! Many people believe they are immune to null user session attacks if they simply disable NetBIOS, but this is not true. Null user sessions are possible because of the Server service and the Server Message Block (SMB) protocol, and in Windows 2000/XP/.NET you can still use these even when NetBIOS is disabled.

Null user session issues have been discussed already in Chapter 27, but you should consider them repeated here. Preventing null user session exploits is an important part of your regimen for securing your network services.

NOTES

Firewalls and Packet Filtering

- As discussed before, personal and perimeter firewalls should filter out unwanted traffic.
- Protocols you should memorize:
  - **SMB**: TCP/139/445
  - **RPC**: TCP/135
  - **LDAP**: TCP/389/636/3268/3269
  - **Kerberos**: TCP/UDP/88
  - *(Continued next slide)* →

SANS Security Essentials – Windows Security

Firewalls and Packet Filtering

After disabling unnecessary services and bindings, you should still firewall the system and network as though all these dangerous services were still running. An earlier chapter discussed firewall theory at length, but there are some Windows-related specifics that should be mentioned here, too.

Windows Network Traffic

There are certain network traffic flows that are characteristic of Windows networks. You should be familiar with their signatures and purposes so that you can recognize them in your packet traces and firewall logs. This list also will be important later when conducting audits. Hackers can use these port numbers to help "fingerprint" your boxes, too.

Server Message Block (SMB): TCP/139/445

Server Message Block (SMB) is the file and printer sharing protocol. When using NetBIOS, SMB operates on TCP/139; without NetBIOS, it uses TCP/445 and is sometimes referred to as the Common Internet File System (CIFS) protocol. All SMB/CIFS packets should be blocked going to or coming from the Internet, unless they are being tunneled through IPSec or a VPN.

Remote Procedure Call (RPC): TCP/135

Remote Procedure Call (RPC) networking is used extensively on Windows networks. Trust relationships, the NetLogon secure channel, Outlook messaging, NTLM pass-through authentication, remote administration, etc., all can use RPC-based sessions. RPC sessions typically begin with a client connection to TCP/135 on the server; then the server will redirect the client to another "ephemeral" high-numbered port for subsequent communications. Be aware, though, that RPC-over-HTTP (TCP/80/443/593) is possible, and RPC-over-SMB (TCP/139/445) is used very commonly, too.

Lightweight Directory Access Protocol (LDAP): TCP/389/636/3268/3269

The Lightweight Directory Access Protocol (LDAP) is the default protocol for searching and editing the Active Directory database. Cleartext LDAP uses TCP/389, while SSL-encrypted LDAP goes over TCP/636. A special portion of the Active Directory database called the "global catalog" also is LDAP-accessible over TCP/3268 (cleartext) and TCP/3269

NOTES

(SSL-encrypted) on domain controllers. LDAP uses Kerberos for authentication, so it is not the case that the cleartext channels send passwords in the clear, too.

Kerberos: UDP/TCP/88

Kerberos is the default authentication protocol on Active Directory networks. It uses UDP/88 primarily; however, when tickets get too large, TCP/88 will be used as well. The Kerberos change password port (TCP/UDP/464) is listening on domain controllers too, but Windows clients still prefer to use an RPC session to change their passwords. Neither the Kerberos administration port (TCP/749) is used nor is the Kerberos de-multiplexor (TCP/2053).

NOTES

More Protocols to Memorize

- **DNS**: UDP/TCP/53
- **NetBIOS**: TCP/UDP/137, UDP/138, TCP/139, TCP/UDP/1512, TCP/42
- **RDP**: TCP/3389
- **IPSec**: UDP/500, Protocols 50 and 51
- **PPTP**: TCP/1723, Protocol 47 (GRE)
- **SQL Server**: TCP/UDP/1433/1434

SANS Security Essentials – Windows Security

Domain Name System (DNS): UDP/TCP/53

Active Directory cannot function without DNS servers. You will see heavy traffic to your DNS servers on both UDP/53 and TCP/53. In general, everything that WINS and NetBIOS did on Windows 9x/NT 4.0 networks is now handled by DNS on Windows 2000/XP/.NET networks.

NetBIOS and WINS: TCP/UDP/137, UDP/138, TCP/139, TCP/UDP/1512, TCP/42

A WINS server maintains a database of NetBIOS-to-IP address mappings just as DNS servers map hostnames to IP addresses. If you have older clients, or if you still have NetBIOS enabled in your LAN, then constantly you will see heavy NetBIOS/WINS traffic. Indeed, NetBIOS is like a constant background noise that you have to exclude from your logs (it's mind-boggling how chatty Windows machines can be). There are many NetBIOS- and WINS-related ports:

- NetBIOS Name Service: TCP/UDP/137
- NetBIOS Datagram Service: UDP/138
- NetBIOS Session Service: TCP/139
- WINS: TCP/UDP/1512
- WINS Replication: TCP/42

Remote Desktop Protocol (RDP): TCP/3389

Terminal Services uses the Remote Desktop Protocol (RDP) to provide remote control of desktops. Windows XP uses the same protocol for its Remote Assistance feature. RDP operates on TCP/3389. (Citrix ICA uses TCP/1494.)

Internet Protocol Security (IPSec): UDP/500, Protocols 50 and 51

Internet Protocol Security (IPSec) is supported natively on Windows 2000/XP/.NET. It is used for authenticating and encrypting packet data, including Layer Two Transport Protocol (L2TP) VPNs. IPSec uses UDP/500 to negotiate sessions, IP protocol number 50 for Encapsulating Security Payload (ESP), and protocol number 51 for Authentication Header (AH). L2TP uses UDP/1701, but you should never see unencrypted UDP/1701 traffic on the wire.

NOTES

Point-to-Point Tunneling Protocol (PPTP): TCP/1723, Protocol 47

Point-to-Point Tunneling Protocol (PPTP) is another VPN protocol. PPTP uses both TCP/1723 and the Generic Routing Encapsulation (GRE) protocol. GRE operates on protocol ID number 47.

Microsoft SQL Server: TCP/UDP/1433/1434

2002 witnessed a rash of published SQL Server exploits. SQL Server listens for queries on TCP/UDP/1433 and is monitored on TCP/UDP/1434. If you use client-server applications with SQL Server, you will see a ton of this traffic. Make sure your external firewall is blocking it too.

NOTES

Personal Firewalls for Windows

- As discussed before, here are some of the more popular personal firewalls:
  - BlackICE (www.iss.net)
  - McAfee Personal Firewall (www.mcafee.com)
  - Norton Personal Firewall (www.symantec.com)
  - Sygate Personal Firewall (www.sygate.com)
  - Tiny Personal Firewall (www.tinysoftware.com)
  - ZoneAlarm (www.zonelabs.com)
- Since this is a Windows course, what about →

SANS Security Essentials – Windows Security

Personal Firewalls for Windows

There are many excellent personal firewall products available on the market. Again, firewalls were discussed in an earlier chapter, so, before discussing Microsoft's flavor, let's just list some of the more popular ones:

- BlackICE (`http://www.iss.net`)
- McAfee Personal Firewall (`http://www.mcafee.com`)
- Norton Personal Firewall (`http://www.symantec.com`)
- Sygate Personal Firewall (`http://www.sygate.com`)
- Tiny Personal Firewall (`http://www.tinysoftware.com`)
- ZoneAlarm (`http://www.zonelabs.com`)

And, of course, there's Microsoft's built-in Internet Connection Firewall.

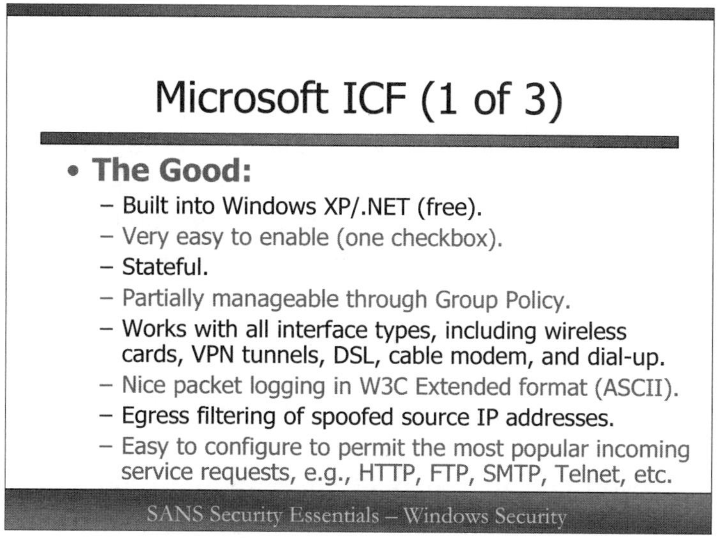

NOTES

Microsoft ICF (1 of 3)

- **The Good:**
  - Built into Windows XP/.NET (free).
  - Very easy to enable (one checkbox).
  - Stateful.
  - Partially manageable through Group Policy.
  - Works with all interface types, including wireless cards, VPN tunnels, DSL, cable modem, and dial-up.
  - Nice packet logging in W3C Extended format (ASCII).
  - Egress filtering of spoofed source IP addresses.
  - Easy to configure to permit the most popular incoming service requests, e.g., HTTP, FTP, SMTP, Telnet, etc.

SANS Security Essentials – Windows Security

Microsoft Internet Connection Firewall

Windows XP/.NET has a built-in firewall called the Internet Connection Firewall (ICF). Let's discuss its pros and cons. On the good side, ICF is built into the operating system, stateful, easy to configure, supported by Microsoft, partially can be managed through Group Policy, and works with all types of interfaces (LAN cards, 802.11 wireless, dial-up connections, VPN tunnels, etc.). The ICF also is compatible with the Internet Connection Sharing service, provides good ASCII text logging in W3C Extended format, performs basic egress filtering to prevent the transmission of packets with spoofed source IP addresses, and easily can be configured to permit the most likely incoming services, e.g., FTP, HTTP, ICMP, SMTP, etc.

The following screenshot is of an ICF log file in W3C Extended format. It's a plain ASCII text file.

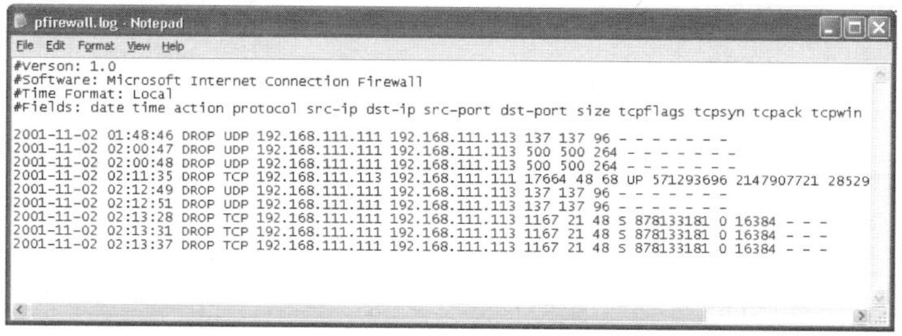

pfirewall.log - Notepad

File Edit Format View Help

```
#Verson: 1.0
#Software: Microsoft Internet Connection Firewall
#Time Format: Local
#Fields: date time action protocol src-ip dst-ip src-port dst-port size tcpflags tcpsyn tcpack tcpwin

2001-11-02 01:48:46 DROP UDP 192.168.111.111 192.168.111.113 137 137 96 - - - - - - - -
2001-11-02 02:00:47 DROP UDP 192.168.111.111 192.168.111.113 500 500 264 - - - - - - - -
2001-11-02 02:00:48 DROP UDP 192.168.111.111 192.168.111.113 500 500 264 - - - - - - - -
2001-11-02 02:11:35 DROP TCP 192.168.111.113 192.168.111.111 17664 48 68 UP 571293696 2147907721 28529
2001-11-02 02:12:49 DROP UDP 192.168.111.111 192.168.111.113 137 137 96 - - - - - - - -
2001-11-02 02:12:51 DROP UDP 192.168.111.111 192.168.111.113 137 137 96 - - - - - - - -
2001-11-02 02:13:28 DROP TCP 192.168.111.111 192.168.111.113 1167 21 48 S 878133181 0 16384 - - -
2001-11-02 02:13:31 DROP TCP 192.168.111.111 192.168.111.113 1167 21 48 S 878133181 0 16384 - - -
2001-11-02 02:13:37 DROP TCP 192.168.111.111 192.168.111.113 1167 21 48 S 878133181 0 16384 - - -
```

You can choose to log dropped packets and/or allowed connections. The logging is good because it includes ports, byte size, TCP flags, TCP synchronize and acknowledgement numbers, TCP window size, ICMP type, and ICMP code.

NOTES

Microsoft ICF (2 of 3)

- **The Bad:**
  - No IDS capabilities (like BlackICE)
  - No application awareness (like ZoneAlarm)
  - No other egress filtering except for blocking spoofed source IP addresses.
  - Difficult to customize incoming service support for complex protocols.
  - Not built into Windows 2000.
  - Can't be managed through Group Policy in 9 out of the 10 ways you would want.

SANS Security Essentials – Windows Security

On the bad side, though, ICF lacks the intrusion detection capabilities and fine-grained flexibility of a BlackICE, lacks the application-awareness of a ZoneAlarm, only does egress filtering to prevent source IP spoofing (nothing else), and often makes impossible configuring incoming support for complex services. ICF also is not built into Windows 2000 and cannot be managed through Group Policy in 9 out of the 10 ways you would want to be able to. Some of the non-Microsoft personal firewalls can be managed centrally, but the details of ICF's configuration cannot. Nor can ICF automatically upload its logs to a central server.

Note

ICF and Windows XP have received some press coverage concerning egress filtering and raw sockets. Two websites where you can read more about those concerns are `http://www.grc.com` and `http://www.grcsucks.com` (in that order).

To be fair, though, the best thing about ICF is that it's built into the operating system and easily enabled. 90% of the security provided by a personal firewall comes from its stateful filtering of incoming packets. The other features of the better non-Microsoft personal firewalls are important, but the value of these features must be weighed against the negatives of licensing, installing, and troubleshooting these firewalls.

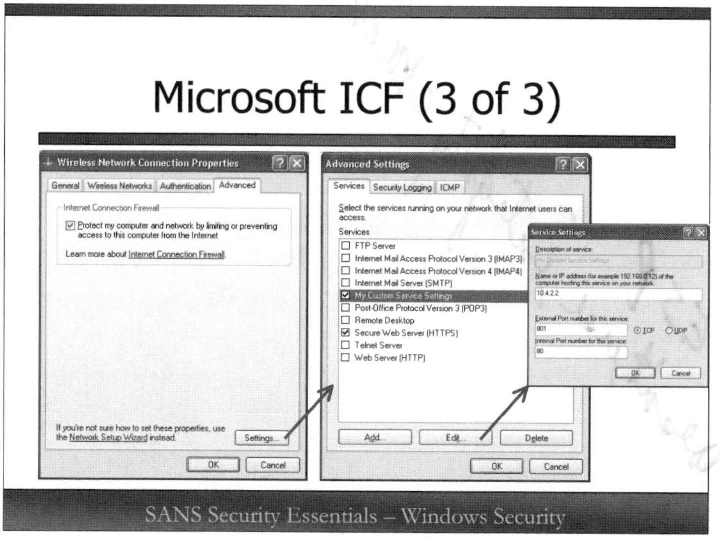

ICF is available only on Windows XP/.NET (not Windows 2000). To enable ICF on a LAN card, wireless interface, dial-up connection, or VPN tunnel, go to the properties of that interface > Advanced tab > check the box to enable ICF. That's it!

If you wish to configure incoming services and logging, then also click the Settings button at the bottom of the Advanced tab. The Services tab of the Advanced Settings dialog box allows you to accept incoming session requests for a variety of protocols. You also can click the Add button to define your own service type and even pass through those incoming requests to other machines on the LAN, like perhaps when you're using Internet Connection Sharing with a DSL or cable modem link.

The Security Logging tab is used to set the log size and location, to enable logging of dropped packets and/or successful connections, or to reset security to

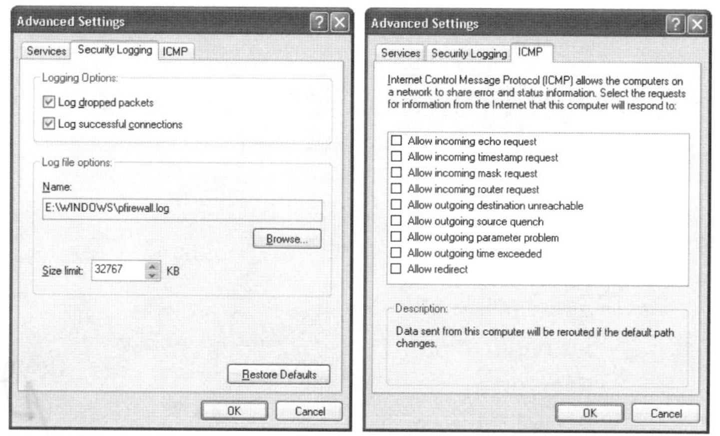

factory defaults. Only the initial packet in a successful session is logged, but *all* dropped packets are logged. The maximum log size is 32MB.

The ICMP tab is for allowing/disallowing a variety of ICMP message types. Unless you have a specific need, it's best to not enable any of them on Internet-facing connections (ICMP is like Britney Spears: *not that innocent*).

NOTES

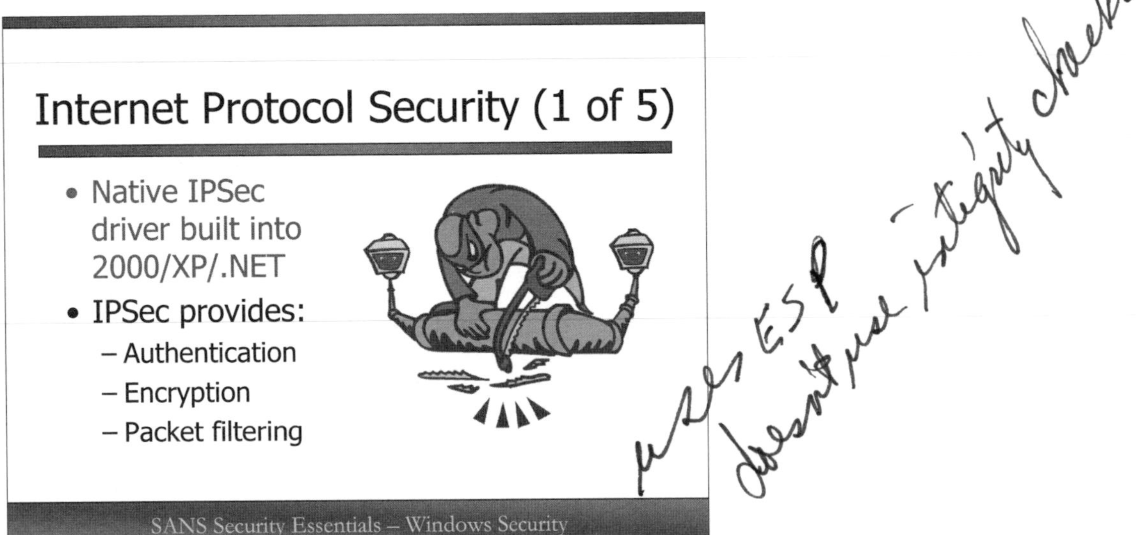

Internet Protocol Security (IPSec)

Internet Protocol Security (IPSec) and Virtual Private Networking (VPN) provide the next layer of security for our network services. After applying hotfixes, disabling bindings and daemons, and firewalling the LAN, whatever traffic is left over must be necessary and important! IPSec helps to secure network services by regulating further who can connect to those services and by encrypting packets on the wire. IPSec also can be used for static packet filtering.

Note

Microsoft's IPSec driver actually was written by Cisco Systems.

IPSECPOL.EXE (2 of 5)

- Command-line IPSec tool (scriptable!)
  - Works with local or remote systems
- **Packet filtering example:**

```
IPSECPOL \\Server -u
IPSECPOL \\Server -f [0+*] (0:80+*::TCP) (0+10.5.5.5)
```

[] = Blocking Rule, () = Allow Rule, * = Any, 0 = My IP's
<*source* :*port*> + <*destination* : *port* : *protocol*>

SANS Security Essentials – Windows Security

IPSec Packet Filtering From the Command Line

IPSec is best known for its encryption capabilities, but it also can be used for static packet filtering. And all IPSec settings can be managed from the command line on both Windows 2000 (IPSECPOL.EXE, *Resource Kit*) and Windows XP/.NET (IPSECCMD.EXE, built in). The tools work on either local or remote systems.

For example, the following single command will block all packets going to or coming from *WebServer*, except for HTTP traffic (TCP/80), and except for the packets to/from the computer at 10.5.5.5:

```
IPSECPOL.EXE \\WebServer -f [0+*]
(0:80+*::TCP) (0+10.5.5.5)
```

The syntax looks strange, but it is not exceedingly difficult. There are three packet-filtering rules being set on the web server. Rules follow the "-f" switch and are enclosed in either square brackets or parentheses. The three rules, and their interpretation, are:

- "[0+*]" means "block all packets whatsoever".
- "(0:80+*::TCP)" means "except for all TCP/80 traffic, which should be allowed through unchanged".
- "(0+10.5.5.5)" means "and except for all packets coming to/from 10.5.5.5; these should also be allowed through unmolested" (presumably 10.5.5.5 is the IP address of the administrator's desktop, from where IPSECPOL.EXE is being run).

Rules which block packets are placed in square brackets, while rules that allow packets are put in parentheses. The plus sign, "+", separates packet source (on the left of it) and destination (on the right). The plus sign also "mirrors" the rule to reverse the source/destination in the rule; non-mirrored rules use the equal sign instead. Hence, the following two filters are equivalent (this also demonstrates how to specify a range of IP addresses by subnet mask):

- -f (0+10.0.0.0/255.0.0.0)
- -f (0=10.0.0.0/255.0.0.0) (10.0.0.0/255.0.0.0=0)

Zero by itself, "0", stands for the computer's own IP addresses, while the asterisk is a wildcard for all IP addresses. That is why "-f [0+*]" blocks everything: "0" is the source; "*" is destination; "[]" means

NOTES

NOTES

block; and "+" causes the rule to be interpreted as equivalent to "-f [0=*] [*=0]."

A port number can follow an optional colon. The port number field can be left blank, and this acts as a wildcard to mean any port number. Another colon can be added at the end of the rule for the protocol type (UDP, TCP or ICMP). Here is a sampling of rules and their interpretations:

- "(0:443+*::TCP)" will allow HTTPS traffic.
- "(0:53+*::UDP)" will allow DNS traffic.
- "[0:+*::ICMP]" will block all ICMP traffic.

To immediately clear all these settings without rebooting or disrupting current packet flows, simply run:

```
IPSECPOL.EXE \\WebServer -u
```

Keep in mind, though, that these are *static* filtering rules, not stateful or dynamic, and there is no detailed logging of packets, as with true firewall products. But because IPSec settings are scriptable, they can be used in scheduled batch files, logon scripts, Active Server Pages, and other custom applications. And what goes for the packet filtering settings also goes for all the encryption and authentication capabilities of IPSec, as well (though these command-line switches get a tad more complex).

The best thing about IPSec in Active Directory environments, though, is that you can push out 100% of your IPSec settings through Group Policy!

IPSec & Group Policy (3 of 5)

- 100% of IPSec settings can be managed through Group Policy!
- **Example:**
  1. Enable IPSec on all computers in the domain.
  2. Require IPSec 3DES encryption only for servers in a particular OU.

Group Policy Management of IPSec

100% of IPSec settings can be managed through Group Policy! This means it is feasible to have custom IPSec configurations for thousands of computers and to change these configurations as often as needed. Each Organizational Unit (OU) could have its own separate IPSec policy; indeed, a valid reason for dividing computer accounts into different OUs is so that you can assign different IPSec policies to them easily.

Group Policy and IPSec are each one-day courses by themselves in the SANS Windows Security Track, so we can't possibly discuss all the options here, but we can walk through an example together. In this example we will enable IPSec on all computers in the domain and configure all the servers in an Organizational Unit to request (or always require) IPSec 3DES encryption for communications with them. This example assumes that all the computers are in an Active Directory domain inside the LAN, and that the computers are all Windows 2000/XP/.NET (Windows 9x/NT do not have native IPSec drivers).

NOTES

NOTES

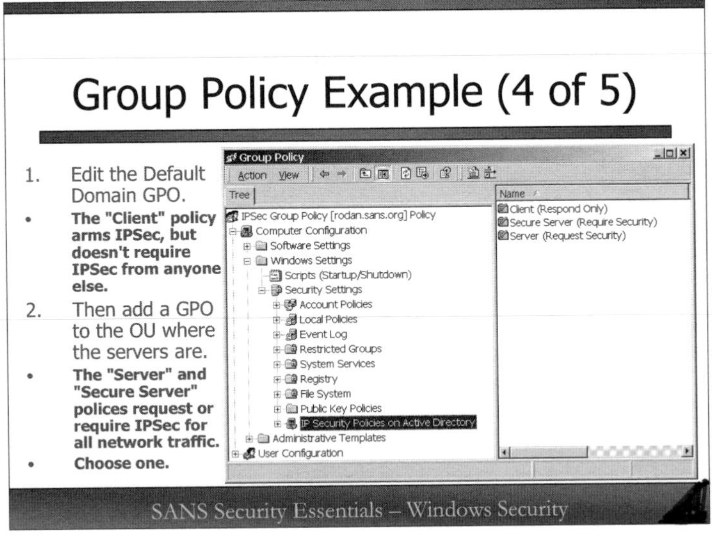

Group Policy Example (4 of 5)
1. Edit the Default Domain GPO.
• The "Client" policy arms IPSec, but doesn't require IPSec from anyone else.
2. Then add a GPO to the OU where the servers are.
• The "Server" and "Secure Server" polices request or require IPSec for all network traffic.
• Choose one.
Group Policy
Client (Respond Only)
Secure Server (Require Security)
Server (Request Security)
SANS Security Essentials – Windows Security

Enable IPSec on all Computers in the Domain

To enable IPSec on all computers in the domain, you will edit the Default Domain Group Policy Object and configure it to arm the IPSec driver on all machines to which it applies (and since it is the Default Domain GPO, it applies to all systems).

To do this, open the Active Directory Users and Computers snap-in > right-click on your domain > Properties > Group Policy tab > highlight the Default Domain Policy > Edit button > navigate to Computer Configuration > Windows Settings > Security Settings > IP Security Policies > right-click on the "Client (Respond Only)" policy > Assign > close the GPO window > OK. That's it!

The "Client (Respond Only)" policy will enable IPSec on a computer, but that computer will not require or request IPSec from any other machine. However, if a client with IPSec enabled connects to a server which does require IPSec, the client will "respond" to any Internet Key Exchange (IKE) negotiation requests the server emits.

Importantly, IPSec is only being "armed" here. It is not the case that enabling IPSec on a computer will cause it to drop all packets not IPSec-encrypted. To enable the IPSec driver simply is to make it willing to negotiate IPSec settings *if some other computer* requests it.

Require IPSec in an Organizational Unit

Now that all computers in the domain are willing to use IPSec, we will next configure all the servers in just one Organizational Unit to require IPSec 3DES encryption for all communications with them (let's imagine they are SQL Servers with health insurance data, and you've got HIPAA auditors breathing down your neck). But no other computers in the LAN will be made to require IPSec.

To require IPSec encryption for all communications with servers in a particular OU, open the Active Directory Users and Computers snap-in > right-click on the desired OU > Properties > Group Policy tab > New button > enter "GPO For IPSec" as the name of the Group Policy Object > highlight your new GPO > Edit button > navigate to Computer Configuration > Windows Settings > Security Settings > IP Security Policies > right-click on the "Secure Server (Require Security)" policy > Assign > close the GPO window > OK.

The "Secure Server (Require Security)" IPSec policy will attempt to use 3DES encryption but will fall back down to regular DES if the client doesn't support 3DES. The policy uses Kerberos authentication and applies to all packets coming in/out of the servers. The “Server (Request Security)” policy will request encryption but will fall back to cleartext packets if the client doesn’t support IPSec at all. This would be appropriate on LANs that still have Windows 9x/NT systems.

NOTES

NOTES

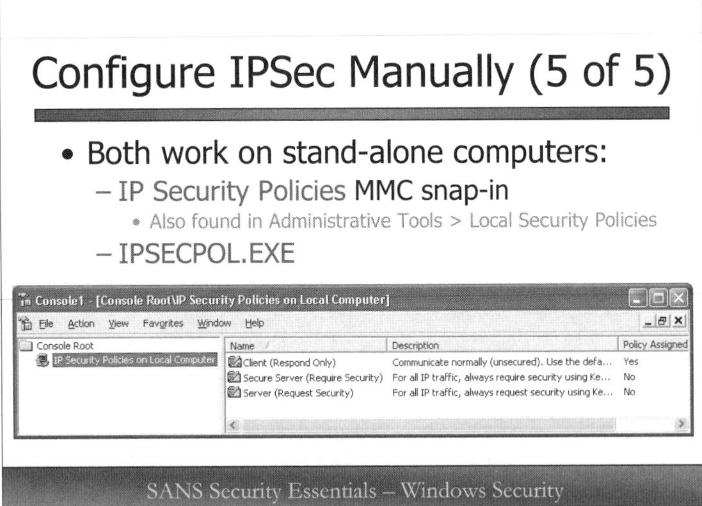

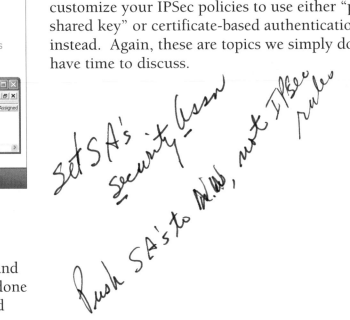

Configure IPSec Without Group Policy

IPSec can be configured on member computers and standalones without Group Policy. This can be done with the command-line tools (`IPSECPOL.EXE` and `IPSECCMD.EXE`) but it is far easier to use the "IP Security Policies" MMC snap-in.

To manage IPSec policies on a single box, open the Local Security Policies applet from the Administrative Tools folder, and go to the "IP Security Policies On Local Machine" container. Here you can right-click on any IPSec policy and select Assign to activate that policy on just this one box. You also can create and customize your own IPSec policies, but that's beyond the scope of this course.

Keep in mind that any local IPSec policies you assign on a box will be overwritten by any IPSec settings pushed out through Group Policy. Also, the default authentication protocol for IPSec is Kerberos, and Kerberos requires an Active Directory domain. If you have standalone systems on which you'd like to use IPSec, then you'll have to customize your IPSec policies to use either "pre-shared key" or certificate-based authentication instead. Again, these are topics we simply don't have time to discuss.

NOTES

Virtual Private Networking (1 of 3)

- **VPN protocol choices:**
  - PPTPv1
  - PPTPv2
  - IPSec and L2TP
- Never use PPTPv1
- PPTPv2 is secure if you use a long complex password or a smart card.
- IPSec/L2TP is the most secure
  - L2TP is a "helper" protocol.

SANS Security Essentials – Windows Security

Virtual Private Networking (IPSec/L2TP and PPTPv2)

If you require secure communications from the Internet into the LAN, though, you probably should deploy a full Virtual Private Networking (VPN) solution. Windows has built-in support for both IPSec/L2TP and PPTP-based VPNs. L2TP, Layer Two Tunneling Protocol, assists IPSec with tasks such as user authentication, encapsulation of non-IP packets, and RADIUS policy enforcement. The Point-to-Point Tunneling Protocol (PPTP), on the other hand, has its own encryption scheme and doesn't use IPSec at all. IPSec/L2TP is more secure, but PPTP VPNs are easier to configure because you don't have to install digital certificates on clients, and there's never any Network Address Translation (NAT) worries.

Never use PPTPv1

If you do plan to use PPTP for your VPN, then it is imperative that you use only PPTPv2. PPTPv1 has dreadful security vulnerabilities and was conclusively ripped to shreds in a famous whitepaper (`http://www.counterpane.com/pptp-paper.html`). Microsoft was embarrassed by this bad press coverage and released PPTPv2 to replace version 1. Not so widely known, however, is that the authors of the original whitepaper wrote an analysis of PPTPv2 as well (`http://www.counterpane.com/pptpv2-paper.html`). This paper is not so widely known because the conclusions are largely positive:

"Microsoft has improved PPTP to correct the major security weaknesses [in PPTPv1]. However, the fundamental weakness of the authentication and encryption protocol is that it is only as secure as the password chosen by the user."

Hence, if you are using PPTP, make sure it is PPTPv2 and that you are enforcing the strongest password policy that you can. For router-to-router VPNs using PPTPv2, the passwords should be complex and 127 characters long. Administrators should be required to have complex and long (30+ characters) passphrases too; or, even better, only permit administrators to authenticate with their smart cards. With smart card authentication to a PPTPv2 gateway, the user's password is ignored, and the VPN encryption keys are randomly generated. PPTPv2 can use up to 128-bit RC4 encryption, so make sure to require this. In the end, however, if you want the best security for your VPN, use IPSec instead. How does one configure these requirements on the client?

NOTES

Virtual Private Networking (2 of 3)

- **VPN Client:**
  - Software built into operating system
  - VPN tunnel is just another interface
- **VPN Gateway:**
  - Routing and Remote Access Service (RRAS)
  - Built into Windows 2000/.NET Server
  - RRAS: VPN gateway, dial-up server, multi-protocol router, NAT, RIPv2, OSPF, RADIUS server, DHCP relay agent, packet filtering, etc.

SANS Security Essentials – Windows Security

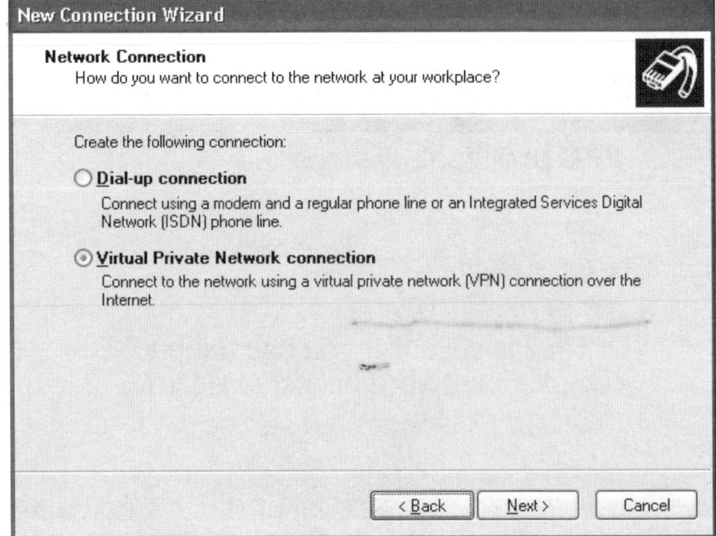
New Connection Wizard
Network Connection
How do you want to connect to the network at your workplace?
Create the following connection:
Dial-up connection
Connect using a modem and a regular phone line or an Integrated Services Digital Network (ISDN) phone line.
Virtual Private Network connection
Connect to the network using a virtual private network (VPN) connection over the Internet.
< Back
Next >
Cancel

VPN Client Built In

Microsoft's VPN client software is built into the operating system. The client software makes the VPN tunnel appear to be just another network adapter card. The operating system treats Ethernet cards, 802.11 wireless cards, dial-up connections, and VPN tunnels all the same: each is just another "interface" through which packets can be sent or received. Your VPN interface will have its own IP address, will appear in the list of adapters when you execute `IPCONFIG`, and can figure into the route table, as well.

To create a VPN interface, go to Control Panel > Network Connections > and run the Make New Connection wizard. The wizard will ask you a few questions about the tunnel (such as the IP address of the VPN gateway) and then create the connection icon for you. Once the icon is created there in the Network Connections folder, you simply double-click it, enter your username and password, and the VPN tunnel is established. You can now use the VPN just as you would any other network adapter card; i.e., there's no other special client software you have to configure.

To require 128-bit PPTPv2 from the client's side, go to Control Panel > Network Connections > right-click your VPN interface icon > Properties > Security tab > select Advanced > Settings button > ensure that only the MS-CHAPv2 option is checked > ensure that "Maximum Strength Encryption (Disconnect If Server Declines)" is selected > OK > OK.

Using MS-CHAPv2 authentication forces the use of PPTPv2. Most of the vulnerabilities in PPTPv1 actually were vulnerabilities in MS-CHAPv1, the authentication and encryption provider. If you were to use a smart card for authentication, you would select "Use Extensible Authentication Protocol

NOTES

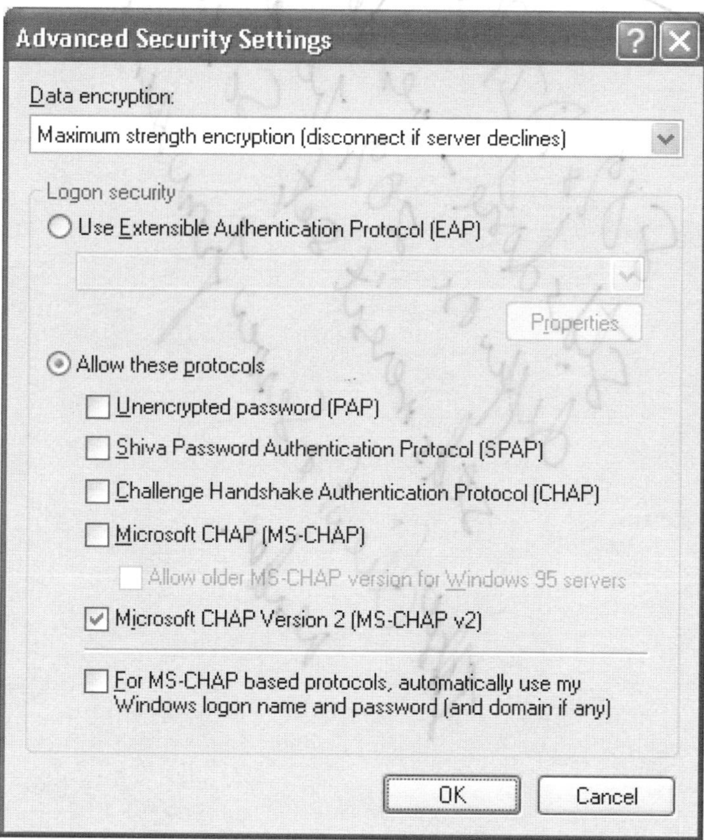

(EAP)" and choose "Smart Card" from the pull-down list. To support this, however, you'll need to set up your own Certificate Server.

But to what is the VPN client connecting?

Routing and Remote Access Service (RRAS)

On the gateway side, Windows 2000/.NET Server has a built-in VPN router called the Routing and Remote Access Service (RRAS). RRAS isn't just a dial-up service; it's also a full multi-protocol router, can perform Network Address Translation (NAT) across

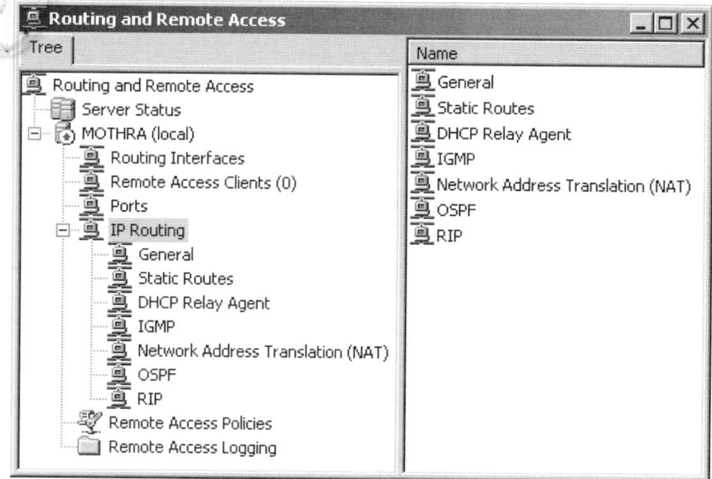

all interface types (including VPNs), and supports the RIPv2 and OSPF routing protocols for all interface types (including VPNs). For authentication, RRAS can be either a RADIUS server or client and uses Active Directory as its authentication provider. It performs static packet filtering on Windows 2000 and dynamic filtering on Windows .NET Server. Even Microsoft's Internet Security and Acceleration Server relies upon RRAS for its VPN functionality.

On Windows 2000/.NET Server, RRAS is configured using the Routing and Remote Access MMC snap-in. You can find this in the Administrative Tools folder.

Configuration of RRAS is somewhat complex and beyond the scope of this book. ActiveLane sells RRAS VPN appliances with wizards to assist in its configuration (`http://www.activelane.com`), but with a little effort you can set up the same thing for less cost. You also can use Windows clients, of course, with many other vendors' VPN gateways, as well.

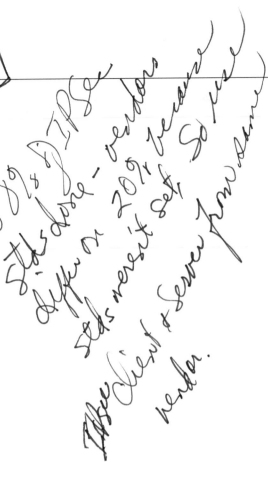

NOTES

Third-Party VPN Solutions (3 of 3)

- Many excellent products out there:
  - Cisco PIX
  - CheckPoint VPN-1/FireWall-1
  - NetScreen
  - Linux FreeS/WAN
  - Many others that can't all be listed here...

SANS Security Essentials – Windows Security

Third-Party VPN Solutions

Many excellent, non-Microsoft VPN solutions are available on the market. Many of these are tightly integrated into the vendor's firewall product too, making a nice package. Some of the more popular VPN solutions are:

- Cisco PIX (`http://www.cisco.com`)
- CheckPoint VPN-1/FireWall-1 (`http://www.checkpoint.com`)
- NetScreen (`http://www.netscreen.com`)
- Linux FreeS/WAN (`http://www.freeswan.org`)

Wireless Security

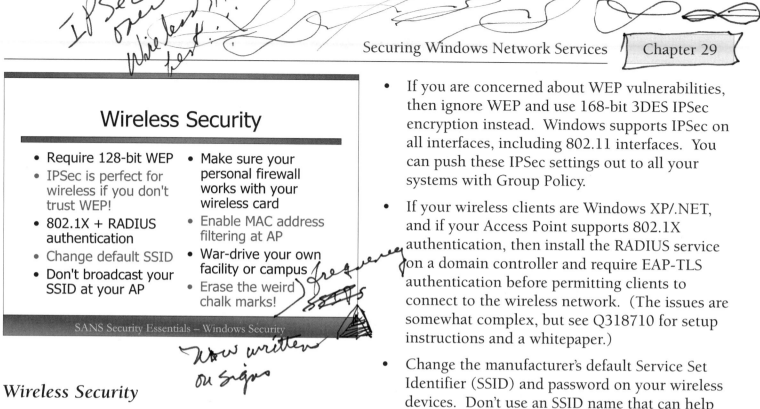

- Require 128-bit WEP
- IPSec is perfect for wireless if you don't trust WEP!
- 802.1X + RADIUS authentication
- Change default SSID
- Don't broadcast your SSID at your AP
- Make sure your personal firewall works with your wireless card
- Enable MAC address filtering at AP
- War-drive your own facility or campus
- Erase the weird chalk marks!

SANS Security Essentials – Windows Security

Wireless Security

Windows 2000/XP/.NET has extensive built-in support for wireless networking. It is easy and tempting to scatter Access Points around the LAN and start handing out 802.11 cards like party favors. But a single unsecured Access Point can open a backdoor around your $75,000 firewall which any teenage hacker with a taste for Pringles can locate.

Wireless security was discussed in a prior chapter, but its importance warrants repetition here as it relates to Windows. Here's a quick overview of the essential steps:

- Despite its imperfections, it is still critical that you enable the strongest Wired Equivalent Privacy (WEP) encryption supported on your Access Points and adapter cards. 128-bit encryption is millions of times stronger than 64-bit encryption.
- If you are concerned about WEP vulnerabilities, then ignore WEP and use 168-bit 3DES IPSec encryption instead. Windows supports IPSec on all interfaces, including 802.11 interfaces. You can push these IPSec settings out to all your systems with Group Policy.
- If your wireless clients are Windows XP/.NET, and if your Access Point supports 802.1X authentication, then install the RADIUS service on a domain controller and require EAP-TLS authentication before permitting clients to connect to the wireless network. (The issues are somewhat complex, but see Q318710 for setup instructions and a whitepaper.)
- Change the manufacturer's default Service Set Identifier (SSID) and password on your wireless devices. Don't use an SSID name that can help identify you or your organization, and don't use weak passwords (of course).
- If your vendor supports it, prevent your Access Point from broadcasting its SSID.
- Enable the Internet Connection Firewall (ICF), or another personal firewall product, to regulate incoming connections to the client's wireless card.
- If your vendor supports it, limit who can associate with your Access Point based on the hardware (MAC) address of the client's wireless card. You'll have to enter every permitted MAC address in a list on all your Access Points (yes, this will be a major pain).

NOTES

NOTES

- Obtain "war driving" software like NetStumbler (`http://www.netstumbler.com`), and war-drive your immediate area to see if you are projecting signals far beyond your building or campus. If possible, physically locate your Access Points so that they provide the necessary internal coverage without being too accessible from the outside. Most wireless card vendors provide diagnostics software which can show a real-time graph of your Access Point's signal strength; use this to better plan the precise locations of your Access Points and to test the range at which war-driving hackers can find you.
- If weird-looking pagan symbols have been written in chalk on the side of your building, erase them quickly and make a donation to a local charity! (To interpret the symbols without losing your soul, see `http://www.warchalking.org`.)

Securing IIS (1 of 11)

- **The most-hacked web server in history!**
- Microsoft's "enable everything" philosophy
  - IIS can be hardened, it just takes elbow grease.
- If possible, use IIS 6.0 with Windows .NET Server:
  - Not installed by default.
  - Must run hardening wizard during installation.
  - Faster.

SANS Security Essentials – Windows Security

Internet Information Server

Perhaps the most hacked Microsoft product is Internet Information Server (IIS). IIS is actually a collection of services that can be installed separately or not, including HTTP, FTP, SMTP, and NNTP. We only care about HTTP here, though. In this section we will discuss a few simple changes to your IIS server that drastically can reduce your vulnerabilities. In fact, IIS can be hardened against virtually all the best-known attacks against it, *even without the patches from Microsoft*. The problem with IIS has been Microsoft's enable-everything philosophy: if an IIS feature *can* be turned on by default, then it *is* turned on by default. Consequently, IIS has been a happy hunting ground for hackers for years! It's taken the six-figure-salary security gurus at Microsoft almost a decade to figure out this, but perhaps the Principle of Least Privilege applies to web servers too. . . .

Choose IIS 6.0 (Windows .NET Server)

Windows .NET Server does not enable IIS 6.0 by default. And when it is enabled, you are compelled to run a hardening wizard which only will install the features you specifically desire. IIS 6.0 runs faster than Windows 2000's IIS 5.0, was designed for ASP.NET and other .NET Framework services from the beginning, and has received the closest security scrutiny that Microsoft can muster (if IIS 6.0 is insecure, then no one will buy into Microsoft's entire ".NET Web Services" business model). Hence, if you have a choice, use IIS 6.0 in Windows .NET Server.

Fortunately, the hardening wizard built into IIS 6.0 can be run on Windows 2000 web servers, as well. We will see it in just a few moments. If you run IIS 4.0 on Windows NT, you have no choice; you must upgrade to IIS 5.0 or 6.0.

NOTES

NOTES

Clean Installation (2 of 11)

1. Ideally, IIS server should be a stand-alone, but a member server can be OK.
2. Start with a fresh OS, the latest Service Pack, and all the latest hotfixes.
3. Uninstall all the other optional components you don't plan to use.
4. Delete all sample files.
5. Remove the Help web site.

SANS Security Essentials – Windows Security

Clean Up the Installation

Start with a fresh install of the operating system, the latest Service Pack, and all the latest hotfixes. Ideally, your Windows box should be a stand-alone server, but it is OK for it to be a domain member. If IIS is a member server, it should not be a member of the main internal domain, but of a special-purpose Active Directory domain created just for the sake of managing your web servers. This IIS domain should be isolated from the internal domain and all traffic scrupulously firewalled.

Whichever IIS version you run, uninstall all the optional components you don't plan on using. On IIS 5.0, go to the Control Panel and use the Add/Remove Programs applet to uninstall all the optional networking components except for IIS.

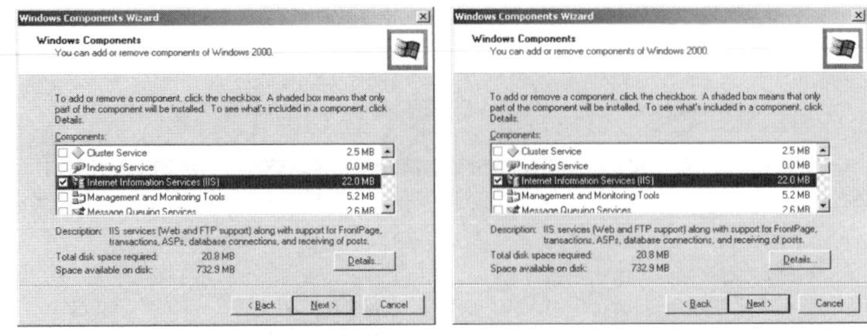

Then, highlight the IIS component in that applet, click the Details button, and uninstall all the IIS sub-components (like SMTP and the Indexing Service) you don't plan to use. The only sub-components you have to have are Common Files, IIS snap-in, and World Wide Web Server.

If you have installed any sample web pages or the IIS Help website, uninstall or delete them now. Without splitting hairs at this point, delete or uninstall everything you can without breaking IIS itself.

Separate NTFS Volumes (3 of 11)

- Separate drive volumes for OS and web content.
- Format NTFS.
- Apply suitable security template to OS volume.
- NTFS permissions for entire web content volume:
  - System: Full Control
  - Administrators: Full Control
  - Everyone: Read & Execute
- Consider explicitly denying write access to the IUSR_Computer account everywhere.

SANS Security Essentials – Windows Security

Separate NTFS Volumes with Minimal Permissions

At a minimum, the operating system should be installed in one drive volume (perhaps C:), and your website files should go into another volume (perhaps D:). Ideally, these should be on separate pairs of mirrored drives, but it's OK to make them merely logical volumes on one hard drive. The volume with the website content should have nothing but website files.

All drive volumes on IIS should be formatted with NTFS. The operating system volume (known as the "boot partition") should have its NTFS permissions reconfigured by applying a suitable INF security template (see Chapter 27). In particular, all the built-in executable tools, such as `TFTP.EXE` and `CMD.EXE`, should have their permissions configured so that only System and Administrators can Read or Execute them.

> *What Is The IUSR Account?*
>
> The IUSR_*ComputerName* account provides the user context under which all anonymous HTTP access to IIS occurs. Granting/denying access to IUSR_*ComputerName* is equivalent to granting/denying access to the billions of potential visitors to your website on earth (and the hackers among them). The account is created automatically when IIS is installed.

The volume with your HTML files, ASP/CGI scripts, and graphics should have nothing but the following NTFS permissions:

- System: Full Control
- Administrators: Full Control
- Everyone: Read & Execute

The important thing is to explicitly grant Write permission to local Administrators and to have everyone else implicitly denied Write access by default (a permission not explicitly granted is interpreted as being implicitly denied). If you explicitly want to deny Write permission to the IUSR_*ComputerName* account to the entire volume, so much the better!

These commonsense changes block all known directory traversal attacks, even without the patches from Microsoft for these types of attacks. IIS respects and enforces NTFS permissions, so don't neglect to configure them in accordance with the Principle of Least Privilege.

NOTES

NOTES

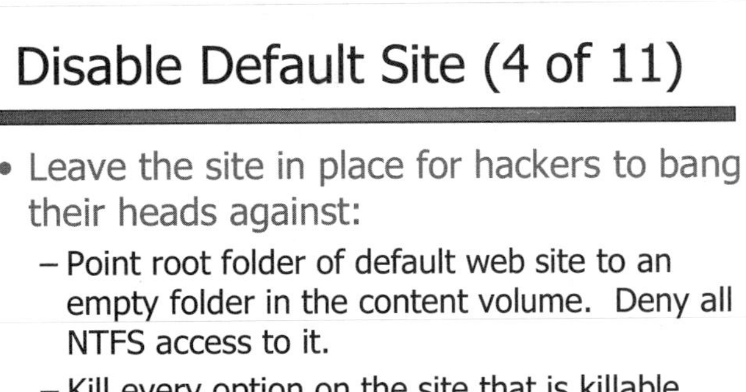

Disable Default Site (4 of 11)
• Leave the site in place for hackers to bang their heads against:
– Point root folder of default web site to an empty folder in the content volume. Deny all NTFS access to it.
– Kill every option on the site that is killable, especially the Execute permission (None).
– Right-click web site > Stop.
SANS Security Essentials – Windows Security

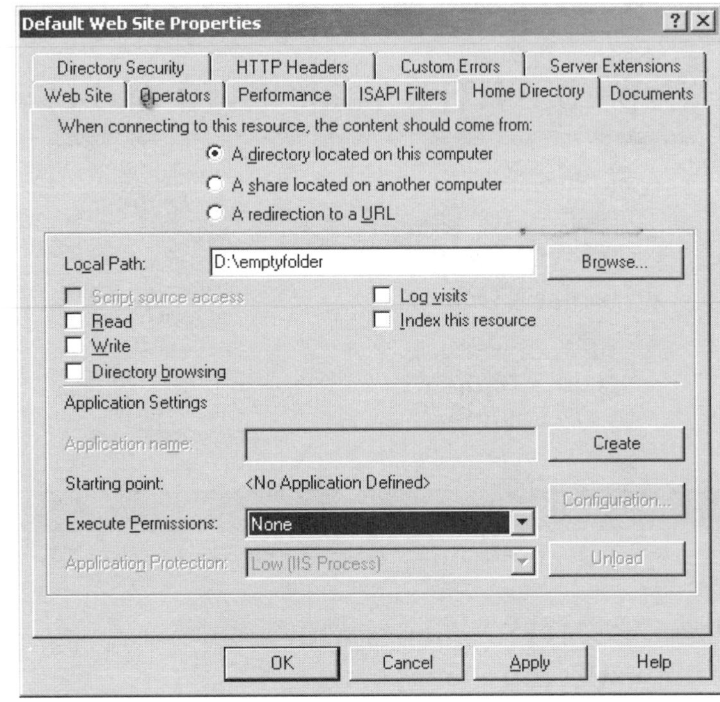

Disable the Default Website

In the Internet Information Services snap-in, found in the Administrative Tools folder, right-click on your Default Website > Properties > Home Directory tab > change the root folder of the website to an empty top-level folder in the volume for website content.

Next, in every property sheet of your Default Website, set every option to disabled/off/restricted/ etc. Don't sweat the details; just kill every feature that looks killable. Well, sweat this detail: make sure that the Execute Permission on the Home Directory tab is set to None. Click OK to save changes.

Next, right-click on your Default Website > select Stop. Your website is totally non-functional. We are going to leave it in place for hackers to bang their heads against. We're also going to leave it in place because some IIS administration tools freak out if the Default Website is gone, and, more importantly, when Windows "fixes" your IIS configuration "errors" (i.e., your hardening changes), the fixes usually are only made to the Default Website. If you create a new website, Windows tends to leave it alone.

NOTES

New Site & Host Headers (5 of 11)

- What is a "host header"? (www.sans.org)
- Make a new web site and make its root folder point towards your content files.
- On this site, require to connect:
  - Particular IP address
  - Particular TCP port (80)
  - Particular host header FQDN
- Why do this? Ask yourself, who does not use host headers when they connect to your site?

SANS Security Essentials – Windows Security

Create a New Website, and Require Host Headers

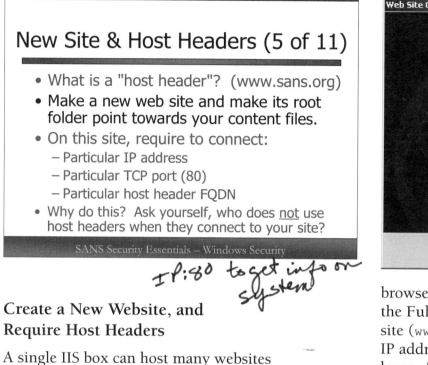

A single IIS box can host many websites simultaneously. When a browser connects to IIS and requests the home page, how does IIS know which website the browser is seeking? There are three ways to make websites distinct from each other:

- Associate a different IP address with each site.
- Associate a different TCP port number with each site.
- Associate a different host header with each site.

When the browser connects to the IIS server, the server will know to which IP address and port number the browser has connected; hence, IIS will know which website the browser wants. If the browser is connecting to "`http://www.sans.org`," the Fully Qualified Domain Name (FQDN) of the site (`www.sans.org`) is resolved through DNS to an IP address; the IP address goes into the network layer of the outgoing packet, but the FQDN *also* is written into the HTTP layer (the payload) of that packet! Hence, the IIS server simply can read the FQDN of the website you want straight out of your request packets. The FQDN is written into the "host header" of your HTTP request to the web server. This is the third way web sites can be kept distinct.

You will create a new website that points towards your content files, and that site will require a particular IP address, a particular port number, and a particular host header. If someone connects to the IIS server and his HTTP request does not include the FQDN of the website in the host header, IIS will

NOTES

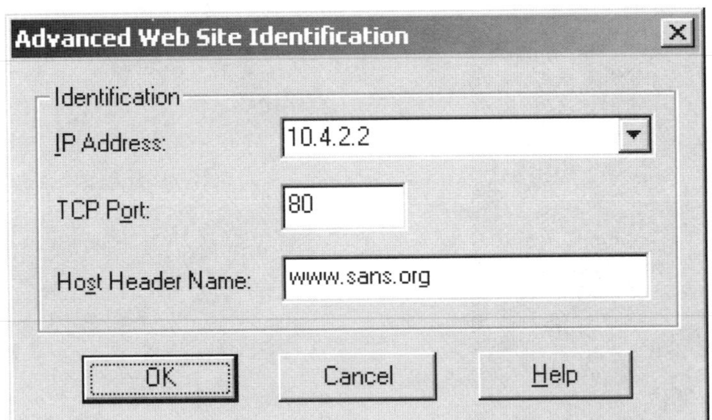

stop processing the request and simply return an error message.

To create a new website with the Web Site Creation Wizard, right-click on your IIS 5.0 web server > New > Web Site > Next > enter any description you wish > Next > select the IP address of your website, select TCP port 80, and enter the FQDN of your website > Next > browse to the path where your website files are in the non-OS volume > Next > Next > Finish.

To configure a website to require a host header, or to confirm that your new website does so, right-click the website > Properties > Web Site tab > Advanced button > highlight the first IP address in the top list > Edit button > enter an IP address, port number and FQDN host header for your site > OK > OK > OK.

Why are we doing all this? Think of all the script-kiddie scanners and IIS worms out there: they don't use host headers; they only connect using the IP address and port number of the HTTP service.

When all these tools and worms connect to your IIS server, to which website will they connect—your Default Website or your new website with the host header? The Default Website, of course; but there's nothing hackable there! The Default Website was killed by you!

This simple change is one of the ways you could have been made immune to the Code Red Worm even before its underlying vulnerability was discovered. This change also will protect you from most automated exploits and scanners that attempt to connect, without the correct FQDN in the host header, to an IIS server.

NOTES

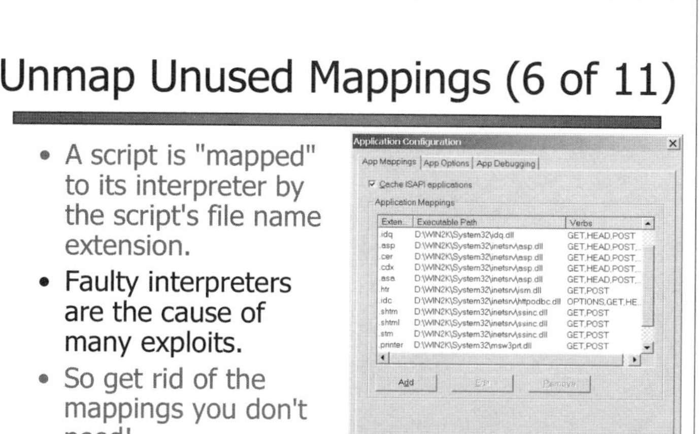

Unmap Unused Mappings (6 of 11)
A script is "mapped" to its interpreter by the script's file name extension.
Faulty interpreters are the cause of many exploits.
So get rid of the mappings you don't need!
Application Configuration
App Mappings
App Options
App Debugging
Cache ISAPI applications
Application Mappings
Add
OK
Cancel
Help
SANS Security Essentials – Windows Security

Unmap Unused Filename Extension Mappings

When an HTTP request for a file arrives at your IIS server, IIS examines the filename extension of the requested file, e.g., .ASP, .GIF, .HTML, .PHP, etc. If that filename extension has been "mapped" to an interpreter, then that file and all the data from the browser's request (GET parameters, cookie contents, header information, form input, etc.) are handed off to that interpreter. The output of this processing is then shot back to the browser as the web page. This is how Active Server Pages (ASPs) and CGI Perl scripts are run.

Now, from a hacker's point of view, the situation is different. To a hacker, you foolishly have configured your server to accept arbitrary input from anonymous people on the Internet, and then you allow this input to be passed into executables (possibly running under System context) as something like command-

Add/Edit Application Extension Mapping
Executable: C:\WINNT\System32\inetsrv\asp.dll
Browse...
Extension: .asp
Verbs
All Verbs
Limit to: GET,HEAD,POST,TRACE
Script engine
Check that file exists
OK
Cancel
Help

line arguments. These executables often are DLLs loaded into the memory address space of the web service itself (INETINFO.EXE). Consequently, all a hacker needs to do is *mangle* this input in just the right way in order to cause memory leaks, 100% CPU utilization, buffer overflows, and a variety of other nasty side-effects. All this is possible because of these filename extension mappings to their script interpreters in IIS! Hence, unmap your *unused* filename extension mappings.

To edit your extension-to-interpreter mappings, right-click on your website > Properties > Home Directory tab > Configuration button. The property sheet displays a list of filename extensions on the left-hand side and their associated interpreters in the middle. Simply highlight and remove every mapping you are not using. Don't worry; if you need to reinstate a mapping tomorrow, simply click Add. Which mappings do you have to have in order to host static web pages? None!

There are dozens of past exploits that require these mappings in order to work, and you can bet that

NOTES

tomorrow new ones will be discovered. The Code Red Worm, for example, requires the .IDA mapping; get rid of it, and you are 100% immune to the Code Red Worm. The Internet Printing Service buffer overflow exploit requires the .PRINTER mapping. The HTR scripts buffer overflow requires the .HTR mapping. Almost all the Active Server Page exploits require the .ASP mapping, and so on.

Folders Not to Have (7 of 11)

- Certain folders are constantly scanned for vulnerabilities.
- In general, be wary of well-known URL paths, e.g., /exchange
- Don't use or have:
  /scripts
  /cgi-bin
  /MSADC
  /Printers
  /IISHelp
  /IISSamples

SANS Security Essentials – Windows Security

Virtual Folders Not to Have

You should not have or use any folders named:

- scripts
- cgi-bin (or cgibin)
- MSADC
- Printers
- IISHelp
- IISSamples

If you do, delete or rename them. These folders are so ubiquitous that they constantly are scanned and relied upon by automated tools/worms. Simply not having the *MSADC* folder, for example, protects a machine from the Rain Forrest Puppy RDS exploit. And, in general, avoid using the default folder names for popular services; e.g., the Outlook Web Access site for Exchange Server installs in the *Exchange* folder by default, but by using a different folder name, you can be spared when the next "OWA Worm" spreads because the worm will not know where you are keeping the pages.

NOTES

NOTES

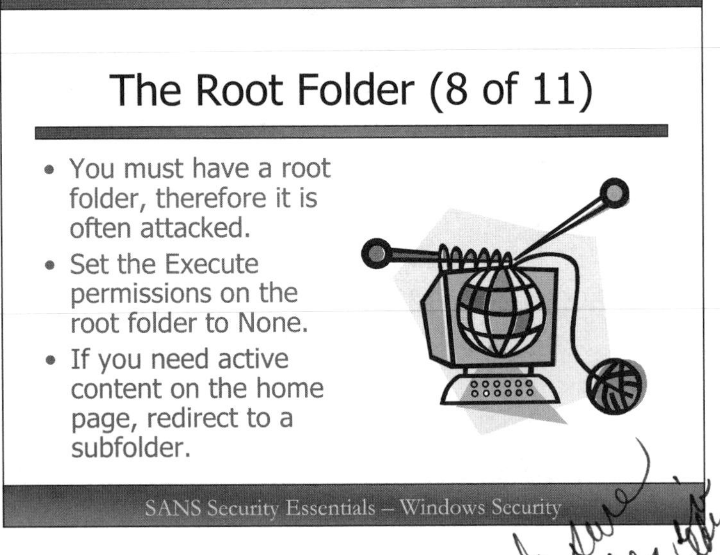

The Root Folder (8 of 11)
• You must have a root folder, therefore it is often attacked.
• Set the Execute permissions on the root folder to None.
• If you need active content on the home page, redirect to a subfolder.
SANS Security Essentials – Windows Security

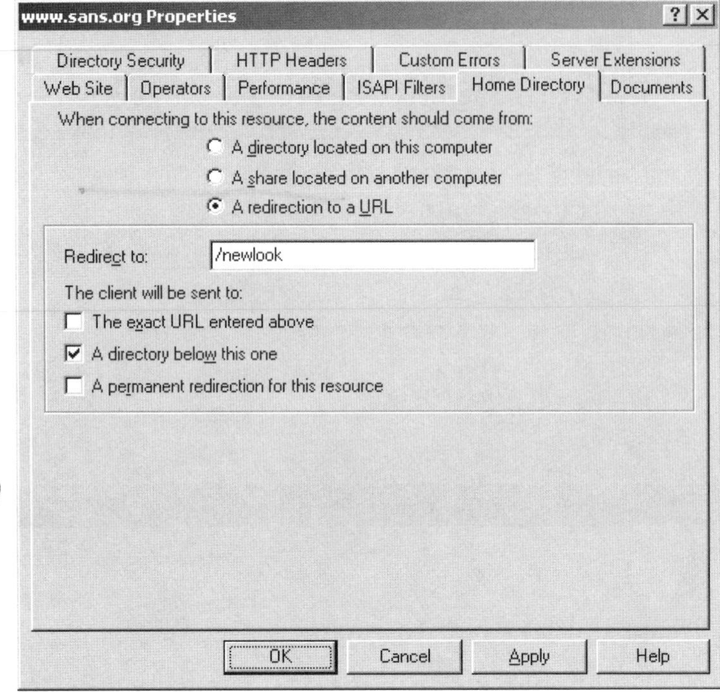

The Root Folder

Every website must have a top-level or "root" folder. If at all possible, set the Execute permissions to None on the root folder. This will not be possible on sites where you must support scripts in the top-level folder, but it's good for security. Why?

When a new scripting-related exploit is discovered, the worms and tools that use the exploit will be hard-coded to run the exploit against all the well-known IIS folders (Scripts, Exchange, MSADC, IISSamples, etc.) and against the root folder because you have to have a root folder. The Code Red Worm, for example, ran its exploit against the root folder. But had the execute permissions been set to None on the root folder of a Code Red-targeted box, the worm would have been ineffective against it.

To set the execute permissions, right-click any folder (or the website itself for the root folder) > Properties > Home Directory tab > select the desired execute permissions from the pull-down list.

In fact, you can have the equivalent of scripts in the root folder: simply redirect all requests aimed at the root folder to a subfolder instead, and enable the Scripts permission in the subfolder. Worms and scanners virtually never follow HTTP redirects.

To redirect requests to the root folder to a subfolder, right-click the root folder > Properties > Home Directory tab > select "A Redirection To A URL" at the top > enter the name of the subfolder preceded by a forward-slash, e.g., "/subfolder" > check the "Directory Below This One" box > OK.

NOTES

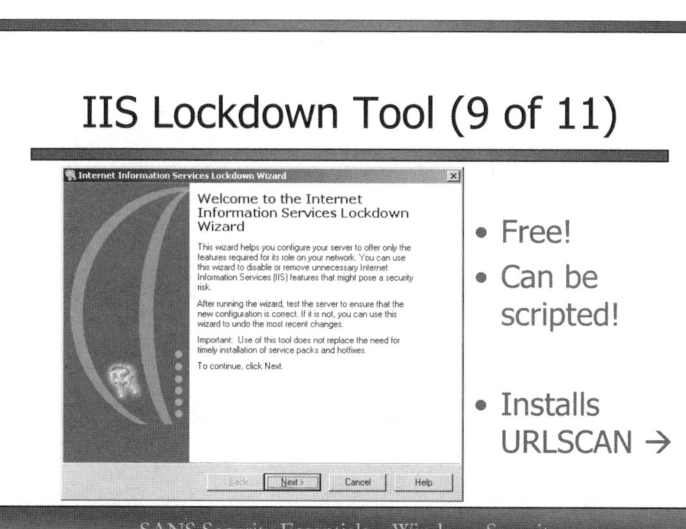

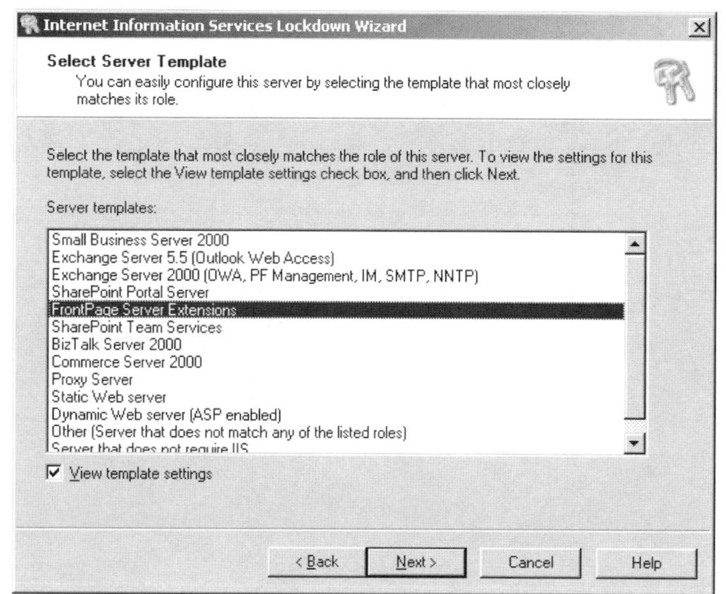

IIS Lockdown Tool

The IIS Lockdown Tool is a free utility from Microsoft that is easy to use and implements many of the security changes this chapter recommends. The tool works on both IIS 4.0 and 5.0 and can be downloaded here:

```
http://www.microsoft.com/technet/security/
tools/locktool.asp
```

Version 2.1 and later supports a command-line switch to read its input from an answer file, thus making it possible to automate the application of the tool to multiple servers with a batch file. To run the program in graphical mode, simply double-click it.

In graphical mode, the tool prompts the user to choose the type of server on which IIS is installed, e.g., an Exchange Server, Commerce Server, BizTalk Server, server with FrontPage Extensions, etc. This information is used to customize the hardening the server receives so that functionality is, hopefully, not lost.

Make sure to check the "View template settings" box so that you will not be unpleasantly surprised. The next page gives you the option to uninstall unneeded services.

You can also choose exactly which changes you would (not) like to be made to your system by the tool. For example, your dangerous script mappings can be remapped to a DLL that simply returns a "404 File Not Found" error message.

The tool also can remove many of the dangerous folders discussed above, as well as other things.

Additionally, the tool can install and configure URLSCAN based on the type of server chosen.

NOTES

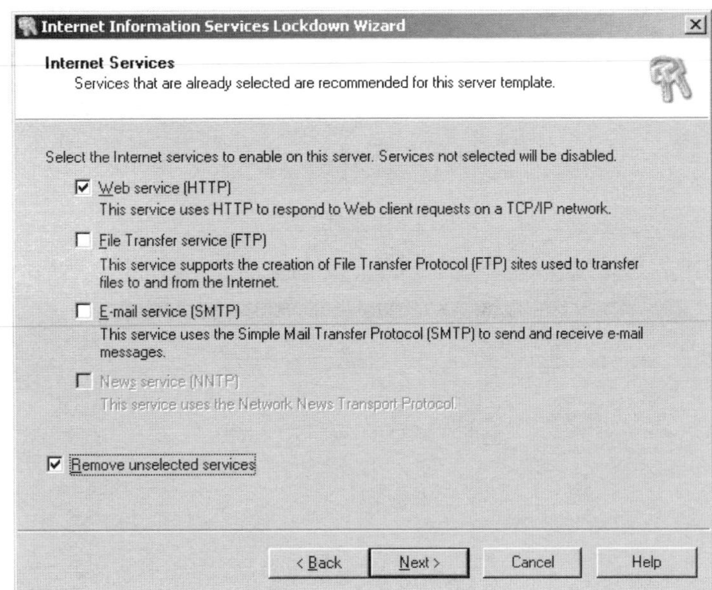
Internet Information Services Lockdown Wizard
Internet Services
Services that are already selected are recommended for this server template.
Select the Internet services to enable on this server. Services not selected will be disabled.
Web service (HTTP)
This service uses HTTP to respond to Web client requests on a TCP/IP network.
File Transfer service (FTP)
This service supports the creation of File Transfer Protocol (FTP) sites used to transfer files to and from the Internet.
E-mail service (SMTP)
This service uses the Simple Mail Transfer Protocol (SMTP) to send and receive e-mail messages.
News service (NNTP)
This service uses the Network News Transport Protocol.
Remove unselected services
< Back
Next >
Cancel
Help

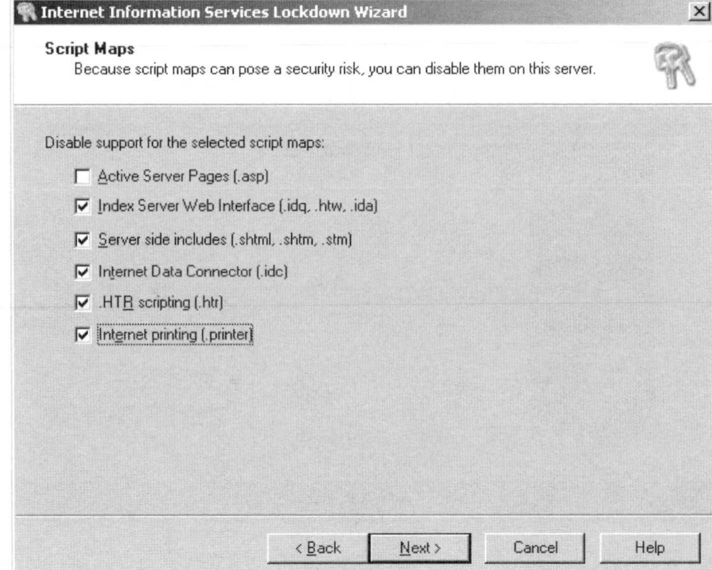
Internet Information Services Lockdown Wizard
Script Maps
Because script maps can pose a security risk, you can disable them on this server.
Disable support for the selected script maps:
Active Server Pages (.asp)
Index Server Web Interface (.idq, .htw, .ida)
Server side includes (.shtml, .shtm, .stm)
Internet Data Connector (.idc)
.HTR scripting (.htr)
Internet printing (.printer)
< Back
Next >
Cancel
Help

URLSCAN will be discussed in the next section. If in doubt, do not install URLSCAN, or else you can find yourself in a troubleshooting quagmire.

So why don't we just run the tool and skip the explanations in the foregoing slides? Because the tool doesn't do everything that needs to be done, and if you rely on the tool exclusively, you are dependent on it (and its limitations). For example, just running the IIS Lockdown Tool won't harden your web applications or tell you how to customize your URLSCAN settings.

NOTES

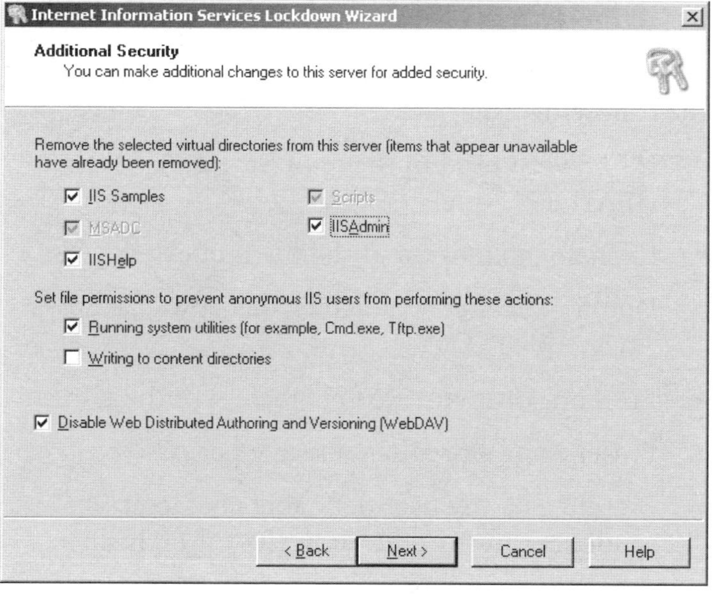
Internet Information Services Lockdown Wizard
Additional Security
You can make additional changes to this server for added security.
Remove the selected virtual directories from this server (items that appear unavailable have already been removed):
IIS Samples
Scripts
MSADC
IISAdmin
IISHelp
Set file permissions to prevent anonymous IIS users from performing these actions:
Running system utilities (for example, Cmd.exe, Tftp.exe)
Writing to content directories
Disable Web Distributed Authoring and Versioning (WebDAV)
< Back
Next >
Cancel
Help

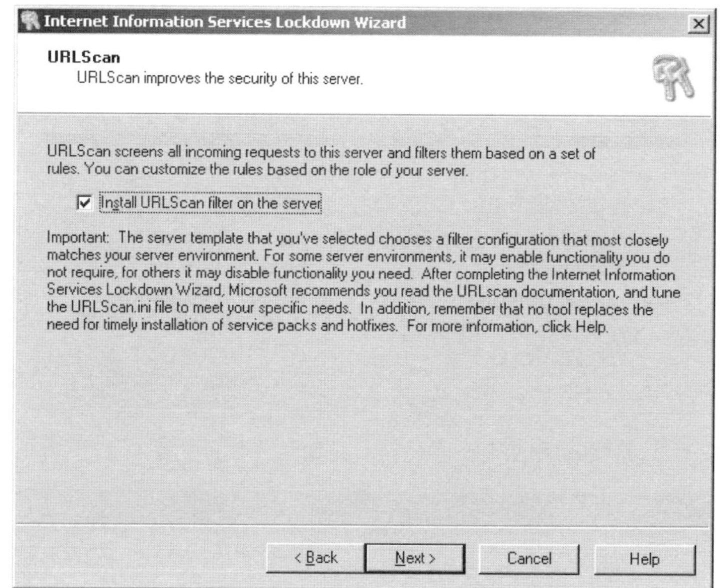
Internet Information Services Lockdown Wizard
URLScan
URLScan improves the security of this server.
URLScan screens all incoming requests to this server and filters them based on a set of rules. You can customize the rules based on the role of your server.
Install URLScan filter on the server
Important: The server template that you've selected chooses a filter configuration that most closely matches your server environment. For some server environments, it may enable functionality you do not require, for others it may disable functionality you need. After completing the Internet Information Services Lockdown Wizard, Microsoft recommends you read the URLscan documentation, and tune the URLScan.ini file to meet your specific needs. In addition, remember that no tool replaces the need for timely installation of service packs and hotfixes. For more information, click Help.
< Back
Next >
Cancel
Help

NOTES

URLSCAN (10 of 11)

- Screens all HTTP requests to IIS.
- Rejects invalid requests and returns "404" error.
- Writes dropped requests to URLSCAN.LOG
- Can change the "Server:" string in IIS headers.
- Rejection Criteria:
  - HTTP Verb
  - Filename Extension
  - Encoding Patterns
  - Non-ASCII Characters
  - Multiple Periods in URL
  - HTTP Headers
  - *Any user-definable string!*
- Third-Party URLSCAN:
  - SecureIIS Application Firewall (www.eEye.com)

SANS Security Essentials – Windows Security

URLSCAN.DLL: Application-Layer Firewall

The IIS Lockdown Tool installs a DLL named "URLSCAN.DLL." URLSCAN inspects incoming HTTP requests to the web server and blocks any requests that match any of the user-definable patterns in a configuration file used by URLSCAN. Also, URLSCAN screens all requests to the web server and returns the "404 File Not Found" error message, if the request is threatening in any way. Because the patterns it screens for are user-configurable, it can be updated quickly as new threats are discovered.

URLSCAN comes as a part of the IIS Lockdown Tool, but you also can download it separately from

```
http://www.microsoft.com/technet/security/
tools/URLscan.asp
```

Rejection Criteria

URLSCAN can reject HTTP requests based on any of the following criteria:

- HTTP verb used in the request, e.g., GET, HEAD, PUT, etc.
- Filename extension of the file requested
- Double-encoded characters, e.g., "%252e" → "%2e" → "."
- Presence of non-ASCII characters in the URL
- Presence of more than a single period
- Presence of any user-definable character sequences in the URL or in the HTTP header

Optionally, when a request is rejected, information about the request can be written to a text log file (urlscan.log). Each entry in the log lists the request's date, time, source IP address, URL, and a user-friendly explanation for why the request was rejected.

The URLSCAN's configuration settings are stored in a plain text file named "URLSCAN.INI." The configuration file is commented thoroughly and easy to edit without breaking other functionality. A moderately detailed understanding of HTTP is required for the more advanced features, but most of the settings are fairly straightforward. For example, changing the "Server:" string in HTTP headers is a simple, single-line edit.

NOTES

Changing the "Server:" String in HTTP Headers

URLSCAN also can change the "Server: Microsoft-IIS/5.0" line in the header of the server's responses, or remove the "Server:" line entirely. This is important because automated scanning tools look for this header to generate lists of accessible IIS targets. By changing this string, the IIS server will not appear on these lists and will appear to be a server of a different type and model, e.g., "Server: Apache/1.3.19 (Unix)."

Third-Party Filters

The best-known third-party tool which screens HTTP requests is eEye's "SecureIIS Application Firewall" (`http://www.eEye.com`). This tool, though not free, is easier to configure than URLSCAN, is supported by its vendor, and has been hardened by developers who *really* know web application security.

NOTES

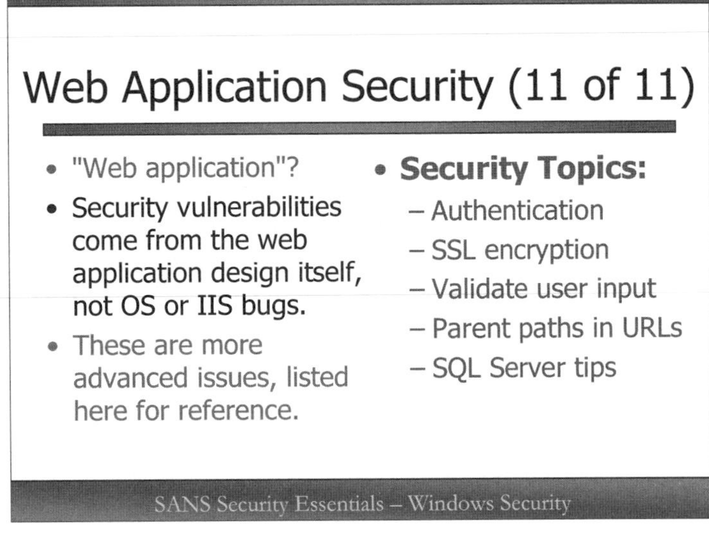

Web Application Security (11 of 11)
• "Web application"?
• Security vulnerabilities come from the web application design itself, not OS or IIS bugs.
• These are more advanced issues, listed here for reference.
• Security Topics:
– Authentication
– SSL encryption
– Validate user input
– Parent paths in URLs
– SQL Server tips
SANS Security Essentials – Windows Security

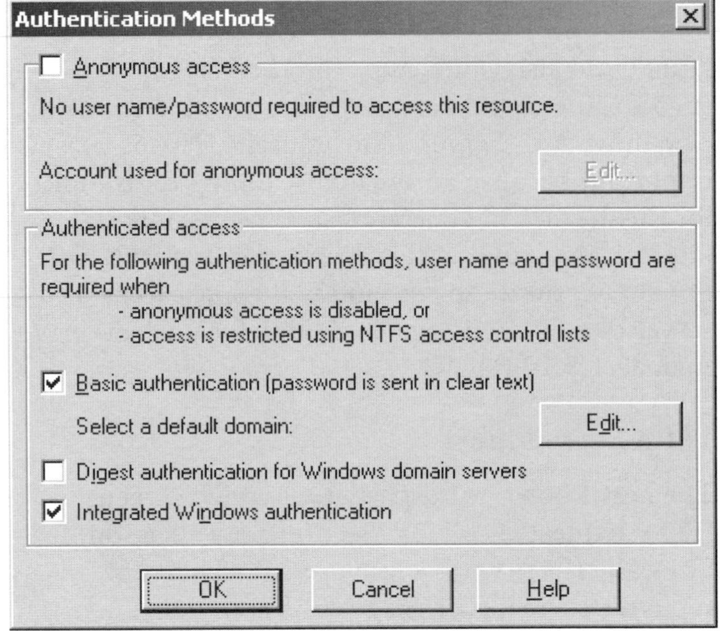

Web Application Security

A "web application" is a set of scripts and executables on a web server which together provide a service, like being able to read/send e-mail through web forms, trade stocks, manage one's bank account, or manage a Human Resources database on SQL Server. Web application security has a lot to do with the design of the application itself as opposed to bugs in the HTTP daemon or the operating system.

Require Authentication

It is trivially easy to require authentication on a folder or file in IIS. It requires no custom scripting. IIS uses Active Directory for its accounts database, and, once a user has authenticated, IIS is aware of that user's group memberships and, therefore, can enforce NTFS permissions. You should require authentication on sensitive web applications, like the IIS Administration website, and on virtual folders to restricted files.

To require user authentication on a folder or file, right-click it > Properties > Security tab > click the top Edit button > uncheck the box next to Anonymous Access > check the box for Basic authentication > OK > OK. Basic authentication was selected because it is compatible with all browsers; however, basic authentication also sends passwords unencrypted. Fortunately, SSL can be used to encrypt the channel.

SSL Encryption

Secure Sockets Layer (SSL) encryption can encrypt strongly all data transmitted between browser and server. After installing a digital certificate, you can

NOTES

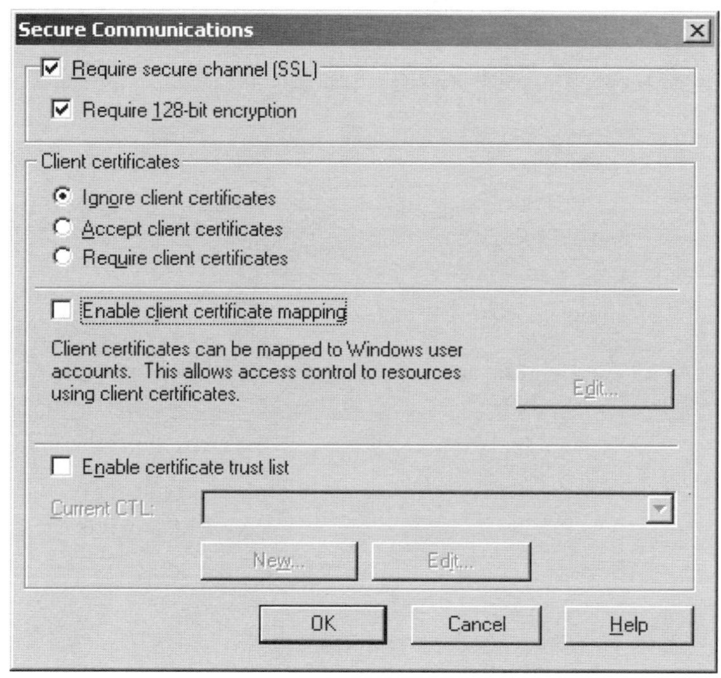

require SSL encryption on any folder or file. To do so, right-click the item > Properties > Security tab > bottom Edit button > check the Require Secure Channel box > OK > OK.

If you don't check the "Require 128-bit Encryption" box, the browser might only negotiate a 40-bit session key. If your data or passwords are particularly sensitive, make sure to require 128-bit encryption.

SSL should be used whenever basic authentication is required. Importantly, remember that your credentials are cached in your browser and sent automatically for every page that requests authentication. A common mistake is to use SSL on the initial connection to the web server (when the dialog box appears for the username and password) but then to continue requiring basic authentication on subsequent folders/files even though SSL is no longer being used.

SSL also should be used on any forms for submitting personal data, such as credit card numbers or birth dates. Actually, it is perfectly safe to download the form in cleartext, but the data should be posted back up to the web server using SSL when the Submit button is clicked. Examine your HTML to ensure that the form method reads `Action="https://...."`

Validate User Input

Especially if your IIS server provides access to a back-end database, you must validate all user input that malicious users can modify. To "validate" input is to check that the data is of the expected length, type, and format and that it does not contain any potentially harmful commands or characters.

In a cross-site scripting attack, for example, a malicious user posts HTML code into a form on your website; the HTML code contains client-side JavaScript that performs unwanted actions when someone else views that posted data. Hence, all HTML data should be cleansed from user input before it is processed by IIS any further. Other dangerous items that should be cleansed from input include SQL keywords ("INSERT," "SELECT," "WHERE," etc.) and the command-line symbols for piping ("|") and redirection (">").

The best general-purpose technique for validating user input is through the use of regular expressions in server-side scripts. (Don't perform input validation on the client's side except as a

NOTES

convenience to the user.) For example, the following VBScript function takes form input and deletes everything found after any pipe symbols found in the data:

```
Function CleanOutTextAfterPipe(sInput)

    If Not IsObject(oRegExp) Then Set
oRegExp = New RegExp

    oRegExp.Pattern = "^(.+)\|(.+)"

    CleanOutTextAfterPipe =
oRegExp.Replace(sInput,"$1")

End Function
```

Similar functions could clean out HTML code, dangerous SQL keywords, unformatted binary garbage, etc.

Disable Support for Parent Paths

One type of input validation is so important that it's built into IIS as an option. When you enter "`cd ..`" in a command-prompt window, you "move up" one directory in the folder hierarchy. You also could enter "`cd ..\..\..\winnt\system32`" to move up three levels in the hierarchy and down into the \system32 folder.

This technique also can be used with web pages! For example, a number of IIS 4.0 sample pages (showcode.asp, viewcode.asp, codebrws.asp) permitted attackers to view the contents of other files with URLs like this:

```
http://10.0.0.1/msadc/Samples/SELECTOR/
showcode.asp?source=/msadc/Samples/../../
../../../../Inetpub/Scripts/myscript.pl
```

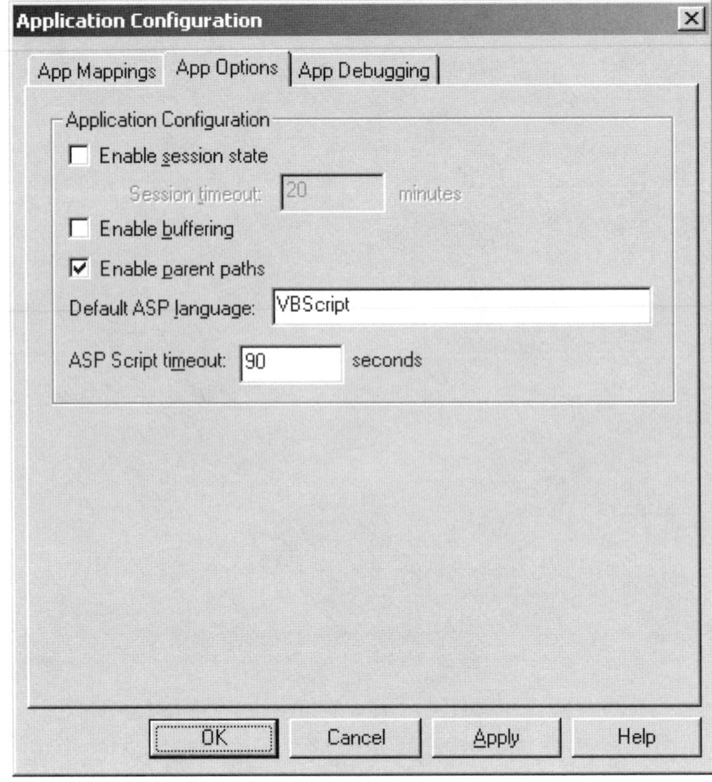

The "`/..`" notation is dangerous because it permits a script to break out of its working folder into its "parent paths" and down into other folders. If possible, disable the use of "`/..`" in scripts on your web server. To disable the use of parent path syntax, go to the properties of a website > Home Directory Tab > Configuration button > App Options tab > uncheck the box labeled "Enable Parent Paths."

Note that you can still use the "`/..`" notation to access static content, such as GIF files; you simply won't be able to use it with dynamic content, such as scripts or custom DLLs.

NOTES

SQL Server 2000 Security Tips

Many IIS web servers act as front-ends to Microsoft SQL Server databases behind them. The data in these SQL Servers are the real wealth of your organization, not the IIS boxes themselves. You may not be the database administrator, but it is important, nonetheless, to mention a few critical security measures for SQL Server that can save your job:

- Avoid installing SQL Server on the IIS server itself. Place the SQL Server behind the firewall or, ideally, on a separate service subnet to which the firewall regulates access. Block all external access to the database servers themselves, especially TCP ports 1433 and 1434.
- Assign a long, random password to the SQL Server system administrator ("sa") account. The password is blank by default. The sa account has the SysAdmin role on the server, so secure all other accounts that have this role as well, such as members of the local Administrators group. In general, be paranoid about any accounts which have any of the sensitive roles on the server (e.g., ServerAdmin, SecurityAdmin, db_owner, etc.).
- Use Integrated Windows authentication instead of mixed/standard authentication. The former relies upon Active Directory and Kerberos, while the latter relies upon the authentication mechanisms built into the SQL Server itself (a legacy feature from the old Sybase days of the product).
- Avoid permitting IIS to send raw SQL commands to the database server. Instead, scripts on IIS should validate user input, then pass that cleaned input to procedures stored on the SQL Server itself (where the input data can be checked again). You'll get better performance using stored procedures, too.

NOTES

Terminal Services (1 of 3)

- Remote control of virtual desktops.
- Terminal Services on Windows 2000/.NET Server:
  - Application Server Mode (requires user licenses)
  - Remote Administration Mode (two admins only)
- Windows XP Remote Desktop.
- Windows XP Remote Assistance.
  - Invitation files are sent via e-mail or Windows Messenger
  - Invitations have a TTL and require a password
- Download free thin-client software from Microsoft.

SANS Security Essentials – Windows Security

Terminal Services and Remote Desktop

Terminal Services provides graphical remote control of virtual desktops running on Windows 2000/XP/.NET. It is similar to Symantec pcAnywhere or VNC in that it makes a remote desktop appear in a local application window (you can click the Start menu, see icons, etc.), except that you don't connect to "the" desktop of the remote box; you connect to a "virtual" desktop hidden in the RAM of the Terminal Server. Hence, when you connect to a remote system, it is not the case that anyone sitting at that computer will see your typing and mouseclicks; in fact, a single Windows 2000/.NET Terminal Server could be running scores of virtual desktops simultaneously, each desktop separate and protected from the others.

Terminal Services on Windows 2000/.NET Server

Terminal Services is installed on Windows 2000/.NET Server as another optional networking component using the Add/Remove Programs applet in Control Panel. When installed, you'll have to choose its licensing mode: remote administration or application server. If you choose application server licensing, then any user can connect, but she'll require a special license from Microsoft. If you choose remote administration mode, you don't have to purchase any additional licenses, but only Administrators can connect to the box (and only two at a time).

Terminal Services on Windows XP Professional

Terminal Services on Windows XP Professional is called "Remote Desktop." You enable/disable it using the System applet in Control Panel > Remote

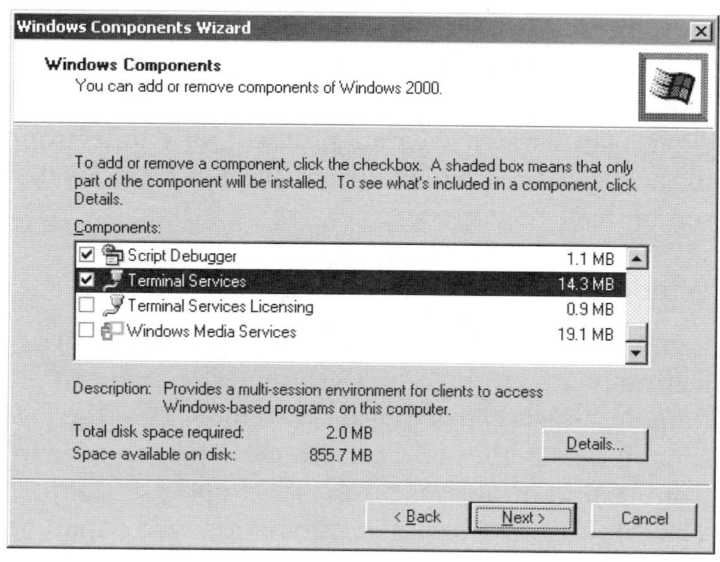

tab. Needless to say, disable it, if you don't plan to use it.

Remote Desktop prevents any user account with a blank password from connecting. By default, only local Administrators can connect, but in the System applet you can add other accounts, and you don't have to buy more licenses. If you are a non-administrative user, you only can connect when either no one is logged on at the remote system or when you are logged on there. If you already are logged on, the remote machine's visible desktop becomes locked. If you are a member of the local Administrators group, you can connect to any machine, but this action will forcibly log off any interactively logged-on user there.

Thin-Client Applications for Connecting

Windows XP Professional and Windows .NET include a thin-client application for connecting to

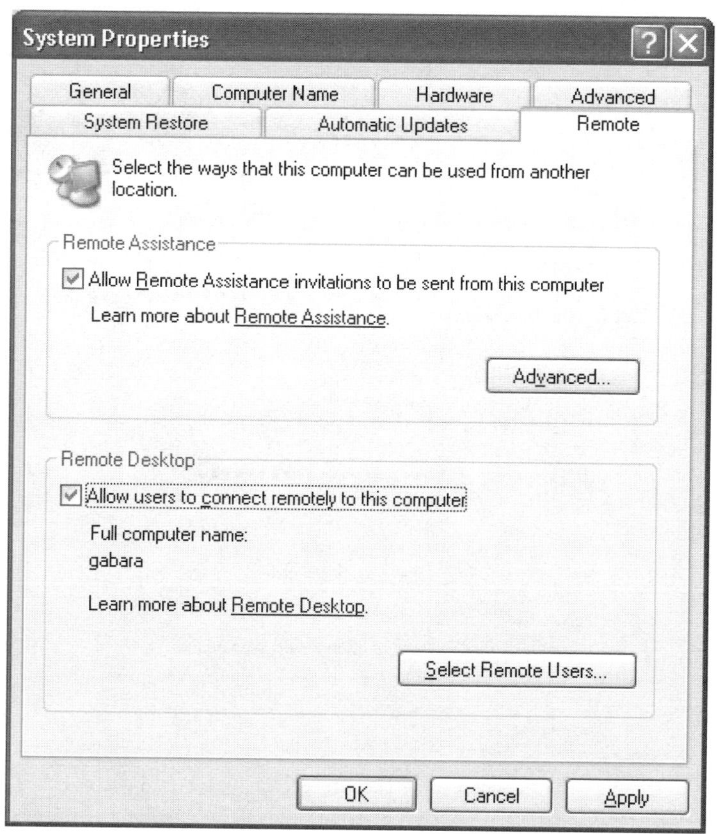

remote desktops by default. Launch the client by going to the Start menu > All Programs > Accessories > Communications > Remote Desktop Connection. Enter the IP address or computer name of the target, and you're ready to go! You also can click the Options button in the initial window to configure screen resolution, color depth, connection speed optimizations, and other settings.

For Windows 2000, it's important to get the latest version of the client for performance and security reasons. Download from `http://www.microsoft.com/windows2000/downloads/recommended/TSAC/`,

NOTES

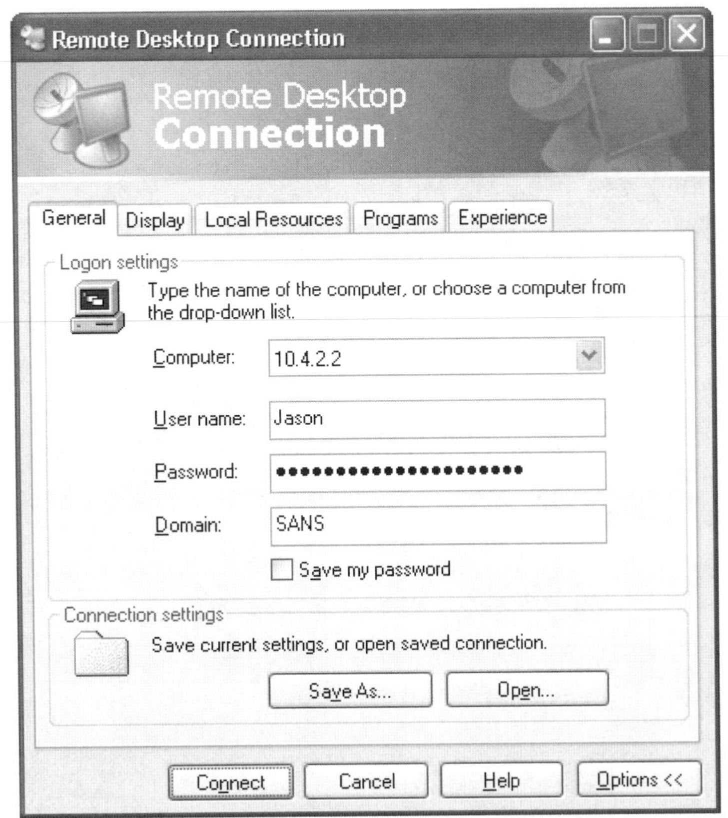

and make sure to select "MSI Package" from the selection list. Once installed, you'll have a new program group: Start menu > Programs > Terminal Services Client.

There even is an ActiveX control version of the client that can be loaded into web pages! Download the control, along with sample web pages for displaying it, from the same URL just above. This version is called the "Terminal Services Advanced Client" and by default creates a virtual directory on your website named /tsweb. Hence, browsers would connect to, for example, "`http://www.sans.org/tsweb/`," and the client will load into the web page displayed. The user would then enter the IP address of the machine to be controlled. (The ActiveX control is downloaded with HTTP, but the client uses its own separate protocol for connecting to the target box, which doesn't have to be the web server itself.)

Windows XP Remote Assistance

Remote Assistance is a Windows XP Professional feature related to Remote Desktop. The intent of Remote Assistance is to use the Remote Desktop capabilities to allow a trusted remote person to help troubleshoot problems on the local user's desktop. The local user will send an "invitation" via e-mail or Windows Messenger to the other person; the other person, who must be running Windows XP/.NET, double-clicks the attachment in the invitation e-mail, which opens up a special Remote Desktop connection to the desktop of the person who sent the invitation. Both the local and remote users see the same active desktop, and, if granted permission, the remote user can even take control of the mouse and keyboard.

From the local Windows XP desktop you send a Remote Assistance invitation by going to the Start menu > All Programs > Accessories > System Tools > Remote Assistance. This launches a wizard to walk you through the process. You can choose to send the invitation via Windows Messenger or Microsoft Outlook or choose to create a separate invitation file on the hard drive. You'll choose for how long the invitation is good (1 minute to 99 days) and the password the remote user must enter when connecting to the local system. This password must

NOTES

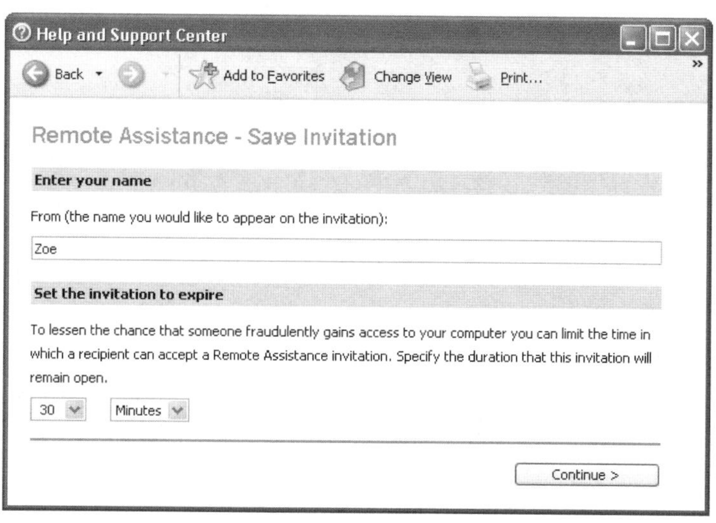

be communicated to the remote user through some other channel, e.g., by phone.

When the remote user receives the invitation, he or she simply double-clicks the attached file to connect to the local user's computer using Remote Desktop.

You enable/disable the ability to send invitations using the System applet in Control Panel > Remote tab.

NOTES

Remote Desktop Protocol (2 of 3)

- RDP operates on TCP/3389.
- Three RDP encryption levels are available:
  - Low: 56-bit RC4 <u>to</u> the server, but no encryption for packets <u>from</u> the server.
  - Medium: 56-bit RC4 for all packets.
  - High: 128-bit RC4 for all packets.
- Older client software only used 40-bit RC4 for the Low and Medium levels (bug).
- Terminal Server can require High level.

SANS Security Essentials – Windows Security

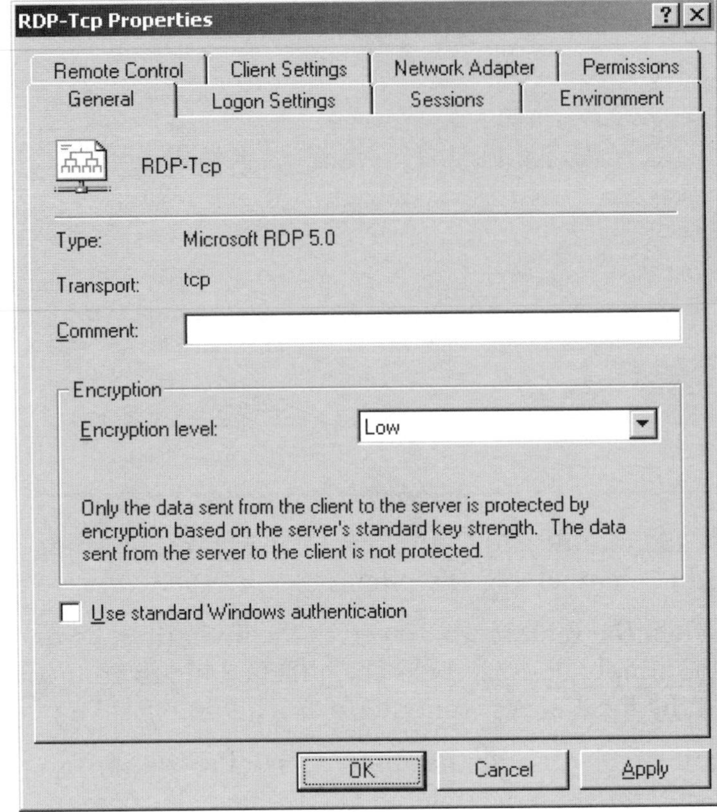

Remote Desktop Protocol (RDP)

Terminal Services and Remote Desktop both use the Remote Desktop Protocol (RDP) on TCP port 3389. Windows XP/.NET always uses 128-bit RC4 encryption, but Windows 2000 clients require Service Pack 2 or later to enable high encryption (they use 56-bit RC4 without it).

For security and performance reasons, it is important to use the latest version of the client and to install the latest Service Pack and hotfixes. There have been a number of published RDP vulnerabilities that have been fixed via Service Packs or hotfixes.

Also, Terminal Services on Windows 2000/.NET Server should be configured to require high encryption. There are three settings possible on the server:

- Low. 56-bit RC4 encryption of data sent to the Terminal Server, including passwords. However, data received from the server is cleartext. Only use this on intranets or through VPN tunnels. (Important: If you are using an older version of the client, the encryption is only 40-bit. This also is true for the Medium level.)
- Medium (Default). 56-bit RC4 encryption of all data.
- High. 128-bit RC4 encryption of all data.

To configure your Terminal Server to require 128-bit (High) encryption, open the Terminal Services Configuration snap-in in the Administrative Tools folder > Connections > right-click the RDP-Tcp icon > Properties > General tab > select High from the list > OK.

NOTES

NOTES

RDP Best Practices (3 of 3)

- Apply latest Service Pack and hotfixes.
- Block unwanted TCP/3389 traffic at firewall.
- Get latest version of thin client software from Microsoft.
- Require 128-bit (High) RDP encryption at server.
- Use IPSec or a VPN instead of RDP encryption when data is sensitive (or if you simply don't trust RDP security).
- Disable Remote Desktop and Remote Assistance on workstations if not needed (Group Policy can do this).
- Require password and a short TTL for Remote Assistance invitations (Group Policy can do this).
- Investigate Citrix MetaFrame as an alternative.

SANS Security Essentials – Windows Security

Best Practices for Terminal Services

The following is a summary of the security best practices for both Terminal Services on Windows 2000/.NET Server and Remote Desktop on Windows XP. Not all recommendations can be discussed in detail here, but it's important to list them nonetheless.

- Apply the latest Service Packs and hotfixes on both the RDP client and server.
- Make sure to block all TCP 3389 traffic at the firewall.
- Get the latest version of the Terminal Services thin-client from Microsoft's website for Windows 2000. This comes in MSI package format for easy deployments.
- Require 128-bit RC4 (High) encryption at the Terminal Server.
- Consider using IPSec or a VPN instead of the RDP encryption if you are concerned about future vulnerabilities.
- Disable Remote Desktop and Remote Assistance on all Windows XP systems where you do not intend to use these features. Fortunately, this can be done through Group Policy.
- If you allow users to send Remote Assistance invitations, set the invitation expiration timer to a relatively short value (3 to 24 hours), and require a password to connect. These options also can be configured through Group Policy.
- If you will be using Terminal Services on Windows 2000/.NET Server for more than just remote administration, consider using Citrix MetaFrame to benefit from its enhanced management and security capabilities (`http://www.citrix.com`). Citrix also provides thin-clients for virtually all platforms desired, including Linux, Solaris, and the Macintosh.

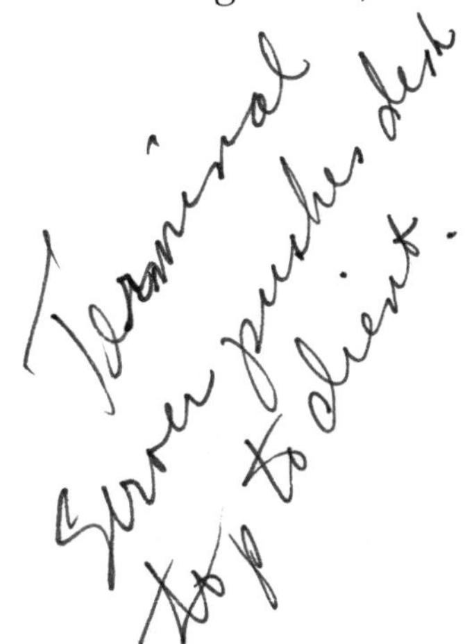

Summary

- Best way to secure a service.
- Firewalls.
- IPSec.
- Virtual Private Networking.
- Wireless Security.
- IIS Security:
  - Clean install
  - Default website
  - Host headers
  - Script mappings
  - IIS Lockdown Tool
  - URLSCAN
- Terminal Services
  - Remote Desktop
  - Remote Assistance
  - RDP

SANS Security Essentials – Windows Security

Summary

The purpose of this chapter was to describe some general techniques for securing network services and to discuss specific hardening steps for wireless networks, IIS and Terminal Services in particular. Especially for IIS, the goal is to create a "bastion host," i.e., a specially-hardened box that, hopefully, will withstand tomorrow's new batch of exploits and attack tools. We're doomed to failure, of course; but there's a huge difference between failing occasionally and getting hacked every other day of the week.

The best way to secure a service, of course, is to uninstall it. Short of that, you also can disconnect any network adapter card bindings to it, filter all packets to/from it with a personal firewall, and encrypt its packets with IPSec. If the service is accessible over an 802.11 wireless LAN, then make sure you enable WEP encryption, change your default SSID, don't broadcast your SSID, and consider using 802.1X authentication.

IIS probably is the most-hacked web server in the world, so it is imperative that you harden those boxes. A few simple changes can improve your threat exposure drastically: delete unused files; use NTFS permissions; have separate volumes for the OS and for web site content; require host headers; unmap unused ISAPI Extensions; and install URLSCAN. Running the IIS Lockdown Tool will scan for vulnerabilities and install URLSCAN for you too.

Terminal Services is very popular, but it's also dangerous because it grants complete remote control over the target system. And it's built into Windows XP as the Remote Assistance feature. Use only high encryption for the RDP protocol; apply the latest hotfixes; disable RDP, if you're not going to use it; and train users to send password-protected invitations with short TTL's only to people whom they know and trust. Hopefully this will prevent your systems from being "owned" by hackers.

Speaking of which, if hackers did get control over one of your servers, how would you know it? Of course, if they deface your website with pictures of the Borg Queen in a bikini, it's going to be easy to tell, but more "elite" hackers will just silently take control. . . . And if you did discover the compromise, how would you analyze the box to figure out what they've done? Do you have a baseline against which you can compare your current settings and operational state? Of course you do! You've been doing regular audits!

NOTES

NOTES

Chapter 30

Automation and Auditing

NOTES

NOTES

Automation and Auditing
SANS Security Essentials V:
Windows Security
SANS Security Essentials – Windows Security

Automation and Auditing

Auditing is the gathering and analysis of detailed information about our own networks. But why audit at all? What's the point? Besides, isn't it . . . *boring*?

The Cuckoo's Egg is a novel about a network administrator who, in the course of investigating a 75-cent billing error, discovered a hacker who had been sifting through classified American military networks for *months* during the Cold War. The hacker had been gathering anti-ballistic-missile secrets and selling them to the KGB. The story tells how the administrator helped trace the hacker back to his base in Germany and expose the entire espionage ring. The story is fascinating, but it's also true! It was written by the network administrator himself, Clifford Stoll. *The Cuckoo's Egg* really is a detective story, but instead of a crime scene with a dead body, there's a network and the hidden world behind it. *The Cuckoo's Egg* is an auditing story.

Auditing is an umbrella term that covers a number of related information-gathering and analysis activities. In this chapter we will discuss the most important of these activities as they relate to Windows security, namely:

- Verifying Policy Compliance
- Vulnerability Scanning and Penetration Testing
- Creating Baseline System Snapshots
- Gathering Ongoing Operational Data
- Employing Change Detection and Analysis

These topics each are vast in themselves, so we'll simply examine the essentials.

First, though, let's examine automation—everything you can do with Windows that does not require a mouse. Automation is how to get your work done more quickly and easily. In short, it's how to accomplish things with scripts, command-line tools, and the Task Scheduler. The good news is that Windows 2000/XP/.NET can be managed almost entirely through command-line tools and scripts.

Automation and auditing go together because if you can't automate your audits, then the auditing just doesn't get done, or, it's done only sporadically or superficially. Besides, learning automation techniques is how you can get *paid more* for *doing less*. And it's fun!

In this chapter, then, we will begin with a discussion of the automation resources available to you; then we'll put these resources to work in auditing our Windows servers.

NOTES

Automation

- 95% of what can be done with graphical tools can be done from the command line or with scripts.
- A vast amount of auditing data can be extracted.
- Let's discuss:
  - Support Tools
  - Resource Kits
  - Scripts
  - Third-Party Tools
  - Task Scheduler

SANS Security Essentials – Windows Security

Automation

Among the command-line tools that come with the OS, the Support Tools, and the *Resource Kit*, you will be able to manage virtually every aspect of your computer without touching your mouse. 95% of what can be done with the graphical tools, such as in Control Panel, can be done from the command line instead. And for auditors, the quantity of information that is extract*able* through scripts and command-line tools is immensely vast. But what are the available tools?

NOTES

The Support Tools

- On the Windows installation CD-ROM:
  - CD:\Support\Tools\Setup.exe
- Download latest version from MS:
  - Updated for each Service Pack
  - Sometimes new tools are included
- Table in your book lists the most useful Support Tools for auditing/security.

SANS Security Essentials – Windows Security

The Support Tools

The Windows 2000 Server installation CD-ROM has a set of supplemental management tools called the "Support Tools." They can be installed by running `CD:\Support\Tools\Setup.exe`. You also should obtain the latest version of the Support Tools for your Service Pack level; get the latest version from `http://www.microsoft.com/windows2000/downloads/servicepacks/`, and then select your Service Pack number.

There are a number of utilities in the Support Tools, but the following table lists the most interesting command-line tools for security/auditing. A few are in bold because they especially are needed.

Command-Line Security/Auditing Support Tools	
Acldiag.exe	Display permissions on Active Directory objects, including the calculated effective permissions for a particular user or group.
Dnscmd.exe	Manage virtually every aspect of DNS servers.
Dsacls.exe	Manage Active Directory permissions.
Filever.exe	Dump detailed file version/creation information.
Kill.exe	Forcibly terminate processes.
Netdiag.exe	Low-level query networking components.
Netdom.exe	View and manage computer accounts and NetLogon channels.
Nltest.exe	Multi-purpose domain controller management utility.
Reg.exe	Search, change, or save registry information on remote systems.
Remote.exe	Run commands on remote servers.
Sdcheck.exe	Display permission information on Active Directory objects.
Tlist.exe	Display very detailed process information (local system only).
Wsremote.exe	Run a console application on a remote server.

NOTES

Resource Kits

- Packed with tools and scripts!
- There are Resource Kits for IIS, SMS, SQL Server, Exchange, FrontPage, etc.
- Mandatory that you obtain it:
  - Get it used! (eBay, Amazon, etc.)
  - http://www.reskit.com
- **Your book lists tables of the best tools**
  - **Especially see XCACLS.EXE and WMIC.EXE**

SANS Security Essentials – Windows Security

The Windows 2000/.NET Server Resource Kit

The Windows 2000 Server *Resource Kit* is filled with command-line tools that can be leveraged for the scripting of auditing and security. The *Resource Kit* more or less is a mandatory purchase for managing Windows 2000/XP/.NET systems. Don't buy the *Resource Kit* at the bookstore, though; try to find it used at eBay, Amazon, or a discount technical bookstore like `http://www.bookpool.com`. Many failed dot-com companies are selling their inventories, including unregistered copies of the *Resource Kit*, dirt cheap.

Also, make sure to visit `http://www.reskit.com` for *Resource Kit* updates and on-line documentation. At this website you can access the text of the *Resource Kits* and download most of their tools for free. Resource Kits are available for Windows 2000 Server and Workstation, Windows .NET Server, Windows XP, SMS Server, SQL Server, Exchange Server, IIS, Small Business Server, FrontPage Extensions, etc. This website is a Windows auditor's goldmine.

The Windows 2000 Server *Resource Kit* has many tools and scripts, too many, in fact, for easy browsing. The next few tables, therefore, list the most useful of the command-line tools for security/auditing, so you quickly can locate them. Because even these lists are a bit long, the best auditing tools also are in bold.

Command-Line *Resource Kit* Tools for Users, Groups, Rights and Permissions	
Usrtogrp.exe	Addusers to groups based on text file input.
Addusers.exe	Create and delete user accounts based on text input file.
Ntrights.exe	Grant or revoke user rights on remote computers.
Permcopy.exe	Copy share permissions from one shared folder to another.
Perms.exe	Calculate permissions of a user/group to a folder/file.
Svcacls.exe	Read and set permissions on services on remote systems.
Subinacl.exe	Show or replace NTFS/registry permissions and owners.
Xcalcs.exe	Get or set NTFS permissions, with flexible options.

Command-Line *Resource Kit* Tools for Remote Execution of Commands	
Rcmd.exe	Client/server utility for executing commands on remote systems.
Rclient.exe	Client/server utility similar to Telnet.
Shutdown.exe	Shutdown or restart remote systems.
Rshsvc.exe	Server-side of Rsh.exe remote execution utility.
Rsh.exe	Execute commands on remote servers running Rshsvc.exe.

Command-Line *Resource Kit* Tools for Auditing and the Registry	
Auditpol.exe	Modify audit policy on remote computers.
Cconnect.exe	Write all user logon activities to a SQL database.
Netsvc.exe	List and manage visible/hidden services on remote machines.
Nlmon.exe	List domain and trust information.
Typeperf.exe	Write real-time Performance Monitor counter data to stdout.
Wc.exe	Win32-version POSIX word count utility.
Touch.exe	Win32-version POSIX file last access date updater.
Pulist.exe	List processes running on remote systems.
Rassrvmon.exe	Monitor and log RRAS server activity.
Rasusers.exe	List all user accounts with dial-permission on remote computers.
Regdmp.exe	Dump registry key/value data to stdout.
Regfind.exe	Search and/or replace registry data.
Regini.exe	Modify registry entries with a text file.
Sc.exe	Low-level query and control of services on remote systems.
Scanreg.exe	Search registry for key or value name.
Sclist.exe	List running services on remote systems.
Instsrv.exe	Install/uninstall services on remote systems.
Showpriv.exe	Show the user rights granted to a user or group.
Showacls.exe	Show NTFS permissions on folders and files.
Showgrps.exe	List the groups to which a user belongs.
Showmbrs.exe	List the members of a group.
Snmputil.exe	Query SNMP agents from the command line.
Srvcheck.exe	List shares and their permissions on remote systems.
Srvinfo.exe	Dump a variety of information from a remote system.
Where.exe	Find folders/files on local or remote file systems.

Command-Line *Resource Kit* Tools for Batch Files	
Autoexnt.exe	Enable a startup batch script, with no user logon required to run script.
Clip.exe	Copy data from StdIn to the clipboard.
Forfiles.exe	Operate only on selected file types, e.g., .TXT files only.
Freedisk.exe	Allow action if a certain percentage of disk space is free.
Gettype.exe	Return operating system type and version.
Sleep.exe	Make a batch script sleep for a specified period.
Choice.exe	Prompt user to make a choice during batch file execution.
Now.exe	Echo the current date and time.
Qgrep.exe	Quick GREP, with many optional arguments to control search.
Setx.exe	Set environmental variables.
Su.exe	Execute command under the context of a different user.
Timeout.exe	Cause a batch script to wait a period of time then continue.
Waitfor.exe	Batch file utility which either waits for or sends a signal across the network to coordinate the activities of multiple remote computers running batch files calling this utility.
Whoami.exe	Return the domain and username of the current user.

Windows XP/.NET is even more manageable from command-line tools than Windows 2000. A full listing of the new Windows XP/.NET tools is not possible here, but the following table is a list of some of the more interesting ones.

Auditor's Swiss Army Knife: WMIC.EXE

Windows XP/.NET includes a command-line tool named `WMIC.EXE` that can be used to get or set

NOTES

Sampling of New Tools in Windows XP/.NET or their Support Tools	
BinDiff.exe	Compare two files at the binary level; includes option to do bulk comparison of all files in two folders and their subfolders.
DiskPart.exe	Manage partitions, disk volumes, mirrors, mount points, etc.
DriverQuery.exe	List drivers and related information with filters (more verbose).
DS*.exe	DSget.exe, DSadd.exe, DSmod.exe, DSmove.exe, DSquery.exe, and DSrm.exe manage objects in directory databases, such as Active Directory.
EventCreate.exe	Write custom events to any local/remote Event Log.
EventTriggers.exe	Automatically execute a chosen command when an event of a specifiable description/ID/source/ etc. occurs in a local or remote Event Log.
FSutil.exe	Manage file system properties, such as quotas, hard links, reparse points, 8.3 name generation, etc.
GPResult.exe	Display Resultant Set of Policy (RSoP) for a particular user and computer from the command line (new version).
IPsecCmd.exe	Command-line IPSec management tool (replaces IPSecPol.exe).
LogMan.exe	Manage Event Trace Session logs and Performance logs.
NetSh.exe	Improved networking configuration tool (try "netsh.exe diag gui" on Windows XP/.NET).
OpenFiles.exe	List opened files on local/remote systems.
ReLog.exe	Resample existing Performance log files.
Sc.exe	Improved service controller tool (new version).
SchTasks.exe	Manage scheduled tasks on local/remote systems (replaces at.exe)
TaskKill.exe	Kill processes and process trees (more flexible than Kill.exe).
TaskList.exe	List processes and related information with filters (more verbose than 2000 version).
TypePerf.exe	Write real-time Performance data to ASCII file or console.
Wmic.exe	Command-line WMI query and configuration tool. This definitely is a tool you should know about!

configuration data for a *very* wide variety of settings. If you are an auditor, you must get to know this tool.

The following for `WMIC.EXE` are the command-line switches, which should be taken as an indication of the tool's power (see the Windows XP Help center for more information). Note that you can run the tool against remote Windows XP/.NET systems using the "/node" switch. Many of the commands will work on Windows 2000 as well, but the tool is intended for Windows XP/.NET.

The most interesting switches for auditing are in bold. To get a feel for the tool quickly, for each item in bold, execute "`wmic.exe` **`bolditem`** `list full.`"

```
WMIC.EXE /?
```

The following global switches are available:

/NAMESPACE	Path for the namespace the alias operates against.
/ROLE	Path for the role containing the alias definitions.
/NODE	Servers the alias will operate against.
/IMPLEVEL	Client impersonation level.
/AUTHLEVEL	Client authentication level.
/LOCALE	Language id the client should use.
/PRIVILEGES	Enable or disable all privileges.
/TRACE	Outputs debugging information to stderr.
/RECORD	Logs all input commands and output.
/INTERACTIVE	Sets or resets the interactive mode.
/FAILFAST	Sets or resets the FailFast mode.
/USER	User to be used during the session.
/PASSWORD	Password to be used for session login.
/OUTPUT	Specifies the mode for output redirection.
/APPEND	Specifies the mode for output redirection.

/AGGREGATE Sets or resets aggregate mode.

/?[:<BRIEF|FULL>] Usage information.

For more information on a specific global switch, type: `switch-name /?`

The following alias/es are available in the current role:

ALIAS	- Access to the aliases available on the local system
BASEBOARD	- Base board (also known as a motherboard) management.
BIOS	- Basic input/output services (BIOS) management.
BOOTCONFIG	- Boot configuration management.
CDROM	- CD-ROM management.
COMPUTERSYSTEM	- Computer system management.
CPU	- CPU management.
CSPRODUCT	- Computer system product information from SMBIOS.
DATAFILE	- DataFile Management.
DCOMAPP	- DCOM Application management.
DESKTOP	- User's Desktop management.
DESKTOPMONITOR	- Desktop Monitor management.
DEVICEMEMORYADDRESS	- Device memory addresses management.
DISKDRIVE	- Physical disk drive management.
DISKQUOTA	- Disk space usage for NTFS volumes.
DMACHANNEL	- Direct memory access (DMA) channel management.
ENVIRONMENT	- System environment settings management.
FSDIR	- Filesystem directory entry management.
GROUP	- Group account management.
IDECONTROLLER	- IDE Controller management.
IRQ	- Interrupt request line (IRQ) management.
JOB	- Provides access to scheduled jobs.
LOADORDER	- Management of services and their dependencies.
LOGICALDISK	- Local storage device management.
LOGON	- LOGON Sessions.
MEMCACHE	- Cache memory management.
MEMLOGICAL	- System memory management.
MEMPHYSICAL	- Computer system's physical memory management.
NETCLIENT	- Network Client management.
NETLOGIN	- Network login information of a particular user.
NETPROTOCOL	- Protocols management.
NETUSE	- Active network connection management.
NIC	- Network Interface Controller (NIC) management.
NICCONFIG	- Network adapter management.
NTDOMAIN	- NT Domain management.
NTEVENT	- Entries in the NT Event Log.
NTEVENTLOG	- NT eventlog file management.
ONBOARDDEVICE	- Management of adapter devices in the motherboard.
OS	- Installed Operating System/s management.
PAGEFILE	- Virtual memory file swapping management.
PAGEFILESET	- Page file settings management.
PARTITION	- Management of partitioned areas of a physical disk.
PORT	- I/O port management.
PORTCONNECTOR	- Physical connection ports management.
PRINTER	- Printer device management.
PRINTERCONFIG	- Printer device configuration management.
PRINTJOB	- Print job management.
PROCESS	- Process management.
PRODUCT	- Installation package task management.
QFE	- Quick Fix Engineering.
QUOTASETTING	- Setting information for disk quotas on a volume.
RECOVEROS	- Information gathered from memory when the OS fails.

NOTES

NOTES

REGISTRY	-	Computer system registry management.
SCSICONTROLLER	-	SCSI Controller management.
SERVER	-	Server information management.
SERVICE	-	Service application management.
SHARE	-	Shared resource management.
SOFTWAREELEMENT	-	Management of a software product installed.
SOFTWAREFEATURE	-	Management of subsets of SoftwareElement.
SOUNDDEV	-	Sound Device management.
STARTUP	-	Management of commands that run automatically.
SYSACCOUNT	-	System account management.
SYSDRIVER	-	Management of the system driver for a base service.
SYSTEMENCLOSURE	-	Physical system enclosure management.
SYSTEMSLOT	-	Management of ports, slots, and peripherals.
TAPEDRIVE	-	Tape drive management.
TEMPERATURE	-	Data management of the temperature sensor.
TIMEZONE	-	Time zone data management.
UPS	-	Uninterruptible power supply (UPS) management.
USERACCOUNT	-	User account management.
VOLTAGE	-	Voltage sensor data management.
VOLUMEQUOTASETTING	-	Management of disk quota settings.
WMISET	-	WMI service operational parameters management.

For example, to find out the number of the last Service Pack applied to the computer with IP address 10.4.2.2, you could run this command:

```
wmic.exe /node:10.4.2.2 OS get
ServicePackMajorVersion
```

To get a list of its shared folders:

```
wmic.exe /node:10.4.2.2 SHARE list brief
```

To dump a list of the programs that automatically execute because they are listed in the registry's Run key:

```
wmic.exe /node:10.4.2.2 STARTUP list full
```

In these commands you can get one particular value from a category of information ("get ServicePackMajorVersion") or do a brief/full listing of all the values from that category ("list brief"). Entering "`wmic.exe /?`" can display the categories (OS, SHARE, STARTUP, etc.).

Network Configuration Tools

- Networking settings are some of the most important data to include in your audits.
- These are your best tools →

- **WMIC.EXE**
- **NETSH.EXE**
- **NETDIAG.EXE**
- GETMAC.EXE
- IPCONFIG.EXE
- ROUTE.EXE
- NET.EXE
- NETSTAT.EXE
- NBTSTAT.EXE

SANS Security Essentials – Windows Security

Command-Line Network Configuration Tools

It was especially difficult to work with networking settings from the command line in Windows 9x/NT. In Windows 2000/XP/.NET, however, virtually every networking setting can be queried or reconfigured through one of the following tools:

- WMIC.EXE
- NETSH.EXE
- NETDIAG.EXE
- GETMAC.EXE
- IPCONFIG.EXE
- ROUTE.EXE
- NET.EXE
- NETSTAT.EXE
- NBTSTAT.EXE

Note

Execute "`hh.exe ntcmds.chm`" to bring up the Windows XP Help section on the new command-line tools.

`NETDIAG.EXE` mainly is a troubleshooting tool that can run a variety of tests and dump the output to the command shell. Execute "`netdiag.exe /?`" to see the available tests. Just execute "`netdiag.exe /v`" to run all of them. Execute "`netdiag.exe /test:`*`testname`*` /v`" to run a particular test and show even more data.

`NETSH.EXE` was modeled on the Cisco Command-Line Interface in both purpose and feel. Execute "`netsh.exe`" to get to the *netsh*> prompt. Enter "`?`" to see the commands available in this context. Enter "`int`" to go into the *netsh-interface*> context, then enter "`ip`" to go into the *netsh-interface-ip*> context. In this context you can get or set the IP configuration of your network adapter cards (enter "`set ?`" and "`show ?`" to see the commands). Notice that with the "`set machine `*`IPaddress`*" command you can execute all these commands on a remote box at *IPaddress* as well.

`GETMAC.EXE` retrieves the hardware and IP addresses of remote computers, even on the other side of routers. Output can be formatted in a variety of ways for easy searching.

If you're not familiar with `NET.EXE` already, then execute "`net.exe /?`". This will show the list of subcommands `NET.EXE` supports; for each possible subcommand displayed, you can enter "`net.exe `*`subcommand`*` /?`" for more information, (e.g.,

NOTES

NOTES

"`net.exe accounts /?`"). For auditing, `NET.EXE` can be used to show shared folders, drive mappings, account and group information, and running services. However, for anything `NET.EXE` can do, there are other tools that can do it better.

The other tools have been around for some time now. `NETSTAT.EXE` can show all listening ports, `IPCONFIG.EXE` a variety of IP settings, `ROUTE.EXE` the route table, and `NBTSTAT.EXE` NetBIOS-related data. See their command-line switches for more information.

NOTES

NT Forensics toolkit

Excellent Third-Party Tools

- Foundstone
  - Forensic Toolkit (many file system analysis tools)
  - NTLast (query the Event Logs)
  - FPort (shows listening ports and their processes)
  - ScanLine (port scanner and banner grabber)
- SomarSoft
  - DumpSec, DumpEvt, DumpReg
- Pedestal Software
  - Great library of general-purpose tools
  - Scriptable COM objects for these tools too

SANS Security Essentials – Windows Security

Excellent Third-Party Tools

There are many excellent command-line tools from non-Microsoft vendors, as well. Most of these are freeware or shareware. Three especially good sources are the following:

- Foundstone (`www.foundstone.com`)
- SomarSoft (`www.somarsoft.com`)
- Pedestal Software (`www.pedestalsoftware.com`)

Foundstone (`www.foundstone.com`)

At the Foundstone website, make sure to at least get the Forensic Toolkit, NTLast, FPort, and ScanLine. Currently, all of them are free.

The Forensic Toolkit (composed of AFind, HFind, SFind, FileStat, and Hunt) mainly is a set of tools for filesystem analysis; you can do things like generate a list of all files accessed within a certain date range (without modifying those last-accessed dates), show all hidden files, show alternative data streams, and audit what information is extractable through a null session.

NTLast helps you to scan through Event Logs quickly for things like the last 20 failed/successful logons on a local or remote system. The comma-delimited output can be redirected to a text file for easy analysis or import.

FPort prints a table of your listening TCP/UDP ports and the executables attached to them ("`NETSTAT.EXE -AN`" does not show the executable or process ID).

ScanLine is a very effective command-line port scanner and banner grabber. It is nice to have when WinPcap issues cause problems when trying to run the Windows version of nmap. ScanLine does not do operating system fingerprinting, however.

SomarSoft (`www.somarsoft.com`)

SomarSoft has three great *free* tools: DumpSec, DumpReg, and DumpEvt. DumpEvt dumps Event Logs into plain ASCII text files. DumpReg dumps the registry to a plain ASCII text file. And guess what DumpSec does? That's right! DumpSec can dump NTFS permissions and audit settings to a text file, but it can also dump user, group, and replication information, too.

Pedestal Software (`www.pedestalsoftware.com`)

Pedestal Software's NTSEC Tools are not free, but they are perhaps the best commercial command-line

NOTES

tools for managing NTFS permissions, NTFS audit settings, registry values, registry key permissions, shared folder permissions, services, drivers, users, and groups. They also support a scriptable COM interface for VBScript and Perl scripts.

NOTES

Scripting Support

- Windows 2000/XP/.NET was specifically designed to be scriptable because MS wants to compete with Linux/Solaris/BSD.
- Perl, Python, JavaScript or VBScript
  - See http://www.activestate.com
- Your book lists the more interesting scripts from the Resource Kit.

SANS Security Essentials – Windows Security

Scripting Support

It was difficult to script the management of Windows 9x/NT; you were often compelled to use only the graphical tools or to purchase third-party toolsets. Windows 2000/XP/.NET, on the other hand, was specifically designed for command-line and scripts-based management because Microsoft wants to compete head-on with Linux, Solaris, BSD, and the other *nix-flavored operating systems (which have wonderful scriptability). Virtually every aspect of the operating system, file system, IIS, Active Directory, Exchange Server, SQL Server, the Office applications, etc. can be managed through custom scripts. For example, your scripts can use the same Windows Management Instrumentation (WMI) interface that the above `WMIC.EXE` tool uses. And these scripts can be written in Perl, Python, JavaScript, or VBScript.

Note

See `http://www.activestate.com` for free Perl and Python interpreters designed for Windows. Even better, ActiveState's PerlNET makes it possible to write Perl components that plug into the .NET Framework, e.g., for ASP.NET web sites.

The Windows 2000 Server *Resource Kit* includes dozens of VBScripts for system administration. Most of these scripts work with either local or remote systems (even if "local or remote" is not specified in the description below). The great thing about scripts, from the *Resource Kit* or elsewhere, is that they are *scripts*: you can see the source code or simply use the scripts like regular command-line tools. The following table is not an exhaustive list but a sampling of the scripts on the *Resource Kit* CD-ROM. The more interesting ones are in bold.

NOTES

Windows 2000 *Resource Kit* Sample Administration Scripts	
BackUpEventLog.vbs	Uses WMI to backup an Event Log to a text file.
ChkUsers.vbs	Checks a domain for users whose properties satisfy a specified criterion.
ClassifyMembers.vbs	Lists the members of a container object or group object in an active directory. It returns the AdsPaths of the member objects, grouped according to their class types.
ClearEventLog.vbs	Uses WMI to clear the System Event Log.
Clone*.vbs	Categorizes a variety of scripts used to clone users, groups, printers and other items from one domain in another domain.
CompSys.vbs	Lists the properties of a computer system, including system type, domain, primary owner, network server mode, and infrared mode.
CreateGroups.vbs	Creates multiple user groups in a domain. Properties of these user groups can be set as the groups are created.
CreateUsers.vbs	Creates multiple user accounts in a domain. Properties of the user accounts can be set as the accounts are created.
DeleteService.vbs	Uses WMI to permanently delete a service from the local system.
Device.vbs	Manages all aspects of device drivers on a local/remote system.
DisplayOld.vbs	Queries the directory for stale (unused) user and computer accounts based on the number of days since the user account or computer account has logged on to the domain. If an output file is specified, it is written out using the LDIF format, enabling the administrator to delete the unused accounts using the LDIFDE import/export utility.
DisplayRID.vbs	Lists the current RID Operations Master, the total number of RIDs remaining, the starting number for the next RID Pool, and for each domain controller, the starting number for its RID Pool, the next RID number to be issued, and the percentage of its RID Pool that has been consumed.
EnableDhcp.vbs	Enables DHCP for a network adapter on a computer.
EventLogMon.vbs	Monitors Windows 2000 event log events on a computer and displays them in a command window or output file.
Exec.vbs	Executes a command or stop a process on a computer, local or remote.
ListAdapters.vbs	Lists the properties of all network adapters.
ListDCs.vbs	Finds all domain controllers of a domain with an LDAP provider.
ListMembers.vbs	Lists members of any container object or group object in an active directory, returning the ADsPaths of the member objects. It differs from ClassifyMembers.vbs in that the member object class can be specified, so that the member objects of only the specified class are listed. If no classes are specified, all members of the object are listed but are not grouped by class.
ModifyLDAP.vbs	Creates, modifies, assigns, and deletes the Lightweight Directory Access Protocol (LDAP) Administration Policies to domain controllers.
ModifyUsers.vbs	Modifies the properties of multiple user accounts.
NetworkProtocol.vbs	Displays the network protocols running on a specified computer, local or remote, and lists selected properties for each protocol.
ProtocolBinding.vbs	Displays information about protocol bindings on a local or remote system.
Ps.vbs	Lists all processes currently running on a computer, local or remote, and their properties. Will show full path of executable but not username of owner.
PsTop.vbs	Lists processes according to CPU usage in descending order.
Restart.vbs	Restarts, logs off, powers off, or shuts down a local or remote computer. Command line switches allow you to specify the time until restart, and to force the operation if desired.

NOTES

SchemaDiff.vbs	Compares the schema on two different forests. It notes differences in the schema version number, compares the number of classes, checks that the mandatory and optional attributes are the same for each class, and checks that the syntax and range match for each attribute.
Search.vbs	Performs a search against a local or remote LDAP server, with options to control DN path, class type, query depth, and other LDAP-specific search parameters.
Service.vbs	Lists services on a computer or administer services on a computer from the command line or a batch file. Administrative functions include starting, stopping, installing, removing, and configuring a service.
Share.vbs	Lists or creates (directory) shares on a computer, local or remote.
Startup.vbs	Enumerates the startup programs on a computer, local or remote.
Subnet_ops.vbs	Adds, deletes, and lists all the subnets of the current domain. You also can use it to set the location property on a subnet object. This is useful if your organization has enabled location tracking, a feature for finding printers using it's location in Active Directory.
SystemAccount.vbs	Displays system account information.
UserAccount.vbs	Displays user account information with optional property filters.
UserGroup.vbs	Adds multiple users to a group or deletes multiple users from a group.
EventQuery.vbs	Queries Event Logs on local/remote systems and filters output (comes with Windows XP/.NET).

NOTES

Push Scripts With Group Policy

- Group Policy can distribute scripts to machines and have the scripts run at:
  - Startup
  - Shutdown
  - Logon
  - Logoff
- Each OU could have its own custom set of scripts, written in different languages.

SANS Security Essentials – Windows Security

Push Out Scripts with Group Policy

It bears repeating in this context that Group Policy can push out scripts to machines automatically. And because Group Policy Objects can be linked to individual Organizational Units, each OU could have its own custom set of scripts.

These scripts can be executed at startup, shutdown, logon, or logoff. They can be written in any language for which the necessary interpreter is installed. Windows 2000/XP/.NET includes interpreters for batch files, Jscript, and VBScript by default, but interpreters for Perl and Python can be installed, as well.

You can push out as many scripts as you wish, and you can mix scripts written in different languages in a single category; e.g., your logoff scripts might include one batch file, two Perl scripts, and three VBScripts. Domain controllers multi-master replicate scripts to each other automatically using the File Replication Service (FRS). Logon/logoff scripts execute in the context of the user, while startup/shutdown scripts execute in the context of the local System account.

NOTES

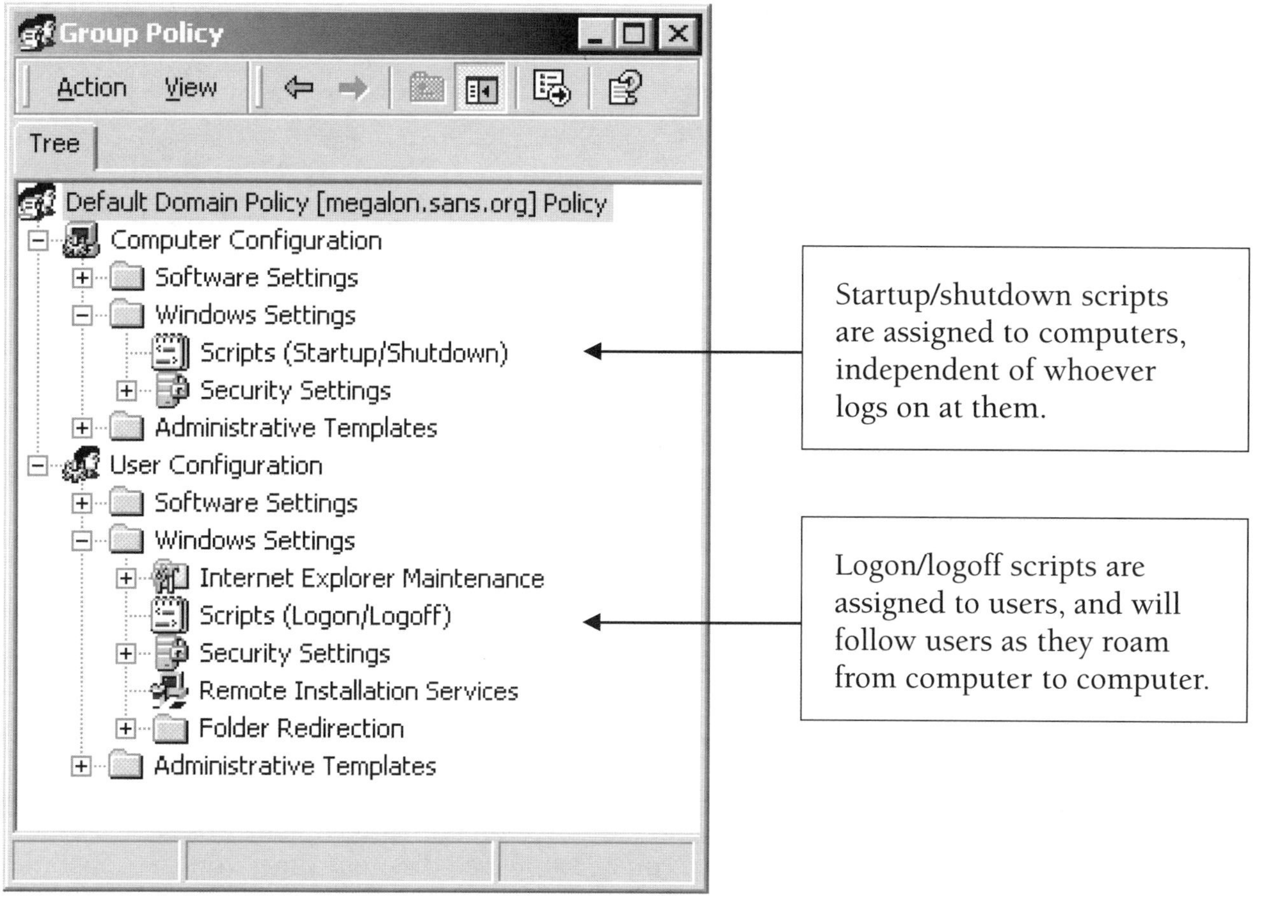
Group Policy
Action View
Tree
Default Domain Policy [megalon.sans.org] Policy
Computer Configuration
Software Settings
Windows Settings
Scripts (Startup/Shutdown)
Security Settings
Administrative Templates
User Configuration
Software Settings
Windows Settings
Internet Explorer Maintenance
Scripts (Logon/Logoff)
Security Settings
Remote Installation Services
Folder Redirection
Administrative Templates
Startup/shutdown scripts are assigned to computers, independent of whoever logs on at them.
Logon/logoff scripts are assigned to users, and will follow users as they roam from computer to computer.

NOTES

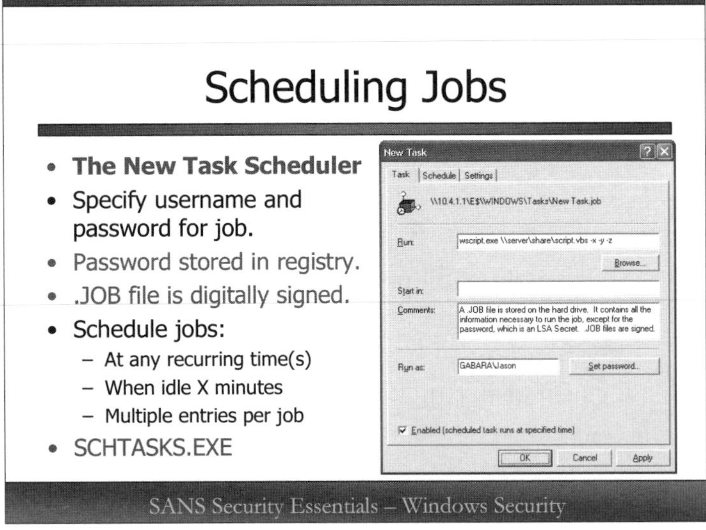

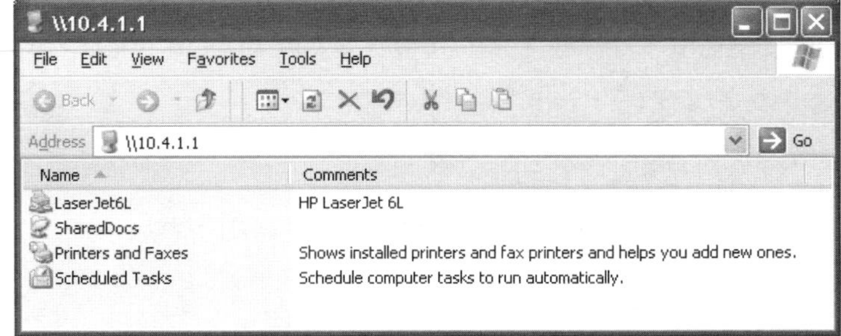

Scheduling Jobs

Through command-line tools and custom scripts, you can automate your work. What we need now is a way to run these tools/scripts automatically on a recurring basis. Enter the new Task Scheduler!

The old Windows NT 4.0 Scheduler service is gone. It has been completely replaced. The new Task Scheduler in Windows 2000/XP/.NET has been redesigned to be more flexible and secure. For example, all scheduled jobs are stored on the hard drive as .JOB files, so NTFS permissions apply to them. JOB files are digitally signed by the OS, which will refuse to run them if their signatures are corrupted, and JOB files do not contain passwords. Every scheduled job must run under the context of the username/password of some user (not the local System account), and these passwords are encrypted and stored in the LSA Secrets portion of the registry.

(Only Administrators can access the registry's LSA Secrets.)

To access the scheduled jobs on a local or remote system, go to the Run line and execute "`\\IPaddress`" or "`\\computername`." This will show the shared folders and printers on that computer, including the Scheduled Tasks folder. In that folder you can right-click on any task to manage it, or you can right-click in the window itself and select New > Scheduled Task to create one.

You also can manage jobs from the command-line on local/remote systems with the Windows XP/.NET `SCHTASKS.EXE` tool. A single job can be scheduled to run at a hundred different times (on the Schedule tab, check "Show Multiple Schedules"), and each time can be scheduled on the basis of the following intervals: daily, weekly, monthly, once, at system startup, at logon, or when the computer has been idle for *X* number of minutes.

NOTES

Note

One of Microsoft's script interpreters can take the network (UNC) path to a remote script to execute it, e.g., "`wscript.exe \\server\share\script.vbs`." This causes the script to be downloaded from the share and executed locally. This is handy because you can keep a master shared folder of all scripts which only you can access and then run them from there.

Keep in mind that if you change the password for an account used to run scheduled jobs, the JOB files are not updated with the new password. This must be done manually. If you need to schedule jobs running with administrative privileges, consider creating a special account for this and assigning it a very long and complex passphrase (50+ characters) so that it doesn't have to be changed as often; no one is logging onto their desktop with this account, so it's not inconvenient to use a very long password. Make sure to audit all access to this account.

NOTES

Auditing

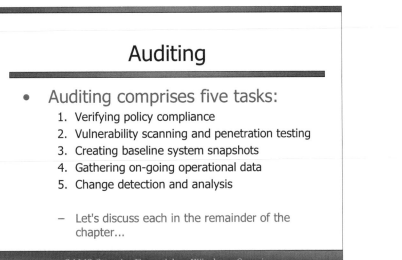

- Auditing comprises five tasks:
  1. Verifying policy compliance
  2. Vulnerability scanning and penetration testing
  3. Creating baseline system snapshots
  4. Gathering on-going operational data
  5. Change detection and analysis

  – Let's discuss each in the remainder of the chapter...

SANS Security Essentials – Windows Security

Auditing

Auditing is a critical duty security administrators should perform but often do not. For the purposes of this course, auditing your Windows systems is comprised of five activities:

- Verifying policy compliance
- Vulnerability scanning and penetration testing
- Creating baseline system snapshots
- Gathering on-going operational data
- Change detection and analysis

There is overlap between the activities; e.g., your policy might require regular vulnerability scans, but these categories are useful. Let's discuss each of these activities in the remainder of the chapter.

NOTES

Verifying Policy Compliance
• Policies are written documents describing your rules and procedures for enforcing network security.
• Two ways to audit policy compliance:
1. Maintain and check written change logs.
2. Examine the machines themselves
– Let's look at some tools for doing this →
– We've seen many of them already!
SANS Security Essentials – Windows Security

Verifying Policy Compliance

As the security administrator, it is your job to develop and enforce a number of written security policies. These documents describe and explain such issues as the password policy, lockout policy, anti-virus policy, and acceptable use. It will be a part of your audits to verify that the measures described in these documents actually are being followed.

One way to do this is to have a log available where the relevant administrators can enter information about actions taken in compliance with various policies. For example, you might have a shared folder with an Excel spreadsheet for each server managed by IT; every time a change is made or a check is performed, the person involved should enter the date, time, his/her name, and notes describing the change/check into the spreadsheet. Script the backup of the spreadsheets to occur every night, and name each backed up file after the current date.

These spreadsheets will aid in troubleshooting and provide some accountability for those charged with policy compliance. The information in the spreadsheets can be correlated with the on-going gathering of operation data to help dissuade devious administrators from entering false records in the spreadsheets. Part of your auditing procedure will be to check that the appropriate entries have been made in the spreadsheets; since this is the primary purpose of the spreadsheets' existence, you should add columns in the spreadsheet for matching records of tasks completed with the policies that mandate those tasks. This will aid in sorting and scripting the checking of this data. If you would like to use a web-based application to make the data-gathering and analysis easier, all the better!

Another way to audit policy compliance is to examine the relevant computers themselves. Fortunately, it often is the same tool that is used to enforce a policy which can be used to verify policy compliance. Let's look at some of these tools.

NOTES

HFNETCHK.EXE
• Scan remote systems for missing hotfixes (seen it before).
• Provides a model of what we want:
– Scheduled script.
– Analyzes or processes the data for us.
– Returns the results from remote systems in a convenient manner (e-mail, SMB, FTP).
– The results are in a form that's easy to work with and store (ASCII text).
SANS Security Essentials – Windows Security

HFNETCHK.EXE

An audit to verify that all the latest patches have been applied on Internet-accessible systems should be performed at least every week. The audit could be performed with the same tool used to know which patches needed to be applied in the first place: `HFNETCHK.EXE` (this is a good example of how auditing and hardening are two sides of the same coin). How could we put our new automation skills to work here?

Write a script that uses `HFNETCHK.EXE` to scan your servers over the network and have its output redirected to a text file. Your script will examine this file, extract the names of the computers missing patches, and automatically e-mail you the list. All this sounds complicated, but the scripting is relatively easy (the scripting seminar in the Windows Security Track covers this). Schedule this script to run every night, and you'll be doing a wonderful job staying on top of patches—with only a few hours of up-front work!

This script is a good example of for what we're aiming for: a scheduled script that gathers important security information, analyzes or processes that information in some way (so you don't have to do it manually), and returns the results back to you in a manner which is easy to work with or permanently store. The easiest data to work with is plain ASCII text, which is easy to store because it is highly compressible, and text files can be returned to you conveniently through internal e-mail, SMB, or FTP. The next step, not covered in this course, would be to import that ASCII data into SQL Server or Microsoft Access. And that could be scripted, too!

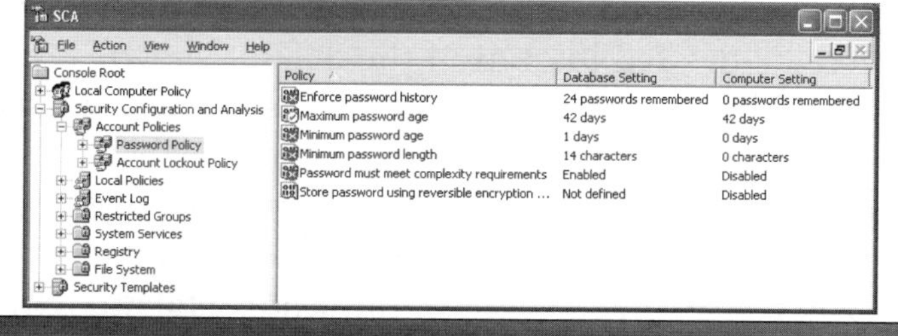

Security Configuration and Analysis

The Security Configuration and Analysis (SCA) snap-in applies security templates to systems to reconfigure NTFS permissions, password/lockout policies, Event Log settings, security options, etc. We've seen this tool already. But not only can the SCA snap-in *apply* templates; it also can *compare* a computer's current configuration against a template and produce a report.

In the snap-in, after you create a database and import a template into it, instead of right-clicking on the tool and selecting "Configure Computer Now," simply select "Analyze Computer Now." No changes will be made to the system whatsoever. Once complete, the SCA will show all the folders in the template and all the policy icons in each folder; if the policy icon has a red X on it, that means the computer's configuration does not match the setting in the template for that policy; if the policy icon has a green checkmark, then the current setting matches the template; and if the icon is just plain blue, then the template didn't specify a setting for that policy one way or the other.

The SCA snap-in produces a textual report of this analysis, as well. The full path to this text file is displayed after you select "Analyze Computer Now." You also can opt to show this in the SCA snap-in itself, if you right-click the snap-in and choose "View Log File." The drawbacks of the SCA snap-in, though, are that it's a graphical tool, and it doesn't work over the network. Fortunately, there's a command-line version of the SCA snap-in.

NOTES

NOTES

SECEDIT.EXE

- Command-line version of the SCA snap-in.
- Can compare a system against a template and produce a text file report.
- Still cannot run against remote systems:
  - Put SECEDIT.EXE and template in shared folder
  - Batch file will map drive letter to share
  - Batch file will run SECEDIT.EXE for the audit
  - Batch file will copy its output file to share
  - Schedule batch file to run on audited servers

SANS Security Essentials – Windows Security

SECEDIT.EXE

`SECEDIT.EXE` is a command-line version of the SCA snap-in. It can do anything the snap-in can do (and more). Unfortunately, it still can't compare templates against remote machines, but a simple batch file can, nonetheless, greatly aid in the process. Store the tool and your templates in a shared folder along with a batch file. The batch file, when run, will map a local drive letter to that share, compare the local system against one of the templates using `SECEDIT.EXE` while redirecting its output to a text file, and then copy that output file to a subdirectory in the share named after the computer.

In the above screenshot, the Generic.inf template is used to create a database named "dbase.sdb," which didn't exist beforehand, and compare the current system against it. Another command-line switch,

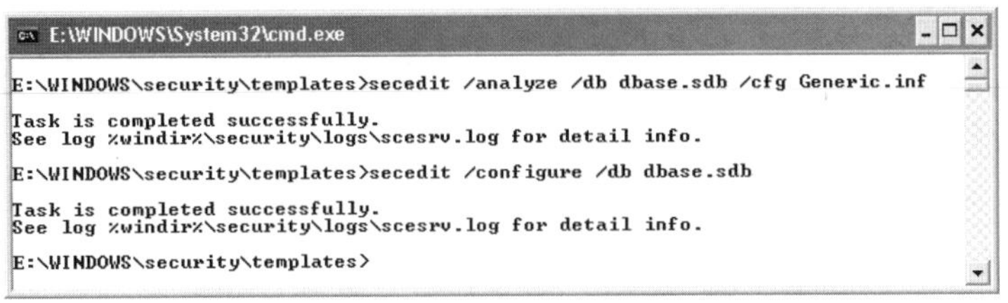

`/log`, could have been used to save the output log anywhere desired instead of the default shown above. The second command just uses the raw database file without specifying the template to reconfigure the machine. The database file was created, in this example, with the first command; alternatively, you could have built the database with the SCA snap-in and then used `SECEDIT.EXE` to apply it or audit with it.

E:\WINDOWS\System32\cmd.exe
E:\WINDOWS\security\templates>secedit /analyze /db dbase.sdb /cfg Generic.inf
Task is completed successfully.
See log %windir%\security\logs\scesrv.log for detail info.
E:\WINDOWS\security\templates>secedit /configure /db dbase.sdb
Task is completed successfully.
See log %windir%\security\logs\scesrv.log for detail info.
E:\WINDOWS\security\templates>

NOTES

MS Baseline Security Analyzer

- Scans Windows NT/2000/XP/.NET, IIS, SQL Server, and Internet Explorer.
- Local or remote systems
  - Takes a range of IP addresses to scan
- Report details the scan and describes how to correct the problems found.
- MBSACLI.EXE

SANS Security Essentials – Windows Security

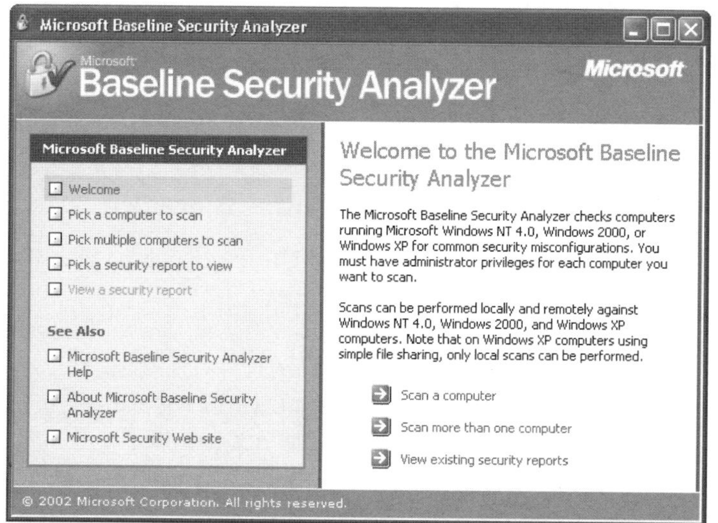

Microsoft Baseline Security Analyzer (MBSA)

The Microsoft Baseline Security Analyzer (MBSA) is a free auditing tool from Microsoft that can scan Windows NT-SP4/2000/XP/.NET, IIS 4.0/5.0, SQL Server 7.0/2000, and Internet Explorer 5.01 and later. It must be run from Windows 2000/XP/.NET, though. What does the MBSA do?

In Overview, the MBSA Sports the Following Features:

- Can scan a single machine or multiple remote machines by IP address or Active Directory domain membership.
- Can be run as a command-line tool (`MBSACLI.EXE`) with switches for which machine(s) to scan, which test(s) to perform, and how the output file should be saved.
- Does not require special agent software on scanned hosts.
- Checks the Service Pack level.
- Uses `HFNETCHK.EXE` to query for missing hotfixes.
- Checks that all drive volumes are using NTFS.
- Checks that the passwords of local accounts are not blank, identical to the user's name, identical to the machine's name, and is not "password," "admin," "administrator," or "sa."
- Lists disabled and locked-out accounts.
- Lists any accounts with passwords that never expire.
- Verifies that the Guest account has been disabled.
- Warns if null user sessions are permitted (RestrictAnonymous) and, on Windows XP,

NOTES

whether permissions assigned to Everyone also apply to anonymous users.

- Checks that password-less automatic logon is not enabled.
- Verifies that Event Log auditing is enabled.
- Lists all shared folders and their permissions.
- Lists the members of the local Administrators group if there are more than two.
- Warns if Internet Explorer and Microsoft Outlook security "zones" are set too lax.
- Alerts if Microsoft Office macro support is enabled.
- Warns if either IIS or SQL Server is installed on a domain controller.
- Warns if any of the following services are installed at all: IIS FTP, IIS HTTP, IIS SMTP, Telnet Server, or the Remote Access Service Manager. (You can modify the list of services this options warns on.)

The MBSA also performs security checks when certain dangerous services are installed. Perhaps the most dangerous service is IIS. (If scanning remote IIS servers, then the box doing the scanning must have the IIS Common Files installed too, but the IIS HTTP/FTP services don't have to be running.) For IIS security, the MBSA will:

- Ascertain whether or not the IIS Lockdown Tool has ever been run on the machine.
- Check that all sample files and the help website are not present.

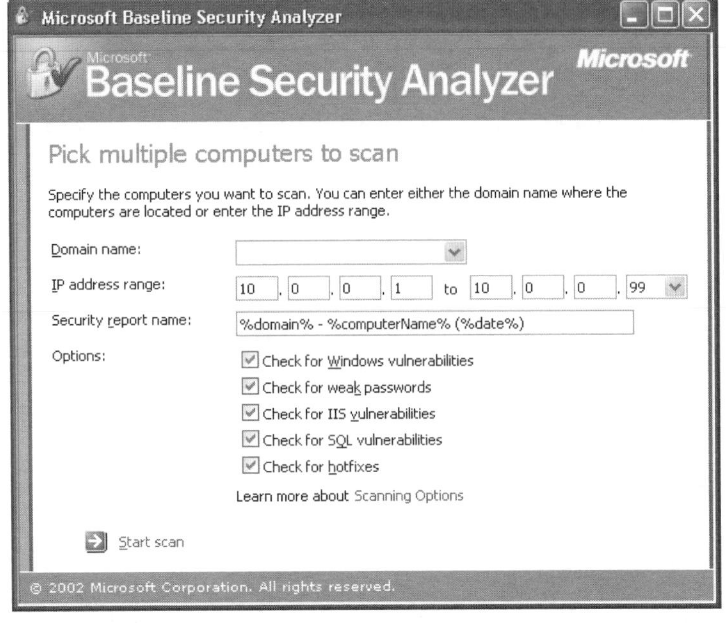

- Warn if the MSADC, IISADMPWD, or SCRIPTS virtual folders are still present.
- Notify if the dangerous "parent paths" (../../..) web application feature is enabled.
- Check that logging is turned on.

Another dangerous service is SQL Server. It's dangerous because it is often exposed to the Internet (if only indirectly through IIS) and because the data it manages may be extremely valuable to the company. For SQL Server security, the MBSA will:

- Verify that the password of the system administrator (sa) account is not in any temp files, is not blank, is not "password," and is not "sa."
- Check the NTFS permissions on critical folders used for database files.

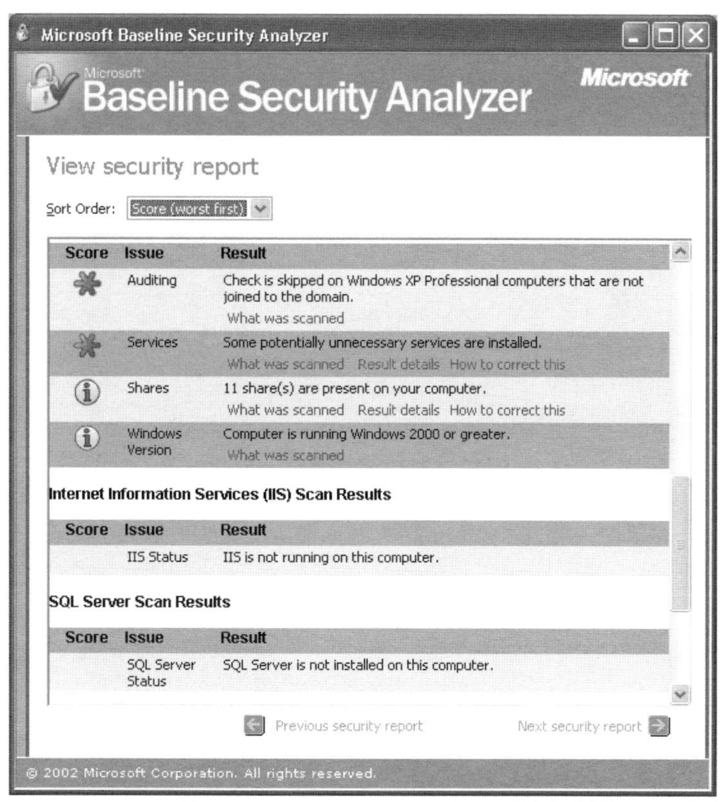

- Warn if old-style Mixed Mode authentication is being used instead of Integrated Windows authentication.
- List all accounts and groups that have the SysAdmin role in SQL Server.
- Check critical registry key permissions that could be used to compromise the server.
- Verify that only the SysAdmin database role has the CmdExec execution right.
- Verify that the service account used by SQL Server is not the local System account or an account which is a member of any administrative groups.
- Check that the local Administrators group has the SysAdmin role in SQL Server.
- List all the databases to which the Guest account has at least read access.

Download the MBSA

The MBSA can be downloaded from Microsoft's website (2.5 MB). It's best simply to search on the full name of the tool, but the last known good URL is `http://www.microsoft.com/technet/security/`. You must install the MBSA on Windows 2000/XP/.NET, and it's best if your scanning system itself has IIS installed, if you will be scanning other IIS servers.

Running the MBSA Graphical Version

Launch the MBSA from the Start menu > All Programs > Microsoft Baseline Security Analyzer. In the page that appears, click "Pick A Computer To Scan" on the left-hand side, enter the IP address in the box on the right, then click "Start Scan." Scanning a single machine requires about two minutes, unless there are very many local accounts on it. You also can enter a range of IP addresses and scan each machine.

Once finished, you will see a summary report. The report will have hyperlinks to describe what was scanned (click on "What Was Scanned"), to show detailed results (click on "Result Details"), and instructions for fixing the problems discovered

NOTES

(click on "How To Correct This"). Past reports are kept, so you can come back later to review them.

Running the MBSA Command-Line Version

The command-line version has straightforward switches (see "MBSACLI.EXE /?"). For example, the following will scan every computer in a range of IP addresses and save the output to a text file:

```
Mbsacli.exe /r "10.1.1.1-10.1.1.200" /f
"c:\file.txt"
```

You can view the details of the report either with the graphical MBSA or by first listing the available reports (`/l`) and then redirecting one (`/ld`) from the command line to a reports file:

```
Mbsacli.exe /l

Mbsacli.exe /ld "WebServer1(11-12-2002)" >
reports.txt
```

In some respects, the MBSA is both an auditing tool and a basic vulnerability scanner.

NOTES

Vulnerability Scanners

- Vulnerability Scanners:
  - CyberCop
  - HackerShield
  - Internet Scanner
  - Nessus
  - NetRecon
  - Retina
  - Secure Scanner
  - STAT Scanner
- Penetration Testing:
  - IBM
  - @Stake
  - Foundstone
  - Predictive Systems

SANS Security Essentials – Windows Security

Vulnerability Scanning and Penetration Testing

Auditing for policy compliance verifies that certain well-known precautions have been taken to secure the system. But this doesn't actually check for the vulnerabilities themselves. By analogy, a restaurant is audited by the local Health Department to ensure the restaurant is following well-known precautions against food poisoning, but that Department doesn't actually send professional tasters there to sample every dish on the menu to see whether they get sick.

Unless you are an expert programmer with *lots* of free time, it's impractical to try to write your own vulnerability scanner. Fortunately, there are commercial tools available that can do this for you. These tools are updated periodically by their vendors with the latest vulnerability information, and many work over the network to test large numbers of system efficiently. Here are the web sites for some of the more popular commercial general-purpose scanners:

- CyberCop (`http://www.nai.com`)
- HackerShield (`http://www.bindview.com`)
- Internet Scanner (`http://www.iss.net`)
- Nessus (`http://www.nessus.org`) — Freeware!
- NetRecon (`http://www.axent.com`)
- Retina (`http://www.eEye.com`)
- Secure Scanner (`http://www.cisco.com`, formerly "NetSonar")
- STAT Scanner (`http://www.statonline.com`)

A "red team" or "tiger team" that attempts to hack into your network with your permission is just an extension of your vulnerability scanning efforts. The software scanners above do penetration testing, but they don't actually break in! Besides, a skilled team of "ethical hackers" will be creative, resilient, subtle, and devious in ways which no push-button vulnerability scanner will ever match. Security experts also can be hired to analyze application source code, scrutinize your firewall design, and evaluate physical defenses. These services don't come cheap, though, and make sure you trust (that is, you can sue) the company if necessary. A few companies that offer penetration testing and code analysis services are:

- IBM (`http://www.ibm.com`)
- @Stake (`http://www.atstake.com`)
- Foundstone (`http://www.foundstone.com`)
- Predictive Systems (`http://www.predictive.com`)

NOTES

Creating Snapshots (1 of 3)
• Capture the running state of a computer at an instant in time:
– Provides a baseline for comparison with future snapshots ("before" and "after")
– Detect system compromises
– Show what changes have occurred
– Aid in troubleshooting
– Potentially act as legal evidence
SANS Security Essentials – Windows Security

Creating Baseline System Snapshots

For mission-critical internal servers and servers exposed to the Internet, your auditing efforts also should include creating periodic system snapshots. A "system snapshot" is a collection of data that documents the configuration and running state of the machine at a point in time. Its purpose is to provide a baseline against which later snapshots can be compared in order to detect changes. Presumably we'll have a "before" snapshot, when we assume the machine is working fine and has not been compromised, and an "after" snapshot, taken after problems began or after a suspected compromise or just because it's time for another audit. The "before" and "after" snapshots can be compared so that only the differences are listed. This process is useful for troubleshooting, but we mainly wish to use these snapshots to detect intrusions, to know how our adversaries have modified our systems (rootkits, trojans, etc.), and to provide forensics evidence that *might* be admissible in a court of law.

Can't We Just Use Tape Backups?

An ideal snapshot of a server, you would think, would be a binary image or full tape backup of its hard drive. This often is required for forensics, but binary images and backup archives suffer from a few shortcomings: they produce too much data to be stored easily; that data cannot be compared against other such snapshots quickly or easily; and they only capture the state of the file system. For example, they ignore other critical data, such as listening ports and running processes.

Fortunately, we are already making regular backups of our critical servers. So whatever advantages these backups provide for auditing, we should view them as fulfilling this role in addition to providing disaster recovery. Knowing this emphasizes the importance of permanently shelving some of our backups. If you are using tape backups, then perhaps once a month (or at least once per quarter) you should select one of the full backups, remove the tab which permits writing to the tape, and put that tape into permanent storage. If you are burning archives to DVD disks, this is even more convenient.

Because the purpose of a snapshot is to provide a baseline for comparison, we want to capture data in a form which easily is compared against other snapshots; we want that data to be highly compressible for long-term storage; and we want to be able to automate the entire snapshot-making

NOTES

process. What fits the bill? Plain ASCII text files produced by custom scripts and command-line tools are perfect for system snapshots. Through scripts and command-line tools you can gather almost any type of data you wish from Windows 2000/XP/.NET. It's trivial to redirect this data to a text file, and large text files can be compressed to a fraction of their original size.

Note

Tip: Store your ASCII snapshot files in an NTFS folder with compression enabled so that you don't have to monkey around with Zip files or other archive software. The compression will be transparent to your auditing tools.

How to Structure the Data

The purpose of making a snapshot is to have it for later comparison with prior snapshots; hence, the names of the snapshot files and their internal structure should be geared to this end.

The names of snapshot files should include the computer's name, its "type," and the date. For example, a snapshot file might be named "SERVER42_externalwebserver_11-28-02.txt." The "type" field is for your own categorization scheme, whatever that may be, to assist in working with the files (because you may soon have hundreds of them).

The snapshot data should begin with a well-formatted header that includes the computer's name, the date and time, the script used to create the snapshot, the username and domain of the person running the script, and any other identifying information you'll later need.

The body of the snapshot should be divided into sections that are labeled uniquely and standardized across as many of the snapshots as possible. In practice, this means you should try to use the same script each time. If you modify the script to gather more data, have that data *appended* to the end of the script's output. Again, anticipate how file-comparison tools or other auditing scripts will later try to use this data; make your snapshots as "digestible" as possible to software; i.e., make it well-formatted and standardized.

NOTES

Snapshot Contents (2 of 3)
• User Properties
• Group Memberships
• Shared Folders
• Account Policies
• User Rights
• Processes
• Drivers
• Service Settings
• Network Configuration
• Listening Ports
• Environmental Variables
• All Registry Values
• All NTFS DACLs
• Per-Folder Byte Counts
• IIS Metabase
• Anything useful!
SANS Security Essentials – Windows Security

What Information Should be in a Snapshot?

Ideally, a snapshot should include all the information necessary to help discover precisely what changes an expert-level intruder with administrative privileges has covertly made to your system. This almost is impossible, but it's the goal for which to shoot. Hence, a good snapshot should include:

- All local user accounts, with as many of their properties as possible.
- All local groups and their memberships, especially the local Administrators group.
- Shared folders, their local paths, and their permissions.
- Local audit, lockout, and password policies.
- List of all user rights and the various users/ groups who have these rights on the machine.
- List of running processes and their properties.
- List of drivers and their properties.
- Running services and the startup settings (Automatic, Manual or Disabled) of all services, running or not.
- All networking configuration settings, including IP addresses, route table, NetBIOS names, DNS/ WINS servers, IPSec configuration, etc.
- Environmental variables.
- The entire registry, or at least the HKEY_LOCAL_MACHINE hive and all of its subkeys.
- List of all files, or at least the files in %SYSTEMDRIVE%, including their sizes, last-modified dates, and file attributes (especially the hidden files).
- List of all folders with the number of files in each folder and the total number of bytes consumed by all the files in each folder.
- Dump of all NTFS permissions, or at least the NTFS permissions of everything under %SYSTEMROOT%.
- If SQL Server is installed, then include lists of all the users and groups who occupy the various "roles" in SQL Server, especially the SysAdmin role.
- If IIS is installed, then include a copy of the entire metabase. (The "metabase" is IIS's own separate registry.)

Example Batch Script (3 of 3)

- Source of batch script is in your book.
- SNAPSHOT.BAT > server42.11-23-02.txt
  - Output about 15 to 30MB in size.
  - 5 to 12 minutes to run on typical box.
- Only uses tools from the OS, Support Tools, and Resource Kit.

SANS Security Essentials – Windows Security

Example Batch Script

Here's a sample batch script that can get you started. It will produce a snapshot between 15 and 30 MB in size, and will take 5 to 12 minutes to run on a typical machine.

The script, `SNAPSHOT.BAT`, only works on Windows 2000/XP/.NET, but much of it can be adapted to NT. It relies only on tools built into the 2000/XP/.NET operating systems, available on the Windows 2000 Server CD-ROM (\Support\Tools\), or the Windows 2000 Server *Resource Kit*. Many of the commands are redundant to give you a choice, and, in real life, you should modify the list of drives/folders it includes in its snapshots to include what you want. Comments start with "REM." The script writes to standard out, so redirect the data to a file, e.g., `snapshot.bat > SERVER42.WebServer.11-23-02.TXT`.

```
SNAPSHOT.BAT

@ECHO OFF
ECHO Computer: %COMPUTERNAME%
ECHO Date: %DATE%
ECHO Time: %TIME%
ECHO Batchfile: %CD%\%0
ECHO User: %USERNAME%@%USERDOMAIN%
ECHO.
ECHO.
ECHO ++++++++++++++++++++++++++++++++++++++++++
ECHO [Operating System Version]
ECHO ++++++++++++++++++++++++++++++++++++++++++
ver
cscript.exe listos.vbs
ECHO ++++++++++++++++++++++++++++++++++++++++++
ECHO [Users, Groups, And Memberships]
ECHO ++++++++++++++++++++++++++++++++++++++++++
addusers.exe /s:; /d %TEMP%\adduserstempfile.txt
1>nul
type %TEMP%\adduserstempfile.txt
del %TEMP%\adduserstempfile.txt 1>nul
ECHO ++++++++++++++++++++++++++++++++++++++++++
ECHO [Password And Lockout Policies]
ECHO ++++++++++++++++++++++++++++++++++++++++++
net.exe accounts
ECHO ++++++++++++++++++++++++++++++++++++++++++
ECHO [Local Audit Policy]
ECHO ++++++++++++++++++++++++++++++++++++++++++
auditpol.exe
ECHO ++++++++++++++++++++++++++++++++++++++++++
ECHO [Shared Folders And Their Permissions]
```

NOTES

NOTES

```
ECHO +++++++++++++++++++++++++++++++++++++++++++
srvcheck.exe \\%computername%
net.exe share
ECHO +++++++++++++++++++++++++++++++++++++++++++
ECHO [Processes]
ECHO +++++++++++++++++++++++++++++++++++++++++++
wmic.exe PROCESS list full
pulist.exe
cscript.exe ps.vbs
ECHO +++++++++++++++++++++++++++++++++++++++++++
ECHO [Drivers]
ECHO +++++++++++++++++++++++++++++++++++++++++++
wmic.exe SYSDRIVER list full
drivers.exe
cscript.exe device.vbs
ECHO +++++++++++++++++++++++++++++++++++++++++++
ECHO [Services]
ECHO +++++++++++++++++++++++++++++++++++++++++++
net.exe start
sc.exe queryex
ECHO +++++++++++++++++++++++++++++++++++++++++++
ECHO [Networking Configuration]
ECHO +++++++++++++++++++++++++++++++++++++++++++
ipconfig /all
netstat -an
route print
cscript.exe protocolbinding.vbs
netdiag.exe /v
nbtstat -n
ECHO +++++++++++++++++++++++++++++++++++++++++++
ECHO [IPSec Configuration]
```

```
ECHO +++++++++++++++++++++++++++++++++++++++++++
netdiag.exe /test:ipsec /debug
ECHO +++++++++++++++++++++++++++++++++++++++++++
ECHO [Environmental Variables]
ECHO +++++++++++++++++++++++++++++++++++++++++++
set
ECHO +++++++++++++++++++++++++++++++++++++++++++
ECHO [Dump Registry Keys]
ECHO +++++++++++++++++++++++++++++++++++++++++++
regdmp.exe HKEY_LOCAL_MACHINE
ECHO +++++++++++++++++++++++++++++++++++++++++++
ECHO [Byte And File Count For Folders]
ECHO +++++++++++++++++++++++++++++++++++++++++++
diruse.exe "C:\"
diruse.exe /S "%SYSTEMROOT%"
diruse.exe /S "%PROGRAMFILES%"
ECHO +++++++++++++++++++++++++++++++++++++++++++
ECHO [Hidden Files With Last-Modified Dates]
ECHO +++++++++++++++++++++++++++++++++++++++++++
dir %SYSTEMDRIVE% /A:H /S /ON /T:W /N
ECHO +++++++++++++++++++++++++++++++++++++++++++
ECHO [Non-Hidden Files With Last-Modified Dates]
ECHO +++++++++++++++++++++++++++++++++++++++++++
dir %SYSTEMDRIVE% /A:-D /S /ON /T:W /N
ECHO +++++++++++++++++++++++++++++++++++++++++++
ECHO [All Files With Version And Attributes Data]
ECHO +++++++++++++++++++++++++++++++++++++++++++
filever.exe %SYSTEMDRIVE% /s /b /v
ECHO +++++++++++++++++++++++++++++++++++++++++++
ECHO [NTFS Permissions]
ECHO +++++++++++++++++++++++++++++++++++++++++++
```

```
showacls.exe /s %SYSTEMDRIVE%
ECHO ++++++++++++++++++++++++++++++++++++++++++
ECHO [Dump IIS 5.x Configuration]
ECHO ++++++++++++++++++++++++++++++++++++++++++
cscript.exe adsutil.vbs ENUM_ALL /W3SVC
REM ******************************************
REM   Tools Required And Their Sources
REM ******************************************
REM ADDUSERS.EXE   Windows 2000 Server Resource Kit.
REM AUDITPOL.EXE   Windows 2000 Server Resource Kit.
REM DEVICE.VBS     Windows 2000 Server Resource Kit.
REM DRIVERS.EXE    Windows 2000 Server Resource Kit.
REM LISTOS.VBS     Windows 2000 Server Resource Kit.
REM PROTOCOLBINDING.VBS
REM                Windows 2000 Server Resource Kit.
REM PS.VBS         Windows 2000 Server Resource Kit.
REM PULIST.EXE     Windows 2000 Server Resource Kit.
REM REG.EXE        Windows 2000 Server Resource Kit.
REM SC.EXE         Windows 2000 Server Resource Kit.
REM SHOWACLS.EXE   Windows 2000 Server Resource Kit.
REM SRVCHECK.EXE   Windows 2000 Server Resource Kit.
REM FILEVER.EXE    Windows 2000 Support Tools.
REM NETDIAG.EXE    Windows 2000 Support Tools.
REM ADSUTIL.VBS    Built into Windows 2000/XP/.NET.
REM METABACK.VBS   Built into Windows 2000/XP/.NET.
REM WMIC.EXE       Built into Windows XP/.NET,
REM                can't run locally on Windows 2000.
REM CSCRIPT.EXE    Built-in interpreter
                   (no need to install)
```

The uppercase words in percentage signs—e.g., %SYSTEMDRIVE%—are environmental variables which are translated when the script is run. You can see your variables and their mappings by opening a command-prompt window and executing "`set`." The command-line switches "`1>nul`" and "`2>nul`" redirect standard-out and error-out, respectively, into a black hole so that this data will not be captured in the snapshot file itself.

A more advanced script would gather its data over the network from remote systems, but that would require a more flexible scripting language, like Perl or VBScript, to do it effectively. However, all of the data the `SNAPSHOT.BAT` script captures (and more) could be gathered remotely.

But what to do with all this data? Let's hold off on that for a moment because we're not done gathering data yet!

NOTES

Gathering Ongoing Data

- Fill the gaps between the snapshots!
- Event Viewer logs:
  - Application
  - Security
  - System
  - Directory Service (domain controllers)
  - DNS Server (DNS servers only)
  - File Replication Service (domain controllers)
- Research Event ID numbers in Google.

SANS Security Essentials – Windows Security

Gathering Ongoing Operational Data

A snapshot is a picture of your server at an instant, and having "before" and "after" snapshots can help you track down changes; but snapshots don't explain *how* those changes occurred. To fill in the gaps between snapshots, we need to keep a running journal of everything that happens. For the purposes of this course, the two "daily diaries" we care about are the Event Logs and the logging that IIS performs.

Windows Event Logs

All Windows 2000/XP/.NET systems have three Event Logs named Application, Security, and System. You can view the contents of these binary logs with the Event Viewer snap-in: Administrative Tools > Event Viewer > click on a log. On a domain controller, you also will have logs named Directory

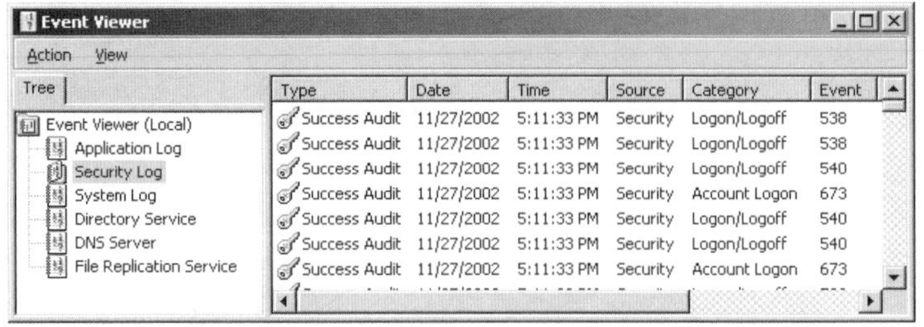

Service and File Replication Service. If you have DNS installed, you'll also have a DNS Server log.

Double-click an event icon in one of the logs to bring up its property sheet. Here you can see the event's date, time, source, user, computer, category, and event ID number. The description field in the middle may also include a few lines or paragraphs of text, including a hyperlink on which you may click to obtain more information from Microsoft about that type of event.

Often the best way to research an entry, though, is to do a search in Google on the words "Windows Event ID *XXXX*," where *XXXX* is the event ID number in question. If you want to go straight to the source, then try `http://search.microsoft.com`. There's also an entire website devoted to Event Log analysis: `http://www.EventID.net`! If you'd rather have a local reference, then the *Resource Kit* has an "Error And Event Messages Help" section, but it's generally not more detailed than what you can find on the Internet.

The System log mainly is for OS troubleshooting. Here you'll find entries related to service start/stop/failures, device driver issues, status reports of background maintenance operations, etc. The Application log is where applications and third-

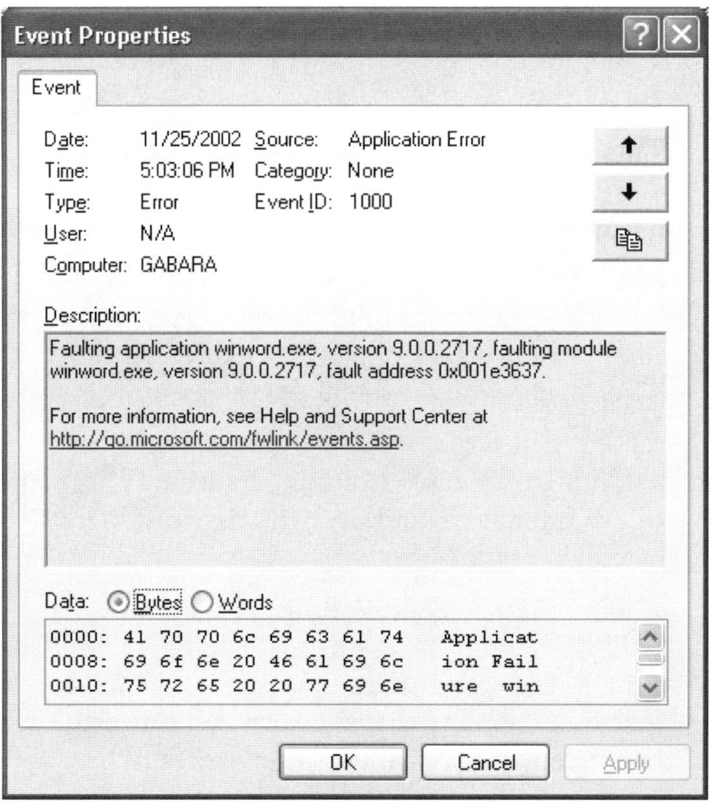

party developers can write anything they wish. We have little control over what goes here; it is entirely up to the original programmers of the software in question.

Note

If you'd like to write your own entries to the Event Logs with a command-line tool, see `LOGEVENT.EXE` from the *Resource Kit*. It can write to local or remote systems.

But what about the Security log? By default, that log will be empty unless you specifically choose to enable security auditing.

NOTES

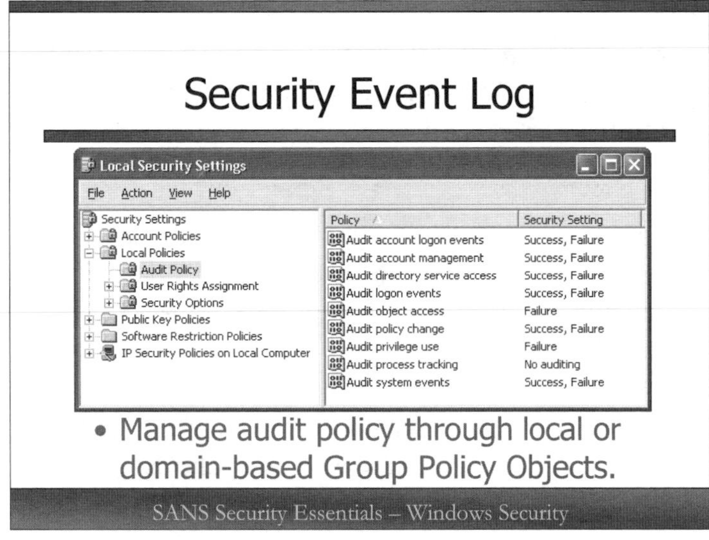

Enabling Logging to the Security Event Log

To enable logging to the Security log, go to Administrative Tools > Local Security Settings > Local Policies > Audit Policy. Here you can choose to log successful and/or failed events of certain types. The types of events are listed below, with recommendations in parentheses for which events to log:

- Audit Account Logon Events (Success, Failure): This tracks authentication requests processed by the domain controllers, even when the access is not to the domain controller itself. Think of DCs as providing a service for the sake of other machines on the network (checking usernames and passwords). This category logs whenever that service is provided. When this policy is enabled on non-domain controllers, then it applies only to the local accounts on those machines; hence, it only applies to authenticated access to those machines with local accounts.
- Audit Account Management (Success, Failure): This monitors user and group tasks, such as account creation, deletion, modification, and group membership changes.
- Audit Directory Service Access (Success, Failure): This is required to begin logging access to Active Directory objects as defined on those objects' individual System Access Control Lists (SACLs).
- Audit Logon Events (Success, Failure): This tracks interactive and over-the-network logons to the computer itself.
- Audit Object Access (Failure): This is required to begin logging access to NTFS folders and files, registry keys, and shared printers. It is not the case that enabling this category will cause all filesystem, registry, and printer access to be logged. Rather, enabling the category makes it possible to have the SACLs on those objects not do anything.
- Audit Policy Change (Success, Failure): Tracks changes to the audit policies themselves and changes to user rights assignments.
- Audit Privilege Use (Failure): Monitors the exercise of certain user rights on the machine, e.g., take ownership, change system time, etc.
- Audit Process Tracking (Not Defined): This is rarely enabled and usually only by programmers who are debugging their own code. This category tracks program execution, process

NOTES

loading and unloading, filesystem handle creation and release, indirect object access, and other low-level OS behaviors. Enabling this category will cause a vast amount of extra log data and will slow down the system considerably.

- Audit System Events (Success, Failure): Tracks system startup, shutdown, and other system-wide events. This also records clearing of the System and Security logs.

Group Policy

All audit policy settings on both servers and workstations can be remotely configured through Group Policy. Audit policy is set under Computer Configuration > Windows Settings > Security Settings > Local Policies > Audit Policy. Hence, when you need to configure audit settings throughout your domain, Group Policy is the way to do it.

If you'd rather manage audit policies on remote systems from the command line, use the `AUDITPOL.EXE` tool from the Windows 2000 Server *Resource Kit*.

NOTES

NTFS, Registry & Printer SACLs

- Two steps to enable object auditing:
  1) Enable the "Audit Object Access" policy
  2) Configure the object SACLs desired
- System Access Control Lists (SACLs)
  - Differ for different types of objects
  - Can be inherited, just like permissions

SANS Security Essentials – Windows Security

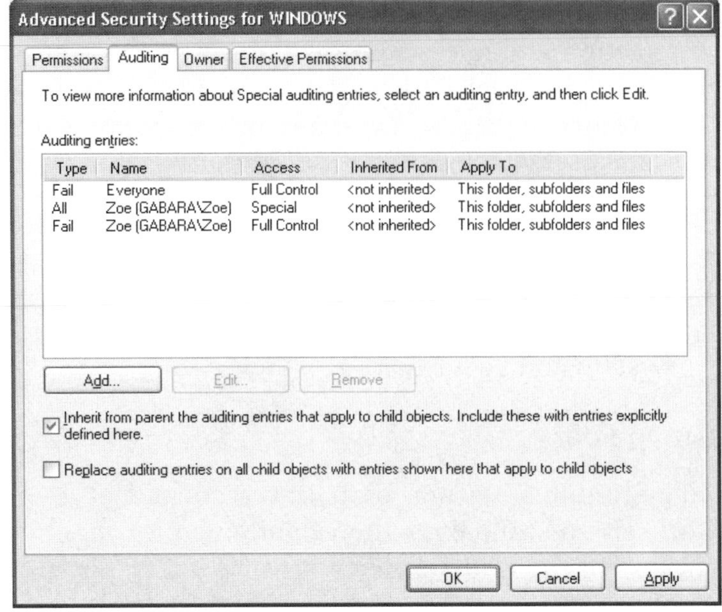

NTFS, Registry and Printer SACLs

Even if you do enable "Audit Object Access" above for both success and failure, nothing extra will be logged. Auditing access to NTFS files/folders, registry keys, and printers is a two-step process. First you enable "Audit Object Access" in the computer's audit policy; then you go to the individual files, folders, keys, and printers you want to monitor and configure their System Access Control Lists (SACLs). An object's SACL defines exactly which users and groups should have their interaction with the object logged. Moreover, you can choose exactly what types of interaction will be logged, too.

Let's configure the SACL of an NTFS file as an example. Right-click any NTFS file on your system and go to Properties > Security tab > Advanced button > Auditing tab. The Auditing tab is where you configure a folder or file's SACL. Now, click the Add button and select a user or group whose interaction with this file you want to track (when in doubt, always audit the Everyone group). Once you've selected a user/group, a dialog box appears asking you exactly which types of actions you want to monitor, e.g., Successful Delete, Failed Read, Failed Execute File, Successful Change Permissions, and so on. The two columns of checkboxes for Successful and Failed actions correspond to the auditing of successful or failed events in the "Audit Object Access" policy above; if you don't enable one of those categories in the policy, then that category of action (Successful or Failed) simply is not logged, no matter what checkboxes are checked in the SACL.

NOTES

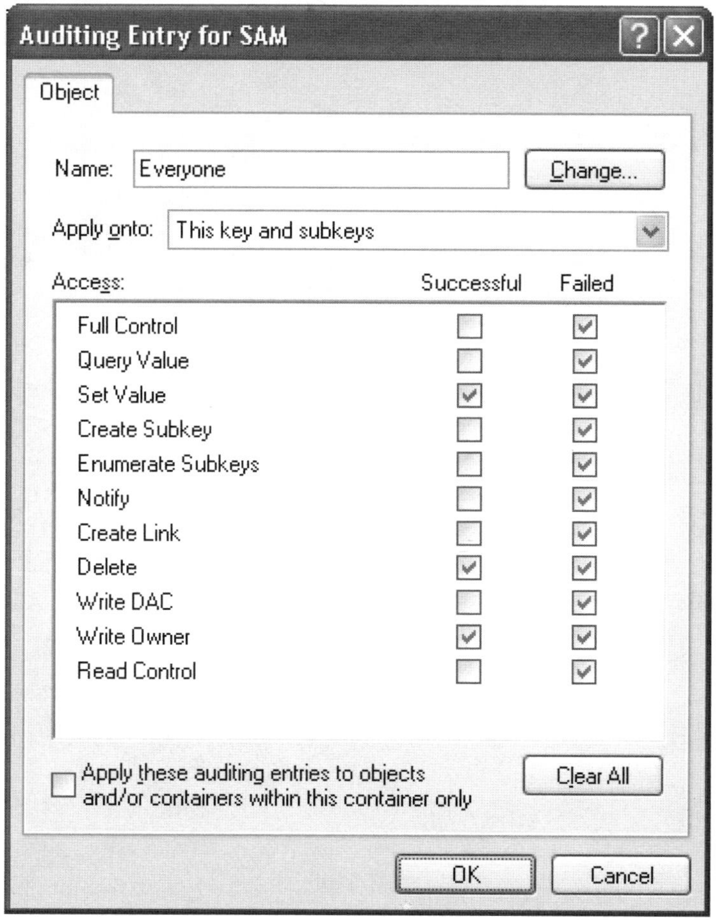

Auditing Entry for SAM

Object

Name: Everyone — Change...

Apply onto: This key and subkeys

Access:	Successful	Failed
Full Control		✓
Query Value		✓
Set Value	✓	✓
Create Subkey		✓
Enumerate Subkeys		✓
Notify		✓
Create Link		✓
Delete	✓	✓
Write DAC		✓
Write Owner	✓	✓
Read Control		✓

Apply these auditing entries to objects and/or containers within this container only — Clear All

OK Cancel

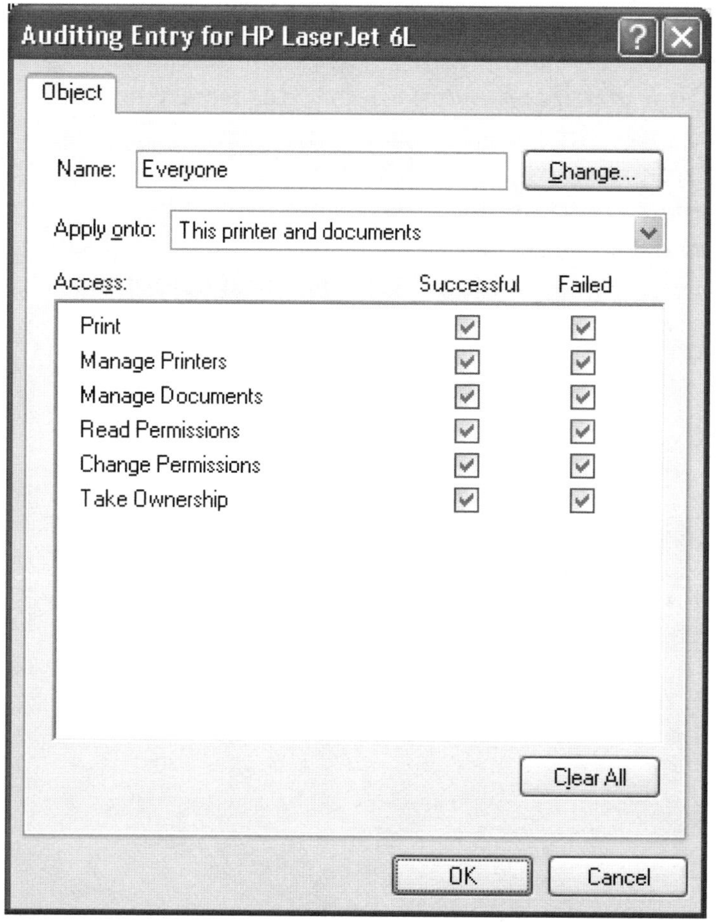

Auditing Entry for HP LaserJet 6L

Object

Name: Everyone — Change...

Apply onto: This printer and documents

Access:	Successful	Failed
Print	✓	✓
Manage Printers	✓	✓
Manage Documents	✓	✓
Read Permissions	✓	✓
Change Permissions	✓	✓
Take Ownership	✓	✓

Clear All

OK Cancel

The same is true for registry keys and printers. To audit access to a registry key, open `REGEDT32.EXE` > Edit menu > Permissions > Advanced button > Auditing tab. (In Windows 2000 it's the Security menu instead.) For printer icons, right-click the printer > Properties > Security tab > Advanced button > Auditing tab.

Note

If you have no Security tab, then pull down the Tools menu in Windows Explorer > Folder Options > View tab > and uncheck the box at the bottom labeled "Use simple file sharing."

There are many actions that can be audited, and the list is different whether you are auditing a folder, file, key, or printer (you interact with them in

NOTES

different ways, after all). Importantly, notice that both NTFS and registry SACLs can inherit settings from their parent containers. This is very helpful because, by using inheritance, you can define the audit settings you want at a top-level folder or key and have those settings apply to everything underneath it. If you need to edit those SACLs, you only have to make a single change at the top-level container.

What Objects Should be Audited?

- The more you log, the slower your server's performance:
  - Avoid flooding logs with useless data.
  - Anticipate how an attacker would leave a trail and audit to collect that data.
  - Audit proprietary data (the jewels).
- Apply SACLs with security templates!

SANS Security Essentials – Windows Security

What Objects Should be Audited?

Don't audit access to the entire hard drive and registry; this will slow your computer down by more than 50%. Beyond that advice, however, only general suggestions can be given because every environment, server, and workstation is different. You should audit what you're interested in! Here are some general suggestions:

- Try to limit the scope of your object auditing as much as possible without missing the data you really need. The more you log, the slower your machine will run, and the quicker your log files will grow.
- The wealth of your organization lies in its proprietary data, so audit all successful and failed actions of the Everyone group on those files. This would include databases, documents, spreadsheets, source code files, customer lists, scripts, and HTML files on the web servers, Outlook personal storage (.PST) files, etc. This will produce a lot of data, but, if not the jewels of the company, why do object auditing at all?
- Avoid auditing Read/List access, except on the most sensitive files and folders; otherwise, your logs will be flooded with data.
- Avoid auditing Execute actions on binaries, except for administrative tools and other dangerous software, e.g., `REGEDIT.EXE`; `NTBACKUP.EXE`; the shortcuts in the Administrative Tools folder, `CMD.EXE`, etc. An exception would be for Internet servers where an extremely high level of paranoia is justified, but you still should selectively omit auditing the binaries that you expect and *want* to be executed, e.g., script interpreters on IIS. For the type of server being audited, try to anticipate which files an intruder would most likely access, and make sure to audit *those* at a minimum.
- In general, audit Delete, Create Files/Write Data, Create Folders/Append Data, Write Attributes, and Change Permissions for the %SYSTEMROOT% and %PROGRAMFILES% folders and their subdirectories by the Everyone group. If an application or service writes temporary files to any of those subdirectories instead of using %TEMP%, then prune your SACLs to ignore them selectively.
- Temporary folders are attractive to hackers because it is easier to hide things there, but you must be careful when auditing them. In general,

NOTES

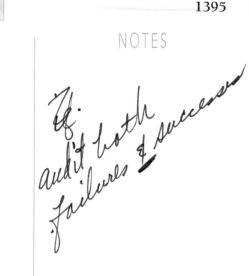

Q: audit both failures & successes

NOTES

only audit the Change Permissions, Write Attributes, and Write Extended Attributes actions in temp folders in order to avoid flooding the logs with useless data. In general, it's better to periodically search temp folders for well-known hacking tools than to try to audit all interactions. You also can use the *Resource Kit*'s `DIRUSE.EXE` tool to alert you if any monitored temp folder exceeds *X* number of megabytes in total content.

- In general, the Take Ownership and Change Permissions actions should be audited on all files, all hard drives.
- Mainly for political reasons, printers should have all of their actions audited for the Everyone group. Even busy print servers don't generate more than a few thousand events each day, and the need to archive these events is small, even if you work for Kinko's.
- It usually is not worth the effort to configure extensive registry key SACLs by hand. Configure registry SACLs with security templates that have been designed by others and then customized by you.

Security Templates (Again)

Remember INF security templates? When applied, a security template can reconfigure NTFS and registry SACLs, as well (but not printer SACLs). You should have a separate template for each type of server you will be auditing. The template will have a number of SACLs defined already by the vendor from which you obtained it (Microsoft, NSA, SANS, CIS, etc.) plus all the custom SACLs you've added for your particular environment. Pre-configured templates are especially useful for registry key SACLs. Exactly which keys have bad default audit settings? How would you know this without weeks of research and effort?

These security templates can be applied, of course, with the Security Configuration and Analysis snap-in, the `SECEDIT.EXE` command-line tool, or Group Policy.

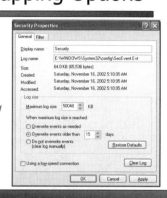

Log Size and Wrapping Options

- Each log is finite and can be sized separately.
- Maximum log size: 4.2GB
  - 1MB is about 7500 events.
- Appropriate log size will be determined by the rate of new events and your wrapping options →

SANS Security Essentials – Windows Security

Log Size and Wrapping Options

A security template also can be used to set the maximum size and wrapping options for your Event Logs. Event Logs are stored in the %SYSTEMROOT%\System32\Config folder. The names of the log files are self-explanatory: `APPEVENT.EVT`, `SYSEVENT.EVT`, and `SECEVENT.EVT`. Event Logs are assigned maximum sizes beyond which they are not permitted to grow. What happens, then, when they fill up?

To change your Event Log size and wrapping options without applying a template, open the Event Viewer from the Administrative Tools folder > right-click a log > Properties > General tab. The default size is 512K. Each log can be increased in size to a maximum of 4,194,240K (about 4.2GB). When setting the maximum size, Windows does not reserve the necessary free space. Rather, the log will grow on the file system as necessary up to the maximum size or when the drive runs out of free space (whichever comes first). 1MB of log space holds about 7500 events. How big should the logs be? Well, set them each initially to at least 50MB, but the size really is determined by your wrapping requirements.

When a log file fills to its maximum capacity, that log file's wrapping options engage. There are three wrapping options:

- Overwrite Events As Needed
- Overwrite Events Older Than *X* Days (number of days is configurable)
- Do Not Overwrite Events (Clear Log Manually)

Paranoid environments should always clear the log manually after an application or custom script archives the log. For run-of-the-mill workstations inside the LAN, events can be overwritten as necessary for the sake of convenience. However, for critical servers and systems exposed to the Internet, events only should be overwritten if they are older than *X* days. On the assumption that you are making full backups once per week, *X* should be set to 15 days. In general, we want at least two full backups to have archived an event before that event is overwritten. If events are written faster than you can back them up, then you must either make more frequent backups and reduce *X*, increase the maximum size of the log files, or deploy a log consolidation system.

NOTES

NOTES

Log Consolidation

- There's no built-in Windows syslog.
- Tools to consolidate Event Logs as text data for easy import into databases:
  - DumpEL.exe (Resource Kit)
  - SomarSoft DumpEvt.exe
  - Custom scripts (examples in Resource Kit)
  - Adiscon EventReporter and WinSyslog
  - Aelita EventAdmin
- Microsoft Operations Manager

SANS Security Essentials – Windows Security

Log Consolidation

Each Windows machine has its own separate Event Logs, but there's nothing built into Windows to consolidate them automatically into one centralized database on the network; i.e., there's no *Microsoft Syslog*. But analysis of Event Logs is assisted greatly by having a central copy of all event data. And it's important for security to move event data off of vulnerable systems as quickly as possible (the first thing a skilled hacker will do after compromising a server is clear its Event Logs).

Just as with snapshots, an Event Log is best stored as plain ASCII text. Text is easy to compress, easy to search, easy to filter, easy to import into a database, easy . . . *everything!* So how can we get Event Log data into textual form?

- Microsoft DumpEL.EXE. The Windows 2000 *Resource Kit* includes a command-line utility named Dump Event Log (DumpEL.EXE). DumpEL is used to dump the contents of a log to an ASCII text file. This file can be tab-separated or space character-separated. The exported logs can be on a local or remote system. DumpEL also can filter the events exported, based on source service or event ID number. If no output file is specified, DumpEL will send data to stdout; hence, the data can be piped or redirected as desired. Unfortunately, DumpEL cannot clear log files.
- SomarSoft DumpEvt.EXE. DumpEvt (`http://www.somarsoft.com`) is a command-line utility similar to DumpEL, but with some advantages. DumpEvt can alter the Event Log data so that it will be imported more easily in SQL, Access, Oracle, and other databases, given the peculiar requirements of each database, e.g., time-date stamp format. DumpEvt can dump only previously un-DumpEvt-dumped data in order to avoid duplicates. Binary data can be dumped, even from remote machines. (Make sure to check out the DumpSec and DumpReg tools too!) And, yes, DumpEvt can clear the log files.
- WMI Scripts. Custom scripts or programs can use the Windows Management Instrumentation (WMI) interface to dump or clear the contents of event logs, as well. WMI scripts also can receive Event Log data as they are being generated on remote systems in near real-time. See the scripts that accompany the *Resource Kit* for examples.

- Adiscon EventReporter and WinSyslog. If you wish to forward Windows Event Log data into a Unix Syslog daemon, there now are numerous utilities for this. One example is Adiscon's EventReporter (`http://www.adiscon.com`). Adiscon also offers a Syslog server, called WinSyslog, which installs on Windows and will accept in-coming syslog data from, for example, routers and Unix hosts. (On the topic of Syslog integration with Windows, see `http://www.counterpane.com/log-analysis.html`.)
- Aelita EventAdmin. Aelita's EventAdmin (`http://www.aelita.com`) collects event data from Windows, Novell, and Unix systems and collects them all in a central database.

Microsoft Operations Manager ("MOM Server")

Actually, Microsoft does have a product for centralizing log data, but it's not free. Microsoft Operations Manager (MOM) watches over and nurtures your servers by continuously extracting their Event Logs and other auditing data, storing that data in a central database, scanning the data for user-definable patterns, raising alerts or initiating user-definable actions when these patterns are found, and providing a set of analysis tools to help rationalize and explain any data of interest to you.

There are special add-on "Management Packs" for IIS, SQL Server, Exchange Server, Active Directory domain controllers, and the .NET Enterprise Servers which have built-in expertise of those products as well. A MOM server also can act as a syslog server to routers and Unix/Linux hosts, issue and receive SNMP trap messages, and collect Performance Monitor data from Windows machines.

Through a multi-tiered architecture, Microsoft claims that a load-balanced and clustered array of MOM servers can handle hundreds of millions of events per day. The agent software required on each monitored host also can be pushed out and reconfigured hands-free. All of this might sound too good to be true but, the product has been around (and tested) for some time. It originally was developed by NetIQ (`http://www.netiq.com`).

For more information or a time-limited evaluation copy of MOM, see `http://www.microsoft.com/mom/`.

NOTES

NOTES

IIS Logging

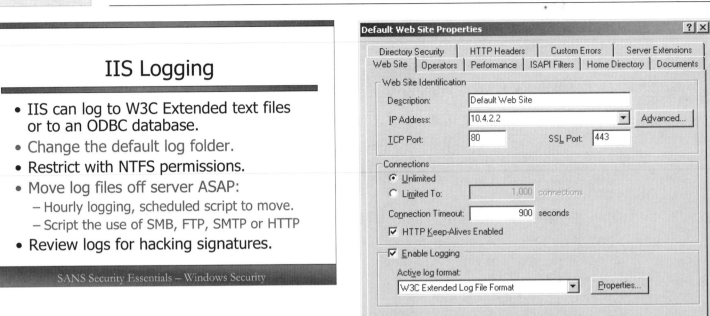

- IIS can log to W3C Extended text files or to an ODBC database.
- Change the default log folder.
- Restrict with NTFS permissions.
- Move log files off server ASAP:
  - Hourly logging, scheduled script to move.
  - Script the use of SMB, FTP, SMTP or HTTP
- Review logs for hacking signatures.

SANS Security Essentials – Windows Security

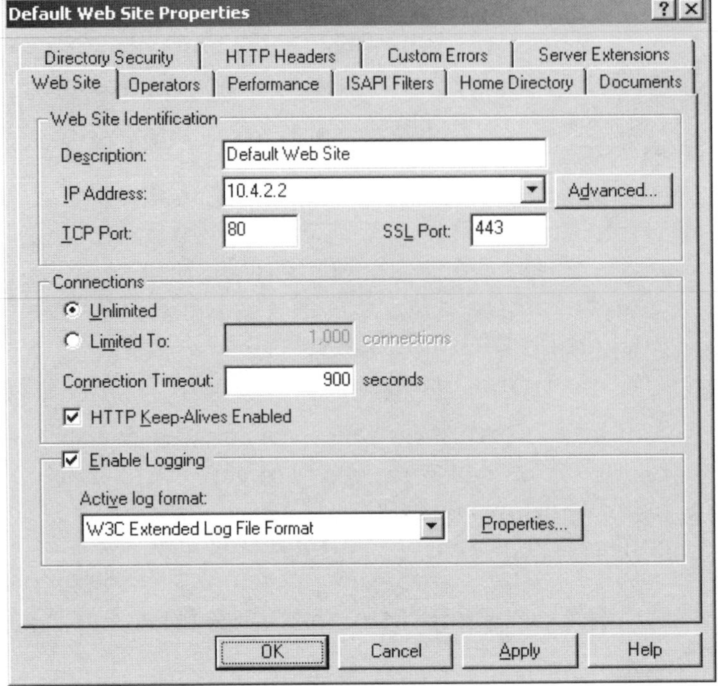

IIS Logging

There are many other sources of audit data that could be discussed, but perhaps the most important to mention is the logging provided by Internet Information Server. Your IIS servers will be probed and attacked regularly, so it's critical that you keep good logs.

IIS log data can be written to local ASCII text files or remote ODBC database servers. Logging can be enabled/disabled on a per-site, per-folder, or per-file basis. Enabling logging is a two-step process. First, you enable the capability to log at the website. Second, you go to each folder/file that you do not wish to be logged and disable the logging. This is necessary because everything will be logged by default.

To enable logging on a website, go to the Properties of the website > Web Site tab > check the Enable Logging box > select W3C Extended Log File Format > OK.

Next, you can enable/disable logging on a per-folder or per-basis by right-clicking on the item > Properties > Directory or File tab > (un)check the Log Visits box > OK.

Securing IIS Log Files

If local logfiles are used instead of an ODBC database, the default storage folder is \%SYSTEMROOT%\System32\LogFiles\, underneath which each HTTP site will have its own subfolder. The subfolder is named after the site; e.g., the

NOTES

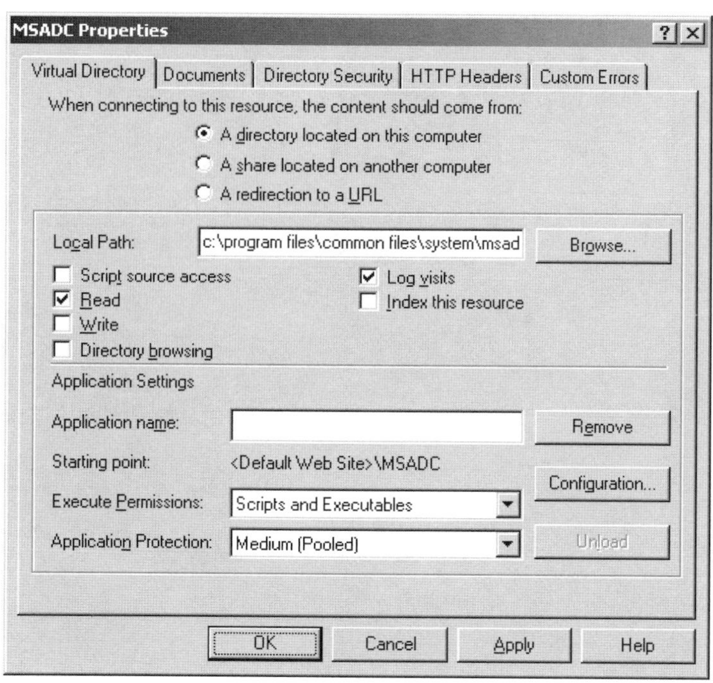

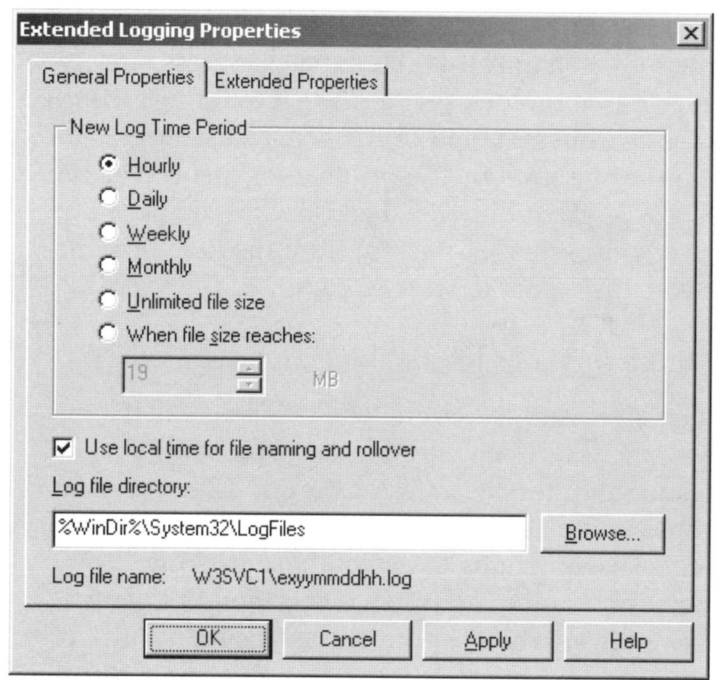

Default Website's logfile folder would be \%SYSTEMROOT%\System32\LogFiles\W3SVC1\. You should move the default location, however, so that an attacker can't leverage this. To move the logging folder, right-click on your website > Properties > Web Site tab > click the Properties button for logging > General Properties tab > click Browse to select a new folder.

NTFS permissions on these folders should be Allow:Full Control to System and Administrators and Deny:Full Control to the IUSR_*ComputerName* account that IIS uses to represent remote anonymous users (and any other users or groups you don't trust). You also should audit all successful and failed access by the Everyone group, as well (don't worry; you won't get a new event every time IIS writes to the log, only when IIS opens and closes handles to it).

Move Logs Off the Server ASAP

The log files should be moved off the IIS server as quickly as possible. A nice option is to configure a new log to be created every hour, and then schedule a script to run ten minutes after the hour to move the last log off the machine. Logging intervals are defined on the same property sheet above for changing the log folder location (select "Hourly," and check the box labeled "Use local time for file naming and rollover").

How you move the logs is up to you: FTP, mapped drive letter to shared folder, HTTP, SMTP, SSH, etc. HTTP is probably the easiest: configure a virtual

NOTES

website whose root is the logging folder; bind that site only to a non-routable private address (e.g., 10.1.1.1, and block that at the firewall too); require NTLM authentication to the site; restrict access to the site so that only the internal loghost server can access it; grant only Read access; and then use the command-line HTTP client from the *Resource Kit*, `HTTPCMD.EXE`, to download a copy of the log file.

Search the Logs for Hacking Signatures

If an adversary is tickling your IIS server in a bad way, there will be traces of that vulnerability scanning in the logs. Using Perl or VBScript, you could automatically scan last hour's log file using regular expressions to detect those hacking signatures and to alert you when found. If your IIS logs indicate that a successful intrusion occurred, it's time to get your magnifying glass out and rename your dog "Doctor Watson."

NOTES

Change Detection & Analysis

- Skilled hackers will leave only very subtle traces of their intrusions.
- Tools to work with snapshot files:
  - LIST.EXE (like the Linux *less*)
  - FC.EXE (prints differences between files)
  - WINDIFF.EXE (graphical FC.EXE)
- But what about all the other audit data? →

SANS Security Essentials – Windows Security

Change Detection and Analysis

The whole point of gathering all this snapshot and logging data is to be able to detect covert changes to our systems and explain how the changes were made. Detection and analysis enables you to stop the spread of further damage, to hopefully repair the damage that already has been done, and to learn what vulnerability made it possible in the first place so that you can prevent it from happening again.

Detecting Changes

If hackers have formatted your hard drives, this is easy to detect, but other changes will be invisible unless you specifically look for them. This is where comparing the current snapshot against earlier ones really helps. What's the best way to do the comparison?

You always can do an "eyeball audit" with two copies of Notepad side-by-side, a snapshot in each. But Notepad is an anemic text viewer. A vastly better one is `LIST.EXE`, from the *Resource Kit* (similar to *less* on Linux boxes). LIST opens large (100+ MB) files instantly because it doesn't load the entire file first. It works entirely from keyboard input (type "?" to see the commands). LIST includes the ability to search multiple files, and you easily can jump from one match to the next and back again. With multiple files open, you can toggle between them without losing your place in each, and you can bookmark various lines in these files, too; so you can jump from one bookmark to the next. And hitting "H" will switch to hexadecimal edit mode. (I know these "advanced features" sound boring, but if you work with large text files regularly, LIST makes life easier.)

But eyeball audits can't be automated, even with LIST. Fortunately, there are other tools that can compare two similar text files and print only their differences. One of these is a built-in tool named `FC.EXE`. FC works from the command line. It takes two files, compares them, and prints each set of mismatches, along with their line numbers. That's it! With the line numbers you can open the files in LIST, if necessary, and jump straight to that line number. If the output of FC is itself hundreds of lines long, redirect it to a file, and open it in LIST too.

A graphical version of FC is `WINDIFF.EXE` from the Support Tools (and it can work from the command-line too). WINDIFF highlights the mismatching lines from the files in different colors, and you can

NOTES

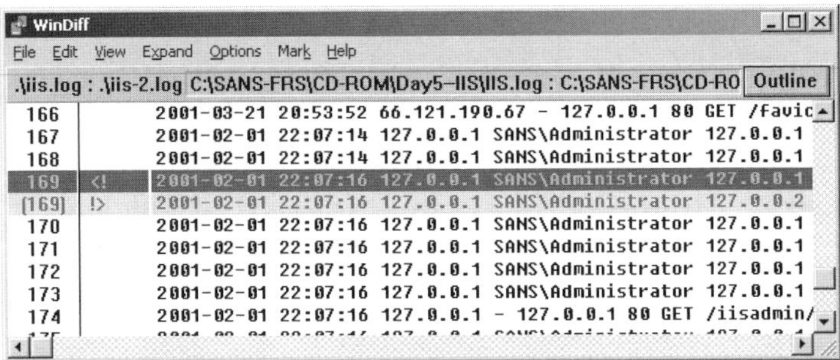

jump back and forth between mismatches easily. It's like FC and LIST combined into one tool. A similar tool with more features is `CSDIFF.EXE` (`http://www.componentsoftware.com`), and it's free!

WinDiff
File Edit View Expand Options Mark Help
.\iis.log : .\iis-2.log C:\SANS-FRS\CD-ROM\Day5–IIS\IIS.log : C:\SANS-FRS\CD-RO
Outline
166 2001-03-21 20:53:52 66.121.190.67 - 127.0.0.1 80 GET /favic
167 2001-02-01 22:07:14 127.0.0.1 SANS\Administrator 127.0.0.1
168 2001-02-01 22:07:14 127.0.0.1 SANS\Administrator 127.0.0.1
169 <! 2001-02-01 22:07:16 127.0.0.1 SANS\Administrator 127.0.0.1
(169) !> 2001-02-01 22:07:16 127.0.0.1 SANS\Administrator 127.0.0.2
170 2001-02-01 22:07:16 127.0.0.1 SANS\Administrator 127.0.0.1
171 2001-02-01 22:07:16 127.0.0.1 SANS\Administrator 127.0.0.1
172 2001-02-01 22:07:16 127.0.0.1 SANS\Administrator 127.0.0.1
173 2001-02-01 22:07:16 127.0.0.1 SANS\Administrator 127.0.0.1
174 2001-02-01 22:07:16 127.0.0.1 - 127.0.0.1 80 GET /iisadmin/

The limitations of these tools, though, are that the snapshots must be formatted very similarly to each other, if you're to avoid hundreds of mismatches, and they only can detect changes in snapshots. What about all the *other* ongoing data we're collecting!

NOTES

Host-Based IDS (1 of 2)

- HIDS monitors the system state in real-time and alerts to changes
  - Not free and not easy to manage.
- Popular HIDS vendors for Windows:
  - CyberSafe Centrax
  - Dragon Squire
  - Pedestal Software INTACT
  - Symantec Intruder Alert
  - TripWire

SANS Security Essentials – Windows Security

Host-Based Intrusion Detection Systems

Making snapshots is easy, mandatory, and something reliable on which you can always fall back, but wouldn't it be nice if the state of your system were monitored continuously for important changes so that you could be alerted in real-time? That's what Host-Based Intrusion Detection Systems (HIDS) can do for you. A HIDS does not analyze live packets on the wire like Snort or ISS RealSecure (these are Network-Based IDS products); instead, a HIDS will monitor any changes to the Event Logs, file system, user accounts, groups, audit policies, security settings in the registry, etc. Network IDS products usually cannot detect completely new attacks; a HIDS, on the other hand, does not attempt to detect the attack mechanism itself, but instead seeks to detect the changes a non-trivial attack will make (by analogy, instead of trying to anticipate the million different ways a cat can be skinned, why not just periodically *check the cat*?).

Unfortunately, unlike using snapshots, HIDS products are not free and not simple to deploy. Nevertheless, they can be useful weapons in your arsenal. Here are some of the more popular HIDS products for Windows:

- Centrax (`http://www.cybersafe.com`)
- Dragon Squire (`http://www.enterasys.com`)
- Entercept (`http://www.clicknet.com`)
- INTACT (`http://www.pedestalsoftware.com`)
- Intruder Alert (`http://enterprisesecurity.symantec.com`)
- TripWire (`http://www.tripwire.com`)

NOTES

Analysis of Changes (2 of 2)

- But no matter how good your HIDS and no matter how detailed your snapshots, it still takes a human being to analyze this data and come up with a plan to prevent the harm from occurring again.
- You are what makes HIDS and snapshots useful in the first place.

SANS Security Essentials – Windows Security

Analysis of Changes

Snapshots and HIDS products can alert you to important changes to the configuration of your machine, but it takes a human being to investigate the change and find an explanation for it. It also takes a human being to discover the scope of the damage and to devise measures to prevent it from happening again. So no matter how expensive your HIDS or complete your snapshots, ***you*** are still what makes having these things useful.

Hopefully your snapshots and your general knowledge of the operating system will provide everything you need to track down the extent of the damage and come up with a plan for stopping it in the future. In many respects, this course was designed to help you do just this.

NOTES

Summary

- **Automation:**
  - Support Tools
  - Resource Kit
  - 3rd-Party Tools
  - Scripting
  - Task Scheduler
- **Auditing:**
  - Policy Compliance
  - Vulnerability Scanning
  - System Snapshots
  - Ongoing Auditing
  - IIS Logging
  - HIDS

→

SANS Security Essentials – Windows Security

Summary

The purpose of this chapter was to introduce you to Windows auditing and automation. We audit our networks so that we can discover vulnerabilities before the bad guys do, to detect harmful changes, and to discover the scope of the harm so that we might repair it and prevent it from happening again.

Auditing as a process comprises a variety of activities, including verifying policy compliance, vulnerability scanning, collecting system snapshots, gathering log data, detecting changes, and analyzing how and why those changes occurred. We looked at a script for making snapshots and discussed tools for working with them.

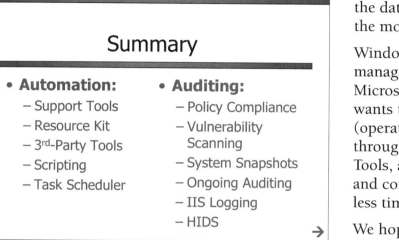

Automation tools and scripts are terribly important for doing audits well. The more the auditing process can be automated, the more standardized the data gathered, the more useful that data is, and the more consistently the audits will be performed.

Windows 2000/XP/.NET was designed to be as manageable from the command-line and scripts as Microsoft could make it because Microsoft now wants to compete head-on with Unix/Linux/Solaris (operating systems that are highly manageable through automation). The *Resource Kit*, the Support Tools, and many web sites provide wonderful scripts and command-line utilities to help us do more in less time.

We hope that these resources and the skills you are learning now will enable you to secure your networks and expand your professional horizons.

NOTES

Unix Security

NOTES

Unix Security

SANS Security Essentials VI

Unix Security Agenda

Chapter 31: Patch and Software Management

Chapter 32: Minimizing System Services

Chapter 33: Logging and Warning

Chapter 34: User Access Control

Chapter 35: System Configuration

Chapter 36: Unix Backup Utilities

SANS Security Essentials – Unix Security

NOTES

Free Security Resources

- Course based on Unix security benchmarks from the Center for Internet Security:
  - Step-by-step guides for improving host security
  - Free auditing tools to measure compliance
  - Volunteer-driven, consensus-based effort

http://www.CISecurity.org/

SANS Security Essentials – Unix Security

Additional Free Security Resources

This section follows a step-by-step process for securing a Unix system. The outline for this process is based on the Unix security benchmark documents published by the Center for Internet Security (`http://www.CISecurity.org/`). These benchmark documents represent the consensus of dozens of organizations from all sectors of industry, government, and academia as to a set of standard security settings for various operating system platforms—RedHat/Mandrake Linux, Solaris, HP-UX, various Windows operating systems, and even Cisco IOS. In addition to providing step-by-step guidelines for securing these operating systems, the Center also provides free auditing tools for testing system compliance with the benchmark standards.

NOTES

Patch and Software Management

SANS Security Essentials VI:
Unix Security

SANS Security Essentials – Unix Security

Patching and Software Management

Computer security experts agree that staying up-to-date on patches for known vulnerabilities is one of the most critical issues for keeping your system secure. Yet many widespread, automated attacks have succeeded in recent years because there are so many unpatched systems connected to the Internet and available to would-be attackers. This chapter looks at the problems raised by the patch management process on various Unix-like operating systems and presents concrete examples on how to keep systems up-to-date.

Patch management on many systems is also deeply intertwined with the problem of managing the software that makes up the operating system. This includes software from the OS vendor and from third-party software utilities (both commercial and freely-available). Many of these third-party software utilities can significantly improve system security. Staying up-to-date by downloading these tools in source code form, and then compiling and installing them manually requires significant effort. This chapter will also cover how to obtain many of these tools in pre-packaged, pre-compiled formats that can be easily installed and maintained using tools provided by the operating system vendor.

The Patch Process

Beyond the purely technical issues of dealing with each vendor's specific patch installation procedure, an organization typically encounters many higher-level issues when planning how to manage patches across their enterprise. Good patch maintenance takes an enormous amount of effort in any organization, causing some sites to question whether they should expend these resources at all, or just leave their systems in their factory default configuration. There are also business continuity issues when untested patches cause applications, or the system itself, to stop functioning normally. Some patches even require a system reboot after installation, so scheduling downtime on mission-critical systems becomes an issue. Also, administrators must find a way to be notified of new patches from their vendor and be able to obtain those patches conveniently.

The Need for Patches

- New exploits are being discovered and distributed all the time
- Vendors release patches to correct these problems
- Unpatched systems are one of the most common reasons for successful attacks

The Case for Patches

Computer security is never "static"—it's always a moving target. Every day it seems like half a dozen or more new vulnerabilities are released on BUGTRAQ and other security-related mailing lists. Each of these issues creates a need for one or more vendors to issue patch updates to their operating systems or other software in order to prevent system compromises.

At this point, it falls to the system administrator to download and install these patches or software upgrades on the appropriate systems. Unfortunately there are millions of systems out there where the administrators are unaware or simply too busy to obtain and install these software updates. The result is a large number of Internet-connected systems that are running vulnerable software.

This is a significant issue because there are individuals and groups on the Internet today actively scanning the network for vulnerable systems and exploiting these systems' weaknesses to gain unauthorized access. Consider:

- Throughout 1999 and 2000, thousands of Solaris systems were compromised via well-known vulnerabilities in the ToolTalk database server (`rpc.ttdbserverd`) and calendar server (`rpc.cmsd`) processes. Linux systems running vulnerable `rpc.statd` processes were also targeted. The attackers deployed a variety of distributed denial-of-service attack tools that were to cause massive interruptions of service for several major e-commerce sites.
- In early 2001, a self-propagating worm called Ramen targeted Linux systems with vulnerable print servers, FTP servers, and `rpc.statd` daemons. This worm was not overtly destructive, but cleanup from an infection could be costly. The worm also mutated into other, more destructive versions.
- Late in 2001, another self-propagating worm known as the Lion worm went after Linux systems running vulnerable versions of BIND (the Internet standard DNS implementation). Lion was significantly more malicious than Ramen, going so far as to install a system back door and rootkit onto the infected machines.

In all cases, the vulnerabilities being exploited by these attacks had been widely publicized for several months, and in some cases, over a year before the actual compromises began in any significant

NOTES

numbers. Vendors had released patches for these vulnerabilities within weeks of the vulnerabilities being reported. Nevertheless, there were still thousands of vulnerable machines to be infected when the vulnerabilities began to be actively exploited.

Administrators and IT organizations regularly complain about the costs associated with maintaining up-to-date patches across all of the systems they are responsible for. Certainly these costs are significant. However, the cost of cleaning up after a major security incident, plus the costs of lost productivity, and potential loss of reputation will almost always outweigh the cost of ongoing patch maintenance.

NOTES

Finding Out About Patches

- Vendor Web/FTP Sites:
  - Problem: must remember to check regularly
  - Need to go here to download actual patches
- Mailing Lists:
  - Info comes to your mailbox automatically
  - Both vendor-managed lists and BUGTRAQ
  - Still need to download/install patches yourself

SANS Security Essentials – Unix Security

Patch Notification and Downloads

Vendor patches are generally made available via a central Web or FTP site run by that vendor. However, administrators must manually download patches from these Internet sites. Theoretically, the administrator could simply check these sites on a regular basis for new information in order to stay up-to-date on patches. In practice, this solution isn't workable since it relies on already overburdened administrators taking time to manually check multiple sites for new information. Most administrators would prefer some sort of automatic notification of new vulnerabilities and corresponding vendor patches.

There are a number of different Internet mailing lists where new vulnerabilities and exploits are discussed, and announcements regarding patches and bug fix releases are made by vendors. Subscription instructions for various mailing lists (along with URLs for some vendor patch sites) are summarized at the end of this chapter.

The BUGTRAQ mailing list is a popular location for disclosing newly discovered vulnerabilities and exploit code for a wide variety of applications and operating systems. While BUGTRAQ is often the best place to get early warning of new vulnerabilities, the breadth of topics covered on the list means that a given vulnerability or discussion thread may not be interesting to a particular site. Filtering out the noise on this list is therefore a problem.

Information carried on BUGTRAQ typically gets reported in different forms by other services. Computer Emergency Response Teams (particularly the CERT Coordination Center located at Carnegie Mellon University) issue advisories for vulnerabilities that were initially reported on BUGTRAQ, as well as on vulnerabilities that were discovered and reported to vendors or the various worldwide CERTs. The SANS Institute publishes regular vulnerability summaries as part of their SANS News Services.

OS vendors also have security update announcement lists that individuals and organizations can subscribe to. The advantage to these lists is that they are targeted for a specific platform. However, it may be several days after a given exploit is published on BUGTRAQ, or some other forum, before the vendor can prepare a patch and make an announcement to their security mailing list. During this waiting period, sites may be able to mitigate the vulnerability by disabling

NOTES

certain services, configuring firewalls to block access, and making appropriate system configuration changes—but only if the site is monitoring the list where the exploit was originally published. Note that many vendors also announce security updates to the BUGTRAQ mailing list, in addition to their own vendor-specific security alert mailing list.

Patching In Practice

Every single OS vendor in the world today seems to provide a slightly different mechanism for maintaining patches on their systems. Each of these mechanisms has its pros and cons. This section looks in some detail at the RedHat patch management scheme and points out some of its failings. It is also interesting to take a look at how other operating systems including—Solaris and the Open Source BSD releases—handle the patch process, and to compare these systems with RedHat.

NOTES

Patching: The RedHat Way

- Gotta catch 'em all:
  ftp://updates.redhat.com/<vers>/en/os/noarch/*.rpm
  ftp://updates.redhat.com/<vers>/en/os/i386/*.rpm
- An RPM per day keeps the bad guys away:

```
mkdir /tmp/updates
cd /tmp/updates
wget ftp://updates.redhat.com/7.2/en/os/noarch/\*.rpm
wget ftp://updates.redhat.com/<vers>/en/os/i386/\*.rpm
rpm -F *.rpm
```

SANS Security Essentials – Unix Security

The RedHat Linux Patch Scheme

Patches for RedHat are distributed as RedHat Package Manager (RPM) files. RPM files are collections of software binaries and related configuration files, documentation, etc. RPM files are in a special archive format that allows them to be installed, updated, and manipulated with the `rpm` utility provided with the operating system.

Each RedHat version has its own set of patch directories at the `updates.redhat.com` FTP site. Patches are further subdivided into directories by the processor type the binaries run on—for example, Intel-type chips versus processors like Alpha and Sparc. There is also a "`noarch`" directory that contains patches that apply to all systems regardless of hardware platform. Typically, these are updates to configuration files or documentation, rather than programs in the OS.

While this distribution structure may sound complicated, it is relatively easy to download and install all of the available updates for a given system with just a few commands. For example, on a RedHat 7.3 system running on an Intel processor, the administrator simply runs:

```
mkdir /tmp/updates
cd /tmp/updates
wget ftp://updates.redhat.com/7.3/en/os/
noarch/\*.rpm
wget ftp://updates.redhat.com/7.3/en/os/
i386/\*.rpm
rpm -F *.rpm
```

Notice that in addition to the `noarch` patches, the administrator must also download the patches in the `i386` directory. In fact, most of the RedHat patches for Intel architectures are in this last directory.

Once the RPM files have been collected in one directory, the patches should be applied to the system with the `rpm -F` command (`-F` for "freshen" or update). The `rpm` command will be covered in greater detail later in this chapter. We will also look at how to use other `rpm` options to more carefully install special OS kernel patches provided by RedHat.

Be aware that not all of the RPMs downloaded from `updates.redhat.com` will contain security-related fixes. Some will be bug fixes or functionality updates that do not have any particular impact on the security of the system.

NOTES

Issues with the RedHat Way

- Lack of patch "bundles" means painful individual patch download process
- Patches as RPMs makes figuring out current system patch level more difficult
- To be fair, RedHat does include support for (mostly) free `up2date` software
- Unfortunately, no way to easily save old version in case "back out" is required

SANS Security Essentials – Unix Security

Downsides of RedHat Patch Scheme

The RedHat patch management scheme has a number of limitations, especially when compared to the patch management systems used by more mature commercial Unix-like operating systems:

- There is no single document that describes all of the patches available for a given RedHat release. In particular, there is no single document that tells an administrator which security patches are required for a given release. RedHat does collect all of its security vulnerability announcements on a single Web page for each OS release, but the actual RPMs to download must be manually culled from each individual security announcement.
- Patches are distributed as individual RPM files, rather than in pre-packaged bundles of critical patches. This can make downloading patches a time-consuming hit and miss proposition.
- Patches to system RPMs are reflected in minor version number updates to the individual RPM files. This makes it difficult for administrators to know whether they are up-to-date on system patches, since they must laboriously compare version numbers against the `updates.redhat.com` site.
- Once an RPM has been updated with the `rpm -F` command, there is no way to easily revert to the previous version of the software. This can be a significant problem when a patch inadvertently disables a critical piece of functionality on the system.

To be fair, RedHat has tried to make the patching process easier by providing software called `up2date`. This is an automated tool for keeping up-to-date on software releases and patches. The service is free if you buy RedHat on CD-ROM, but does require the administrator to register information about themselves and the configuration of their systems with RedHat. `up2date` does not fully address the issues above, however—particularly the back out problem when an administrator needs to revert to the previous version of a software package.

NOTES

Compare with Solaris

- Patch clusters available from:
  `ftp://sunsolve.sun.com/pub/patches/`
- Installation a snap (backup is automatic):
```
unzip -qq 8_Recommended.zip
cd 8_Recommended
./install_cluster [-nosave]
```
- Check current patch level with `showrev -p`

SANS Security Essentials – Unix Security

Other Patch Schemes

For purposes of comparison, it is interesting to consider how another more mature Unix-like operating system handles the issues raised above. Consider Solaris:

- Sun publishes and maintains a combined patch report for each operating system release. This document lists all of the patches available for the given OS version, and also calls out specific critical groups of patches, such as security related updates. The patch report file is `Solaris<vers>.PatchReport` and is available in the same FTP directory as the patch files themselves (`ftp://sunsolve.sun.com/pub/patches/`).
- Sun also maintains a standard Recommended bundle of patches for each OS version that can be downloaded as a single archive file. The archive contains the patch files themselves, and also an automated install script for installing all of the patches in the archive in the correct dependency order. It should be noted that the Recommended Patch Cluster does not always include all of the security patches available for a particular release. This is sometimes due to the time lag needed for QA on new security patches, and sometimes because the security patch is not deemed to be widely useful to most of Sun's customers (perhaps because it only applies to a rarely used component of the operating system). The administrator is encouraged to review the patch report file for their particular OS security patches not included in the "Recommended Patch Cluster" and are clearly identified in this document.
- Each patch file has a unique code number and version associated with it. The Solaris `showrev -p` command displays exactly which patches are installed on the system. This means the administrator can easily compare the output of `showrev -p` with the patch report file for a particular OS version and know whether or not the system is up-to-date. Sun also provides an automated tool called `patchdiag`, which is similar in principal to RedHat's `up2date` utility. However, `patchdiag` is available only to paying Sun support customers.
- When a patch is installed on a Solaris system, the default is for the old version of the software to be archived in a special system directory. This allows the administrator to easily back out a

NOTES

patch that harms some necessary functionality on the system. Of course, keeping backup copies of files that have known security problems could be a security problem too. Also, the saved versions of various files consume disk space that may be required by other applications. The administrator may choose to disable this save feature on a patch-by-patch basis as desired.

So it appears that the RedHat system may have some shortcomings as compared to the system used by Solaris, HP-UX, and other commercial Unix-like operating systems. It should be noted, however, that some Unix-like operating systems—in particular FreeBSD, NetBSD, and OpenBSD—distribute patches in source code form and require the admin to compile and install them manually. RedHat's RPM-based mechanism is certainly a vast improvement over source code only patches! It turns out that RPMs are also useful in other ways, as covered in the next section.

Software Management

There is a good reason why RedHat's RPM-based patch management system does not have the features that some other patch management systems have. The truth is that RPMs were primarily intended as a software distribution scheme, and not really as a patch management tool. This section provides a detailed look at how to use the `rpm` utility to manage operating system packages and third-party software under RedHat, and pointers to similar functionality for other Unix-like operating systems.

NOTES

RPMs Aren't Just for Patches...

- RPMs are really a way to manage/distribute software in binary (and source code) form
- Downloading pre-compiled software means you save time and effort
- Usual warnings about pre-compiled software apply:
  - Only use trusted archive sites (see notes)
  - Always check PGP signatures!

SANS Security Essentials – Unix Security

The Truth About RPMs

Most Linux distributions are just collections of various freely-available software packages grouped around a common operating system kernel. The developers of these free software packages are producing updates on irregular schedules and distributing the source code from hundreds of different sites across the Internet. If administrators were forced to constantly be on the lookout for updated software, and then be required to download the source code, compile, and install the tools manually, it would be impossible to run a large network of Linux systems. RPMs were developed as an easy way to distribute pre-compiled software from a central location. Note that many Linux distributions besides RedHat now use the RPM format, although Debian and some other versions use a different mechanism that has very similar functionality.

Now that Linux has become popular and gained market share, many other software packages are available on the Internet in RPM format. This can be a convenient way for administrators to obtain and install other useful security tools (for example, the Nessus vulnerability scanner) that are not included with the base operating system. This gives the administrator a leg up when trying to get critical tools installed and functioning on their systems.

Whenever you download any software, you are trusting that the tool has not been maliciously modified to include a Trojan horse or exploit code. This is true for both software in source code form and pre-compiled software packages like RPMs. Many administrators seem to feel that software downloaded in source code form is somehow safer than pre-compiled software. But this is only true if the site takes the trouble to carefully review that source code before compiling and installing the software. While many sites have explicit written policies requiring such code reviews, in practice these policies seem to be honored much more in the breach than in the observance.

When downloading third-party software from the Internet, always follow good common sense security practices:

- Only use trusted archive sites. For RPMs, this would be sites like `redhat.com`, `freshrpms.net`, and `rpmfind.net`, or various software project home pages like `nessus.org`.

NOTES

- Always verify the cryptographic checksums on files you download. Use PGP whenever possible, since PGP signatures are extremely difficult to spoof if managed properly by the software maintainer. At least check the MD5 signature provided with the software archive.

It appears that many administrators still are not bothering to confirm the checksums on software and patches they download. In May 2002, attackers breached the server for `monkey.org` and planted back doors in the source code for the popular Dsniff, Fragroute, and Fragrouter tools. Dug Song, the developer of these software tools, reports that nearly 2,000 copies of the tools were downloaded before the problem was noticed and reported. Several years earlier, attackers planted a Trojan horse in the source code for the popular Washington University FTP daemon (WU-FTPD). This Trojan went undiscovered for months and the infected source code was automatically mirrored to many different Internet archive sites before the problem was noticed and resolved.

Managing Software Package RPMs

Earlier, the `rpm -F` command was used to install new patches. However, the `rpm` utility actually has an enormous number of other options for querying, installing, removing, and verifying software packages on the system.

NOTES

Using the RPM Utility

What software is currently installed?

`rpm --query --all` (also `rpm -qa`)

Check the version of a particular package:

```
$ rpm -q openssh                                    (see notes)
openssh-2.5.2p2-5
```

What files are in that package?

`rpm -q --list openssh-2.5.2p2-5` (also `rpm -ql`)

Which package does this file belong to?

```
$ rpm -q --file /usr/bin/ssh-keygen    (also rpm -qf)
openssh-2.5.2p2-5
```

SANS Security Essentials – Unix Security

Keeping Track of Software: rpm --query

`rpm --query` is used for checking the version numbers and contents of packages and files installed via the RPM mechanism. `rpm --query --all` shows a (very long) list of all packages installed on the system. This list could be compared against the contents of the patch directories at `redhat.com` to determine which patch RPMs should be installed on the local system. Note that common `rpm` command options can usually be abbreviated, so `rpm --query -all` becomes `rpm -qa`.

`rpm -q` can also be used to obtain version information about a single package:

```
$ rpm -q openssh

openssh-2.5.2p2-5
```

The above command only displays information about the RPM whose base name (the part before the version numbers) exactly matches the string "`openssh`". However, many software utilities like OpenSSH are actually installed as several separate RPMs. Consider the output of the command below:

```
$ rpm -qa | grep openssh

openssh-askpass-gnome-2.5.2p2-5

openssh-clients-2.5.2p2-5

openssh-2.5.2p2-5

openssh-server-2.5.2p2-5

openssh-askpass-2.5.2p2-5
```

The administrator would want to update all of these related RPMs simultaneously. This technique is extremely useful for keeping an eye on a group of related RPM files.

`rpm -q` can also be used to get information about the contents of a particular RPM. `rpm --q –list` (also `rpm -ql`) shows all the files that belong to a particular RPM that's been installed on the system. Administrators thinking about removing a given RPM—perhaps to eliminate a security vulnerability associated with the software—can use `rpm -ql` to check the contents of the RPM to verify that no critical software or other data would be removed.

`rpm -q --file` (`rpm -qf`) reports which RPM a particular file belongs to—sort of the logical inverse of `rpm -ql`. `rpm -qf` can be used by administrators when they have identified a potentially dangerous executable or other file in the system that needs to be removed. Administrators should always track

NOTES

down the RPM the file belongs to with `rpm -qf` and then remove the RPM, rather than removing the individual file. Otherwise there is a risk of disrupting or confusing the system's RPM database.

Using the RPM Utility (cont.)

Check installed software for tampering:

```
$ rpm -V net-tools-1.57-6
S.5....T   /bin/netstat
S.5....T   /sbin/ifconfig
```

Installing software (three choices):

```
rpm -i nessus-*.rpm      (install new software)
rpm -F openssh-*.rpm     (freshen pre-existing software)
rpm -U nmap-*.rpm        (install/update, remove old vers.)
```

Remove unwanted packages:

```
rpm --erase gcc-2.96-81          (also rpm -e)
```

SANS Security Essentials – Unix Security

NOTES

Verifying Software Integrity: rpm --verify

Tripwire is an integrity-checking tool for detecting when critical files and programs have been modified on a system. If the administrator suspects that the system has been compromised, but the system does not have a valid Tripwire database, `rpm --verify` (`rpm -V`) can be used to check the programs on the system against the machine's local RPM database. `rpm -Va` will check all packages on the system, but be warned that this takes a long time.

Consider the following example:

```
$ rpm -V net-tools

S.5....T   /bin/netstat

S.5....T   /sbin/ifconfig
```

`rpm -V` is reporting that there's something wrong with the `netstat` and `ifconfig` commands. This is a very bad sign since these are binaries that are often replaced by attackers after a successful break-in. The output indicates that the file sizes (`S`), MD5 checksums (`5`), and last modified times (`T`) are all different from their expected values.

In order for `rpm -V` to report correctly, the attacker must not have modified the system's local RPM database. Tripwire has a similar issue with regards to its own integrity database. When investigating a compromised system, the administrator may wish to copy the RPM database from a similar but uncompromised machine onto the local system. Indeed, the administrator could build a brand new system from the RedHat media in order to get a pristine RPM database for use in the investigation. System RPM database files are found in `/var/lib/rpm`.

Software Installation: rpm [--install | --upgrade | --freshen]

There are three options for installing software RPMs:

- `rpm --install` (`rpm -i`) installs a new RPM file, but leaves the old version of the RPM (if any) installed as well. This can lead to confusion and unexpected system behavior.
- `rpm --upgrade` (`rpm` -U) installs a new RPM file and automatically removes any previous version of the software that might exist. This makes `rpm -U` almost always preferable to `rpm -i` for installing software.
- `rpm --freshen` (`rpm -F`) functions similarly to `rpm -U` in that it installs new software and removes the old version from the system.

NOTES

> However, `rpm -F` only installs the new RPM if there is an older version currently installed on the machine. This makes `rpm -F` ideal for patch installation, since the administrator would not want a patch to install new and potentially dangerous or unnecessary software onto the system.

In short, always install patches using `rpm -F`. Install all other new software with `rpm -U`.

Removing Software Packages: rpm --erase

Removing software can help improve the overall security of the system. For example, the administrator might choose to remove the GNU C compiler (`gcc`) from the system in order to make it more difficult for attackers to install malicious software on the system. Certainly there is no good reason to have a functional C compiler on a production system such as a Web server or FTP server. RPMs can be removed with `rpm --erase` (`rpm -e`).

Note that older versions of the rpm utility used `rpm -u` (uninstall) for removing packages. The problem was that this form of the command was too close to the `-U` (update) option. Many administrators accidentally shot themselves in the foot by unintentionally uninstalling RPMs instead of updating them! Thus, `--uninstall` was changed to `--erase` to avoid problems.

NOTES

`pm --query` (-q)
Check software versions and contents
	• List all RPMs on system
	`rpm -qa`
	• Show version for single package
	`rpm -q openssh`
	• Show versions of related packages
	`rpm -qa | grep openssh`
	• Show contents of package
	`rpm -ql openssh`
	• What package does this file belong to?
	`rpm -qf /usr/bin/ssh-keygen`

`prpm --verify` (-V)
Check software integrity
	• Check all packages (takes a long time)
	`rpm -Va`
	• Check a single package
	`rpm -V net-tools`

`rpm --install` (-i)
`rpm --update` (-U)
`rpm --freshen` (-F)
Install and update software
	• Installing new software
	`rpm -i nessus-*.rpm`
	• Update current software with new version
	`rpm -U openssh-*.rpm`
	• Install patch updates
	rpm –F *.rpm

`rpm --erase` (-e) Remove unwanted software	• Remove a package `rpm -e ircii`

NOTES

Lesson: Kernel Patch RPMs

ftp://updates.redhat.com/<vers>/en/os/`uname -m`/*.rpm

- Architecture-specific patches ("rpm -F")
- Install kernel patches with "rpm -i" to avoid crashes, and allow "back out"
- Install the right kernel for your system:

```
# rpm -qa | grep kernel
kernel-2.4.18-7
# rpm -i kernel-2.4.18-10.i686.rpm
```

- Also have to update boot loader config file

SANS Security Essentials – Unix Security

Earlier in the chapter we looked at the commands typically used to download and install patches from the updates.redhat.com FTP site. In fact, for Intel-based machines there is a third directory of patches on this site especially for the specific processor type of a given machine. The "uname -m" command will output this processor type—typically using a string like "i686".

Administrators can download these patches with the command:

```
wget ftp://updates.redhat.com/7.3/en/os/
'uname -m'/\*.rpm
```

Most of these patches can simply be installed with the normal "rpm -F" mechanism we covered earlier. However, the architecture-specific patch directory also includes patches to the Linux kernel that must be installed more carefully.

The kernel patches are the ones with names like "kernel-2.4.18-10.i686.rpm", "kernel-smp-2.4.18-10.i686.rpm", and "kernel-bigmem-2.4.18-10.i686.rpm". Typically, only one of these RPMs will be installed on a given system, because each represents a specialized kernel for a particular type of system ("kernel-smp" is for multi-processor systems, "kernel-bigmem" for systems with large amounts of memory, etc.). Administrators should use the command "rpm -qa | grep kernel" to figure out which of these RPMs is currently installed on the local system.

It is important to know which of these RPMs the current system is using because kernel patches should only be installed with "rpm -i", rather than the usual "rpm -F" mechanism. Patching a running kernel with "rpm -F" leads to unexpected system behavior and can render the system unbootable in the future. Also, using "rpm -F" makes it impossible to revert back to the old kernel if the new kernel is unable to boot or causes other problems. Using "rpm -i" means that both the old kernel and the new version will be available on the system so that administrators can switch back and forth as necessary. Kernel files are carefully grouped into special directories on the system named for the kernel version number so that multiple versions of the Linux kernel can exist on the same system at the same time.

Once the new kernel RPM has been installed, administrators may manually have to edit their /etc/grub.conf or /etc/lilo.conf files to tell the system boot loader which version of the kernel to

NOTES

boot from. For example, /etc/grub.conf will typically contain lines like:

```
title Red Hat Linux
  root (hd0,0)
  kernel /boot/vmlinuz-2.4.18-7 ro root=/
  dev/hda1
  initrd /boot/initrd-2.4.18-7.img
```

The administrator simply changes the version numbers on the last two lines shown above to reflect the version number of the new RPM that was just installed. For example, after installing "kernel-2.4.18-10.i686.rpm" all of the "2.4.18-7" strings in the lines above should be changed to "2.4.18-10". Once this change has been made, the system should be rebooted.

After the system has been running the new kernel version for some time without problems, the older version of the kernel can be removed with "rpm -e". Since the kernel is large, this will recover an enormous amount of free space on the system.

NOTES

Fun With Dependencies

- Nothing is ever easy:

```
# rpm -F openssh-*.rpm
error: failed dependencies:
libc.so.6(GLIBC_2.2.4) is needed by openssh-server-…
```

- Use `rpm -qf` to figure out other packages that must be freshened first
- Good rule of thumb is to keep up-to-date on library updates (glibc, gtk+, gnome, etc.)

SANS Security Essentials – Unix Security

Dealing with Dependency Issues

Many dependencies exist between the various software packages that make up the operating system. The `rpm` utility forces the administrator to update software in the correct dependency order. Due to the deeply nested nature of some dependency relationships, this can be somewhat tricky.

Consider the example of trying to upgrade to the latest OpenSSH RPMs. The administrator first downloads the necessary RPMs from `updates.redhat.com`, but gets an unpleasant surprise when trying to install these RPMs with `rpm -F`:

```
# rpm -F openssh-*.rpm
error: failed dependencies:
libc.so.6(GLIBC_2.2.4) is needed by
openssh-server-3.1p1-2
```

The error indicates that the RPM containing the file `libc.so.6` must be updated. The question is, which RPM is this exactly? `rpm -qf` shows which RPM a given file belongs to, but only if the exact pathname of the file is known. At this point, the administrator may have no idea where the `libc.so.6` file resides in the system.

Ultimately, the administrator is forced to use several different modes of the `rpm –query` command. First the administrator can use `rpm -qla` to list all files on the machine. Since this list is very long, the output is filtered with the `grep` command:

```
# rpm -qla | grep libc.so.6
/lib/i686/libc.so.6
/lib/libc.so.6
/usr/i386-glibc21-linux/lib/libc.so.6
```

It appears that there are three different files on the system named `libc.so.6`, so it is not clear exactly which of these files the original `rpm -F` command was objecting to.

However, now that the full path names of these files are known, the administrator can use the `rpm -qf` command to find out which RPMs the files belong to:

```
# rpm -qf /lib/i686/libc.so.6 /lib/
libc.so.6 \
/usr/i386-glibc21-linux/lib/libc.so.6
glibc-2.2.1-13
```

```
glibc-2.2.1-13

compat-glibc-6.2-2.1.3.2
```

Certainly the administrator should download and install updated versions of the above RPMs. However, there may be other related RPMs that need to be installed as well:

```
# rpm -qa | grep glibc

glibc-2.2.1-13

compat-glibc-6.2-2.1.3.2

glibc-profile-2.2.1-13

glibc-common-2.2.1-13

glibc-devel-2.2.1-13
```

This, then, is the complete list of RPMs that the administrator should look into upgrading. Having installed these RPMs, the administrator can go back and install the OpenSSH RPMs with the original `rpm -F` command.

Of course, the `glibc-*` RPMs might have dependencies on other RPMs in the system. Or the administrator might find, once the `glibc-*` RPMs have been updated, that there are other dependencies to address before the new OpenSSH updates can be installed. This becomes an ongoing burden.

In fact, most RPMs on the system are dependent upon the `glibc-*` RPMs being up-to-date, so it is always a good idea to keep current with these RPMs. Other critical RPMs for dependencies are the `gtk+-*` and `gnome-*` RPMs, which are used by many GUI-based utilities.

NOTES

NOTES

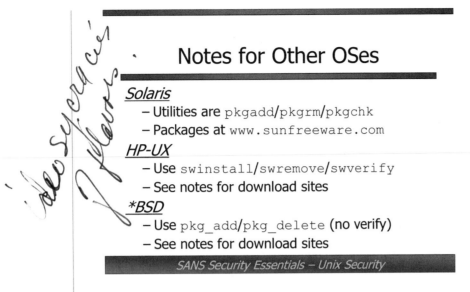

Notes for Other OSes

Solaris
- Utilities are `pkgadd`/`pkgrm`/`pkgchk`
- Packages at `www.sunfreeware.com`

HP-UX
- Use `swinstall`/`swremove`/`swverify`
- See notes for download sites

**BSD*
- Use `pkg_add`/`pkg_delete` (no verify)
- See notes for download sites

SANS Security Essentials – Unix Security

A Brief Look at Other Operating Systems

RedHat was certainly not the first Unix-like operating system to distribute pre-compiled software in easy-to-install archive formats. Most modern Unix systems have their own systems for managing system software:

- Solaris provides the `pkgadd` and `pkgrm` utilities for installing and removing system software. The `pkgchk` command performs a similar function to `rpm -V`, though Solaris uses a weaker (more easily spoofed) checksumming algorithm than MD5. Many useful utilities are available in Solaris `pkgadd` format from the `www.sunfreeware.com` Web site.
- HP-UX uses the `swinstall`, `swremove`, and `swverify` commands for managing system software. Pre-packaged software for HP-UX systems can be found at `devresource.hp.com` and `hpux.cs.utah.edu`.
- The FreeBSD, NetBSD, and OpenBSD projects each maintain a set of software ports for their respective operating systems, which may be downloaded from the appropriate project Web site. The administrator uses the `pkg_add` and `pkg_delete` commands to install and remove software. No verification function is provided, however.

Software installation instructions for other operating systems can be found by consulting appropriate vendor documentation.

NOTES

Summary: Lessons Learned

- Unpatched systems are a compromise waiting to happen
- Keep up-to-date on security patches by monitoring vendor mailing lists
- Careful use of pre-compiled software is an easy way to get up and running quickly
- Software installation utilities can often be used to check for signs of tampering

SANS Security Essentials – Unix Security

Summary

Staying up-to-date on vendor security patches is critical for maintaining system security. Well-known vulnerabilities are now being exploited by automated tools, which are even being distributed as virus payloads to attack systems on internal protected enterprise networks. The only way to fix many of these exploitable vulnerabilities is to apply the appropriate vendor patches. Of course, the organization must know about the vulnerability and the patch in order to update their systems. Subscribing to various security-related mailing lists and sites ensures that you will receive automatic notification when new exploits and fixes are published.

There are so many useful third-party tools available on the Internet today that it is becoming a full-time job just managing all of this extra software. Most modern Unix-like operating systems have an easy installation mechanism for third-party software tools distributed in binary format. Of course, installing software in binary form makes it easier for attackers to distribute binaries with malicious code inside. Always use well-known trustworthy archive sites and be sure to validate downloads against a PGP signature if possible, or at least an MD5 checksum.

In addition to adding and removing software from your system, package management tools can also be used to verify software against the system's local package database. In the event of a compromise (assuming the attacker hasn't modified the local database), you can use these tools to verify the integrity of the binaries on your system and discover what files the attacker may have changed. This is not a replacement for a dedicated integrity-checking tool like Tripwire, but can be useful in an emergency when other mechanisms are unavailable.

NOTES

URL Summary

BUGTRAQ
http://online.securityfocus.com/cgi-bin/sfonline/subscribe.pl
Searchable archives also at http://www.securityfocus.com/

CERT Advisories
http://www.cert.org/contact_cert/certmaillist.html
Archives at http://www.cert.org/advisories/

SANS News Services
http://www.sans.org/sansnews

SANS Security Essentials – Unix Security

Security Mailing Lists, Patches, Third-Party Software

- *BUGTRAQ*

  `http://online.securityfocus.com/cgi-bin/sfonline/subscribe.pl`

  Searchable archives also at `http://www.securityfocus.com/`

- *CERT Advisories*

  `http://www.cert.org/contact_cert/certmaillist.html`

  Archives at `http://www.cert.org/advisories/`

- *SANS News Services*

  `http://www.sans.org/sansnews`

  In particular, the weekly Security Alert Consensus summarizes vulnerabilities provided by a variety of sources and can be customized to report only on the specific operating systems in use at a particular site.

- *RedHat*

  Various mailing lists at `http://www.redhat.com/mailing-lists/`

  In particular, `http://www.redhat.com/mailing-lists/redhat-announce-list/index.html`

  Patches found at `ftp://updates.redhat.com/<vers>/en/os/*`

  RPMs from `ftp://ftp.redhat.com/pub/redhat/linux/<vers>/en/os/`

  Other RPM sources include `freshrpms.net` and `rpmfind.net`

- *Solaris*

  Security bulletins archived at `http://sunsolve.sun.com/security`

  Subscribe to security-alert mailing list by sending e-mail to `security-alert@sun.com` with the command `subscribe cws <address>` in the `Subject:` line (***not*** the body) of the message.

  Patches at `ftp://sunsolve.sun.com/pub/patches/`

Pre-compiled packages at
`http://www.sunfreeware.com`

- *HP-UX*

  Subscribe to mailing lists at `http://us-support.external.hp.com/digest/bin/doc.pl/` (free registration required)

  Patches can be found under same URL

  Pre-compiled packages from `http://devresource.hp.com/` and `http://hpux.cs.utah.edu/`

- *BSD Releases*

  All information is at appropriate project sites

  `http://www.freebsd.org`

  `http://www.netbsd.org`

  `http://www.openbsd.org`

NOTES

Chapter 32

Minimizing System Services

NOTES

Minimizing System Services

SANS Security Essentials VI:
Unix Security

SANS Security Essentials – Unix Security

Minimizing System Services

In the previous chapter, we discussed the importance of keeping up-to-date on patches to close known security holes. But patches only protect systems from vulnerabilities that are *already known*. Turning off or disabling services protects the system from vulnerabilities that may not have yet been discovered or reported. This is one of the most important pieces of the Unix security puzzle.

This chapter looks at some of the common system services that run under Unix and covers:

- Describing known security holes in some of the more dangerous services
- Disabling certain services that may not be needed
- Restricting access to network services based on the IP address of the source of the connection

The High-Level View

Before taking a detailed look at all of the different services that can run on a Unix system, it is worth taking a step back and considering the larger picture. Why should an organization disable unused services? If most system services are disabled, is keeping up-to-date on system patches still a priority? How does an administrator determine which services are required and which are not? How are services started in the Unix environment? As for the first of these questions, let's make the argument for disabling services by means of a simple example.

NOTES

Why This is Critical

- You leave work at 6pm on Friday
- A `telnetd` exploit is released at 6:30pm
- Do you have a good Monday or not?

That depends on whether you chose to disable the dangerous service before the problem surfaced!

SANS Security Essentials – Unix Security

A Hypothetical Example

In July 2001, vulnerabilities were disclosed in the telnet service (a remote login service for Unix systems and many other devices). The vulnerability allowed the attacker to gain privileged access on remote systems running the Telnet service.

Now suppose the vulnerability and exploit code were released on BUGTRAQ at 6:30 p.m. on Friday, July 1. All over the United States, administrators have left their jobs early to enjoy the long July 4th Independence Day holiday weekend with their families. After a long weekend of barbeques, immoderate drinking, and late night fireworks displays the administrators return to their jobs and see the vulnerability reports. Suddenly there are two distinct groups of administrators: happy admins and unhappy admins.

The unhappy administrators work for organizations with systems running the Telnet service. They know that attackers have had more than 72 hours to locate, target, and compromise systems all over the organization's networks. These administrators can expect to spend hours (if not days) looking for evidence of system compromises, cleaning up after security incidents, and deploying patches to all of their potentially affected machines.

The happy administrators, on the other hand, had decided months earlier to turn off the Telnet service and use something more secure—like the SSH service, which will be covered shortly. These admins read the vulnerability report and know that they have dodged the bullet. The quick-thinkers among this group will even notify their management about the potential vulnerability that has been avoided, and use the incident to reinforce the value of the site's security posture.

NOTES

Do I Still Need to Patch?

- Even if you manage to disable *everything* you still need to keep up on patches:
  - Prevent local exploits by unprivileged users
  - In case you re-enable services in the future
- And, of course, it's unlikely that you'll be able to turn off every service...

SANS Security Essentials – Unix Security

Are Patches Still Necessary?

While we may accept the previous example as an argument for disabling services, some sites may also see hardening their systems by shutting off exploitable services as an excuse not to maintain good patch discipline on their machines. After all, if a site is planning to disable all unneeded services that might be used to compromise their systems, is patch maintenance still important? Absolutely!

Consider:

- It is highly unlikely that a site will be able to completely disable every service and still have a usable computing environment. Patches must be maintained for at least those services that are required by the business mission of the organization.
- The organization might choose to re-enable a service in the future. For example, the site might decide that it needs to set up an anonymous FTP server to share information with customers. If the system's FTP server binary has known vulnerabilities because patches have not been kept up-to-date, then the organization has a significant problem waiting to be exploited.
- There are a number of exploits that allow authorized users on the system to gain unauthorized access. Patches must be maintained to protect from these insider attacks.
- Patches for one vulnerability have been known to inadvertently correct other undiscovered vulnerabilities. Even functionality-related patches have occasionally resulted in unexpected security fixes.

For all these reasons, keeping systems secure requires keeping up with patches from vendors and also turning off unneeded services. This kind of Defense in-Depth is one of the cornerstones of good information security.

NOTES

The Golden Rule

If you don't need it, turn it off...

If you're not sure, turn it off and see what breaks!

SANS Security Essentials – Unix Security

Ideology vs. Business Goals

The next question is, how can administrators determine which services can be safely shut off on their systems? The proper attitude to take when disabling services on a system is:

If a service is not needed, turn it off...

When in doubt, turn the service off and see what breaks!

Sites should change their thinking from "this service might be dangerous, it should probably be disabled" to "is there one good reason why this service should be running?" The idea is to only run services that can be justified as being mission-critical.

Of course, whether or not a given service is needed or mission-critical is subjective based on the business needs of the organization. In these cases, the right choice is rarely an absolute technical decision. There may be many technologies available to accomplish similar functionality, but some of the alternatives may be so difficult to manage or use that they are unacceptable even though these solutions may provide higher levels of security.

For example, it is not absolutely necessary to run the NFS file sharing service. There are other ways in Unix to share the same file across many machines—such as the `rdist` tool, which copies files from a central server to one or more machines. However, it is difficult to imagine a distributed workstation cluster using `rdist` to keep users' home directories in synch across multiple machines where users might be working on files on many different systems.

The organization needs to make the call between absolute security and ease of use. Having made that call, the organization can look for additional ways to mitigate security problems caused by this decision. For example, the organization should use good NFS administration practices to protect their file servers and data, keep up-to-date on NFS-related patches, and deploy a strong firewall architecture around their enterprise network to protect corporate NFS servers and clients.

Also remember that this decision can and will be different for different parts of the network. NFS might be fine on an internal network protected by a strong firewall. On the other hand, it may be preferable to force administrators to distribute files using `rdist` via SSH on Internet connected machines like Web and FTP servers. These systems are more easily accessible to external attackers, and

NOTES

they are also typically more critical to the business mission of the organization. A higher level of security is certainly desirable.

In addition to reducing the number of potential security vulnerabilities on the system, turning off services also improves system performance and reliability. Less memory and CPU time will be devoted to services that are not really being used. The system will boot faster because there are fewer services to start at boot time. The system will also be more reliable, since there are fewer processes running, and thus less that could go wrong.

How Are Services Started

- Under Unix, generally two ways:
  1. At boot time
  2. Automatically by `inetd`
- We'll cover each group separately
- Sys Admin has control over which services are run, syntax varies depending on OS

SANS Security Essentials – Unix Security

How Unix Services Are Started

Controlling the services running on a Unix system requires an understanding of how these services are started by the operating system. Unix services are generally started in one of two ways:

- Some services are started automatically at boot time by the system initialization process, `init`. Unless interrupted by the system administrator or some other external force, these processes will generally run unattended until the system is shutdown or rebooted. Such processes are generally referred to in Unix parlance as system *daemons*.
- Other processes are started by the system "Internet daemon", `inetd`, on an as-needed basis. Processes started by `inetd` are always network-oriented services, but certain network services run as separate daemon processes on the system and are not controlled by `inetd` (e.g., Web servers and other sorts of high-volume network servers).

Various programs also run at certain times of the day by the Unix `cron` service. `cron` security issues will be covered in detail in a later chapter.

Regardless of which Unix variant the system is running, the administrator always has total control over which services will and will not run on the system. Of course, different vendors provide different tools for controlling system services.

The rest of this chapter is devoted to looking at the various services that are commonly found on a Unix system. First, common boot-time services will be discussed, and the facilities for disabling these services—both at boot time and on-the-fly—will be introduced. Next, the chapter covers the common network services run via `inetd`, how to control these utilities, and how to provide simple IP address-based access controls.

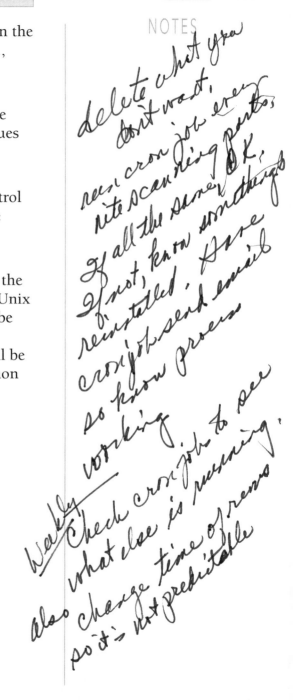

NOTES

NOTES

Boot Services

SANS Security Essentials – Unix Security

Services Started at Boot Time

NOTES

Boot Services to Watch Out For

- *File Sharing* – NFS and Samba
- *Naming* – NIS/NIS+, LDAP, DNS/BIND
- *Other RPC services* and the `portmapper`
- *Internet* – Web, Email, `inetd`
- *Printing*
- *Network* – Routing, SNMP
- *Local* – GUI Logins, Volume Mgrs, TTYs

SANS Security Essentials – Unix Security

Unix systems can run a bewildering variety of services, many of which have well-known security issues. Unfortunately, many Unix vendors still ship their operating systems in an "everything enabled by default" configuration, leaving the task of shutting things off to the administrator.

Before looking at exactly how to disable services, here is a review of some of the common Unix based services started at boot time and the security issues associated with each.

NOTES

NFS

- Convenient, but generally only appropriate in a strongly firewalled environment

- Use all available security features:
  - Restrict access by address/hostname
  - Export read-only/"`nosuid`" where possible
- Beware of vendor implementation mistakes

SANS Security Essentials – Unix Security

File Sharing - NFS and Samba

NFS is the standard way Unix systems share files with one another. Samba is an Open Source tool that allows Unix systems to share files with Windows systems using standard Windows Shared Message Block (SMB) protocols.

It is difficult to imagine running a network of computers without the ability to easily share files. However, both NFS and the Windows SMB file sharing system use weak authentication that makes it relatively easy for attackers to steal or modify data on file servers. Both NFS and SMB are protocols that should only be used on networks that are well protected by a strong firewall defense.

NFS actually gives the file server administrator a number of important features to help improve NFS security. Historically, however, administrators have not taken advantage of these features, leaving their systems wide-open to exploitation and relying on network layer defenses (firewalls, etc.) for protection. Again, Defense in-Depth is a good policy, and server administrators should take advantage of NFS security features whenever possible.

Some security facilities provided by NFS include:

- The server administrator may specify a list of host names or IP addresses that are permitted to access a given file system. If no such list is specified, then anybody who can reach the file server is allowed to mount the file system remotely. Always specify an access list!
- The file system may be shared in read-only mode. This may be appropriate for file systems containing third-party software tools like the `/usr/local` directory.
- Another option is the "`nosuid`" option, which means that the "set-UID" bit on the binaries in the exported file system is ignored (more on set-UID in Chapter 35). This is often a good option to set on file systems containing user home directories, since it prevents malicious users creating set-UID files on their local system and using them to attack other machines in the environment.

The RedHat NFS implementation also allows the administrator to do access control using TCP Wrappers ("`man mountd`" for more information). This gives an extra layer of protection beyond network-based firewalls and the standard NFS access control mechanisms described above. Note however, that this facility is not widely implemented in other Unix versions.

Historically, there have been a number of implementation mistakes in various vendor NFS offerings. The freely available `nfsbug` program can be used to check for many of these known issues. `nfsbug` can be obtained from `ftp://ftp.cs.vu.nl/pub/leendert/nfsbug.shar`.

NOTES

NOTES

NIS, LDAP, and DNS

- Significant security issues:
  - Sensitive information disclosure
  - Spoofing
  - Denial-of-service
  - Buffer overflows
- Protect name servers and deploy redundancy throughout network
- Utilize security configuration parameters for each service as appropriate

SANS Security Essentials – Unix Security

Naming Services - DNS, NIS, and LDAP

Unix systems will generally employ one or more "naming services", including NIS (the Networked Information service, formerly "Yellow Pages" or "YP"), LDAP (the Lightweight Directory Access Protocol), or DNS (the Domain Name Service). All of these services supply databases of information that can be accessed from all systems on the network. The closest analogues in the Windows universe are WINS and Active Directory.

NIS was originally developed by Sun Microsystems but was widely adopted in the Unix community, and later by many non-Unix vendors. NIS was designed to allow administrators to centrally manage common system configuration files, such as the system password database, and network configuration files like `hosts` and `services`. Clients could simply look this information up over the network, rather than the administrator having to make changes on every single system. This is an enormous win from the perspective of administrative convenience and had a lot to do with the early success of network computing.

LDAP is merely a specification on how to access generic data across a network from some central server. The information stored on that server, and the way the data is organized, is completely up to the local site, though certain standard schemas have been developed and are widely used. Many sites are now using LDAP as an alternative to NIS for storing information about users (including passwords), hosts, and other network devices. Unix LDAP implementations can even interoperate with Windows Active Directory servers.

DNS is the way IP address and host name information is shared on the Internet. Sites maintain DNS servers that hold information about local hosts at that site, and consult the DNS servers at other organizations for information about their hosts. When a user types "`www.sans.org`" into their Web browser, their local DNS server consults the DNS servers for `sans.org` in order to find the correct IP address for the HTTP connection. Since sites have to maintain DNS servers in order to communicate with the outside world, most sites will also use DNS as the standard way of sharing IP address and hostname information with internal hosts as well.

Clearly all of these services are potentially dealing with passwords, network data, and other sensitive information. Unfortunately, all of these services have well-known security issues associated with

them. Let's examine four of these problems in more detail: unauthorized information sharing, spoofing, denial of service attacks, and buffer overflows.

Unauthorized Information Sharing

Attackers like to obtain information from networked databases. With NIS this is almost trivial—any user with access to the `ypcat` command can dump the contents of any database on the NIS server. In the case of the password database, the information returned usually includes the users' encrypted password strings, which can be fed into a password cracking tool in order to compromise the users' accounts.

DNS servers allow "zone transfers" so that backup servers can download DNS information for a site in case the primary server goes down. Unfortunately the default is to allow *any host* to do a zone transfer—even machines that are not actual backup DNS servers. This information allows the attacker to target specific machines, because administrators often name hosts according to the platform type (`linuxpc-01`, `linuxpc-02`, etc.) or function (`oracle.mydomain.com`). It also provides a map of hosts that are likely to be active on the network.

Similarly, network surveys have shown huge numbers of sites running LDAP servers, which are accessible from the Internet and which contain sensitive information like passwords. In many cases there is no form of access control, so anybody capable of locating the server could get at least read-only access to the contents of the LDAP database.

Spoofing

Typically there is little or no authentication between client and server in these naming service protocols. For example, when a client makes a DNS request, if an attacker can send back a spoofed response before the actual DNS server gets a chance to reply, the client will believe the bogus information. This could have a significant security impact if the client is validating network connections based on host names ("only allow connections from the machine `foo.bar.com`"), because the client needs to convert the IP address of the remote end of the connection to a host name via DNS. If the attacker can convince the client that their IP address corresponds to the trusted host, they may be able to gain unauthorized access.

The situation with NIS is even worse. In many NIS implementations, clients will broadcast to the network at boot time in order to find an NIS server. If an attacker can send a response packet to the client before the actual NIS server does, the client will bind itself to the attacker's server and send all of its NIS requests to that malicious host. This means that the attacker could now feed the client bogus password information (or bogus host information as in the aforementioned DNS attack) and compromise the machine.

Denial-of-Service

If all of the hosts on a network are depending on a central server for authentication or network information, then taking that central server off the network will usually cause serious problems,

NOTES

potentially taking an entire network down. The most common denial-of-service attack against naming services is to simply barrage the server with legitimate requests—ideally requests that cause the server to search a large portion of its databases.

In January 2001, all of Microsoft's public DNS servers were located on the same network segment behind a single set of routers. When a configuration change on those routers blocked access to the DNS servers from the Internet, Microsoft's public Web sites became inaccessible because no external organizations were able to resolve the IP address for `www.microsoft.com`, et al. After the cause of the outage was revealed, attackers brought down the same routers with a denial-of-service attack, resulting in another outage for Microsoft's sites. Microsoft has since distributed its DNS infrastructure across many different provider networks to help prevent future outages.

Buffer Overflows

Various implementations of these networked naming services have suffered from buffer overflow issues that have allowed attackers to gain unauthorized access to remote servers. Since the year 2000, many buffer overflow attacks have been reported against NIS servers (particularly the `yppasswdd` utility, which allows users to change their passwords remotely) and the Internet standard DNS implementation, BIND (the Berkeley Internet Name Daemon).

An attacker who has compromised a site's NIS, LDAP, or DNS server is now well positioned to compromise other hosts on the network via bogus information sent to client systems. An attacker with control of a site's DNS server can also redirect other Internet users away from the organization's actual Web and FTP servers—perhaps to malicious servers run by the attacker, or to the servers of a competitor, or to a site that causes public embarrassment (e.g., a pornographic site).

With all of these security issues in mind, there are some basic steps administrators can take to help protect themselves:

- For all naming services, keep up-to-date on vendor patches. This has been particularly critical for BIND lately as many exploits are being discovered, published, and widely exploited. Also be sure to deploy appropriate redundant servers, widely distributed throughout the network, to help prevent denial-of-service attacks.
- NIS should only be run on networks that are well-protected by a strong network firewall infrastructure. Avoid sharing information via NIS with other sites. Also, if the vendor's implementation allows the administrator to specify a list of known good NIS servers to each client, take advantage of this feature rather than relying on the default broadcast mechanism for finding servers. Some vendor implementations allow the server to filter client requests based on IP address, so the server will only honor requests from legitimate local network clients. Consult appropriate vendor documentation for more information.

NOTES

- Depending on the implementation used, LDAP servers and clients may support some form of mutual authentication. It is also becoming common for LDAP implementations to support SSL for encrypted communication between client and server. Take advantage of these features if available. Always protect LDAP servers with strong firewalls; do not allow general access to LDAP servers from remote sites. Also consider carefully exactly what information is going into the local LDAP database. Many sites overload the database with extraneous and potentially damaging information, such as personal data from HR files. Always have a mission-critical justification before adding any additional data to the site's LDAP schemas.
- BIND allows the server administrator to run the name server as an unprivileged user and in a captive `chroot()` environment (like an anonymous FTP server). This is highly recommended in order to help protect a site in the event of as yet unknown buffer overflows and other remote compromise attacks. Restrict zone transfer access to only legitimate backup name servers.

NOTES

RPC Services

- Lots of different RPC-based services:
  - NFS and NIS/NIS+, `rpc.rstatd`
  - CDE/KDE and other windowing-related helpers
  - `sadmind`, `rpc.ttdbserverd`, `rpc.cmsd`
- Plenty of buffer overflows– DDoS attacks a result of systems w/ vulnerable RPC apps
- These services are not appropriate for "Internet facing" production servers

SANS Security Essentials – Unix Security

RPC Services and the Portmapper

The Unix Remote Procedure Call (RPC) mechanism is a convenient way of developing client-server applications. Many common Unix services are implemented with RPCs, including NFS and NIS. Similarly, many Unix vendors use RPCs to enable functionality in their CDE/KDE windowing environments or particular GUI applications. Examples include `rpc.ttdbserverd` under Solaris, which enables Sun's "Tool Talk" framework for various applications, or the calendar manager server, `rpc.cmsd`, for appointment scheduling.

Unfortunately, many of these applications have had a history of buffer overflow problems. The distributed denial-of-service attacks were made possible largely by Solaris and Linux systems being compromised by buffer overflows in RPC-based services: `rpc.ttdbserverd` and `rpc.cmsd` under Solaris, and `rpc.statd` (an NFS-related utility) for Linux. The distributed attack tools were loaded onto the compromised hosts and later used to bring down many high-profile Internet sites in early 2000.

RPC services communicate with one another via a service called the portmapper. This is the `portmap` process on most Unix systems, and `rpcbind` under Solaris. Historically, it has been easy to spoof the portmapper, potentially allowing the attacker to replace a legitimate service with a malicious one—for example, a malicious NIS server that allows the attacker to compromise other hosts on the network.

There are some common-sense steps that can be taken to help protect a site from vulnerabilities in RPC-based services:

- Many RPC-based services are either completely unnecessary (e.g., Sun's Calendar Manager at a site that uses Microsoft Exchange for this purpose) or duplicate existing command-line functionality. Unnecessary services should be disabled. It is never appropriate to use these RPC-based services on Internet connected hosts such as Web and FTP servers.
- Keep up-to-date on vendor patches. The distributed denial-of-service attacks mentioned earlier would not have been nearly as serious if sites had kept their systems up-to-date and prevented the initial system compromises.
- Protect systems running RPC-based services with strong network firewalls. RPC-based services are particularly difficult to firewall because they tend to bind to random ephemeral ports. However, the portmapper always uses

port 111 (both TCP and UDP), and NFS tends to use ports 2049 and 4045 (again, both TCP and UDP). Access to these ports should certainly be tightly controlled. Also, attempts to spoof the portmapper generally use a source IP address of `127.0.0.1`, the network "loopback" address. Network devices should be configured to drop packets sourced from this address (and in fact the entire `127.0.0.0` network), which should never appear on the wire in normal communications.

- If the vendor's implementation allows it, configure the portmapper to restrict client access by IP address, ala TCP Wrappers. RedHat systems have this functionality built in to their `portmap` implementation. Solaris users can download a replacement `rpcbind` with this functionality from `ftp://ftp.porcupine.org/pub/security/`.

NOTES

NOTES

Web Servers

- To demonstrate "Internet readiness" many systems ship with a Web server enabled
- If you're not serving Web pages then you should shut the Web server off
- Practice secure Web server administration
  - Run server as unprivileged user
  - Restrict access by IP address/password
  - Beware CGIs and other executable code

SANS Security Essentials – Unix Security

Web Servers

Since the popularization of the Web in the mid-90s, most Unix systems ship with a Web server as part of the base OS install—usually Apache. Often this Web server is enabled at boot time by default. Even worse, in some cases vendors ship this Web server with some sample CGI applications that may contain security holes. This includes such holes as allowing remote users to run arbitrary commands on the Web server!

Obviously, if the machine does not need to be serving up Web pages then the Web server should be disabled. The Apache project team has also put together a "Security Tips" document for Web server administrators (available from `http://www.apache.org/docs/misc/security_tips.html`). Some of the more critical suggestions from this document include:

- *Never* run Web servers as the Unix administrative user, `root`. Always create a special unprivileged user for the Web server to run as.
- Where possible, restrict access to Web documents by IP address or by requiring a password.
- Beware CGI programs and other server side executables (PHP, Java, etc.)—more Web security issues have been the result of these kinds of vulnerable scripts than any other single factor.
- Never put the source code for these executable programs anywhere in your document tree. Always locate CGIs in a special directory with restricted access. This is done by making sure you use the Apache "ScriptAlias" option to set up the CGI bin directory outside of the normal docroot (as opposed to using the ExecCGI option to put CGIs in the docroot). Then make sure that the normal directory permissions on the CGI bin dir require special access to add CGIs.

NOTES

E-mail

- 99.9% of machines don't need to be running an email server:
  - Mail daemon receives mail from *other* hosts
  - Local mail clients run server binary from disk
- Simple configuration:
  - Config relays outgoing email to central server
  - Turn off mail daemon
  - Process queue periodically via `cron`

SANS Security Essentials – Unix Security

E-mail

Typical Unix-like operating systems ship with an e-mail server enabled. In most cases, this is the standard Unix e-mail server, Sendmail. Some Linux distributions are starting to ship with the Postfix e-mail system instead, since many administrators have a perception that Postfix is more secure than Sendmail.

Since almost every Unix system ships with the Sendmail daemon enabled, many administrators think that you have to be running Sendmail if users want to be able to send e-mail from the system. It turns out that *this is completely incorrect.*

In fact, when e-mail is sent out from a machine, the mail client software simply runs the `sendmail` executable directly from the disk. The Sendmail daemon that is running on the system is not directly involved at all. The Sendmail daemon only has two purposes:

- The daemon listens on TCP port 25 for *incoming* e-mail from other systems.
- Periodically the daemon will check the mail queues for messages that were not transmitted immediately, usually because of a short-term network outage. These messages will be forwarded to their destination or left in the queue if the destination is still unreachable.

Most sites are set up so that incoming e-mail only goes to a handful of machines. On the other 99.9% of the systems on the network, there is no reason to have a daemon listening on TCP port 25 for incoming e-mail. The only thing this daemon could do is provide a potential point of compromise for an external attacker with a mail server exploit. Disabling the Sendmail daemon on these machines is a huge security enhancement.

Care must be taken that queued messages are still processed periodically, however. The administrator has two options here. Sendmail can be run as a daemon that only processes the queue but does not listen on TCP port 25 for incoming mail by simply dropping the "`-bd`" switch from the `sendmail` invocation in the system's boot scripts. On RedHat this can be accomplished by setting "`DAEMON=no`" in `/etc/sysconfig/sendmail`. The other alternative is to not run the Sendmail daemon at all, but instead run "`sendmail -q`" from `cron` regularly to flush the mail queues. The administrator will still need to create a working Sendmail configuration file for the system. The details for creating a Sendmail

NOTES

configuration file under RedHat are covered in the sidebar.

Staying up-to-date on Sendmail versions and vendor patches is still critical, even when the Sendmail daemon is disabled on the machine. Security flaws in the `sendmail` executable have often been a mechanism for local unprivileged users to gain extra access rights on the system. Sendmail's entire architecture has been significantly revamped in recent releases to help prevent these issues, but not all operating system vendors have caught up with the latest release.

Creating sendmail.cf on RedHat

Creating a working Sendmail configuration file for RedHat systems is reasonably straightforward.

First, create a file called `/etc/mail/sendmail.mc` with the following lines:

```
include('/usr/share/sendmail-cf/m4/cf.m4')
OSTYPE('linux')
FEATURE('nullclient', 'mailhub')
MASQUERADE_AS(yourdomain.com)
```

Be sure to change `mailhub` and `yourdomain.com` to be the name of the mail server and the local domain name for the site, respectively.

Once the `sendmail.mc` file has been created, build the actual Sendmail configuration file by running:

```
cd /etc/mail
mv sendmail.cf sendmail.cf-old
m4 sendmail.mc >sendmail.cf
```

The next time a mail client invokes `sendmail` to send out a piece of e-mail, the new configuration file will be used automatically.

For this procedure to work, administrators must ensure that the `sendmail-cf` RPM is installed on their systems. Note that the `sendmail.cf` file could be created on one system that has this RPM installed, and then copied to other systems as necessary.

NOTES

Unix Printing

- Buffer overflow problems
- Printing system often runs as privileged user and isn't careful about queue dirs
- Typical security problems have included:
  - Overwrite any file on the system
  - Print any file (e.g., `/etc/shadow`)
  - Execute arbitrary commands with privilege

SANS Security Essentials – Unix Security

Printing

The Unix printing facility has historically had significant security problems. Many years ago these problems were magnified because the printing system ran with full administrative privileges. Thankfully, modern Unix systems now run the printing service as an unprivileged user to help reduce the impact of security issues.

Common security issues with Unix printing include:

- Buffer overflow problems in the Unix print daemon, which seem to have been particularly common lately. The Ramen worm propagated itself across Linux systems by exploiting vulnerable Linux print servers, among other things.
- In older eras, when disk space was expensive, the print system needed to be able to handle large print jobs that didn't fit in the system print queues. In these cases, the print system would simply make a link from the print queue directory to the actual file to be printed. If the print job actually resided in a user's home directory, or some other place a malicious user had access to, the user could simply replace the original file with a link to some other file on the system. The printing service would then print the file that it had been redirected to.

When the printing service ran with administrative privileges, this meant that malicious users could print any file on the system—for example the system password database! Now a malicious user can only print files that are readable by the special "line printer" user, `lp`, but this level of access could still be used to steal a user's print jobs flowing through the printer's queues. These print jobs could contain sensitive or proprietary information.

- The printing system may use print filters to convert output from one form to another before printing (for example, converting text files to Postscript). Some printing systems allowed the user to specify their own print filters. This would allow an attacker to run arbitrary commands as whatever user the print system is running as. Modern print systems generally restrict the choice of filters and the location of these files to the system administrator.

Common sense security rules apply to the Unix printing service:

- Disable the printing service if you have no need to print from your Unix systems.

NOTES

- Be sure to keep up-to-date on vendor patches.
- Consider deploying centralized print servers that are only accessible by administrators. Print jobs submitted from client systems should be immediately copied over to the print servers rather than being spooled directly from the client's. This shortens the time period that print jobs actually reside on client systems, and causes filter processing to be done on the more secure centralized print servers.
- Consider upgrading to LPRng (available from `http://www.LPRng.org/`), which is a modern printing system written with security in mind. In a heterogeneous environment, switching to LPRng can be worthwhile from an administrative perspective since it means that all systems will have a common printing interface (rather than a hodge-podge of solutions from different vendors). Some Linux distributions are now shipping with LPRng as their standard printing system.

Of course, physical security is always important as well. Remember to make secure document shredding bins are widely available for disposing of sensitive output.

NOTES

Routing

- By default, many Unix systems start up a *dynamic routing daemon*
- Routing daemon modifies route table based on info received via network
- Route updates are usually accepted without authentication or verification
- Static routing avoids these issues entirely

SANS Security Essentials – Unix Security

Network Routing

The Unix operating system kernel maintains a table of network routes that tells the machine how to direct network traffic leaving the host. By default, many Unix systems will start a dynamic routing daemon (`routed` or `in.routed` on many Unix systems) at boot time. This is a process that listens on the network for routing updates from nearby routers and changes the operating system routing table accordingly.

Unfortunately, in most cases these route updates have no built-in authentication mechanism. An attacker can send out bogus routing updates that cause the system to redirect traffic either to a non-existent router (denial-of-service attack) or to the attacker ("man in the middle" attack).

Rather than doing dynamic routing, the administrator has the option of configuring routes into the operating system routing table manually. This is typically referred to as *static routing*. Often the system only requires a single default route to the closest network router. On many Unix systems the IP address of this default router is usually placed in a configuration file to be set at boot time. This configuration file is often `/etc/defaultrouter`, though under Linux the administrator sets the `GATEWAY=` parameter in the `/etc/sysconfig/network-scripts/ifcfg-*` files.

Setting a default route at boot time will often automatically disable the dynamic routing daemon on the host. Sometimes this daemon will need to be disabled with a separate manual process.

Static routing is preferred from a security perspective but can make administration more difficult, and also make it harder for systems to automatically fail over to a backup router. However, most routers now implement some sort of "hot standby" protocol (such as Cisco's HSRP). The best advice seems to be to use a static default route on the end systems and let the routers handle fail-over.

NOTES

SNMP

- Remote system monitoring daemon used by many network management tools
- Massive number of insecurities disclosed in Feb 2002– *patch, patch, patch!*
- If you must run an SNMP daemon, experts say change default "community string"

SANS Security Essentials – Unix Security

SNMP

Many Unix systems now ship with an SNMP daemon enabled by default. This allows administrators to monitor systems using common network management tools like HP Openview and MRTG. On the other hand, if the site is not currently using one of these tools, the only thing an SNMP daemon on the host accomplishes is giving potential attackers large amounts of data about the system and its configuration. Disable the SNMP daemon unless it is actively being used.

If the SNMP daemon is running on a host, experts recommend using something other than the default community string value of "`public`". The community string is a weak password that the remote machine uses to request information from the local SNMP daemon. Under RedHat, set the community string in the file `/etc/snmp/snmpd.conf`. Also avoid allowing remote read-write access to the machine's SNMP daemon—only permit read-only access.

In February 2002, a huge number of vulnerabilities were reported in the standard SNMP implementation used by many vendors. This included most Unix vendors, Windows systems, and network devices, such as routers and switches. It is vitally important that sites obtain and deploy the appropriate vendor patches. Specific information on patches for various vendor systems can be found in CERT Advisory CA-2002-03 (`http://www.cert.org/advisories/CA-2002-03.html`).

GUI Logins

- Many systems fire off a user-friendly X Windows based login screen
- Underlying app (`xdm`) supports XDMCP protocol to provide remote login services
- Often configured to allow remote login window access to the world
- Control access via system `Xaccess` file

SANS Security Essentials – Unix Security

GUI Logins

It is common these days to see a graphical login type window on most desktop Unix systems. This actually presents two potential layers of security issues.

First is that the underlying X Windows server, which supports the Unix windowing environment, is a complicated piece of software with generally weak authentication and a history of security issues. If the system is not a desktop machine, it is probably best to avoid running the windowing system at all. This means disabling these GUIs on Web servers, name servers, database servers, et al.

It may even be appropriate to completely remove the windowing software from these systems, since there have been exploits caused by set-UID programs distributed as part of various vendor GUI implementations.

For desktop systems that must run these login GUIs, there is another level of potential security issues. The underlying application that runs the login window (`xdm` or some other application) typically also supports a protocol called X Display Manager Control Protocol (XDMCP). XDMCP allows remote devices (such as X terminals) to request similar login services from the local machine.

By default, most Unix systems are configured to allow *any* remote system to request a login from the local host. This is probably not the desired behavior. In order to ignore remote login requests, modify the system `Xaccess` file, which is `/etc/X11/xdm/Xaccess` file on Linux. Any lines that contain a "`*`" (a wildcard meaning "match any host") should have the "`*`" replaced with "`!*`" ("do not match any host").

NOTES

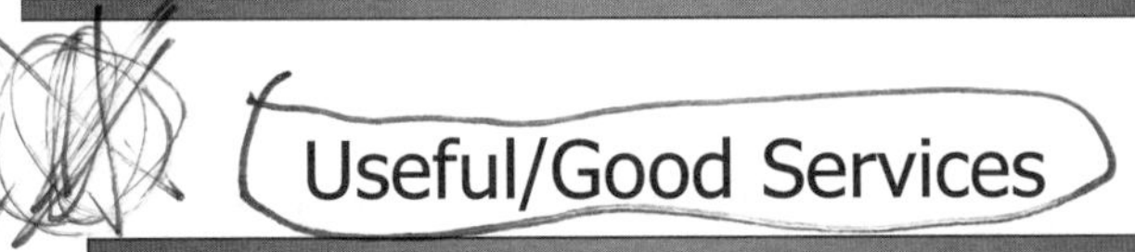

- SSH for secure, encrypted logins
- NTP for time synchronization
  - Correlate data from different logging sources
  - Avoid disruptions due to incorrect time
- `cron` for running tasks at scheduled times
- Syslog for capturing logging events

SANS Security Essentials – Unix Security

Good and Useful Services

It may appear at this point that it is unsafe to run *any* service on a Unix system. However, there are a number of services that should generally *always* be running on a machine:

- SSH is the secure remote login and file transfer mechanism for Unix. SSH communications are encrypted, and SSH supports several alternate forms of authentication stronger than simple usernames and passwords. Free, portable SSH implementations are now available and most Unix vendors are starting to include SSH in their base operating system installs.
- NTP is used to keep system clocks in synch with each other across a network. NTP is widely supported by Unix systems, Windows systems, and most network devices. After a security incident, when investigators are trying to correlate log events from hosts, routers, firewalls, and intrusion detection systems, it is critical that all of the log file timestamps match. Time synchronization is also important for time-based security software like Kerberos or even when using a file sharing protocol like NFS. More information on setting up NTP can be found at `http://www.deer-run.com/~hal/ns2000/ntp2.pdf`.
- `cron` automatically runs programs at times of the day specified by the system administrator or the users on the system. It is difficult to imagine running a Unix system without this feature, because without it all administrative tasks would have to be done manually. `cron` security issues are covered in detail in a later chapter.
- Syslog is the system logging daemon for Unix systems. It collects logging information from local and remote processes and either puts that information into log files on the local disk or relays the information to other systems. Syslog is covered in detail in the next chapter.

The next section covers how the administrator actually manages these services on a running system.

NOTES

OK, Great! But...

- As an administrator you want to:
  - Prevent services from running at boot time
  - Re-enable services that have been disabled
  - Start/stop services "on the fly"
- The bad news is that *every* Unix OS seems to do this a bit differently

SANS Security Essentials – Unix Security

Controlling Boot Services

The administrator needs the ability to control which services will be started at boot time and which will not. In addition, it is convenient to be able to stop and start services on the fly without rebooting the system. Unfortunately, different vendors provide different utilities for performing these actions. This section will look closely at the utilities for managing the boot process under RedHat and then briefly discuss the differences between the RedHat tools and other operating systems.

In order to understand how to control services at boot time, however, it is first necessary to understand the high-level process by which Unix systems boot.

NOTES

How Unix Systems Boot

1. Start the boot loader
2. Kernel initialization and execution
3. Spawn "~~spontaneous~~" processes (`init`)
4. Let `init` run system start-up scripts

SANS Security Essentials – Unix Security

The Unix Boot Process

The boot process can be divided into four general sections:

1. First, a boot loader is executed in order to prepare the system to begin executing the Unix kernel code. On Intel systems, the boot loader is actually run from the first few sectors of the disk by the system BIOS when the machine is powered on. On proprietary hardware platforms, the boot loader is often installed in a non-volatile memory device (NVRAM).
2. Second, the boot loader executes the Unix operating system kernel. The kernel is a large piece of software responsible for initializing and managing the system's hardware resources. The kernel handles communication between the applications running on the system and the hardware devices (disk drives, keyboard, mouse, graphics card, etc.) attached to the machine.
3. Third, the kernel then starts up some initial system processes that then allow other processes on the system to be run. This includes the processes that manage the virtual memory system, and the process scheduler that handles dividing CPU time between all of the jobs running on the system. Most importantly, the kernel runs a program called `init` that starts every other service on the system.
4. Fourth, `init` then runs one or more start-up scripts, which actually start the programs and services that most users interact with on a functional Unix system. `init` is the process that actually runs all of the system services that have been discussed so far.

almost Everything in Ascii script files

NOTES

RedHat `init` Process

- First run `/etc/rc.d/rc.sysinit`
- Then step through a series of "run levels":
  - 1 – "single user" administrative mode
  - 2 – multi-user mode w/o NFS
  - 3 – enable NFS, etc.
  - 4 – not used (for local customization)
  - 5 – start GUI login
- FYI: "`init 0`" halts system, "`init 6`" triggers a reboot

SANS Security Essentials – Unix Security

The RedHat init Process

Under RedHat, the `init` process first runs the `/etc/rc.d/rc.sysinit` script. This script is responsible for initializing the system network interfaces, mounting local file systems, and performing other basic system initialization tasks.

Next, the `init` process steps through a series of up to five *run levels*. At each run level, different OS processes are started:

1. Run level 1 is single user administrative mode. At this level, only administrative access at the system console is allowed and most of the standard Unix services are not yet running. Single user mode is most commonly used for correcting problems that are preventing the system from operating normally and for making clean backups of the system.
2. Run level 2 is normal multi-user mode for the system, except that `inetd`, NFS, and other common network services are generally not running yet. This level might be appropriate for a system that is not networked.
3. At run level 3, all of the standard network services are fully initialized. This is an appropriate run state for server-class machines, and other non-desktop hosts.
4. RedHat does not use run level 4. The intention is to allow sites to add their own custom services at run level 4 if desired.
5. At run level 5, the GUI login screen is started. This is the standard run level for desktop systems.

Again, RedHat desktop systems generally boot all the way to run level 5 where the GUI login screen is turned on. In order to avoid running the GUI login screen, the system can be booted to run state 3 or 4, depending on whether the local site chose to configure special daemons at run level 4. The default run level that the system boots to is configured in `/etc/inittab`.

After the system has gone through all of its run levels, the `init` process also executes a script called `/etc/rc.d/rc.local`. While the administrator is free to put start-up instructions in this file, the preferred method is to introduce scripts into one of the normal system run states.

The administrator can also run the `init` program once the system has booted and change the system's run level on the fly. "`init 1`" would drop the

NOTES

machine to single user mode. This is a good state for the system to be in when trying to make a clean backup of the system, though it means that the system will basically be offline during the backup process. "`init 0`" actually halts the operating system completely. "`init 6`" causes the system to reboot and come back up to the default run level listed in `/etc/inittab`. Note that all Unix systems also implement `halt` and `reboot` commands, which are equivalent to "`init 0`" and "`init 6`" respectively.

NOTES

RedHat Start-Up Scripts

- Start-up scripts in `/etc/rc.d/init.d`
- Generally one script for each boot service or configuration task
- Scripts take both "`start`" and "`stop`" arguments– useful for clean shutdowns

SANS Security Essentials – Unix Security

each level has a directory

System Boot Scripts

NOTES

Running Scripts at Boot Time

- Each run level has corresponding /etc/rc.d/rc*X*.d directory
- Links are made from rc*X*.d directories to scripts in /etc/rc.d/init.d
- Links are named S*nn*... (run script with "start" argument) or K*nn*... ("stop")
- Numbers are used so that scripts are run in proper order

SANS Security Essentials – Unix Security

The /etc/rc.d/init.d directory contains dozens of scripts, each one of which is generally responsible for starting a particular service—Apache, Sendmail, the SNMP daemon, etc. These scripts can be run with either a "stop", "start", or "restart" argument. Running the script with the "start" argument performs any special initialization tasks and then runs the service. "stop" shuts the service down cleanly. "restart" first stops and then restarts the service.

With the boot scripts all piled into /etc/rc.d/init.d, the init program needs a way to figure out which scripts to run at which point in the boot process. Each run level has its own directory under /etc/rc.d—/etc/rc.d/rc1.d, /etc/rc.d/rc2.d, /etc/rc.d/rc3.d, etc. The init program searches each of these directories in turn.

Each directory is made up of a set of links (pointers) back to the scripts in /etc/rc.d/init.d. However, the links in the /etc/rc.d/rc*.d directories have a special naming convention: the letter "S" or "K", followed by two digits, followed by a script name (usually the name of the script in /etc/rc.d/init.d). For example, the name of the link back to the Sendmail start script is "S30sendmail".

A link name that begins with "S" tells init to invoke the script that the link points to with the "start" argument. A link name beginning with "K" means invoke the script with the "stop" argument ("K" is short for "kill"). The two digits in the link name are used to sort the directory so that the scripts are run in the correct order. Usually gaps are left in the numbering scheme to allow local administrators to add their own scripts.

One way for administrators to control which services get started at boot time is to manually add and delete links from the various /etc/rc.d/rc*.d directories. Fortunately, RedHat provides a more convenient interface for managing these directories.

chkconfig To The Rescue!

- Don't mess with those ugly rc*X*.d dirs!
- chkconfig is a simple interface for controlling what gets run at boot time

```
# chkconfig --list sendmail
sendmail  0:off 1:off 2:on  3:on  4:on  5:on  6:off
# chkconfig --level 2345 sendmail off
# chkconfig --list sendmail
sendmail  0:off 1:off 2:off 3:off 4:off 5:off 6:off
# chkconfig sendmail reset
# chkconfig --list sendmail
sendmail  0:off 1:off 2:on  3:on  4:on  5:on  6:off
```

SANS Security Essentials – Unix Security

Controlling RedHat Boot Scripts—chkconfig

RedHat supplies the `chkconfig` command as a simple command-line interface for managing the scripts in the `/etc/rc.d/rc*.d` directories.

`chkconfig --list` with no arguments gives a list of all of the services that are configured on the system—whether they are configured to run by default or not. Running `chkconfig --list` for a particular service just lists information for that service:

```
# chkconfig --list sendmail

sendmail  0:off 1:off 2:on  3:on  4:on
5:on  6:off
```

The output indicates that the Sendmail daemon is turned on for run states 2-5. It is shut off in run state 1—single user mode—and of course shut down when the system is halted or rebooted.

`chkconfig` can also be used to enable or disable services at boot time. "`chkconfig sendmail off`" disables Sendmail at boot time:

```
# chkconfig --level 2345 sendmail off

# chkconfig --list sendmail

sendmail  0:off 1:off 2:off 3:off 4:off
5:off 6:off
```

The `--level` option is used to specify the run states that Sendmail should be disabled in. By default `chkconfig` only affects run states 3-5, but Sendmail should also be shut off in run state 2—hence the use of `--level`.

As might be expected, `chkconfig --level 2345 sendmail on` would re-enable the Sendmail daemon. `chkconfig --reset sendmail` resets the on/off settings to the OS defaults:

```
# chkconfig sendmail reset

# chkconfig --list sendmail

sendmail  0:off 1:off 2:on  3:on  4:on
5:on  6:off
```

SGI fans may recognize `chkconfig` as being derived from IRIX.

NOTES

always reboot after changes to make sure it'll work.

NOTES

But What About Right Now?

- `chkconfig` settings only apply at reboot!
- To shut down a service immediately, use the scripts in `/etc/rc.d/init.d`

```
# /etc/rc.d/init.d/sendmail stop
Shutting down sendmail: [  OK  ]
# /etc/init.d/httpd stop; /etc/init.d/httpd start
Stopping httpd: [  OK  ]
Starting httpd: [  OK  ]
# /etc/init.d/httpd restart
Stopping httpd: [  OK  ]
Starting httpd: [  OK  ]
```

SANS Security Essentials – Unix Security

Controlling Services On-the-Fly

`chkconfig` only changes the settings in the `/etc/rc.d/*` directories. Changes made with `chkconfig` will only take effect at the next reboot. Often the administrator wants to stop or start a service without having to reboot the entire system.

Recall that the scripts in the `/etc/rc.d/init.d` directory can take "`stop`", "`start`", and "`restart`" arguments. The admin can simply run the appropriate script from this directory in order to turn on or shut down a particular service.

For example, shutting off Sendmail can be accomplished by running `/etc/rc.d/init.d/sendmail stop`:

```
# /etc/rc.d/init.d/sendmail stop
Shutting down sendmail: [  OK  ]
```

Actually, RedHat has made a link from `/etc/init.d` to `/etc/rc.d/init.d`—`/etc/init.d` being the normal Unix standard. To save typing, the above command could be abbreviated to `/etc/init.d/sendmail stop`.

In some cases, the administrator wants to stop and restart a service that has become wedged, or to cause the daemon to re-read its configuration files. The administrator could perform this action by issuing a "`stop`" followed by a "`start`":

```
# /etc/init.d/httpd stop; /etc/init.d/httpd start
Stopping httpd: [  OK  ]
Starting httpd: [  OK  ]
```

However, it is usually easier to just use "`restart`":

```
# /etc/init.d/httpd restart
Stopping httpd: [  OK  ]
Starting httpd: [  OK  ]
```

NOTES

Other Unix Variants

Solaris
- Scripts in /etc/init.d, /etc/rc?.d
- Must remove rc?.d links manually

HP-UX
- Scripts in /sbin/init.d, /sbin/rc?.d
- Enable/disable with files in /etc/rc.config.d

BSD
- Boot scripts are /etc/rc, /etc/rc.local
- Enable/disable with /etc/rc.conf

SANS Security Essentials – Unix Security

Other Operating Systems

The chkconfig interface is probably one of the most convenient mechanisms available for managing the boot process on a system. Unfortunately it is also the least widely used. Other operating systems generally make life harder on system administrators:

- Solaris is the operating system that actually most closely implements the "System V, Release 4" Unix standard. Boot scripts are located in /etc/init.d. The startup directories for init are /etc/rc1.d, /etc/rc2.d, etc. There is no chkconfig script under Solaris, so to disable or enable services at boot time, the administrator must manually manage the links in the /etc/rc*.d directories. Note that Solaris startup scripts also do not generally implement the "restart" option for restarting services on-the-fly—the administrator must first issue a "stop" and then a "start".
- HP-UX uses /sbin/init.d, /sbin/rc1.d, /sbin/rc2.d, etc. for holding boot scripts. However, the HP-UX boot scripts look at configuration files in /etc/rc.config.d to decide whether or not a given service should start. For example, to disable Sendmail at boot time, put the string SENDMAIL_SERVER=0 in /etc/rc.config.d/mailservs.
- BSD Unix systems jam all of their startup tasks into two scripts. init runs the /etc/rc script, which handles most system start-up tasks. /etc/rc, in turn, invokes /etc/rc.local to run site-specific daemons. New services must be added by manually editing the /etc/rc.local script. The administrator can use /etc/rc.conf to configure which processes get started at boot time. However, there is no way to start and stop services on the fly other than manually finding the process in the process table and killing the daemon by hand.

With this discussion about boot time services out of the way, it is time to look at the second standard way of starting services on a Unix system: inetd and xinetd.

NOTES

inetd and xinetd

SANS Security Essentials – Unix Security

inetd and xinetd Based Services

`inetd`—and its more modern replacement `xinetd` (pronounced "zye-net-dee")—are just another service that is started at boot time. Their job on a Unix system is to start other network-oriented services on an as-needed basis. However, many of the services that are launched by `inetd`/`xinetd` have a history of security problems.

This section covers information about `inetd` and `xinetd` and how to configure and manage them, and also looks at some of the more common services started by `inetd`/`xinetd` and the security issues surrounding those services.

Since the services run by `inetd`/`xinetd` are networked-based, it is also appropriate to look at how to filter access to these services by IP address.

NOTES

What Are They?

- inetd and xinetd are "super servers" which start other services as needed:
  - Saves system resources
  - Programmers are bad at writing network code
- Most common network services under Unix are started by inetd/xinetd
- Some services run independently for performance reasons

SANS Security Essentials – Unix Security

inetd vs. xinetd

A typical Unix system is capable of supporting a wide variety of network-oriented services. However, only a few of these services may actually be used at any given site. Having a large number of idle services running all the time is wasteful of system resources: even if the service is not actively being used, it is still consuming memory, a slot in the process table, etc.

`inetd` (and later `xinetd`) was created to act as a super server that would launch various other network services on request. Many of the common Unix network services are actually started by `inetd`/`xinetd`—Telnet, FTP, `rlogin`/`rsh`/`rcp`, TFTP, etc.

This saves system resources because it means that the network services run via `inetd` will only be executed when needed. `inetd` also saves programmers the trouble of writing complex network code to handle network connection setup in each network daemon. Historically, programmers have been bad at this.

However, there is a performance penalty at each new connection when a service is started by `inetd` because `inetd` must first spawn a copy of itself in memory (*forking* in the Unix parlance), then execute the daemon process being requested (`telnetd`, `ftpd`, etc.). This "fork and execute" process adds a slight amount of latency on each new connection. This is not normally a big deal for most network services, but can cause performance problems for certain high-volume network services such as Web servers and e-mail servers. When performance is an issue, developers generally choose to create stand-alone network daemons that are started at boot time rather than via `inetd`/`xinetd`.

NOTES

inetd vs. xinetd

- inetd is the "original":
  - Simple admin with single configuration file
  - Requires TCP Wrappers for IP-based ACLs
  - Still widely used
- xinetd is "new and improved":
  - More complex admin, more features
  - Built-in IP-based filtering
  - Common on recent Linux distros

SANS Security Essentials – Unix Security

inetd was the original Unix network super server, and is still widely used on most Unix systems. inetd has a simple configuration file and is not capable of doing much more than firing off various network servers on request. Features like IP-based access control have to be accomplished via external programs like TCP Wrappers.

xinetd was originally developed as an Open Source replacement for inetd. xinetd can be installed on most Unix systems, and is now standard on RedHat and many other Linux distributions. xinetd has added many extra built-in features over standard inetd including:

1. more logging options
2. built-in IP address based access control
3. redirection of services to services on other ports or other systems
4. built-in support for warning banners
5. resource thresholds (only run so many copies of the service at one time, throttle services if the machine goes above a certain load, etc.)

All of these new features mean that configuring xinetd is a bit more complicated than configuring inetd.

Services Controlled by inetd/xinetd

Let's review some of the common services controlled by inetd/xinetd and discuss known security problems with these services. Following this review, we will look at how to disable unnecessary services and restrict access to the rest.

NOTES

Login Services

Standard Unix "login" type services:
- telnet and ftp
- BSD-style rlogin/rsh/rcp

Problem: clear-text protocols
- Passwords and other data can be sniffed
- Sessions can be hijacked

Other problems:
- Weak .rhosts authentication for r-cmds
- Passwords in .netrc files for FTP

SANS Security Essentials – Unix Security

Login Services—Telnet, FTP, r-Commands

Login services generally refer to the utilities for accessing systems over the network and transferring files back and forth. Telnet and FTP were the original Unix tools for accomplishing these tasks. BSD Unix later added the so-called *r-commands*—rlogin, rsh, and rcp—which now appear on all Unix systems.

The problem with all of these standard Unix login and file transfer services is that they all use *clear text protocols*. Everything the user types into their telnet session (including passwords) and all the data they get back from the remote system (such as the contents of sensitive files, and their e-mail) can be sniffed off the network by anybody who cares to listen.

The other problem with clear text protocols is that they can be *hijacked* by an external attacker—meaning the attacker can take over the network connection and run commands on the remote system the user was connected to. Typically the attacker will wait until the user logs into the system and gets privileged access before taking over the user's session. At this point, the attacker has unlimited access to the system and can install back doors and other exploit code that will allow them to gain access in the future.

The r-commands also allow users to set up trust relationships using .rhosts files in their home directories. .rhosts files list remote machines from which the user can log into the local system without providing a password. Unfortunately, this means that users are allowed to replace the already weak standard username/password authentication with an authentication scheme based on IP addresses and hostnames. Addresses and hostnames can be spoofed by an attacker and used to gain unauthorized access.

FTP allows users to create .netrc files in their home directory. These are essentially automatic login scripts for accessing remote FTP servers. However, since these scripts need to automate the login process, .netrc files often contain passwords for the remote system in clear text. Discovering this information would certainly allow the attacker to compromise the remote system. Unfortunately users also have a tendency to use the same password everywhere: the password in the .netrc file may in fact be the user's password on the local system as well.

NOTES

Some form of login service is necessary for the remote administration of systems on a network. It is not really conceivable to administer a large network of systems without the ability to log into those systems remotely and issue commands, and without the ability to transfer files from system to system.

NOTES

The Free Alternative: SSH

- To administer a system remotely you need:
  - Remote login access
  - File transfer ability
- SSH accomplishes this securely:
  - Full, strong crypto
  - Support for strong authentication
  - Admin control over `.rhosts` support
  - Connection forwarding an extra bonus

SANS Security Essentials – Unix Security

SSH is a free alternative for `rlogin`, `rsh`, and `rcp` that accomplishes the goal of allowing remote login access and file transfers without all of the security issues associated with the older, clear text login services. All SSH sessions are fully encrypted, so eavesdropping and sniffing are not a problem. Encryption also prevents session hijacking attacks. SSH allows the administrator to easily control whether or not users are allowed to use the `.rhosts`-style hostname/address based authentication scheme—many sites are choosing to disable this feature completely. Note that unlike the BSD r-commands, the SSH daemon normally runs as a stand-alone service that is started at boot time, rather than being started by `inetd`/`xinetd`.

SSH also has a number of useful features not present in the standard Unix clear text login protocols. It has built-in support for stronger forms of authentication, including Kerberos, public key based authentication, and support for SecurID, and other token cards. SSH also allows users to tunnel other protocols over their SSH login sessions. For example, it is possible to run a GUI-based application on a remote system and have the window appear on the local machine, but in fact have all data flow through the encrypted SSH session.

SSH runs on Unix systems, Windows devices, and even network equipment like routers and switches. Sites that still use clear text login protocols should immediately begin phasing them out and start using SSH exclusively. Note that there are insecurity issues with version 1 of the SSH protocol—sites should only use SSH clients and servers that support SSH v2 if at all possible. For more information on SSH, including where to find free clients for various platforms, see the Internet SSH FAQ at `http://www.employees.org/~satch/ssh/faq/`.

NOTES

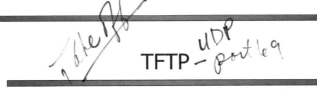

TFTP

- Trivial File Transfer Protocol designed to allow diskless workstations to boot
- Permits file transfers without requiring username or password
- Early versions very insecure, but significant improvements have been made
- Still, don't run TFTP unless you need to

SANS Security Essentials – Unix Security

TFTP

TFTP was developed as a mechanism for diskless workstations, X-terminals, etc. to download their bootstrap code from a central server. The problem is that TFTP was designed so that devices could reboot easily in an unattended fashion, without a user or operator standing by to enter a password. Thus, TFTP requires no authentication before transferring files.

Some early TFTP implementations allowed any file on the TFTP server to be read and transferred to the requesting device. Even worse, many TFTP servers ran the TFTP daemon with full administrative privileges. This allowed remote attackers to grab any file on the system if it was running a TFTP daemon, including the system password database, which could then be fed into a password cracking utility. These days, TFTP servers have much stricter access controls: they run as unprivileged users and are restricted to reading and writing files in a single directory.

However, TFTP is now used by routers, switches, and other network devices to transfer backup copies of configuration information over the network to the TFTP server. These configuration files can contain passwords and SNMP community strings, firewall rule sets, and other sensitive information. And, of course, system bootstrap code for diskless devices is also interesting to an attacker. Imagine the attacker being able to plant a Trojan boot program into all network-bootable devices. So even though the TFTP server is restricted to accessing a single directory, that directory can contain very sensitive information.

It is important that sites disable TFTP on all machines except those that absolutely need it. These days most Unix systems ship the TFTP service disabled by default. A site's TFTP servers should be protected by a strong firewall, and only authorized system and network administrators should be granted access to TFTP server machines.

NOTES

finger

- finger allows a user to get information about users on a remote system
- Such information can help an attacker who wants to attack your machine
- Several other finger-related security issues have been discovered (and fixed)
- Turn it off if you don't need it...

SANS Security Essentials – Unix Security

Finger

The finger program allows a user to get information about who is logged into either the local machine or some other system on the network:

```
% finger @foo.sysiphus.com
Login  Name           TTY      Idle  When  Where
alice  Alice Rogers   console        Wed   22:51
alice  Alice Rogers   pts/5    2:37  Sat   07:48   bar.sysi...
```

This information could be extremely useful to an attacker. For example, users show an annoying tendency to use their name, username, or some permutation thereof for their password. Thus, an attacker might be able to guess passwords based on this information. Also, knowing when a user tends to be logged in can help an attacker plan when to attack a given system. The attacker might plan their attack for when the user is normally logged in so that the system administrator does not see anything out of the ordinary; or the attacker might plan their attack for an abnormal time to escape detection by the user. If the attacker sees a user logged in from a remote system—as shown in the second line of output—the attacker might try to test whether or not there is a .rhosts-style trust relationship set up with that remote machine that can be exploited to gain access.

The server that is started by inetd/xinetd to handle finger requests, fingerd, has also had its share of buffer overflows. In fact, a buffer overflow in fingerd was one of the exploits used by the Morris Worm in 1988, to propagate it from system to system. This may have been the first widespread buffer overflow attack in history.

Frankly, the utility of the finger service is far outweighed by the risks of running it. From an information warfare perspective, there is no good reason to run a service that gives away so much information to a potential attacker. Sites should disable fingerd wherever possible, and especially on machines that are accessible from the Internet.

used by Mitnick to learn trust config.

NOTES

Small Services

- "Small" services are `echo`, `chargen`, `daytime`, `time`, and `discard`
- Called "small" services because they listen on low port numbers
- Can be used as a denial-of-service or for network mapping

- Not generally useful and can be disabled without impacting system

SANS Security Essentials – Unix Security

"Small Services"

`inetd/xinetd` also runs a number of diagnostic services that were originally created to aid in network debugging:

- `echo`—simply echoes back anything that is typed at it
- `chargen`—generates a stream of characters upon connection
- `daytime`—prints the Unix standard date string and exits
- `time`—prints the internal Unix time and exits
- `discard`—throws away all characters typed at it

These services are generally referred to as the small services because they listen on smaller port numbers—all of them appear below port 20, except `time`, which listens on port 37. These services generally respond to both TCP and UDP requests.

One problem with the small services is that they can be used for denial of service attacks. For example, an attacker can forge a network packet to set up a communication stream between the `echo` port on one machine and the `chargen` port on another. The machines will shoot packets back and forth at each other until one is rebooted or its `inetd/xinetd` process is killed. If the attacker sets up enough of these channels, the target system will become unusable.

These services also function much like a `ping`—a remote user sends a packet to one of these services and gets a response back if the machine is live. This means an attacker can use these services to map a remote network and figure out which IP addresses are being used by live systems. Some sites will go out of their way to block the standard ICMP-based `ping` command but forget to block these services!

While these sorts of services were useful for debugging in the early days of the Internet, they are not widely utilized today. They should be disabled wherever possible. Note that even network devices like Cisco routers sometimes run these services (these services can be disabled on a Cisco router with the commands `no service tcp-small-servers` and `no service udp-small-servers`—this is the default for Cisco IOS v12.x).

Other Problem Children

- History of buffer overflow issues:
  - imapd/popd – email access servers
  - comsat – enables biff email notifications
  - talk/ntalk – two person network chat
- Of these services, only IMAP and POP servers are potentially useful
- If you are going to run these services, be sure to keep up-to-date on patches

SANS Security Essentials – Unix Security

POP and IMAP

POP (the Post Office Protocol) and IMAP (the Internet Message Access Protocol) allow users to access their Unix mailboxes remotely using e-mail clients like Netscape, Microsoft's Internet Explorer, Outlook, Eudora, etc. Historically, the popular POP and IMAP servers have had many instances of buffer overflow problems. It is vital to keep up-to-date on releases and patches from the software vendor. Obviously, POP and IMAP servers should only be enabled on mail servers that need to allow remote client access to user mailboxes.

comsat

The `comsat` daemon is what enables local Unix users running the `biff` command to get notifications when e-mail arrives in their mailbox. `comsat` is another fairly buggy service that has a history of buffer overflow problems. Actually, the Unix command shell can be configured to notify users when new mail arrives, so the `biff` command is not strictly necessary. This means that the `comsat` service can be disabled without a significant loss of functionality.

talk and ntalk

`talk` and `ntalk` were the original network chat applications. These services seem to have been largely supplanted by IRC and Instant Messaging, but many Unix systems still ship with `talk/ntalk` enabled by default. Again, these are services with a history of buffer overflow problems and should probably be disabled if they are not actively being used.

So it appears that many of the services mentioned here are candidates for being disabled. The question is how does the administrator go about doing this? The answer is different depending on whether the OS vendor ships the standard `inetd`, or the newer `xinetd`. Filtering connections based on source IP address is also handled differently for each daemon.

NOTES

NOTES

Service Config With `inetd`

- Config file is `/etc/inetd.conf`
- Normal entry:

```
tftp  dgram udp wait root  /usr/sbin/in.tftpd
  in.tftpd -s /tftpboot
```

- With TCP Wrappers support:

```
tftp  dgram udp wait root  /usr/sbin/tcpd
  /usr/sbin/in.tftpd -s /tftpboot
```

- Disable service by "commenting out" line or by removing from `inetd.conf`

SANS Security Essentials – Unix Security

inetd Configuration with TCP Wrappers

`inetd` uses a single configuration file called `/etc/inetd.conf`, or `/etc/inet/inetd.conf` on some Unix systems. Each service started by `inetd` has a one-line configuration entry in the file similar to the one shown here:

```
tftp  dgram udp wait root  /usr/sbin/
in.tftpd

  in.tftpd -s /tftpboot
```

Note that this example would normally appear as a single line in the `inetd.conf` file

The meaning of the various columns in the `inetd.conf` is as follows:

- The first column says what network port to listen on. Port name to port number mappings are kept in the `/etc/services` file (`tftp` is port 69/udp).
- The next two columns say whether the service is TCP or UDP-based. The entries should be either "`dgram udp`" or "`stream tcp`".
- The next column is either `wait` or `nowait`, depending on whether the daemon process should hang around after the initial network connection has finished. Most services are `nowait` type services, meaning `inetd` should fire off a new daemon for each new network connection.
- The next column is the full path the binary `inetd` should run, and the rest of the line contains the command line arguments `inetd` should use when invoking the daemon. Note that the name of the daemon process is repeated as the first argument—this is the name that will appear in the process table entry for the process.

It is always a good idea to use TCP Wrappers with `inetd` to provide IP-based access control, as well as additional logging about each connection. To enable TCP Wrappers support, replace the path name to the daemon `inetd` would normally invoke with the path of the TCP Wrappers `tcpd` binary:

```
tftp  dgram udp wait root  /usr/sbin/tcpd

  /usr/sbin/in.tftpd -s /tftpboot
```

Notice that the argument list for `tcpd` now starts with the full path name of the actual daemon binary. `tcpd` will run this binary, assuming the IP-based access control lists (ACLs) configured by the administrator are passed. All of the normal command-line arguments to the daemon are then replicated from the original `inetd.conf` entry.

NOTES

NOTES

ACLs w/ TCP Wrappers

/etc/hosts.allow ("good" hosts):

```
ALL: 192.168.1.0/255.255.255.0
in.ftpd: ALL
sshd: 216.15.51.194, 130.58.66.123
```

/etc/hosts.deny ("bad" hosts):

```
ALL: ALL
```

Order of evaluation is *critical:*

- hosts.allow read before hosts.deny
- "First match and exit" behavior

SANS Security Essentials – Unix Security

TCP Wrappers use two different files for access control. First, tcpd checks the /etc/hosts.allow file for patterns that match machines that should be granted access. Next, tcpd checks /etc/hosts.deny for machines that should not be allowed to connect to the local system. If a match is not found in either file, then access is granted.

Since tcpd logs each connection, some sites actually use TCP Wrappers just for the logging feature and do not actually create hosts.allow/hosts.deny for access control. With neither a hosts.allow nor a hosts.deny file, all connections will be allowed since there are no lines to match in either file.

For access control purposes, the usual tactic is to list all allowed connections in hosts.allow and then block all access in hosts.deny. Since hosts.allow is read first, and since tcpd will stop looking at rules as soon as a matching rule is found ("first match and exit" behavior), this is the easy way to write the so-called *default deny stance*—where everything not explicitly permitted by hosts.allow is denied.

Consider the following example hosts.allow file:

```
ALL: 192.168.1.0/255.255.255.0

in.ftpd: ALL

sshd: 216.15.51.194, 130.58.66.123
```

In the first line of this example, any machine on the 192.168.1.0 network is granted access to any service—at least any service that is currently enabled in inetd.conf and filtered with TCP Wrappers. It would appear that this 192.168.1.0 network is the local trusted LAN. The second line would seem to indicate that this machine is an anonymous FTP server because any host on the Internet is allowed access to the FTP daemon. The third line grants SSH access to a couple of addresses not on the local network. Perhaps these are the IP addresses of the system administrators' home networks so that they can troubleshoot problems late at night and on weekends.

hosts.deny then simply has a blanket deny everything rule that blocks access to ALL services from ALL IP addresses:

```
ALL: ALL
```

Anything that was not matched by the rules in hosts.allow is going to be dropped by this rule.

Service Config With `xinetd`

- Global defaults in `/etc/xinetd.conf`
  - Logging parameters
  - Load thresholds, max concurrent processes
  - Where to find service entries
- Per-service entries in `/etc/xinetd.d`
  - One file per service
  - Per-service parameters override defaults
- IP-based ACLs can be set in either file

SANS Security Essentials – Unix Security

NOTES

xinetd Configuration

As mentioned earlier, `xinetd` configuration is a bit more complicated than configuring services in `inetd`. The usual `xinetd` configuration starts with a file called `/etc/xinetd.conf`. This file defines some defaults for all services. Typically these parameters include items like how to log information and how much to log, and how many simultaneous processes `xinetd` should start at a given time. This file also defines a directory that contains the configuration information for individual services.

Here is a sample `xinetd.conf` file from a RedHat system:

```
defaults
{
    instances          = 60
    log_type           = SYSLOG authpriv
    log_on_success     = HOST PID
    log_on_failure     = HOST
    cps                = 25 30
}
includedir /etc/xinetd.d
```

`instances` is the maximum number of simultaneous daemons `xinetd` is willing to spawn. `log_type` is telling `xinetd` that messages should be logged via the standard Unix Syslog system logging service, and the messages should be sent to the `authpriv` facility (more on Syslog facility names in the next chapter). On successful connections (`log_on_success`) both the remote hostname/IP address and the process ID of the daemon process servicing the connection are logged. On failed connections (`log_on_failure`) log the remote host/IP address. `cps` is used to throttle the number of incoming connections: the first number is the maximum number of connections per second the daemon will handle before disabling the service, and the second number is the number of seconds to disable the service for when the threshold is reached. The final configuration directive shown here, `includedir`, tells `xinetd` where to find the configuration files that list information about specific services.

NOTES

Sample xinetd Service File

```
service tftp
{
   only_from     = 192.168.1.0/24
   socket_type   = dgram
   protocol      = udp
   wait          = yes
   user          = root
   server        = /usr/sbin/in.tftpd
   server_args   = -s /tftpboot
   disable       = yes
}
```

SANS Security Essentials – Unix Security

The per-service configuration files, which in this example are in /etc/xinetd.d, define pretty much the same information that appears in the standard inetd.conf entries shown previously. These per-service configuration files can also override the default values that were set in /etc/xinetd.conf.

Here is a sample service configuration file for the TFTP service:

```
service tftp
{
   only_from          = 192.168.1.0/24
   socket_type        = dgram
   protocol           = udp
   wait               = yes
   user               = root
   server             = /usr/sbin/in.tftpd
   server_args        = -s /tftpboot
   disable            = yes
}
```

Notice that the information in the socket_type, protocol, wait, user, server, and server_args fields are essentially identical to the entries seen earlier in the standard inetd.conf file.

xinetd does not require TCP Wrappers for IP address-based access control: the only_from field is a built-in mechanism for accomplishing the same thing. This example indicates that only machines on the 192.168.1.0 network are allowed to connect to the TFTP daemon.

The administrator can define IP-based access control for all services by putting only_from configuration directives in /etc/xinetd.conf. Access control for individual services is accomplished via only_from fields in the appropriate per-service configuration file in /etc/xinetd.d. Defining ACLs for individual services gives more flexibility, but is more complicated to administer. As a compromise, the administrator could define some standard default access control policy in /etc/xinetd.conf and then override that policy as necessary for particular services via the files in /etc/xinetd.d.

NOTES

Updating Running [x]inetd

- Changes made to the `inetd`/`xinetd` config files don't take effect immediately
- Must use `kill`/`pkill` to send a `HUP` signal to the running `inetd`/`xinetd` process
- Note that older versions of `xinetd` use `USR2` signal instead

SANS Security Essentials – Unix Security

Controlling inetd/xinetd Services

In order to disable a service from being started by `inetd`, the administrator can either remove its configuration entry from `inetd.conf` entirely or comment it out by putting a "#" sign at the beginning of the configuration line.

Similarly, `xinetd`-based services can be disabled simply by removing the appropriate per-service configuration file from `/etc/xinetd.d`. `xinetd` also supports a `disable` field. Setting this to `yes` is similar to commenting an entry out of the `inetd.conf` file—it prevents the service from being started by `xinetd`. RedHat ships with service configuration files for a number of network daemons, but almost all of them have `disable` set to `yes` so they are not started by default.

Once `inetd` or `xinetd` configuration files have been updated, the administrator must signal the running daemon to re-read the new configuration files and adjust itself appropriately. `inetd` and `xinetd` have been written so that the administrator does not actually need to stop and restart the daemon to get this to happen. If the daemon were restarted, any network connections that were already in progress would be shut down.

Sending a `HUP` signal to `inetd` or `xinetd` causes the daemon to re-read its configuration files and reset itself. Note that earlier versions of `xinetd` used the `USR2` signal for this purpose, but recent versions have switched to using `HUP`, because this is the Unix standard. On Linux systems, the easiest way to send a process a signal is with the `pkill` command:

```
pkill -HUP xinetd
```

On other operating systems that do not implement the `pkill` command, the administrator must go through a two-step manual process:

```
# ps -ef | grep inetd

root   138     1  0   May 02 ?      0:00 /
usr/sbin/inetd -s

root  8122  8121  0 18:31:12 pts/2 0:00
grep inetd

# kill -HUP 138
```

First the administrator runs the `ps` command, sending its output into the `grep` command, which will pull out all lines which match the string `inetd`. The process ID of the `inetd` process can be found in the second column. The administrator uses this

NOTES

value as an argument to the `kill` command, which is used to send the process a `HUP` signal.

Note that it is not necessary to restart `inetd` after changes to the TCP Wrappers `hosts.allow` and `hosts.deny` files. These files are consulted on each new network connection, so changes will be picked up automatically.

NOTES

Delete or Disable?

Q: Should the admin simply disable a service or completely remove the config entry?

A: *Remove it!*

Reason 1: Bogus `inetd.conf` *entries:*

```
imap  stream tcp nowait root  /bin/sh  /bin/sh -i
```

Reason 2: Exploits have been known to automatically enable disabled services!

SANS Security Essentials – Unix Security

Delete vs. Disable

One common question is whether the administrator should just disable services—either by commenting them out in `inetd.conf` or with the `disable` field in the `xinetd` configuration files—or whether the admin should completely remove the configuration information for a given service from all configuration files. While there is some amount of debate on this subject, removing the entries seems to be the right answer for a couple of reasons:

- Often after a system compromise, the attacker will leave behind a back door entry in `inetd.conf` similar to the following:

```
imap  stream tcp nowait root /bin/sh /bin/sh -i
```

  What this entry says is that when somebody connects to the standard IMAP port on the system (143/tcp) inetd should spawn the program /bin/sh –i. This program is simply an interactive command shell. No authentication of any kind will be done, so the person connecting to this port just gets an interactive shell prompt. Notice also that this service is configured to run as the all-powerful root user, so this entry gives immediate, unauthenticated administrative access to the system.

  Now if this entry were added to a standard inetd.conf file, which typically has dozens of lines in it, it is unlikely that anybody would notice this entry for a very long time. On the other hand, if the inetd.conf file only contained five or six lines for absolutely necessary services, then this line would immediately stand out.

- The other problem with just disabling services is that certain exploit kits (e.g., the T0rn rootkit) automatically re-enable certain services like Telnet and `rlogin` that may have been simply disabled by the administrator. If the services have been removed completely, then this part of the exploit kit does not work.

So it appears that the best advice is to remove unused configuration entries. The administrator may wish to make a backup copy of these configuration files, however, just in case they need to re-enable a service at some point in the future.

NOTES

One Final Thought

- If you're not running any services from `inetd`/`xinetd`, turn the daemon off!

Remember – If you don't need it, turn it off!

SANS Security Essentials – Unix Security

Note that if no services end up being configured to run via `inetd`/`xinetd`, then the administrator should simply stop the daemon from being started at boot time. Remember that all the administrator really needs to manage the system remotely is login access and file transfer ability. Since both of these tasks can be accomplished securely via SSH, it may not be necessary to use any `inetd`/`xinetd` based services at all.

NOTES

Summary: Lessons Learned

- *If you don't need it, turn it off!*
- Disabling unneeded services protects you from exploits you don't know about (yet)
- Certainly replace old clear-text login and file transfer protocols with SSH
- May be possible to do without [x]inetd

SANS Security Essentials – Unix Security

Summary

Disabling unused services is one of the most important tasks in helping to defend Unix systems from as yet unknown vulnerabilities. Remember the golden rules of service minimization:

If a service is not needed, turn it off...

When in doubt, turn the service off and see what breaks!

Disabling unused services improves a system's security posture, and it can also make the system perform better and be more reliable.

Of the services run by inetd/xinetd, the most commonly used services are the standard login and file transfer protocols: Telnet, FTP, and the BSD "r-commands". However, SSH is in all ways a better replacement for these protocols. This is primarily because SSH communications are encrypted, which prevents eavesdropping and session hijacking attacks. Organizations should seriously look into replacing all of the old standard clear-text login protocols with SSH v2.

Having done this, a site may find that you have no real reason to run inetd or xinetd and can just shut these services off completely. Remember that reducing configuration files so that they only include the absolutely required services makes systems much easier to audit on an ongoing basis and can help stop certain automated exploits.

NOTES

Chapter 33

Logging and Warning

NOTES

NOTES

Logging and Warning

SANS Security Essentials VI:
Unix Security

SANS Security Essentials – Unix Security

Logging and Warning

This chapter covers two different topics: system logging and system warning banners. Most of the chapter is devoted to looking at the various logging facilities common to Unix operating systems and logging techniques that will help improve security and provide more information in the event of a system compromise. The second section looks at ways in which the administrator can configure systems to display warning banners before granting access to various login services on the system.

Both of these topics are somewhat "passive" approaches to improving the overall security of the system and usually are more of a factor **after** a successful compromise than they are in preventing a compromise initially. For these reasons, administrators may have a tendency to pay scant attention to these topics when configuring their systems. However, complete and trustworthy system logs are critical for understanding what has happened on a given system, and warning banners may be required in some jurisdictions in order to prosecute an individual successfully under local computer crime statutes. So take care to configure system logging and system warning banners appropriately.

NOTES

Logging

Logging

Unix systems provide several different styles of logging. Most of this section is devoted to a discussion of the standard Unix Syslog facility and information on managing the logs written by the Syslog daemon, `syslogd`. However, we also will look at other common logging options, including "system accounting" and "process accounting," that can help administrators gain a deeper understanding of what is happening on their systems.

Before looking at specific types of logging available to the administrator, though, let's first examine why logging is so critical and cover some high-level guidelines for good logging practices.

NOTES

Why is Logging Important?

Cliff Stoll's discovery of a $0.75 accounting error leads to international investigation

- Good logging practices:
  - Gather all the info you can
  - Use automated analysis/reporting tools
  - Log to multiple machines when possible

SANS Security Essentials – Unix Security

The Importance of Good Logging

Logging is very much about the old "What if the tree falls in the forest, and there is nobody around to hear?" syndrome. System problems and break-ins may occur without any obvious errors or other symptoms being apparent to the system's users or administrators. Only after the system's logs are reviewed do the trouble signs become apparent.

Of course, overworked administrators rarely have time to do a good job of reviewing the system log files on all of the machines for which they are responsible. Also, there is the tendency to become bored with the review process and simply miss critical items in the system logs. So one of the important tenets of good log administration is to shift the burden of reviewing the logs onto an automated program like Swatch or LogSentry (freely available at `http://www.psionic.com/products/logsentry.html`). These programs will monitor system logs automatically and report only the "interesting" events to the system administrator.

As attackers become increasingly sophisticated, they also are becoming more adept at modifying system logs to cover their tracks. Another important principal of good logging practice is that the system administrator should log as much information as possible, even information that is not directly security-related, like system usage and performance metrics. This makes it more difficult for an attacker to hide all of the evidence of his exploits and may "trip up" an inexperienced attacker who may be unfamiliar with local logging policies and procedures.

This point is driven home in Cliff Stoll's book, *The Cuckoo's Egg*. Cliff describes his electronic pursuit of a person who had been breaking into systems all over the world. These break-ins had gone completely undetected until one of Cliff's systems which was running a special proprietary accounting software package in order to charge users for time sharing resources detected a seventy five cent discrepancy in one of the monthly reports. Cliff's research into this apparent "bug" in the accounting system set off an entire chain of deductions that ultimately led to a major law enforcement investigation, arrest, and incarceration.

NOTES

Multiple Machines? Why?

- An attacker who subverts your system can remove evidence from local files
- Having a second copy of the logs on a secure machine allows you to find "diffs"
- Central log server lets you notice probes against multiple machines
- Don't lose information when a single machine's disk crashes

SANS Security Essentials – Unix Security

The final rule for good logging is to log information to multiple systems wherever possible. Attackers who break into a system and gain administrative access can modify any file on the system. In particular, the attackers are going to be motivated to remove any traces of their break-in from the system logs. Even if the break-in is detected, the administrator may not have enough information to figure out how the break-in was accomplished. This means it is going to be much harder to lock the attackers out of systems in the future.

Now suppose that the logging information was kept not only on the local system but also on a central "log server" machine. The system administrator now can go to that central log server, extract the logs which came from the compromised machine, and then compare that copy of the logs with the logs on the compromised system. Unix has a program called `diff`, which will display only the lines that are different between two files—in this case, the "different" lines would be exactly those log entries that the attacker thought were important enough to delete! These are, of course, precisely the entries the administrator wants to see.

Another bonus from centralized logging is that the administrator may be able to see "patterns" that affect the entire computing infrastructure. For example, the TCP Wrappers logs from all machines on the network, when collected together in one place, may show that somebody is probing the `telnet` port on all of the local systems. Possibly this is some sort of a network mapping attack prior to an active attack on the machines.

The central log server should be a very secure machine to which only a small number of administrators have access. Obviously, the machine will require a lot of disk storage, and perhaps even a RAID array for reliability.

Syslog

- syslogd runs as a daemon and accepts messages from local programs
- syslogd can also listen on port 514/udp for messages from other machines
- Final destination of messages is controlled in /etc/syslog.conf

SANS Security Essentials – Unix Security

Syslog

Syslog is the standard Unix logging mechanism. The Syslog daemon, syslogd, is started at boot time to receive logging messages from other processes on the system and redistribute them to various local log files. Messages even can be forwarded to remote systems, displayed on users' terminal windows, or sent to specific system devices (such as a serial port that has a printer attached to it).

The Syslog daemon generally will listen for incoming messages on two different channels. For messages within the system, syslogd reads from a special device called /dev/log (which technically is an object called a "Unix domain socket" rather than a normal kernel device). syslogd also can listen on UDP port 514 for messages from other systems. In addition to receiving messages from other machines, syslogd is capable of sending its own messages to other systems and even forwarding messages from one system to another.

It should be noted, however, that syslogd happily will accept messages from any source, without any sort of authentication. One denial-of-service attack is to fill up a system's logging partition with bogus messages. This can help an attacker hide her real activity from the administrator. Be sure that your corporate firewall blocks external connections on UDP port 514.

The only system(s) that should be listening for Syslog messages from the network are your central log server(s). On many Unix systems, on the one hand, the default behavior for syslogd is to listen on UDP port 514, and you may not be able to disable this "feature." On the other hand, the syslogd that ships with RedHat systems actually requires a special option be set to enable listening on UDP port 514 for messages from other systems. The administrator must add the -r option to the SYSLOGD_OPTIONS variable in /etc/sysconfig/syslog—this is **not** enabled by default. Then the Syslog daemon must be restarted (/etc/init.d/syslog restart).

In the Syslog universe, every log message is tagged with a "facility" value that describes to what aspect of the system the message applies (a message from the system kernel, the cron daemon, the e-mail system, etc.) and a "priority" value that gives the severity of the message. The Syslog configuration file, /etc/syslog.conf, uses these facility/priority pairs to decide on the final destination of each message. Let's examine these concepts in more detail to understand how to configure the Syslog subsystem.

NOTES

NOTES

Message Facilities

- kern – kernel errors
- user – messages from user processes
- mail – messages from mail servers
- cron – messages from cron/at jobs
- daemon – other system daemons
- auth – authentication warnings
- authpriv – "private" auth info *[Linux]*
- local[0-7] – other services as needed

SANS Security Essentials – Unix Security

Facility and Priority

Common Syslog Message Facilities

kern - kernel errors

user - messages from user processes

mail - messages from mail servers

cron - messages from cron/at jobs

daemon - other system daemons

auth - authentication warnings

authpriv - "private" auth info [Linux only]

local[0-7] - other services as needed

Syslog defines several different message facilities. The most common ones are listed above, but other facility names may be defined, as well (man syslog.conf for more information). A given process defines what facility it will use when it opens up communications with syslogd—i.e., the facility that the program uses is entirely up to the application developer—but certain conventions exist.

The kern facility is used for messages from the system kernel—these messages often are important. Older e-mail servers tended to use the user facility for sending Syslog messages but now use the mail facility. Most user messages can be ignored, but messages sent to the mail facility should be captured for debugging the mail system. The daemon facility is used by other system daemons (named, NTP, etc.) except for cron, which has its own special Syslog facility. auth is used by programs that are part of the Unix authentication system—login and su, for example. These messages are very important, but some Unix systems (notably Solaris) are not configured to capture these messages by default. Linux also has added a non-standard authpriv facility for security messages that are sensitive ("private") and only should be written to files that are not readable by normal users.

The local0, ..., local7 facilities are reserved for use by programs written locally at a given site. However, many vendors have co-opted these facilities for their own purposes. For example, by default Cisco routers with Syslog logging enabled will log on the local7 facility. RedHat uses local7 for capturing system boot messages. System administrators often are surprised when they start capturing messages from one of these facilities because all of a sudden they start "seeing" messages of which they were completely unaware!

Message Priorities

`emerg` – system is unusable
`alert` – take action immediately
`crit` – critical condition
`err` – general error condition
`warn` – system warnings
`notice` – normal but significant condition
`info` – "FYI" or informational messages
`debug` – debugging output

SANS Security Essentials – Unix Security

Syslog Message Priorities

`emerg` – system is unusable

`alert` – take action immediately

`crit` – critical condition

`err` – general error condition

`warn` – system warnings

`notice` – normal but significant condition

`info` – "FYI" or informational messages

`debug` – debugging output

In addition to the various Syslog facilities, there are eight defined Syslog priority levels, shown here in descending order of severity. Unfortunately, strong conventions have not been established as far as what constitutes, say, an "emergency" versus a "critical condition," so these descriptions are at best suggestions. Not every programmer follows these guidelines religiously, so deciding what level of messages to log often is a matter of intuition on the part of the administrator. `emerg`, `err`, `notice`, and `info` probably are the most commonly used priorities.

NOTES

NOTES

/etc/syslog.conf

```
# Log all kernel messages to the console.
kern.*                              /dev/console

# Log anything (except mail) of level info or higher.
# Don't log private authentication messages!
*.info;mail.none;authpriv.none      /var/log/messages

# The authpriv file has restricted access.
authpriv.*                          /var/log/secure

# Everybody gets emergency messages
*.emerg                             *

# Save boot messages also to boot.log
local7.*                            /var/log/boot.log
```

SANS Security Essentials – Unix Security

The syslog.conf *File*

The `/etc/syslog.conf` file is written in two columns. The first column is a semi-colon delimited list of facility/priority combinations, and the second column is where messages that match those parameters should be sent.

It is critical to remember two things when editing the `syslog.conf` file:

- It is absolutely **imperative** that the whitespace between the two columns is made up of **tab** characters only. If not, then the file will not be parsed correctly, and no logging at all may be done. One common mistake is doing a cut'n'paste operation from an example file in one window to a file being edited in another window—the cut'n'paste operation usually transforms the tabs into spaces, causing significant problems.
- Syslog logs all messages for the given facility **at the listed priority and higher**. If the administrator specifies `auth.info`, for example, then all `auth` messages of `info` priority and above will be logged to the location given in the `syslog.conf` entry. Actually, the Linux Syslog daemon allows the administrator to use the special `auth.=info` syntax in `syslog.conf` to say "only log `auth.info` messages and no higher priorities."

This is very non-standard and normally not implemented by the Syslog daemon on other Unix systems.

Here is a sample `syslog.conf` file that resembles the one commonly found on RedHat systems:

```
# Log all kernel messages to the console.
kern.*          /dev/console

# Log anything (except mail) of level info or higher.
# Don't log private authentication messages!
*.info;mail.none;authpriv.none     /var/log/messages

# The authpriv file has restricted access.
authpriv.*      /var/log/secure

# Everybody gets emergency messages on their tty
*.emerg         *

# Save boot messages also to boot.log
local7.*        /var/log/boot.log
```

NOTES

Facilities may be specified with a wildcard ("*"), and `<facility>.none` may be used to suppress messages from certain facilities when a wildcard is specified. Notice in the example above that `mail.none` is used to suppress messages from the mail system, and `authpriv.none` is used so that private security messages do not go into the common log files. Also as shown above, wildcards can be used for priority values, although specifying `<facility>.debug` accomplishes the same thing since Syslog usually logs messages of the specified priority and higher to the specified destination.

The most common destination for log messages is a local file on the system. However, messages may be sent to a device: in the example above, messages from the kernel are being sent to `/dev/console`, which will cause each message to appear on the system's console terminal. The administrator also might connect a printer to one of the system's serial devices and send log messages to that device in order to capture a hard-copy log automatically. Messages also may be sent to another machine using the `@<hostname>` or `@<ipaddr>` syntax. Hostnames are more convenient since the administrator will not have to modify `syslog.conf` every time the IP address of the log host changes, but IP addresses are more secure since DNS can be spoofed to redirect logs erroneously. Messages also can be sent to the terminal of a particular user, if that user happens to be logged in at the time. In the example above, emergency messages are being sent to all ("*") users on the system, but the file also could list an individual user, such as `root` or the system administrator's account.

Since this example is based on an excerpt from `syslog.conf` from an actual RedHat system, it is worth noting that this configuration could be improved in a couple of respects. First, it seems like a good idea to log both `authpriv.*` **and** `auth.*` to `/var/log/secure`. Also, the administrator may want to suppress `authpriv.emerg` messages from being written to all users' terminals—use "`*.emerg;authpriv.none`" in the example above.

NOTES

Alternate syslog.conf Idea

```
kern.*          /var/log/kern
kern.*          @loghost

auth.*          /var/log/auth
auth.*          @loghost

mail.*          /var/log/mail
mail.*          @loghost

daemon.*        /var/log/daemon
daemon.*        @loghost
```

[... continue pattern for other facilities ...]

SANS Security Essentials – Unix Security

In this example, all messages sent to a given facility are logged to a separate log file for that specific facility. Those messages also are transmitted to a central machine named `loghost`.

It is also worth pointing out that Syslog allows the administrator to send the same message(s) to multiple different destinations. And remember that one of the principles of good logging is to log messages to a local file on the system and to a remote log server as well.

For this reason, some sites choose to go with a somewhat simpler `syslog.conf` file:

```
kern.*          /var/log/kern
kern.*          @loghost
auth.*          /var/log/auth
auth.*          @loghost
daemon.*        /var/log/daemon
daemon.*        @loghost
[… continue pattern for other facilities …]
```

Other syslogd Notes

- pkill -HUP syslogd after modifying syslog.conf file
- syslogd will not create new files– create empty files before restarting

SANS Security Essentials – Unix Security

Administering Syslog

Whenever a change is made to syslog.conf, the administrator must send the running syslogd process a "hang up" (HUP) signal, similar to the procedure covered in the last chapter for making changes to inetd.conf. On RedHat systems, the administrator simply can pkill -HUP syslogd. On other systems that do not have a pkill command, the administrator must use ps, grep, and kill:

```
# ps -ef | grep syslogd
  root   212     1  0   May 02 ?     0:00
syslogd -m 0
  root  8666  8121  0 10:50:10 pts/2 0:00
grep syslogd
# kill -HUP 212
```

Aside from re-reading its configuration file, syslogd also will close any log files it may be writing to and re-open all files listed in /etc/syslog.conf. It is important to note that syslogd will not create new log files if they do not exist—the messages which would be sent to these non-existent log files simply will be discarded. Thus, it may be necessary to create an empty log file before restarting syslogd, if a new log file destination has been added in syslog.conf. Empty files can be created on a Unix system with either the touch <filename> or cp /dev/null <filename> commands.

NOTES

NOTES

"Rotate" Log Files!

- Syslog will happily append data to a log file until the disk fills up
- Need to "rotate" files regularly:
  - Move current file to new name
  - Create new empty log file
  - Restart `syslogd`
  - Optionally `compress`/`gzip` old log file
- "Standard" tends to be weekly rotation, keeping the previous four weeks

SANS Security Essentials – Unix Security

"Rotating" Log Files

Syslog will continue accepting messages and writing data to log files until told to do otherwise or until the file system fills up, at which point any new log messages are discarded. It is, therefore, extremely important to "rotate" log files on a regular basis, meaning move the old log file aside, and start a new one. Then the old log file can be compressed and/or moved to off-line storage.

While different sites have different needs depending on how much data they log, available disk space, etc., the "standard" schedule usually is rotating log files weekly and keeping the last four weeks of previous log information on-line. Sites often simply will throw away older logs, though some sites have procedural or even legal reasons to keep log files for longer periods of time—years in some cases.

Note that there is a "correct" procedure that should be followed to rotate a log file so that data is not lost during the switch:

1. Use the Unix `mv` command to rename the current log file. The standard convention is to move `<logfile>` to `<logfile>.0`—the old `<logfile>.0` is renamed `<logfile>.1` beforehand, etc. The `mv` command is used because renaming the file in this way does not impact the `syslogd` process that is still writing data to the file.
2. Create a new empty `<logfile>`
3. Send the `HUP` signal to the `syslogd` process. This causes `syslogd` to stop writing and close the connection to the old log file—the one that was renamed with the `mv` command. `syslogd` then opens `<logfile>`, which is, of course, the new empty log file that was just created.

Doing things in this fashion means that no logging information will be lost during the switchover. Of course, performing this process manually is both time-consuming and error-prone. Having a tool that automatically rotates system logs is a huge boon to administrators.

There are a number of free scripts and tools that will rotate log files appropriately available on the Internet—a Web search for "rotate logs" will turn up many different options. Vendors also are starting to include log rotation programs with their operating systems. For example, Sun is incorporating their `logadm` tool for managing logs into Solaris 9.

NOTES

RedHat logrotate

- logrotate run from /etc/cron.daily
- Config file is /etc/logrotate.conf
  - Sets frequency, number of logs to keep
  - Choose compression here if desired
- Logfile configs in /etc/logrotate.d
  - Which files to rotate
  - Pre- and post-rotation commands to run
  - Override defaults from logrotate.conf

SANS Security Essentials – Unix Security

RedHat ships with a program called logrotate that already is set up to do rotation on the standard log files used by the RedHat system. If logging is started in another location, though, the administrator will need to make sure to rotate the new log file regularly.

logrotate is set up to run out of cron as part of the regular cron.daily task list. Even though logrotate is being run daily, it does not necessarily rotate the log files each time it is run. The /etc/logrotate.conf file sets a default frequency for rotating the log files, though this can be overridden for specific files. logrotate.conf allows the administrator to set other defaults, such as whether the old log file should be compressed to save space.

For each individual log file to be rotated, there also is a configuration file entry in the /etc/logrotate.d directory. These configuration files can override the default values from logrotate.conf. The per-log-file configuration entries also can specify any special commands that need to be run before or after the log files are rotated. For example, files being written by Syslog require the administrator to HUP the syslogd process, but files written by the Apache Web server require restarting the Web server to open the new log files. The administrator also might want to run some sort of usage reporting script on the old Apache log file before compressing it—triggering this reporting script also could be set up in the logrotate configuration file for the Web server logs.

NOTES

Security Issues with Syslog

- Denial of service:
  - Anybody can spam your Syslog port
  - Overwhelm daemon, fill up logging area
  - Block access to 514/udp
- Buffer overflows:
  - Potential remote root compromise
  - Can be triggered via other apps and without direct system access by attacker

SANS Security Essentials – Unix Security

Syslog Security Issues

As mentioned earlier, one of the biggest problems with Syslog is that it will accept messages over the network from any host that is able to reach the Syslog port (UDP port 514) on the local system. This means that an attacker can continuously send a large volume of messages at the Syslog daemon non-stop until either the daemon is overwhelmed and cannot log any other messages or until the partition where the logging is happening fills up. Make sure that network firewalls block outside access to UDP port 514. If the vendor provides `syslogd` option to prevent the daemon from listening on UDP port 514 entirely, then make use of that option in addition to employing network-based firewalls.

The Syslog daemon has a history of buffer overflow problems (for specific examples, search the BUGTRAQ archives or Mitre CVE database for "syslog"). One fact that makes Syslog buffer overflow issues so dangerous is that an attacker need not have direct network access to the system whose Syslog daemon is being compromised. For example, Sendmail logs a plethora of data via Syslog—an attacker may be able to construct an e-mail message, send it to an internal mail server behind an organization's firewall, and trigger a buffer overflow in Syslog via the message logged by Sendmail about the attacker's message! It is critical to keep up-to-date on vendor patches for `syslogd` to help avoid exposure to these buffer overflow issues.

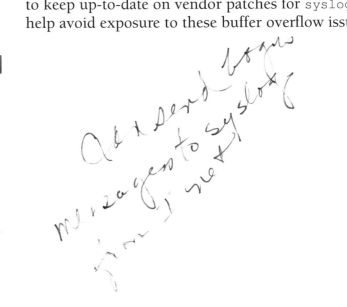

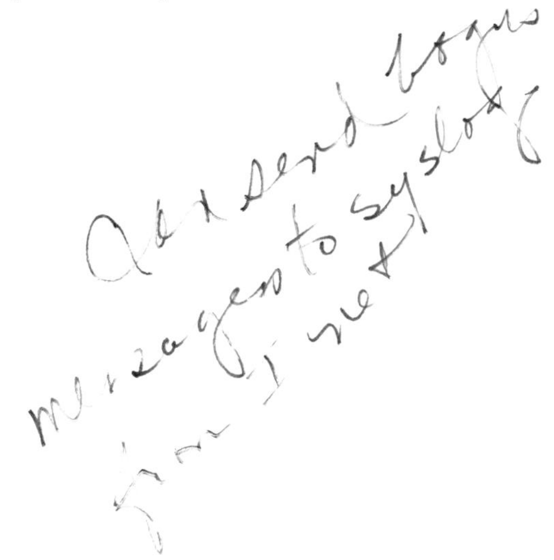

NOTES

System Accounting

- Gathers data on system resource usage:
  - CPU and memory utilization, paging
  - Disk and file I/O, TTY activity
  - System calls, semaphore activity, ...
- Useful for performance tuning, capacity planning, justifying new hardware
- Detect intruders due to unexpected departures from system "baseline"

SANS Security Essentials – Unix Security

System Accounting

System accounting was developed primarily as a performance-monitoring tool for Unix systems. When system accounting is enabled, every 10 or 20 minutes a `cron` job runs (depending on the particular Unix OS) that collects statistics on system parameters, such as CPU utilization, memory usage, and disk I/O. This data is archived into daily log files that can be queried interactively by the system administrator. Nightly summary reports also are produced automatically.

From a performance-monitoring perspective, this data gives the system administrator an historical view of the performance curve of the system. Administrators can use the data to provide system performance metrics to management and justify additional hardware resources required to avoid anticipated system bottlenecks. The data also may reveal system bottlenecks that can be fixed easily—for example, a frequently accessed file or file system on a slow disk drive could be moved to a faster disk or "striped" file system to improve performance.

From a security perspective, system accounting provides a baseline for the "normal" performance curve of the system. If the system deviates from this baseline, that may be an indication of malicious activity on the system.

For example, suppose a system's CPU runs at about 60% utilization every day, from 8am to 7pm, and then drops back to nothing outside of business hours, except for a brief spike during the system's normal backup window. One morning, the system administrator looks at the previous day's performance report and notices a second CPU spike outside of normal business hours. Maybe that "extra" spike was a denial-of-service attack that was part of an IP spoofing attack, or a "smurf" attack in progress, or an attacker running a password-cracking program on the system. Like Cliff Stoll and his 75 cent accounting error, relatively small departures from the "normal" performance curve for a system may indicate larger problems.

NOTES

System Accounting for RedHat

- Enabled automatically when you install the `sysstat` RPM
- `/usr/lib/sa/sa1` run every 10 minutes to collect data
- `/usr/lib/sa/sa2` run from `cron.daily` to produce nightly reports
- Data archived in `/var/log/sa`–removed automatically after one week!

SANS Security Essentials – Unix Security

System Accounting Under RedHat

System accounting is enabled automatically on RedHat systems by installing the `sysstat` RPM. This RPM is on the RedHat install media and can be downloaded from `redhat.com`. More work may be required to enable system accounting on other operating systems. For example, Solaris requires the administrator to load the `SUNWaccr` and `SUNWaccu` packages (if not installed already) and do some manual configuration. HP-UX systems usually have the system accounting tools installed by default, but administrator intervention is required to enable accounting.

The data collection script for system accounting under RedHat is `/usr/lib/sa/sa1` (possibly other path names on other Unix systems). It is run every 10 minutes via `cron`, as configured by the `/etc/cron.d/sysstat` file. Data collected by this script is stored in files under `/var/log/sa` called sa<dd>, where <dd> is the day of the month. One data file for a 24-hour period is about 140K—roughly a megabyte of data per week.

The `/usr/lib/sa/sa2` script is run nightly from `cron` per the `/etc/cron.daily/sysstat` file. This script generates the nightly report file /var/log/sa/sar<dd>, where again <dd> is the day of the month. Nightly report files are roughly 185K in size (or another 1.25MB/week) but compress very well for archiving.

Note that the `sa2` script also removes all data files and nightly report files that are older than one week from `/var/log/sa`. It often is useful to keep this data around longer than one week. In fact, some sites archive this data for years in order to do long-term trend analysis on system performance data. The system administrator must manually set up some process to archive this data into another directory, however. Even if the `sa2` script were prevented from removing files, the files would still be overwritten on a monthly cycle because the file names are only differentiated by the day of the month.

NOTES

Dealing with Data

- Data written in binary format– use `sar` command to produce text reports
- How to produce graphs/charts from `sar`:
  - Import into spreadsheet
  - Use `gnuplot` or other Unix utility
  - Some systems also provide `sag` utility
- Will need to develop some archiving scheme to keep data longer than a week

SANS Security Essentials – Unix Security

Using System Accounting Data

The system accounting data files are written in a binary format that is not easily interpreted by the standard Unix text manipulation tools like `awk` and Perl. The `sar` command can be used to query the accounting files and produce text reports, however, which later can be parsed by other tools. Charts and graphs can be produced either by importing the output of `sar` into a spreadsheet or by feeding this output into a utility like `gnuplot` (for more information see `http://www.ucc.ie/gnuplot/gnuplot.html`).

Some Unix systems, notably Solaris, also ship with a utility called `sag` that can produce on-screen graphs from system accounting data. However, the `sag` tool must be run inside a window (such as an `xterm`) that is capable of emulating a graphics terminal, such as a Tektronix device.

NOTES

Process Accounting

- Kernel can log data about every process that runs on the system
- Can be selectively enabled and disabled:

```
# /sbin/accton /var/log/pacct
# cd /log/adm
# ls -l pacct
-rw-r--r--    1 adm    adm      64 May 12 11:41 pacct
# lastcomm
ls         root   stdin    0.01 secs Sun May 12 11:41
# ls -l pacct
-rw-r--r--    1 adm    adm     192 May 19 11:42 pacct
# /sbin/accton
```

SANS Security Essentials – Unix Security

Process Accounting

Process accounting is a mechanism originally developed for time-sharing Unix systems to allow system owners to do charge-backs based on system resource usage. When process accounting is enabled, every command that executes on the system is logged, along with the username of the user who started the process, the controlling terminal device, and other metrics like the amount of CPU and memory consumed and the amount of disk (and other) I/O.

While the CPU, memory, and I/O information is not particularly useful from a security perspective, having a log of all of the commands run by all of the users on the system is an obvious win. However, only the command names are logged—neither the full path name of the command nor the command line arguments are preserved. So the administrators know that a given user ran a program called `vi`, but they do not know if the user was editing an innocuous file or some critical system configuration file, or even running a password-cracking program that the user had simply renamed `vi`. Of course, in this latter case, looking at the CPU utilization metrics probably will reveal that something strange is happening because password crackers consume enormous amounts of CPU, and editors normally do not.

To utilize process accounting under RedHat, the administrator must install the `psacct` RPM. Process accounting can be turned on and off at will using the `/sbin/accton` command. `accton <filename>` starts process accounting and puts the logged data in the `<filename>` specified—if no `<filename>` is specified, then the default `/var/log/pact` is used. Running `accton` a second time turns off process accounting. Note that if `/sbin/accton` is installed, then RedHat enables process accounting automatically at boot time via the `/etc/rc.d/rc.sysinit` script.

Once process accounting is enabled, the kernel logs 64 bytes of data for each process that runs to completion on the system. As with system accounting, process accounting data is written in a binary format. Text output can be retrieved with the `lastcomm` command, which allows the administrator to search for specific commands, all commands run by a specific user, or all commands executed on a particular terminal device.

Note that Solaris and HP-UX machines use a command called `acctcom`, rather than `lastcomm`, for viewing process accounting data. These systems also provide other commands for analyzing this data, generating charge-back reports, etc. See the `accton` manual page on these systems for more information.

NOTES

Warnings

- Process accounting can cause a 10-20% percent performance degradation
- 64 bytes of data logged per process– this can be a lot of data on some hosts
- Process accounting *enabled by default* under RedHat 7.x
- Data is logged when process finishes– some processes may not be logged

SANS Security Essentials – Unix Security

64 bytes of data may not seem like a lot until one considers running process accounting on a Web server or another system that does millions of transactions per day. Also note that simply logging the data can cause significant (10-20%) performance degradation on the system. In particular, the disk that is the logging device becomes a "hot-spot" in the file system; therefore, make sure this log is on a fast disk, striped file system, or perhaps even a "silicon disk."

Remember that if the `psacct` RPM is installed, RedHat systems enable process accounting by default. Since many sites end up installing this RPM, they may end up incurring an unnecessary performance drain on their systems. Of course, if the site has been running process accounting without noticing the performance impact, then there probably is no reason to disable it. Still, some sites prefer to edit the `rc.sysinit` script to prevent process accounting from being enabled at boot time and only enable it manually if they detect malicious activity on the system. Of course this means that the commands run by attackers before their presence is detected will not be logged.

Also note that process logging only happens when the process terminates. Some processes, such as daemons which only terminate when the system reboots, or even a password-cracking tool which runs forever and never terminates, may never get logged.

NOTES

Other logging

- utmp and wtmp files keep track of logins– query with who/last
- btmp (Linux) keeps track of failed logins– query with lastb
- *Problem with btmp:*
  - Users get "out of sequence" and type their password at the login prompt
  - Clear text password now visible in btmp
  - Remove btmp file to prevent logging entirely

SANS Security Essentials – Unix Security

Login History with utmp, wtmp, and btmp

When a user logs into a Unix system, login records usually are written to the `utmp` and `wtmp` files, which are found in `/var/log` on most Unix systems (but in `/var/adm` on Solaris and HP-UX). Note that there is no mandatory or automatic mechanism in the operating system for forcing `utmp` and `wtmp` logging—the application developer must manually choose to implement it. For this reason, some login sessions may not be logged to the `utmp`/`wtmp` files, but the "standard" Unix login mechanisms—`login`, `telnet`, `rlogin`, SSH, etc.—generally update the `utmp` and `wtmp` files properly for each login.

NOTES

Sample `last` Output

```
$ last
pomeranz  pts/10  associates.deer- Wed May  1 15:46   still logged in
albert    pts/23  bullwinkle.deer- Wed May  1 15:31   still logged in
randy     pts/10  buck.deer-run.co Wed May  1 15:29 - 15:37  (00:07)
gale      pts/33  216.15.51.198    Wed May  1 15:09 - 15:09  (00:00)
che       pts/1   moose.deer-run.c Wed May  1 15:03   still logged in
mason     pts/23  caribou.deer-run Wed May  1 14:59 - 15:19  (00:20)
helen     pts/21  faun.deer-run.co Wed May  1 14:53   still logged in
helen     pts/29  faun.deer-run.co Wed May  1 14:50   still logged in
josh      pts/32  206.82.40.251    Wed May  1 14:48   still logged in
mary      pts/24  doe.deer-run.com Wed May  1 14:40   still logged in
cathy     pts/24  elk.deer-run.com Wed May  1 14:29 - 14:38  (00:08)
cathy     pts/24  elk.deer-run.com Wed May  1 14:24 - 14:25  (00:00)
```
[... output goes on and on ...]

SANS Security Essentials – Unix Security

The `utmp` file is a record of the users currently logged into the system. The file is written in a binary format but can be viewed with the `who` and `finger` commands. The `wtmp` file is a record of all logins to the system. The contents of this file can be viewed with the `last` command.

RedHat systems also can keep track of failed login attempts in the `btmp` file (this functionality is not widely implemented in other Unix systems). Note that users sometimes get "out of sequence" and end up typing their password into the username portion of the login. Since the `btmp` file stores the username that the user tried to log in with, the `btmp` file often ends up containing the clear text passwords for some users, which is an obvious security problem. Simply removing the `/var/log/btmp` file stops the system from keeping these logs. The contents of the `btmp` file can be viewed with the `lastb` command.

NOTES

Higher Levels of Logging

- Solaris/HP-UX allow "kernel-level" auditing
- Every system call can be logged:
  - Can show *exactly* what has happened on host
  - Enormous amounts of data must be dealt with
  - Potential system performance impact
  - No good tools for analyzing audit trail
- Must be enabled manually by admin
- Some "fine-tuning" required

SANS Security Essentials – Unix Security

Higher Levels of Logging

To meet US Government security standards at the so-called "C2" level or above, higher levels of logging and audit trail are required for systems. While this level of logging is not available for RedHat systems, Solaris and HP-UX both provide very high levels of audit logging at the kernel level.

When this level of logging is enabled, the system kernel is capable of logging every system call invoked by any and all processes on the system. While the administrator is able to specify exactly which system calls are "interesting" enough to be logged, even minimal logging can result in huge audit log files in a very short amount of time. Dealing with this data and archiving it for extended periods of time are difficult issues. And, like process accounting, simply logging this much information for each process on the system can be a performance drain on the machine.

For these reasons, this level of auditing is not enabled by default under either Solaris or HP-UX. On Solaris, the administrator must run the `/etc/security/bsmconv` script to enable auditing. HP-UX systems must be converted to "trusted mode" with the `/usr/lbin/tsconvert` command before auditing can be enabled.

Turning on kernel-level auditing can have unexpected consequences for the system—under Solaris, enabling kernel-level auditing disables the auto-mounting of CD-ROMs and floppy disks, and "trusted mode" under HP-UX disables NIS support. For more information on kernel-level auditing and related issues, consult the appropriate vendor documentation.

So far we have examined the various types of logging that are available on Unix systems. Now we turn our attention to presenting appropriate warning banners to users of the system. Note that in some jurisdictions, administrators are required to warn potential users that logging is taking place.

NOTES

Warning Banners

SANS Security Essentials – Unix Security

Warning Banners

The subject of warning banners— whether they should be used, where they should be used, and what their content should be—actually provokes enormous debate in the security community. Part of the reason for this confusion is that the legal ramifications of various sorts of warning banners have yet to be clearly defined in the law in most areas of the world.

It is important somebody with appropriate legal training review any warning banners for their appropriateness in the local jurisdiction. The warning banners also should conform with site policies and guidelines. One size definitely does not fit all here.

NOTES

Why?

- Possible legal ramifications:
  - Having "Welcome" in a login message is thought to be a bad idea
  - May need to warn people about their expectations of privacy
- Also replaces default banners which disclose OS version, hostname, etc.

SANS Security Essentials – Unix Security

The Content of Warning Banners

Various organizations and individuals have attempted to encapsulate what should go into a well-written warning banner. For example, the US Department of Defense (DoD) has issued a memo that all warning banners should at least include:

- The name of the organization which owns the system;
- The fact that the system is subject to monitoring;
- That such monitoring is in compliance with local statutes;
- That use of the system implies consent to such monitoring.

The concern is that in some areas of the world, monitoring and logging are not permissible without the consent of the parties being monitored—in this case, the users of the system. Monitoring without consent may mean that any evidence collected as a result of the monitoring may be inadmissible. In some cases, monitoring without consent actually can get the organization or individual system administrator doing the monitoring into legal hot water!

The site also may want to indicate in its warning banners that evidence of unauthorized use of the system may be reported to law enforcement agencies. The site also may want to add a note to the effect that unauthorized use will be prosecuted vigorously.

There is some amount of debate about having the world "welcome" appear in login banners. Some have argued that the word "welcome" somehow implies that the organization is giving free rein to anybody who wants to come at your system. While this interpretation seems far-fetched, it probably is a good idea to drop "welcome" and other similar greetings from login banners.

The default login banners used by many OS utilities often display the OS name, version number, and/or host name. Replacing these banners with locally developed messages can help hide this information from potential attackers. On the other hand, tools like Nmap allow remote attackers to discover the OS type and version number of the local system without looking at the system login banners, so this is a relatively minor security enhancement.

NOTES

US DoJ Warning Message

```
This system is for the use of authorized users only.
Individuals using this computer system without authority, or in
excess of their authority, are subject to having all of their
activities on this system monitored and recorded by system
personnel.

In the course of monitoring individuals improperly using this
system, or in the course of system maintenance, the activities
of authorized users may also be monitored.

Anyone using this system expressly consents to such monitoring
and is advised that if such monitoring reveals possible
evidence of criminal activity, system personnel may provide the
evidence of such monitoring to law enforcement officials.
```

SANS Security Essentials – Unix Security

Sample Warning Banners

The warning banner shown here originally was developed by the US Department of Justice (DoJ) but now is used widely by many different organizations. This message lays out several important precepts:

- The system is for authorized uses only—this means authorized users doing the things that they are supposed to be doing on the system and nothing else. Not only are unauthorized users not welcome, but so are authorized users using the system "in excess of their authority."
- Per the DoD guidelines, the warning tells people that authorized and unauthorized uses of the system may be monitored. Use of the system implies consent to this monitoring.

US DoJ Warning Banner

This system is for the use of authorized users only. Individuals using this computer system without authority, or in excess of their authority, are subject to having all of their activities on this system monitored and recorded by system personnel.

In the course of monitoring, individuals improperly using this system, or in the course of system maintenance, the activities of authorized users also may be monitored.

Anyone using this system expressly consents to such monitoring and is advised that if such monitoring reveals possible evidence of criminal activity, system personnel may provide the evidence of such monitoring to law enforcement officials.

- Any of the data that is collected can be shared with law enforcement officials under the appropriate circumstances.

This seems to cover most of the important bases, though it is rather verbose.

NOTES

The Short Form

Authorized uses only.
All activity may be monitored and reported.

Sometimes a message that fits on an 80-character line is desirable. A shorter message that conveys the gist of the US DoJ message shown here might be:

```
Authorized uses only.  All activity may be
monitored and reported.
```

Note the first sentence is "Authorized **uses** only," not "users." This is an attempt to cover both the case of unauthorized users as well as authorized users exceeding their authority.

Again, always check with your local legal counsel and site security officer before adopting either of these warning messages.

NOTES

Where to Put This Warning?

/etc/motd – Only displayed *after* login

/etc/issue – Displayed before local logins

/etc/issue.net – Displayed before telnet login prompt *[Linux only!]*

Don't forget about GUI login screens!

SANS Security Essentials – Unix Security

How to Display Warning Banners

There are several standard places where these warning messages can be displayed. The /etc/motd ("message of the day") file is displayed to users **after** they log in. Experts generally agree that it is much more important to display these banners **before** the user (or attacker) gets the opportunity to login.

Most Unix systems have an /etc/issue file which is displayed before the login prompt on the system console or a physical serial line (like when connecting via a terminal or modem). RedHat systems also use another file called /etc/issue.net, which is displayed before logins via the telnet application. Similarly, in the SSH server configuration file, sshd_config, the administrator can set the Banner option to the name of a file containing a warning banner. RedHat systems set this to /etc/issue.net by default.

Another place to put these warning messages is on the standard console GUI login screen. The generic software for displaying these login screens is an application called xdm. The administrator can set the warning string with the xlogin*greeting parameter in the system's Xresources file. This file can be in one of many different directories, depending on the operating system, but common directories include /etc/X11/xdm, /usr/lib/X11, or /usr/dt/config.

Linux systems generally will use either a GNOME or KDE login service instead of xdm. For GNOME, set the warning banner via the Welcome parameter in /etc/X11/gdm/gdm.config. For KDE set GreetString in the system kdmrc file, which could be /etc/X11/xdm/kdrmrc, /usr/share/config/kdmrc, or /usr/share/config/kdm/kdmrc, depending on the version of Linux being used.

It probably is appropriate to go ahead and set the warning banner in all of these files, even the /etc/motd file. This covers all the bases, in case any of these login services gets enabled at any time, and /etc/motd provides some level of warning when it is not possible to provide a warning prior to login.

NOTES

What About Other Net Services?

- `xinetd` has built-in banner option
- TCP Wrappers can display banners

- Problems:
  - Need to be careful that banner doesn't interfere with normal protocol
  - Banner must be formatted appropriately

SANS Security Essentials – Unix Security

Banners for Network Login Services

While RedHat supports `/etc/issue.net`, other Unix systems generally do not have a built-in mechanism for displaying warning banners prior to telnet logins. Even RedHat does not supply a mechanism for supplying warnings for other networked login services like FTP and `rlogin`.

The one thing that is common to all of these networked login services is that they are started by `inetd` or `xinetd` (depending, of course, on which daemon the OS vendor chooses to supply). `xinetd` has built-in support for displaying banners. If the system uses `inetd`, then TCP Wrappers can be used to display a banner before starting a particular service—even if TCP Wrappers is not being used for IP address-based access control.

NOTES

Deep Wizardry

Luckily, TCP Wrappers package comes with an automated way to make good banners:

```
# cd /usr/share/doc/tcp_wrappers-7.6
# mkdir /etc/banners
# cp Banners.Makefile /etc/banners/Makefile
# cd /etc/banners
# echo 'Authorized uses only…' >prototype
# make
```

SANS Security Essentials – Unix Security

The only difficulty is that different protocols require the banner to be formatted and presented in a particular way, or clients will be unable to connect to the server. And, of course, the format is different for each and every individual login protocol. The good news is that TCP Wrappers comes with an automated mechanism for creating properly formatted banners for `rlogin`, `telnet`, and `ftp`. This mechanism can be used to create appropriate banners, even if the banners end up being displayed by `xinetd` rather than by TCP Wrappers via `inetd`.

The procedure for creating the banners looks like this:

```
# cd /usr/share/doc/tcp_wrappers-7.6
# mkdir /etc/banners
# cp Banners.Makefile /etc/banners/
Makefile
# cd /etc/banners
# echo 'Authorized uses only…' >prototype
# make
```

First the administrator creates a directory called `/etc/banners`, which ultimately will hold the completed banners. The `Banners.Makefile` file is copied into this directory from the TCP Wrappers documentation tree. For non-Linux systems, this file can be found in the TCP Wrappers source distribution. This "`Makefile`" contains Unix commands that will produce the banners automatically.

The text for the warning banner must be put in a file called `prototype` in the `/etc/banners` directory. It probably is best to use a one-line warning message of some sort—longer messages may interfere with some protocols. The `make` command reads the contents of `Makefile` and executes the instructions it finds there. When `make` is finished running, there will be three new files in the directory called `in.rlogind`, `in.telnetd`, and `in.ftpd`. Each file contains the appropriate banner for the given service.

Now the question is how to use these banner files?

NOTES

Using These Banners

- For inetd/TCP Wrappers, in hosts.allow:

```
ALL: 192.168.1.0/255.255.255.0 : banners /etc/banners
```

- Use banner option for xinetd configs:

```
service login
{
    server = /usr/sbin/in.rlogind
    banner = /etc/banners/in.rlogind
    only_from = 192.168.1.0/24
    [...]
```

SANS Security Essentials – Unix Security

For TCP Wrappers, banners can be enabled via the third field in the hosts.allow file:

```
ALL: 192.168.1.0/255.255.255.0 : banners
/etc/banners
```

The banners directive tells tcpd to look in the specified directory (/etc/banners in this example) for a file named for the particular service being accessed. So, if a telnet connection is being attempted, the in.telnetd daemon would be invoked, and TCP Wrappers would look for a banner file called /etc/banners/in.telnetd. If the file exists, then its contents are displayed before TCP Wrappers executes the daemon. If the file does not exist, then TCP Wrappers simply invokes the appropriate daemon without complaining.

For xinetd, simply edit the service configuration file in /etc/xinetd.d and add a line with the banner option:

```
service login
{
    server = /usr/sbin/in.rlogind
    banner = /etc/banners/in.rlogind
    only_from = 192.168.1.0/24
    [... rest of file not shown ...]
```

Note that the full path name of the banner file must be specified. This is different from the TCP Wrappers case, where only the banner directory was specified.

Like /etc/issue.net under RedHat, other OS vendors may have other proprietary mechanisms for displaying warning banners for various services. For example, under Solaris the administrator can set the BANNER option in /etc/default/telnetd and /etc/default/ftpd to display banners for these services. And similar to SSH, some network daemons have their own built-in warning banner mechanisms—such as the Washington University FTP daemon (WU-FTP), which has its own banner option in its standard ftpaccess configuration file. The best advice is to consult the appropriate documentation from both the OS vendor and the software provider(s).

NOTES

Summary: Lessons Learned

- Log as much information as possible–better shot at noticing unexpected activity
- Syslog remote logging:
  - Log to a secure central log server
  - Protect `514/udp` on non-loghost machines
- Display appropriate warning banners *before* logins wherever possible

SANS Security Essentials – Unix Security

Summary

In summary, logging is good, and more logging always is better. Remember the point is to log as much as possible in order to have a better chance of attackers failing to cover all of their tracks. Small clues—like a 75 cent accounting error—may add up when detecting attacks on local systems.

Logging to multiple destinations often is a good idea. Secure, centralized logging provides a backup for data that may have been deleted locally from the compromised system. Also, centralized logging can help spot patterns, like network mapping attacks or concerted attacks against many systems in an enterprise, that would not be detected by just looking at the log files on a single machine.

Syslog can transmit log messages to another system over the network and therefore can be used to relay messages to a remote log server. However, these messages are received and stored by the remote system without any authentication, so an attacker can overwhelm network log servers without too much trouble. If possible, close off the Syslog port (UDP port 514) on systems that are not log servers, and make sure firewalls limit access on this port, particularly from external systems.

Logging and monitoring may require that users be warned of this activity in advance. Displaying warning banners can help set "ground rules" for both authorized and unauthorized system users. Again, be sure to pass these warning banners by local legal counsel and to get them approved for compliance with local policies and procedures by the site security officer or somebody else with authority to approve these messages.

NOTES

Chapter 34

User Access Control

NOTES

NOTES

User Access Control

SANS Security Essentials VI:
Unix Security

NOTES

Quick Look at What's Coming

- Overview of Unix password management
- Passwords for boot process
- Limiting `root` logins to system console
- Disable `.rhosts` support globally

This chapter is devoted to critical issues related to controlling user access to a Unix system. The bulk of the chapter covers the Unix account and password system. Beyond that, however, we will take a look at special precautions necessary for protecting the Unix administrative or "superuser" account. We also will discuss how to guard against local and remote users bypassing the normal user access restrictions on the system, including how to protect the system boot process from abuse by unauthorized individuals who have physical access to the system, and how to control the insecure `.rhosts` access mechanism used by the `rlogin`, `rsh`, and `rcp` networked login services.

NOTES

The Unix Password System

SANS Security Essentials – Unix Security

Unix User Accounts

A basic overview of how Unix accounts are structured and how the operating system stores account information is necessary before we can look at how to manage users, restrict accounts, and apply other sorts of access controls. The basic Unix account structure actually is very simple—in fact, one of the criticisms of the basic Unix security model is the lack of "granularity" of access control provided to the administrator. As we also will see, many of the administrative functions provided by other operating systems (such as forcing password changes at next login, and keeping a "history" of previously used user passwords) are not widely implemented on Unix systems.

NOTES

Usernames and Passwords

- Every user has an assigned username and password
- Usernames and passwords are case-sensitive
- Usernames generally limited to eight characters for backwards compatibility

SANS Security Essentials – Unix Security

User Names, User IDs, and Passwords

Every user on the system has an identity assigned to her in the form of a unique username. Associated with each username is a password that the user must enter in order to be able to log into the system.

Usernames can contain any alphanumeric characters and are case-sensitive. Thus, "`Alice`" and "`alice`" are different usernames. Most Unix installations stick to all lower-case usernames by convention, just to avoid confusion. Older Unix systems assumed that usernames would be eight characters or less—even modern Unix operating systems may contain certain programs that will abort when encountering a user name longer than eight characters. Many sites have adopted an "eight characters or less" username policy just to be on the safe side.

Eight or less lower-case-only characters is a rather restrictive username space. This often becomes an issue in mixed Unix and Windows environments when the administrators want users to have a common username for both their Windows and Unix logins. The more restrictive Unix standard often becomes the "lowest common denominator" requirement for selecting usernames.

Unix passwords also are case sensitive. We probably all are familiar with the common mistake of attempting to enter a password with the caps-lock key on. Unix systems generally allow passwords to be made up of any printable character: alphanumeric characters, punctuation marks, and even spaces. Some Unix systems allow non-printable control sequences in passwords, as well.

NOTES

Usernames vs. User IDs

- Usernames are purely for the convenience of human beings
- Unix systems store ownership info in terms of User IDs (UIDs)
- Commands like `chown` will accept either usernames or UIDs

SANS Security Essentials – Unix Security

Each username on the system also is associated with a numeric user ID (UID) value. All usernames, UIDs, and passwords are stored (along with other information about the user's account) in the system account database. On most Unix systems, this database actually is two files: `/etc/passwd` and `/etc/shadow`. We will examine the format of these files in some detail later on in this chapter.

What is important to understand for right now is that as far as the Unix operating system is concerned, the UID entry for the user in the system account database is what is important, not the username. Usernames are only for the convenience of the human beings who use the system. All data about file and directory ownerships is stored internally in the operating system by UID.

The primary purpose of the `/etc/passwd` file, in fact, is to allow the system to relate UIDs to usernames for the convenience of users and administrators on the system. If a user's entry is deleted from the `passwd` file, Unix commands still will display the numeric UID on files that were owned by that user but will be unable to associate that UID number with a more human-readable username. Unix commands that deal with file ownership generally accept either usernames or UIDs as arguments.

Originally, the maximum possible UID value on a Unix system was 65,535 (UIDs were "signed" two-byte quantities). And, of course, some UIDs are already reserved by the operating system. Fortunately or unfortunately, we have reached a point now where large Unix installations are dealing with total user populations of over 65,000 users. In these cases not all users can have unique user IDs.

It turns out that this can cause serious problems, especially when sharing files between systems using protocols like NFS. Remember that Unix access controls are based on UIDs and not usernames: if two users share the same UID and can cross-mount each other's home directories, then they can access each other's files!

NOTES

UIDs and Networked File Systems

- John has UID 500 on his machine
- Mary has UID 500 on her machine
- Administrator mounts John's home directory on Mary's machine via network
- Mary can read all of John's files!

Moral: if you're using NFS, make sure you ensure unique UIDs!

SANS Security Essentials – Unix Security

For example, let's suppose John and Mary have Linux running on their laptops. They create accounts for themselves using the `useradd` program, which by default starts assigning UIDs to new accounts with UID 500. Since both are the first user accounts on "their" systems, each one gets UID 500. Now John and Mary want to share files with each other. John exports his home directory so Mary can see it via NFS. Mary is surprised when she does a directory listing of John's home directory, and all of the files show up as being owned by her! Actually, all of the files are owned by UID 500, which on Mary's system is the UID that corresponds to user `mary`. The situation would be reversed if John mounted Mary's home directory on his machine where his `/etc/passwd` file says that user `john` is UID 500.

Now think about a company where there are more than 65,535 Unix users. The only thing to do is to divide the user community up into smaller organizational units, each of which can have unique UIDs within their own community. Typically this is done along pre-existing organizational divisions: engineering has their user accounts and UIDs, the sales team another, etc. As long as file sharing between these groups is not an issue, things work out fine. Still, managing to keep usernames and UIDs unique in a large company often can be an enormous effort.

Newer Unix operating systems are starting to support 32-bit UIDs in order to deal with this problem. However, the fact that there are still so many Unix systems out there with only a maximum UID of 65,535 means that most sites stick with this lower limit for backwards-compatibility reasons.

NOTES

The Superuser

- Unix systems have an "all or nothing" security model
- Superuser access provides ability to control all files, processes, and devices
- By convention, the superuser account is named `root`

SANS Security Essentials – Unix Security

The Unix Superuser

The Unix security model recognizes two classes of users: normal users who can only manipulate their own data, and a single all-powerful "superuser" who can do anything to any object on the system. The superuser can read any file, change the permissions and ownership on any file, delete any file, change user passwords at will, start and stop processes, and add and remove devices. The goal of an attacker trying to break into a Unix system is to get superuser access because then he "owns" the system.

Over the years, Unix has received a certain amount of justifiable criticism for this "all or nothing" security model. Recently, Unix operating system vendors have started implementing more granular sorts of access controls at the kernel level. In this new model, superuser power is broken up into several specialized "roles" that are capable of performing specific administrative tasks. For example, an administrator could be given authority over only the commands and files required for setting up new user accounts or for managing printers. It is ironic that the original, more trivial Unix security model was developed originally in reaction **against** earlier operating systems (notably Multics) that had exactly the same sorts of complicated security models now being re-introduced into Unix.

From the early days of Unix, the primary superuser account has been the `root` user. People familiar with the Windows environment may find it simplest to think of the Unix `root` account as being equivalent to `Administrator` under Windows. Unix users tend use "`root`" and "superuser" interchangeably.

NOTES

UIDs and the Superuser

- *Any* account with UID 0 has superuser privileges
- Other UID 0 accounts may exist besides the `root` account– usually locked
- Attackers often try to create new UID 0 accounts to get root access

SANS Security Essentials – Unix Security

However, the superuser account just as easily could be called "`mack`" or "`buddy.`" As far as the Unix operating system is concerned, any account with UID 0 has superuser privileges. Some sites even go so far as to grant certain users administrative rights to the system by setting the UID on their accounts to 0. This is a terrible idea, however, since it ruins any possibility of auditability on the system: nobody will be able to tell which of these users crashed the system or removed some critical file. Plus, any one of those accounts might have an easily guessable password that will allow some outside attacker unlimited access to your system. Furthermore, even trivial mistakes by these users—like accidentally deleting the wrong directory—can cripple the machine.

Some Unix operating systems include a few UID 0 accounts besides `root` for special purposes. Generally these accounts will be set up so either that interactive logins are impossible, that the account has an invalid password, or that logging into the account runs some special program which performs a certain task rather than giving interactive command access. A favorite tactic of attackers is to change the configuration on UID 0 accounts that are normally locked in order to have a "back-door" to access the system as the superuser. Audit extra UID 0 accounts on a regular basis, or remove them from the system entirely if they are not needed.

Another ploy on systems with large account databases is to add accounts with UID 0 buried someplace in the middle of the database. Administrators may not notice the new account, and again the attacker has a "back-door" to superuser access on the system.

The following command will display the entries from the `/etc/passwd` file, sorted numerically by UID:

```
sort -t: -k 3,3n /etc/passwd
```

UID 0 accounts will appear at the top of the list, making it easy to spot rogue UID 0 accounts and see if any of the standard UID 0 accounts have been tampered with. It also helps administrators spot other accounts where duplicate UIDs may have been assigned incorrectly.

Becoming Superuser

- Log in as `root`
  - Bad! No accountability
- Use `/bin/su` command
  - Better audit trail
- Limited access with `sudo`
  - Excellent audit trail and fine-grained controls

SANS Security Essentials – Unix Security

Unix systems generally provide three legitimate ways of getting superuser access. In the Unix lingo this typically is referred to as "going `root`."

The first mechanism is to log into the system as `root` with the `root` password. This generally is thought to be a bad idea since there is no way to know exactly **who** is using the `root` password. If the system crashes right after somebody logs in as `root`, whom should the administrator track down to find out what happened?

It occasionally is necessary to log in as `root` on the system console when there is no other way to access the system in an emergency, but the system console should be the only place where `root` logins are allowed. In particular, **never** allow root logins over the network—particularly when using insecure channels like `telnet` or `rlogin` from which an attacker with a password sniffer can grab the `root` password. Later in this chapter we will be looking at how to restrict `root` logins to the system console device only.

I Had Always Heard This Was Switch User

The second standard way of getting `root` access is with the command: `/bin/su` or `/usr/bin/su`, depending on the version of Unix. This command actually allows a normal user to become any other user on the system, as long as she knows the other user's password. However, `su` most commonly is used to become `root`. In fact, running `su` without specifying an alternate username defaults to "`su root`." Every time a user runs the `su` command, information about the attempt is logged in the system logs, whether the attempt succeeded or failed. This way, administrators can find out who did what in the case of system problems and detect when users are trying to gain unauthorized access.

It is considered "good practice" to always type the full pathname of the `su` program; i.e., type "`/bin/su`" and not just "`su`." This helps to avoid getting trapped by Trojan horse `su` programs designed to capture the root password. If an attacker were able to get his malicious `su` program into a directory that appeared before `/bin` or `/usr/bin` in the administrator's executable search path, problems could result.

NOTES

A third mechanism for granting root access on Unix systems is the `sudo` tool, maintained at `http://www.courtesan.com/sudo/`. The `sudo` command allows a user to run a single command with `root` privilege as long as he has a proper listing in the `/etc/sudoers` file created by the system administrator.

`sudo` has a number of advantages over the normal Unix `su` command:

- `sudo` prompts users for their own passwords rather than the root password. At many sites that use `sudo`, most of the users and administrators may not even know the root password for the systems on which they work! This makes life easier when administrators and users leave the company, since the root password no longer has to be changed on all systems.
- `sudo` allows for very fine-grained access controls. The administrator may specify a list of specific commands that a given user may execute with superuser privileges and even in some cases specify which command-line options may be used.
- `sudo` produces a much higher level of logging than the normal `su` command. Every command executed via `sudo` is logged in great detail.

Now most of the newer Open Source Unix operating systems include `sudo` by default. For operating systems that do not, the source code is widely available and compiles easily on many different platforms. `sudo` is easy to install and configure and is well worth using.

/etc/passwd and /etc/shadow

- /etc/passwd stores "public" user info:

```
bob:x:500:500:Bob Smith:/home/bob:/bin/bash
```

- /etc/shadow stores secret information:

```
bob:$1$N4N4Z.eu$odU29tg/Epm4a…:11817:0:99999:7:::
```

- /etc/shadow format varies for each OS
- It's critical that /etc/shadow is only readable by the superuser!

SANS Security Essentials – Unix Security

The Unix Account Database

Unlike many other operating systems, Unix account information typically is stored in simple flat text files. The standard files for holding account information on most Unix systems are /etc/passwd and /etc/shadow. The /etc/group file stores additional information about group membership and privileges (more on this shortly).

/etc/passwd contains the "public" information that all processes need to be able to see about users on the system. This file generally is readable by any user or process on the system.

Here is a typical entry from /etc/passwd:

```
bob:x:500:500:Bob Smith:/home/bob:/bin/bash
```

Notice that the different fields in the account entry are separated by colons. The seven fields in the password file correspond to the following information: (1) the username, (2) an unused field, (3) the UID, (4) the user's group ID, (5) the user's full name, (6) the path to the user's home directory, and (7) the default command shell that is run for the user when she logs in.

In the early days of Unix, the second unused field used to hold an encrypted form of the user's password. Bitter experience taught Unix administrators that having encrypted password strings in a file that anybody could read made it easy for attackers to steal these strings and run password cracking tools against them. In order to thwart this problem, the user's password information and other private administrative information for the user's account was moved to the /etc/shadow file. This file is readable only by the superuser, which is fine since all of the processes that need to use the user's password (like programs which do system logins) run with root privileges.

Here is a sample /etc/shadow entry:

```
bob:$1$vbiQmaqc$kq47Tox3y9amXkPumoLLu0:
11920:0:99999:7:::
```

Like the /etc/passwd file, the /etc/shadow file is colon-delimited. The first two fields of the shadow file always are the username and the encrypted representation of the user's password. The remaining fields are used to hold various pieces of administrative information, depending upon the Unix operating system being used. We will look at how Linux and Solaris systems make use of these fields later in the chapter.

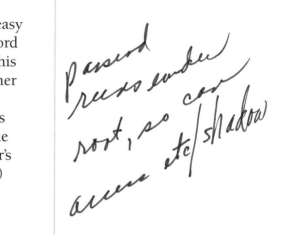

NOTES

NOTES

A Quick Word About Groups

- Users are assigned to a default group according to their /etc/passwd entry
- Users may also belong to other groups as defined in /etc/group

```
wheel:x:10:root,bob,alice
```

- groups command tells you which groups you are currently a member of
- Some groups have special privileges

SANS Security Essentials – Unix Security

While a user's UID defines his primary access rights and privileges on the system, Unix groups are a way of allowing access to a related group of users on the system. Unix groups often are used by software development teams or other groups whose respective users need to share files and other data while working together on a project. Files created by a particular developer will be owned by that user, but the file also has a group ownership, which can correspond to the team with whom that developer is working. As we will see in the next chapter, different levels of access rights can be defined for both the owner of the file and the "group owner" of the file.

Each user belongs to at least one group— the "primary" group defined in that user's /etc/passwd entry. A user may belong to other groups as well, as defined in the /etc/group file. Like the passwd file, the /etc/group file is used primarily to relate human-readable group names to group IDs (GIDs) for use by the operating system.

Here is a sample /etc/group entry:

```
wheel:x:10:root,bob,alice
```

Again, /etc/group is colon-delimited just like the passwd and shadow files. The fields in the /etc/group entry are: (1) the group name, (2) an unused field, (3) the GID, and (4) a list of users who are members of the given group (this list may be empty).

A single user may appear in the group lists for many different groups in the /etc/group file. When users log in, they are given the group privileges of their primary group from the /etc/passwd file plus all of the other group privileges of the groups in which they are listed in the /etc/group file. Users can run the groups command to learn which groups of which they are members.

Note that like the /etc/passwd file, the second unused field in /etc/group used to be a password entry. This field no longer is used on modern Unix systems: older Unix systems allowed users to "log in" to certain groups once they had accessed the system. Since users now inherit group privileges simply by being listed in the member list in the fourth field of the /etc/group entry, these passwords no longer are required. There is no /etc/shadow equivalent for the group file.

Certain groups have special privileges. On some Unix systems the operator group is allowed to run the privileged commands that backup and restore files. On BSD systems, members of the wheel group—the "big wheels" on the system—are the only people on the system allowed to use the su command to become root. If the wheel group has no members, then any user may su to root as long as he knows the root password. Group privileges vary with the version of Unix being used, so consult appropriate vendor documentation for more information.

NOTES

NOTES

Different OS, Different Encryption

- DES56 (Solaris, HP-UX, AIX, ...):
  - Old way, still "lowest common denominator"
  - No longer computationally intensive
  - Silently truncates passwords at 8 characters
- MD5 (Linux, BSDs), Blowfish (OpenBSD):
  - Can use long passwords
  - Much harder to compute than DES56

SANS Security Essentials – Unix Security

Password Encryption Algorithms

While different Unix systems may use different forms of encryption to protect user passwords, what is important to know is that all of these encryption systems utilize what are referred to as "one-way hash functions." This means that data may be translated into an encrypted version with these routines, but it is "computationally difficult" (impossible) to reverse the encryption and get the original data back out. So there is no way for administrators to know easily what a user's password is. The best administrators can do is change the password to something that they do know.

Similarly, when a user logs into a Unix system, the process that is verifying the user's password cannot decrypt the password field from the user's `/etc/shadow` entry. Instead, the login process encrypts the password that the user types in and compares the encrypted version against the encrypted data from `/etc/shadow`. Then, if the encrypted strings match, the user entered the correct password. When attackers are "cracking" passwords, they simply are encrypting random strings, trying to find in `/etc/shadow` an encrypted string that matches one of the encrypted strings they have computed. Since the attackers know what string they used to create the encrypted string that matched a user's `/etc/shadow` entry, they know what the given user's password must be.

The original algorithm that was used by Unix systems for creating encrypted password hashes was based on the 56-bit "Data Encryption Standard" (DES56 for short) that originally was developed for the US government. This algorithm still is used today by the older commercial Unix operating systems like Solaris, HP-UX, and AIX.

One of the limitations of this hashing algorithm is that it is unable to handle more than 8 characters of data at a time, so passwords on these systems are truncated silently at 8 characters. If a user types in "`thisisareallylongpassword`," the system treats this as the password "`thisisar`." This means an attacker only has to try guessing strings of up to 8 characters in order to crack passwords on these systems, limiting the amount of work required to "crack" passwords on these machines.

The other big problem with DES56, of course, is that it no longer is computationally difficult for modern computers. Even older PCs in use today still can encrypt as many as 50,000 strings per second with the DES56 password-hashing algorithm. This again shortens the amount of time that an attacker needs to spend when "cracking" passwords.

Modern, Open Source Unix systems use better algorithms. Linux systems use MD5 by default, and OpenBSD systems use the Blowfish algorithm. One advantage that these algorithms have over DES56 is that users can enter very long passwords. Also, these algorithms are much more difficult to compute: in practice, MD5 is at least 10 times more computationally intensive and Blowfish more than 100 times more difficult. Both of these factors mean that "cracking" passwords encrypted with these algorithms is much more difficult for an attacker.

Unfortunately, it is administratively convenient to be able to "share" password information between various systems on a network, such as when a site is using NIS. However, this means that all systems have to agree on the password-hashing algorithm that will be used. Since the Solaris, HP-UX, and AIX systems on the network only understand DES56, most sites end up falling back to this less secure "lowest common denominator" hashing algorithm.

How can the administrator tell which password-hashing algorithm currently is being used in the account database? The easiest way simply is to look at the encrypted password hashes in the `/etc/shadow` file (or equivalent). The sidebar shows the standard encrypted password format for the three commonly used password-hashing algorithms—clearly the differences are obvious just from the length of the various encrypted strings.

Password Hash Formats

DES56 -- `bob:clWzbbBDUYi2Q:...`

MD5 -- `bob:$1$vbiQmaqc$kq47Tox3y9amXkPumoLLu0:...`

Blowfish -- `bob:$2a$06$cIuiVKvWgRc5HtYhvomZh.dqzLyCP2p8bOmTZf7ybm89OXW.B32U6:...`

No matter which password-hashing algorithm the system uses, the resulting encrypted strings are always the same fixed length: the shortest strings are those produced by the DES56 hashing algorithm, only 13 characters. Also, each hash contains only characters from a small subset of the possible printable character set. No matter what the hashing algorithm, the characters `!`, `*`, and `=` are never valid in these encrypted password hashes.

All of this becomes relevant when the administrator wants to block a user account.

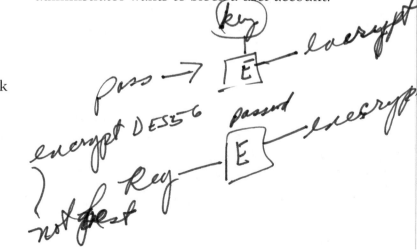

NOTES

NOTES

"Blocking" Accounts

- Standard encrypted password strings are fixed length and use limited character set
- Edit /etc/shadow and use an invalid password string to block logins
- Can also set an invalid shell in /etc/passwd for additional protection
- *Never* use an empty password string in /etc/shadow!

SANS Security Essentials – Unix Security

Blocking Accounts

When administrators wish to block logins to a particular account, they simply edit /etc/shadow and change that user's encrypted password hash to any string that could not be a valid hash value. This typically means choosing a short string, less than the standard 13 character DES56 hash length, which also contains one or more "invalid" characters. Standard choices are strings like "=NP=" or "*BLOCKED*" or sometimes just "*," though the longer strings are easier to pick out in a large password database. Never under any circumstances use an empty field in the /etc/shadow file: an empty field means that user is allowed to log in without providing any password at all!

In addition, administrators often will set the user's shell in the last field of /etc/passwd to an invalid or non-existent executable like /bin/false or /nosuchshell. Even if a valid password hash were put into /etc/shadow for the blocked account, logins still will not be allowed as long as the shell is invalid in /etc/passwd. Also, administrators now can tell if the account is supposed to be blocked just by looking at the /etc/passwd file, rather than having to look at /etc/shadow with administrative privileges.

Of course, an attacker with administrative privileges on the system might replace this "invalid" shell binary with an actual copy of a valid shell executable, opening a potential back door. For this reason, many administrators like to use /dev/null as an invalid shell. /dev/null obviously is not a valid shell executable, and if this system device is replaced by a copy of a shell executable, then the system stops working properly. This then alerts administrators that there is a problem on the system.

In a similar vein, there also is a freely available program called noshell that is designed as an invalid shell for blocking accounts. The extra feature of the noshell program is that it logs an alert message via Syslog if it ever gets executed. This means that even if a blocked account suddenly is enabled with a valid password, the noshell program will still block access and also alert the system administrators that this unexpected access is occurring.

"System" Accounts

- Unix operating systems tend to come with a lot of dummy accounts for various apps
- Typically, these are accounts with low UID numbers (Linux convention is UID < 500)
- Attackers will sometimes activate these accounts as "back doors" into the system
- If you're not using a particular service or app, then remove (or block) the account

SANS Security Essentials – Unix Security

Unix systems typically will ship with a number of accounts that are associated with a particular application on the system rather than an individual user. For example, NFS uses the special "`nobody`" user; Oracle requires an "`oracle`" database administrator account; and the system might have an "`apache`" or "`www`" user set up for running the Web server. These accounts typically will be given low UID numbers to distinguish them from other accounts in the password file. The Linux convention is to reserve UIDs 0-499 for these kinds of system accounts. Other Unix systems often reserve UIDs less than 100.

Usually the default `/etc/shadow` file from the vendor ships with these accounts disabled and with an invalid password entry, but attackers commonly will try to insert as a back door valid password strings in these system account entries. Setting invalid shells on these accounts in `/etc/passwd` where possible is a good idea, as is regularly auditing the system `passwd` and `shadow` files for changes to these accounts.

Disabling the account may be preferable to deleting the account altogether. In most cases, each of these system accounts "owns" one or more files and directories on the system. If the account were completely deleted from the `passwd` and `shadow` files, then the original UID for that account might end up getting re-assigned to a different user. Remember that Unix systems store file ownership information by UID. By reassigning the UID to a new user on the system, the administrators have created a situation where the new user now "owns" the operating system files that were created for the previous system account. If these files are critical configuration files, directories, or system devices, then the user might be able to get increased privileges on the system.

A similar argument can be made for blocking rather than deleting user accounts when a user leaves the organization or no longer requires access to the system. Typically that user will leave behind some number of files and directories she owns. Administrators want to avoid UID overlaps, but it also can be useful to know who originally created a file long after that individual has moved on.

Of course, having large numbers of blocked accounts in the `passwd` and `shadow` files makes it harder to audit these files for malicious changes, so some sites opt for a strict policy of purging old user accounts and data from their systems soon after a user leaves. Similarly, if the system administrator is certain that a given non-user account no longer owns any files on the system, that account may be deleted from the `passwd` and `shadow` files.

NOTES

NOTES

Typical Password Security Features

- Password expiration and "aging"
- Password "history"
- Minimum password lengths
- Force wide variety of character types
- Check new passwords against dictionary
- Lock out accounts after multiple failures

The bad news is that Unix systems have historically been bad at providing these...

SANS Security Essentials – Unix Security

Password Administration Features

Beyond being able to block accounts simply, administrators generally expect certain "standard" functionality for managing user accounts and passwords:

- Administrators should be able to force passwords to expire on a regular basis—be it monthly, quarterly, or on some other schedule—and force users to change their old passwords.
- Furthermore, users should be forced to use their new password for some period of time, perhaps a week, before being allowed to change it again. This "password aging" feature forces users to get comfortable with the new password rather than immediately change the password back to an old password.
- As an extra layer of security, the system should be able to keep a "history" or record of previous passwords for a given user and not allow that user to re-use an old password.
- The system should enforce a minimum password length and also force users to select passwords that contain some minimum number of upper-case characters, numbers, and non-alphanumeric characters.
- Passwords also should be checked against a "dictionary" of easily guessable passwords or strings that commonly are hit by the standard password "cracking" tools.
- The administrator also should be able to set a given account to be disabled after a certain number of failed logins. Obviously, though, this feature could be used as a denial-of-service attacks against that account—**never** enable this feature on administrative accounts.

The bad news is that Unix systems historically have not had a good track record as far as supporting many of these features. Certainly RedHat does better in this department than many Unix systems, but administrators coming to Unix from other platforms often are disappointed by the lack of features available to them.

NOTES

Expiration and Aging

- "Extra" /etc/shadow fields used:

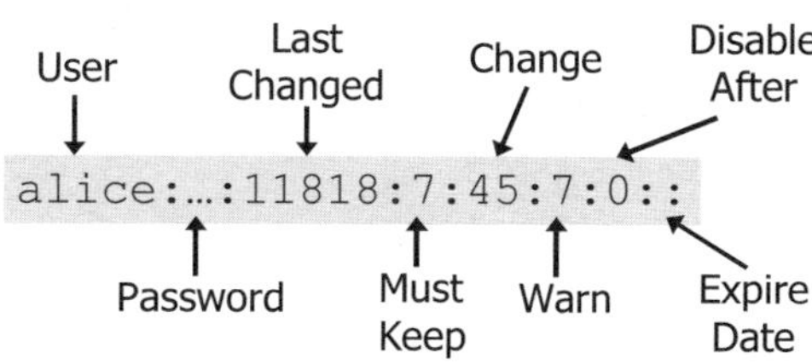

SANS Security Essentials – Unix Security

Password Expiration and Aging

It was noted earlier that the "extra" fields in /etc/shadow were used to hold different kinds of administrative information, depending on which flavor of Unix was being used. Some Unix operating systems use these fields to hold password administration information. The scheme described here is used by both RedHat and Solaris. Further RedHat documentation can be found in /usr/share/doc/shadow-utils-*/HOWTO file on most RedHat systems.

Here is another sample /etc/shadow entry with the password hash not shown for the sake of clarity:

```
alice:…:11818:7:45:7:0::
```

After the encrypted password string in the second field, there are seven additional fields that are described as follows:

```
username:passwd:last:may:must:warn:expire:
disable:reserved
```

These seven "extra" fields are used to control password expiration, aging, and account expiration as follows:

- The third field (last) is the date the password was last changed. This date is represented as a number of days since January 1, 1970, the start of the Unix "epoch."
- The fourth field (may) is how many days must elapse after the last changed date before the password may be changed by the user. This is the so-called password "aging" value or hold-down limit. In the example above, Alice must wait a week before being able to change her password again.
- The fifth field (must) is how many days after the last changed date the password will expire. This site apparently expires passwords every 45 days. When the password expires, the user is forced to change her password at her next login.
- The sixth field (warn) is how many days before the next expiration date the user is warned that he will have to change his password soon. These warnings appear at login time. In this example, warnings will start appearing a week before the expiration date.
- The seventh field (expire) is how many days after the expiration date the account is completely disabled. Setting this to 0 means the account is disabled as soon as the password

NOTES

expires, so the user had better change her password ahead of the expiration time!

- The eighth field (`disable`) is an absolute date that the account expires. For example, the administrator can give a user an account until the end of the month and then have it shut down automatically. Again, this date is expressed as a number of days since January 1, 1970, although RedHat and Solaris provide commands for setting this value using more human-readable date formats.

Note that administrators also may block accounts by setting the eighth "disable" field to zero. On the one hand, however, changing the password hash to something invalid in `/etc/shadow` and/or using an invalid shell in `/etc/passwd` probably is more self-documenting. On the other hand, if there ever comes a time when the account must be re-enabled, setting the password hash to an invalid value means that the user's original password has been lost.

NOTES

System Defaults

- In /etc/login.defs:
  - PASS_MAX_DAYS, PASS_MIN_DAYS
  - PASS_WARN_AGE
  - Also PASS_MIN_LEN
- In /etc/default/useradd:
  - INACTIVE
- Default settings only apply to new users–must use chage on existing accounts

SANS Security Essentials – Unix Security

Clearly, setting these values for various users on the system by manually editing the /etc/shadow file is the wrong way to go. The probability of making an error and corrupting the shadow file or accidentally blocking or enabling an account in error is too great. Fortunately, the operating system provides better interfaces for setting these values.

If the site is using the RedHat useradd program to create new accounts, then defaults for all of these values may be set in either the /etc/login.defs file, or in one case the /etc/default/useradd file. In /etc/login.defs, PASS_MAX_DAYS is the default expiration interval for passwords, expressed as a number of days. By default RedHat sets this to 99999, so passwords effectively never expire. PASS_MIN_DAYS is the number of days for the password "aging" threshold. This value is set to 0 by default. PASS_WARN_AGE is the advance expiration notice threshold in days. This is set to a week by default, which probably is fine.

login.defs also happens to include the PASS_MIN_LEN parameter, which is the minimum password length expressed as a number of characters. The default is 5, which is probably too low even if the site is using DES56 style passwords that are truncated at eight characters. Six characters seems to be the generally agreed upon minimum password standard, and sites may want to increase this to 8 or more if they are using MD5 passwords exclusively.

The only default that is not in login.defs is the number of days in which the account should be deactivated after the password expires . This default is set using the INACTIVE parameter in /etc/default/useradd. This parameter can be set either by editing the /etc/default/useradd file directly or by executing the useradd -D -f <val> command as the root user.

Obviously, these defaults only will apply to new accounts, and even then only if the account is created with the useradd program. Administrators who wish to change these values for other accounts must use the chage command as the root user. Running chage <username> with no further arguments starts an interactive mode, where the administrator is prompted for the various values. chage also allows these values to be set on the command line for use in administrative scripts (for more information, read the on-line manual page for the chage command).

Note that Solaris keeps its defaults in the /etc/default/passwd file. Also, instead of chage, Solaris administrators must use the passwd command to set these values for existing accounts.

NOTES

What is PAM?

- PAM = "Pluggable Authentication Modules"
- Standard programming interface for how services should handle logins/passwords
- Centralized to allow "easy" reconfiguration:
  - Use different types of authentication
  - Enforce good password rules
- Supported by many Unix systems, but not generally portable between OS versions

SANS Security Essentials – Unix Security

Additional Functionality with pam_cracklib

One buzzword that always seems to come up when discussing Unix authentication is PAM, which stands for "Pluggable Authentication Modules." PAM is a system developed to make it easier for developers and administrators to reconfigure how their systems should handle user authentication.

The basic idea is that all of the code for doing logins and changing passwords has been pulled out of various Unix applications like `login`, `rlogind`, `ftpd`, and `xdm` and replaced with calls to the PAM "abstraction layer." Essentially, the application no longer looks up the user's account in the `/etc/shadow` file to get the password. Instead, the application developer calls the "validate this user" function from the PAM libraries and lets that routine take care of it.

The advantage to this system is that administrators are then free to replace the underlying authentication scheme with anything they want, as long as it conforms to the PAM "standard interface" definitions. So, instead of usernames and passwords, the site could choose to use token cards, Kerberos, or some other authentication scheme. Since the routines for changing passwords also are handled via PAM interface, administrators additionally can also use PAM to insert their own "good password enforcement" routines.

Originally, PAM was developed to be a cross-platform standard. However, PAM has not been embraced universally, even in the Unix community, and different vendor implementations are incompatible. More documentation on the RedHat PAM system can be found by starting with the `/usr/share/doc/pam-*/html/pam.html` file installed on most RedHat systems.

NOTES

pam_cracklib

- Enabled in /etc/pam.d/system-auth
- Enforces good password checks:
  - Check against dictionary
  - New password must differ from current word
  - Require mixed case, non-letter characters
- Documentation sketchy
- Changing defaults confusing

SANS Security Essentials – Unix Security

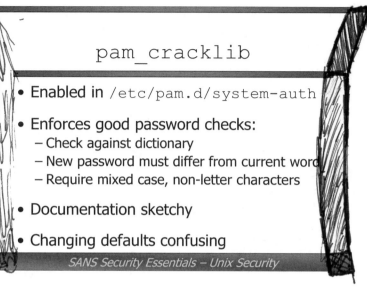

RedHat systems use a PAM module called pam_cracklib to enforce some standard "good password" checks on new user passwords:

- The password is checked to make sure it is not too similar to the previous password, for example, the same word with just case changes, or the word reversed.
- Passwords are checked against dictionary files so that the user does not pick an easily guessable password.
- In most cases, pam_cracklib requires that the password contain at least some non-letter characters and/or case changes.

Unfortunately, pam_cracklib has a number of shortcomings, not the least of which is very incomplete and confusing documentation. The dictionaries used by pam_cracklib, /usr/lib/cracklib_dict.*, are in a binary database format to speed up word searches. Unfortunately, the documentation does not say which format is used or how to make updates to these files. This makes it difficult for administrators to add their own word lists.

The requirements for non-letter characters and case changes actually is handled by a somewhat odd "scoring system." Passwords are required to be a minimum number of characters, but shorter passwords are allowed if the password contains mixed case or non-letter characters by giving "extra credit" towards the minimum length for each of these "special" characters. Also, if the users picks long enough passwords, they can enter one that is all lower case letters, which may not be the desired behavior.

At least some of the default configuration settings for pam_cracklib can be changed by modifying the /etc/pam.d/system-auth file. What documentation there is can be found in the /usr/share/doc/pam-*/html/pam-6.html file on most RedHat systems.

While pam_cracklib may not be a perfect solution in many respects, be aware that most Unix systems do not even provide this much functionality for strong password enforcement. pam_cracklib is being ported to the BSD operating systems, and other vendors may have implemented their own proprietary solutions. Consult the appropriate vendor documentation for the system for further information.

NOTES

Things You Can't Do

- Lock out accounts after failed logins
- Force password change at next login (in any sensible way)
- Keep user password "history"

SANS Security Essentials – Unix Security

Features That Are Not Available

As for the other "standard" account administration features discussed earlier, most Unix systems simply have not implemented them. For example, Unix systems generally do not give administrators the ability to lock out accounts after a certain number of failed logins. Some vendors may have implemented their own proprietary mechanisms for doing this, and other third-party vendors sell add-on software that can provide this feature.

Similarly there also is no good way for the administrator to force a user to change his password the next time he logs in. One option would be for the administrator to set the "password last changed" field on the user's account backwards, so that the password expiration limit has passed. The `chage` command on RedHat does allow the administrator to set this value. Of course, the administrator must also be careful to avoid the "expire account if password remains unchanged" threshold, which would completely lock the users out of their accounts. Whatever the case, this approach only can be regarded as something of a kludge.

Unix systems also generally do not support keeping a password "history" to force users to choose passwords that they have not already used. `pam_cracklib` claims to have this feature, but it apparently does not. Other third-party software may be available to address this feature.

All of the security features discussed in this section are entirely useless, however, if an attacker with physical access to the system is able to manipulate the system boot process to bypass the system's standard access controls. The next section looks at how to protect the boot sequence from unauthorized tampering.

NOTES

Physical Access = Compromise?

- Somebody who has physical access to your machine could break in:
  - Boot "single user mode" and get root shell
  - Boot off floppy/CD-ROM
- Password protecting your boot process can help prevent this
- Need to make sure the system can still reboot normally without password

SANS Security Essentials – Unix Security

Boot-Level Access Control

An attacker with physical access to a machine can reboot the system simply by powering the system off or pulling out the power cord, if nothing else. Once the system starts its boot process, the attacker sitting at the system console can enter boot commands to cause the system to boot in a non-standard fashion.

One approach is to force the system into "single-user" administrative mode. While most modern Unix systems now require the person sitting at the console to enter the superuser password before being granted single-user access, RedHat by default gives the single-user `root` shell prompt without requiring a password. As we will see, however, it almost is trivial to force RedHat to prompt for the `root` password in single-user mode.

If single-user mode is password protected, then the next best alternative for the attacker is to force the system to boot off a copy of the vendor installation media. In other words, the attacker is not booting from the standard OS installation on the system's local hard drives but rather is running the minimal operating system installation provided by the vendor for installing new systems. However, once the system is booted into this minimal OS image, the attacker typically can mount the file systems from the machine's local hard drive and make changes to those file systems with `root` privilege. This means the attacker can change the system's normal `root` password and have complete access to the machine once it has rebooted to its regular OS image. Unix system administrators often will use this technique to legitimately break into systems that they own when the `root` password has been lost or forgotten.

The boot loaders commonly shipped with Linux systems can be configured to require a password before allowing the standard boot commands to be changed. This means that the attacker would have to know this boot-level password in order to force the system to boot from vendor media in the CD-ROM drive (the system's "standard" boot command should boot the system from the OS image on the local hard drive). Administrators do need to be careful that the regular boot process may go on without requiring somebody be present to enter a password, however. Imagine what would happen if a system crashed and required somebody to enter a password before rebooting, but that system was 3000 miles away in a locked data center! The system would be down until somebody could get on an airplane and get to the machine in person.

NOTES

Force Single-User Password

- Rebooting into single-user mode gives `root` shell, no password required
- Can require `root` password by adding this line to `/etc/inittab`:

```
sum:S:wait:/sbin/sulogin
```

- Most Unix operating systems require `root` password by default for single-user mode

SANS Security Essentials – Unix Security

Requiring a Single-User Password

In Chapter 32, we mentioned that running the command "`init 1`" as root will drop the system into single-user mode. But how can an attacker who has crashed the system or an administrator doing legitimate work at the system console cause the machine to come up in single-user mode during the reboot process?

The method is slightly different depending on which of the standard Linux boot loaders the system is using. If the system is using the older LILO (LInux LOader) program, then a "`lilo:`" prompt should appear during the boot process. When this prompt appears, simply enter the command "`boot single`" to cause the system to reboot into single-user mode.

If the system is using GRUB (the GRand Unified Boot-loader), things are slightly more complicated. During the GRUB boot process, a screen appears showing the different boot choices available (unless the system is in a "dual-boot" configuration, there will probably only be one choice here). When this screen appears, hit the "`e`" key to edit the default boot command. Now use the arrow keys to select the line which begins "`kernel /boot/…`" and hit "`e`" again to edit this line. In the line editing mode, simply add the word "`single`" to the end of this line and hit `<return>` to exit editing mode. Now just type "`b`" to boot the system, and it will come up in single-user mode.

Forcing RedHat to require the `root` password before granting single-user access is almost trivial. Simply add the following line to `/etc/inittab`:

```
sum:S:wait:/sbin/sulogin
```

The value in the first field is irrelevant; it just has to be some 2-4 character string that is disparate in `/etc/inittab`. Here we are using "`sum`" for "Single-User Mode."

`/sbin/sulogin` is a command that prompts for the `root` password and then starts the standard Unix command shell, if the correct password is entered. The rest of the `inittab` entry above says to run the `/sbin/sulogin` command whenever the system enters single-user mode, the meaning of the "`S`" in the second field above, and to `wait` around for this command to exit before proceeding with the rest of the normal multi-user boot process.

Requiring the `root` password for single-user access is easy to do and is a relatively significant security enhancement to the system because it forces the attacker to at least prepare by bringing along a bootable CD-ROM or floppy disk. This helps prevent “casual” break-ins and “keeps the honest people honest.” It is a mystery why RedHat—a company which seems to care about system security in many other respects—does not make this `inittab` configuration standard for all of its releases. Certainly administrators should make sure to add the above line to all of their RedHat systems.

Boot-Level Passwords

In order to password-protect the standard system boot process, the administrator must modify the configuration of the standard system boot loader. Linux systems typically will use one of two standard boot loaders: the older LILO (LInux LOader) program or the newer GRUB (GRand Unified Boot-loader). LILO was the standard boot-loader for RedHat up through v7.1. After this release, GRUB became the standard, although LILO still is available for those who want to use it.

NOTES

NOTES

LILO – The Older Boot Loader

- Add to /etc/lilo.conf:
  password=<*password*>
  restricted
- Run /sbin/lilo command:
  # **/sbin/lilo**
  Warning: /etc/lilo.conf should be readable only for root if using PASSWORD
- Protect /etc/lilo.conf:
  # **chown root:root /etc/lilo.conf**
  # **chmod 600 /etc/lilo.conf**

SANS Security Essentials – Unix Security

The LILO configuration file is /etc/lilo.conf. To enable a boot-level password, administrators should add the following two lines to the **top** of this file:

```
password=<password>
restricted
```

<password> should be replaced with whatever password the administrator wishes to use. The restricted keyword means that the password only is required when entering non-standard boot commands. The normal system boot process can proceed without somebody being present to enter the password.

When the lilo.conf file is changed, the /sbin/lilo command must be run as root in order to install the changes. However, after the password directive has been added to lilo.conf, running the lilo command often produces a warning message:

```
# /sbin/lilo
Warning: /etc/lilo.conf should be readable
only for root if using PASSWORD
```

Consider that /etc/lilo.conf now contains a sensitive system password in clear-text format. Only the system administrators should be able to read lilo.conf and see this password, so the lilo command is warning the admin to make sure lilo.conf is readable only by the root user.

The following two commands will accomplish this:

```
# chown root:root /etc/lilo.conf
# chmod 600 /etc/lilo.conf
```

The chown and chmod commands will be covered in more detail in the next chapter, in which we discuss file permissions and access control.

NOTES

GRUB – The Brave New World

- Add to `/etc/grub.conf`:
  `password` *<password>*
- Don't need to run any special commands to pick up changes
- Set secure permissions on `grub.conf`!
- Newer versions of GRUB support MD5 hashed passwords!

SANS Security Essentials – Unix Security

GRUB the Free Software Foundation's "Grand Unified Bootloader" (GRUB, for short) is a new boot loader meant to be a replacement for LILO. It looks like some non-Linux systems may start using GRUB as well.

The GRUB configuration file is `/etc/grub.conf`. Setting up a boot-level password for GRUB is as easy as adding this line to the `grub.conf` file:

```
password <password>
```

Note that unlike `lilo.conf`, there is no equals ("=") sign between the `password` keyword and the actual password string `<password>`. Also, no `restricted` keyword is required. The GRUB password is required only when the user at the console tries to modify the default boot command. Changes made to `grub.conf` take effect automatically at the next reboot, so there is no special command the administrators need to run to load their changes.

While it is still a good idea to make sure that `grub.conf` is readable only by the `root` user, newer versions of GRUB support using MD5 hashed password strings instead of clear text passwords in `grub.conf`. To use an MD5 hash rather than a clear text password, simply add the "`--md5`" option to the line above:

```
password --md5 <md5hash>
```

The question now is how can an administrator create an MD5 hash of her preferred password to use here? The `grub` command that ships with the operating system has an `md5crypt` mode that allows the administrator to compute these strings:

```
# grub
grub> md5crypt
Password: ********
Encrypted: $1$14mqH/
$brx3ZzY8x49UZrW3IyVhq/
grub> quit
```

"Cut and paste" the resulting encrypted string into `grub.conf` file, and everything should work fine!

Note that Unix systems that run on proprietary hardware (e.g., Sun Sparc architecture machines) often will have their boot loader reside in an NVRAM chip or other non-volatile storage device, rather than existing as an executable on the local hard drive. In these cases it usually is necessary to set the boot-level password by changing parameters in this non-volatile storage area. For example, Solaris ships with an `eeprom` command that allows the administrator to interact with the system

NOTES

NVRAM device. "`eeprom security-mode=command`" will force the system to require a password for non-standard boot commands. Running this command prompts the administrator for the password that will be used—this password itself is stored in another variable on the NVRAM chip.

Digression: BIOS Passwords

- Intel-based systems allow you to set a password in the system BIOS
- As soon as system is powered up, password must be entered
- Machine will no longer reboot unattended, but may be appropriate for laptops, etc.
- Forgetting this password can be a hassle!

SANS Security Essentials – Unix Security

NOTES

BIOS Passwords

One problem with Intel-based machines is that the system BIOS actually gets involved in the boot process before the LILO or GRUB boot-loader. The BIOS has a list of devices that it will probe in order to find a boot-loader program to execute. The BIOS may first check the floppy and/or CD-ROM drives before executing the GRUB or LILO boot loader from the system's hard drive. This means an attacker simply could insert a bootable floppy or CD-ROM into the drive and reboot the machine. The BIOS will find and execute the boot-loader from the attacker's media rather than off the system's hard drive, and the boot-level password that the administrator configured will be completely bypassed.

So one thing to do is to change the default BIOS boot order for the system. When the system is first powered on, the BIOS can be accessed directly, typically by hitting the `<delete>` key. One of the configuration options available should be the default order to use when checking devices for boot-loader programs. Of course, even if the administrator configures the system always to execute the boot-loader from the local hard drive first, an attacker with physical access to the system always could get into the BIOS configuration and change this default search order.

It actually is possible for the administrator to set a BIOS-level password in addition to any boot-loader password they may have configured. This is a hardware-level password that is completely independent of the operating system and is configured onto the machine (so BIOS passwords can be used to protect Windows systems as well). Once a BIOS password is set, this password must be entered as soon as the system is powered on.

However, this means that the system will no longer reboot after a power outage, unless somebody is there to enter the BIOS password. So, while BIOS passwords might be appropriate on a laptop system, or even a machine in an unguarded area, they probably should not be used on "server" type machines—particularly machines that already are in locked data center environments.

Also, if the BIOS password is lost or forgotten, then the machine becomes unbootable. The system BIOS usually is a memory module protected with a battery to preserve the BIOS settings when the machine is powered down. Removing this battery from the BIOS chip on the system motherboard will usually "blank" the BIOS and return it to its factory-default

NOTES

settings. However, in addition to removing the BIOS password, resetting the BIOS in this way also may cause the system to lose important BIOS settings that were set up by the system manufacturer. The system may end up being unbootable even after the BIOS password has been cleared.

NOTES

What Password Should You Use?

- *DO NOT* use the system root password:
  - Don't want this sitting around in config files
  - You'll forget to change boot password when you update system root password
- Use a consistent password and stick with it
- Remember, primary purpose of boot-level security is to thwart outsiders

SANS Security Essentials – Unix Security

What Password to Use?

So the question now becomes, what password should a site choose as its standard boot-loader and/or BIOS password? Some sites think that using the system `root` password is a good idea, but actually this turns out to be a bad idea for a couple of reasons. For one thing, it means that the system `root` password is going to be sitting in `/etc/lilo.conf` or `/etc/grub.conf`—possibly in clear text. This does not seem like a good idea.

The other problem, though, is that when sites change their `root` passwords they often will forget to change the boot-loader password. Six months or a year down the road, the administration staff vainly is trying to remember an old system `root` password so that they can boot the system from the vendor's CD-ROM to perform a system upgrade . . . or worse, so that they can fix the system after the disks have crashed!

The reality is that these passwords primarily are used to discourage outsiders from interfering with local systems. So it probably is best just to choose a consistent boot-loader password that is different from the system `root` passwords across all machines. Give this boot-loader password to anybody with a "need to know."

Having done all we can to protect the system boot process, it also is worth spending some time to protect the system from unauthorized `root` access once it has booted and is running normally. This is the topic of the next section.

NOTES

Restricting Root Access

SANS Security Essentials – Unix Security

Restricting Superuser Access

Earlier in the chapter we mentioned that it was a bad idea to allow administrators to log into the system directly as the `root` user. This generally is referred to as an "anonymous `root` login" because the user does not have to identify herself with her own username before getting `root` access. Why are anonymous `root` logins bad? The reason noted earlier was a loss of accountability. If there is an anonymous `root` login, and the system crashes soon thereafter, how can the administrative staff know who was responsible?

NOTES

Root Login for Emergencies Only

- Anonymous root logins are *bad:*
  - No audit trail, no accountability
  - May allow exhaustive guessing attacks
- Under normal circumstances, log in as normal user and use su/sudo
- Need to allow for root logins on console in case of emergencies

SANS Security Essentials – Unix Security

The other problem with allowing anonymous root logins is that attackers may be able to try logging in repeatedly as root with different passwords until they guess the actual root password. Typically, this sort of behavior will cause alert messages to appear all over the system logs and even on the system console, but this information may be lost if the site does not do a good job of monitoring its systems.

Administrators normally should log in under their own account and then use su or sudo to get root access. In certain emergency situations, it may be necessary to log into the system console as root, typically when the machine is inaccessible via other means. However, direct root logins only should be allowed on the system's physical console device and never over the network.

NOTES

securetty and More

- /etc/securetty lists where anonymous root logins are allowed
  - File should contain only physical ttys associated with the console device
  - Note that this is not the default configuration!
- Other issues:

  - Set "PermitRootLogin no" in sshd_config
  - Also disable root logins for GUI login screens?

SANS Security Essentials – Unix Security

On RedHat systems, the /etc/securetty file lists the devices where anonymous root logins are allowed. The primary console device on a RedHat system is /dev/tty1, so the /etc/securetty file should contain only the line:

```
tty1
```

Note that the default RedHat securetty file contains additional lines that correspond to the system "virtual consoles." Allowing root logins on these devices is not critical for the functioning or administration of the system, and these lines may be deleted safely from the /etc/securetty file.

The standard GNOME and KDE graphical login screens for RedHat do not obey the /etc/securetty file. Disabling root logins via these login screens requires direct modifications to the configuration files for these programs. The configuration file for the GNOME login program, gdm, typically is /etc/X11/gdm/gdm.conf. Set AllowRoot=false and AllowRemoteRoot=false in this file to prevent anonymous root logins. For the KDE login screen, the administrator must edit the kdmrc file, which may appear in any one of several locations, depending on the version of the operating system (/etc/X11/xdm/kdmrc, /usr/share/config/kdmrc, or /usr/share/config/kdm/kdmrc are common locations). The administrator must set AllowRootLogin=false in **two** locations in this file to block anonymous root logins.

Administrators may be concerned about blocking root access via these GUIs. What happens in an emergency when a direct root login is the only way to access the system? Typically RedHat provides "virtual console" support so that a user at the console can access a text-based login in order to get direct root access. These text-based logins occur on standard system terminal (tty) devices and so are under the control of the /etc/securetty file.

Various network login services also may have their own mechanisms for controlling anonymous root logins. For example, SSH uses the PermitRootLogin parameter in the SSH server configuration file, typically /etc/ssh/sshd_config. Setting "PermitRootLogin no" blocks anonymous root logins. It is annoying that the sshd_config file that ships with RedHat has "PermitRootLogin yes" as the default setting. After changing this to "no," send a HUP signal to the running SSH daemon ("pkill -HUP sshd") to force the daemon to re-read its configuration file.

NOTES

RedHat Virtual Consoles

Remember that when a RedHat system boots to run level 5, it starts a GUI login process on the system console. However, what happens if the system's X Windows configuration is broken? The user could be completely locked out of the machine. In fact, this used to be a huge problem in the early days of Linux, when the X Windows implementation was much less stable than it is today.

As a work-around, RedHat provides multiple "virtual" consoles in addition to the standard display with the GUI login screen. The idea behind these virtual consoles is that it allows the user to escape to a text-only login when the standard GUI login is broken. This allows the user to log into the machine and hopefully correct whatever problem is causing the GUI not to function.

The user may access the first console by typing `<ctrl>-<alt>-<F1>`. This provides access to a text-based login running on the primary system console device, `/dev/tty1`. Typically there are five other virtual consoles, accessed with `<ctrl>-<alt>-<F2>` through `<ctrl>-<alt>-<F6>`. `<ctrl>-<alt>-<F7>` switches back to the standard GUI login screen.

NOTES

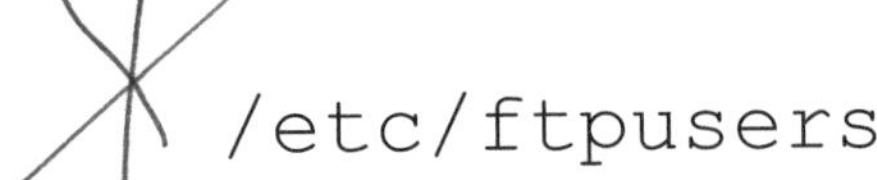

/etc/ftpusers

- ftpusers file is a list of users who are *NOT* allowed to FTP into this machine
- root user should always be listed here
- Probably also want to add all "system" user accounts created for various apps
- May want to add all other users in order to force people to use SSH for file transfer

SANS Security Essentials – Unix Security

Similarly, the system FTP daemon has its own configuration file, /etc/ftpusers, for controlling which users can access the system via FTP. This /etc/ftpusers file actually is mis-named since it is a list of the users who are **not** allowed to log into the system via FTP. Certainly administrators should add "root" to this file to prevent root logins via FTP.

However, it also is probably a good idea to add all of the other "system" accounts—like "oracle," "apache," "nobody," and "daemon"—to the /etc/ftpusers file, as well. There is no reason why these accounts, which do not correspond to real users on the system, should ever be logging in via FTP.

In fact, if the site has chosen to stop using FTP in favor of the more secure scp or sftp protocols provided by SSH, then perhaps **all** of the users in the password file should appear in /etc/ftpusers since nobody should be using FTP on the system at all.

Of course, in this case it probably is advisable to disable the FTP daemon completely, unless the system is an anonymous FTP server or makes data publicly available via FTP. Still, go ahead and create the ftpusers file, even if the FTP daemon has been shut off. This "Defense in-Depth" measure can help protect the system if the FTP daemon ever is re-enabled.

Note that if the system is an anonymous FTP server, it is important that the "ftp" user is **not** in /etc/ftpusers. When anonymous users log in, they are logging in as this "ftp" user. If user "ftp" is prevented from logging in by /etc/ftpusers, then anonymous FTP access is totally blocked.

Having done as much as we can to protect and control root access to the system, it also is important to take appropriate measures to control other access via unprivileged user accounts on the system. In particular, the .rhosts mechanism supported by rlogin, rsh, and rcp probably should be disabled entirely due to the security issues surrounding this weak authentication scheme.

NOTES

Create ftpusers Automatically

- Add all "system" users (UID < 500) to /etc/ftpusers file:

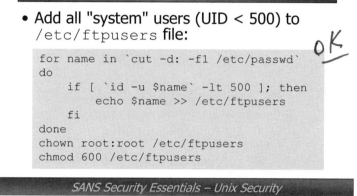

```
for name in `cut -d: -f1 /etc/passwd`
do
    if [ `id -u $name` -lt 500 ]; then
        echo $name >> /etc/ftpusers
    fi
done
chown root:root /etc/ftpusers
chmod 600 /etc/ftpusers
```

SANS Security Essentials – Unix Security

Here is a little bit of shell script that automatically will add all "system" accounts to /etc/ftpusers, assuming the system follows the standard Linux convention of giving these accounts UIDs less than 500:

```
for name in 'cut -d: -f1 /etc/passwd'
do
    if [ 'id -u $name' -lt 500 -a "$name" != "ftp" ]; then
        echo $name >> /etc/ftpusers
    fi
done
chown root:root /etc/ftpusers
chmod 600 /etc/ftpusers
```

The script first pulls all of the usernames out of the /etc/passwd file by using the cut command to extract the first field from all entries. The "for" loop then iterates over each username and uses the id command to find the UID corresponding to that username (although this information could also have been extracted directly from /etc/passwd if desired). If the UID is less than 500, and the user name is not "ftp," the username is appended to /etc/ftpusers.

Since the FTP daemon runs as root, the /etc/ftpusers file may as well be readable only by the root user. There is no reason to disclose which accounts have FTP logins disabled and which do not.

NOTES

Disabling `.rhosts`

Disabling .rhosts

`.rhosts` files essentially comprise a convenience feature, since they allow users to move from system to system over the network without providing a password. But `.rhosts` files allow users to bypass the normal system username and password authentication process, replacing it with an authentication system which is based on IP addresses and host names. Unfortunately it is all too easy to spoof IP addresses or provide false host name information via malicious DNS responses. So host name and IP address information is not a sound basis for access control.

NOTES

The Problem

- `.rhosts` files replace username/password auth with hostname/address-based auth
  - IP addresses can be spoofed
  - Hostname lookups usually rely on DNS which can also be spoofed
- Disabling `.rhosts` globally improves security at the cost of user convenience

Choose security over convenience in this case

SANS Security Essentials – Unix Security

DISABLE

For this reason, most sites now are making the choice of security over convenience in this case and disabling `.rhosts` support on their systems. This choice is simpler now that SSH provides equally convenient access mechanisms that provide much higher levels of security. For example, the `ssh-agent` program and SSH agent forwarding allow users to move easily between systems on the network while still performing strong authentication at each login (for more information, see the `ssh-agent` and `ssh` manual pages). Automated tasks such as `cron` jobs which rely on `.rhosts` files to operate without manual intervention can replace the `.rhosts` mechanism with DSA authentication (again, see the `ssh` manual page).

Some sites attempt to disable `.rhosts` files by running `cron` jobs that periodically remove `.rhosts` files from user home directories. This does not work in the long run, however, because users simply will put the files back as soon as they are removed.

NOTES

Cooking With PAM

- Services obey `/etc/pam.d` config files
- Remove `pam_rhosts_auth` lines:

```
cd /etc/pam.d
for file in *
do
    grep -v rhosts_auth $file > $file.new
    mv $file.new $file
    chown root:root $file
    chmod 644 $file
done
```

SANS Security Essentials – Unix Security

A better approach would disable `.rhosts` functionality globally at the operating system level. On Unix systems which support PAM, `.rhosts` functionality is controlled via the PAM configuration files. Administrators may disable `.rhosts` support entirely simply by removing the appropriate lines from the system's local configuration files.

On RedHat systems, the PAM configuration files for various services appear in `/etc/pam.d`. The PAM module that allows `.rhosts` authentication is `pam_rhosts_auth`. Simply removing any lines from the configuration files in `/etc/pam.d` that reference this module will disable `.rhosts` support. Here is some shell code to do this automatically:

```
cd /etc/pam.d
for file in *
do
    grep -v rhosts_auth $file > $file.new
    mv $file.new $file
    chown root:root $file
    chmod 644 $file
done
```

Note that most of the modules in `/etc/pam.d` do not even mention `pam_rhosts_auth`; so for most of the files in this directory, this code is a "no-op." In fact, the administrator really only has to edit the `/etc/pam.d/rlogin` and `/etc/pam.d/rsh` files to remove all references to `pam_rhosts_auth`.

NOTES

Special Case for SSH

- SSH daemon may not obey system PAM configuration files
- Need to edit `sshd_config`:

```
IgnoreRhosts              yes
RhostsAuthentication      no
RhostsRSAAuthentication   no
```

SANS Security Essentials – Unix Security

SSH is capable of supporting `.rhosts` style authentication. If enabled, the SSH daemon will look for either `.rhosts` or SSH-specific `.shosts` files in the user's home directory. Unfortunately, the system SSH daemon may not obey the PAM system, so it is best to disable explicitly `.rhosts` and `.shosts` support in the SSH server configuration file, which again usually is `/etc/ssh/sshd_config`. Simply set three values as follows:

```
IgnoreRhosts              yes

RhostsAuthentication      no

RhostsRSAAuthentication   no
```

After modifying the SSH server configuration, it is necessary to send a `HUP` signal to the running SSH daemon ("`pkill -HUP sshd`").

NOTES

Extra Insurance

- Many attackers try to put back doors in `hosts.equiv` or root's `.rhosts`/`.shosts`
- Shouldn't work now that we've disabled `.rhosts` support with PAM
- Some sites link these files to `/dev/null` just in case

SANS Security Essentials – Unix Security

Attackers who are trying to exploit the `.rhosts` mechanism to gain access to the system typically will attempt to write the string "+ +" to the `.rhosts` or `.shosts` file in `root`'s home directory (usually `/root` on RedHat systems). "+ +" in a `.rhosts` file is a wildcard meaning "grant access from any user on any remote system." If the system did allow `.rhosts` style access, getting this string into `root`'s `.rhosts` file would give the attacker the ability to remotely execute any command on the local system with root privileges.

Attackers sometimes will try to get this string into the `/etc/hosts.equiv` file, which functions similarly to a global `.rhosts` file for all users on the system. The local system allows logins without a password, as long as the remote system is listed in `hosts.equiv` and as long as the account on the remote system matches the account being accessed on the local machine. "+ +" in this file means that any user on any remote machine can access any user account on the local system without providing a password. However, `hosts.equiv` access does not apply to the `root` account on the local system, so only access to unprivileged accounts is granted, which still could be serious if the local account being accessed were something like the "`oracle`" database administration account.

Even though they have globally disabled `.rhosts` support via PAM (which incidentally also disables support for the `hosts.equiv` file as well), some sites go for extra "Defense in-Depth" and create symbolic links from `root`'s `.rhosts` and `.shosts` files and from `/etc/hosts.equiv` to the system `/dev/null` device. `/dev/null` is the system "bit bucket"—anything written to this device simply is discarded. By linking these configuration files to `/dev/null`, the administrator ensures that anything the attacker attempts to write to these files is thrown away. Here is some simple shell code to create these links:

```
for file in /etc/hosts.equiv /root/.rhosts
/root/.shosts

do

     rm -f $file

     ln -s /dev/null $file

done
```

Of course, the attacker could remove the symbolic link before attempting to write to the file, but most of the automated exploit scripts out there do not go to this extra step.

NOTES

Summary: Lessons Learned

- Control superuser access:
  - Beware unauthorized UID 0 accounts
  - Prevent anonymous `root` logins
- Other account issues:
  - Avoid duplicate UIDs in password file
  - Block access to "system" accounts
- Use appropriate boot-level security
- Disable `.rhosts` support

SANS Security Essentials – Unix Security

Summary

We have covered a number of important access control concepts in this chapter. Password protecting the boot process can help stop attackers with local access to the system from booting from alternate media and bypassing the system's normal access control mechanisms. Certainly the administrator should ensure that the system requires the `root` password before granting access to the system in single-user mode, or else an attacker trivially can reboot the system and gain `root` access at the single-user level.

Anonymous `root` logins reduce accountability and may allow a remote attacker to do a "brute force" password guessing attack on the root password. Anonymous `root` logins only should be allowed on the system console, and administrators should use this access mechanism only in the event of a system emergency. For normal operations, administrators should log in under their own user accounts and then use `su` or `sudo` to get `root` privileges. Also, disable the standard `.rhosts` functionality that allows normal users to bypass normal system username and password authentication.

Remember that any account with UID 0 has superuser privileges on the system. The password file probably should have only a single UID 0 account in it, and that should be the `root` account. In fact, any duplicate UIDs in the password file are a bad idea because it means that any files created by one user can be modified by the other users that share the same UID.

Be sure to keep an eye on "system" accounts that were created for certain applications. These accounts should be blocked so that logins are not possible, but attackers sometimes will attempt to re-activate these accounts as a "back door" into the system.

NOTES

Chapter 35

System Configuration

NOTES

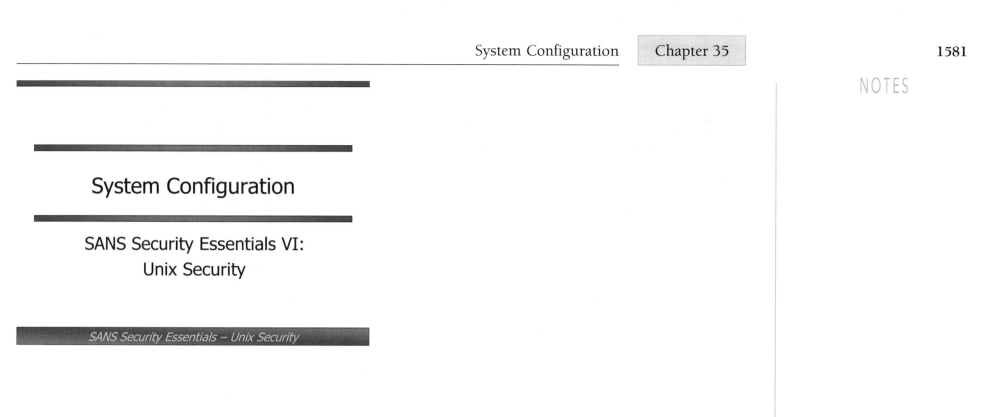

NOTES

System Configuration

SANS Security Essentials VI:
Unix Security

NOTES

Quick Look at What's Coming

- File permissions and ownership
- File system security
- Adjusting kernel parameters
- `cron` security and access control
- Preventing anonymous shutdowns

SANS Security Essentials – Unix Security

This chapter covers some simple settings administrators can make to improve the overall security of their systems. The early part of the chapter covers the basics of access control for individual files and directories in the file system and then moves into controlling security settings on the file system as a whole. Then we look at some simple settings that can be modified at the lowest levels of the operating system to help set reasonable defaults that can protect against denial-of-service attacks and other types of system abuse.

Chapter 32 briefly introduced the system `cron` daemon, which runs jobs for users and administrators at scheduled times of the day. Later in this chapter we will look at additional configuration changes that can be made to improve the security and auditability of the `cron` system.

Chapter 34 discussed how unauthorized tampering with the system boot process may allow local attackers to subvert standard system access controls. However, Linux and other newer Unix systems are starting to provide mechanisms for non-`root` users to shut down or reboot systems in the name of user friendliness. Some sites prefer to prevent normal users from performing these kinds of administrative operations, and so we will end the chapter by looking at how to disable this functionality.

NOTES

File Permissions/Ownership

SANS Security Essentials – Unix Security

File Permissions and Ownership

The last chapter covered Unix user IDs (UIDs) and group IDs (GIDs). Now we will look at how UIDs and GIDs relate to file and directory ownership and how this ownership ties into access rights that can be set on files and directories. It also is important to mention some special types of files and directories for which administrators should look out.

NOTES

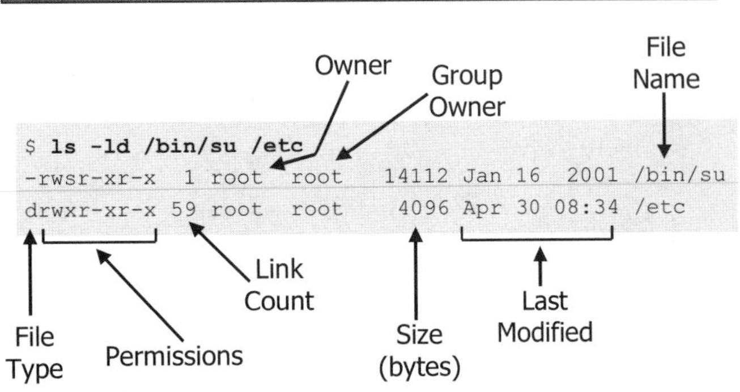

File Attributes

The Unix operating system stores a number of different attributes for files and directories, including the file's owner and group owner and the access control settings on the file. The easiest way to view the attributes for a file is with the "`ls -l`" command, which gives a detailed file listing:

```
$ ls -ld /bin/su /etc

-rwsr-xr-x    1 root     root          18452
Jul 23  2001 /bin/su

drwxr-xr-x   69 root     root           5120
Aug 22 11:36 /etc
```

Note that the "`-d`" option forces the `ls` command to display the file attributes for the actual directories listed—in this case `/etc`—rather than showing the attributes for all of the files in that directory, which is the default.

The first column of the listing is a block of letter codes showing the type of file and the access permissions set on the file. The letter in the first column of this block shows what type of object this is: "`-`" means a regular file, and "`d`" indicates a directory. There are several other letter codes defined for other special types of files, but they are not important for the current discussion. The other nine columns in this initial block of letter codes describe the access permissions on the file, which will be our concern for most of the rest of this section.

The next column in the file listing is the "link count" field. Again, understanding the meaning of the link count field is not critical for this discussion.

The next two columns show the owner of the file and the group owner of the file. These combine with the file access permissions to tell the system who has access to the file.

The fifth column is the file size in bytes. Next comes the last modified time on the file. Note that dates within the last year display the actual time of modification while older dates simply display month, day, and year. This simply is a human readable formatting decision; actual Unix dates are stored in a completely different internal format. The last column displays the file name.

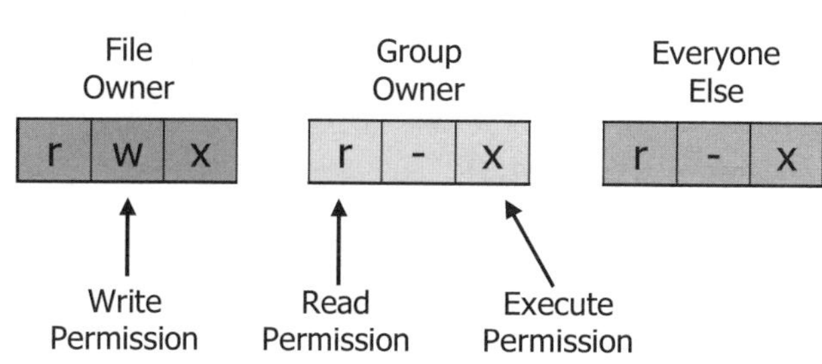

File Permissions

Let's focus our attention on the permission settings in the first column of the "`ls -l`" output. Unix file permissions use a security model with fairly coarse granularity. Only three basic permissions—"read", "write", and "execute"—can be set. Read permissions ("`r`") means the ability to look at or view the contents of a given file and also the ability to make a copy of that file elsewhere on the system. Write permission ("`w`") is the ability to modify the contents of the file. Execute ("`x`") is the ability to run that file as a program. Note that a program file may have execute permissions set without allowing read permissions. Users will be able to execute the program code stored in the file but not "read" the contents of the file to make a copy of that program elsewhere on disk.

Read, write, and execute permissions can be set for three different categories of people: the file's owner, people belonging to the Unix group listed as the group owner of the file, and "everybody else" (or "other"). The first three permission flags shown by "`ls -l`" (after the initial letter which indicates the type of file) are the permissions that are set for the owner of the file. The next group of settings in the middle three columns applies to the group owner of the file. The final three permission flags apply to the "everybody else" category. Note that if a particular permission flag is not set, then a dash ("-") is displayed.

NOTES

NOTES

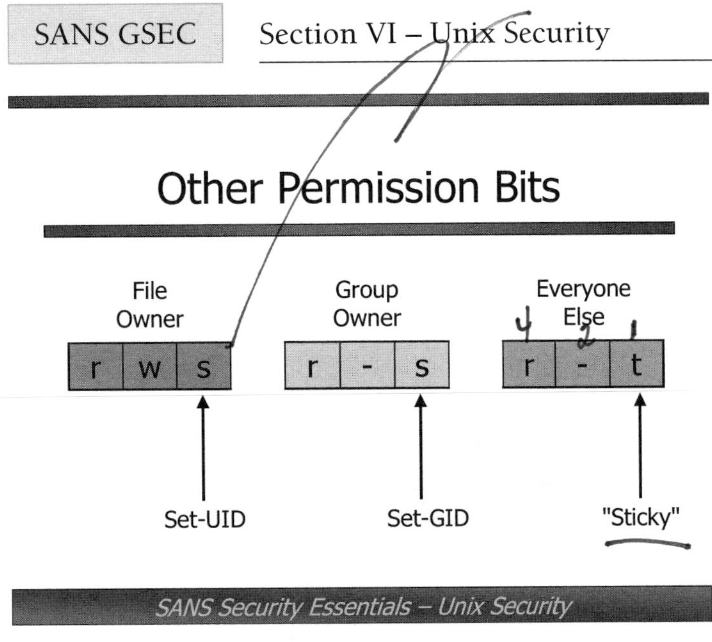

There are three other permission flags that optionally may be set on a file: "set-UID," "set-GID," and "sticky." Since there is no room to display these extra three bits in the "`ls -l`" output, the `ls` command shows these settings by replacing the `x`'s in the normal output. If "set-UID" is set, then an "`s`" is displayed instead of the "`x`" for the file's owner ("set-UID" only makes sense if the file also is executable . . . more on this in a moment). Similarly, "set-GID" is represented by showing an "`s`" instead of an "`x`" for the group owner category. The "sticky" flag is represented as a "`t`" in the very last column of the permissions flags, hiding the "`x`" for the "everybody else" category.

"Set-UID" and "set-GID" are interesting innovations that were created by the original Unix developers. Certain programs need to run with special access privileges not available to normal users. For example, the `passwd` command that allows users to change their passwords needs `root` privileges so it can update the `/etc/shadow` file. The "set user ID" flag (usually shortened to "set-UID" or just "suid") causes a program to run as the owner of the executable, rather than as the user that executed the program. Thus, the `passwd` program is set-UID and owned by `root` so that it can update the `shadow` file when executed by a normal user.

"Set-GID" ("set group ID") functions the same way but only gives the user who executes the program additional group access rights. The Unix commands that are used to print files often are set-GID to a special "line printer" ("`lp`") group that is allowed to copy files into the system's printer queue directories.

The so-called "sticky" flag originally was developed in the early days of Unix on slower machines. The idea was that any program which had the sticky bit set was supposed to "stick around" in the memory of the operating system after the program had finished executing. This was a win on programs that needed to be executed frequently because they did not need to be read back into memory constantly. Modern Unix systems, which use shared libraries, have better caching algorithms, and run on faster hardware, generally ignore the sticky bit on executables. However, the sticky bit now has a different special meaning when applied to directories . . . more on this shortly.

NOTES

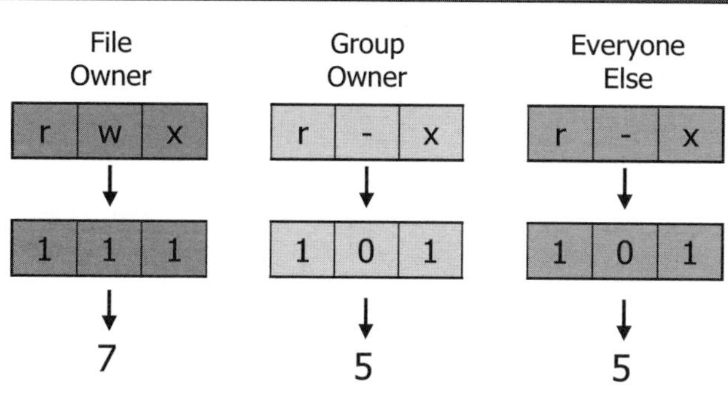

While the `ls` command displays permission settings using the letters "`r`," "`w`," "`x`," etc., the operating system actually stores these settings in a completely different internal format. Unix access permission flags often are referred to as "bits" because their representation in the Unix operating system as binary digits: a one means the given flag is turned on, and a zero means the flag is not set. Since there are three "bits" to be set for each ownership group—read, write, and execute—these permissions usually are represented in octal notation.

Consider the example in the illustration. The owner of the file has read, write, and execute permission: all bits are turned on, so the binary representation is "111," which is octal 7 (4+2+1). The group owner and "other" category only have read and execute set but not write permissions: the binary representation is "101," which is 5 (4+1) in octal notation.

NOTES

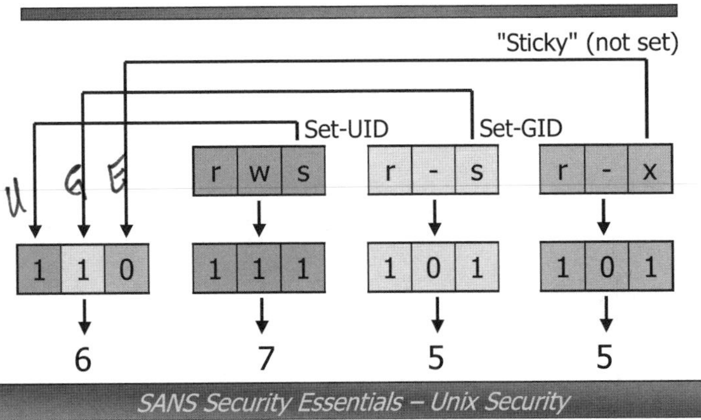

How are the set-UID, set-GID, and sticky "bits" represented? A fourth octal digit representing these values can be put in front of the three octal digits used to represent the read/write/execute permissions for the various ownership categories. In this leading octal digit, set-UID is the leading "most significant" binary digit (4 octal); set-GID is the next bit (2 octal); and "sticky" is the final "least significant" bit (1 octal).

In the illustration above, both the set-UID and set-GID bits are set, but the "sticky" bit is not. The octal representation of the leading digit is therefore 6 (4+2). In addition, read/write/execute is set for the file owner and read/execute is set for the group owner and "everybody else" categories, just as in the previous example. Thus, the complete numeric representation for this file's mode is 6755.

Since this octal notation completely specifies all of the permission bits on a file, it generally is referred to as the "absolute mode" of the file. The "`r`"/"`w`"/"`x`" notation displayed by `ls` usually is referred to as the "symbolic" mode of the file. Unix commands that deal with file permissions usually are able to handle either absolute or symbolic mode.

NOTES

Files vs. Directories

	File	Directory
Read	can read file contents	can get directory listing
Write	can modify file contents	can create/remove files
Execute	may execute file	may access files in directory
Set-UID	file executes with privileges of file's owner	N/A
Set-GID	as above but for group owner	group ownership of new files is inherited
"Sticky"	N/A	only owner may remove files

SANS Security Essentials – Unix Security

File vs. Directory Permissions

Because the Unix file permissions model is so limited, the meaning of each of the permissions flags we have seen so far is "overloaded." In other words, the permissions flags have different behavior depending on whether or not they are being applied to files or directories.

For example, being able to "read" a directory means that the user can run the `ls` command (or other similar commands) to get a listing of the files in the directory. The execute bit on a directory gives the user the ability to change directories into the given directory and to access files out of that directory, but a directory listing cannot be obtained unless the read permissions also are set. Generally speaking, directories need the execute flag turned on to be useful, but sometimes it is appropriate to give execute rights on a directory but not read privileges, such as for the "everybody else" access class. This would allow the owner of the directory to create files in the directory for various users on the system. A user would be able to access "her" file if the owner of the directory told her the explicit name of the file but would not be able to get a directory listing to see the other user's files.

Write permissions on a directory give the ability to change elements of the directory "file." In Unix, directories store file names and pointers to the file contents. So, being able to modify a directory means being able to rename files as well as to add files to the directory and delete files from the directory altogether. This often is confusing to users of other operating systems where "create," "delete," and "rename" privileges are implemented as separate attributes on individual files.

Set-GID has a surprising meaning on directories, as well. If the set-GID bit is set on a directory, and a user creates a new file in that directory, then the group owner of the new file will be the group owner of the directory rather than the primary group to which the user belongs (which would be the normal default behavior). This is useful when using Unix groups as a mechanism for sharing files in a large project because it ensures that new files created in the project tree end up being owned by the special group created for the project.

When the "sticky" bit is set on a directory, then only the owner of a given file may remove that file from the directory. This bit often is set on `/tmp` and other "world-writable" directories to prevent users from stomping on each other's files (either accidentally or purposely). These so-called "world-writable" directories are examples of potential security issues of which administrators should be aware on their systems.

NOTES

Lesson: File vs. Directory Perms

- Some sites try to stop .rhosts files:
  - Create empty .rhosts files in user home dirs
  - Make files owned by root, shut off all perms
- *Problem:* users have write access to their home dir– can remove any file
- Setting "sticky" bit on user home dir doesn't help– user can just unset this

SANS Security Essentials – Unix Security

This discrepancy between file and directory permission settings can be very confusing. Let's take a look at a practical example where things do not work out the way system administrators would like them to.

The previous chapter discussed disabling .rhosts files to improve the overall security of the system. Some sites try to prevent users from creating .rhosts files in their home directories by setting up the user's home directory with an empty .rhosts file that is owned by the root user and on which all permissions are turned off. The user does not have write permissions to the file, so he cannot add his own .rhosts entries to the file.

Remember, however, that the ability to remove a file is controlled by the permissions on the directory that contains the file. Since users have write permissions to their own home directories, they can just remove the root-owned .rhosts file that was created by the administrator and replace it with one of their own.

Aha! If the administrator sets the "sticky bit" on users' home directories, then the users can remove files that only they own and not the root-owned .rhosts file created by the administrator. The only problem with this strategy is that users, because they are the owners of their individual home directories, can reset the permissions on the directory and remove the sticky bit.

There simply is no way for the administrator to succeed at this game. The correct way to stop users from using .rhosts files is to disable them globally using the system PAM configuration files as we discussed in the previous chapter.

NOTES

Look Out: World-Writable Dirs

- World-writable dirs like /tmp used by programs to hold intermediate results
- What if attacker clobbered your program's temporary file and substituted their own?
- Golden rules:
  - Avoid world-writable directories if possible
  - Always set the "sticky" bit if world-writable

SANS Security Essentials – Unix Security

Potentially "Dangerous" Permissions

Unix systems typically have a number of directories that are "world-writable," meaning that write permissions are enabled for the "everybody else" category. In fact, "world-writable" directories generally are configured so that all permissions (read, write, and execute) typically are turned on for all three ownership categories. This means that anybody on the system can create, rename, and delete files at will in these directories. An example of such a directory would be the standard Unix `/tmp` and `/var/tmp` directories, where programs are supposed to write "scratch" data and intermediate results.

Historically, though, world-writable directories have caused enormous security problems. A simple example is the Unix C compiler used to compile programs from source. This compiler usually makes several "passes," in which the source code is transformed from one form to another before being turned into an actual executable. The results from each compiler "pass" are put into temporary files in `/tmp`. Now imagine an attacker quickly substituting a file containing malicious code for one of the files created during a compiler pass—suddenly there is a virus or Trojan horse in the program!

Therefore it is extremely important to ensure that the "sticky bit" is set on all world-writable directories, as is the default for system directories like `/tmp` and `/var/tmp`. With the "sticky bit" set, our attacker would not be able to delete or rename a user's intermediate compiler files to substitute the attacker's Trojan horse code.

Many programs these days simply are avoiding directories like `/tmp` altogether and instead are starting to use their own private temporary directories to which normal users on the system do not have write permissions. For example, the Sendmail e-mail server writes temporary data files containing messages that are currently being processed into a private directory called `/var/spool/mqueue` that is only accessible by the `root` user.

NOTES

Look Out: SUID/SGID Programs

- Double-edged sword:
  - Can't run Unix without SUID/SGID programs
  - However, rogue SUID/SGID programs can easily compromise a machine
- Keep track of the SUID/SGID programs provided with your OS
- Raise an alarm if new or unexpected SUID/SGID programs appear

SANS Security Essentials – Unix Security

Set-UID and set-GID programs historically have been one of the most common weaknesses that attackers have exploited to get privileged access on Unix systems. For example, an attacker may be able to bring a set-UID `root` copy of the Unix command shell onto the system on a CD-ROM or floppy. When the user executes this shell, she instantly gets `root` privileges without providing a password. Set-UID programs with buffer overflows or other coding errors may allow attackers to "escape" from the running program and get an interactive shell.

It may be a good idea to make a list of all of the set-UID and set-GID programs on the system when the machine is installed for the first time. Then periodically scan the system for set-UID and set-GID programs and compare the results against the original list. If "new" set-UID or set-GID programs appear, be suspicious.

All of this, of course, begs the question, "how can administrators scan their file systems for set-UID and set-GID files in the first place?" It also would be nice to be able to locate world-writable directories to confirm that their "sticky bit" is set.

`find` Your Way Around

Find recently modified files:

```
find /etc -mtime -1 -print
```

Find all subdirectories:

```
find /dev -type d -print
```

Run a command on all files:

```
find /dev -type d -exec ls -ld {} \;
```

SANS Security Essentials – Unix Security

Locating Special Files and Directories

Locating any object in the Unix file system typically is done with the `find` command. The `find` command has a syntax that is rather different from most standard Unix commands, so let's first cover some of the basics.

The arguments to the find command generally are divided into three groups: "`find` *<directory>* *<qualifiers>* *<action>*." Here *<directory>* is the path where find should begin working; use "`.`" to start the search from the current directory. *<action>* usually is either `-print`, which simply prints the names of matching files, or `-exec` followed by some other Unix command.

There are many, many *<qualifiers>* that can be used to match different sorts of files. Here are some simple examples:

```
find /etc -mtime -1 -print
find /dev -type d -print
```

The first example would print the names of all files under the `/etc` directory tree and whose "last modified time" (`-mtime`) is less than one day old (`-1`); in other words, all files that have been changed in the last 24 hours. "`-mtime +7`" would show all files whose last modified time is greater than seven days ago; that is, files which have not been changed in the last week. The `-type` qualifier matches files of a particular type: "`d`" for directories, "`f`" for regular files, etc. Attackers love to hide their tools in directories under `/dev` because the huge number of regular files in this directory tends to "hide" new files and directories from the notice of system administrators.

The `-exec` action has a rather strange looking syntax associated with it:

```
find /dev -type d -exec ls -ld {} \;
```

The `-exec` is followed by a normal Unix command line but with a couple of notable exceptions. First, use "`{}`" instead of the normal filename argument to the command that `find` should execute. Every time `find` discovers a file or directory which matches the search criteria, it executes the command specified with `-exec`, except that it substitutes the name of the matching file where the "`{}`" characters are. `find` also requires that the command line after `-exec` be terminated with "`\;`." This allows the `find` command to know when the arguments to `-exec` are done, in case after the `-exec` there are other `find` options that need to get parsed.

NOTES

NOTES

File Modes + `find` = Success!

Show world-writable directories:

```
find / -type d -perm -0002 -ls
```

Find SUID/SGID files:

```
find / -type f \
   \( -perm -04000 -o -perm -02000 \) \
   -print
```

SANS Security Essentials – Unix Security

Now as far as the current task is concerned, the `find` command has a "`-perm`" option for locating files that have certain file permission flags set. "`-perm`" understands both "absolute" and "symbolic" file modes.

Using symbolic mode, here is a `find` command for locating world-writable objects throughout the entire file system, starting from the top or "root" of the file system, the directory "`/`":

```
find / -perm -o=w -print
```

Generally, "world-writable" means that write permissions are enabled for the "everybody else" ownership category. "`o=w`" is how this is represented typically in symbolic mode; the "`o`" stands for "other". "`u=`" is used to specify permissions for the owner ("user") of the file, and "`g=`" is used to specify permissions for the group owner.

The dash before the "`o=w`" means that `find` should display any objects which have **at least** the write bit set for the "other" category but which also may have other permission bits set. Without the dash, the `find` command would only report objects that **exactly** match the permissions specified. It is very unlikely that anything in the file system would have only the write bit set for "other" and no other flags turned on.

Now this same command could be written using "absolute" file modes:

```
find / -perm -0002 -print
```

Again, the dash before the octal permission value means "match at least" these flags, as opposed to "match exactly."

The two `find` commands shown above will display any world-writable file, directory, or other object encountered in the file system. This probably is a good idea since even world-writable files should be discouraged. Users do not want anybody on the system to be able to modify their files, and system configuration and log files should never be world-writable.

However, suppose the administrator only wished to find world-writable directories, perhaps in order to find ones which did not have the "sticky bit" set. This is accomplished easily by combining the "`-type d`" qualifier with either form of the "`-perm`" option:

```
find / -type d -perm -o=w -print

find / -type d -perm -0002 print
```

The `find` command does the expected thing here and only shows objects that match both criteria (a logical "and").

NOTES

More complicated logical expressions can be built up using "and" ("-a"), "or" ("-o"), "not" ("!"), and parentheses. For example, it is possible to write a find command that shows only world-writable directories that do not have the "sticky bit" set:

```
find / -type d \( -perm -o=w -a \! -perm
-o=t \) -print

find / -type d \( -perm -0002 -a \! -perm
-1000 \) -print
```

Parentheses and the "!" character are interpreted as special characters by the Unix command shell. Putting a "backslash" ("\") in front of these characters prevents the Unix shell from evaluating these special characters and instead causes them to be passed into the find command for parsing.

A similar sort of logical grouping could be used to locate files that have either the set-UID or the set-GID bit set:

```
find / -type f \( -perm -u=s -o -perm -g=s
\) -ls

find / -type f \( -perm -4000 -o -perm -2000
\) -ls
```

This certainly is one way the administrator could generate a list of set-UID and set-GID files currently installed on the system. Comparing lists generated with the "-ls" action will tell the administrator not only if new set-UID or set-GID files have been added to the system but also will alert the admin if file attributes on previously installed set-UID and set-GID programs have changed (like the file size or last modified time).

NOTES

Set Perms with chmod & umask

- Can use "symbolic" file modes:

```
chmod u-s myfile          # turn off SUID bit
chmod g+w myfile          # give group write
chmod o-r myfile          # no read for "others"
chmod a-x myfile          # turn off execute
```

- Can also use "absolute" file modes:

```
chmod 666 myfile          # file is "world write"
chmod 600 /etc/lilo.conf  # only owner perms set
chmod 1777 /tmp           # set "sticky bit"
```

- umask is bits *not to set* by default:

```
umask 022           # no write for group/other
umask 077           # only owner has rights
```

SANS Security Essentials – Unix Security

Setting File Permissions

Of course, being able to simply locate problematic files and directories is not enough. Administrators also need to be able to change the permissions on files and directories, such as adding the "sticky bit" to a world writable directory or removing the set-UID bit from an executable. The Unix chmod ("change mode") command is used to set permission flags on files and directories. Like the "-perm" option for the find command, chmod supports both "absolute" and "symbolic" mode.

Symbolic mode is most useful for setting or unsetting specific individual permission flags on a given file:

```
chmod u-s myfile    # turn off SUID bit

chmod g+w myfile    # give group write

chmod o-r myfile    # no read for "others"

chmod a-x myfile    # no execute for all
```

chmod uses the same letters for identifying the ownership categories that find does: "u" ("user") for the file owner permissions, "g" for the group owner, and "o" for the "other" or "everybody else" category. chmod also recognizes "a" ("all"), which means apply the permission setting to all categories. Actually, "a" is the default, so "chmod a-x myfile" and "chmod -x myfile" do the same thing on most Unix systems. The ownership category is followed by a plus or a minus, indicating whether the given flag should be enabled or disabled.

In fact, multiple ownership categories and multiple permission flags can be specified simultaneously. Even commas can be used to specify a list of flags to be set and unset. For example, the command "chmod u+s,go-r myfile" would turn on the set-UID bit on the executable myfile and simultaneously remove the read bit for both the group owner and "other" categories. It is not uncommon to disable read privileges on set-UID binaries because on some Unix systems this may be the only way to prevent users from executing set-UID binaries in a symbolic debugger and potentially obtaining sensitive data.

However, this last chmod command comes perilously close to specifying the entire permission list for myfile. At some point, using "absolute" mode to specify the exact permissions for a file is appropriate:

```
chmod 666 myfile    # file is "world write"

chmod 600 /etc/lilo.conf     # only owner
perms set
```

```
chmod 1777 /tmp      # set "sticky bit" on
/tmp
chmod 4711 myfile    # set-UID executable,
no read
```

Of course, making a file completely world-writable by setting its mode to 666 is dangerous, particularly if the file contains logging information or system configuration data. The second example above comes from the last chapter, where we set the mode on /etc/lilo.conf to 600 to protect the clear text password string stored there. The third example sets the normal permissions on the /tmp directory; everybody on the system has read, write, and execute permissions on the directory, but the "sticky bit" is set so that users cannot clobber each other's files. The last example sets permissions in a similar fashion to the "chmod u+s,go-r myfile" symbolic mode command, though the absolute mode specifies exactly the complete vector of permission flags.

Now by default, the Unix operating system would create all new files mode 666, or 777 for directories and executable files produced by the system compilers. Ideally, users and administrators would like to be able to specify a different default mode for new files and directories they create so that they are not world-writable by default. The umask command allows a user to specify the permission flags that **should not** be enabled by default.

A standard choice is "umask 022," which turns off the write bit for the group owner and "other" categories. Some sites even prefer umask values of 027 ("no write for group owner and no access at all for everybody else") or 077 ("only owner has access"). These more restrictive umask settings give the file's owner the choice of whether or not to allow explicitly other people access to the file. This generally is referred to as giving users "discretionary access control" over their data and is a requirement in many secure environments.

Whatever the site policy on the umask value is, administrators should make sure that this umask value gets into their user's default command shell environments. Either the /etc/profile or the /etc/.login file will get read by the user's login shell by default, and the settings in these files will become part of the user's environment. Putting the umask command in these files is a good idea. If the site also provides default configuration files in user home directories, putting the umask command in these files also is warranted.

It also is important to make sure that the umask value is set for all processes that are started at boot time for the system. After all, it would not be good for system daemons to create log files that were the system default mode of 666. Unfortunately, the trick for setting the boot-time umask for various processes varies from system to system. Under RedHat, the umask command can be inserted into /etc/rc.d/init.d/functions because the commands in this file are executed in all of the other boot scripts in /etc/rc.d/init.d. Under newer Solaris releases, the default umask value for boot-time processes can be set via the CMASK parameter in /etc/default/init.

NOTES

NOTES

User and Group Ownership

- `chown` changes file ownership
  `chown hal /home/hal`
- `chgrp` changes group ownership
  `chgrp other /home/hal`
- Usually, you can do both at once

```
chown hal.other /home/hal          # old BSD
chown root:root /etc/lilo.conf     # modern
```

SANS Security Essentials – Unix Security

Changing File Ownership

Sometimes simply changing the permissions on a file is not enough. Administrators also need the ability to change the owner or group owner of a file or directory. The `chown` ("change owner") and `chgrp` ("change group") commands are used to modify ownership rights to files and directories:

```
chown alice /home/alice

chgrp staff /home/alice
```

In fact, on most Unix systems the `chown` command can set the file owner and group owner simultaneously. The usual syntax looks like "`chown alice:staff /home/alice`," with the format being "`<owner>:<group>`". Older Unix systems may use a period instead of a colon—"`chown alice.staff /home/alice`"—but now this is very rare.

Most Unix systems only allow the superuser to use the `chown` command. Allowing normal users to `chown` files, even files that they own, can be dangerous. For example, a user could create an executable and make it set-UID. If that user were then allowed to change the ownership of that file to `root`, then he would have a set-UID `root` executable that he could use to compromise the system. For this reason, if the `chown` command is allowed to be run by a normal user on a Unix system, the command generally will strip off the set-UID and set-GID bits automatically when the owner of the file is changed.

Allowing users to `chown` their own files can also have an impact on the system if file system quotas are enabled, restricting users to a fixed amount of disk consumption. If normal users can run `chown`, then they can make their files owned by other users on the system, effectively giving themselves "more disk space" by stealing it from other users. Ultimately, this could become a denial-of-service attack, at least as far as the other users on the system are concerned.

It should also be noted that both `chown` and `chgrp` allow the user to specify either usernames and group names or instead to use numeric UIDs and GIDs, or even a combination of the two. Most users and administrators find it more convenient to use human-readable names, however.

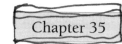

NOTES

File System Security

SANS Security Essentials – Unix Security

File System Security

While the last section focused on ownership and access control on individual files and directories, it also is important to apply security controls to the file system as a whole, and perhaps especially to files and directories that are brought in on removable media, such as floppy disks and CD-ROMs. Before we get to that, however, let's review the basics of the Unix directory structure and how these directories are distributed onto the system's physical disk drives.

NOTES

Logical File System...

/ – root file system, top of directory hierarchy

`/dev`, `/devices` – directory containing "files" used to talk to system devices

`/usr` – primary OS directory, "read-only"

`/var` – contains log files, queues, etc.

`/bin`, `/usr/bin`, `/usr/local`, `/opt` – executable programs, some SUID/SGID

`/home`, `/export/home` – user home dirs

SANS Security Essentials – Unix Security

Unix File System Basics

There used to be a lot of variance in where different files were located in different Unix "flavors," but modern Unix variants have settled down to using the same general file system layout. The top of the file system tree is the "root directory," `/`. Below this directory are various important subdirectory trees.

The `/dev` directory contains the special "device files" that programs running on the system use to communicate with the physical hardware devices controlled by the operating system kernel. Unix systems derived from the AT&T "System V" (SYSV) Unix standard, such as Solaris and HP-UX, often will put these device files into the `/devices` directory but also usually maintain a `/dev` directory for compatibility with other systems.

`/usr` is where most of the critical components of the operating system live, including system binaries, programming libraries and tools, and on-line documentation. This directory structure can be thought of as being "read-only": after the operating system is loaded, not many changes under `/usr` should occur unless the operating system is upgraded or patches are installed. `/var` is where the system keeps frequently changing data, such as log files and temporary queues for system services like e-mail and printing.

While programs provided with the operating system end up in directories like `/usr/bin` and `/usr/sbin`, other programs can be found scattered throughout the system. A standard convention is to put third-party software obtained from the Internet into the `/usr/local` directory. SYSV derived machines systems like Solaris and HP-UX often will put third-party software (particularly commercial software) into `/opt`. Different sites may choose to use a different directory naming scheme for third-party software, however, such as `/pkg` or `/sw`.

User home directories often are found under `/home`. For large Unix networks, though, `/home` often is an NFS mounted directory, and `/export/home` is the directory in which the files physically reside on the file server. Again, many other local conventions exist. Some sites prefer directory names like `/users` or `/u1`, `/u2`, ..., etc.

NOTES

User E-mail

The one piece of critical user data that is not found in the user's home directories is user e-mail. User e-mail usually is found in `/var/mail` or `/var/spool/mail`. Administrators often will back up user home directories carefully but forget to back up user e-mail in `/var`, resulting in unhappy users when the system disks crash. On the other hand, some sites have explicit policies **against** backing up e-mail because they are worried that archived e-mail may be subpoenaed and used against them in a court case (which has happened in a number of high-profile cases in recent years).

NOTES

...and the Physical File System

- The logical Unix file system is made up of multiple physical disk partitions
- Disk partitions are mounted at various points in the file system
- Different security options can be set on each mount point

SANS Security Essentials – Unix Security

While the Unix file system appears to be a single logical entity to the users on the system, it actually is made up of several pieces (called "partitions") that correspond to physical sections of the machine's disk drives. Partitions generally are assigned to critical pieces of the logical directory structure. For example, the system might have one partition for the root file system, another for `/usr`, another for `/var`, and so on. During the boot process, all of these partitions are "mounted" into their proper place to make the file system appear contiguous.

Disk partitions, their mount points, and the options applied to each partition generally are described in a file called `/etc/fstab`. Solaris uses the name `/etc/vfstab` apparently just to be perverse. These file system options in the `/etc/fstab` file allow the administrator to specify different security settings for various partitions.

From a Unix perspective, disk drives have sixteen different partition "slices," either numbered 0-15 or lettered a-p. For example, Linux would use the device named "`hda7`" to specify slice `7` (which technically is the 8th slice since the numbering starts at 0) of the first (disk "`a`") hard disk ("`hd`") on the system. Note that older Unix systems such as Solaris only allow eight physical partitions per drive.

One slice generally is reserved as the "overlap" partition, which represents the entire disk geometry. By convention this usually is the third slice of the disk because early Unix systems required the first slice to be the root file system and the second slice to be the swap space for the virtual memory system. This "overlap" slice should not be used for file systems. Note that not all possible disk partitions need be used. In fact, the administrator might just create a single partition that spans an entire disk and ignore the other slices.

Partitions were created to solve two problems. One was to make it more difficult for problems with one subsystem, such as the logging processes in `/var`, to cause a denial-of-service to other processes, such as compilers writing files in `/tmp`. Partitions are created at system installation time and with a fixed amount of space. If syslogd were to fill up `/var` with spurious log messages, then no more logging could be done until some space was freed up by deleting old log files or removing other data from the `/var` partition. Not being able to log new messages is bad but not as bad as the entire system becoming unusable because the logs consumed all available disk space.

The other reason for partitioning is to make backups easier. Some partitions like `/usr` rarely need to get backed up because they change so infrequently. On the other hand, user home directories might need to get backed up every night.

From a security perspective, however, splitting the Unix file system up into different partitions allows the administrator to set different security options on different parts of the file system. While the exact partitioning scheme for a machine will vary from system to system and site to site, it is important that the root file system, `/usr`, and `/var` be separate partitions in order to apply appropriate security measures to various OS directories. Non-OS data (user data and home directories, plus application data) and third-party applications not supplied by the OS vendor generally should be put into their own partitions so that they do not "pollute" the OS directories.

Some Unix vendors periodically will assert that partitioning is not necessary and that all data should be loaded into a single large partition which spans the entire disk drive. For all of the reasons cited so far, these vendors are dead wrong.

NOTES

NOTES

As Seen by the `df` Command


```
$ df
Filesystem   1k-blocks     Used Available Use% Mounted on
/dev/hda5      3099260  2383084    558744  82% /
/dev/hda1        38859     3485     33368  10% /boot
/dev/hda7      5486908       20   5208164   1% /home
```

SANS Security Essentials – Unix Security

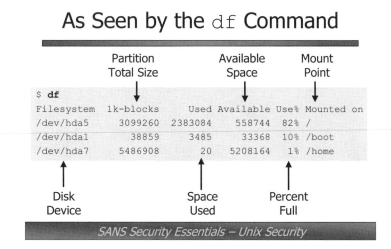

Administrators can display the currently mounted partitions with the `df` command. `df` stands for "disk free," because the command actually was created to help administrators find partitions who were running out of disk space:

```
# df
Filesystem  1k-blocks     Used  Available  Use%  Mounted on
/dev/hda1      256667   108443     134972   45%  /
/dev/hda6     3201980   593908    2445416   20%  /home
/dev/hda     33099292  2665948     275908   91%  /usr
/dev/hda5     2063504   104048     185463   66%  /var
```

The first output column shows the disk device associated with the partition, while the last column shows the piece of the logical file system to which the partition corresponds. Note that `df` only shows currently mounted file systems. Typically, the machine also will have a partition devoted to "swap space" for the virtual memory system. This is a "raw disk" partition which is not mounted into the logical Unix file system; however, this swap partition will have an entry in the `/etc/fstab` file.

The middle columns in the `df` output show the total size of the partition, the amount of disk space currently used, and the amount of free disk space, all reported in 1 kilobyte chunks. The attentive reader will note that the "bytes used" figure plus the "bytes available" amount is not equal to the "total size" number. For performance reasons, standard Unix file systems typically will reserve some 5-10% of the total file system for free space. When a partition gets to 90% full, no user except `root` is allowed to write data into the file system. Note that the "percent of capacity" figure in the second-to-last column of the `df` output takes into account this reserved space. Thus, `df` shows 100% full when the partition actually is only 90-95% full.

NOTES

File System Security Goals

- Protect OS Binaries in `/usr`

- Prevent introduction of SUID programs and unauthorized devices

- Allow other software to be installed

- Discourage denial-of-service attacks

SANS Security Essentials – Unix Security

File System Security Goals

When thinking about file system security, it is useful to keep a few important goals in mind:

- An attacker who compromises a system likely wants to install a "root kit"—a set of binaries that gives the attacker a back-door into the system and helps her escape detection by the system administrator. Typically the binaries that the attacker replaces are OS programs in the `/usr/bin` and `/usr/sbin` directories, so protecting the `/usr` file system is important.
- The administrator also should attempt to stop people from creating or bringing unauthorized set-UID and set-GID programs on the machine. Unauthorized device files can be equally dangerous because they may allow normal users to get what normally is privileged access to disk drives, the system memory, etc., bypassing normal system access controls.
- Conversely, system administrators need to be able to apply patches to the operating system and update software that has been installed on the machine. If they are unable to do this, then the system gradually becomes less "secure" as new exploits that cannot be patched are discovered.
- Also, to avoid denial-of-service attacks, administrators should partition the system carefully. For one thing, this means splitting the file system appropriately; take the earlier example of making `/var` a separate partition so that overwhelming the system logs will not take out the entire machine. However, the administrator also should take care to provide sufficient free space in heavily used partitions to accommodate unexpected growth.

NOTES

File System Security Options

- `ro` – file system is mounted read-only (files and directories can't be modified)
- `nosuid` – SUID/SGID bits are ignored on all programs in the file system
- `nodev` – Unix device files don't work

SANS Security Essentials – Unix Security

A combination of sensible partitioning and appropriate use of file system mount options in the `/etc/fstab` file can help achieve these goals. While there are a lot of different mount options administrators can set on a given file system, there are just a few specific options required to protect the security of file systems on the machine:

- The "`ro`" ("read-only") option causes the Unix operating system kernel to prevent writes or updates to the given file system. When a file system is in "read-only" mode, nobody can update files or directories in that partition, add new files, or delete files.
- The "`nosuid`" option means that the operating system simply ignores the set-UID and set-GID bits on executables in the file system. So, if a user attempts to execute a set-UID program out of a "`nosuid`" file system, the program runs as the user and not as the owner of the program.
- Similarly, "`nodev`" means that special "device files" are ignored in the file system. These are the kinds of files usually found in `/dev` and `/devices` and are used to communicate with the system hardware devices. Device files appearing in other directories usually are a problem, the only exception being special file systems used by anonymous FTP servers and the like (see sidebar for more details).

NOTES

Device Files Outside of /dev

Actually, system device files also occasionally appear in other directories. For example, the directory used by anonymous FTP servers usually contains its own `/dev` directory with copies of various system device files in it.

This is because anonymous FTP uses a special Unix security mechanism called `chroot()`. When a process makes the `chroot()` system call, it locks itself up under one directory in the file system. To the process that calls `chroot()`, it appears as if this directory were the root of the Unix file system. This means that everything the program normally would need from the operating system, including system devices, must be copied into the directory where the process intends to `chroot()` itself.

For a long time, anonymous FTP servers were one of the few Unix processes that made significant use of `chroot()`: after all, administrators do not want anonymous users to be able to see the FTP server's entire file system image. Recently, however, other applications such as Web servers and DNS servers have been taking advantage of the additional security provided by `chroot()`. For example, if an attacker exploits a buffer overflow in a server that is trapped in a `chroot()` directory, the attacker still will not have access to the entire system.

The upshot is that more and more `chroot()` directories are appearing on Unix servers, and each of these directories may contain device files. It is important that the administrator not mount the partitions containing these directories with the "`nodev`" option, or these device files will be unusable, and the `chroot()`ed application will not function properly. It is a good idea to make each one of these `chroot()` directories its own physical partition. Not only does this make it easier for the administrator to apply the "`nodev`" option to other file systems but also helps stop the attacker from filling up the `chroot()` directory as a denial-of-service on the rest of the system.

NOTES

All file systems should either be mounted read-only or `nosuid`.

- `/usr` and `/usr/local` contain SUID/SGID programs but can be read-only
- Most other file systems must be writable, but have no SUID/SGID programs
- / file system contains `/dev`, but all other file systems can be mounted `nodev`

SANS Security Essentials – Unix Security

The basic rule to follow when applying file system options is simple: file systems should either be mounted "`nosuid`" or read-only. Additionally, the "`nodev`" option should be used wherever possible. Set-UID/set-GID executables and system device files should really be restricted to operating system directories that are tightly controlled by the system administrator.

On most Unix systems, the critical set-UID and set-GID programs are all located in directories under the `/usr` file system, with `/usr/bin` and `/usr/sbin` being the most common locations. Some additional third-party set-UID and set-GID programs also may show up in `/usr/local` or `/opt`. However, all of these directories usually can be mounted in "read-only" mode because data usually is not written into these directories; Unix programs tend to write data under the `/var` directory or in scratch directories like `/tmp`. Mounting these file systems read-only helps stop attackers from planting "root kits" into the file system and stops the introduction of rogue set-UID or set-GID files and system devices.

Other file systems typically need to allow write access but should not have any set-UID and set-GID programs showing up in them. Thus, these file systems can be mounted "`nosuid`" to again prevent the introduction of rogue set-UID and set-GID executables.

As far as system device files go, the system devices live in `/dev` and `/devices`, which always are parts of the root file system. It turns out that if the primary system devices are not found in the root file system, the machine usually cannot boot. It is unusual to have device files elsewhere in the file system, so pretty much every other partition except the root file system can be mounted "`nodev`." This means that even if attackers were able to create device files in these file systems, they would not be able to use them. Of course an attacker could still create a malicious device file in the root file system or change the permissions on a device file already in `/dev` or `/devices`, so this is not a "perfect" solution. However, it is a huge improvement over the default situation, which is no security options being set at all.

NOTES

Linux is Not a Perfect World

- / file system is "polluted" with items that really belong under /usr
  - /bin contains critical SUID programs
  - /lib contains system libraries
- Can't mount these directories as separate file systems either
- Limits usefulness of file system options

SANS Security Essentials – Unix Security

Practical Implementation Issues

If all Unix vendors "did the right thing," then the discussion in the previous section would be the end of the story. However, various vendor implementation "choices"—a polite euphemism for "bugs," perhaps—force some revised thinking about file system security options.

For example, Linux systems do not always obey the standard Unix principle of putting OS programs and libraries under /usr. Under RedHat, the su program is installed as /bin/su: if the administrators mount the root file system (which contains the /bin directory) with the "nosuid" option, then they will not be able to use the su command to become root. This makes the system essentially unmaintainable. RedHat also installs a large number of system libraries in /lib. The administrator would like to protect these libraries and the programs in /bin from being corrupted by an attacker, but it is not possible to mount the root file system read-only either because data gets written there throughout the life of the system. "nodev" also is out of the question because of the system device files in /dev.

The bottom line is that administrators cannot set read-only, "nosuid," or "nodev" on the root file system on their RedHat machines. This is too bad, but file system security options still should be applied to other file systems.

NOTES

A Sample /etc/fstab

```
LABEL=/        /       ext2  rw                 1 1
LABEL=/boot    /boot   ext2  rw,nosuid,nodev    1 2
LABEL=/home    /home   ext2  rw,nosuid,nodev    1 2
LABEL=/usr     /usr    ext2  ro,nodev           1 2
LABEL=/var     /var    ext2  rw,nosuid,nodev    1 2
```

- Obeys "nosuid or read-only" rule (where possible)
- Uses nodev option on most file systems
- Separates logging space (/var) and user data (/home) from other system partitions

SANS Security Essentials – Unix Security

Here is a portion of an /etc/fstab file from a RedHat system showing appropriate use of the various mount options:

```
LABEL=/        /       ext2   rw                 1 1

LABEL=/home    /home   ext2   rw,nosuid,nodev    1 2

LABEL=/usr     /usr    ext2   ro,nodev           1 2

LABEL=/var     /var    ext2   rw,nosuid,nodev    1 2
```

This partitioning scheme actually accomplishes most of the important file system security goals discussed earlier. First, of course, the file system is split into multiple partitions. Not only does this allow the administrator to set the various security options appropriately on different partitions but also helps prevent denial-of-service attacks in one partition from impacting the rest of the system.

The /usr file system has been mounted read-only to protect the binaries there from malicious attackers. All file systems except the root file system, and /usr are mounted "nosuid" to prevent the introduction of rogue set-UID and set-GID applications to the extent possible. Furthermore, all file systems except the root file system are taking advantage of the "nodev" option.

either RO or SUID

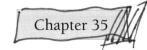

But How Do I Install Patches?

- /usr is now read-only– patch installs fail!
- Admin can set mount options "on the fly":

```
# mount -o remount,rw /usr
  [… install patches …]
# mount -o remount,ro /usr
```

- Of course, an attacker could do this too…

SANS Security Essentials – Unix Security

Of course, one of the other file system security goals was to allow administrators to apply patches easily to the system. How is that going to be possible if the /usr file system is mounted read-only? It turns out that the superuser can run the mount command to turn the read-only flag on or off at will.

The command "mount -o remount,rw /usr" sets the /usr file system to "read-write" mode. No applications running on the system will be interrupted, and a reboot is not required. After patches have been installed, simply "mount -o remount,ro /usr" to make the file system read-only again. Actually, on Solaris, a reboot is required to switch back to read-only mode, which is somewhat annoying.

Of course, an attacker who has gotten root access on the system could do exactly the same sequence of mount commands in order to install his root kit.

Nothing is perfect. However, there are enough automated exploits and inexperienced script kiddie attackers out there to make this security feature worthwhile.

NOTES

NOTES

Careful With CD-ROMs/Floppies!

- Apply `nosuid` and `nodev` options on CD and floppy entries in `/etc/fstab`
- Edit `/etc/security/console.perms` if media shouldn't "auto-mount" for users
- May also want to look at entries for Zip/Jaz drives, flash memory, etc.

SANS Security Essentials – Unix Security

Removable Media Devices

Another way attackers get dangerous files onto the system is via removable media devices, such as CD-ROMs and floppy drives. In fact, many modern Unix systems automatically mount CD-ROMs and floppies for the user as soon as the media is inserted into the drive. This means the attacker could put a set-UID `root` copy of Unix command shell on a floppy disk on one machine, carry it over to another machine, and get `root` access simply by executing the set-UID shell from the floppy.

There really is no reason to allow set-UID and set-GID programs to operate from the system's CD-ROM or floppy drives. Device files on removable media should not be usable, either. RedHat allows the administrator to set the "`nosuid`" and "`nodev`" options for these devices in the `/etc/fstab` file:

```
/dev/fd0   /mnt/floppy auto
noauto,owner,nosuid,nodev              0 0
/dev/cdrom /mnt/cdrom  iso9660
noauto,owner,kudzu,ro,nosuid,nodev  0 0
```

Other operating systems use different configuration files to set similar options: Solaris uses `/etc/rmmount.conf`, etc.

If users do not need to access CD-ROMs and floppies on their systems, the administrator can even choose to disable the "auto-mounting" feature provided by the operating system. To disable this feature on RedHat, edit `/etc/security/console.perms`, and delete any line which contains the string "`floppy`" or "`cdrom`." RedHat's `console.perms` file also contains entries for other types of removable media, including Zip and Jaz drives, flash memory modules, memory sticks, etc. Perhaps these entries also should be removed.

On Solaris systems, CD-ROMs and floppies are mounted by a special "volume manager" process. The easiest way to disable automatic mounting of removable media simply is to prevent this process from being started at boot time by removing the `/etc/rc2.d/S92volmgt` link.

If the administrator disables the auto-mounting feature for CD-ROMs and floppies, then these devices will need to be mounted manually with the `mount` command whenever somebody needs to access data from them. However, the `mount` command can be executed only by the superuser, so somebody with `root` access is going to need to be on hand to perform this operation. One option would be to give specific, trusted users the ability to mount CD-ROMs and floppies via the `sudo` command, rather than give them full `root` privileges on the system.

Protecting file systems with appropriate mount options certainly is one important aspect of tightening the overall security of the system. However, the Unix operating system also allows the administrator to set security-related parameters at an even deeper level of the operating system, as we will see in the next section.

NOTES

NOTES

Kernel Tuning for Security

- The kernel is the primary piece of software that makes up the OS
- Many security-related parameters can be set in the OS kernel:
  - limits on system resource utilization
  - networking parameters
- Very OS-specific– every vendor's kernel configuration interface is different

SANS Security Essentials – Unix Security

Kernel Tuning for Security

The Unix kernel is a large piece of software that makes up the "core" of the operating system. The job of the kernel is to act as an interface between the applications that are running on the system and the hardware devices that make up the machine, including the CPU, memory, disk drives, etc. The typical Unix kernel has dozens, if not hundreds, of different parameters that can be tuned by the administrator to affect system performance, I/O throughput, reliability, and many other aspects of the system's behavior. Some of these parameters also have security implications.

From a security perspective, there really are two different categories of relevant system parameters to address. There are a number of low-level parameters that can be used to set limits on various system resources on both a system-wide and a per-user basis. Tuning these parameters typically helps defeat local denial-of-service attacks that exhaust system resources. The other category of kernel parameters that can be tuned are network-oriented parameters that help the system handle network-based denial-of-service attacks or discard obviously incorrect or malicious network traffic.

Of course, every vendor's kernel is different, and each different Unix OS typically has a different way of allowing the administrator to set various kernel parameters. The best advice here is to consult the appropriate documentation from the vendor.

NOTES

/etc/security/limits.conf

- Allows admin to define sensible limits to help prevent denial-of-service attacks, etc.
- Limits can be hard or soft and apply to individuals, groups, or everybody
- Useful limits for security:
  - Prevent core files– may contain sensitive data
  - Limit number of processes per user

SANS Security Essentials – Unix Security

System Resource Limits

The standard RedHat mechanism for setting system resource limits is the /etc/security/limits.conf file. The limits set in this file actually are enforced via a PAM module call pam_limits (see the "What is PAM?" discussion in the previous chapter for more information about PAM), rather than being set directly in the system's kernel configuration. While other operating systems require the administrator to set these limits in the system kernel, the limits.conf interface provides a great deal more flexibility to the administrator.

However, there are some restrictions on the limits.conf mechanism as far as controlling system resources. First, the limits set in this file do not apply to the superuser, though some might argue that this is a feature. Second, the limits set in limits.conf only apply to actual user login sessions. They do not apply to processes started at boot time or processes started via inetd or cron. The advantage for systems that set these parameters in the system kernel configuration is that the limits then globally would apply to all users and all processes on the system.

The resources that can be managed by /etc/security/limits.conf typically are system process related resources like memory consumption, number of simultaneous processes, maximum CPU time, and maximum number of simultaneous logins. The format of entries in the limits.conf file is:

```
<who>  [hard|soft]  <parameter>  <limit>
```

The first field, <who>, is which user or users to whom the limit applies. This value can be a username: "@<group>" where <group> is some Unix group name from /etc/group or "*," which means the setting applies to all users. The next field is either "hard" or "soft": "soft" means the limit is a default but may be overridden by the user via the ulimit command; "hard" means the limit is absolute. Next comes the name of the parameter that is being set followed by the numeric limit value for that parameter.

From a security and reliability standpoint, a couple of different parameters are worth considering. Administrators may want to limit the number of simultaneous processes allowed for any given user. This prevents a trivial denial-of-service attack where a user spawns so many processes that the system process table fills up, preventing normal users from getting any work done. There are times when junior system programmers who are first learning Unix can

NOTES

make programming mistakes that accidentally cause this problem.

The administrator also may want to limit "core files" on the system. Core files are caused when a program terminates abnormally, dumping its memory image into a world-readable file called "core." This memory image is supposed to be used by the system administrator or software developer to debug the process. However, because the core file contains the complete memory image of the process, it might contain sensitive data like passwords, secret keys, etc. If the administrator limits the size of core files to 0 bytes, they effectively have prevented core files from being created.

The trade-off for disabling core files is that developers and administrators lose information that might have helped them debug problems with a process when it crashes. Perhaps it is appropriate to disable core files on "production" systems but leave them enabled on development and testing systems.

Also, remember that the limits set in /etc/security/limits.conf do not apply to processes started at boot time. This means that even if the administrator disables core files in limits.conf, system daemon processes started at boot time or via inetd may still leave core files behind. Unfortunately, these are the core files that are most likely to contain sensitive data. In order to prevent these processes from leaving behind core files, RedHat systems generally have the "ulimit -c 0" command in the /etc/rc.d/init.d/functions file. Since the functions file is read automatically by every boot script, this limit will apply to all processes started at boot time and all other processes that these system daemons may start (such as daemons started by inetd or xinetd).

In any event, here are entries that might be appropriate for limits.conf:

```
* hard   nproc   128   # limit max procs
  per user

* hard   core      0   # no core files!
```

Both of these entries set limits for all users ("*") on the system. Some sites will allow different limits for different groups of users. One example would be a university that allows unlimited numbers of processes for faculty members but a more restrictive limit for student users. Or a software development shop might not restrict core files for members of the software development and QA teams but disable them for administrative users.

NOTES

Network Tuning

- Various network parameters can be set in /etc/sysctl.conf
- RedHat 7.x systems read settings out of this file at boot time
- Admin can also make changes "on the fly" using the sysctl command:

```
sysctl -p /etc/sysctl.conf          [re-apply file settings]
sysctl -w net.ipv4.ip_forward=0     [set single value]
```

SANS Security Essentials – Unix Security

Network Parameter Tuning

As we mentioned earlier, the other class of configuration parameters to be concerned with are network-oriented parameters in the system kernel. The most straightforward method for working with these parameters on RedHat is via the /sbin/sysctl command.

Setting Parameters with sysctl

"sysctl -a" shows all of the different kernel parameters which can be modified and their current values (as of RedHat 7.2, this list included 238 different parameters). The value of a single parameter can be displayed simply by specifying the parameter name as an argument to the sysctl command, and the value can be modified with "sysctl -w":

```
# sysctl net.ipv4.tcp_max_syn_backlog
net.ipv4.tcp_max_syn_backlog = 256
# sysctl -w
net.ipv4.tcp_max_syn_backlog=4096
net.ipv4.tcp_max_syn_backlog = 4096
```

However, the normal use for the sysctl command is to set parameters at boot time. "sysctl -p <filename>" will apply all of the configuration settings from the specified <filename>. If no file is specified, "sysctl -p" defaults to using the standard system /etc/sysctl.conf file: in this file is where administrators should make updates to the system default values. Note that prior to RedHat 7.x, the /etc/sysctl.conf was not read automatically during the system boot process. On RedHat 6.x and earlier systems, it may be necessary to manually insert the "sysctl -p" command into /etc/rc.d/rc.sysinit.

One challenge with setting network-related kernel parameters is that some parameters apply globally, while others only apply to specific network interfaces on the system. The tcp_max_syn_backlog parameter in the example above is a global setting that applies to all network traffic processed by the system. On the other hand, a parameter like accept_source_route must be applied on an interface-by-interface basis. Even a machine with only a single physical network interface actually has two interfaces on which these parameters must be set: the physical interface itself plus the system internal "loopback" ("lo") interface. And, of course, the administrator even has more

NOTES

/proc/sys/net

The `sysctl` command interacts with the kernel via the special `/proc/sys` pseudo file system. `/proc` appears to be a normal directory structure but in fact does not exist on any physical disk device. Instead, /proc is an illusion created by the system kernel to allow administrators and users on the system to access different kinds of internal information easily from the running system.

For example, all of the network parameters which can be set with the `sysctl` command are represented by something that appears to be a file under `/proc/sys/net/ipv4`. To see the current value of the `tcp_max_syn_backlog` parameter, for example, the administrator simply could:

```
cat /proc/sys/net/ipv4/
tcp_max_syn_backlog
```

This is equivalent to displaying this value with the "`sysctl net.ipv4.tcp_max_syn_backlog`" command. Notice that the periods in the `sysctl` argument correspond to subdirectory boundaries under the `/proc/sys` file system.

In addition, the administrator even can set kernel parameters via `/proc/sys`. To increase the `tcp_max_syn_backlog` parameter to 4096, the administrator can:

```
echo 4096 >/proc/sys/net/ipv4/
tcp_max_syn_backlog
```

Still, the `sysctl` interface probably is easier to use in most cases and saves typing since the administrator does not have to keep typing the `/proc/sys` prefix in front of each parameter. Also, the `/etc/sysctl.conf` interface for setting parameters automatically at boot time is extremely convenient.

work to do on machines with multiple network interface cards.

Thankfully, setting the `net.ipv4.all.accept_source_route` parameter will apply the setting to all network interfaces on the system (as opposed to setting `net.ipv4.eth0.accept_source_route`, which would only set this parameter on the "`eth0`" interface). However, the `net.ipv4.all.*` settings only apply to interfaces that are enabled at the time the `sysctl` command is run. To make a given parameter, the "default" setting for future interfaces that might be initialized, whether later in the boot process, or "on-the-fly" by the administrator. Also, set the `net.ipv4.default.*` version of each parameter. Unfortunately, defaults set in this manner do not apply to currently active interfaces, so it is necessary to set both `net.ipv4.all.<parameter>` as well as `net.ipv4.default.<parameter>`.

NOTES

Security-Related Settings

- Forwarding packets:
```
net.ipv4.conf.ip_forward=0
net.ipv4.conf.all.forwarding=0
net.ipv4.conf.all.mc_forwarding=0
net.ipv4.conf.all.rp_filter=1
```
- Source routing is bad:
```
net.ipv4.conf.all.accept_source_route=0
```
- Beware ICMP redirects:
```
net.ipv4.conf.all.send_redirects=0
net.ipv4.conf.all.accept_redirects=0
```

SANS Security Essentials – Unix Security

Recommended Parameter Settings

Here are some recommended settings for security-related networking parameters in `/etc/sysctl.conf`:

```
net.ipv4.ip_forward = 0
net.ipv4.conf.all.forwarding=0
net.ipv4.conf.all.mc_forwarding=0
net.ipv4.conf.all.rp_filter=1
net.ipv4.conf.all.log_martians=1

net.ipv4.conf.all.accept_source_route=0

net.ipv4.conf.all.send_redirects=0
net.ipv4.conf.all.accept_redirects=0
net.ipv4.conf.default.forwarding=0
net.ipv4.conf.default.mc_forwarding=0
net.ipv4.conf.default.rp_filter=1
net.ipv4.conf.default.log_martians=1

net.ipv4.conf.default.accept_source_route=0

net.ipv4.conf.default.send_redirects=0
net.ipv4.conf.default.accept_redirects=0

net.ipv4.tcp_max_syn_backlog=4096
```

This list appears to be longer than it really is due to the necessity of setting both the `net.ipv4.conf.all.*` and `net.ipv4.conf.default.*` versions of many of the parameters.

Note that each of the parameters listed above will be discussed in more detail in the upcoming sections.

IP Forwarding – ip_forward, forwarding, mc_forwarding

The first two parameters deal with "IP forwarding." A Unix system with multiple network interfaces will act as a network router and actually pass traffic between its interfaces unless IP forwarding is disabled. Consider the case of a Web server with one network interface that is connected towards the public Internet and a second interface connected to a "private" network where some database server or

NOTES

back-end e-commerce infrastructure resides. If this Web server allowed IP forwarding, attackers could route packets through the Web server to attack the systems on the "private" network. IP forwarding usually is inappropriate for host computers, since most organizations rely on dedicated network routers and firewall devices to control network traffic between their various networks.

`net.ipv4.ip_forward=0` disables IP forwarding globally, and `net_ipv4.all.forwarding=0` disables forwarding on all network interfaces. Setting the interface-specific parameter after setting `net.ipv4.ip_forward` is redundant, but it does not hurt either, and "Defense in-Depth" is a good policy to follow. The `net.ipv4.all.mc_forward=0` line also disables the forwarding of multicast traffic. Multicast is rarely used in practice, so multicast forwarding almost always can be disabled safely. Note that IP forwarding (and multicast forwarding) is disabled by default under RedHat and other newer Open Source operating systems but tends to enabled by default on the older commercial Unix systems, such as Solaris.

Impossible Traffic – rp_filter and log_martians

`rp_filter=1` turns on "reverse path filtering" in an attempt to stop packets with spoofed source addresses and other sorts of malicious traffic. When reverse path filtering is enabled in the kernel, every time the system receives a packet over one of its network interfaces, it checks the source address of that packet against its own internal network routing table. The routing table lookup tells the kernel which network interface a reply packet would use to reach the given source address. If the incoming packet is received on a different interface from the one the reply packet would use leaving the system, then the kernel assumes that the source address was spoofed and that the packet was generated by some unauthorized system. The "spoofed" packet is discarded immediately, and no further processing is done.

In practice, reverse path filtering is most useful for discarding spoofed packets that purport to come from the system "`loopback`" interface, which has IP address 127.0.0.1. Many different sorts of network-based attacks rely on convincing the remote system that the attacker's packets were generated from this address. However, packets with this source address should never be coming into the system via its physical network interfaces, since all 127.0.0.1 traffic is handled via the system's internal software loopback ("`lo`") interface. Since the system's network routing table sends all packets for 127.0.0.1 to the "`lo`" interface, a packet with source address 127.0.0.1 received on the system's physical ethernet interface would be discarded if reverse path filtering were enabled.

Reverse path filtering can be a problem on systems that have multiple network interfaces, if the networks to which the machine is attached allow "asymmetric" routing, meaning that packets can travel from machine A to machine B via one sequence of networks but flow back from machine B to machine A via a completely different path. If a machine regularly receives packets from a system on one interface but sends the responses out a different interface, then reverse path filtering is going to discard the incoming packets, effectively terminating network connectivity between the two systems. Asymmetric routing is something that should be avoided for the most part.

Setting `log_martians=1` causes the system to send messages to Syslog when "impossible" traffic is received on a network interface and dropped by the kernel. Seeing these messages in the system log can alert local administrators to a potential network attack in progress. Be aware that sometimes these messages simply can be the result of misconfigured systems on the local LAN, although arguably this is a condition that the local administrators would like to know about as well.

Source Routing – accept_source_route

Setting `accept_source_route=0` causes the system simply to discard any packets that have the "source routing" options turned on. Source routing allows the system that generates a packet to specify a list of gateways through which the packet must travel, and the system receiving such a packet uses the same list of gateways in reverse on the reply packet. Attackers often use this "feature" as part of address spoofing attacks or to route traffic around firewalls and other network security devices. Source routing is never used by "normal" network traffic, so source routed packets always should be discarded.

ICMP Redirects – send_redirects, accept_redirects

ICMP redirect packets cause a system to update its internal network routing table. These packets were intended to allow routers and other network gateways to help nearby systems find better routes to other network devices. However, ICMP redirect traffic is completely unauthenticated, meaning attackers easily can send bogus ICMP redirects that cause a remote system to send traffic to non-existent routers (a denial-of-service attack) or perhaps even to a machine owned by the attacker (a man-in-the-middle attack). Certainly a standard Unix machine that is not acting as a gateway should have no reason to transmit ICMP redirects, so the `send_redirects` parameter should be set to 0. Setting `accept_redirects=0` causes the machine to ignore incoming ICMP redirects from other systems and probably is appropriate for most standard network architectures, where systems simply use a single default router for all traffic.

NOTES

Security-Related Settings (cont.)

- Help protect against SYN floods:
  `net.ipv4.tcp_max_syn_backlog=4096`
- Help stop Smurf attacks (but may annoy your network administrator):
  `net.ipv4.icmp_echo_ignore_broadcasts=1`

SANS Security Essentials – Unix Security

SYN Floods – tcp_max_syn_backlog

Setting the `tcp_max_syn_backlog` parameter to a large number attempts to harden the system against "SYN flood" attacks. In a SYN flood denial-of-service attack, the attacker barrages the system with thousands of TCP packets that appear to be initiating a TCP "three-way handshake" (these initial packets have the TCP "SYN" flag sent, hence the name of the attack). However, the attacker never transmits the final packet to complete each three-way handshake, leaving the system with thousands of pending connections. Eventually, the system's internal kernel buffers used to hold these pending connections fill up, making it impossible for the system to accept new TCP connections and effectively taking the system off the network. Increasing the value of `tcp_max_syn_backlog` increases the number of "slots" available in the kernel to hold these pending connections, making it harder for the attacker to overwhelm the system.

In fact, Linux kernels and many other Unix kernels now will discard the oldest pending connection automatically when the kernel's internal tables fill up and when space is required to service a new connection. This means that it is impossible for an attacker to take a system completely off the network with a SYN flood attack against these kernels. However, an attacker still can barrage the system with enough traffic in a short period of time so that the kernel ends up discarding legitimate connections in order to attempt to service the attacker's bogus attempts. So increasing `tcp_max_syn_backlog` is a good idea anyway.

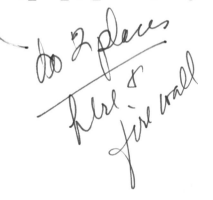

Do 2 places
here & firewall

NOTES

The Great ICMP Echo Debate

Some security experts recommend setting `net.ipv4.icmp_echo_ignore_broadcasts=1`. This setting prevents the system from responding to ICMP Echo (`ping`) packets sent to the network broadcast address. On the one hand, setting this parameter on every system on a network prevents that network from being used as an intermediate or "amplifier" network in a Smurf-style attack. On the other hand, being able to `ping` the local broadcast address and get responses from all live hosts on the network is a legitimate network administration tool.

For hosts on a protected, internal network that is behind multiple layers of firewalls and other network security devices, it is probably sufficient to rely on the network security devices to block malicious broadcast ICMP traffic. In these environments, the convenience of allowing network admins to `ping` the broadcast address and get back useful information seems to outweigh the added security benefit gained by disabling broadcast echo on all systems. However, for machines on a network which is not protected by firewalls and other security devices, such as networks in large hosting facilities or some university networks, disabling responses to broadcast echo requests may be a good idea.

NOTES

Other OSes, Other Parameters

- Other operating systems may allow you to set other network-related options:
  - Improve TCP sequence number randomizer
  - TCP connection timeouts
  - ARP cache timeouts
  - Disable other ICMP message types
- Best advice is to check available documentation from your vendor

SANS Security Essentials – Unix Security

Security Parameters on Other Systems

Other Unix systems may allow administrators to set more or different network security related parameters in the system kernel. Solaris in particular seems to give administrators the most flexibility in configuring various kernel parameters (some would argue that this is more like giving the administrators plenty of rope with which to hang themselves).

For example, we discussed helping to defend against SYN flood attacks by setting `tcp_max_syn_backlog` to increase the number of "slots" available to the kernel to hold pending TCP connections. Another way to harden the system against these sorts of attacks is to tune down the kernel timeout for holding onto these pending connections. In some Unix implementations, this timeout can be as long as three minutes, certainly more time than normally is required for completing the TCP three-way handshake, with even the most distant machines. Setting the timeout value down to one minute or even 30 seconds should allow the machine to discard bogus connections more quickly without impacting normal network traffic. While some Unix implementations allow the administrator to modify this timeout value, there appears to be no way on RedHat systems to do this.

Another important factor in the security of TCP-based network communications is the randomness of TCP sequence numbers chosen for new network connections. If the system does not do a good job of choosing random sequence numbers, then IP spoofing and other sorts of network attacks against the system are much simpler. Some Unix implementations use a rather poor sequence number generation algorithm but do allow the administrator to access kernel variables that can be used to modify this algorithm or even choose an entirely new algorithm to use instead. RedHat uses a reasonable random sequence number generation algorithm by default, so further tweaking by the administrator is not required.

Another class of network attacks rely on the attacker being able to manipulate a system's ARP cache. The ARP cache stores a mapping between the IP addresses and physical layer (ethernet, for example) addresses with which the system has communicated recently. However, ARP update messages, such as ICMP redirects, are completely unauthenticated, allowing attackers to insert spurious ARP information into the caches on nearby systems. In a similar fashion to ICMP redirect attacks, false ARP information could cause systems to send traffic to non-existent destinations as a denial-of-service or to the attacker's machine so that the attacker can act as a "man-in-the-middle" and intercept and modify traffic as it flies by. Some Unix systems allow administrators to reduce the timeout value for keeping information in the ARP cache. This makes the attacker's job much more difficult because he constantly will have to "re-infect" nearby machines with bogus ARP information, and the extra ARP update traffic may help local administrators discover and track down the attacker's system.

Some Unix implementations also allow administrators to disable certain types of infrequently used ICMP messages. ICMP timestamp requests and ICMP netmask requests can function like a "ping" to help attackers find hosts that are active on the network, even if the site might be blocking normal ICMP echo request and echo reply traffic at its firewalls. These requests also can give the attacker additional information that can help them during the actual attack phase of their operation. Both of these types of ICMP messages are examples of network traffic that safely can be ignored by the system without impacting normal network operations.

As always, consult the documentation provided by the Unix vendor for information on exactly what parameter options are available.

NOTES

NOTES

Stack Protection

- Buffer overflows are a common reason for compromised Unix systems
- "Stack protection" helps prevent common forms of buffer overflow
- May not be available for all OSes and/or processor types
- In particular, not available in RedHat due to limitations of the Intel architecture

SANS Security Essentials – Unix Security

Stack Protection

Stack protection, which attempts to prevent certain kinds of buffer overflow attacks, is a kernel feature available to some Unix operating systems. These attacks have been one of the most common sources of remote compromise on Unix systems over the last several years. Buffer overflows are the result of a programming error that allows an attacker to remotely insert malicious code into the memory of a running process and then execute it. Typically this gives the attacker complete access to the system with whatever privileges with which the original process was running, the `apache` user if the attacker exploits a buffer overflow in the system Web server, or worse, the `root` user if some privileged system process were compromised. Since new programs are being written every day, and since even smart programmers make dumb mistakes, it seems unlikely that there ever will be a day when there are no buffer overflow exploits anywhere in the Unix source code base.

The classic buffer overflow attack relies on the attacker inserting his malicious code into areas of memory that normally should not contain executable program instructions. Stack protection, then, is a change to the operating system kernel that marks certain parts of memory as being protected areas where the program instructions reside. If a process attempts to execute instructions from another part of memory, as happens during a buffer overflow attack, the kernel simply shuts down the process rather than executes the malicious instructions. Of course, this could be seen as a denial-of-service attack, particularly if the process being shut down is the system Web server on a production e-commerce site; however, it is better than the alternative of giving the attacker access to the system.

Keep in mind, though, that stack protection not only requires modifications to the Unix kernel but also requires the cooperation of the memory management unit on the system CPU for reasonable performance. The Intel CPU family, which is the most common platform for Linux systems by far, is not cooperative as far as providing appropriate memory management functions to the system kernel to make stack protection easy. Hence, stack protection is not widely implemented in Linux operating systems. Solar Designer has released kernel patches for older Linux kernels that implement stack protection and some other useful security features. These patches are available at www.openwall.com.

Since stack protection can be difficult to implement in Unix kernels running on the Intel architecture, various groups have implemented stack protection at the application level rather than the kernel level. This typically involves modifying the system C compiler to insert additional code into applications during the compilation process. This code detects buffer overflow attacks and causes the application to shut down itself if a problem is detected. An example of this kind of system is the StackGuard patches for GCC, available from www.immunix.org.

Solaris and HP-UX systems, which generally run on proprietary CPUs, have stack protection built into the OS. To enable stack protection on Solaris, add these lines to /etc/system:

```
set noexec_user_stack = 1

set no_exec_user_stack_log = 1
```

On HP-UX 11i simply run the command line "`kmtune -s executable_stack=0 && mk_kernel && kmupdate`" as `root`. On either operating system, a reboot is required to enable stack protection once the appropriate configuration changes have been made.

While rooting around in the internals of the Unix kernel can be an interesting and mind-expanding experience, there still are other security configuration settings at higher levels of the operating system that can be useful. We will examine some of these settings in the remainder of the chapter.

NOTES

NOTES

Cron Security

- `cron` runs commands for users at scheduled times of the day
- `cron` security-related considerations:
  - Keeping a log of jobs executed
  - Restricting administrative access
  - Permissions on "crontabs" and executables

SANS Security Essentials – Unix Security

cron Security

The `cron` system runs programs for users at particular times of the day or on particular days of week or month. `cron` is another Unix mechanism that starts new processes on the system without human intervention, just as the system starts various daemons at boot time, or runs new processes via `inetd`. It is prudent, then, to spend at least a little bit of time worrying about the security of the `cron` system.

Of primary concern are:

- keeping a log or "audit trail" of all `cron` jobs executed on the system
- controlling who has access to add, modify, and delete `cron` jobs on the system
- controlling access to `cron`'s configuration files and directories
- setting appropriate access controls on programs and scripts executed by the `cron` system

All of these issues can be addressed with relatively little effort on the administrators' part.

cron Logging

- RedHat's cron daemon automatically logs information to Syslog
- Default is for cron.* Syslog messages to go to /var/log/cron
- Other operating systems may initiate cron logging in other ways

SANS Security Essentials – Unix Security

Keeping a Log

Obviously, keeping a log of all cron jobs that run on the system will help administrators spot suspicious or potentially malicious cron jobs. This would include cron jobs that appear to be consuming large amounts of CPU time or other system resources, cron jobs running for users who would be unlikely to make use of the cron system, or even cron jobs running as root or other administrative users who were not created by the system administrator. Logging cron jobs also helps the administrator simply spot jobs that are encountering problems or problems with the cron daemon itself.

Happily, RedHat systems are configured to log information about cron jobs by default. The RedHat cron daemon automatically logs information about each cron job to Syslog using Syslog's cron facility (for more information on Syslog, see Chapter 33). RedHat's default syslog.conf file causes these messages to be stored in /var/log/cron.

Other operating systems may require more configuration work on the part of the administrator to enable cron logging. For example, on Solaris systems the administrator must set the "CRONLOG=YES" parameter in /etc/default/cron (though this is the default in recent Solaris releases). The Solaris cron daemon then writes logs to the /var/cron/log file directly rather than logging the messages via Syslog. For other systems, the best advice is to look at the vendor's on-line documentation for the cron daemon with the "man cron" command.

NOTES

NOTES

Administrative Access

- Jobs are created/modified using the crontab and at commands
- Perhaps regular users should not be able to create/modify jobs?
- Use /etc/cron.allow, at.allow:
  - List of users who are allowed to use crontab and at *commands*
  - *Does not* restrict which users can have cron jobs running on their behalf

SANS Security Essentials – Unix Security

Administrative Access

cron jobs can be added, modified, and removed using the crontab command. By default, most Unix systems will allow any user to run the crontab command to manage her own cron entries. The root user always can add, delete, or modify cron jobs for any user on the system. On some systems, administrators may wish to control which users are allowed to set up cron jobs and which are not. In fact, on tightly controlled systems it may be appropriate only for administrators running as root to manage cron jobs, both for the root account and for other users on the system.

Under RedHat, the /etc/cron.allow file is the list of users who are allowed to run the crontab command (any users not listed in this file cannot run crontab). It is important to note that even if a user is not listed in cron.allow, the superuser still can set up cron jobs to run as that user on the system. So cron.allow only controls access to the crontab command for adding, deleting, and modifying cron jobs; it in no way affects the behavior of the cron daemon itself. Again, on tightly controlled systems it may be appropriate to list only the user "root" in this file, meaning only the superuser is allowed to run the crontab command.

If /etc/cron.allow does not exist, then the crontab command will look for a file called /etc/cron.deny. cron.deny is a list of users who specifically should not have access to the crontab command, but any user not listed in this file will be able to run the command normally. If neither cron.allow nor cron.deny exist, then all users can run the crontab command; this is the default configuration for most Unix systems.

This "check cron.deny only if cron.allow does not exist" policy can lead to confusion. The best advice is to do any access control in cron.allow, and simply remove any cron.deny files from the system. Or if the system configuration is more permissive, use cron.deny exclusively, but be careful to get rid of any cron.allow file because it would cause the administrator's settings in cron.deny to be ignored.

Unix systems also have an "at" command that allows users to schedule a particular command to be run one time at some point in the future, rather than on a periodic basis as with cron. Similar to the crontab command, there are at.allow and at.deny files to control which users have the ability to use the at command to schedule jobs. In most cases, the `at.allow` and `cron.allow` files on the system should be configured identically.

Note that while RedHat systems keep the `cron.allow`, `cron.deny`, `at.allow`, and `at.deny` files in the `/etc` directory, other vendor `cron` daemons may look for these files in other directories. The vendor's on-line documentation ("`man crontab`" or "`man at`") should give the proper location of these files for a particular system.

NOTES

NOTES

Config File Permissions

- cron daemon runs as root
- crontab command is SUID root
- May as well make all cron configuration files readable only by root:

```
chown -R root:root /etc/cron* /var/spool/cron
chmod -R 700 /etc/cron* /var/spool/cron
chmod 600 /etc/crontab /etc/cron.d/* \
    /var/spool/cron/* /etc/{cron,at}.allow
```

SANS Security Essentials – Unix Security

Access to cron Configuration Files

The system cron daemon runs as the root user and reads all of its configuration files with root privileges , including the "crontab" ("cron table") files, which store cron entries for individual users on the system. Similarly, the crontab command is set-UID to root so that it can modify user's crontab files. This being the case, all cron configuration files should be owned by root and in fact can be set to be readable only by the superuser, as well. This helps hide information from local attackers regarding what cron jobs are configured to run on the system, a slight, but not insignificant security enhancement. Note that most Unix systems leave their cron configuration files readable by any user on the system by default.

The following commands can be used to set more restrictive permissions on the various cron configuration files found on a RedHat system:

```
chown -R root:root /etc/cron* /var/spool/
cron

chmod -R 700 /etc/cron* /var/spool/cron

chmod 600 /etc/crontab /etc/cron.d/* \

    /var/spool/cron/* /etc/{cron,at}.allow
```

The "-R" ("recursive") option on chown and chmod causes these commands to set not only the permissions or ownership on a single directory but also to set automatically the same permissions or ownership on all files and directories below that point in the file system. Be careful with this option when operating as the superuser; even a small typo can cause enormous problems very quickly!

The RedHat cron system has a needlessly large collection of different configuration files and directories. Most other Unix systems will not require nearly as much reconfiguration on the part of the administrator. In fact, on most Unix systems all cron configuration files are stored in a single directory: usually /var/cron or /var/spool/cron.

NOTES

Executable Permissions

- Admin writes script to run from `root`'s crontab– script still owned by admin
- Admin (or attacker who has broken admin's account) could add malicious code
- Could result in system compromise or denial-of-service attack

Programs run from `cron` should always be owned by the job owner or by root user!

SANS Security Essentials – Unix Security

Access Controls on Executables

While restricting access to `cron` configuration files can help hide information from local attackers, it is even more important to pay careful attention to the permissions and ownership on scripts and other programs that will be executed by the `cron` daemon as various users. The biggest problems in this area tend to crop up when an administrator is creating a shell script that is going to be executed out of `root`'s crontab.

Often the administrator will create and test the script in her own home directory using her normal user ID. Sometimes the administrator will then add the completed script to `root`'s crontab without changing the ownership or permissions on the script or without even moving the script out of her home directory. This means that the script file still can be modified by the administrator or by anybody who manages to compromise the administrator's account. However, the commands in the script file are going to be run via `cron` as the `root` user, so if an attacker can break into the administrator's account and modify the script, he can add any commands he wants to the script and have them executed with superuser privileges. Typically the attacker will insert commands which give him a set-UID copy of the Unix command shell in `/tmp`:

```
cp /bin/sh /tmp/myfile

chown root:root /tmp/myfile

chmod 4755 /tmp/myfile
```

Now all the attacker has to do is wait for `cron` to run the script and then execute the resulting `/tmp/myfile` executable to get `root` access on the system. The attacker then will probably return the administrator's script to its original state, create some other back door for himself on the system, and delete the set-UID executable in order to avoid detection by the system administrator.

Of course, for this attack to be worthwhile, it has to be easier to get access to the administrator's account than it is to get `root` access. It is a truism that it is easier for an attacker to get access as an unprivileged user on a Unix system than it is for the attacker to break the `root` account directly. The usual approach is to take advantage of "local root access" on a system the attacker controls in order to get wider access as a normal user.

To see how this is done, suppose an attacker already has superuser access on some system on an enterprise network. This could be a remote attacker who has

NOTES

managed to find an exploit on one machine, or it could be an "insider" who was given `root` privileges on her local workstation or simply took them because she was able to do something like boot into single-user mode or boot from OS media as we discussed in the previous chapter. Whatever the case, this attacker now can run the `su` command as `root` to become any other user on the system without providing a password. So our attacker simply runs the `su` command to become the system administrator who wrote the `cron` script.

In most large enterprise Unix environments, user home directories are shared between all systems via NFS. While NFS stops a user with `root` access on one machine from manipulating files with `root` privilege on the file server, NFS is designed to allow users to access their own files remotely. In this case, we have an attacker who is now masquerading as the system administrator and would have complete access to all files in the system administrator's home directory. If the script being run from `cron` is still in the admin's home directory, then the attacker simply can insert her malicious commands and be done. If the script were in some other directory, possibly on some other system, the attacker potentially could put a `.rhosts` file in the administrator's home directory and then log into other systems as the administrator in order to modify the script. If `.rhosts` files are disabled, the attacker could put malicious commands into the administrator's startup files so that the next time the administrator logged in, the attacker's commands would be executed to add the malicious code automatically to the target script. There are many similarly devious options open to the attacker at this point.

The short rule for programs and scripts that are being executed from `cron` is that either they should be owned by the user as whom `cron` will be running the program, or they should be owned by the `root` user. However, administrators also need to be careful about the permissions and ownership of the directories that contain these executables. For example, if our administrator had made his script owned by `root` but left the script in his home directory, then the attacker masquerading as the admin simply could move the root-owned `cron` script aside and substitute a file with the original name containing the malicious commands. Remember that it is write permissions on the directory in which a file is contained that give a user the right to rename or delete files in that directory. It always is best to put `cron` jobs that will be executed with `root` privileges in a tightly controlled directory that is only accessible by the `root` user.

In the last chapter we discussed how an attacker with local access to the system could manipulate the system boot process to gain `root` access. Here we are using this as an example of how our attacker might gain local `root` access in order to `su` to the system administrator's user ID. Clearly this is an exploit that gives a local attacker significant leverage. Would it be prudent, then, to make this sort of attack easier by allowing normal users, or even users with no account on the system at all, to reboot the machine at will? It would seem the answer to that question is a resounding "NO!" And yet RedHat makes it possible to do just that. Disabling this "feature" is the topic of the next and final section of this chapter.

NOTES

Who the Heck Thought This Was a Good Idea?

- Seems unreasonable to allow any user on the system to shut the machine down
- But guess what?
  - Ctrl-Alt-Del reboots the system
  - GUI login screens have a "Shutdown" button
- This may be useful on personal laptops if you don't want to give out root password

SANS Security Essentials – Unix Security

Disabling Anonymous Shutdowns

RedHat systems generally provide two different ways for non-root users to shut down and reboot a system. By default the <ctrl>-<alt>-<delete> keyboard sequence will reboot the machine, although this is complicated by the fact that most of the common Linux window managers will trap the <ctrl>-<alt>-<delete> sequence as a signal to log out of the windowing environment instead. It also is the case that the GUI login screen that allows the user to log in usually will have a "Shutdown" button that allows anybody with access to the system's console to shut down or reboot the machine.

Now it might seem "obvious" that the superuser should be the only person allowed to shut down or reboot the machine. However, the reason these features were included in the RedHat operating system was so that users could shut down the operating system on his laptop or personal desktop without requiring superuser access. In fact, it may be reasonable to leave these facilities enabled on these kinds of machines. The administrator also does have the option of giving the user sudo access to accomplish this same shutdown task in a way that provides a higher level of accountability and auditability. It certainly is the case, however, that this sort of "anonymous" shutdown ability should be disabled on "server" type machines that are critical from a network operations standpoint, just to disable a trivial denial-of-service attack if nothing else.

Stopping Ctrl-Alt-Del

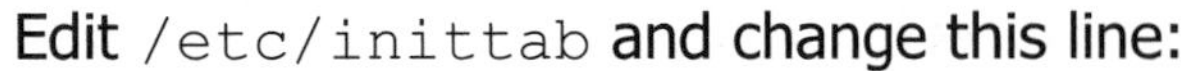

- Edit `/etc/inittab` and change this line:

```
ca::ctrlaltdel:/sbin/shutdown -t3 -r now
```

- New entry might look like:

```
ca::ctrlaltdel:/usr/bin/logger -p auth.info
  "ctrl-alt-del sequence ignored"
```

- Change will take effect at next reboot
- Note that non-Linux/non-Intel platforms may have other conventions

SANS Security Essentials – Unix Security

Disabling the `<ctrl>-<alt>-<delete>` sequence is straightforward. There is a single line in `/etc/inittab` which enables this feature:

```
ca::ctrlaltdel:/sbin/shutdown -t3 -r now
```

It might seem like the best policy simply to remove this line from `/etc/inittab`, but this turns out to be even more dangerous to the system. The `<ctrl>-<alt>-<delete>` sequence is recognized at the BIOS level below the operating. If the `inittab` file does not have some entry that specifically traps this key sequence, then hitting `<ctrl>-<alt>-<delete>` will cause the system to do a hard reboot that may leave the machine's file systems in a corrupted state.

Instead, the best approach would be to change the default `/etc/inittab` entry to one that traps the `<ctrl>-<alt>-<delete>` sequence but does not shut down the system:

```
ca::ctrlaltdel:/usr/bin/logger -p
auth.info "ctrl-alt-del sequence ignored"
```

The sample entry shown above causes the system to log a message via Syslog whenever the `<ctrl>-<alt>-<delete>` sequence is triggered. The system will need to be rebooted for this change to take effect.

Note that other systems running on proprietary hardware may have other keyboard sequences that shut down or abort the operating system. For example, on Sun machines the `<Stop>-<A>` keyboard sequence aborts the operating system. Solaris allows the administrator to disable this keyboard sequence in `/etc/default/kbd`.

NOTES

Disabling Shutdown Buttons

- Need to fix the problem for both GNOME and KDE login screens
- GNOME:
  - File is `gdm.config`
  - Setting is `SystemMenu=false`
- KDE:
  - File is `kdmrc`
  - Setting is `AllowShutdown=None`

SANS Security Essentials – Unix Security

Disabling the "Shutdown" button on the regular GUI login screens is only slightly more challenging than disabling `<ctrl>-<alt>-<delete>`. Again, Linux systems generally will use either the GNOME or KDE login widgets, so the administrator typically will want to make a change in the configuration files for both. The GNOME configuration file usually is `/etc/X11/gdm/gdm.conf`. Here the system administrator sets "`SystemMenu=false`." For KDE, the administrator edits the `kdmrc` file and sets "`AllowShutdown=none`." The `kdmrc` file can appear in any one of several directories, depending on the version of RedHat. Common locations are `/usr/share/config/kdm/kdmrc`, `/usr/share/config/kdmrc`, or `/etc/X11/xdm/kdmrc`.

Of course, even after the administrator has disabled these shutdown features, an attacker with local access to the system still could force the system to reboot simply by removing the power cord from the back of the system. Again, most security measures are not foolproof, but administrators should do the best they can.

Now let's wrap up all of the material we have covered in this chapter.

NOTES

Summary: Lessons Learned

- In the file system:
  - Keep an eye on SUID/SGID programs
  - Partition wisely and use appropriate file system security options
- Take advantage of available kernel parameters that can be tuned for security
- Restrict access to crontabs and log all jobs
- Don't let normal users shut down system

SANS Security Essentials – Unix Security

Summary

"Special" files and directories like set-UID and set-GID programs, world-writable directories, and Unix device files can cause problems. Attackers also can attempt denial-of-service attacks by trying to fill up file systems. Using a sensible partitioning scheme coupled with intelligent use of file system security options can go a long way in making this situation better. Also it is prudent to keep track of the set-UID and set-GID programs and world-writable directories installed with the operating system and take action if changes suddenly occur to these files and directories or if new ones are added.

The Unix kernel typically gives the administrator some hooks for improving security and making the system more robust. RedHat also includes the `/etc/security/limits.conf` mechanism for further restricting system resource access for normal users on the system. The only problem here is locating the appropriate vendor documentation . . . and sometimes in just trying to understand what the documentation is trying to tell you!

Be careful with the security of `cron` configuration files and the programs that `cron` is executing. Where possible, make files owned by `root` and only readable by the root user. Use `cron.allow` and `at.allow` to control who is allowed to create, modify, and delete `cron` and `at` jobs.

And, finally, it probably is a good idea to prevent normal users from shutting down or rebooting the system. Rather than enabling this feature on personal workstations or laptop systems, giving users `sudo` access to shut down the system cleanly provides better access control and a better audit trail.

Chapter 36

Backups and Archiving

NOTES

Backups and Archiving

SANS Security Essentials VI:
Unix Security

SANS Security Essentials – Unix Security

NOTES

Backups and Archiving

It probably seems strange to be covering backups in a book on computer security. After all, backups are one of those dreary "housekeeping" chores that tend to get pushed off onto the junior members of the IT staff. However, in addition to the obvious business continuity reasons, having backups and being able to archive and manipulate file system data is also critical to security professionals, particularly during and after a break-in or other computer security incident.

For one thing, system backups may be the investigator's only tool for discovering what files and directories on the system have been changed or corrupted by the attacker. These backups may be the only way to view the "original" state of the system prior to the break-in. Of course, restoring the backups and doing a comparison against the existing system can be time consuming and difficult; and without knowing exactly when the incident occurred, it can be difficult to decide how far back in the system archives to search for an uncorrupted image of the system. This is one of the reasons why using Tripwire or some other similar integrity-checking tool is so important.

Being able to back up file system data also is critical for computer forensics. Forensic analysis never should be conducted on the actual system that was compromised; the compromised system and all the data on it is evidence that needs to be strictly protected. Instead, the investigator must be able to make multiple copies of the file system data on alternate media and only analyze the copies during the investigation.

This chapter, then, is not a tutorial on how to manage backups in a large enterprise network. The issues around enterprise backups are complex and already have been the subject of several books. Instead, this chapter attempts to provide basic information that an investigator would need to archive or copy data from a single system and later restore and manipulate that data to assist in a computer crime investigation.

NOTES

Three Options

- tar – Portable archive format, easy to use, good for quick backups
- dump/restore – standard full-featured Unix backup utilities
-  dd – Copies raw file system information, can capture "deleted" data

SANS Security Essentials – Unix Security

Unix Data Archiving Options

There are several different commands available under Unix for archiving and later restoring files. The choice of which method to use depends a lot on the situation and the reason for making the archive:

- The `tar` ("tape archive") command takes a list of files and directories and gathers them together into a single file, preserving file attributes like ownership, permissions, and timestamps. The `tar` archive file—"`tar` file" for short—can be written to disk, tape, CD-ROM, or whatever media is handy, and the `tar` format is portable across different Unix platforms and different processor types.
- The `dump` command creates a backup of a Unix partition that later can be recovered using the `restore` program. `dump` and `restore` are the standard basic backup utilities for Unix systems, but the archive format used by these programs tends to be extremely vendor-specific and is not at all portable.
- The `dd` command simply copies raw data from one place to another and also is able to do "on-the-fly" data conversions. Because `dd` can deal directly with raw file system data, it can pick up data that the other Unix archiving methods may miss, including the remnants of files that were deleted from a file system by an attacker.

Unix also supports the `cpio` utility for making archive files. However, `tar` now is the more commonly used utility, in no small part because it is much easier to use than `cpio`. Hence, this chapter will ignore `cpio` and concentrate on the `tar` command instead.

Let's look at some of the "pros and cons" for `tar`, `dump`, and `dd`, along with some hints for the situations in which each is most useful. Hopefully, this will help when trying to decide which option is best for the current archiving need.

NOTES

tar

Pro

- Can be used on "active" file systems
- Byte-order independent format

Con

- Can't span multiple volumes
- Various versions have some limitations

SANS Security Essentials – Unix Security

tar Overview

`tar` is the portable archive format for Unix systems. `tar` files made on one machine can be read almost anywhere, including some Windows-based utilities. This is why so much of the software and source code that is available on the Internet is made into `tar` archives for easy downloading.

`tar` operates by simply working its way through the list of files and directories that the user specifies on the command line. If one of the targets for the archive file is a directory, `tar` recursively descends into the directory and gathers up all files and subdirectories into the archive. Because it gathers files and directories "one-by-one" as it were, the `tar` command can be used to archive file systems that currently are "active"; that is, which have one or more users adding, deleting, or modifying files while the archive is happening. This is very different from the `dump` command, which only should be used on inactive file systems.

One downside to `tar` is that it does not handle splitting a single, large archive across multiple tapes, CD-ROMs, floppies, etc. Some `tar` implementations claim to have this feature, but they usually do not work properly. This used to be more of an issue in the old days, when tapes did not hold much information, but now is a major problem only when attempting to back up or make archival copies from systems that have large disk arrays connected to them. Of course, it usually is possible for the administrator to divide the data manually into several separate archives that will fit on the available media.

Different versions of `tar` also have had various odd and mostly historical limitations. For example, some versions of `tar` cannot handle pathnames longer than some fixed limit, sometimes as low as 100 characters. Some versions will not back up device files or other special sorts of files that may be encountered in the file system. However, GNU `tar` from the Free Software Foundation has none of these limitations and is portable across a wide variety of systems. Most Linux systems use GNU `tar` as their standard `tar` command, but on other Unix platforms, it is a good idea to download, compile, and use it. Source code can be found at `ftp://ftp.gnu.org/gnu/tar/`.

NOTES

dump/restore

Pro

- Supports multiple volumes
- Supports "incremental" backups
- "Interactive" mode for restore

Con

- Format is byte-order dependent
- Can get confused if file system is active
- Can only back up one partition at a time

SANS Security Essentials – Unix Security

dump and restore

dump and restore are the common utilities for doing normal Unix backups. While it is possible to write a dump archive to a disk drive, CD-ROM, or similar media, these commands originally were designed for writing backups to tape, which shows in the command-line options, as we will see later. However, because dump is designed to archive large amounts of data to tapes, the dump command does handle splitting a single large archive across multiple tapes gracefully, if necessary (unlike the tar command). Also, because dump was designed for taking system backups, it also supports the notion of "incremental backups;" that is, the ability to only back up files and directories that have changed since the last backup.

The restore command can be used to bring back an entire dump or to restore selected individual files. As we will see later, restore has a very nice "interactive" mode that allows administrators to view the files in the dump archive as if they were in the Unix file system and selectively mark files which they want to restore.

As we mentioned earlier, the format of the dump archive is incredibly system dependent and not at all portable. Also, dump only works on a single disk partition at a time, so backing up a complete Unix file system generally involves several successive dumps.

The big problem with dump, though, is that it actually dumps the file system using several "passes:" the first pass maps the file system; the next pass dumps the directory structure to tape; and the final pass backs up the actual file information. If the file system changes while the dump is being performed, the backup may be corrupted and useless. This is why dumps should be performed late at night, when nobody is using the system, or in "single-user" mode by an admin on the console of the system.

NOTES

dd

Pro

- May capture data that other tools miss
- Can perform data conversions as well

Con

- Must usually be used with other tools
- Odd command line syntax

The dd Command

dd is not an archiving utility per se, rather a means of copying raw data from one place to another. dd does not care whether it is moving data from a disk drive to a tape drive, from one disk drive to another, copying data between two tape drives, or even moving data over the network to a disk or tape device.

However, dd usually needs to be used in combination with some other utility to interpret the data. Typically this is an archiving command like tar or dump and restore. However, dd also is used simply to make copies of raw file system data, usually so that the copies can be analyzed later with forensic analysis tools, such as the file system utilities that come with the free Coroner's Toolkit (see http://www.fish.com/tct/).

The reason dd is useful in forensic analysis is because it deals with file system data at a lower level than the standard Unix archiving utilities. tar and dump only see files and directories that currently are part of the file system. dd, on the other hand, grabs all data blocks off the disk, including data blocks that currently are not part of any allocated files. However these "free" data blocks may have been part of a file that was removed by the attacker; the original data that was in these blocks will still be readable until these blocks are re-allocated into a newly created file. Good forensic utilities will help the administrator to "undelete" these blocks and piece their contents back together into the original file (which also can be useful for recovering a critical file that accidentally may have been deleted).

Also, dd does have some nice data conversion features that make it possible to migrate data from one type of system to another. Trivial conversions like upper to lower case mapping and vice versa are possible, as are more complex operations like byte swapping and converting EBCDIC based mainframe data to the standard ASCII character set. dd also can help the administrator to skip over bad blocks that are preventing other commands like tar and restore from being able to recover data from an archive.

dd is one of the oldest Unix utilities. In fact, it pre-dates the Unix operating system. As we will see later, it has a funny "non-standard" command line syntax compared to other Unix commands.

With this general information for tar, dump, and dd out of the way, let's examine how to use each utility in detail. Also, in most cases there are some useful "tricks" or standard command lines of which administrators should be aware when using these commands.

NOTES

Digression: Tape Devices

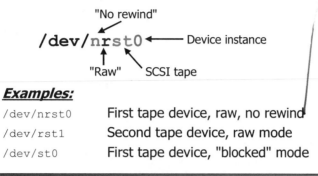

"No rewind"

/dev/nrst0 ← Device instance

"Raw" SCSI tape

Examples:

`/dev/nrst0`	First tape device, raw, no rewind
`/dev/rst1`	Second tape device, raw mode
`/dev/st0`	First tape device, "blocked" mode

SANS Security Essentials – Unix Security

Before looking at specific examples of how to use `tar`, `dump`, and `dd`, it is useful to know how different tape devices are specified under Unix. These days, Unix tape devices usually are named `/dev/st0` on most Unix systems, with systems that have multiple tape devices attached having a `/dev/st0`, `/dev/st1`, and so on. The "`st`" means SCSI-attached tape device. Older tape devices may have a non-SCSI interface, and these generally are accessed via `/dev/mt*` devices ("`mt`" for "magnetic tape").

In some cases, letters appear before the "`st`" device name. These letters indicate different options that affect the behavior of the tape drive. For example, `/dev/nst0` indicates "no rewind" mode for the tape drive. By default, any time a tape device is accessed on a Unix system, the tape is rewound before the command is executed and then automatically rewound again after the operation is completed.

However, if the administrator were trying to dump several partitions to a single large tape, and the tape were rewound to the beginning after each dump, then each dump would overwrite the one before it. Plenty of sites have been burned precisely by this behavior throughout the history of Unix! Since commands exist explicitly for rewinding the tape when needed, it always is good practice to specify the "no rewind" tape device unless absolutely certain that is not what is desired.

`/dev/rst0` would indicate the "raw mode" tape device. "Raw mode" means that data is read and written from the tape one byte at a time, rather than in blocks of data. The standard Unix backup utilities all use raw mode when accessing tapes, and, in fact, if the administrator makes a mistake and does not specify the raw tape device, the backup utility generally will use the "raw" device automatically anyway. Linux systems no longer even have `/dev/rst*` devices: `/dev/st*` on Linux systems is the "raw mode" tape device.

Note that machines based on the AT&T SYSV Unix standard (notably Solaris) use a different device-naming scheme for tapes. "Raw" tape devices on these systems are `/dev/rmt/0`, `/dev/rmt/1`, etc., even if the tape is a SCSI tape. The "no rewind" option appears after the tape number on these systems: e.g., `/dev/rmt/0n`.

The Tao of tar

`tar` has three main mode options:

`-c`	Create a new archive
`-x`	Extract files from archive
`-t`	Show archive table of contents

Other useful options:

`-f`	Specify an archive file or tape dev
`-v`	Verbose mode
`-p`	Preserve owner/access times w/ `-x`

SANS Security Essentials – Unix Security

Using the tar *Command*

`tar` generally operates in one of three major modes: the user is either creating an archive (`-c`), extracting files from an archive (`-x`), or looking at the "table of contents" of an archive (`-t`). These modes are mutually exclusive, so only specify one of `-c`, `-t`, or `-x` per command line.

`tar` has a number of other options, as well. The most important of these is `-f` for specifying to where the archive should be written. The argument to the `-f` option is the name of a tape device or even just a file name where the archive should be created.

The `-v` option turns on "verbose mode." When writing an archive or extracting files from an archive, `-v` causes the name of each file in the archive to be printed. Note that printing each file name significantly slows down the process of reading or writing the archive, so leaving off `-v` when using `-c` or `-x` may be a good idea. When used with the `-t` option, however, verbose mode causes a detailed listing of the archive contents, similar to the output of `ls -l`. This information is useful.

`tar` always stores the owner, permissions, and access times on files in the archive. However, when extracting files from the archive, the extracted files normally will be owned by the user who unpacks the `tar` file, and the original access times will be lost. However, the `-p` option tells tar to "preserve" the original owner and access times of the files when the extraction is done. Note that `-p` only works if the system administrator is running `tar` as the superuser. When using `tar` to capture file system data for forensic analysis, the investigator probably should use `-p` when later extracting the data for review.

NOTES

after -t
tar -xvf

NOTES

Using tar

Dump entire file system to tape:

```
tar -cf /dev/st0 /          # Danger!
```

Extract that same archive:

```
tar -xpf /dev/st0
```

Get a verbose listing of tape contents:

```
tar -tvf /dev/st0
```

Dump a directory to a file on disk

```
tar -cf hal.tar /home/hal   # Danger!
```

SANS Security Essentials – Unix Security

Let's suppose an investigator wishes to make an archive of the entire file system for later analysis. The naïve approach would be a simple command line like:

```
tar -cf /dev/st0 /
```

This command says to create ("`-c`") an archive starting with the root of the file system ("`/`"). The archive should be written to the system tape drive ("`-f /dev/st0`," which got squeezed together with the "`-c`" option to save typing).

There are two problems with this command line. The first problem is that the `tar` command will archive the entire file system happily—even parts of the file system that may be NFS-mounted from other servers—rather than being on the system's local disks. Traversing NFS-mounted directories probably is not desirable, for performance reasons alone if nothing else.

GNU `tar` has a `-l` option that tells the `tar` command to archive only local directories, but this option is not widely implemented in other versions of `tar`. Frankly, this is yet another point in GNU `tar`'s favor. The second problem with the example above is more serious, however . . . more on this in the next section.

First, though, let's look at a couple of other basic `tar` usage examples. Suppose we had a `tar` archive and were not sure what it contained. Checking the contents of an unknown archive is the purpose of the `-t` option:

```
tar -tvf /dev/st0
```

Note that we are using the `-v` option to get the full, detailed listing of the archive contents. It always is a good idea to check the contents of an archive before unpacking it.

Extracting the archive is as simple as:

```
tar -xpf /dev/st0
```

The archive generally is unpacked to from whatever directory the command was executed. It usually is a good idea to unpack the archive into a temporary directory and then copy the files extracted from the archive into whatever directory is required. This avoids the problem of accidentally overwriting existing data.

So far, we have been reading and writing archive files from the system tape device. However, tar archives also can be written to files on disk. Simply specify a file name rather than a tape device after the `-f` option:

```
tar -cf alice.tar /home/alice
```

This would create a file called `alice.tar` that would contain user "`alice`"'s home directory, useful for then copying this directory to another system via the network. Actually, this example shares the same problem that our first example had: the problem of "absolute path names."

NOTES

NOTES

Warning! Absolute Paths!

```
tar -cf hal.tar /home/hal
```

- Standard versions of `tar` will preserve full path names
- When this archive is extracted, `/home/hal` directory gets overwritten!
- Note that GNU `tar` automatically strips off the leading '`/`'

SANS Security Essentials – Unix Security

Absolute Path Name Dangers

It is critical to understand that `tar` preserves complete pathname information from the point in the file system that is specified. This means that if the administrator creates an archive of `/home/alice`, all of the file names in the archive will start `/home/alice/`…. When the administrator later extracts files from that archive, they will be extracted to the exact path name `/home/alice/`… and not into the directory the `tar` from where command was executed. In other words, the contents of the archive will overwrite the current version of the files in the user's home directory! The situation is even worse in the first example above, where the contents of the archive are the entire file system starting from the root directory, "`/`". Warning: Unpacking this archive could over write the entire operating system!

The danger of absolute path names embedded in `tar` archive files is one of the reasons it is so important always to check the contents of an unknown archive file with `-t` before extracting it with `-x`. After all, an attacker could distribute a malicious archive file that attempted to overwrite `/etc/passwd` and `/etc/shadow`. If an administrator naively unpacked this archive as `root`, the attacker could give herself a back-door onto the system.

Being sure always to use GNU `tar` can help here as well. GNU `tar` is smart enough to strip off leading "`/`"s automatically when creating or extracting archive files, thereby forcing the data to get unpacked in the directory from where the `tar` command is executed. This is a huge point in GNU `tar`'s favor.

The "Right" Way To Do It

Dump entire file system to tape:

```
cd /
tar -cf /dev/st0 .
```

Dump a directory to a file on disk:

```
cd /home
tar -cf hal.tar hal
```

SANS Security Essentials – Unix Security

Still, administrators always should try to be careful not to create archives with a leading "/" in path names. The "right" way to archive an entire file system with tar would be:

```
cd /

tar -clf /dev/st0 .
```

First change directories to the top of the file system, and then archive everything from that point downward by specifying the current directory (".") as the starting point for the `tar` archive. Note that we are also using the special `-l` option to GNU `tar` to avoid traversing NFS-mounted directories.

Similarly, the best way to archive specific directories, as in our "archiving a user's home directory" example, would be:

```
cd /home

tar -cf alice.tar alice
```

This method results in all path names in the archive starting with the user's name, "`alice`." This will help the administrator in the future when viewing the table of contents of the archive; it immediately will be obvious which user's files are archived here.

NOTES

NOTES

tar Tricks

Create compressed archive file:

```
tar -cf - hal | gzip > hal.tar.gz
```

Check contents of compressed archive:

```
zcat bind-src.tgz | tar -tf -
```

Extract a compressed archive:

```
zcat bind-src.tgz | tar -xf -
```

The recursive directory copy idiom:

```
tar -cf - hal | (cd /new/dir; tar -xfp -)
```

SANS Security Essentials – Unix Security

tar Tips and Tricks

When writing a `tar` file to disk, it usually is a good idea to compress the data as well. `tar` files generally are slightly larger than the sum of the sizes of the files in the archive. This overhead is due to extra data added by the `tar` archive format itself. Unix makes it easy to combine the archiving and compression operations into a single command line:

```
tar -cf - alice | gzip >alice.tar.gz
```

The first part of the command line invokes `tar` on the directory "`alice`," per our previous example. However, rather than directing the output of `tar` to a tape device or file on disk, we are sending it to "`-`." This is a special marker that tells the `tar` command to send its output (i.e., the archive file) to the "standard output." Normally this means that the contents of the archive file would get blasted to the terminal window of the user running the command, but the pipe ("`|`") takes this output and makes it the input for the `gzip` command, which compresses the data "on-the-fly." The redirect (">") then writes the output of the `gzip` command—a compressed `tar` archive in this case—to the file `alice.tar.gz`.

"`.gz`" is the standard extension for files that have been compressed with the `gzip` utility, although any file name could have been chosen. In fact, `gzip`-ed tar files are so common that the "`.tar.gz`" extension is often shortened to "`.tgz`" just to save a few keystrokes.

Now the question is whether there is an easy way to view the table of contents and extract files from an archive that has been compressed with `gzip`. Both the `-t` and `-x` options to `tar` will accept the "`-f -`" option to read the contents of a `tar` archive from the "standard input." So, all we need is a command to uncompress a `gzip`-ed file "on-the-fly," which is precisely for what the `zcat` command exists:

```
zcat alice.tar.gz | tar -tvf -

zcat alice.tar.gz | tar -xpf -
```

Again, it always is critical to look at the table of contents of an unknown archive before extracting the files in the archive, just to make sure that there are no unexpected files or absolute path names in the archive.

As if there were not enough reasons to use it already, GNU `tar` also has a `-z` option that does all of this `gzip`-style compression with built-in routines. This option allows us to simplify all of our examples so far:

NOTES

```
tar -czf alice.tar.gz alice

tar -tzvf alice.tar.gz

tar -xzpf alice.tar.gz
```

Still, the longer "pipelining" version from the initial examples is useful on systems where GNU `tar` is not available.

`tar` also is useful for copying a directory structure from one disk to another or even just for moving a directory from one part of the file system to another. From the perspective of a forensic analyst, tape drives are cumbersome, but it is easy to carry around a portable disk with a USB or firewire interface that can be connected quickly to a machine and used to snap off a copy of the machine's file system. The advantage to using `tar` for this operation, rather than the normal Unix copy ("`cp`") command, is that `tar` can preserve access times and file ownerships with `-p`, whereas `cp` normally does not.

Let's suppose our user "`alice`" has left the company, and we wish to move her home directory from `/home/alice` to `/graveyard/alice`:

```
cd /home

tar -cf - alice | (cd /graveyard; tar -xpf
-)
```

What basically is happening here is that we are sending the output of the first "`tar -c`" command into the input of the second "`tar -x`" command. The parentheses on the right-hand side of the pipe symbol group the `cd` command and the "`tar -x`" command together so that the files get extracted in `/graveyard`. What happens is that the change directory operation ("`cd /graveyard`") occurs first and then the "`tar -x`" to extract the archive into this directory. Technically what is going on is that the parentheses cause the Unix command shell to spawn a "sub-shell" that executes the two commands we specify together.

`tar` makes it very easy to take quick archive copies of Unix file systems. As such, it is very useful when forensic investigations call for making a rapid copy of the file system for later analysis. For long-term backup and recovery operations, however, `dump` and `restore` may be more appropriate.

dump and restore

While `tar` is the "quick and dirty" way to make an archive of a directory or file system, `dump` and `restore` are much more oriented towards being used as part of a site's normal backup strategy. From a computer forensics standpoint, `dump` actually does capture one additional piece of file system information that `tar` does not: each file's "inode number" in the original file system. While an experienced analyst might be able to use this information to help spot files that have been modified by the attacker (this "inode number" changes if a file is deleted and replaced with a new file), `dump` can be much slower than `tar` and also requires that the file system being dumped not currently be in use in order to get a clean image of the file system. When the situation calls for taking a snapshot of a running system and getting that machine back into "production" use as quickly as possible, `tar` may be preferable.

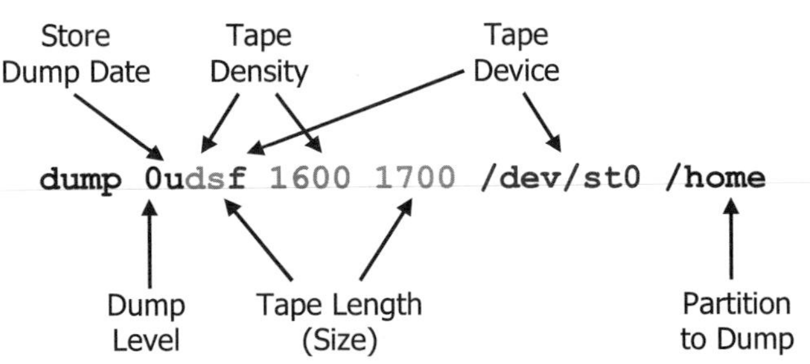

The dump Command

The `dump` command has a somewhat strange command line syntax. Generally, the arguments to the command break down into three sections: "`dump <options> <arguments> <partition-name>`." The first `<options>` chunk specifies the dump level number and all command options with no spaces, no leading dash. The `<arguments>` section is all of the arguments to the options that were specified in the initial `<options>` group; the arguments must be specified in the same order in which the options were given. The last thing on the command line is the file system that should be dumped.

Here is a sample `dump` command:

```
dump 0udsf 1600 1700 /dev/st0 /home
```

In this example, the leading zero in the options block is the "dump level". The "`u`" ("update") option tells `dump` to update the `/etc/dumpdates` file with the date and time of this dump, along with the dump level. Dump levels, and the data and time information stored in `/etc/dumpdates` are the mechanism the dump command uses to perform "incremental" backups— that is, only backing up files that have been modified since the last dump. We will discuss dump levels and incremental backups in much more detail in just a moment.

The "`d`" option specifies the tape "density" in bits per inch, and the "`s`" ("size") option specifies the tape length in feet. These options allow `dump` to calculate whether the dump will fit on one tape or whether multiple tapes ("volumes" in dump-speak) are required. These options were important when tapes were smaller but are not used commonly today. The product of these two values can be used to calculate the total capacity of the tape in bytes: (tape density) * (tape length) * 12 is the total capacity of the tape in bits. Divide by eight to get the total number of bytes the tape will hold. In our example, this tape holds 1600*1700*12/8 bytes. This works out to only 4MB or so, which believe it or not was the capacity of small tapes two decades ago.

Of course, modern tapes have much higher capacities. Since a typical dump is going to fit onto a single tape with room to spare, it is pointless to specify exact tape density and size parameters. The easiest method is to simply specify a very large tape size so that the `dump` command never decides to try and split the backup across multiple tapes:

```
dump 0usf 9999999 /dev/st0 /home
```

Here we are using a tape size of almost 10 million feet. The default density value for dump is 6250 bpi (this number is historical). This works out to a tape that holds almost 90GB of data, actually nearly the correct amount for some modern, high-density tape drives.

"`f`" specifies the name of a tape device or file, just like when using `tar`. Also like `tar`, `dump` allows the administrator to dump to the "-" file, meaning the "standard output." This means that `dump` can be used as part of a shell pipeline, just as we did with `tar`, so that `dump` images can be compressed "on-the-fly" with commands like `gzip`.

NOTES

NOTES

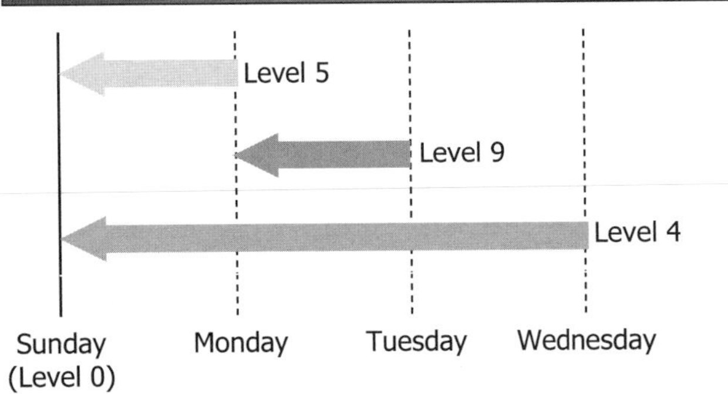

Dump Levels and Incremental Backups

Now that we've covered the basic options for the `dump` command, let's take a more detailed look at the meaning of the "dump level" and its relationship to "incremental" backup activity. Dump levels range from 0-9. A "level 0" dump backs up all data in the dumped file system, and is often referred to as a "full dump." Picking a higher number performs an "incremental" dump, which will only back up the files that have been modified since the last dump of a lower number. Remember that the "`u`" option to the `dump` command writes the dump level and a timestamp to the `/etc/dumpdates` file in order to keep track of exactly when the last dump of each level was performed. By using this information, the `dump` command is able to back up only the appropriate files during an incremental backup.

Consider the illustration above. Suppose an administrator starts off the weekly backup schedule with a level 0 dump at midnight on Sunday night. On Monday at midnight, the admin runs off a level 5 dump: this dump captures all of the files that have been modified since the level 0 dump was done on Sunday night. If Tuesday night's dump is a level 9 dump, then this backup only captures the changes since the level 5 dump the night before. Now if Wednesday's dump is a level 4 dump, this captures everything that has been changed since the original level 0 dump on Sunday night.

In some sense the level 5 and level 9 tapes are now redundant, since the level 4 tape should contain all of the information that was captured by the level 5 and level 9 dumps. However, suppose that the system had been compromised during the day on Wednesday, in between the level 9 and level 4 dumps. Suddenly those level 5 and level 9 dump tapes are very important, because they contain the last "good" image of the file system before the compromise took place. Also, from a data integrity perspective, the level 9 tape might contain the last known copy of a particular file that was deleted on Wednesday before the level 4 dump was run. So don't be hasty when discarding "redundant" dump tapes.

Incremental dumps are most often used as part of a site's normal backup strategy in order to limit the amount of time and media that are spent on backups. For computer forensic purposes, however, security analysts typically always want a full "level 0" dump of the entire file system to analyze. While it always is a good idea to use the "`u`" option when following the normal system backup schedule, security professionals taking system dumps for forensic analysis or in other "special circumstances" probably will want to leave the "u" option off their command lines, specifically so that these "special" level 0 dumps do not interfere with the system's normal backup activities.

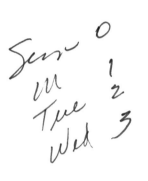

NOTES

NOTES

dump Examples

Normal use with large tape drives:

```
dump 0usf 9999999 /dev/nst0 /home
```

Do an "incremental" dump:

```
dump 5usf 9999999 /dev/nst0 /home
```

Yes, you can dump to a file:

```
dump 0sf 9999999 - /home | \
  gzip >home.dump.gz
```

SANS Security Essentials – Unix Security

So, the standard command to do a full dump of a file system to tape as part of a site's regular backup schedule would be:

```
dump 0usf 9999999 /dev/nst0 /home
```

The above command line uses the "`u`" flag to update the `/etc/dumpdates` file. If this were a special dump for forensic purposes, simply leave off the "`u`" option.

Notice that the command line shown above uses the `/dev/nst0` "no rewind" tape device. One common practice for large tapes is to start the tape with a "level 0" backup of a file system and then follow that with daily incremental backups:

```
dump 5usf 9999999 /dev/nst0 /home
```

Tapes then get swapped out on a weekly or monthly basis, depending on the site's backup and retention policies.

However, using tape is becoming less and less common. These days, dumps often are done to a file:

```
dump 0usf 9999999 - /home | gzip
>home.dump.gz
```

This file could be copied to another system for archival storage or, perhaps, burned onto a CD-ROM or DVD-ROM (depending on the size of the dump file). Of course, the system needs enough free disk space to hold the dump file that gets written by this command; and obviously the dump file cannot be written to the file system that is being backed up, or the archive will get corrupted.

NOTES

Restoring an Entire Partition

```
# restore -rf /dev/st0
Warning! lost+found: File exists
# rm restoresymtable
```

- Restore most recent level 0 dump, then overlay incremental dumps
- Deleted files have a tendency to "reappear" after restore

SANS Security Essentials – Unix Security

Restoring Data

The simplest use of the `restore` command is to bring back an entire file system image from a single dump with the "`restore -r`" command:

```
# restore -rf /dev/st0

Warning! lost+found: File exists

# rm restoresymtable
```

Note that if the dump image were split across multiple tapes, `restore` automatically would prompt the administrator to put each volume into the tape drive when appropriate.

The warning message from `restore` shown in the example indicates that the `restore` is overwriting a file that already exists in the file system. Typically, "`restore -r`" is used after a disk crash to bring back the lost data into the empty file systems of a new disk drive. However, even a new "empty" Unix file system contains the special `lost+found` directory, so this warning message is normal. Note that after the restore is completed, `restore` leaves a file behind called `restoresymtable`, an uninteresting file which may be deleted safely.

Now suppose that the last "level 0" dump was four weeks ago, and in the intervening time several incremental backups have been created. In order to completely restore the most current file system image, the administrator must restore the level 0 dump and then restore all of the active incremental dumps in order by date. This has significant implications for sites planning their backup strategies: how many restores and how much time is going to be required to recover any given file system completely? In order to speed up the recovery process, "level 0" dumps need to be done with more frequency.

Another interesting outcome of this need to "overlay" incremental backups to re-create the file system is that users may complain that they deleted a file days or weeks ago, but that it "came back" after the restore. A dump is a snapshot of the file system at a particular instant: if one of the incremental dumps happened to capture the file system before the user deleted his file, then the file is "put back" when the restore occurs. The more frequently the site does dumps, the more likely this sort of thing is to happen.

NOTES

Interactive Restore

```
# cd /tmp
# restore -if /dev/st0
restore> cd mail
restore> ls
erin        hal         laura
restore> add hal                    Add file(s) to restore list
restore> extract                    Begin restore process
   [...]
Specify next volume #: 1            Wait for restore to happen
set owner/mode for '.'? [yn] n      Always answer no!
# mv mail/hal /var/mail/hal
```

SANS Security Essentials – Unix Security

As we mentioned earlier, the `restore` command also has an interactive mode ("`restore -i`") that allows administrators to bring back only specific files from a dump archive. This can be particularly useful after security incidents, since it would allow the administrator to bring back just a certain log file, or the original copies of `/etc/passwd` and `/etc/shadow`, or a user's mailbox that may have been corrupted by the attacker.

Here is a sample interactive `restore` session, in which the administrator is recovering a user's mailbox from a dump image of the `/var` partition:

```
# cd /tmp
# restore -if /dev/st0
restore> cd mail
restore> ls
alice          bob          eve
restore> add eve
restore> extract
     [...]
Specify next volume #: 1
set owner/mode for '.'? [yn] n
#
```

When initially invoked, "`restore -i`" reads the directory structure information saved by the first pass of the dump and then puts the administrator into interactive mode at a "`<restore>`" prompt. Interactive mode in `restore` operates like a crippled Unix command shell. The administrator can `cd` around the dump image and use `ls` to get directory listings. However, "`ls -l`" and other options generally do not work: only file names are displayed.

When the administrator locates a file he wishes to restore, the special "`add`" command puts that file on the pending list of files to be extracted. Once the administrator has tagged all the files he wants to pull back, the "`extract`" command starts the actual restore process.

Now `restore` is expecting that we still are living in a world where backups are split across multiple tapes, which almost certainly is not the case. Nevertheless, `restore` prompts the user for which tape volume should be read first. Note that the message that has been removed from the example above in order to save space suggests that the user start reading from the last volume and work backwards, which is the most efficient approach for multi-volume dumps. However, since most dumps these days fit on a single tape, simply specify volume 1, the current and only volume, when prompted.

At this point the tape will spin, and `restore` will extract the specified files from the archive file. The last prompt from `restore` asks the administrator if he wants to set the owner and permissions on the current directory to match the owner and permissions of the root directory of the dump archive on tape. Since the `restore` most likely is happening in some other directory than the file system that was dumped originally, **always** answer "no" to this question, or else the permissions and ownership of the temporary directory where the restore is happening will be corrupted. The most common mistake in interactive restores is to do the restore in `/tmp` and accidentally reset the permissions on this directory so that it is no longer world-writable. For this reason, it usually is a good idea to make a subdirectory in `/tmp` for doing the restore: even if the administrator accidentally resets the permissions on the subdirectory, there is no real harm done.

If the administrator were recovering this mailbox because the user had accidentally deleted it and needed the data recovered, it would now be up to the admin to copy the recovered file manually into its normal location in the `/var/mail` directory. The admin would have to use `chown` and `chmod` to set the correct ownership and permissions on the file.

The dd *Command*

Unlike the `tar`, `dump`, and `restore` commands, which are designed specifically for backing up and archiving file system data, the `dd` command simply is for moving raw data from one place to another. `dd` appears to be very mysterious at first because it has very different command line syntax from other Unix commands, but it is a very simple-minded program.

NOTES

NOTES

Using dd

Creating boot floppies:

```
dd if=boot.img of=/dev/fd0
```

Copy raw disk data to tape:

```
dd if=/dev/rsd0a of=/dev/st0
```

Copy raw disk image to data file:

```
dd if=/dev/rsd0a of=/var/tmp/data
```

Tape-to-tape copy:

```
dd if=/dev/st0 of=/dev/st1
```

SANS Security Essentials – Unix Security

Basic dd Usage

Probably the most common use for dd these days is creating "boot floppies" for OS installs. Some older PC BIOS are unable to boot from CD-ROM: in order to install Linux or some other Open Source operating system onto the machine, it must first be booted from a floppy so that the CD-ROM based OS can be loaded. Most of these Unix operating systems will ship a bootable floppy image in a file on their CD-ROM, but this image must be copied onto a blank floppy with dd:

```
dd if=boot.img of=/dev/fd0
```

The "if=" argument specifies the "input file" that dd will copy, in this case the boot.img file off the vendor's CD-ROM. As one might expect, "of=" is the "output file" or destination for the copied data, the system floppy disk device, /dev/fd0, in this case.

For forensic purposes, however, the most common use for dd is to transfer file system images in the other direction: off the local hard drive to some other media like a tape, another disk device, or even a file in some other file system. For example, the following dd command would dump a file system image from a single disk partition to a local tape device:

```
dd if=/dev/hda1 of=/dev/st0
```

The file system image written to the tape drive would have to be read off the tape and transferred to an empty disk partition on another machine before the data could be analyzed effectively. dd would be the appropriate command for this operation as well.

If the administrator were able to attach a second disk drive directly to the system, dd simply could move the data directly from one disk to another. Assuming the system's primary drive is /dev/hda, and the second disk is /dev/hdb, the command might look like:

```
dd if=/dev/hda1 of=/dev/hdb1
```

This command would need to be repeated for each partition on the primary disk in order to capture all of the data.

dd can even move data from a disk device and write it to a regular file someplace else on the disk:

```
dd if=/dev/hda1 of=/var/tmp/dd-output
```

The dd-output file could then be copied over the network to another system, where it could be unpacked into an empty partition and analyzed.

One problem with this approach is the size of the archive file created: the output file is going to be as large as the total size of the partition that is being dumped, not just the amount of space currently allocated to files. This is because dd grabs not only the data blocks that make up the files currently in the file system but also the "free" data blocks that not yet have been allocated to files. Make sure that there is enough space in the destination file system before executing the dd command. It may be a good idea to compress the file as it is being written:

```
dd if=/dev/hda1 of=- | gzip >/var/tmp/dd-
output.gz
```

As with tar, dump, and restore, the special output file "-" means send the output of dd to the "standard output."

The other problem with using dd to dump file system data into a file in another partition is that this operation may clobber important file system evidence in the destination file system. The primary purpose of capturing a file system dump with dd is to get at the information in "free" (unallocated) data blocks that may once have been part of files in the file system but have since been deleted. Every time data is written into a file, however, data blocks are pulled back off the "free" list in that partition, allocated to the new file, and overwritten with the new file's contents. By dumping our file system image to /var, we may be overwriting some of the deleted data in this partition with our own evidence! In a criminal investigation, modifying the state of the file system during the investigation is almost certainly going to make the file system evidence inadmissible. So, the best course of action is to dump the file system image to a tape or another disk drive whenever possible.

One last common use for dd is to make tape-to-tape copies on systems with two tape drives:

```
dd if=/dev/st0 of=/dev/st1
```

If file system evidence were written to tape during a forensic investigation, this would be a way to make copies for multiple analysts. This also is a useful mechanism for duplicating backup tapes so that one set of backups can be kept off-site in case of disaster.

NOTES

NOTES

Converting Data

Swapping byte order:

```
dd if=/dev/st0 of=- conv=swab | tar xpf -
```

Converting old mainframe data:

```
dd if=/dev/st0 of=asc.dat conv=ascii,lcase
```

Skip over bad tape blocks:

```
dd if=/dev/st0 of=- conv=noerror,sync | \
  tar xpf -
```

SANS Security Essentials – Unix Security

While dd is normally used to move data between systems of the same type, dd also allows administrators to do data conversion "on-the-fly" to help facilitate migrating data between different types of systems.

One useful conversion is byte swapping. Older SGI machines were famous for writing tapes with the "wrong" byte order, which would prevent the tapes from being read on other Unix systems. The work-around was to use dd to read the data off the tape and swap the byte ordering at the same time:

```
dd if=/dev/st0 of=- conv=swab | tar -xpf -
```

The "conv=" flag is used to specify the desired conversion operation, and "swab" is the byte swapping operator.

dd also can be used to convert all upper case characters in its input file to lower case characters, or vice versa:

```
dd if=myfile of=newfile conv=lcase
```

Here we are making a copy of the file myfile with all of the upper case letters converted to lower case ("conv=lcase"). This conversion often is useful when dealing with large data sets produced on mainframe type systems. Note that "conv=ucase" would have converted all of the lower case letters to upper case.

dd can also help convert mainframe data by converting the EBCDIC character set to the standard ASCII character set used on Unix systems:

```
dd if=/dev/st0 of=ascii_data conv=ascii
```

Actually, multiple data conversion options can be specified simultaneously. It may be desirable to both convert our EBCDIC data to ASCII and also shift the characters to all lower case:

```
dd if=/dev/st0 of=ascii_data
conv=ascii,lcase
```

There is a conversion option to go from ASCII to EBCDIC ("conv=ebcdic"), but it seems unlikely that anybody would use this option much these days.

Probably the most useful conversion operation, however, does not, strictly speaking, modify any data. The "conv=noerror" option can be used to skip over bad blocks in the input file. This is critical because a bad block on a tape, for example, will prevent tar or restore from being able to read

NOTES

the tape image, making the archive useless. In reality, though, if the bad block were skipped, the rest of the data probably could be read and recovered.

Here is a sample command line that makes use of "conv=noerror":

```
dd if=/dev/st0 of=- conv=noerror,sync |
tar xpf -
```

The "sync" conversion tells dd to replace the data skipped because of the bad block with an equal number of NULL (ASCII 0) characters. Without the "sync" option, "noerror" would just skip the bad blocks, which might confuse the tar or restore program.

NOTES

The Real Use for dd

```
ssh otherhost \
  dump 0usf 9999999 - /home | \
  dd if=- of=/dev/nst0
```

- Implies that the machine otherhost trusts the tape server as root
- Performance can be improved with compression and weaker crypto

SANS Security Essentials – Unix Security

Writing Data Over the Network

The everyday use for dd, however, is as part of shell pipelines that copy data from one system to another over the network. The most common reason for doing this is for networked backups.

Since it would be expensive and impractical to install a tape drive for every system on the network, it often is necessary to dump one machine's file systems to a tape drive on another host. The most secure way to do this is with SSH:

```
ssh <host> dump 0usf 9999999 - /home | dd
if=- of=/dev/nst0
```

This command would be run on the machine that has the tape drive attached to it (the "tapehost"). "<host>" needs to be replaced with the host name or IP address of the system that needs to be backed up (the "dumphost").

The dump command is identical to examples we have seen earlier, except here the command will be running via SSH on the dumphost machine. When the dump command sends the dump archive to the "standard output," that data is transported by SSH across the network back to the tapehost machine, where it becomes the output of the ssh command running on the local system. This output is fed into the dd command that reads data from the "standard input" ("if=-") and writes it to the local "no rewind" tape device, /dev/nst0.

Now in order for this command to function properly, there has to be a "trust relationship" set up between the tapehost and the dumphost. When using rsh in the old days of Unix, this meant creating a .rhosts file in root's home directory on the dumphost, so that the tapehost could execute remote commands on that system as root. One of the reasons to use SSH instead of rsh is that SSH supports better ways of granting remote root access for commands. For more information, read the on-line SSH manual pages for details on "DSA Authentication."

In any event, it is critical to prevent unauthorized access to the tapehost machine. Since all of the systems that are backed up to this host must allow the tapehost to execute remote commands with root privilege, an attacker who has control of the tapehost system will have free reign on these remote machines. Also, of course, an attacker with access to the tapehost system would be able to steal data directly off the backup tapes in the local tape drive.

The primary advantage to using SSH is that the data between the dumphost and the tapehost will be encrypted as it flies over the network. Unfortunately, the overhead for doing the encryption makes the backup take much longer than if the data had been sent over the network in the clear. SSH does allow the administrator to select less secure encryption methods that are faster to compute and therefore create less overhead. The local site needs to decide on the best trade-off between security and performance.

Writing data over the network to another host also can be useful for capturing forensic data. For example, in the last section we talked about the dangers of writing file system dumps into the local file system on a machine that was being investigated. On the other hand, it may not be possible to attach an extra disk drive or tape device to the compromised system without modifying or rebooting the system and causing important evidence to be lost.

In order to avoid this problem, the data from the local file systems could be shunted over the network to an unused partition on some other system:

```
dd if=/dev/hda1 of=- | ssh <host> dd if=-
of=/dev/hdb1
```

Here `<host>` would be the name or IP address of the remote system with the spare disk partition. As in the networked backup example above, at least a temporary "trust relationship" must be set up so that the SSH command will be allowed to write the data on the remote system as `root`. However, be careful because an attacker with control of the local machine possibly could exploit this "trust relationship" to attack the remote system where the forensic evidence is being gathered.

Dealing with Large Tapes

We have mentioned throughout this section that most tape drives have the capacity to hold multiple `tar` or `dump` archives. For systems with limited disk capacity, it is possible to dump all of the partitions on the system and even keep several days worth of incremental backups all on the same tape. This saves a lot of administrator time that would otherwise be spent changing tapes. However, having written multiple archives to a single tape, administrators need the ability to jump to the right archive to recover the data for which they are looking. Fortunately, Unix makes this relatively straightforward.

NOTES

NOTES

Working With Large Tapes

- These days tapes are capable of holding several days worth of backups
- *Always* use the "no rewind" tape device!
- However, the admin must be able to skip to the right tape location for restores…

SANS Security Essentials – Unix Security

Multiple Archives Per Tape

The key for getting multiple archives on a single tape is always to use the "no rewind" tape device (e.g., `/dev/nst0`). Each backup will run to completion and leave the tape heads positioned at the end of the backup file that was just written. The next time a `tar` or `dump` archive is written to the tape, that archive file will be written onto the tape right after the previous one. Do not attempt to restore data or interact with the tape device in any fashion as long as data needs to be appended onto the tape. Any operations on the tape device may end up causing the tape to be rewound or the tape to be repositioned, possibly overwriting previous archives the next time the regular backup process writes something to the tape.

The other problem is to ensure that the backup process does not run off the end of the tape in the middle of an archive, or else that backup will be useless. Also, reaching the end of tape automatically causes the tape to be rewound, so subsequent archives will start overwriting data from the beginning of the tape.

Unfortunately, when multiple archives have been written to a single tape, the standard Unix `tar` and `dump` utilities are unable to warn the administrator when the end of tape is near because these commands have no way to know how much data has been written to the tape already. It is up to the administrator to come up with some method for keeping track of how much data has been written to the tape and how much space is left.

Often the easiest thing to do is err on the side of caution. If the administrator is backing up a 4GB partition (which probably is not completely full anyway) to a tape drive that holds 60GB, then only do 15 dumps before changing the tape. Be aware that many tape drive vendors who quote a "capacity" for their tape drives use compression factors that are based on ideal circumstances. If the tape drive vendor is saying that its 30GB tapes hold 60GB with compression, it probably is best to assume that the tapes hold only 45-50GB.

NOTES

The mt Command

`mt -f /dev/nst0` *command*

command is one of:

status	Give tape status
rewoffl	Rewind and eject tape
rew	Rewind tape to beginning
fsf *n*	Skip forward *n* archive files
bsf *n*	Go back *n* archive files

SANS Security Essentials – Unix Security

Rewinding and Repositioning Tapes

Eventually the tape will fill up and need to be rewound and removed from the tape drive. Also, if the administrator ever needs to recover data from the tape in the future, she will need a way to jump to the proper archive file.

The mt ("magnetic tape") command is used to rewind tapes and also to reposition the tape so that a particular archive file can be read. The format of the mt command is simple: "mt -f /dev/nst0 <command>", where <command> is any one of a number of different commands, depending on what options the given vendor has chosen to implement.

Regardless of the version of Unix, "mt -f /dev/st0 rew" will cause the tape to rewind. Actually, this command is somewhat redundant since accessing the tape via the /dev/st0 device will cause the tape to rewind automatically before the "mt" command even gets a chance to run. "mt -f /dev/st0 rewoffl" not only rewinds the tape but also causes it to be ejected from the tape drive. This is useful for automated backup scripts, in which the administrator wants the tape to be ejected so that it will not get reused accidentally after the backup is complete.

"mt -f /dev/nst0 fsf <n>" will cause the tape drive to "fast forward" and skip over the next <n> archive files on the tape. This is how administrators can jump to a specific archive on the tape to do their restores. It is critical to use the "no rewind" tape device here; otherwise the mt command will forward the tape the specified number of archive files, but then the tape drive will automatically rewind the tape to the beginning after the mt operation completed!

There is another tricky problem with "fsf" of which to be aware. Suppose the administrator wanted to recover data from the third archive on the tape. The correct mt command to use would be "mt -f /dev/nst0 fsf 2". Notice that the command here is "fsf 2," not "fsf 3": the administrator wants to skip over the first two archive files and leave the tape positioned at the beginning of the third archive file to start the restore.

The safest way to jump "backwards" on a tape probably is just to rewind the tape to the beginning, and then use the "fsf" option to skip forward to the desired archive.

NOTES

A Useful Shell Script

```
#!/bin/sh

PARTITIONS=`df -k | awk '/^\/dev\// { print $6 }'`

mt -f /dev/st0 rew
for $part in $PARTITIONS
do
     dump 0usf 9999999 /dev/nst0 $part
done
mt -f /dev/st0 rewoffl
```

SANS Security Essentials – Unix Security

Here is a "quick and dirty" shell script for automatically dumping all local disk partitions to a tape drive attached directly to the system:

```
#!/bin/sh

PARTITIONS='df -k | awk '/^\/dev\// {
print $6 }''

mt -f /dev/st0 rew

for $part in $PARTITIONS

do

    dump 0usf 9999999 /dev/nst0 $part

done

mt -f /dev/st0 rewoffl
```

First, we send the output of the `df` command through an `awk` filter that looks for lines beginning with "`/dev/`", indicating file systems on local disk devices. `awk` then prints the partition name (mount point) from the sixth column of the `df` output. This output from the `awk` command actually is assigned into the variable `$PARTITIONS`, which will be used later in the script.

Next we use the `mt` command to make sure the tape is rewound to the beginning. Once the tape is rewound, we simply dump each partition listed in the `$PARTITIONS` variable in turn to the "no rewind" tape device. Once all of the dumps have been completed, we again use the `mt` command to rewind and eject the tape.

The tape should be labeled with the date, the system name, and the order in which the partitions were written to the tape. It also is a good idea to indicate on the tape that the archives were written using `dump` rather than `tar` so that other people would know what command to use to recover the data. Also, remember to keep the tape safe from strong magnetic fields and other environmental hazards.

NOTES

Restoring a File System

```
# mt -f /dev/st0 rew
# mt -f /dev/nst0 fsf 2
# cd /var
# restore -rf /dev/nst0
Warning! lost+found: File exists
# rm restoresymtable
# mt -f /dev/st0 rewoffl
```

SANS Security Essentials – Unix Security

Recovering Data: An Example

Suppose we had a tape that had multiple backups of different partitions from a single system written to it using the `dump` command. Now, assume that we wish to restore the image of the `/var` partition from the third archive on the tape.

Step one is to insert the tape into the drive and then make sure we are at the beginning of the tape by issuing the "`mt -f /dev/st0 rew`" command. Also make sure that we have changed directories to the directory on the local system to where we want the restore to occur.

Now skip the tape forward to the beginning of the third archive:

```
mt -f /dev/nst0 fsf 2
```

At this point the tape should be in the correct position, and we can start our `restore` command:

```
restore -rf /dev/nst0
```

Note that it is critical in both these commands to use the "no rewind" tape device, `/dev/nst0`.

That essentially completes the `restore` operation. However, we now can remove the `restoresymtable` file left behind by the restore operation ("`rm restoresymtable`"). Also, we should rewind and eject the tape to prevent it from accidentally being overwritten by another user on the system:

```
mt -f /dev/st0 rewoffl
```

Be sure to put the tape back in whatever storage area is used for holding backup tapes, so it is not just lying around for anybody to steal.

That pretty much finishes the basics of archiving and recovering data on Unix systems. While there is plenty more to learn, the examples we have seen so far should be enough to handle "emergency" sorts of backup and recovery operations that arise.

NOTES

Summary: Lessons Learned

- Use the "no rewind" tape device to put multiple volumes on a single tape
- `tar`/`dump` via `rsh`/`ssh` can be used to move data over the network
- `tar` can be used to copy directories within a system, preserving timestamps
- `dd` can sometimes be used to recover "deleted" data

SANS Security Essentials – Unix Security

Summary

The standard archiving commands on Unix systems are `tar` and `dump` and `restore`. `tar` is best suited for taking quick archives and for writing archives that will be used on many different Unix systems. `dump` and `restore` are intended more for regular system backup operations and only should be used on file systems that are not being modified currently. The `dd` command can be used to capture "raw" file system data, which includes unallocated data blocks that may have the remnants of previously deleted files in them. Special tools will be needed to access this data, however.

`tar`, `dump`, `restore`, and `dd` are capable of reading and writing data not only to and from tape drives but also to and from regular files. These commands also can interact with the Unix "standard input" and "standard output" channels, so they can be combined with other Unix utilities like the `gzip` utility for compressing data "on-the-fly." Also, the output of one `tar` command can be used as the input of a second `tar` command in order to copy entire directory structures within the file system while still preserving file ownerships and access times. Data on the "standard input" and "standard output" also can be redirected across the network using tools like SSH.

When writing multiple archives to a single tape, always be careful to specify the "no rewind" tape device, usually `/dev/nst0`. Otherwise the tape will rewind before and after each tape operation, usually causing the previous data to be overwritten.

NOTES

Wrap Up

SANS Security Essentials – Unix Security

NOTES

References

Peter Salus, A Quarter Century of Unix, Addison-Wesley, ISBN 0-201-54777-5

Nemeth et al, Unix System Administration Handbook, Prentice Hall, ISBN 0-13-151051-7

McKusick et al, The Design and Implementation of the 4.4 BSD Operating System, Addison-Wesley, ISBN 0-201-54979-4

Kernighan and Pike, The Unix Programming Environment, Prentice Hall, ISBN 0-13-937681-X

Garfinkel and Spafford, Practical Unix and Internet Security, O'Reilly and Assoc, ISBN 1-56592-148-8

SANS Security Essentials – Unix Security

Books

Peter Salus, *A Quarter Century of Unix*, Addison-Wesley, ISBN 0-201-54777-5 *[Comment: An entertaining an anecdotal history of the growth of Unix, written by the people who were there.]*

Nemeth et al, *Unix System Administration Handbook*, Prentice Hall, ISBN 0-13-151051-7 *[Comment: Still the best general book on the basics of Unix system administration.]*

McKusick et al, *The Design and Implementation of the 4.4 BSD Operating System*, Addison-Wesley, ISBN 0-201-54979-4 *[Comment: The classic and authoritative reference on Unix internals. Applicable to all versions of Unix.]*

Kernighan and Pike, *The Unix Programming Environment*, Prentice Hall, ISBN 0-13-937681-X *[Comment: An older book, but still a good introduction to the Unix command shell]*

Garfinkel and Spafford, *Practical Unix and Internet Security*, O'Reilly and Assoc, ISBN 1-56592-148-8 *[Comment: Somewhat dated, but still a reasonably good general book on Unix security.]*

NOTES

URL Summary

BUGTRAQ
http://online.securityfocus.com/cgi-bin/sfonline/subscribe.pl
Searchable archives also at http://www.securityfocus.com/

CERT Advisories
http://www.cert.org/contact_cert/certmaillist.html
Archives at http://www.cert.org/advisories/

SANS News Services
http://www.sans.org/sansnews

SANS Security Essentials – Unix Security

Security Advisories, Mailing Lists, Patches and Software

BUGTRAQ

`http://online.securityfocus.com/cgi-bin/sfonline/subscribe.pl`

Searchable archives also at `http://www.securityfocus.com/`

CERT Advisories

`http://www.cert.org/contact_cert/certmaillist.html`

Archives at `http://www.cert.org/advisories/`

SANS News Services

`http://www.sans.org/sansnews`

RedHat:

Various mailing lists at `http://www.redhat.com/mailing-lists/`

In particular, `http://www.redhat.com/mailing-lists/redhat-announce-list/index.html`

Patches found at `ftp://updates.redhat.com/<vers>/en/os/*`

RPMs from `ftp://ftp.redhat.com/pub/redhat/linux/<vers>/en/os/`

Other RPM sources include `freshrpms.net` and `rpmfind.net`

Solaris:

Security bulletins archived at `http://sunsolve.sun.com/security`

Instructions for subscribing to security mailing list at the bottom of each bulletin

Patches at `ftp://sunsolve.sun.com/pub/patches/`

Pre-compiled packages at `http://www.sunfreeware.com`

HP-UX:

Subscribe to mailing lists at `http://us-support.external.hp.com/digest/bin/doc.pl/`
(free registration required)
Patches can be found under same URL

Pre-compiled packages from `http://devresource.hp.com/` and `http://hpux.cs.utah.edu/`

NOTES

BSD Releases:

All information is at appropriate project sites- `http://www.freebsd.org`, `http://www.netbsd.org`, `http://www.openbsd.org`

NOTES

Other URLs

General info documents–

The Center for Internet Security
`http://www.CISecurity.org/`

The SANS Reading Room:
`http://rr.sans.org/unix/unix_list.php`

The Unix "Rosetta Stone"
`http://bhami.com/rosetta.html`

Internet RFC documents
`http://www.ietf.org/rfc.html`

SANS Security Essentials – Unix Security

Other Resources

General info documents

The Center for Internet Security:
`http://www.CISecurity.org/`

The SANS Reading Room:
`http://rr.sans.org/Unix/unix_list.php`

The Unix "Rosetta Stone":
`http://bhami.com/rosetta.html`

Internet RFC documents:
`http://www.ietf.org/rfc.html`

Tips and Info for Specific Apps

NTP – `http://www.deer-run-com/~hal/ns2000/ntp2.pdf`

SSH – `http://www.employees.org/~satch/ssh/faq/`

Apache – `http://www.apache.org/docs/misc/security_tips.html`

Home Pages for Various Free Software Packages

Logsentry (automatically reports "interesting" log events via e-mail) – `http://www.psionic.com/products/logsentry.html`

sudo (give limited root access) – `http://www.courtesan.com/sudo/`

LPRng (more secure replacement for standard Unix print services) – `http://www.lprng.org/`

TITAN (OS hardening tool for Linux/Solaris) – `http://www.fish.com/titan/`

Bastille (OS hardening tool for Linux) – `http://www.bastille-linux.org/`

Coroner's Toolkit (forensic analysis tools for Unix systems) – `http://www.fish.com/tct/`

Commercial Software

VMware (run Unix in a virtual machine window– for Unix and Windows) – `http://www.vmware.com/`

Docs on kernel parameters for various OS flavors:

Linux – `http://www.linuxhq.com/kernel/v2.4/doc/networking/ip-sysctl.txt.html`

NOTES

Solaris (general) – `http://docs.sun.com/ab2/coll.707.1/SOLTUNEPARAMREF/`

Solaris (networking) – `http://www.sun.com/software/solutions/blueprints/1200/network-updt1.pdf`

NOTES

Docs!

- Password aging, `/etc/shadow`:

  `/usr/share/doc/shadow-utils-*/HOWTO`

- PAM documentation, `pam_cracklib`:

  `/usr/share/doc/pam-*/html/pam.html`
  `/usr/share/doc/pam-*/html/pam-6.html#ss6.3`

SANS Security Essentials – Unix Security

Linux PAM and Password Management Info

Password expiration/aging, `/etc/shadow` format:
`/usr/share/doc/shadow-utils-*/HOWTO`

PAM documentation, `pam_cracklib`:
`/usr/share/doc/pam-*/html/pam.html`

NOTES

Appendices

NOTES

Appendix F

Glossary of Terms

NOTES

Appendix F - Glossary of Terms

Word	Definition
3-way handshake	Machine A sends a packet with a SYN flag set to Machine B. B acknowledges A's SYN with a SYN/ACK. A acknowledges B's SYN/ACK with an ACK.
Access Control	Access Control ensures that resources are only granted to those users who are entitled to them.
Access Control List (ACL)	A mechanism that implements access control for a system resource by listing the identities of the system entities that are permitted to access the resource.
Access Control Service	A security service that provides protection of system resources against unauthorized access. The two basic mechanisms for implementing this service are ACLs and tickets.
Access Management	Access Management is the maintenance of access information which consists of four tasks: account administration, maintenance, monitoring, and revocation.
Access Matrix	An Access Matrix uses rows to represent subjects and columns to represent objects with privileges listed in each cell.
Account Harvesting	Account Harvesting is the process of collecting all the legitimate account names on a system.
ACK Piggybacking	ACK piggybacking is the practice of sending an ACK inside another packet going to the same destination.
Active Content	Program code embedded in the contents of a web page. When the page is accessed by a web browser, the embedded code is automatically downloaded and executed on the user's workstation. Ex. Java, ActiveX (MS)
Activity Monitors	Activity monitors aim to prevent virus infection by monitoring for malicious activity on a system, and blocking that activity when possible.
Address Resolution Protocol (ARP)	Address Resolution Protocol (ARP) is a protocol for mapping an Internet Protocol address to a physical machine address that is recognized in the local network. A table, usually called the ARP cache, is used to maintain a correlation between each MAC address and its corresponding IP address. ARP provides the protocol rules for making this correlation and providing address conversion in both directions.
Advanced Encryption Standard (AES)	An encryption standard being developed by NIST. Intended to specify an unclassified, publicly-disclosed, symmetric encryption algorithm.
Algorithm	A finite set of step-by-step instructions for a problem-solving or computation procedure, especially one that can be implemented by a computer.
Applet	Java programs; an application program that uses the client's web browser to provide a user interface.
ARPANET	Advanced Research Projects Agency Network, a pioneer packet-switched network that was built in the early 1970s under contract to the US Government, led to the development of today's Internet, and was decommissioned in June 1990.
Asymmetric Cryptography	Public-key cryptography; A modern branch of cryptography in which the algorithms employ a pair of keys (a public key and a private key) and use a different component of the pair for different steps of the algorithm.
Asymmetric Warfare	Asymmetric warfare is the fact that a small investment, properly leveraged, can yield incredible results.
Auditing	Auditing is the information gathering and analysis of assets to ensure such things as policy compliance and security from vulnerabilities.

NOTES

Authentication	Authentication is the process of confirming the correctness of the claimed identity.
Authenticity	Authenticity is the validity and conformance of the original information.
Authorization	Authorization is the approval, permission, or empowerment for someone or something to do something.
Autonomous System	One network or series of networks that are all under one administrative control. An autonomous system is also sometimes referred to as a routing domain. An autonomous system is assigned a globally unique number, sometimes called an Autonomous System Number (ASN).
Availability	Availability is the need to ensure that the business purpose of the system can be met and that it is accessible to those who need to use it.
Backdoor	A backdoor is a tool installed after a compromise to give an attacker easier access to the compromised system around any security mechanisms that are in place.
Bandwidth	Commonly used to mean the capacity of a communication channel to pass data through the channel in a given amount of time. Usually expressed in bits per second.
Banner	A banner is the information that is displayed to a remote user trying to connect to a service. This may include version information, system information, or a warning about authorized use.
Basic Authentication	Basic Authentication is the simplest web-based authentication scheme that works by sending the username and password with each request.
Bastion Host	A bastion host has been hardened in anticipation of vulnerabilities that have not been discovered yet.
BIND	BIND stands for Berkeley Internet Name Domain and is an implementation of DNS. DNS is used for domain name to IP address resolution.
Biometrics	Biometrics use physical characteristics of the users to determine access.
Bit	The smallest unit of information storage; a contraction of the term "binary digit;" one of two symbols—"0" (zero) and "1" (one) — that are used to represent binary numbers.
Block Cipher	A block cipher encrypts one block of data at a time.
Boot Record Infector	A boot record infector is a piece of malware that inserts malicious code into the boot sector of a disk.
Border Gateway Protocol (BGP)	An inter-autonomous system routing protocol. BGP is used to exchange routing information for the Internet and is the protocol used between Internet service providers (ISP).
Bridge	A product that connects a local area network (LAN) to another local area network that uses the same protocol (for example, Ethernet or token ring).
British Standard 7799	A standard code of practice and provides guidance on how to secure an information system. It includes the management framework, objectives, and control requirements for information security management systems.
Broadcast	To simultaneously send the same message to multiple recipients. One host to all hosts on network.
Broadcast Address	An address used to broadcast a datagram to all hosts on a given network using UDP or ICMP protocol.
Browser	A client computer program that can retrieve and display information from servers on the World Wide Web.
Brute Force	A cryptanalysis technique or other kind of attack method involving an exhaustive procedure that tries all possibilities, one-by-one.
Buffer Overflow	A buffer overflow occurs when a program or process tries to store more data in a buffer (temporary data storage area) than it was intended to hold. Since buffers are created to contain a finite amount of data, the extra information - which has to go somewhere - can overflow into adjacent buffers, corrupting or overwriting the valid data held in them.

NOTES

Business Continuity Plan (BCP)	A Business Continuity Plan is the plan for emergency response, backup operations, and post-disaster recovery steps that will ensure the availability of critical resources and facilitate the continuity of operations in an emergency situation.
Business Impact Analysis (BIA)	A Business Impact Analysis determines what levels of impact to a system are tolerable.
Byte	A fundamental unit of computer storage; the smallest addressable unit in a computer's architecture. Usually holds one character of information and usually means eight bits.
Cache	Pronounced *cash*, a special high-speed storage mechanism. It can be either a reserved section of main memory or an independent high-speed storage device. Two types of caching are commonly used in personal computers: *memory caching* and *disk caching*.
Cache Cramming	Cache Cramming is the technique of tricking a browser to run cached Java code from the local disk, instead of the internet zone, so it runs with less restrictive permissions.
Cache Poisoning	Malicious or misleading data from a remote name server is saved [cached] by another name server. Typically used with DNS cache poisoning attacks.
Cell	A cell is a unit of data transmitted over an ATM network.
Certificate-Based Authentication	Certificate-Based Authentication is the use of SSL and certificates to authenticate and encrypt HTTP traffic.
Chain of Custody	Chain of Custody is the important application of the Federal rules of evidence and its handling.
Challenge-Handshake Authentication Protocol (CHAP)	The Challenge-Handshake Authentication Protocol uses a challenge/response authentication mechanism where the response varies every challenge to prevent replay attacks.
Checksum	A value that is computed by a function that is dependent on the contents of a data object and is stored or transmitted together with the object, for the purpose of detecting changes in the data.
Cipher	A cryptographic algorithm for encryption and decryption.
Ciphertext	Ciphertext is the encrypted form of the message being sent.
Circuit Switched Network	A circuit switched network is where a single continuous physical circuit connected two endpoints where the route was immutable once set up.
Client	A system entity that requests and uses a service provided by another system entity, called a "server." In some cases, the server may itself be a client of some other server.
Collision	A collision occurs when multiple systems transmit simultaneously on the same wire.
Competitive Intelligence	Competitive Intelligence is espionage using legal, or at least not obviously illegal, means.
Computer Emergency Response Team (CERT)	An organization that studies computer and network INFOSEC in order to provide incident response services to victims of attacks, publish alerts concerning vulnerabilities and threats, and offer other information to help improve computer and network security.
Computer network	A collection of host computers together with the sub-network or inter-network through which they can exchange data.
Confidentiality	Confidentiality is the need to ensure that information is disclosed only to those who are authorized to view it.
Configuration Management	Establish a known baseline condition and manage it.
Cookie	Data exchanged between an HTTP server and a browser (a client of the server) to store state information on the client side and retrieve it later for server use. An HTTP server, when sending data to a client, may send along a cookie, which the client retains after the HTTP connection closes. A server can use this mechanism to maintain persistent client-side state information for HTTP-based applications, retrieving the state information in later connections.

NOTES

Corruption	A threat action that undesirably alters system operation by adversely modifying system functions or data.
Cost Benefit Analysis	A cost benefit analysis compares the cost of implementing countermeasures with the value of the reduced risk.
Covert Channels	Covert Channels are the means by which information can be communicated between two parties in a covert fashion using normal system operations. For example by changing the amount of hard drive space that is available on a file server can be used to communicate information.
Cron	Cron is a Unix application that runs jobs for users and administrators at scheduled times of the day.
Crossover Cable	A crossover cable reverses the pairs of cables at the other end and can be used to connect devices directly together.
Cryptanalysis	The mathematical science that deals with analysis of a cryptographic system in order to gain knowledge needed to break or circumvent the protection that the system is designed to provide. In other words, convert the cipher text to plaintext without knowing the key.
Cryptographic Algorithm or Hash	An algorithm that employs the science of cryptography, including encryption algorithms, cryptographic hash algorithms, digital signature algorithms, and key agreement algorithms.
Cryptography	Cryptography garbles a message in such a way that anyone who intercepts the message cannot understand it.
Cut-Through	Cut-Through is a method of switching where only the header of a packet is read before it is forwarded to its destination.
Cyclic Redundancy Check (CRC)	Sometimes called "cyclic redundancy code." A type of checksum algorithm that is not a cryptographic hash but is used to implement data integrity service where accidental changes to data are expected.
Daemon	A program which is often started at the time the system boots and runs continuously without intervention from any of the users on the system. The daemon program forwards the requests to other programs (or processes) as appropriate. The term *daemon* is a Unix term, though many other operating systems provide support for daemons, though they're sometimes called other names. Windows, for example, refers to daemons and *System Agents* and *services*.
Data Custodian	A Data Custodian is the entity currently using or manipulating the data, and therefore, temporarily taking responsibility for the data.
Data Encryption Standard (DES)	A widely-used method of data encryption using a private (secret) key. There are 72,000,000,000,000,000 (72 quadrillion) or more possible encryption keys that can be used. For each given message, the key is chosen at random from among this enormous number of keys. Like other private key cryptographic methods, both the sender and the receiver must know and use the same private key.
Data Aggregation	Data Aggregation is the ability to get a more complete picture of the information by analyzing several different types of records at once.
Data Mining	Data Mining is a technique used to analyze existing information, usually with the intention of pursuing new avenues to pursue business.
Data Owner	A Data Owner is the entity having responsibility and authority for the data.
Data Warehousing	Data Warehousing is the consolidation of several previously independent databases into one location.
Datagram	Request for Comment 1594 says, "a self-contained, independent entity of data carrying sufficient information to be routed from the source to the destination computer without reliance on earlier exchanges between this source and destination computer and the transporting network." The term has been generally replaced by the term packet. Datagrams or packets are the message units that the Internet Protocol deals with and that the Internet transports. A datagram or packet needs to be self-contained

NOTES

	without reliance on earlier exchanges because there is no connection of fixed duration between the two communicating points as there is, for example, in most voice telephone conversations. (This kind of protocol is referred to as connectionless.)
Decapsulation	Decapsulation is the process of stripping off one layer's headers and passing the rest of the packet up to the next higher layer on the protocol stack.
Decryption	Decryption is the process of transforming an encrypted message into its original plaintext.
Defacement	Defacement is the method of modifying the content of a website in such a way that it becomes "vandalized" or embarrassing to the website owner.
Defense In-Depth	Defense In-Depth is the approach of using multiple layers of security to guard against failure of a single security component.
Denial of Service	The prevention of authorized access to a system resource or the delaying of system operations and functions.
Dictionary Attack	An attack that tries all of the phrases or words in a dictionary, trying to crack a password or key. A dictionary attack uses a predefined list of words compared to a brute force attack that tries all possible combinations.
Diffie-Hellman	A key agreement algorithm published in 1976 by Whitfield Diffie and Martin Hellman. Diffie-Hellman does key establishment, not encryption. However, the key that it produces may be used for encryption, for further key management operations, or for any other cryptography.
Digest Authentication	Digest Authentication allows a web client to compute MD5 hashes of the password to prove it has the password.
Digital Certificate	A digital certificate is an electronic "credit card" that establishes your credentials when doing business or other transactions on the Web. It is issued by a certification authority. It contains your name, a serial number, expiration dates, a copy of the certificate holder's public key (used for encrypting messages and digital signatures), and the digital signature of the certificate-issuing authority so that a recipient can verify that the certificate is real.
Digital Envelope	A digital envelope is an encrypted message with the encrypted session key.
Digital Signature	A digital signature is a hash of a message that uniquely identifies the sender of the message and proves the message hasn't changed since transmission.
Digital Signature Algorithm (DSA)	An asymmetric cryptographic algorithm that produces a digital signature in the form of a pair of large numbers. The signature is computed using rules and parameters such that the identity of the signer and the integrity of the signed data can be verified.
Digital Signature Standard (DSS)	The US Government standard that specifies the Digital Signature Algorithm (DSA), which involves asymmetric cryptography.
Disassembly	The process of taking a binary program and deriving the source code from it.
Disaster Recovery Plan (DRP)	A Disaster Recovery Plan is the process of recovery of IT systems in the event of a disruption or disaster.
Discretionary Access Control (DAC)	Discretionary Access Control consists of something the user can manage, such as a document password.
Disruption	A circumstance or event that interrupts or prevents the correct operation of system services and functions.
Distance Vector	Distance vectors measure the cost of routes to determine the best route to all known networks.
Distributed Scans	Distributed Scans are scans that use multiple source addresses to gather information.
Domain	A sphere of knowledge, or a collection of facts about some program entities or a number of network points or addresses, identified by a name. On the Internet, a domain consists of a set of network

NOTES

	addresses. In the Internet's domain name system, a domain is a name with which name server records are associated that describe sub-domains or host. In Windows NT and Windows 2000, a domain is a set of network resources (applications, printers, and so forth) for a group of users. The user need only to log in to the domain to gain access to the resources, which may be located on a number of different servers in the network.
Domain Name	A domain name locates an organization or other entity on the Internet. For example, the domain name "www.sans.org" locates an Internet address for "sans.org" at Internet point 199.0.0.2 and a particular host server named "www". The "org" part of the domain name reflects the purpose of the organization or entity (in this example, "organization") and is called the top-level domain name. The "sans" part of the domain name defines the organization or entity and together with the top-level is called the second-level domain name.
Domain Hijacking	Domain hijacking is an attack by which an attacker takes over a domain by first blocking access to the domain's DNS server and then putting his own server up in its place.
Domain Name System (DNS)	The domain name system (DNS) is the way that Internet domain names are located and translated into Internet Protocol addresses. A domain name is a meaningful and easy-to-remember "handle" for an Internet address.
Due Care	Due care ensures that a minimal level of protection is in place in accordance with the best practice in the industry.
Due Diligence	Due diligence is the requirement that organizations must develop and deploy a protection plan to prevent fraud, abuse, and additional deploy a means to detect them if they occur.
DumpSec	DumpSec is a security tool that dumps a variety of information about a system's users, file system, registry, permissions, password policy, and services.
Dumpster Diving	Dumpster Diving is obtaining passwords and corporate directories by searching through discarded media.
Dynamic Link Library	A collection of small programs, any of which can be called when needed by a larger program that is running in the computer. The small program that lets the larger program communicate with a specific device such as a printer or scanner is often packaged as a DLL program (usually referred to as a DLL file).
Dynamic Routing Protocol	Allows network devices to learn routes. Ex. RIP, EIGRP Dynamic routing occurs when routers talk to adjacent routers, informing each other of what networks each router is currently connected to. The routers must communicate using a routing protocol, of which there are many to choose from. The process on the router that is running the routing protocol, communicating with its neighbor routers, is usually called a routing daemon. The routing daemon updates the kernel's routing table with information it receives from neighbor routers.
Eavesdropping	Eavesdropping is simply listening to a private conversation which may reveal information which can provide access to a facility or network.
Echo Reply	An echo reply is the response a machine that has received an echo request sends over ICMP.
Echo Request	An echo request is an ICMP message sent to a machine to determine if it is online and how long traffic takes to get to it.
Egress Filtering	Filtering outbound traffic.
Emanations Analysis	Gaining direct knowledge of communicated data by monitoring and resolving a signal that is emitted by a system and that contains the data but is not intended to communicate the data.
Encapsulation	The inclusion of one data structure within another structure so that the first data structure is hidden for the time being.

NOTES

Encryption	Cryptographic transformation of data (called "plaintext") into a form (called "cipher text") that conceals the data's original meaning to prevent it from being known or used.
Ephemeral Port	Also called a transient port or a temporary port. Usually is on the client side. It is set up when a client application wants to connect to a server and is destroyed when the client application terminates. It has a number chosen at random that is greater than 1023.
Escrow Passwords	Escrow Passwords are passwords that are written down and stored in a secure location (like a safe) that are used by emergency personnel when privileged personnel are unavailable.
Ethernet	The most widely-installed LAN technology. Specified in a standard, IEEE 802.3, an Ethernet LAN typically uses coaxial cable or special grades of twisted pair wires. Devices are connected to the cable and compete for access using a CSMA/CD protocol.
Event	An event is an observable occurrence in a system or network.
Exponential Backoff Algorithm	An exponential backoff algorithm is used to adjust TCP timeout values on the fly so that network devices don't continue to timeout sending data over saturated links.
Exposure	A threat action whereby sensitive data is directly released to an unauthorized entity.
Extended ACLs (Cisco)	Extended ACLs are a more powerful form of Standard ACLs on Cisco routers. They can make filtering decisions based on IP addresses (source or destination), Ports (source or destination), protocols, and whether a session is established.
Extensible Authentication Protocol (EAP)	A framework that supports multiple, optional authentication mechanisms for PPP, including clear-text passwords, challenge-response, and arbitrary dialog sequences.
Exterior Gateway Protocol (EGP)	A protocol which distributes routing information to the routers which connect autonomous systems.
False Rejects	False Rejects are when an authentication system fails to recognize a valid user.
Fast File System	The first major revision to the Unix file system, providing faster read access and faster (delayed, asynchronous) write access through a disk cache and better file system layout on disk. It uses inodes (pointers) and data blocks.
Fault Line Attacks	Fault Line Attacks use weaknesses between interfaces of systems to exploit gaps in coverage.
File Transfer Protocol (FTP)	A TCP/IP protocol specifying the transfer of text or binary files across the network.
Filter	A filter is used to specify which packets will or will not be used. It can be used in sniffers to determine which packets get displayed, or by firewalls to determine which packets get blocked.
Filtering Router	An inter-network router that selectively prevents the passage of data packets according to a security policy. A filtering router may be used as a firewall or part of a firewall. A router usually receives a packet from a network and decides where to forward it on a second network. A filtering router does the same, but first decides whether the packet should be forwarded at all, according to some security policy. The policy is implemented by rules (packet filters) loaded into the router.
Finger	A protocol to lookup user information on a given host. A Unix program that takes an e-mail address as input and returns information about the user who owns that e-mail address. On some systems, finger only reports whether the user is currently logged on. Other systems return additional information, such as the user's full name, address, and telephone number. Of course, the user must first enter this information into the system. Many e-mail programs now have a finger utility built into them.
Fingerprinting	Sending strange packets to a system in order to gauge how it responds to determine the operating system.
Firewall	A logical or physical discontinuity in a network to prevent unauthorized access to data or resources.
Flooding	An attack that attempts to cause a failure in (especially, in the security of) a computer system or other data processing entity by providing more input than the entity can process properly.

NOTES

Forest	A forest is a set of Active Directory domains that replicate their databases with each other.
Fork Bomb	A Fork Bomb works by using the fork() call to create a new process which is a copy of the original. By doing this repeatedly, all available processes on the machine can be taken up.
Form-Based Authentication	Form-Based Authentication uses forms on a webpage to ask a user to input username and password information.
Forward Lookup	Forward lookup uses an Internet domain name to find an IP address
Forward Proxy	Forward Proxies are designed to be the server through which all requests are made.
Fragment Offset	The fragment offset field tells the sender where a particular fragment falls in relation to other fragments in the original larger packet.
Fragment Overlap Attack	A TCP/IP Fragmentation Attack that is possible because IP allows packets to be broken down into fragments for more efficient transport across various media. The TCP packet (and its header) are carried in the IP packet. In this attack the second fragment contains incorrect offset. When packet is reconstructed, the port number will be overwritten.
Fragmentation	The process of storing a data file in several "chunks" or fragments rather than in a single contiguous sequence of bits in one place on the storage medium.
Frames	Data that is transmitted between network points as a unit complete with addressing and necessary protocol control information. A frame is usually transmitted serial bit by bit and contains a header field and a trailer field that "frame" the data. (Some control frames contain no data.)
Full Duplex	A type of duplex communications channel which carries data in both directions at once. Refers to the transmission of data in two directions simultaneously. Communications in which both sender and receiver can send at the same time.
Fully-Qualified Domain Name	A Fully-Qualified Domain Name is a server name with a hostname followed by the full domain name.
Gateway	A network point that acts as an entrance to another network.
gethostbyaddr	The gethostbyaddr DNS query is when the address of a machine is known and the name is needed.
gethostbyname	The gethostbyname DNS quest is when the name of a machine is known and the address is needed.
GNU	GNU is a Unix-like operating system that comes with source code that can be copied, modified, and redistributed. The GNU project was started in 1983 by Richard Stallman and others, who formed the Free Software Foundation.
Gnutella	An Internet file sharing utility. Gnutella acts as a server for sharing files while simultaneously acting as a client that searches for and downloads files from other users.
Hardening	Hardening is the process of identifying and fixing vulnerabilities on a system.
Hash Function	An algorithm that computes a value based on a data object thereby mapping the data object to a smaller data object.
Header	A header is the extra information in a packet that is needed for the protocol stack to process the packet.
Hijack Attack	A form of active wiretapping in which the attacker seizes control of a previously established communication association.
Honey pot	Programs that simulate one or more network services that you designate on your computer's ports. An attacker assumes you're running vulnerable services that can be used to break into the machine. A honey pot can be used to log access attempts to those ports including the attacker's keystrokes. This could give you advanced warning of a more concerted attack.
Hops	A hop is each exchange with a gateway a packet takes on its way to the destination.

NOTES

Host	Any computer that has full two-way access to other computers on the Internet. Or a computer with a web server that serves the pages for one or more Web sites.
Host-Based ID	Host-based intrusion detection systems use information from the operating system audit records to watch all operations occurring on the host that the intrusion detection software has been installed upon. These operations are then compared with a pre-defined security policy. This analysis of the audit trail imposes potentially significant overhead requirements on the system because of the increased amount of processing power which must be utilized by the intrusion detection system. Depending on the size of the audit trail and the processing ability of the system, the review of audit data could result in the loss of a real-time analysis capability.
HTTP Proxy	An HTTP Proxy is a server that acts as a middleman in the communication between HTTP clients and servers.
HTTPS	When used in the first part of a URL (the part that precedes the colon and specifies an access scheme or protocol), this term specifies the use of HTTP enhanced by a security mechanism, which is usually SSL.
Hub	A hub is a network device that operates by repeating data that it receives on one port to all the other ports. As a result, data transmitted by one host is retransmitted to all other hosts on the hub.
Hybrid Attack	A Hybrid Attack builds on the dictionary attack method by adding numerals and symbols to dictionary words.
Hybrid Encryption	An application of cryptography that combines two or more encryption algorithms, particularly a combination of symmetric and asymmetric encryption.
Hyperlink	In hypertext or hypermedia, an information object (such as a word, a phrase, or an image; usually highlighted by color or underscoring) that points (indicates how to connect) to related information that is located elsewhere and can be retrieved by activating the link.
Hypertext Markup Language (HTML)	The set of markup symbols or codes inserted in a file intended for display on a World Wide Web browser page.
Hypertext Transfer Protocol (HTTP)	The protocol in the Internet Protocol (IP) family used to transport hypertext documents across an internet.
Identity	Identity is whom someone or what something is, for example, the name by which something is known.
Incident	An incident as an adverse network event in an information system or network or the threat of the occurrence of such an event.
Incident Handling	Incident Handling is an action plan for dealing with intrusions, cyber-theft, denial of service, fire, floods, and other security-related events. It is comprised of a six step process: Preparation, Identification, Containment, Eradication, Recovery, and Lessons Learned.
Incremental Backups	Incremental backups only backup the files that have been modified since the last backup. If dump levels are used, incremental backups only backup files changed since last backup of a lower dump level.
Inetd (xinetd)	Inetd (or Internet Daemon) is an application that controls smaller internet services like telnet, ftp, and POP.
Inference Attack	Inference Attacks rely on the user to make logical connections between seemingly unrelated pieces of information.
Ingress Filtering	Ingress Filtering is filtering inbound traffic.
Interrupt	An Interrupt is a signal that informs the OS that something has occurred.
Information Warfare	Information Warfare is the competition between offensive and defensive players over information resources.

NOTES

Input Validation Attacks	Input Validations Attacks are where an attacker intentionally sends unusual input in the hopes of confusing an application.
Integrity	Integrity is the need to ensure that information has not been changed accidentally or deliberately, and that it is accurate and complete.
Integrity Star Property	In Integrity Star Property a user cannot read data of a lower integrity level then their own.
Internet	A term to describe connecting multiple separate networks together.
Internet Control Message Protocol (ICMP)	An Internet Standard protocol that is used to report error conditions during IP datagram processing and to exchange other information concerning the state of the IP network.
Internet Engineering Task Force (IETF)	The body that defines standard Internet operating protocols such as TCP/IP. The IETF is supervised by the Internet Society Internet Architecture Board (IAB). IETF members are drawn from the Internet Society's individual and organization membership.
Internet Message Access Protocol (IMAP)	A protocol that defines how a client should fetch mail from and return mail to a mail server. IMAP is intended as a replacement for or extension to the Post Office Protocol (POP). It is defined in RFC 1203 (v3) and RFC 2060 (v4).
Internet Protocol (IP)	The method or protocol by which data is sent from one computer to another on the Internet.
Internet Protocol Security (IPsec)	A developing standard for security at the network or packet processing layer of network communication.
Internet Standard	A specification, approved by the IESG and published as an RFC, that is stable and well-understood, is technically competent, has multiple, independent, and interoperable implementations with substantial operational experience, enjoys significant public support, and is recognizably useful in some or all parts of the Internet.
Intranet	A computer network, especially one based on Internet technology, that an organization uses for its own internal, and usually private, purposes and that is closed to outsiders.
Intrusion Detection	A security management system for computers and networks. An IDS gathers and analyzes information from various areas within a computer or a network to identify possible security breaches, which include both intrusions (attacks from outside the organization) and misuse (attacks from within the organization).
IP Address	A computer's inter-network address that is assigned for use by the Internet Protocol and other protocols. An IP version 4 address is written as a series of four 8-bit numbers separated by periods.
IP Flood	A denial of service attack that sends a host more echo request ("ping") packets than the protocol implementation can handle.
IP Forwarding	IP forwarding is an Operating System option that allows a host to act as a router. A system that has more than 1 network interface card must have IP forwarding turned on in order for the system to be able to act as a router.
IP Spoofing	The technique of supplying a false IP address.
ISO	International Organization for Standardization, a voluntary, non-treaty, non-government organization, established in 1947, with voting members that are designated standards bodies of participating nations and non-voting observer organizations.
Issue-Specific Policy	An Issue-Specific Policy is intended to address specific needs within an organization, such as a password policy.
ITU-T	International Telecommunications Union, Telecommunication Standardization Sector (formerly "CCITT"), a United Nations treaty organization that is composed mainly of postal, telephone, and telegraph authorities of the member countries and that publishes standards called "Recommendations."

NOTES

Jitter	Jitter or Noise is the modification of fields in a database while preserving the aggregate characteristics of that make the database useful in the first place.
Jump Bag	A Jump Bag is a container that has all the items necessary to respond to an incident inside to help mitigate the effects of delayed reactions.
Kerberos	A system developed at the Massachusetts Institute of Technology that depends on passwords and symmetric cryptography (DES) to implement ticket-based, peer entity authentication service and access control service distributed in a client-server network environment.
Kernel	The essential center of a computer operating system, the core that provides basic services for all other parts of the operating system. A synonym is *nucleus*. A kernel can be contrasted with a shell, the outermost part of an operating system that interacts with user commands. *Kernel* and *shell* are terms used more frequently in Unix and some other operating systems than in IBM mainframe systems.
Lattice Techniques	Lattice Techniques use security designations to determine access to information.
Layer 2 Forwarding Protocol (L2F)	An Internet protocol (originally developed by Cisco Corporation) that uses tunneling of PPP over IP to create a virtual extension of a dial-up link across a network, initiated by the dial-up server and transparent to the dial-up user.
Layer 2 Tunneling Protocol (L2TP)	An extension of the Point-to-Point Tunneling Protocol used by an Internet service provider to enable the operation of a virtual private network over the Internet.
Least Privilege	Least Privilege is the principle of allowing users or applications the least amount of permissions necessary to perform their intended function.
Legion	Software to detect unprotected shares.
Lightweight Directory Access Protocol (LDAP)	A software protocol for enabling anyone to locate organizations, individuals, and other resources such as files and devices in a network, whether on the public Internet or on a corporate Intranet.
Link State	With link state, routes maintain information about all routers and router-to-router links within a geographic area, and creates a table of best routes with that information.
List Based Access Control	List Based Access Control associates a list of users and their privileges with each object.
Loadable Kernel Modules (LKM)	Loadable Kernel Modules allow for the adding of additional functionality directly into the kernel while the system is running.
Log Clipping	Log clipping is the selective removal of log entries from a system log to hide a compromise.
Logic Gate	A logic gate is an elementary building block of a digital circuit. Most logic gates have two inputs and one output. As digital circuits can only understand binary, inputs and outputs can assume only one of two states, 0 or 1.
Loopback Address	The loopback address (127.0.0.1) is a pseudo IP address that always refer back to the local host and are never sent out onto a network.
MAC Address	A physical address; a numeric value that uniquely identifies that network device from every other device on the planet.
Malicious Code	Software (e.g., Trojan horse) that appears to perform a useful or desirable function, but actually gains unauthorized access to system resources or tricks a user into executing other malicious logic.
Malware	A generic term for a number of different types of malicious code.
Mandatory Access Control (MAC)	Mandatory Access Control controls is where the system controls access to resources based on classification levels assigned to both the objects and the users. These controls cannot be changed by anyone.

NOTES

Masquerade Attack	A type of attack in which one system entity illegitimately poses as (assumes the identity of) another entity.
Measures of Effectiveness (MOE)	Measures of Effectiveness is a probability model based on engineering concepts that allows one to approximate the impact a give action will have on an environment. In Information warfare it is the ability to attack or defend within an Internet environment.
Monoculture	Monoculture is the case where a large number of users run the same software, and are vulnerable to the same attacks.
Morris Worm	A worm program written by Robert T. Morris, Jr. that flooded the ARPANET in November, 1988, causing problems for thousands of hosts.
Multi-Cast	Broadcasting from one host to a given set of hosts.
Multi-Homed	You are "multi-homed" if your network is directly connected to two or more ISP's.
Multiplexing	To combine multiple signals from possibly disparate sources, in order to transmit them over a single path.
National Institute of Standards and Technology (NIST)	National Institute of Standards and Technology, a unit of the US Commerce Department. Formerly known as the National Bureau of Standards, NIST promotes and maintains measurement standards. It also has active programs for encouraging and assisting industry and science to develop and use these standards.
Natural Disaster	Any "act of God" (e.g., fire, flood, earthquake, lightning, or wind) that disables a system component.
Netmask	32-bit number indicating the range of IP addresses residing on a single IP network/subnet/supernet. This specification displays network masks as hexadecimal numbers. For example, the network mask for a class C IP network is displayed as 0xffffff00. Such a mask is often displayed elsewhere in the literature as 255.255.255.0.
Network Address Translation	The translation of an Internet Protocol address used within one network to a different IP address known within another network. One network is designated the *inside* network and the other is the *outside*.
Network-Based IDS	A network-based IDS system monitors the traffic on its network segment as a data source. This is generally accomplished by placing the network interface card in promiscuous mode to capture all network traffic that crosses its network segment. Network traffic on other segments, and traffic on other means of communication (like phone lines) can't be monitored. Network-based IDS involves looking at the packets on the network as they pass by some sensor. The sensor can only see the packets that happen to be carried on the network segment it's attached to. Packets are considered to be of interest if they match a signature.Network-based intrusion detection passively monitors network activity for indications of attacks. Network monitoring offers several advantages over traditional host-based intrusion detection systems. Because many intrusions occur over networks at some point, and because networks are increasingly becoming the targets of attack, these techniques are an excellent method of detecting many attacks which may be missed by host-based intrusion detection mechanisms.
Network Mapping	To compile an electronic inventory of the systems and the services on your network.
Network Taps	Network taps are hardware devices that hook directly onto the network cable and send a copy of the traffic that passes through it to one or more other networked devices.
Non-Printable Character	A character that doesn't have a corresponding character letter to its corresponding ASCII code. Examples would be the Linefeed, which is ASCII character code 10 decimal, the Carriage Return, which is 13 decimal, or the bell sound, which is decimal 7. On a PC, you can often add non-printable characters by holding down the Alt key, and typing in the decimal value (i.e., Alt-007 gets you a bell). There are other character encoding schemes, but ASCII is the most prevalent.
Non-Repudiation	Non-repudiation is the ability for a system to prove that a specific user and only that specific user sent a message and that it hasn't been modified.

NOTES

Term	Definition
Null Session	Known as Anonymous Logon, it is a way of letting an anonymous user retrieve information such as user names and shares over the network or connect without authentication. It is used by applications such as explorer.exe to enumerate shares on remote servers.
Octet	A sequence of eight bits. An octet is an eight-bit byte.
One-Way Encryption	Irreversible transformation of plaintext to cipher text, such that the plaintext cannot be recovered from the cipher text by other than exhaustive procedures even if the cryptographic key is known.
One-Way Function	A (mathematical) function, f, which is easy to compute the output based on a given input. However given only the output value it is impossible (except for a brute force attack) to figure out what the input value is.
Open Shortest Path First (OSPF)	Open Shortest Path First is a link state routing algorithm used in interior gateway routing. Routers maintain a database of all routers in the autonomous system with links between the routers, link costs, and link states (up and down).
OSI	OSI (Open Systems Interconnection) is a standard description or "reference model" for how messages should be transmitted between any two points in a telecommunication network. Its purpose is to guide product implementers so that their products will consistently work with other products. The reference model defines seven layers of functions that take place at each end of a communication. Although OSI is not always strictly adhered to in terms of keeping related functions together in a well-defined layer, many if not most products involved in telecommunication make an attempt to describe themselves in relation to the OSI model. It is also valuable as a single reference view of communication that furnishes everyone a common ground for education and discussion.
OSI layers	The main idea in OSI is that the process of communication between two end points in a telecommunication network can be divided into layers, with each layer adding its own set of special, related functions. Each communicating user or program is at a computer equipped with these seven layers of function. So, in a given message between users, there will be a flow of data through each layer at one end down through the layers in that computer and, at the other end, when the message arrives, another flow of data up through the layers in the receiving computer and ultimately to the end user or program. The actual programming and hardware that furnishes these seven layers of function is usually a combination of the computer operating system, applications (such as your Web browser), TCP/IP or alternative transport and network protocols, and the software and hardware that enable you to put a signal on one of the lines attached to your computer. OSI divides telecommunication into seven layers. The layers are in two groups. The upper four layers are used whenever a message passes from or to a user. The lower three layers (up to the network layer) are used when any message passes through the host computer or router. Messages intended for this computer pass to the upper layers. Messages destined for some other host are not passed up to the upper layers but are forwarded to another host. The seven layers are: Layer 7: The application layer...This is the layer at which communication partners are identified, quality of service is identified, user authentication and privacy are considered, and any constraints on data syntax are identified. (This layer is *not* the application itself, although some applications may perform application layer functions.) Layer 6: The presentation layer...This is a layer, usually part of an operating system, that converts incoming and outgoing data from one presentation format to another (for example, from a text stream into a popup window with the newly arrived text). Sometimes called the syntax layer. Layer 5: The session layer...This layer sets up, coordinates, and terminates conversations, exchanges, and dialogs between the applications at each end. It deals with session and connection coordination. Layer 4: The transport layer...This layer manages the end-to-end control (for example, determining whether all packets have arrived) and error-checking. It ensures complete data transfer. Layer 3: The network layer...This layer handles the routing of the data (sending it in the right direction to the right destination on outgoing transmissions and receiving incoming transmissions at the packet

NOTES

	level). The network layer does routing and forwarding. Layer 2: The data-link layer...This layer provides synchronization for the physical level and does bit-stuffing for strings of 1's in excess of 5. It furnishes transmission protocol knowledge and management. Layer 1: The physical layer...This layer conveys the bit stream through the network at the electrical and mechanical level. It provides the hardware means of sending and receiving data on a carrier.
Overload	Hindrance of system operation by placing excess burden on the performance capabilities of a system component.
Packet	A piece of a message transmitted over a packet-switching network. One of the key features of a packet is that it contains the destination address in addition to the data. In IP networks, packets are often called *datagrams*.
Packet Switched Network	A packet switched network is where individual packets each follow their own paths through the network from one endpoint to another.
Partitions	Major divisions of the total physical hard disk space.
Password Authentication Protocol (PAP)	Password Authentication Protocol is a simple, weak authentication mechanism where a user enters the password and it is then sent across the network, usually in the clear.
Password Cracking	Password cracking is the process of attempting to guess passwords, given the password file information.
Password Sniffing	Passive wiretapping, usually on a local area network, to gain knowledge of passwords.
Patch	A patch is a small update released by a software manufacturer to fix bugs in existing programs.
Patching	Patching is the process of updating software to a different version.
Payload	Payload is the actual application data a packet contains.
Penetration	Gaining unauthorized logical access to sensitive data by circumventing a system's protections.
Penetration Testing	Penetration testing is used to test the external perimeter security of a network or facility.
Permutation	Permutation keeps the same letters but changes the position within a text to scramble the message.
Personal Firewalls	Personal firewalls are those firewalls that are installed and run on individual PCs.
Ping of Death	An attack that sends an improperly large ICMP echo request packet (a "ping") with the intent of overflowing the input buffers of the destination machine and causing it to crash.
Ping Scan	A ping scan looks for machines that are responding to ICMP Echo Requests.
Ping Sweep	An attack that sends ICMP echo requests ("pings") to a range of IP addresses, with the goal of finding hosts that can be probed for vulnerabilities.
Plaintext	Ordinary readable text before being encrypted into ciphertext or after being decrypted.
Point-to-Point Protocol (PPP)	A protocol for communication between two computers using a serial interface, typically a personal computer connected by phone line to a server. It packages your computer's TCP/IP packets and forwards them to the server where they can actually be put on the Internet.
Point-to-Point Tunneling Protocol (PPTP)	A protocol (set of communication rules) that allows corporations to extend their own corporate network through private "tunnels" over the public Internet.
Poison Reverse	Split horizon with poisoned reverse (more simply, poison reverse) does include such routes in updates, but sets their metrics to infinity. In effect, advertising the fact that there routes are not reachable.
Polyinstantiation	Polyinstantiation is the ability of a database to maintain multiple records with the same key. It is used to prevent inference attacks.
Polymorphism	Polymorphism is the process by which malicious software changes its underlying code to avoid detection.

NOTES

Port	A port is nothing more than an integer that uniquely identifies an endpoint of a communication stream. Only one process per machine can listen on the same port number.
Port Scan	A port scan is a series of messages sent by someone attempting to break into a computer to learn which computer network services, each associated with a "well-known" port number, the computer provides. Port scanning, a favorite approach of computer cracker, gives the assailant an idea where to probe for weaknesses. Essentially, a port scan consists of sending a message to each port, one at a time. The kind of response received indicates whether the port is used and can therefore be probed for weakness.
Possession	Possession is the holding, control, and ability to use information.
Post Office Protocol, Version 3 (POP3)	An Internet Standard protocol by which a client workstation can dynamically access a mailbox on a server host to retrieve mail messages that the server has received and is holding for the client.
Practical Extraction and Reporting Language (Perl)	A script programming language that is similar in syntax to the C language and that includes a number of popular Unix facilities such as *sed, awk,* and *tr*.
Preamble	A preamble is a signal used in network communications to synchronize the transmission timing between two or more systems. Proper timing ensures that all systems are interpreting the start of the information transfer correctly. A preamble defines a specific series of transmission pulses that is understood by communicating systems to mean "someone is about to transmit data". This ensures that systems receiving the information correctly interpret when the data transmission starts. The actual pulses used as a preamble vary depending on the network communication technology in use.
Pretty Good Privacy (PGP)™	Trademark of Network Associates, Inc., referring to a computer program (and related protocols) that uses cryptography to provide data security for electronic mail and other applications on the Internet.
Private Addressing	IANA has set aside three address ranges for use by private or non-Internet connected networks. This is referred to as Private Address Space and is defined in RFC 1918. The reserved address blocks are: 10.0.0.0 to 10.255.255.255 (10/8 prefix) 172.16.0.0 to 172.31.255.255 (172.16/12 prefix) 192.168.0.0 to 192.168.255.255 (192.168/16 prefix)
Program Infector	A program infector is a piece of malware that attaches itself to existing program files.
Program Policy	A program policy is a high-level policy that sets the overall tone of an organization's security approach.
Promiscuous Mode	When a machine reads all packets off the network, regardless of who they are addressed to. This is used by network administrators to diagnose network problems, but also by unsavory characters who are trying to eavesdrop on network traffic (which might contain passwords or other information).
Proprietary Information	Proprietary information is that information unique to a company and its ability to compete, such as customer lists, technical data, product costs, and trade secrets.
Protocol	A formal specification for communicating; an IP address the special set of rules that end points in a telecommunication connection use when they communicate. Protocols exist at several levels in a telecommunication connection.
Protocol Stacks (OSI)	A set of network protocol layers that work together.
Proxy Server	A server that acts as an intermediary between a workstation user and the Internet so that the enterprise can ensure security, administrative control, and caching service. A proxy server is associated with or part of a gateway server that separates the enterprise network from the outside network and a firewall server that protects the enterprise network from outside intrusion.
Public Key	The publicly-disclosed component of a pair of cryptographic keys used for asymmetric cryptography.
Public Key Encryption	The popular synonym for "asymmetric cryptography".

NOTES

Public Key Infrastructure (PKI)	A PKI (public key infrastructure) enables users of a basically unsecured public network such as the Internet to securely and privately exchange data and money through the use of a public and a private cryptographic key pair that is obtained and shared through a trusted authority. The public key infrastructure provides for a digital certificate that can identify an individual or an organization and directory services that can store and, when necessary, revoke the certificates.
Public-Key Forward Secrecy (PFS)	For a key agreement protocol based on asymmetric cryptography, the property that ensures that a session key derived from a set of long-term public and private keys will not be compromised if one of the private keys is compromised in the future.
QAZ	A network worm.
Race Condition	A race condition exploits the small window of time between a security control being applied and when the service is used.
Radiation Monitoring	Radiation monitoring is the process of receiving images, data, or audio from an unprotected source by listening to radiation signals.
Reconnaissance	Reconnaissance is the phase of an attack where an attackers finds new systems, maps out networks, and probes for specific, exploitable vulnerabilities.
Reflexive ACLs (Cisco)	Reflexive ACLs for Cisco routers are a step towards making the router act like a stateful firewall. The router will make filtering decisions based on whether connections are a part of established traffic or not.
Registry	The Registry in Windows operating systems in the central set of settings and information required to run the Windows computer.
Request for Comment (RFC)	A series of notes about the Internet, started in 1969 (when the Internet was the ARPANET). An Internet Document can be submitted to the IETF by anyone, but the IETF decides if the document becomes an RFC. Eventually, if it gains enough interest, it may evolve into an Internet standard.
Resource Exhaustion	Resource exhaustion attacks involve tying up finite resources on a system, making them unavailable to others.
Response	A response is information sent that is responding to some stimulus.
Reverse Address Resolution Protocol (RARP)	RARP (Reverse Address Resolution Protocol) is a protocol by which a physical machine in a local area network can request to learn its IP address from a gateway server's Address Resolution Protocol table or cache. A network administrator creates a table in a local area network's gateway router that maps the physical machine (or Media Access Control - MAC address) addresses to corresponding Internet Protocol addresses. When a new machine is set up, its RARP client program requests from the RARP server on the router to be sent its IP address. Assuming that an entry has been set up in the router table, the RARP server will return the IP address to the machine which can store it for future use.
Reverse Engineering	Acquiring sensitive data by disassembling and analyzing the design of a system component.
Reverse Lookup	Find out the hostname that corresponds to a particular IP address. Reverse lookup uses an IP (Internet Protocol) address to find a domain name.
Reverse Proxy	Reverse proxies take public HTTP requests and pass them to back-end webservers to send the content to it, so the proxy can then send the content to the end-user.
Risk	Risk is the product of the level of threat with the level of vulnerability. It establishes the likelihood of a successful attack.
Risk Assessment	A Risk Assessment is the process by which risks are identified and the impact of those risks determined.
Rivest-Shamir-Adleman (RSA)	An algorithm for asymmetric cryptography, invented in 1977 by Ron Rivest, Adi Shamir, and Leonard Adleman.

NOTES

Role Based Access Control	Role based access control assigns users to roles based on their organizational functions and determines authorization based on those roles.
Root	Root is the name of the administrator account in Unix systems.
Rootkit	A collection of tools (programs) that a hacker uses to mask intrusion and obtain administrator-level access to a computer or computer network.
Router	Routers interconnect logical networks by forwarding information to other networks based upon IP addresses.
Routing Information Protocol (RIP)	Routing Information Protocol is a distance vector protocol used for interior gateway routing which uses hop count as the sole metric of a path's cost.
Routing Loop	A routing loop is where two or more poorly configured routers repeatedly exchange the same packet over and over.
RPC Scans	RPC scans determine which RPC services are running on a machine.
Rule Set Based Access Control (RSBAC)	Rule Set Based Access Control targets actions based on rules for entities operating on objects.
S/Key	A security mechanism that uses a cryptographic hash function to generate a sequence of 64-bit, one-time passwords for remote user login. The client generates a one-time password by applying the MD4 cryptographic hash function multiple times to the user's secret key. For each successive authentication of the user, the number of hash applications is reduced by one.
Safety	Safety is the need to ensure that the people involved with the company, including employees, customers, and visitors, are protected from harm.
Scavenging	Searching through data residue in a system to gain unauthorized knowledge of sensitive data.
Secure Electronic Transactions (SET)	Secure Electronic Transactions is a protocol developed for credit card transactions in which all parties (customers, merchant, and bank) are authenticated using digital signatures, encryption protects the message and provides integrity, and provides end-to-end security for credit card transactions online.
Secure Shell (SSH)	A program to log into another computer over a network, to execute commands in a remote machine, and to move files from one machine to another.
Secure Sockets Layer (SSL)	A protocol developed by Netscape for transmitting private documents via the Internet. SSL works by using a public key to encrypt data that's transferred over the SSL connection.
Security Policy	A set of rules and practices that specify or regulate how a system or organization provides security services to protect sensitive and critical system resources.
Segment	Segment is another name for TCP packets.
Sensitive Information	Sensitive information, as defined by the federal government, is any unclassified information that, if compromised, could adversely affect the national interest or conduct of federal initiatives.
Separation of Duties	Separation of duties is the principle of splitting privileges among multiple individuals or systems.
Server	A system entity that provides a service in response to requests from other system entities called clients.
Session	A session is a virtual connection between two hosts by which network traffic is passed.
Session Hijacking	Take over a session that someone else has established.
Session Key	In the context of symmetric encryption, a key that is temporary or is used for a relatively short period of time. Usually, a session key is used for a defined period of communication between two computers, such as for the duration of a single connection or transaction set, or the key is used in an application that protects relatively large amounts of data and, therefore, needs to be re-keyed frequently.

NOTES

Shadow Password Files	A system file in which encryption user password are stored so that they aren't available to people who try to break into the system.
Share	A share is a resource made public on a machine, such as a directory (file share) or printer (printer share).
Shell	A Unix term for the interactive user interface with an operating system. The shell is the layer of programming that understands and executes the commands a user enters. In some systems, the shell is called a command interpreter. A shell usually implies an interface with a command syntax (think of the DOS operating system and its "C:>" prompts and user commands such as "dir" and "edit").
Signals Analysis	Gaining indirect knowledge of communicated data by monitoring and analyzing a signal that is emitted by a system and that contains the data but is not intended to communicate the data.
Signature	A Signature is a distinct pattern in network traffic that can be identified to a specific tool or exploit.
Simple Integrity Property	In Simple Integrity Property a user cannot write data to a higher integrity level than their own.
Simple Network Management Protocol (SNMP)	The protocol governing network management and the monitoring of network devices and their functions. A set of protocols for managing complex networks.
Simple Security Property	In Simple Security Property a user cannot read data of a higher classification than their own.
Smartcard	A smartcard is an electronic badge that includes a magnetic strip or chip that can record and replay a set key.
Smurf	The Smurf attack works by spoofing the target address and sending a ping to the broadcast address for a remote network, which results in a large amount of ping replies being sent to the target.
Sniffer	A sniffer is a tool that monitors network traffic as it received in a network interface.
Sniffing	A synonym for "passive wiretapping."
Social Engineering	A euphemism for non-technical or low-technology means—such as lies, impersonation, tricks, bribes, blackmail, and threats—used to attack information systems.
Socket	The socket tells a host's IP stack where to plug in a data stream so that it connects to the right application.
Socket Pair	A way to uniquely specify a connection, i.e., source IP address, source port, destination IP address, destination port.
SOCKS	A protocol that a proxy server can use to accept requests from client users in a company's network so that it can forward them across the Internet. SOCKS uses sockets to represent and keep track of individual connections. The client side of SOCKS is built into certain Web browsers and the server side can be added to a proxy server.
Software	Computer programs (which are stored in and executed by computer hardware) and associated data (which also is stored in the hardware) that may be dynamically written or modified during execution.
Source Port	The port that a host uses to connect to a server. It is usually a number greater than or equal to 1024. It is randomly generated and is different each time a connection is made.
Spam	Electronic junk mail or junk newsgroup postings.
Spanning Port	Configures the switch to behave like a hub for a specific port.
Split Key	A cryptographic key that is divided into two or more separate data items that individually convey no knowledge of the whole key that results from combining the items.
Split Horizon	Split horizon is a algorithm for avoiding problems caused by including routes in updates sent to the gateway from which they were learned.

NOTES

Spoof	Attempt by an unauthorized entity to gain access to a system by posing as an authorized user.
SQL Injection	SQL injection is a type of input validation attack specific to database-driven applications where SQL code is inserted into application queries to manipulate the database.
Stack Mashing	Stack smashing is the technique of using a buffer overflow to trick a computer into executing arbitrary code.
Standard ACLs (Cisco)	Standard ACLs on Cisco routers make packet filtering decisions based on Source IP address only.
Star Property	In Star Property, a user cannot write data to a lower classification level without logging in at that lower classification level.
State Machine	A system that moves through a series of progressive conditions.
Stateful Inspection	Also referred to as *dynamic packet filtering*. Stateful inspection is a firewall architecture that works at the network layer. Unlike static packet filtering, which examines a packet based on the information in its header, stateful inspection examines not just the header information but also the contents of the packet up through the application layer in order to determine more about the packet than just information about its source and destination.
Static Host Tables	Static host tables are text files that contain hostname and address mapping.
Static Routing	Static routing means that routing table entries contain information that does not change.
Stealthing	Stealthing is a term that refers to approaches used by malicious code to conceal its presence on the infected system.
Steganalysis	Steganalysis is the process of detecting and defeating the use of steganography.
Steganography	Methods of hiding the existence of a message or other data. This is different than cryptography, which hides the meaning of a message but does not hide the message itself. An example of a steganographic method is "invisible" ink.
Stimulus	Stimulus is network traffic that initiates a connection or solicits a response.
Store-and-Forward	Store-and-Forward is a method of switching where the entire packet is read by a switch to determine if it is intact before forwarding it.
Straight-Through Cable	A straight-through cable is where the pins on one side of the connector are wired to the same pins on the other end. It is used for interconnecting nodes on the network.
Stream Cipher	A stream cipher works by encryption a message a single bit, byte, or computer word at a time.
Strong Star Property	In Strong Star Property, a user cannot write data to higher or lower classifications levels than their own.
Sub Network	A separately identifiable part of a larger network that typically represents a certain limited number of host computers, the hosts in a building or geographic area, or the hosts on an individual local area network.
Subnet Mask	A subnet mask (or number) is used to determine the number of bits used for the subnet and host portions of the address. The mask is a 32-bit value that uses one-bits for the network and subnet portions and zero-bits for the host portion.
Switch	A switch is a networking device that keeps track of MAC addresses attached to each of its ports so that data is only transmitted on the ports that are the intended recipient of the data.
Switched Network	A communications network, such as the public switched telephone network, in which any user may be connected to any other user through the use of message, circuit, or packet switching and control devices. Any network providing switched communications service.
Symbolic Links	Special files which point at another file.

NOTES

Symmetric Cryptography	A branch of cryptography involving algorithms that use the same key for two different steps of the algorithm (such as encryption and decryption, or signature creation and signature verification). Symmetric cryptography is sometimes called "secret-key cryptography" (versus public-key cryptography) because the entities that share the key.
Symmetric Key	A cryptographic key that is used in a symmetric cryptographic algorithm.
SYN Flood	A denial of service attack that sends a host more TCP SYN packets (request to synchronize sequence numbers, used when opening a connection) than the protocol implementation can handle.
Synchronization	Synchronization is the signal made up of a distinctive pattern of bits that network hardware looks for to signal that start of a frame.
Syslog	Syslog is the system logging facility for Unix systems.
System Security Officer (SSO)	A person responsible for enforcement or administration of the security policy that applies to the system.
System-Specific Policy	A System-specific policy is a policy written for a specific system or device.
T1, T3	A digital circuit using TDM (Time-Division Multiplexing).
Tamper	To deliberately alter a system's logic, data, or control information to cause the system to perform unauthorized functions or services.
TCP Fingerprinting	TCP fingerprinting is the user of odd packet header combinations to determine a remote operating system.
TCP Full Open scan	TCP Full Open scans check each port by performing a full three-way handshake on each port to determine if it was open.
TCP Half Open scan	TCP Half Open scans work by performing the first half of a three-way handshake to determine if a port is open.
TCP Wrapper	A software package which can be used to restrict access to certain network services based on the source of the connection; a simple tool to monitor and control incoming network traffic.
TCP/IP	A synonym for "Internet Protocol Suite;" in which the Transmission Control Protocol and the Internet Protocol are important parts. TCP/IP is the basic communication language or protocol of the Internet. It can also be used as a communications protocol in a private network (either an Intranet or an Extranet).
TCPDump	TCPDump is a freeware protocol analyzer for Unix that can monitor network traffic on a wire.
TELNET	A TCP-based, application-layer, Internet Standard protocol for remote login from one host to another.
Threat	A potential for violation of security, which exists when there is a circumstance, capability, action, or event that could breach security and cause harm.
Threat Assessment	A threat assessment is the identification of types of threats that an organization might be exposed to.
Threat Model	A threat model is used to describe a given threat and the harm it could to do a system if it has a vulnerability.
Threat Vector	The method a threat uses to get to the target.
Time to Live	A value in an Internet Protocol packet that tells a network router whether or not the packet has been in the network too long and should be discarded.
Tiny Fragment Attack	With many IP implementations it is possible to impose an unusually small fragment size on outgoing packets. If the fragment size is made small enough to force some of a TCP packet's TCP header fields into the second fragment, filter rules that specify patterns for those fields will not match. If the filtering implementation does not enforce a minimum fragment size, a disallowed packet might be passed because it didn't hit a match in the filter. STD 5, RFC 791 states: Every Internet module must be able to forward

	a datagram of 68 octets without further fragmentation. This is because an Internet header may be up to 60 octets, and the minimum fragment is 8 octets.
Token-Based Access Control	Token based access control associates a list of objects and their privileges with each user. (The opposite of list based.)
Token-Based Devices	A token-based device is triggered by the time of day, so every minute the password changes, requiring the user to have the token with them when they log in.
Token Ring	A token ring network is a local area network in which all computers are connected in a ring or star topology and a binary digit or token-passing scheme is used in order to prevent the collision of data between two computers that want to send messages at the same time.
Topology	The geometric arrangement of a computer system. Common topologies include a bus, star, and ring. The specific physical, *i.e.,* real, or logical, *i.e.,* virtual, arrangement of the elements of a network. *Note 1:* Two networks have the same topology if the connection configuration is the same, although the networks may differ in physical interconnections, distances between nodes, transmission rates, and/or signal types. *Note 2:* The common types of network topology are illustrated
Traceroute (tracert.exe)	Traceroute is a tool the maps the route a packet takes from the local machine to a remote destination.
Transmission Control Protocol (TCP)	A set of rules (protocol) used along with the Internet Protocol to send data in the form of message units between computers over the Internet. While IP takes care of handling the actual delivery of the data, TCP takes care of keeping track of the individual units of data (called packets) that a message is divided into for efficient routing through the Internet. Whereas the IP protocol deals only with packets, TCP enables two hosts to establish a connection and exchange streams of data. TCP guarantees delivery of data and also guarantees that packets will be delivered in the same order in which they were sent.
Transport Layer Security (TLS)	A protocol that ensures privacy between communicating applications and their users on the Internet. When a server and client communicate, TLS ensures that no third party may eavesdrop or tamper with any message. TLS is the successor to the Secure Sockets Layer.
Triple DES	A block cipher, based on DES, that transforms each 64-bit plaintext block by applying the Data Encryption Algorithm three successive times, using either two or three different keys, for an effective key length of 112 or 168 bits.
Triple-Wrapped	S/MIME usage: data that has been signed with a digital signature, and then encrypted, and then signed again.
Trojan Horse	A computer program that appears to have a useful function, but also has a hidden and potentially malicious function that evades security mechanisms, sometimes by exploiting legitimate authorizations of a system entity that invokes the program.
Trunking	Trunking is connecting switched together so that they can share VLAN information between them.
Trust	Trust determine which permissions and what actions other systems or users can perform on remote machines.
Trusted Ports	Trusted ports are ports below number 1024 usually allowed to be opened by the root user.
Tunnel	A communication channel created in a computer network by encapsulating a communication protocol's data packets in (on top of) a second protocol that normally would be carried above, or at the same layer as, the first one. Most often, a tunnel is a logical point-to-point link— i.e., an OSI layer 2 connection— created by encapsulating the layer 2 protocol in a transport protocol (such as TCP), in a network or inter-network layer protocol (such as IP), or in another link layer protocol. Tunneling can move data between computers that use a protocol not supported by the network connecting them.
UDP Scan	UDP scans perform scans to determine which UDP ports are open.

NOTES

Unicast	Broadcasting from host to host.
Uniform Resource Identifier (URI)	The generic term for all types of names and addresses that refer to objects on the World Wide Web.
Uniform Resource Locator (URL)	The global address of documents and other resources on the World Wide Web. The first part of the address indicates what protocol to use, and the second part specifies the IP address or the domain name where the resource is located. For example, http://www.pcwebopedia.com/index.html .
Unix	A popular *multi-user*, *multitasking* operating system developed at Bell Labs in the early 1970s. Created by just a handful of programmers, Unix was designed to be a small, flexible system used exclusively by programmers.
Unprotected Share	In Windows terminology, a "share" is a mechanism that allows a user to connect to file systems and printers on other systems. An "unprotected share" is one that allows anyone to connect to it.
User	A person, organization entity, or automated process that accesses a system, whether authorized to do so or not.
User Contingency Plan	User contingency plan is the alternative methods of continuing business operations if IT systems are unavailable.
User Datagram Protocol (UDP)	A communications protocol that, like TCP, runs on top of IP networks. Unlike TCP/IP, UDP/IP provides very few error recovery services, offering instead a direct way to send and receive datagrams over an IP network. It's used primarily for broadcasting messages over a network. UDP uses the Internet Protocol to get a datagram from one computer to another but does not divide a message into packets (datagrams) and reassemble it at the other end. Specifically, UDP doesn't provide sequencing of the packets that the data arrives in.
Virtual Private Network (VPN)	A restricted-use, logical (i.e., artificial or simulated) computer network that is constructed from the system resources of a relatively public, physical (i.e., real) network (such as the Internet), often by using encryption (located at hosts or gateways), and often by tunneling links of the virtual network across the real network. For example, if a corporation has LANs at several different sites, each connected to the Internet by a firewall, the corporation could create a VPN by (a) using encrypted tunnels to connect from firewall to firewall across the Internet and (b) not allowing any other traffic through the firewalls. A VPN is generally less expensive to build and operate than a dedicated real network, because the virtual network shares the cost of system resources with other users of the real network.
Virus	A hidden, self-replicating section of computer software, usually malicious logic, that propagates by infecting—i.e., inserting a copy of itself into and becoming part of—another program. A virus cannot run by itself; it requires that its host program be run to make the virus active.
Vulnerability	A flaw or weakness in a system's design, implementation, or operation and management that could be exploited to violate the system's security policy.
War Chalking	War chalking is marking areas, usually on sidewalks with chalk, that receive wireless signals that can be accessed.
War Dialer	A computer program that automatically dials a series of telephone numbers to find lines connected to computer systems, and catalogs those numbers so that a cracker can try to break into the systems.
War Dialing	War dialing is a simple means of trying to identify modems in a telephone exchange that may be susceptible to compromise in an attempt to circumvent perimeter security.
War Driving	War driving is the process of traveling around looking for wireless access point signals that can be used to get network access.
Web of Trust	A web of trust is the trust that naturally evolves as a user starts to trust other's signatures, and the signatures that they trust.

NOTES

Web Server	A software process that runs on a host computer connected to the Internet to respond to HTTP requests for documents from client web browsers.
WHOIS	An IP for finding information about resources on networks.
Windowing	A windowing system is a system for sharing a computer's graphical display presentation resources among multiple applications at the same time. In a computer that has a graphical user interface (GUI), you may want to use a number of applications at the same time (this is called task). Using a separate window for each application, you can interact with each application and go from one application to another without having to reinitiate it. Having different information or activities in multiple windows may also make it easier for you to do your work. A windowing system uses a window manager to keep track of where each window is located on the display screen and its size and status. A windowing system doesn't just manage the windows but also other forms of graphical user interface entities.
Windump	Windump is a freeware tool for Windows that is a protocol analyzer that can monitor network traffic on a wire.
Wired Equivalent Privacy	A security protocol for wireless local area networks defined in the standard IEEE 802.11b.
Wireless Application Protocol	A specification for a set of communication protocols to standardize the way that wireless devices, such as cellular telephones and radio transceivers, can be used for Internet access, including e-mail, the World Wide Web, newsgroups, and Internet Relay Chat.
Wiretapping	Monitoring and recording data that is flowing between two points in a communication system.
World Wide Web ("the Web", WWW, W3)	The global, hypermedia-based collection of information and services that is available on Internet servers and is accessed by browsers using Hypertext Transfer Protocol and other information retrieval mechanisms.
Worm	A computer program that can run independently, can propagate a complete working version of itself onto other hosts on a network, and may consume computer resources destructively.
Wrap	To use cryptography to provide data confidentiality service for a data object.
Zone Transfer	A zone transfer is when a DNS server performs a complete dump of the database for a domain and sends the information from the primary DNS server to the secondary DNS servers.

NOTES

References:

http://real.cotse.com/cgi-bin/Dict

http://whatis.techtarget.com/

http://www.google.com/

http://www.pcwebopedia.com

http://www.its.bldrdoc.gov/projects/telecomglossary2000

http://www.freesoft.org/CIE/RFC/bynum.cgi?2828

http://www.clock.org/~jss/glossary/index.html

http://www.deer-run.com, Hal Pomeranz

RFC 1858

RFC 2080

NOTES

Appendix G

Acronym List

NOTES

Appendix G - Acronym List

3DES	Triple DES (NIST)
3G	Third Generation (telephony)
ABM	Asynchronous Balanced Mode
ACE	Access Control Entry
ACK	Acknowledgement Field Valid flag (TCP) *or* Acknowledgement number
ACL	Access Control List
ACM	Association for Computing Machinery
AD	Active Directory (Microsoft)
ADCE	Active Directory Client Extensions
ADSL	Asymmetrical Digital Subscriber Line
AES	Advanced Encryption Standard (NIST)
AFS	Andrew File System
AH	Authentication Header (IPsec)
ALE	Annualized Loss Expectancy
ALT	ALTernate
AMAP	Application Mapping tool
AMD	AutoMounteD (Unix)
AMEX	American Express
ANSI	American National Standards Institute
AP	Access Point (WLAN)
APOP	Authenticated Post Office Protocol
ARIN	American Registry for Internet Numbers
ARM	Asynchronous Response Mode
ARO	Annualized Rate of Occurrence
ARP	Address Resolution Protocol
ARPANET	Advanced Research Projects Agency Network
AS	Authentication Server
ASAP	As Soon As Possible
ASCII	American Standard Code for Information Interchange
ASIC	Application Specific Integrated Circuit
ASP	Active Server Page (Microsoft)
ASR	Automatic System Recovery
AT	Administration Tools
ATM	Asynchronous Transfer Mode *or* Automatic Teller Machine
AV	Anti-Virus
AXFR	Zone Transfer
b	Bit
B	Byte (8 bits)
BCP	Business Continuity Plan
BDC	Backup Domain Controller (Microsoft Windows NT)
BER	Bit Error Rate
BGP	Border Gateway Protocol
BIA	Business Impact Analysis
BID	BlackICE Defender
BIND	Berkeley Internet Name Daemon
BIOS	Basic Input/Output System (Microsoft)
BITS	Background Intelligent Transfer Service
BMP	Bitmap File Format (Microsoft)
BO	Back Orifice
BOF	Back Officer Friendly
BOOTP	Bootstrap Protocol
Bps, b/s	Bits per second
BS	British Standard
BSD	Berkeley Software Distribution
BSI	British Standard Institute
BSS	Basic Service Set
CA	Certificate Authority (PKI)
CACM	Communications of the ACM
CAST	Carlisle Adams, Stafford Tavares
CAT	Category
CBC	Cipher Block Chaining mode
CCITT	Consultative Committee for International Telegraphy and Telephony
CCTV	Closed Circuit Television

NOTES

CD	Compact Disk
CDE	Common Desktop Environment
CDFS	Compact Disk File System
CDMA	Code Division Multiple Access
CDPD	Cellular Digital Packet Data
CDROM	Compact Disk Read-Only Memory
CEO	Chief Executive Officer
CER	Crossover Error Rate
CERN	A French acronym for the European Laboratory for Particle Physics
CERT	Computer Emergency Response Team (deprecated name)
CFB	Cipher FeedBack mode
CGI	Common Gateway Interface
CHAP	Challenge-Handshake Authentication Protocol
chargen	Character Generation Service
CIA	Confidentiality, Integrity, and Availability
CID	Consensus Intrusion Database
CIDF	Common Intrusion Detection Framework
CIDR	Classless Interdomain Routing
CIFS	Common Internet File System
CIO	Chief Information Officer
CIRT	Computer Incident Response Team
CIS	Cerberus Information Security
CLR	Common Language Runtime (Microsoft)
CN	Common Name
CNN	Cable News Network
CO	Central Office
COM	Component Object Model (Microsoft)
COMEX	Commodity Exchange
COPS	Community Oriented Policing Services
CPU	Central Processing Unit
CRC	CyclicalRredundancy Check
CRII	Code Red II Worm
CRL	Certificate Revocation List (PKI)
CRYPT	Unix Password Algorithm

CS	Code Segment
CSE	Communications Security Establishment (Canada)
CSMA/CA	Carrier Sense Multiple Access with Collision Avoidance
CSMA/CD	Carrier Sense Multiple Access with Collision Detection
CSO	Chief Security Officer
Ctrl	Control
CVE	Common Vulnerabilities and Exposures
DAC	Discretionary Access Control
DACL	Discretionary Access Control List
DAD	Destruction, Alteration, and Disclosure
DARPA	Defense Advanced Research Projects Agency (US)
DBS	DOS Boot Sector
DC	Domain Components
DC	Domain Controller (Microsoft)
DCE	Data Communications Equipment
DCT	Discrete Cosine Transform
DDE	Dynamic Data Exchange
DDoS	Distributed Denial of Service
DEA	Data Encryption Algorithm
DEC	Digital Equipment Corp. (now Compaq)
DeCSS	De-Contents Scrambling System
DEFCON	DEFense CONdition
DEL	DELete
DES	Data Encryption Standard (NIST)
DESTPORT	DESTination PORT
DF	Don't Fragment flag (IP)
DH	Diffie-Hellman
DHCP	Dynamic Host Configuration Protocol
DLCI	Data Link Connection Identifier
DLL	Dynamic Linked Library
DMZ	Demilitarized Zone
DN	Distinguished Name (PKI)
DNS	Domain Name System or Service
DNSSEC	Domain Name System Security

NOTES

DOJ	Department of Justice (US)
DoS	Denial of Service
DOS	Disk Operating System (PC)
DRP	Disaster Recovery Plan
DSA	Data Signature Algorithm
DSDM	Dynamic Systems Development Method
DSL	Digital Subscriber Line
DSS	Digital Signature Standard (NIST)
DSSS	Direct Sequence Spread Spectrum
DTE	Data Terminal Equipment
DTK	Deception Toolkit (Cohen)
DVD	Digital Versatile Disc
EAP	Extensible Authentication Protocol
EBCDIC	Extended Binary Coded Decimal Interchange Code (IBM)
ECB	Electronic Code Book mode
ECC	Elliptic Curve Cryptography
ECDLP	Elliptic Curve Discrete Logarithm Problem
ECDSA	Elliptic Curve Digital Signature Algorithm
EDGAR	Education Department General Administrative Regulations
ECPA	Electronic Communications Privacy Act
EER	Equal Error Rate
EF	Exposure Factor
EFS	Encrypting File System
EGP	Exterior Gateway Protocol
EGS	European Global System (wireless)
EIA	Electronic Industries Alliance (was Electronic Industries Association)
EICAR	European Institute for Computer Anti-Virus Research
EIGRP	Extended Interior Gateway Routing Protocol (Cisco)
EMS	Enterprise Management System
ERD	Emergency Repair Disk (Microsoft)
ESP	Encapsulating Security Payload (IPsec)
ESS	Extended Service Set
EU	European Union

EV	Event Viewer (Microsoft Windows NT/2000)
EVT	Event Viewer File Format (Microsoft)
FAA	Federal Aviation Administration (US)
FAQ	Frequently Asked Questions
FAR	False Accept Rate
FAT	File Allocation Table (Microsoft)
FBR	Floppy Boot Record
FC	File Compare Command (DOS)
FCS	Frame Check Sequence
FDDI	Fiber Distribution Data Interface (ANSI)
FEC	Forward Error Correction
FFS	Standard Berkeley Fast File System
FHSS	Frequency-Hopping Spread Spectrum
FIFO	First In, First Out Queue
FIN	Finish Flag (TCP)
FIPS	Federal Information Processing Standard (US)
FQDN	Fully-Qualified Domain Name
FR	Frame Relay
FRS	File Replication Service (Microsoft)
FRR	False Reject Rate
FTP	File Transfer Protocol
FW-1	Firewall-1 (Checkpoint)
FYI	For Your Information
G	Giga; 1,000,000,000 = 10^9 (bit rate) or 1,073,741,824 = 2^{30} (storage)
GAO	Government Accounting Office (US)
Gb	Giga-bits
GCFW	GIAC Certified Firewall Analyst
GCHQ	Government Communication Headquarters (UK)
GECOS	General Electric Comprehensive Operating System
GHz	Giga-Hertz
GIAC	Global Information Assurance Certification
GIAC-TC	Global Information Assurance Certification-Training Center
GID	Group Identifier (Unix)
GIF	Graphic Interchange Format (Compuserve)

GIMP	GNU Image Manipulation Program
GLB	Gramm Leach Bliley Act. (US)
GNU	GNU's Not Unix
GPL	GNU Public License
GPO	Group Policy Object (Microsoft)
grep	Get Regular Expression and Print
GRUB	Grand Unified Bootloader
GSM	Global System for Mobile Communications
GUI	Graphical User Interface
HDLC	High-Level Data Link Control (ISO)
HIDS	Host-based Intrusion Detection System
HIPAA	Health Insurance Portability and Accountability Act
HKLM	HKEY_LOCAL_MACHINE (Microsoft)
HMAC	Hashed Message Authentication Code
HR	Human Resources
HSRP	Hot Standby Router Protocol (Cisco)
HTML	Hypertext Markup Language
HTTP	Hypertext Transfer Protocol
HTTPS	HTTP over SSL
HUP	Hang-Up
HVAC	Heating, Ventilation, And Cooling
Hz	Hertz; cycles per second
I/O	Input/Output
IANA	Internet Assigned Numbers Authority
IASIW	Institute for the Advanced Study of Information Warfare
IBM	International Business Machines Corp.
ICE	Information Concealment Engine (Encryption)
ICF	Internet Connection Firewall (Microsoft)
ICMP	Internet Control Message Protocol
ICQ	Internet Call to Quarters, derived from military and ham radio CQ, or "call to quarters" signal; also derived from phrase "I seek you"
ICSA	International Computer Security Association
ICV	Integrity Check Value (IPsec)
ID	Identifier *or* Intrusion Detection

IDC	International Data Corp.
IDE	Integrated (or Intelligent) Drive Electronics
IDEA	International Data Encryption Algorithm
IDS	Intrusion Detection System
IE	Internet Explorer (Microsoft)
IEC	International Electrotechnical Commission
IEEE	Institute of Electrical and Electronics Engineers
IETF	Internet Engineering Task Force
IGMP	Internet Group Management Protocol
IGP	Interior Gateway Protocol
IHL	Internet Header Length (IP)
IIS	Internet Information Server (Microsoft)
IKE	Internet Key Exchange (IPsec)
IMAP	Internet Message Access Protocol
IOS	Internetwork Operating System (Cisco)
IP	Internet Protocol or Instruction Pointer
IPsec	IP Security Protocol
IPv4	IP Version 4
IPv6	IP version 6
IPX	Internet Work Packet Exchange Protocol (Novell)
IQUERY	Inverse query
IRC	Internet Relay Chat
IRDP	Internet Router Discovery Protocol
ISAKMP	Internet Security Association and Key Management Protocol (IPsec)
ISDN	Integrated Services Digital Network
ISM	Internet Service Manager (Microsoft) or Internet System Manager
ISN	Initial Sequence Number (TCP)
IS	Information Systems
ISO	International Organization for Standardization or Internet Security Officer
ISP	Internet Service Provider
ISS	Internet Security Systems, Inc.
IT	Information Technology
ITU	International Telecommunication Union (formerly CCITT)

NOTES

NOTES

ITU-T	International Telecommunication Union Telecommunication Standardization Sector
IW	Information Warfare
JPEG	Joint Photographic Experts Group (ISO)
k, K	kilo; 1,000 = 10^3 (bit rate; usually 'k') or 1,024 = 2^{10} (storage; usually 'K')
KDC	Key Distribution Center (Keberos)
KDE	K Desktop Environment
L2F	Layer 2 Forwarding
L2TP	Layer 2 Tunneling Protocol
L6	Bell Telephone Laboratories Low-Level Linked List Language
LAN	Local Area Network
LC3	L0phtCrack v3
LDAP	Lightweight Directory Access Protocol
LFSR	Linear Feedback Shift Register
LILO	Linux Loader
LKM	Loadable Kernel Modules
LM	LAN Manager (Microsoft)
LSB	Least Significant Bit
LSOF	List Open Files (tool)
M	Mega; 1,000,000 = 10^6 (bit rate) or 1,048,576 = 2^{20} (storage)
MAC	Mandatory Access Control
MAC	Message Authentication Code
MAC	Media Access Control
MAN	Metropolitan Area Network
MB	Mega Bytes
Mb	Mega-bit
Mbps	Mega-bit per second
MBR	Master Boot Record
MBSA	Microsoft Baseline Security Analyzer
MD2	Message Digest 2
MD4	Message Digest 4
MD5	Message Digest 5
ME	Windows ME
MIB	Management Information Base

MIME	Multipurpose Internet Mail Extensions
MINIX	MINi-unIX
MIT	Massachusetts Institute of Technology
MMC	Microsoft Management Console (Microsoft)
MO	Method of Operations
MOE	Measure Of Effectiveness
MOM	Microsoft Operations Manager
MP3	MPEG Audio Layer 3
MPEG	Motion (or Moving) Picture Experts Group (ISO)
MPLS	Multiprotocol Label Switching
MS	Microsoft
MSAU	Multistation Access Unit
MSB	Most Significant Bits
MTA	Metropolitan Transit Authority (Boston)
MTU	Maximum Transmission Unit
NAI	Network Associates, Inc.
NAPT	Network Address and Port Translation
NASL	Nessus Attack Scripting Language
NAT	Network Address Translation
NCSA	National Computer Security Association (now the ICSA)
NDA	Non-Disclosure Agreement
NDS	NetWare Directory Services (Novell)
NetBIOS	Network Basic Input/Output System (Microsoft)
NFPA	National Fire Protection Association
NFR	Network Flight Recorder
NFS	Network File System
NIC	Network Interface Card
NIDS	Network-Based Intrusion Detection System
NIPC	National Infrastructure Protection Center
NIS	Network Information Service
NIST	National Institute of Standards and Technology (US)
NMAP	Network Mapping Tool
NNTP	Network News Transfer Protocol
NRM	Normal Response Mode
NSA	National Security Agency (US)

NSWC	Naval Surface Warfare Center (US Navy)
NT	Windows NT
NT4SP2	Windows NT 4.0 Service Pack 2
NTFS	Windows NT File System (Microsoft Windows NT/ 2000)
NTLM	Windows NT LAN Manager (Microsoft)
NTLM2	Windows NT LAN Manager version 2 (Microsoft)
NTP	Network Time Protocol
NVRAM	Non-Volatile Random Access Memory
ODBC	Open Database Connectivity (Microsoft)
OEM	Original Equipment Manufacture
OFB	Output FeedBack Mode
OI	Order Information
OOB	Out of Band
OPSEC	Operations Security
OS	Operating System
OSI	Open Systems Interconnect
OSPF	Open Shortest Path First
OSR2	Windows 95 Service Release
OU	Organization Unit
OUI	Organizationally Unique Identifiers
PAM	Pluggable Authentication Modules
PAN	Personal Area Network
PAP	Password Authentication Protocol
PARMS	Parallel Algebraic Recursive Multilevel Solver
PBR	Partition Boot Record
PBX	Private Branch Exchange
PC	Personal Computer
PDA	Personal Data Assistant
PDC	Primary Domain Controller (Microsoft Windows NT)
PEM	Privacy Enhanced Email
PGP	Pretty Good Privacy
PHP	PHP: Hypertext Preprocessor
PI	Payment Information
PID	Process Identifier (Unix)
PIM	Personal Information Management

PIN	Personal Identification Number
PING	Packet InterNet Groper
PKC	Public Key Cryptography
PKI	Public Key Infrastructure
POP	Point Of Presence
POP3	Post Office Protocol v3
POST	Power On Self Test
PPP	Point-to-Point Protocol
PPTP	Point-to-Point Tunneling Protocol
PSH	Push Flag (TCP)
PSYOP	Psychological Operation
PVC	Permanent Virtual Circuits
PWB	Programmers' Workbench
QA	Quality Assurance
QoS	Quality of Service
qotd	Quote-of-the-Day Service (Unix)
QS	Quality System Requirements
R&D	Research and Development
RA	Risk Analysis *or* Risk Assessment
RADIUS	Remote Authentication Dial In User Service
RAID	Redundant Array of Independent Disks
RAM	Random Access Memory
RARP	Reverse Address Resolution Protocol
RAS	Remote Access Server (Microsoft Windows NT/2000)
RC4	Rivest Cipher (or Ron's Code) #4
RC6	Rivest Cipher (or Ron's Code) #6
RDP	Remote Desktop Protocol (Microsoft)
RDS	Remote Data Service (Microsoft)
RF	Radio Frequency
RFC	Request for Comments (IETF)
RFP	Request for Proposal
RIAA	Recording Industry Association of America
RID	Relative Identifier
RIP	Routing Information Protocol
RO	Read-Only
ROI	Return On Investment

NOTES

NOTES

ROM	Read-Only Memory
ROT	Rotation Forward (Ciphers)
RPC	Remote Procedure Call
RPM	Red Hat Package Manager
RRAS	Routing and Remote Access Service
RSA	Rivest, Shamir, and Adleman
RSBAC	Rule Set Based Access Control
RST	Reset Flag (TCP)
RW	Read-Write
S/KEY	S/KEY One-Time Password System (Bellcore, now Telcordia)
SA	Security Associations
SACL	System Access Control List
SAINT	Security Administrator's Integrated Network Tool
SAM	Security Account Manager (Microsoft Windows NT/ 2000)
SANS	SysAdmin, Network, Security
SARA	Security Auditor's Research Assistant
SAT	Security Access Token (Microsoft)
SATAN	Security Administrator's Tool for Analyzing
SBS	Small Business Server (Microsoft) *or* Step-by-Step (SANS)
SCA	Security Configuration and Analysis (Microsoft)
SCAT	Security Configuration and Analysis Tool (Microsoft Windows 2000)
SCCS	Source Code Control System
SCM	Security Configuration Manager
SCO	Santa Cruz Organization
SCSI	Small Computer System Interface (ANSI)
SCU	System Configuration Utility (Microsoft Windows NT/ 2000)
SDK	Software Development Kit
SDCL	Synchronous Data Link Control
SEC	Securities and Exchange Commission (US)
SEQ	Sequence Number
SESAME	Secure European System for Applications in a Multi-vendor Environment

SET	Secure Electronic Transaction (MasterCard, Visa, et al.)
SF	Syn/Fin Data Flag
SFC	System File Checker
SGI	Silicon Graphics Indy
SHA	Secure Hash Algorithm (NIST)
SHS	Secure Hash Standard (NIST)
SID	Security ID Number (Microsoft)
SIGGEN	Special Interest Group for natural language GENeration
SKC	Secret Key Cryptography
SKEME	Secure Key Exchange Mechanism
SKIP	Simple Key-Management for Internet Protocols (Sun Microsystems)
SLE	Single Loss Expectancy
SLIP	Serial Line IP
SMB	Server Message Block
S/MIME	Secure Multipurpose Internet Mail Extensions
SMTP	Simple Mail Transfer Protocol
SNA	Systems Network Architecture
SNAPLEN	Snapshot Length
SNAT	Source Network Address Translation
SNMP	Simple Network Management Protocol
SOA	Start of Authority
SOHO	Small Office/Home Office
SOP	Standard Operating Procedure
SP	Service Pack (Microsoft)
SPF	Shortest Path First algorithm
SPI	Security Profile Inspector for Unix Networks
SPX	Sequenced Packet Exchange
SQL	Structured Query Language
SSH	Secure Shell
SSI	Server Side Includes
SSID	Service Set Identifier (IEEE 802.11b)
SSL	Secure Sockets Layer (Netscape)
STP	Shielded Twisted Pair

STS	Station To Station
SGID	Set Group Identifier
SUID	Set User Identifier
SUS	Software Update Services (Microsoft)
SVC	Switched Virtual Circuit
SVRx	Unix System V Revision *x*
SW	Software
SYN	Synchronize Sequence Number Flag (TCP)
Syslog	System Logger
SYSV	System V Unix
TACACS	Terminal Access Controller Access Control System
tar	Tape Archive (Unix)
TCP	Transmission Control Protocol
TFN	Tribe Flood Network
TFN2K	Tribe Flood Network 2000
TFTP	Trivial File Transfer Protocol
TGS	Ticket Granting Server (Keberos)
TGT	Ticket Granting Ticket Request (Keberos)
TLS	Transport Layer Security
TOC	Time of Check
TOS	Type of Service (IP)
TOU	Time of Use
TP	Transformation Procedure
TSIG	Transaction signature (DNS)
TTL	Time To Live (IP)
TTY	Teletypewriter
UAPRSF	Urgent, Ack, Push, Reset, Syn, Finish flags (TCP)
UDP	User Datagram Protocol
UID	User Identifier (Unix)
UNC	Universal Naming Convention
UNIX	From UNICS (Uni-plexed Information and Computing System)
UPS	Uninterruptible Power Supply
URG	Urgent Data Flag (TCP)
URL	Uniform Resource Locator
US	United States

UTP	Unshielded Twisted Pair
VAX	Virtual Address eXtension
VBS	VisualBASIC Script (Microsoft)
VCI	Virtual Channel Identifier
VDSL	Very high bit rate Digital Subscriber Line
VGanyLAN	Virtual Grade any Local Area Network
VLAN	Virtual Local Area Network
VM	Virtual Machine
VoIP	Voice over IP
VPI	Virtual Path Identifier
VPN	Virtual Private Network
VxDS	Virtual Device Driver
W	Watt (unit of power)
W2K	Windows 2000
W3C	Word Wide Web Consortium
WAN	Wide Area Network
WAP	Wireless Application Protocol
WEP	Wired Equivalent Privacy (IEEE 802.11b)
WINS	Windows Internet Name Service (Microsoft)
WLAN	Wireless Local Area Network
WM97	Word Macro Virus
WMI	Windows Management Instrumentation (WMI)
WMLscript	Wireless Markup Language (WML) Scripting Language
WSH	Window Scripting Host
WTLS	Wireless Transport Layer Security
WWW	World Wide Web
XDM	X Display Manager
XDMCP	X Display Manager Control Protocol
XML	Extensible Markup Language
XOR	Exclusive OR
Y2K	Year 2000
YMMV	Your Mileage May Vary
YP	Yellow Pages (Network Information Service)

NOTES

NOTES

Appendix H

URL List

NOTES

Appendix H - URL List

Section 1	
802.11a Article in eWeek	http://www.eweek.com/article/0,3658,s%253D714%2526a%253D21038,00.asp
Amap	http://www.thehackerschoice.com/
ATM – Asynchronous Transfer Mode	http://www.ece.wpi.edu/courses/ee535/hwk11cd95/bkh/vpi_vci.html
ATM Internetworking	http://www.cisco.com/warp/public/614/12.html
Bugtraq	http://www.securityfocus.com
CERT	http://www.cert.org
Cisco	http://www.cisco.com
Commonly exploited ports	http://www.simovits.com/nyheter9902.html
Dynamic Solutions International	http://www.dynamsol.com
ExtremeTech	http://www.extremetech.com
Frame Relay	http://www.cisco.com/univercd/cc/td/doc/cisintwk/ito_doc/frame.htm
IEEE (OUI List)	http://standards.ieee.org/regauth/oui/oui.txt
Linksys	http://www.linksys.com
LSOF	http://www.online.securityfocus.com/tools/1008
MAC Vendor Codes	http://standards.ieee.org/regauth/oui/index.shtml
McAfee	http://www.mcafee.com
Microsoft, Network+ Certification Training Kit	http://www.microsoft.com/mspress/books/sampchap/5507c.asp
NMAP introduction	http://www.nmap.org/nmap/p51-11.txt
NMAP manual	http://www.nmap.org/nmap/nmap_manpage.html
NMAP source	http://www.nmap.org/nmap
NMAP Windows port	http://www.eeye.com/html/Research/Tools/nmapNT.html
Network Associates PGP	http://www.pgp.com
Network Flight Recorder, Inc	http://www.nfr.net
Network ICE	http://www.networkice.com
NTBugtraq	http://www.ntbugtraq.com
Ping War	http://www.fantastica.com/digilex/pingwar.html
Psionic Software	http://www.psionic.com
Symantec (Norton)	http://www.symantec.com
TCPDump	http://www.tcpdump.org

NOTES

Tcpdump	http://ee.lbl.gov
TCP/IP Stack Fingerprinting	http://www.nmap.org/nmap/nmap-fingerprinting-article.html
Token Bus Network	http://www.webopedia.com/TERM/T/token_bus_network.html
The SANS Institute	http://www.sans.org
SANS Twenty Most Critical Internet Security Vulnerabilities	http://www.sans.org/top20.htm
United Nations environmental protection organization	http://www.uneptie.org
Vulnerabilities in VLAN Implementations?	http://www.sans.org/newlook/resources/IDFAQ/vlan.htm
Windump	http://netgroup-serv.polito.it/windump
Wiring Tutorial for 10BaseT UTP	http://www.netspec.com/helpdesk/wiredoc.html
Zone Labs	http://www.zonelabs.com

NOTES

Section 2	
Achilles	http://www.digizen-security.com/projects.html
Air France Espionage – Claypro	http://www.claypro.com/CTF/ESPIONAGE.html
Air France Espionage – Opsec	http://www.opsec.org/OPSJournal93/035.html
Anti-Ballistic Missile Story – USAF	http://www.airpower.maxwell.af.mil/airchronicles/apj/apj97/win97/parrin.html
Anti-Ballistic Missile Story – Daily Record	http://www.the-daily-record/past_issues/02_feb/010214dr3.html
Anti-Ballistic Missile Story – Time	http://www.time.com/time/nation/articles/0,8599,49263,00.html
Attrition.org	http://www.attrition.org/
Bloomberg, NYC Mayoral Race	http://www.cnn.com/2002/ALLPOLITICS/03/30/bloomberg.mayor/
Brutus	http://www.hoobie.net/brutus
CERT formation	http://www.cert.org/kb/aircert/motivation.html
CERT – Melissa Macro Virus	http://www.cert.org/advisiories/CA-1999-04.html
CERT – Virus Protection	http://www.cert.org/tech_tips/virusprotection.html
Contingency Planning – Compaq	http://nonstop.compaq.com/view.asp?IOID=4492
Contingency Planning – DRII	http://drii.org
Contingency Planning – Massachusetts	http://www.state.ma.us/y2k/Archive/projplanning/businesscontinuity plan_template.htm
Contingency Planning – MIT	http://web.mit/edu/security/www/pubplan.htm
Contingency Planning – Treasury Board of Canada	http://www.cio-dpi.gc.ca/emf-cag/busconplan/bconplan_e.asp
Contingency Planning – U. Cal	http://www.ucop.edu/facil/eps/continuity.html
Contingency Planning – U. Sydney	http://www.personal.usyd.edu/au/~stephen/network/disaster3.shtml
Contingency Planning – U. Wales	http://www.swan.ac.uk/uws/y2k/bcplan.htm
CIS Password Policy tool	http://www.cisecurity.org
Chinese Crackers dampen WinXP Celebration	http://www.vnunet.com/News/1126503
Code Blue	http://www.wired.com/news/technology/0,1282,46624,00.html
Code Red II Analysis	http://www.eeye.com/html/Research/Advisiories/AL20010804.html
Code Red II Information	http://www.cert.org/incident_notes/IN-2001-09.html
Code Red and China link - GAO	http://www.gao.gov/new.items/d011073t.pdf
Code Red and China link – The Guardian	http://www.guardian.co.uk/internetnews/story/0,7369,545072,00.html
Code Red and Patch information	http://www.microsoft.com/technet/trrview/default.asp?url=/technet/security/bulletin/MS01-033.asp
Code Red Removal – Microsoft	http://www.microsoft.com/technet/security/tools/redfix.asp
Code Red Removal – nsclean	http://www.nsclean.com/cr2kill.html

NOTES

Code Red Removal – Symantec	http://www.symantec.com/avcenter/venc/data/codered.removal.tool.html
Computer Economics – Terrorism	http://www.usatoday.com/money/finance/2001-10-29-network-russian-hacker.htm
Cosmos 954 crash – Dnd	http://www.dnd.ca/menu/Fourth) Dimension/2002/jan02/jan25_fd_e.htm
Cosmos 954 crash – Ssimicro	http://www.ssimicro.com/~ufoinfo/satelitte.html
Counterfeit Microsoft Software – Paul Stamatis	http://www.inforworld.com/articles/hn/xml/01/10/26/011026hncounterfeit.xml
Crack	ftp://ftp.cerias.purdue.edu/pub/tools/Unix/pwdutils/crack
Crack Information	http://www.users.dircon.co.uk/~crypto/
DDoS Attacks – Cloud Nine	http://zdnet.com/2100-1105-837412.html
Deception Toolkit	http://all.net
DES crypt() Function	http://www.usenix.org/events/usenix99/provos/provos_html/node13.html
Diffuse Project Info. Security Stds	http://www.diffuse.org/secure.html
DumpSec	http://www.somarsoft.com
DumpSec	http://www.systemtools.com
DVD Decryption Loses	http://www.idsa.com/2_14_2002.html
Editing Tools	http://www.microsoft.com
Election 2002 Attack	http://www.computerworld.com/cwi/story/0,1199,NAV47_STO53489,00.html
FAA Security	http://abcnews.go.com/sections/us/DailyNews/faa_computers001015.html
Federal Search guidelines (US)	http://www.usdoj.gov/criminal/cybercrime/searching.html
Foxnews DDoS attack	http://www.vnunet.com/News/1132665
Hacking Exposed	http://www.hackingexposed.com
HTTP Basic Authentication Encode and Decode	http://www.securitystats.com/tools/base64.asp
ICSA study	http://www.icsalabs.com/html/library/whitepapers/crime.pdf
Institute for Security Technology Studies	http://www.ists.dartmouth.edu
Internet Storm Center	http://www.incidents.org
ISO 17799 Service & Software Dir	http://www.iso17799software.com
John the Ripper	http://www.openwall.com/john
Kevin Mitnick	http://www.zdnet.com/zdnn/stories/news/0,4586,2634540,00.html
L0phtCrack	http://www.securitysoftwaretech.com
LC4	http://www.atstake.com/research/lc3/
Levy Copyright Enforcement Case	http://www.wired.com/news/print/0,1294,32919,00.html
Microsoft Network Client	http://www.microsoft.com/technet

NOTES

Mitnick attack	http://www.gulker.com/ra/hack/tsattack.html
Morris Worm	http://www.software.com.pl/newarchive/misc/Worm/darbyt/pages/worm.html
NAI	http://www.nai.com
Nessus	http://www.nessus.org
NIST	http://www.nist.gov
Npasswd	ftp://ftp.cc.utexas.edu/pub/npasswd
NT Security	http://www.windows2000faq.com
Nuclear Information Attacks – Paknews	http://paknews.com/sp-hack1.html
Nuclear Information Attacks – Indian-Express	http://www.indian-express.com/full_story.php?content_id=3562
Passwd+	ftp://ftp.dartmouth.edu/pub/security
Password Cracking Wordlists	ftp://ftp.ox.ac.uk/pub/wordlists/
Pwdump	ftp://samba.anu.edu.au/pub/samba/pwdump/
Pwdump2	http://razor.bindview.com/tools/index.shtml
Pwdump2	http://www.webspan.net/~tas/pwdump2
Pwdump3e	http://www.ebiz-tech.com/html/pwdump.html
Qualcomm Laptop Story	http://news.cnet.com/news/0-1004-200-2804480.htm
Randall Schwartz Story	http://www.lightlink.com/spacenka/fors/
RFC 2196 Site Security Handbook	http://www.ietf.org/rfc/rfc2196.txt?number=2196
RFC 2504 User's Security Handbook	http://www.ietf.org/rfc/rfc2504.txt?number=2504
Russian Federal Security Service Investigation	http://www.ds-osac.org/edb/cyber/news/story.cfm?KEY=6830
Sample Security Policy (Cisco)	http://www.cisco.com/warp/public/126/secpol.html
SANS Security Policy Project	http://www.sans.org/newlook/resources/policies/policies.htm
SANS Model Security Policies	http://www.sans.org/infosecFAQ/policy/policy_list.htm
Schwartz Story – Password Cracking	http://www.lightlink.com/spacenka/fors/
SecurityFocus	http://www.securityfocus.com
Security Guide Link	http://csrc.ncsl.nist.gov/isptg/html/ISPTG.html
SirCam Information	http://www.symantec.com/avcenter/venc/data/w32.sircam.worm@mm.html
SirCam Information – CERT	http://www.cert.org/advisiories/CA-2001-22.html
Smurf Amplifier Sites	http://www.netscan.org
Snort	http://www.snort.org
Space Shuttle Atlantis – Hacking Incident	http://www.usatoday.com/life/cyber/tech/cti189.htm
Strong Passwords for NT	http://www.microsoft.com/technet/security
Stunnel	http://www.stunnel.org
SYSKEY	http://www.microsoft.com/technet

Terrorist Target Choices	http://www.cdi.org/terrorism/targets-methods.html
Trojan Port Numbers	http://www.sans.org/newlook/resources/IDFAQ/oddports.htm
Virus Hoax Catalog – F-Secure	http://www.f-secure.com/news/hoax.htm
Virus Hoax Catalog – Hoaxbuster	http://hoaxbuster.ciac.org
Virus Hoax Catalog – McAfee	http://www.mcafee.com/hoax
Virus Hoax Catalog – Symantec	http://www.symantec.com/avcenter/hoax.html
Virus Hoax Catalog – TrendMicro	http://www.trendmicro.com/vinfo/hoaxes/hoax.html
Whisker/Libwhisker	http://www.wiretrip.net/rfp/p/doc.asp/i2/d21.htm
White House (US)	http://www.whitehouse.gov
Zen and the Art of the Internet	http://sunland.gsfc.nasa.gov/info/guide/The_Internet_Worm.html
Zone Alarm	http://www.zonelabs.com

NOTES

NOTES

Section 3	
Contents	Address
ACID	http://www.cert.org/kb/acid/
ActivePorts	http://www.ntutility.com
ADODB	http://php.weblogs.com/adodb/
Adore worm	http://www.sans.org/y2k/adore.htm
Apache	http://www.apache.org
BlackICE	http://www.blackice.iss.net
Bugtraq	http://www.securityfocus.com
Caligula	http://www.securiteam.com
CalliSoft's Personal Firewall	http://www.standingguard.com/pdf/Productsheetpfwclient-UK
Cerberus	http://www.cerberus-infosec.co.uk/cis.shtml
Cerias	http://www.cerias.purdue.edu
CIDF	http://www.isi.edu/gost/brian/cidf/
CIDF	http://www.gidos.org
Coast	ftp://coast.cs.purdue.edu
Computer Economics	http://www.computereconomics.com
Computer Fraud and Abuse Act (US)	http://www.usdoj.gov/criminal/1030_new.html
Computer Misuse Act (UK)	http://www.hmso.gov.uk/acts/acts1990/Ukpga_19900018_en_1.htm
Computer Misuse Act (UK)	http://safety.ngfl.gov.uk/ukonlines/document.php3?D=d10
ConSeal	http://www.consealfirewall.com
Criminal Code of Canada	http://www.rcmp-grc.gc.ca/scams/cpu-cri.htm
Criminal Code of Canada	http://www.catalaw.com/logic/docs/ds-3421.htm
Criminal Code of Canada	http://ist.waterloo.ca/~reggers/misc/CRIMINAL.CODE.html
CVE	http://cve.mitre.org
Cybercrime Convention (Europe)	http://www.cybercrime.gov/crycoe.htm
Cybercrime Convention (Europe)	http://press.coe.int/cp/2001/875a(2001).htm
Deception Tool Kit	http://www.all.net/dtk
Dragon Squire	http://www.enterasys.com/ids/squire
DTK Deception Toolkit	http://www.all.net
Egress Filtering – CERT	http://www.cert.org/advisories/CA-1996-21.html
Egress Filtering – SANS	http://rr.sans.org/sysadmin/egress.php
Ethereal	http://www.ethereal.com
Evolving Firewalls	http://techupdate.zdnet.co.uk/story/0,,t481-s2120765,00.html

NOTES

Exploitation of Vulnerabilities in Microsoft SQL Server	http://www.cert.org/incident_notes/IN-2002-04.html
Fport	http://www.foundstone.com/rdlabs/tools.php
Gartner	http://www.gatner.com
GD	http://www.boutell.com/gd/
Gnutella	http://www.sans.org/y2k/gnutella.htm
Google	http://www.google.com
Gibson Research Corporation	http://www.grc.com
Hacking Web Site	http://www.antionline.com
Hacking Web Site	http://www.sabotage.org
Honeypots	http://project.honeynet.org/
Hping Downloads	http://www.kyuzz.org/antirez/hping2
Information Technology Act (India)	http://www.mit.gov.in/itbill2000.pdf
Internet Security Systems	http://www.iss.net/xforce/alerts.html
Legion	http://www.nmrc.org/files/snt/
Libpcap	http://www.tcpdump.org
Lion Worm	http://www.sans.org/y2k/lion.htm
MacSSH	http://pro.wanadoor.fr/chombier/
Mantrap	http://www.symantec.com/press/2002/n020717a.html
MySQL	http://www.mysql.com
Nessus	http://www.nessus.org
NetStumbler	http://www.netstumbler.com
Network Address Translation	http://www.howstuffworks.com/nat.htm/printable
Network Taps	http://www.sans.org/newlook/resources/IDFAQ/switched.htm
NFR Security	http://www.nfr.net
Nmap Unix Version	http://www.insecure.org/nmap/
Nmap Win NT Version	http://www.eeye.com/html/Research/Tools/nmapnt.html
NSWC Web Page	http://www.nswc.navy.mil/ISSEC
NukeNabber	http://www.dynamsol.com/puppet/nukenabber.html
OpenSSH	http://www.openssh.org
Out of Band Attacks	http://www.winplanet.com/features/reports/netexploits/index2.html
Packet Filtering – Obfuscation	http://www.obfuscation.org/ipf/ipf-howto.txt
Packet Filtering – OpenBSD	http://www.deadly.org/pf-howto/html/
Packet Filtering – SANS	http://rr.sans.org/firewall/packet_filter.php
Packet Filters	http://www.burningvoid.com/iaq/firewall-type.html
Personal Firewalls	http://www.networkcomputing.com/1116/1116f3.html

NOTES

PIPEDA (Canada)	http://www.privcom.gc.ca/legislation/02_06_01_e.asp
Packet Filtering for Firewall Systems	http://www.cert.org/tech_tips/packet_filtering.html
Phonesweep	http://www.sandstorm.net
PHP	http://www.php.net
Psionic Port Sentry	http://www.psionic.com/abacus/portsentry
PuTTY	http://www.chiark.greenend.org.uk/~sgtatham/putty/
Queso and Friends	http://www.apostols.org/projectz/queso/
Ramen Worm	http://www.sans.org/y2k/ramen.htm
RIPA (UK)	http://www.homeoffice.gov.uk/ripa/index.html
RIPA (UK)	http://www.homeoffice.gov.uk/oicd/ioc.html
RIPA (UK)	http://www.privacyinternational.org/countries/uk/surveillance
RIPA (UK)	http://news.bbc.co.uk/1/hi/uk/670092.stm
RFC 1918	http://www/ietf.org/rfc/rfc1918.txt
RFC 2663	http://www/ietf.org/rfc/rfc2663.txt
RFC 2766	http://www/ietf.org/rfc/rfc2766.txt
RFC 2827	http://www/ietf.org/rfc/rfc2827.txt
RFC 2993	http://www/ietf.org/rfc/rfc2993.txt
RFC 3022	http://www/ietf.org/rfc/rfc3022.txt
RFC 3235	http://www/ietf.org/rfc/rfc3235.txt
Risk Assessment	http://www.nswc.navy.mil/ISSEC
Saint	http://wwdsilx.wwdsi.com/saint/
SANS	http://www.sans.org
SARA	http://www-arc.com/sara/index.html
Security Events	http://www.mynetwatchman.com
Security Events	http://www.dshield.org
Security Events	http://www.incidents.org
Security Focus	http://www.securityfocus.com
SHADOW & CIDER	http://www.nswc.navy.mil/ISSEC/CID
Snort	http://www.snort.org
Snort (Win32 version)	http://www.datanerds.net/~mike/snort.html
SnortSnarf	http://www.silicondefense.com/software/snortsnarf.index.html
Security Profile Inspector	http://www.cert.mil/resources/security_tools.htm
SPI	http:://ciac.llnl.gov/cstc
Spoofed IP Address DDoS Attacks	http://rr.sans/org/threats/spoofed.php
Stack Smashing	http://online.securityfocus.com/archive/1/5667

NOTES

SVChost.exe	http://support.microsoft.com/support/Kb/articles/Q250/3/20.asp
Swatch	http://www.oit.ucsb.edu/~eta/swatch
Swatch with Snort	http://www.lug-burghausen.org/projects/Snort-Statistics/t1.html
Swatch with Snort – Spitzner	http://www.spitzner.net/swatch.html
Symantec Virus Encyclopedia	http://securityresponse.symantec.com/avcenter/vinfodb.html
Synscan	http://www.psychoid/lam3rz/de/synscan.html
Tcpdump	http://www.tcpdump.org
TCPWrappers	ftp://ftp.porcupine.org/pub/security/index.html
Telecommunications Act - Australia	http://www.alp.org.au/media/0902/20002179.html
Telecommunications Act – Australia	http://www.efa.org.au/Issues/Privacy/tia_bill2002.html
Telecommunications Act - Australia	http://www.voicecallcentral.com/help/acc/index.html?page=source/legal/australia.htm
SANS/FBI Top Twenty List	http://www.sans.org/top20.htm
Tripwire	http://www.Tripwiresecurity.com/
Tripwire	ftp://coast.cs.purdue.edu/pub/tools/Unix/Tripwire/
Unprotected Share Worm	http://www.project.honeynet.org/papers/worm/
War Dialer	http://www.sandstorm.net
Win95 Patch	http://support.microsoft.com/support/kb/articles/Q168/7/47.asp
Winpcap	http://winpcap.polito.it
X-force	http://www.iss.net

NOTES

Section 4	
AES	http://www.nist.gov/aes
Caesar Cipher	http://www.trincoll.edu/depts/cpsc/cryptography/caesar.html
CIAC Notes	http://ciac.llnl.gov/ciac/notes/Notes04c.shtml
comp.virus FAQ	http://www.faqs.org/faws/computer-virus/faq
Cracking Caesar's Cipher	http://www-math.cudenver.edu/~wcherowi/courses/m5410/exsubcip.html
Crypto Timeline	http://emmy.nmsu.edu/crypto/public_html/Timeline.html
Evolution of Malicious Agents	http://www.zeltser.com/agents
F-Secure – CIH Info	http://www.europe.f-secure.com/v-descs/cih.shtml
F-Secure – Nimda	http://www.europe.f-secure.com/v-descs/nimda.shtml
ICSA Anti-Virus Certification	http://www.icsa.net/html/certification/index.shtml
ICSA Anti-Virus Testing	http://www.icsalabs.com/html/communities/antivirus
IIS Buffer Overflow	http://cve.mitre.org/cgi-bin/cvename.cgi?name=CAN-2001-0500
Intl PGP 6.5.xi	http://www.pgpi.org
Jsteg	http://linkbeat.com/files/
Key Lengths	http://www.counterplane.com/keylength.html
Macro Viruses	http://online.securityfocus.com/infocus/1278
McAfee – CIH Virus	http://vil.nail.com/vil/content/v_10300.htm
McAfee – CodeRed worm	http://vil.nai.com/vil/content/v_99142.htm
McAfee – PeachyPDF Virus	http://vil.nai.com/vil/content/v_99179.htm
McAfee – Perrun	http://vil.nail.com/vil/content/v_99522.htm
Melissa Virus Advisory	http://www.cert.org/advisories/CA-1999-04.html
Melissa Virus FAQ	http://www.cert.org/tech_tips/Melissa_FAQ.html
MIME Header vulnerability	http://cve.mitre.org/cgi-bin/cvename.cgi?name=CAN-2001-0154
Mimicry Applet	http://www.wayner.org/texts/mimic
OPSEC basics	http://www.nswc.navy.mil/ISSEC/Docs/Ref/GeneralInfo/opsec_basics.html
PGP	http://web.mit.edu/network/pgp.html
PGP key server – MIT	http://pgp.mit.edu
References	http://www.eetimes.com/story/OEG20010226S0080
References	http://www.idg.net/crd_wireless_411385_103.html
References	http://www.mobileworld.org/info_security.html
References	http://www.networkmagazine.com/article/NMG20001106S0004
References	http://www.niksula.cs.hut.fi/~jiitv/bluesec.html
References	http://www.niksula.cs.hut.fi/~mkomu/docs/wirelesslansec.html

NOTES

References	http://www.nwfusion.com/buzz2000/buzz-wireless.html
References	http://www.sans.org/infosecFAQ/wireless/threats.htm
References	http://www.tml.hut.fi/Opinnot/Tik-110.501/1997/wireless_lan.html
References	http://www.vnunet.com/News/601800
References	http://www.wlana.com/learn/security.htm
References	http://www.zdnet.com/zdnn/stories/news/0,4586,2597657-1,00.html
sadmind/IIS worm	http://www.cert.org/advisories/CA-2001-11.html
SANS Digests	http://www.sans.org/newlook/digests
SANS Intrusions list	http://www.incidents.org/intrusions
SecurityFocus Incidents list	http://online.securityfocus.com/archive/75
Snow	http://www.darkside.com/au/snow/
Sophos – FunLove	http://www/sophos.com/virusinfo/articles/powerpuff.html
Spam Mimic	http://www.spammimic.com
Stego Tools	http://www.stegoarchive.com
Stego Tools	http://www.wayner.org/books/discrypt2/links.html
Stego Tools	http://members.tripod.com/steganography/stego.html
Stego Tools	http://members.tripod.com/steganography/stego/software.html
S-Tools	ftp://idea.sec.dsi.unimi.it/pub/security/crypt/code/s-tools4.zip
Symantec – Discount Virus Hoax	http://securityresponse.symantec.com/avecenter/venc/data/discount.hoax.html
Symantec Security Response – Klez Virus	http://securityresponse.symantec.com/avcenter/venc/data/w32/klez.gen@mm.html
Symantec Security Reponse – Understanding Virus Behavior	http://securityresponse.symantec.com/avcenter/reference/virus.behavior.under.win.nt.pdf
Trend Micro	http://download.antivirus.com/ftp/white/policywp.pdf
Virus and Hoax Information	http://nai.com
Virus and Hoax Information	http://www.antivirus.com
Virus and Hoax Information	http://www.cert.org
Virus and Hoax Information	http://www.hoaxkill.com
Virus and Hoax Information	http://hoaxbusters.ciac.org
Virus and Hoax Information	http://www.f-secure.com/v-descs
Virus and Hoax Information	http://www.nonprofit.net/hoax/
Virus and Hoax Information	http://www.snopes2.com
Virus and Hoax Information	http://www.sophos.com/virusinfo/
Virus and Hoax Information	http://www.trusecure.com
Virus and Hoax Information	http://www.symantec.com/avcenter

NOTES

Virus and Hoax Information	http://www.virusbtn.com
Virus and Hoax Information	http://www.vmyths.com
Virus Bulletin – Simile	http://www.virusbtn.com/resources/viruses/indepth/simile.xml
VPN Resources	http://vpn.shmoo.com/
VPN Resources	http://www.antd.nist.gov/itg/cerberus
VPN Resources	http://www.antd.nist.gov/itg/plutoplus
VPN Resources	http://www.enteract.com/~lspitz/pubs.html
VPN Resources	http://www.ietf.org/html.charters/ipsec-charter.html
VPN Resources	http://www.openssh.com
VPN Resources	http://www.usenix.org/publications/login/1999-12/features/harmful.html (req. USENIX membership)
VPN Resources	http://www.xs4all.nl/~freeswan
ZDNet – CIH Virus	http://www.zdnet.com/products/stories/reviews/0,4161,2553837,00.html

NOTES

Section 5	
.NET	http://www.microsoft.com/net/
.NET security	http://www.foundstone.com/microsoft/dotnet
Active Directory	http://www.microsoft.com/activedirectory/
Active Directory Client Extensions	http://www.microsoft.com/windows2000/server/evaluation/news/bulletins/adextension.asp
ActiveLane	http://www.activelane.com
Adiscon	http://www.adiscon.com
Aelita	http://www.aelita.com
article on NTFS file streams	http://www.sans.org/newlook/alerts/NTFS.htm
Backup Express	http://www.syncsort.com
Bindview Corporation	http://www.bindview.com
Bindview Corporation – Razor	http://razor.bindview.com
Bookpool	http://www.bookpool.com
Bootable CDs	http://www.nu2.nu/bootablecd/
BrightStor ARCserve	http://www.ca.com
Brute Force Kerberos Cracker	http://ntsecurity.nu
bug list, user2sid & sid2user tools	http://www.ntbugtraq.com
Centrax	http://www.cybersafe.com
Checklists, Bulletins, Tools, Downloads	http://www.microsoft.com/technet/security
Checkpoint	http://www.checkpoint.com
Citrix	http://www.citrix.com
Cisco	http://www.cisco.com
CLR for Linux/Unix	http://www.go-mono.com
Component Object Model (COM)	http://www.microsoft.com/com/tech/com.asp
CSDIFF	http://www.componentsoftware.com
DumpEvt	http://www.systemtools.com/somarsoft
Entercept	http://www.clicknet.com
ERD Commanders, NTFSDOs Tools Source	http://www.sysinternals.com
Event Log Analysis	http://www.eventid.net
Event Log Integration with syslog	http://www.counterplan.com/log-analysis.html
Freeswan	http://www.freeswan.org
Foundstone	http://www.foundstone.com
FW-1 DNS hole	http://www.securityfocus.com/archive/1/10972
Galaxy	http://www.commvault.com

NOTES

Ghost	http://www.symantec.com/ghost
Hfcheck	http://www.microsoft.com/Downloads/Release.asp?ReleaseID=24168
IANA port assignments	http://www.iana.org/assignments/port-numbers
IBM	http://www.ibm.com
ICF Review	http://www.grc.com
ICF Review	http://www.grcsucks.com
InstallShield	http://www.installshield.com
International Organization for Standards	http://www.ISO.ch
Internet Engineering Task Force	http://www.ietf.org
Internet Standards	http://www.normos.org
Intruder Alert	http://enterprisesecurity.symantec.com
Inzider	http://ntsecurity.nu
KB Alertz	http://www.kbalertz.com
Legato	http://www.legato.com
L0phtCrack	http://www.atstake.com
Microsoft Download Site	http://www.microsoft.com/downloads/
Microsoft IIS Lockdown Tool	http://www.microsoft.com/technet/security/tools/locktool.asp
Microsoft Operations Manager	http://www.microsoft.com/mom/
Microsoft Search engine	http://search.microsoft.com
Microsoft Security Bulletin	http://www.microsoft.com/technet/security/bulletin/MS01-013.asp
Microsoft Security Hotfixes	http://www.microsoft.com/security
Microsoft Security Tools	http://www.microsoft.com/technet/security/tools.asp
Microsoft Service Packs	http://www.microsoft.com/windows2000/downloads/servicepacks/
Microsoft Software Update Services	http://www.microsoft.com/windows2000/windowsupdate/sus/
Microsoft URLScan	http://www.microsoft.com/technet/security/tools/URLscan.asp
Microsoft Windows 2000 Remote Desktop Client	http://www.microsoft.com/windows2000/downloads/recommended/TSAC/
Netrecon	http://www.axent.com
Netscreen	http://www.netscreen.com
NT Bugtraq	http://www.ntbugtraq.com
NTFS-DOS	http://www.sysinternals.com
NTObjectives Tools	http://www.foundstone.com/rdlabs/tools.php
Null User Sessions	http://www.microsoft.com/technet
OmniBack II and Data Protector	http://www.hp.com
Packetstorm	http://packetstormsecurity.nl
PatchWork	http://grc.com/pw/patchwork.htm

NOTES

Pedestal Software	http://pedestalsoftware.com
Perl or Python Interpreters	http://www.activestate.com
Polaris Group	http://www.polarisgroup.com
Possible Trojans	http://www.simovits.com/nyheter9902.html
PPTP v1 Review	http://www.counterplane.com/pptp-paper.html
PPTP v2 Review	http://www.counterplane.com/pptpv2-paper.html
Predictive Systems	http://www.predictive.com
Qfecheck	http://www.microsoft.com/technet/support/kb.asp?ID=282784
Resource Kit	http://www.reskit.com
St. Bernard Software	http://www.stbernard.com
Setting Registry Keys	http://www.microsoft.com/technet
Shavlik Technologies	http://www.shavlik.com
Somarsoft	http://www.somarsoft.com
STAT Scanner	http://www.statonline.com
Sygate Personal Firewall	http://www.sygate.com
SystemScanner	http://www.iss.net
Tiny Personal Firewall	http://www.tinysoftware.com
UltraBac	http://www.ultrabac.com
Veritas	http://www.veritas.com
VirtualPC	http://www.connectix.com
VMWare	http://www.vmware.com
Warchalking	http://www.warchalking.org
Win 2k Resource Kit	http://www.microsoft.com/windows2000/techinfo/reskit/tools/default.asp
Windows Installer	http://www.wise.com
Windows Resource Kit	http://www.microsoft.com/windows/default.asp
Windows Update	http://windowsupdate.microsoft.com
Writing a Custom Password Filter	http://www.microsoft.com/technet

NOTES

Section 6	
Apache Security Tips	http://www.apache.org/docs/misc/security_tips.html
Bugtraq mailing lists archives	http://www.securityfocus.com
Center for Internet Security	http://www.cisecurity.org
CERT Advisories	http://www.cert.org/advisories
CERT SNMP Advisory	http://www.cert.org/advisories/CA-2002-03.html
Coroner's Toolkit	http://www.fish.com/tct
Deer Run Associates	http://www.deer-run.com
FreeBSD	http://www.freebsd.org
gnuplot	http://www.ucc.ie/gnuplot/gnuplot.html
HP Packages	http://devresouce.hp.com
HP Packages	http://hpux.cs.utah.edu
Internet SSH FAQ	http://www.employees.org/~satch/ssh/faq/
Linux stack protection	http://www.openwall.com
LogSentry	http://www.psionic.com/products/logsentry.html
LPRng	http://www.lprng.org
NetBSD	http://www.netbsd.org
Nfsbug	ftp://ftp.cs.vu.nl/pub/leendert/nfsbug.shar
NTP setup	http://www.deer-run.com/~hal/ns2000/ntp2.pdf
OpenBSD	http://www.openbsd.org
Redhat updates	ftp://updates.redhat.com
Rpcbind	ftp://ftp.porcupine.org/pub/security/
SANS News Services	http://www.sans.org/sansnews
Solaris Packages	http://www.sunfreeware.com
Solaris patches	ftp://sunsolve.sun.com/pub/patches/
StackGuard	http://www.immunix.org
Sudo	http://www.countesan.com/sudo/
SyslogNG	http://www.balabit.hu/products/syslog-ng
Tar	ftp://ftp.gnu.org/gnu/tar/

Index

NOTES

NOTES

Index

Page numbers in italic refer to tables or boxed text. Page numbers preceded by the letter A refer to Appendix pages in Volume 2. Acronyms are spelled out in the Acronym List starting on page A151 in Volume 2.

A

NOTES

NOTES

NOTES

B

NOTES

NOTES

C

NOTES

NOTES

D

NOTES

NOTES

NOTES

E

NOTES

NOTES

G

NOTES

NOTES

NOTES

I

NOTES

NOTES

NOTES

J

NOTES

K

L

NOTES

NOTES

NOTES

NOTES

N

NOTES

O

NOTES

NOTES

NOTES

NOTES

NOTES

Q

R

NOTES

NOTES

NOTES

NOTES

S

NOTES

NOTES

NOTES

NOTES

NOTES

T

NOTES

NOTES

U

NOTES

NOTES

NOTES

V

NOTES

W

NOTES

NOTES

NOTES

NOTES

X

Y

Z

NOTES

NOTES

NOTES

NOTES